THE REALITIES OF AGING
AN INTRODUCTION TO GERONTOLOGY

FIFTH EDITION

Cary S. Kart
The University of Toledo

Allyn and Bacon
Boston · London · Toronto · Sydney · Tokyo · Singapore

To the Memory of
Eleanor and Irving Kart

Editor-in-Chief, Social Sciences:
  Karen Hanson
Editorial Assistant: Jennifer Jacobson
Marketing Manager: Karon Bowers
Production Administrator: Annette Joseph
Production Coordinator: Holly Crawford

Editorial-Production Service:
  Lynda Griffiths, TKM Productions
Photo Researcher: Susan Duane
Composition Buyer: Linda Cox
Manufacturing Buyer: Megan Cochran
Cover Administrator: Linda Knowles

Copyright © 1997, 1994, 1990, 1985, 1981 by Allyn & Bacon
A Viacom Company
160 Gould Street
Needham Heights, MA 02194

Internet: www.abacon.com
America Online: keyword: College Online

Library of Congress Cataloging-in-Publication Data

Kart, Cary S. (Cary Steven).
  The realities of aging : an introduction to gerontology / Cary S.
Kart. — 5th ed.
    p.   cm.
  Includes bibliographical references and index.
  ISBN 0-205-19154-1
    1. Gerontology.   I. Title.
HQ1061.K36   1996
305.26–dc20   96-24588
                                                                        CIP

Printed in the United States of America
10   9   8   7   6   5   4   3   2   01   00   99   98   97

Photo Credits: p. 11: Tony Neste; p. 38: Earl Dotter/Impact Visuals; p. 48: Eileen Hohmuth-Lemonick; p. 79: Robert Harbison; p. 103: Jim Whitmer/FPG; p. 122: Mike Valeri/FPG; p. 151: Will Faller; p. 186: Richard Harrington/FPG; p. 219: Lisa Law/Image Works; p. 255: Eileen Hohmuth-Lemonick; p. 292: Elizabeth Crews/Stock Boston; p. 324: Mary Ellen Lepionka; p. 348: Martha Tabor/Impact Visuals; p. 371: Owen Franken/Stock Boston; p. 381: Will Faller; p. 410: Ulrike Welsch; p. 441: Ron Chapple/FPG; p. 467: Michael Weisbrot/Image Works; p. 497: H. Armstrong Roberts; p. 527: Loren Santow/Impact Visuals.

CONTENTS

PREFACE

Allyn and Bacon deserves a thank you for providing me with a fifth opportunity to present *The Realities of Aging*. The field of gerontology continues to grow rapidly and my efforts in this edition have focused on keeping current. This is a considerably more difficult task than in the past, as gerontology has strengthened its multidisciplinary identity.

A survey of gerontology programs carried out by the Association for Gerontology in Higher Education (AGHE) and the University of Southern California (USC) has identified four courses as most commonly offered in gerontological instruction programs in institutions of higher education in the United States. Some would describe these four courses as representing a core curriculum in gerontology. The courses are Social Gerontology, Psychology of Aging, Biology/Physiology of Aging, and Sociology of Aging. From my biased perspective, the Fifth Edition of *The Realities of Aging* remains the text of choice for an introductory course in gerontology, precisely because it has strengths in social gerontology and the sociology of aging, the biology/physiology of aging, and the psychology of aging.

The basic structure of this book has been retained from the Fourth Edition. Part I introduces the study of aging and consists of three chapters. Chapter 1 discusses 10 myths about aging. Chapter 2 defines the field of gerontology, presents a history of aging, and includes updated material on methodological issues current in aging research. Chapter 3 presents the population dynamics and demographic characteristics of the aged, updated to include the most current data. Part II presents material on the biomedical aspects of aging. Chapters 4 and 5 are devoted to the biological aspects of aging. Chapter 6 describes the health status of the elderly population.

Part III places aging in psychological and sociological perspective. Separate chapters are devoted to the psychological aspects of aging (Chapter 7) and to sociological theories of aging (Chapter 9). Chapter 8 bridges the psychological and sociological approaches to aging. Part IV looks at the relationship between the aged and society. Chapter 10 presents material on the family life of older people, whereas Chapters 11, 12, and 13 deal, respectively, with the economics of aging; work, retirement, and leisure; and the politics of aging. Chapter 14 deals with the relationship between religion and aging.

Part V deals with special issues of concern for older people: the problems of racial and ethnic aging (Chapter 15); living environments (Chapter 16); long-term care (Chapter 17); health policies for the aged in the United States (Chapter 18); and death and dying (Chapter 19). The future of the field and career opportunities are discussed in an epilogue.

Revised chapters from the Fourth Edition were read in various stages of development by Ruth Dunkle and Eileen and Seamus Metress. Much of what is good here comes from their collective wisdom. These same individuals deserve a special thank you for the chapters they have contributed to this volume. Finally, I wish to thank the reviewers of this edition: Daniel J. Klenow, North Dakota State University; Russell A. Ward, State University of New York at Albany; and Sharon Wilson, Lorain County Community College.

These are not the best of times in higher education. Budgets are tight and resources scarce. Nevertheless, the University of Toledo continues to be a productive environment for me. The Department of Sociology, Anthropology and Social Work has a hard-working, productive faculty and staff, as well as conscientious and congenial students, making it a rewarding place in which to work.

By the time this edition appears, Michelle will have put up with about 28 years of this—and it has not been easy! Through it all, she has remained a caring and loving partner, while at the same time pursuing her own career. I really have been lucky! In the preface to an earlier edition, I wrote that Renee is old enough for me to start thinking about her using this text in a college course. That time has now come and gone, as has her graduation from law school. Finally, there will be someone in the family to read the fine print in these book contracts! Jeremy is progressing through his college career, with errors of judgment, large and small, behind him. The future is his to create. In any case, I have reason to be a proud father!

With the recent death of my mother, the family circle narrows. May Ina (my sister), Charlie, Stacey (Rutgers), Jamie (Delaware), and Illisa remain healthy, happy, and prosperous; and Grandpa Max and Grandma Sylvia stay active and in good health. Finally, this Fifth Edition is formally dedicated to the memory of my mother and father, Eleanor and Irving Kart.

CHAPTER 1

FIRST THE GOOD NEWS...
THE MYTHS OF AGING

According to Greek mythology (Hamilton, 1942, p. 428), Aurora, the goddess of the Dawn, was in love with Tithonus, a Trojan. Aurora asked Zeus to make Tithonus immortal, and Zeus agreed. But Aurora did not think to ask Zeus to allow Tithonus to retain his youthfulness. For a while, the lovers lived happily, but then the consequences of Aurora's error began to appear. Tithonus's hair turned gray, and soon he could move neither hand nor foot. He prayed for death, but there was no release for him. At last, in pity, Aurora left him alone in his room, locking the door behind her. As one version of the story goes, Tithonus still lies in that room, babbling endlessly.[1]

The legend of Tithonus reflects a number of themes relevant to contemporary life in the United States, not the least of which is the prevalent fear of old age and its concomitant hardships and infirmities. Some see this fear of growing old as the root of a negative attitude toward aging and old age, and of the tendency on the part of many Americans to avoid the word *old* and substitute euphemisms such as *golden years*. Surveys of individuals aged 18 years and over conducted by the National Council on Aging show that, on average, Americans believe that the problems of older people are more severe than their own problems (Ferraro, 1992). Ferraro (1992) reports that these surveys show that most Americans believe the problems of older people are more serious than do older persons themselves.

Dr. Robert N. Butler (1975), winner of the Pulitzer Prize for his book *Why Survive? Being Old in America*, coined the term *ageism* to describe this negative attitude

---

[1]Another version of the story maintains that Tithonus shrank in size until Aurora, with a feeling for the natural fitness of things, turned him into a skinny and noisy grasshopper.

toward aging and the aged. He equates ageism with racism and sexism and defines it as "a process of systematic stereotyping and discrimination against people because they are old" (Butler, 1987, p. 22). Just as racism has generated unfortunate stereotypes of members of different racial groups, so too has ageism fostered unfortunate myths about old people and the aging process. Moreover, like racism, ageism has roots in the early American experience.

According to historian David Hackett Fischer (1977), colonial America was a place in which age, not youth, was exalted and venerated, honored, and obeyed. This respect for older people found expression in a variety of forms, including the iconography of Puritanism, the distribution of honored seats in the meeting-houses of Massachusetts, and the patterns of office holding in church and state. Fashions were also designed to flatter age, and census data suggest that people attempted to enhance their status by reporting themselves as older than they actually were.

This era of *gerontophilia* was succeeded by a period of transformation (1780–1820) during which attitudes toward old age began to change. In the nineteenth century, Fischer (1977) argues, there was truly a revolution in age relations in the United States, evidenced by new expressions of contempt for the aged (such as *old fogey* and *geezer*), by the appearance of mandatory retirement policies, and by the development of a cult of youth in literature.

Fischer (1977) attributes the beginnings of this era of *gerontophobia* to two important factors. The first is demographic. Declines in both birth and death rates along with increases in life expectancy—long-term trends beginning in the colonial period—changed the age composition of the population in the United States. Old people increased in numbers as well as in the proportion of the population they constituted. Second, and perhaps more important according to Fischer, is the radical expansion of the ideas of equality and liberty that occurred during the late eighteenth and early nineteenth centuries. These ideas altered forever the conception of the world on which the old order had rested. Not only did the aged suffer the apparent misfortune of being identified with the old order but they were also a constant reminder of what the new order hoped to avoid: dependence, disease, failure, and sin (Cole, 1983).

Ageism is a cultural phenomenon whose acceptance is long-standing and crosscuts differences in age, region, and social class. Some theories of prejudice against racial and religious minorities also seem to help explain ageist attitudes in the United States. According to Levin and Levin (1980), people who hold unfavorable attitudes toward the aged are also apt to dislike blacks, the mentally ill, and the physically disabled. Laws (1995) argues that, more than prejudice, ageism is a form of oppression that limits those who are the object of that oppression and shapes the perceptions of those who hold ageist attitudes.

Ageism may be passed from generation to generation by means of socialization and other processes of transmission of culture. For example, Covey (1991) has analyzed the extent to which older people have historically been characterized as avaricious and miserly in Western art and literature. He reminds his readers of Dickens's 1843 classic, *A Christmas Carol,* which introduces the charac-ter of Ebenezer Scrooge, who has become the contemporary archetype of the old miser.

In examining the artworks of the "old-age painter," European artist Hubert von Herkomer (1849–1914), McLerran (1993) argues that the positive images of aged seamstresses depicted in his popular late-nineteenth century woodcuts and paintings were ageist in nature. They provided support for the view in England at that time that individuals could be redeemed by the work they per-formed. McLerran asserts that these images promoted the idea that the elderly were as able-bodied and capable of their own support as anyone else. Conse-quently, aged individuals who could not support themselves were deemed immoral and undeserving of help unless they agreed to a life of enforced labor in a squalid poorhouse. Seemingly, no account was made for diminishment of physical capacity that might accompany advanced age. From McLerran's per-spective, the presentation of positive stereotypes of the aged were used in Victo-rian England to support an ageism that allowed for the institutionalization of the aged poor. The aged poor women in Herkomer's paintings were "doomed to conditions of squalor by an ideology of labor which allows no compromise" (p. 770). They were, in Victorian eyes, "saved by the hand that is not stretched out" (p. 770).

Cohen and Kruschwitz (1990) have examined popular sheet music published in the United States between 1830 and 1980 and found considerably more negative than positive sentiment about aging and old age. The 1912 song "Old Joe Has Had His Day" reflects a sad acceptance of old age:

> The marks are creeping on
> My hair is turning grey
> The springtime of life has faded
> With the flow'rs that grow by the way
> We, like roses, must wither and fade
> There's nothing comes to stay
> The allotted time is drawing near
> "Old Joe has had his day."

In a more contemporary vein, Paul Simon's song "Old Friends" presents an equally sad view of old age:

> Old friends,
> Sat on their park bench like bookends,
> A newspaper blows through the grass
> Falls on the round toes
> Of the high shoes
> Of the old friends ...
> Can you imagine us
> Years from today
> Sharing a park bench quietly?

How terribly strange to be 70,
Old friends,
Memory brushes the same years,
Silently sharing the same fears.[2]

How is ageism perpetuated today? One way is through so-called common-sense observations. Everyday aphorisms ("You can't teach an old dog new tricks") reflect a common sense that is negative as well as inconsistent with scientific knowledge. Scientific knowledge can also reinforce negative stereotypes about old people. This was especially the case in the early post–World War II period, as the study of aging began to develop (see Chapter 2). As Steffl (1978) points out, "Early research described characteristics of . . . aged congregated in poor farms, nursing homes, and state mental hospitals leading to a general picture of impaired elderly." Add to this picture the testimony of physicians and social workers, whose elderly clients were (and are) often physically and socially dependent. Finally, as Tibbitts (1979) suggests, the private agencies and public program bureaucracies helped perpetuate negative stereotypes by pleading with Congress for legislation on behalf of "the impaired, deprived, dependent elderly."

Myths and stereotypes of the elderly may also be transmitted through the mass media. Virtually all analyses of the content of television programming show an underrepresentation of older people in comparison to their numbers in the total population, as well as a striking imbalance in the ratio of older males to females (Kubey, 1980). According to Davis and Davis (1985), only 10 percent of the people on television over 65 years of age are female, whereas, in reality, in the United States and virtually every other setting in the world, elderly women outnumber elderly men. Moreover, with some exceptions, the image of older people in television has been generally negative. Even network and TV news shows often portray the elderly as victims of disasters, such as hurricanes or tornadoes, for example, or as having some serious problem (homelessness or lack of access to health care) that is the basis for a human-interest story or editorial commentary.

Public affairs and talk shows have been an island of exception in this sea of negativity. Generally, they have presented the greatest percentages of older people and the most positive image of the elderly. This is reflected in high ratings of authority and esteem given to older politicians, journalists, and business executives who appear on such programs. These authoritative old people are overwhelmingly male (e.g., David Brinkley or Hugh Downs).

Television is not the only mass medium in which stereotypes about old people have been found. Researchers have examined themes of aging as they have appeared in diverse media from children's books and fairy tales (Chinen, 1987; Peterson & Karnes, 1976; Robin, 1977), to poetry (Sohngen & Smith, 1978), newspapers (Buchholz & Bynum, 1982), and literature (Holstein, 1994).

---

[2]Copyright © 1968 Paul Simon. Used by permission of the Publisher.

GROWING TO BE AN OLD WOMAN: AGING AND AGEISM
Shevy Healey

In my late fifties, and then my sixties, I heard, "I can't believe you're that old. You don't look that old." At first that felt like a compliment. Then I became a bit uneasy. It reminded me of early pre-feminist days when I was complimented by some men for being "smarter," "more independent" than those "other" women. What was I now—a token "young"?

Slowly other experiences began to accumulate, reminding me of a real change in my life status.

First, I moved. And while I found easy acceptance among older people in the community, when younger people talked to me they invariably would say something like, "You remind me of my grandmother." Grandmother?! I felt labelled and diminished somehow.

. . . I looked in the mirror and saw lots of wrinkles. I had a hard time fitting that outward me with the me inside. I felt like the same person, but outside I looked different. I checked into a face lift, with much trepidation. What a seduction took place in that doctor's office! He told me he would make me less strange to myself. I would look more like I felt! I became frightened by the whole process. Who was I then? This face? What I felt like inside? How come the two images were not connected? My own ageism told me that how I looked outside was ugly. But I felt the same inside, not ugly at all.

. . . Finally, death entered my life as a direct reality. My oldest friend died of cancer three years ago. My father died two years ago after what turned out to be needless surgery. Another close friend died last month after a year of struggling with a massive stroke. The realization hit me that I can expect this kind of personal contact with death to occur with greater and greater frequency.

Not just by chronological age, but life itself was telling me that I was becoming an older/old woman!

. . . Think of all the adjectives that are most disrespectful in our society. They are all part of the ageist stereotyping of old women: pathetic, powerless, querulous, complaining, sick, weak, conservative, rigid, helpless, unproductive, wrinkled, asexual, ugly, unattractive, and on, ad nauseum. There is, by the way, an exception to this, and that is the stereotype of the wise old woman. She, of course, never complains, is never sick, and although no one really would want to *be* with her, occasionally it might be fine to sit at her feet!

How did this happen, this totally denigrating picture of old women?: To understand this phenomenon we must look at sexism, for ageism is inextricably tied to sexism and is the logical extension of its insistence that women are only valuable when they are attractive and useful to men.

Under the guise of making themselves beautiful, women have endured torture and self mutilation, cramped their bodies physically, maimed themselves mentally, all in order to please and serve men better, as men defined the serving, because only in that service could women survive.

. . . As we alter and modify our bodies in the hopes of feeling good, we frequently achieve instead an awful estrangement from our own bodies. In the attempt to meet that arbitrary external standard, we lose touch with our own internal body messages, thus alienating ourselves further from our own sources of strength and power.

What does this have to do with aging and ageism? Having spent our lives estranged from our own bodies in the effort to meet that outer patriarchal standard of beauty, it is small wonder that the prospect of growing old is frightening to women of all ages. We have all been trained to be ageist. By denying our aging we hope to escape the penalties placed upon growing old. But in so doing we disarm ourselves in the struggle to overcome the oppression of ageism.

...We have systematically denigrated old women, kept them out of the mainstream of productive life, judged them primarily in terms of failing capacities and functions, and then found them pitiful. We have put old women in nursing "homes" with absolutely no intellectual stimulation, isolated from human warmth and nurturing contact, and then condemned them for their senility. We have impoverished, disre-

spected, and disregarded old women, and then dismissed them as inconsequential and uninteresting. We have made old women invisible so that we do not have to confront our patriarchal myths about what makes life valuable or dying painful.

Having done that, we then attribute to the process of aging *per se* all the evils we see and fear about growing old. It is not aging that is awful, nor whatever physical problems may accompany aging. What is awful is how society treats old women and their problems. To the degree that we accept and allow such treatment we buy the ageist assumptions that permit this treatment.

Source: "Growing to Be an Old Woman: Aging and Ageism" by Shevy Healy is reprinted by permission of the publisher from *Women and Aging* ed. Jo Alexander et al., published by CALYX Books, 1986.

Some research does indicate a positive shift in attitudes toward older persons. Austin (1985) reports a sample of midwestern university students more accepting of close relationships with older people than of close relationships with people who are disabled, including the blind, paraplegics, and the mentally retarded. Austin proposes that people have developed more positive attitudes toward old age in recent years as more older people have become visible in productive roles. This does not suggest that ageist attitudes have disappeared in U.S. society, only that, vis-à-vis other groups, older people are seen as productive and conforming to societal values.

Some exceptions to the generally negative television image of older people have also appeared in recent years. Bell (1992) recently analyzed the images of aging presented in five prime-time television programs in which older persons played a major character. These included *The Golden Girls, Murder She Wrote, In the Heat of the Night, Matlock,* and *Jake and the Fatman.* (A number of these programs are in syndication and continue to appear as reruns on local television stations.) Rather than appearing "comical, stubborn, eccentric, and foolish," Bell argues that the older characters portrayed in these programs are stereotyped more positively, appearing powerful, affluent, healthy, socially and mentally active, and widely admired. Also, during the late 1980s and into the 1990s, Hollywood put forth successful films with themes related to aging. These included *Driving Miss Daisy* (1989), *Avalon* (1990), *Fried Green Tomatoes* (1991), *The Joy Luck Club* (1993), *Grumpy Old Men* (1993), and *Nobody's Fool* (1994). A number of these films also gave esteemed older actors and actresses an opportunity to display their creative talents.

Holtzman and Akiyama (1985) compared the frequency and quality of the portrayal of older characters on Japanese and U.S. television programs most often watched by children. They found that U.S. television portrayed older characters more frequently and more positively than did Japanese television. This was particularly surprising given commonly held beliefs about the cultural importance of older persons in non-Western cultures.

Should one be concerned about the relationship between television viewing and ageism? Passuth and Cook (1985) caution about exaggerating this relationship. In response to the question, "Does heavy television viewing make a consistently negative contribution to the public's knowledge and attitudes about older persons?," they answer "no." Only for adults under age 30 do Passuth and Cook report a modest relationship between heavy television viewing and low levels of knowledge levels about aging; for adults 30 years of age and older, no such relationship is reported. From the researchers' point of view, other socializing institutions and contexts must be examined to understand how knowledge and attitudes about aging and older people are developed.

Whether television is implicated or not, some research does suggest that many young children already possess well-defined negative attitudes toward older people and the aging process (Corbin, Kagan, & Metil-Corbin, 1987). Programmatic efforts may be required, however, to overcome these negative attitudes. Fernandez-Pereiro and Sanchez-Ayendez (1992) report on a pilot project in the Dominican Republic that focuses on early childhood development but enlists older people as an important educational resource. The project includes specific activities to give children a positive view of older people and of the aging process. The theory is that knowledge of the aging process and the development of positive attitudes toward old age can contribute to the improvement of intergenerational relationships, combat stereotypes that promote ageism, and prepare children for a more realistic approach to their own aging.

The theory may work. Aday and colleagues (Aday, Sims, & Evans, 1991) matched fourth-graders with elderly subjects from a center for senior citizens in a nine-month intergenerational project on aging. Students developed significantly more positive views toward the elderly and these were maintained after a one-year follow-up. One student summarized what had been learned in the project as follows: "Older people are basically the same as us. They have a heart, they have feelings, and they depend on someone to help them when they need help" (p. 380).

Still, ageism can be a subtle and flexible foe. According to Binstock (1983), a past president of the Gerontological Society of America, new distortions of the reality of older people have appeared to provide the foundation for the emergence of the aged as a scapegoat for a variety of economic and political frustrations in U.S. society. These distortions, identified by Binstock as classic examples of "tabloid thinking," include the belief that annual federal budget deficits in the United States in the range of $200 billion and more during the 1980s and into the 1990s resulted from insatiable demands by older people for additional Social Security and health benefits. From this view, current generations of younger workers are taxed at a burdensome level in order to support social programs for the elderly (Villers Foundation, 1987).

According to the Budget Committee of the U.S. House of Representatives (1986), however, were it not for Medicare and Social Security, the budget deficit would be *substantially greater*. The committee notes that Social Security and Medicare swung substantially out of deficit to balance during the 1980s, while the rest of the budget plunged deeply into deficit. Like many contemporary analysts, Martin Feldstein, former chair of President Reagan's Council of Economic Advisors, identified the major causes of the federal deficit increase since 1981 as including sustained increases in military spending and substantial federal tax decreases, *not* programs for the elderly.

The increase in the elderly population has created demand for federal, state, and local programs to benefit this group. It is important to remember, however, that the biggest of these programs—Social Security, Medicare, veterans' and civil service pensions—are not welfare programs. They are entitlements to which the elderly (and their employers) have contributed throughout their working years. Old people and the programs that benefit them cannot be held accountable for the massive federal budget deficits that have burdened the economy since 1981.

Binstock (1983) identifies three important consequences for U.S. society of this scapegoating of the aged. First, it diverts attention from other public policy issues, including unemployment and the federal budget deficit. Second, it produces conflict between generations as representatives of the young and the old battle for scarce resources. Third, it diverts attention from long-standing issues of equity and justice in public programs of support for older people.

One aim of this book is to refute negative stereotypes and present a more realistic view of aging in the United States—a view that is more positive than many students of aging have admitted. Treat the following list of 10 statements about old people and the aging process as a quiz. Read each item carefully and indicate whether you believe it to be true or false.

_____ **1.** Senility inevitably accompanies old age.

_____ **2.** Most old people are alone and isolated from their families.

_____ **3.** The majority of old people are in poor health.

_____ **4.** Old people are more likely than younger people to be victimized by crime.

_____ **5.** The majority of old people live in poverty.

_____ **6.** Old people tend to become more religious as they age.

_____ **7.** Older workers are less productive than younger ones.

_____ **8.** Old people who retire usually suffer a decline in health and early death.

_____ **9.** Most old people have no interest in, or capacity for, sexual relations.

_____ **10.** Most old people end up in nursing homes and other long-term care institutions.

If you answered "false" to all 10 statements, you have a perfect score; "true" responses indicate misconceptions about old people and the aging process.

DEBUNKING THE MYTHS

MYTH 1: Senility Inevitably Accompanies Old Age

Cervantes wrote the second part of *Don Quixote* in his sixty-eighth year. Verdi composed the opera *Falstaff* in his eightieth year. Barbara McClintock, a noted geneticist, won a National Medal of Science at age 68, the first MacArthur Laureate Award at age 79, and a Nobel Prize in Physiology at age 81. Goethe completed *Faust* when he was 83 years old; Bach dictated the final chorale to *Art of the Fugue* from his deathbed in his mid-sixties; Marcel Duchamp, considered by many art professionals to be the greatest artist of the twentieth century, was productive right up to his death in his eighty-first year (Simonton, 1990; Pritikin, 1990); and heartthrob actor Paul Newman received an Academy Award nomination for Best Actor for the 1994 movie, *Nobody's Fool,* in his seventieth year.

These are individuals whose quality of achievement was not diminished by age. This myth is part of the conventional view that aging brings with it a decline in intelligence, memory, learning, and creativity. Yet, empirical evidence shows that these relationships are quite complex, and decline is anything but inevitable. Age-related changes in learning ability appear to be quite small, even after the keenness of the senses has begun to decline. Similarly, although creativity seems to peak in the forties, the age-related decline thereafter is such that creators in their sixties and seventies will still be generating new ideas at a rate exceeding their rate in their twenties (Dennis, 1966). Memory and learning are functions of the central nervous system. Thus, when there is impairment, it is often due to some disease (e.g., arteriosclerosis) or an associated condition; one should not assume that some typical process of normal aging is at work.

MYTH 2: Most Old People Are Alone and Isolated from Their Families

Research on the history of family relations in the United States and Europe has contradicted myths about a so-called Golden Age in the family relations of older people in days past. Apparently, those extended families (three or more generations living together) that have become part of the folklore of modern society rarely existed in the past (Laslett, 1977). Historical research has similarly dispelled the myth of the contemporary American nuclear family isolated from adult children and other kin. Nuclear family members continue to maintain strong traditional and reciprocal relations, and the expectation that family and kin carry the major responsibilities for the care of aged relatives is still strong in the United States. However, there is growing concern that families do not have the necessary supports available to discharge these responsibilities (Litwak, 1985).

As Hareven (1994) asserts, the family has ceased to be the only available source of support for dependent members. Starting in the nineteenth century and continuing through the twentieth century, the family has surrendered to the public sector functions of social welfare it previously controlled. Increasingly, there are ambiguities about who exactly provides what for the elderly.

> On the one hand, family members assume that the public sector carries the major responsibilities of care for the aged; on the other hand, the public sector assumes that the family is responsible for the major supports. This confusion in the assignment of responsibilities often means that old people are caught between the family and the public sector without receiving proper supports from either. (Hareven, 1994, p. 456)

Compounding these ambiguities is a revolution in the demography of intergenerational family life, with individuals growing older in more diverse familial settings than ever before (Bengtson, Rosenthal, & Burton, 1990). Shanas (1980) estimates that about 50 percent of people over age 65 are members of four-generation families, and Hagestad (1988) reports that 20 percent of women who died after the age of 80 were great-great-grandmothers, members of five-generation families.

Changes in the configurations of families have also resulted from increases in divorce and remarriage. As Furstenberg (1981) points out, however, divorce has not necessarily reduced the extent or strength of ties between older family members and kin. Ties with grandparents do survive divorce, especially when the grandparents have had close contact with the grandchildren before divorce. Also, with remarriage, the kinship pool expands with the addition of new relatives, without the relinquishment of existing ones (Furstenberg, 1981).

Most older people live near, but not with, their children and interact with them frequently. And most older people prefer it this way. Assistance in the form of goods and services, as well as financial aid, flows both from adult children to their parents and from the parents to their children. Grandparents and older family members may provide care for young children within the extended family network, and adult children may act as caregivers to parents and other relatives with chronic illnesses and/or cognitive deficits.

Despite the commitment to independent living in nuclear households, in virtually all ethnic and racial groups, these households expand to include other kin in times of need, especially when older parents and widowed mothers are unable to maintain themselves in separate households (Hareven, 1994). In the National Survey of Families and Households, only 7 percent of Americans aged 55 and older with a surviving parent reported that the parent was living with them at the time of the survey, yet about one in four of those in their late fifties had an aged parent live with them for some time in their lives (Hogan, Eggebeen, & Snaith, 1994). Pelham and Clark (1987) state that Hispanic and Asian widows are more likely to be living with other family members than white and African American widows. The large household size and larger number of offspring among Hispanic widows suggests that they may have more active support systems than do other racial and ethnic groups.

MYTH 3: The Majority of Old People Are in Poor Health

I recently asked a group of third-year medical students what proportion of older people they believed were sick and institutionalized. The consensus was that more than half the older population are in ill health, and perhaps half of that population (25 percent of the total) are in institutions. *This simply is not the case.* These answers reflected the fact that in their clinical experiences, these medical students come into contact with only sick and disabled elderly persons.

The majority of older people do *not* have the kinds of health problems that limit their ability to be employed or manage their own households. Only about 5 percent of those age 65 and over can be found in an old-age institution on a given day. Data from the National Health Interview Surveys, conducted annually by the National Center for Health Statistics to assess the health status and needs of the noninstitutionalized population in the United States, consistently show about two-thirds of those 65 years of age and older reporting their health status in positive terms (good, very good, or excellent); about one-third report themselves as being in fair or poor health (Cohen, Van Nostrand, & Furner, 1993). Although the

Most older people are healthy and have few limitations in activities.

proportion of older adults who rate their health in positive terms seems to decline with age, more than 60 percent of the oldest-old (those 85 years of age and over) continue to evaluate their health status positively.

Self-assessment of health status is one important measure of the health status of a population; another is how that population is functioning. Wiener and associates (1990) explain that across 11 different national surveys, 5 to 8 percent of community-dwelling elderly receive help in one or more of the activities of daily living (ADLs): bathing, dressing, moving out of beds and chairs, toileting, and eating. Hing and Bloom (1990) define *functional dependency* as needing help in at least one of seven ADLs or one of seven instrumental activities of daily living (IADLs). IADLs include preparing meals, shopping, managing money, using the telephone, getting outside, and doing light or heavy housework. Under this definition, Hing and Bloom estimate 6.7 million elderly, or less than one in four, are functionally dependent. Functional dependencies are more prevalent among women than men, among African Americans and Hispanics than whites, and increase with age. Still, what is clear is that the vast majority of individuals 65 years of age and older live independently in the community with no functional dependencies!

MYTH 4: Old People Are More Likely than Younger People to Be Victimized by Crime

Concerns about crimes against elderly Americans are quite high—especially among elderly Americans themselves. Many surveys show that old persons are more fearful of crime than younger persons. This concern appears to stem from the popular belief that elderly persons are victimized more often than others and suffer more serious consequences as a result. Yet, no evidence supports this belief.

National and local surveys show that the elderly are actually *less* likely to be victimized than are younger persons, in all crime categories. Data from the National Crime Survey for 1992, for example, show that when compared with rates of victimization against person 12 years old and over, the elderly have lower rates of victimization in all categories of crime (U.S. Bureau of the Census, 1995, Table 318). Further, differences in rates of victimization of the elderly and the general population are so great that even factoring in substantial underreporting by older people does not equalize the rates of victimization. For example, the rate of victimization of the elderly by robbery was only about one-quarter that for the total 12-year-old and over population in 1992. The elderly were victimized by larceny theft at a rate only 28 percent of that for the total population in 1992.

Despite these comparisons of rates of actual criminal victimization between the elderly and the general population, there is no getting away from the fact that many older people are fearful of crime. For some, this fear is so great that they can be described as living under virtual house arrest. And, for certain subgroups of elderly people, there is some reality to these fears. Many urban aged persons, including minority elderly, live in central-city neighborhoods where the crime rate is high. Many of these same elderly persons live alone and rely on public transportation, which makes them available for victimization. Add reduced strength and diminished vision to the equation, and it is easy to understand why some elderly people feel particularly vulnerable to crime, even though the national crime data suggest such fears are disproportionate to the reported levels of victimization.

MYTH 5: The Majority of Old People Live in Poverty

It used to be easy to write about the economic problems of the old. The situation today, though more complex, is much improved. For example, in 1992, while 12.9 percent of those 65 years of age and older in the United States had incomes below the poverty threshold, 14.5 percent of the total U.S. civilian noninstitutionalized population could be similarly characterized. Many private and public programs have been developed in recent decades to deal with the economic problems of old age. According to Schulz (1995), these programs include the following:

1. There have been substantial increases in Social Security old-age benefits in the recent years—a faster rate of climb than inflation in the same period.
2. Private pension plans have spread widely and grown rapidly, with increased benefit levels.
3. Public health insurance and nutrition programs have been created.
4. Property tax and other tax-relief laws have been legislated in virtually all states.
5. The Supplemental Security Income (SSI) Program, which now covers more than twice as many low-income elderly as did the now abolished-old age assistance plan, has raised benefit levels above previous levels of old-age assistance.

However, there are subgroups among the elderly who continue to show relatively high rates of impoverishment. More than one in four (26.8 percent) elderly women living alone or with nonrelatives had income below the poverty threshold in 1992.

Part of the complexity in analyzing the economic situation of the aged stems from the fact that they receive money income from so many available sources. Wages and salaries, retirement benefits, veterans' benefits, unemployment insurance, worker's compensation, public assistance, dividends, interest, rents, royalties, private pensions, and annuities are only some of their sources of money income. In recent years, the composition of total income of the elderly has shifted slightly toward earnings and pensions and away from property income and Social Security benefits (Radner, 1991). Approximately three out of four aged Americans own homes, and most have substantial equity in these homes. Finally, the elderly receive indirect or in-kind income in the form of goods and services that they obtain free or at reduced cost. Medicare, food stamps, and housing subsidies are examples of programs that provide in-kind benefits to older people.

MYTH 6: Old People Tend to Become
More Religious as They Age

Religion serves a variety of functions in human societies. It defines the spiritual world and provides explanations for events and occurrences that are difficult to comprehend. Further, it helps integrate people into the broader community in at least two ways. First, institutionally based religious services provide a physical meeting ground for unattached and disaffiliated people. Second, religious ideas arise out of the collective experience of individuals. As a result, the content of religious belief systems expresses a vision of a shared fate of believers, a community of individuals with otherwise diverse interests and aspirations. Thus, religion functions both to maintain social control and to provide social support in times of need.

Do these functions change over time, as individuals and their families age and move through individual and family developmental periods? Bahr (1970) suggests that the relationship between aging and religiosity be interpreted with reference to four distinct models: traditional, lifetime stability, family life cycle, and progressive disengagement. Much research supports the lifetime stability model (Levin, 1989). On the one hand, findings suggest that *organizational* religious involvement, such as attendance at religious services, is stable over the life course, with some slight decline at advanced ages, especially among those who are disabled. On the other hand, indicators of *nonorganizational* religious involvement, such as watching religious television shows or praying at home, remain stable as people age, with some slight chance of increase among the very old and disabled to offset declines in organizational involvement.

MYTH 7: Older Workers Are Less
Productive Than Younger Ones

This myth, based on misconceptions about the aging process and the employment of older people, is often raised by proponents of mandatory retirement. The argument assumes that older persons, as a group, may be less well suited for work than younger workers because older people do not learn new skills as well as younger persons do, older workers are less flexible with respect to changes in work schedules and regimens, and declining physical and mental capacity are found in greater proportion among older persons.

These arguments are not based on fact. Many studies indicate that older workers produce a quality of work that is as good as or better than that of younger workers. In addition, older workers bring significant benefits to the workplace, including flexibility in scheduling, low absenteeism, high motivation, and mentoring of younger workers. There is no reason to expect a decline in intellectual capacities with age and every reason to assume that older workers in good health are capable of learning new skills when circumstances require it.

Still, the employment situation of older Americans is quite varied (Quinn & Burkhauser, 1990). Since 1950, when nearly half of all men aged 65 and over were in the labor force, the rates of labor-force participation have decreased dramatically. Today, only about 17 percent of older men are in the labor force. The trends for older women are less dramatic, with little change evident in work force participation over the past two decades. Those elderly people who do work are likely to work part time, and the proportion of the elderly working part time has increased over the last 20 years to almost 50 percent of men and 60 percent of women. Those elderly people still in the labor force are three times more likely to be self-employed than is the general population, and almost twice as likely as those aged 55 to 64. A recent study suggests that the official counts greatly underestimate the actual number of self-employed elderly persons (Haber, Lamas, & Lichtenstein, 1987).

Interestingly, the declining birth rate (discussed in Chapter 3) will mean a proportionately smaller labor force supporting a larger retiree population early in the next century. The potentially problematic economics of this situation could be alleviated by inducing older workers to *remain* in the labor force and retirees to *return* to the workplace. According to one study, reported on in *Working Age,* a newsletter published by the American Association of Retired Persons (AARP), less than 10 percent of U.S. companies have formal hiring policies or programs to recruit retirees to return to the workplace. Nevertheless, as recently as 1991, 46 percent of U.S. businesses reported employing retirees. Most of these people had retired from other firms (AARP, 1993).

Obstacles to change in the labor-force participation rates of the elderly remain great, however. Jondrow, Brechling, and Marcus (1987) argue that many, perhaps most, workers would like to retire gradually. Most do not because they cannot. Part-time wage rates are generally much lower than full-time compensation, and only a small minority of firms permit phased retirement.

MYTH 8: Old People Who Retire Usually Suffer a Decline in Health and Early Death

It is widely held that retirement has an adverse affect on health. Most people have heard at least one story about a retiree who "went downhill fast." The way the story usually goes is that the individual carefully plans for retirement, only to become sick and die within a brief period of time—and the story is the same regardless of whether the retirement is mandatory or voluntary.

One problem with such stories is that they are never clear what the health status of the retiree was before retirement. Another problem is that most retirees themselves are older, and although the majority of old people do not have major health problems, it is true that older people have a greater risk of illness than younger people do. In a well-known study, *Retirement in American Society,* Streib and Schneider (1971) conclude that retired people are no more likely to be sick than are people of the same age who are still on the job. That is, *health declines appear to be associated with age, not with retirement!* In fact, as some researchers have pointed out, unskilled workers and others who work in harsh environments and in high-risk occupations may show *improvements* in health following retirement.

MYTH 9: Most Old People Have No Interest in, or Capacity for, Sexual Relations

Sexual interests, capacities, and functions change with age. Nevertheless, older men and women in reasonably good health can have active and satisfying sex lives. Verwoerdt and colleagues (1969a, 1969b) at Duke University studied 254 men and women ranging from 60 to 94 years of age and found no age-related decline in the incidence of sexual interest. In fact, interest may persist indefinitely. Most important, these researchers found that sexual behavior patterns of the later years correlate with those of the younger years. If there was interest and satisfying activity in the early years, there is likely to be continuing interest and satisfying activity in the later years as well.

Some decline in sexual activity among the old is due to old people's acceptance of stereotypes about the sexless older years. Elderly people may feel shame and embarrassment about having sexual interests. Further, some older people relate normal changes in sexual functioning and impotence, and so avoid sexual opportunities because they fear failure. Fulton (1988) suggests that some responsibility for acceptance of sexuality among the aged must rest with those in the helping professions. As he indicates, "Support and encouragement of sexual behavior should be given without embarrassment or evangelization" (p. 282).

Older people need not duplicate the sexual behavior of youth in order to enjoy their sexual experiences. Sex is qualitatively different in the later years. Sexual activity in the elderly may fulfill the human need for the warmth of physical closeness and the intimacy of companionship. Older people should be encouraged to seek this fulfillment.

MYTH 10: Most Old People End Up in Nursing Homes and Other Long-Term Care Institutions

Most old people do *not* end up in nursing homes. The 1990 U.S. Census reports about 5 percent of the elderly population residing in old-age institutions of one kind or another. Still, this does not mean that the odds of being institutionalized are 1 in 20. The Census only gives a picture of the institutional population at one point in time.

In 1976, Palmore (1976) of Duke University reviewed the cases of 207 individuals from the Piedmont, North Carolina, area who were studied in the Duke First Longitudinal Study of Aging beginning in 1955 until their deaths prior to the spring of 1976. He observed that 54 of the 207 persons, or 26 percent, had been institutionalized in some type of extended-care facility one or more times before death. On the basis of this and other findings, Palmore concluded that, among normal elderly persons living in the community, the chance of institutionalization before death would be about one in four. Other researchers, using different populations and different methods, have substantiated these findings. This suggests that three in four aged persons have no reason to view a nursing home stay as inevitable.

SUMMARY

This brief chapter opened with a look at the legendary Tithonus, an unfortunate man who suffered the infirmities of old age endlessly. Actually, this myth appears in the middle of a Homeric hymn describing an adventure of Aphrodite, the goddess of Love (Evelyn-White, 1936). It seems that Aphrodite had considerable power over other gods. She was often able to beguile them into mating with mere mortals, an act considered demeaning. To temper her arrogance, Zeus managed to infect her with desire for Anchises, a handsome Trojan (and a mortal himself).

Aphrodite arranged a rendezvous with Anchises, but after the lovemaking, Anchises, concerned about his ability to sustain a love affair with the goddess, begged Aphrodite to do something to preserve his good health. At first, Aphrodite seemed sympathetic to Anchises, but then she recounted to him the legend of Tithonus. She emphasized that she would not want Anchises to be deathless if he had to suffer the fate of Tithonus. Unwilling to grant him "youthful immortality," Aphrodite finally turned down Anchises's request with these words: "But as it is, harsh old age will soon enshroud you— ruthless old age which stands someday at the side of every man, deadly, wearying, dreaded even by the gods" (cited in Evelyn-White, 1936).

Although most people in U.S. society *do* live to experience old age (about 79 percent of those born today can expect to reach age 65; almost 71 percent can expect to reach age 70), not many expect to endure as Tithonus has. And although some in the United States do experience the harsh and ruthless old age that Aphrodite described for Anchises, many do not. Further, the debunking of prevalent myths about aging and the aged does not require that old people reflect the mirror opposite of ageism: Old people do not have to be intellectually gifted, happy, wealthy, and sexually active. Rather, the myths of aging discussed here simply suggest the diversity of aging experiences represented in society. The rest of this book explores the biological, psychological, and social factors that contribute to this wide range in the experience of old age.

STUDY QUESTIONS

1. Is the myth of Tithonus relevant to aging in contemporary society? How so?

2. Define the term *ageism*. What are its origins and how is it perpetuated today? Does television play a special role in maintaining myths about the aged? Why or why not? Does television have a role in combatting these myths? How so?

3. Why do gerontologists argue that senility is not an inevitable part of the aging process?

4. A common misconception is that most old people are alone and isolated from their families. Present evidence to the contrary.

5. What is the health status of people 65 years of age and older in the United States? Discuss this in terms of their ability to work and carry out other daily activities, their risks of being institutionalized, and their capacity for sexual relations.

6. Why has analyzing the economic position of older people become so complex? What has occurred in recent decades to improve the economic position of older people relative to the population as a whole?

REFERENCES

Aday, R. H., Sims, C. R., & Evans, E. (1991). Youth's attitudes toward the elderly: The impact of intergenerational partners. *Journal of Applied Gerontology, 10* (3), 372–384.

American Association of Retired Persons. (1993). Small businesses hire retirees. *Working Age, 9* (3), 2.

Austin, D. R. (1985). Attitudes toward old age: A hierarchical study. *Gerontologist, 25* (4), 431–434.

Bahr, H. (1970). Aging and religious disaffiliation. *Social Forces, 49,* 59–71.

Bell, J. (1992). In search of discourse on aging: The elderly on television. *Gerontologist, 32* (3), 305–311.

Bengtson, V., Rosenthal, C., & Burton, L. (1990). Families and aging: Diversity and heterogeneity. In R. H. Binstock & L. K. George (Eds.), *Handbook of aging and the social sciences,* 3rd ed. San Diego, CA: Academic Press.

Binstock, R. H. (1983). The aged as scapegoat. *Gerontologist, 23* (2), 136–143.

Buchholz, M., & Bynum, J. E. (1982). Newspaper presentation of America's aged: A content analysis of image and role. *Gerontologist, 22* (1), 83–88.

Butler, R. (1975). *Why survive? Being old in America.* New York: Harper & Row.

Butler, R. (1987). Ageism. In G. Maddox (Ed.), *The encyclopedia of aging.* New York: Springer.

Chinen, A. B. (1987). Fairy tales and psychological development in late life: A cross-cultural hermeneutic study. *Gerontologist, 27* (3), 340–352.

Cohen, E. S., & Kruschwitz, A. L. (1990). Old age in America represented in nineteenth and twentieth century popular sheet music. *Gerontologist, 30* (3), 345–354.

Cohen, R. A., Van Nostrand, J. F., & Furner, S. E. (1993). *Health data on older Americans, 1992.* DHHS Pub. No. (PHS)93-1413. Hyattsville, MD: National Center for Health Statistics.

Cole, T. R. (1983). The "enlightened" view of aging: Victorian morality in a new key. *Hastings Center Report, 13* (3), 34–40.

Corbin, D. E., Kagan, D. M., & Metil-Corbin, J. (1987). Content analysis of an intergenerational unit in aging in a sixth grade classroom. *Educational Gerontology, 13,* 403–410.

Covey, H. C. (1991). Old age and historical examples of the miser. *Gerontologist, 31* (5), 673–678.

Davis, R., & Davis, J. (1985). *TV's image of the elderly.* Lexington, MA: Lexington Books.

Dennis, W. (1966). Creative productivity between the ages of 20 and 80 years. *Journal of Gerontology, 21,* 1–8.

Evelyn-White, H. G. (1936). *Hesiod, The Homeric hymns and Homerica.* London: William Heinemann.

Fernandez-Pereiro, A., & Snachez-Ayendez, M. (1992). LinkAges: Building bridges between children and the elderly. *Ageing International, 19* (2), 10–14.

Ferraro, K. F. (1992). Self and older-people referents in evaluating life problems. *Journal of Gerontology, 47* (3), S105-114.

Fischer, D. H. (1977). *Growing old in America.* New York: Oxford University Press.

Fulton, G. B. (1988). Sexuality in later life. In C. S. Kart, E. K. Metress, & S. P. Metress. *Aging, health and society.* Boston: Jones and Bartlett.

Furstenberg, F. F., Jr. (1981). Remarriage and intergenerational relations. In R. W. Fogle et al. (Eds.), *Aging: Stability and change in the family.* New York: Academic.

Haber, S. E., Lamas, E. J., & Lichtenstein, J. H. (1987). On their own: The self-employed and others in private business. *Monthly Labor Review, 72,* 716–724.

Hagestad, G. O. (1988). Demographic change and the life course: Some emerging trends in the family realm. *Family Relations, 37,* 405–410.

Hamilton, E. (1942). *Mythology.* Boston: Little, Brown.

Hareven, T. (1994). Aging and generational relations: A historical and life course perspective. In J. Hagan & K. S. Cook (Eds.), *Annual review of sociology* (Vol. 20). Palo Alto, CA: Annual Reviews.

Hing, E., & Bloom, B. (1990). *Long-term care for the functionally dependent elderly.* Vital and Health Statistics, Series 13, No. 104, DHHS Pub. No. (PHS)90–1765. Hyattsville, MD: Public Health Service.

Hogan, D. P., Eggebeen, D. J. & Snaith, S. M. (1994). The well-being of aging Americans with very old parents. In T. K. Hareven (Ed.), *Aging and generational relations over the life course: A historical and cross-cultural perspective.* Berlin: Walter de Gruyter.

Holstein, M. (1994). Taking next steps: Gerontological education, research, and the literary imagination. *Gerontologist 34* (6), 822–827.

Holtzman, J. M., & Akiyama, H. (1985). What children see: The aged on television in Japan and the United States. *Gerontologist, 25* (1), 62–67.

Jondrow, J., Brechling, F., & Marcus, A. (1987). Older workers in the market for part-time employment. In S. H. Sandell (Ed.), *The problem isn't age: Work and older Americans.* New York: Praeger.

Kubey, R. (1980). Television and aging: Past, present, and future. *Gerontologist, 20,* 16–35.

Laslett, P. (1977). *Family life and illicit love in earlier generations.* Cambridge, England: Cambridge University Press.

Laws, G. (1995). Understanding ageism: Lessons from feminism and postmodernism. *Gerontologist, 35,* 112–118.

Levin, J. S. (1989). Religious factors in aging, adjustment and health: A theoretical review. In W. M. Clements (Ed.), *Religion, aging and health.* New York: Haworth (for the World Health Organization).

Levin, J., & Levin, W. C. (1980). *Prejudice and discrimination against the elderly.* Belmont, CA: Wadsworth.

Litwak, E. (1985). *Helping the elderly: The complementary roles of informal networks and formal systems.* New York: Guilford.

McLerran, J. (1993). Saved by the hand that is not stretched out: The aged poor in Hubert von Hurkomer's *Eventide: A Scene in the Westminster Union. Gerontologist, 33* (6), 762–771.

Palmore, E. (1976). Total chance of institutionalization among the aged. *Gerontologist, 16,* 504–507.

Passuth, P. M., & Cook, F. L. (1985). Effects of television viewing on knowledge and attitudes about older people: A critical reexamination. *Gerontologist, 25* (1), 69–77.

Pelham, A. O., & Clark, W. F. (1987). Widowhood among low income racial and ethnic groups in California. In H. Lopata (Ed.), *Widows, Vol. 2: North America.* Durham, NC: Duke University Press.

Peterson, D. A., & Karnes, E. L. (1976). Older people in adolescent literature. *Gerontologist, 16,* 225–231.

Pritikin, R. (1990). Marcel Duchamp, the artist, and the social expectations of aging. *Gerontologist, 30* (5), 636–639.

Quinn, J. F., & Burkhauser, R. V. (1990). Work and retirement. In R. H. Binstock & L. K. George (Eds.), *Handbook of aging and the social sciences* (3rd ed.). San Diego, CA: Academic Press.

Radner, D. (1991). Changes in incomes of age groups, 1984–89. *Social Security Bulletin, 54* (12), 2–28.

Robin, E. P. (1977). Old age in elementary school readers. *Educational Gerontology, 2,* 275–292.

Schulz, J. H. (1995). *The economics of aging* (5th ed.). Westport, CT: Auburn House.

Shanas, E. (1980). Older people and their families: The new pioneers. *Journal of Marriage and the Family, 42,* 9–15.

Simonton, D. K. (1990). Creativity in the later years: Optimistic prospects for achievement. *Gerontologist, 30* (5), 626–631.

Smith, M. C. (1976). Portrayal of elders in prescription drug advertising: A pilot study. *Gerontologist, 16,* 329–334.

Sohngen, M., & Smith, R. J. (1978). Images of old age in poetry. *Gerontologist, 18,* 181–186.

Steffl, B. M. (1978). Gerontology in professional and pre-professional curricula. In M. Seltzer, H. Sterns, & T. Hickey (Eds.), *Gerontology in higher education: Perspectives and issues.* Belmont, CA: Wadsworth.

Streib, G., & Schneider, C. (1971). *Retirement in American society.* Ithaca, NY: Cornell University Press.

Tibbitts, C. (1979). Can we invalidate negative stereotypes of aging? *Gerontologist, 19* (1), 10–20.

U.S. Bureau of the Census. (1995). *Statistical abstract of the United States: 1995* (115th ed.). Washington, DC: U.S. Government Printing Office.

U.S. House of Representatives, Committee on the Budget. 1986. *President Reagan's fiscal year 1987 budget.* Washington, DC: U.S. Government Printing Office.

Verwoerdt, A., Pfeiffer, E., & Wang, H. S. (1969a). Sexual behavior in senescence. I. *Journal of Geriatric Psychiatry, 2,* 163–180.

Verwoerdt, A., Pfeiffer, E., & Wang, H. S. (1969b). Sexual behavior in senescence. II. *Geriatrics, 24,* 137–154.

Villers Foundation. (1987). *On the other side of easy street: Myths and facts about the economics of old age.* Washington, DC: Author.

Wiener, J. M., Hanley, R. J., Clark, R., & Van Nostrand, J. F. (1990). Measuring the activities of daily living: Comparisons across national surveys. *Journals of Gerontology: Social Sciences, 45* (6), S229–237.

CHAPTER 2

THE STUDY OF AGING

Concerns about aging and death are found in the written and oral records of societies dating back many thousands of years. One of the most prominent themes reflects the belief that extended life is neither possible nor desirable; another, by contrast, refers to the desirability of attempting to lengthen life (Gruman, 1966). Clearly, the latter has been the most prevalent throughout history.

Three different themes represent the quest for the prolongation of life. The *antediluvian theme*—the belief that in the past, people lived much longer—is best exemplified in the book of Genesis, which records the life spans of 10 Hebrew patriarchs who lived before the Flood. Noah lived for 950 years, Methuselah for 969 years, Adam for 930 years, and so on. The *hyperborean theme* involves the idea that in some remote part of the world there are people who enjoy remarkably long lives. According to the traditions of ancient Greece, a people live *hyper Boreas* ("beyond the north wind"): "Their hair crowned with golden bay-leaves they hold glad revelry; and neither sickness nor baneful eld mingleth among the chosen people; but, aloof from toil and conflict, they dwell afar" (Pindar in Gruman, 1966, p. 22).

Finally, the *fountain theme* is based on the idea that there is some unusual substance that has the property of greatly increasing the length of life (Gruman, 1966). The search for the Fountain of Youth in 1513 by Juan Ponce de Leon (who accidentally discovered Florida instead) is a good example of this rejuvenation theme. According to the earliest account of Ponce de Leon's adventure, published by a Spanish official in the New World in 1535, the explorer was "seeking that fountain of Biminie that the Indians had given to be understood would renovate or resprout and refresh the age and forces of he who drank or bathed himself in that fountain" (Lawson, 1946, in Gruman, 1966).

These themes remain current. The fascination with reportedly long-lived peoples such as the Abkhasians of the Georgian Republic of Russia (see Chapter 5) reflects a modern-day hyperborean theme. Similarly, any student of U.S. billboard and television advertising will recognize the fountain theme. Skin creams, hair colorings, body soaps, foods, and vitamins are all depicted as unusual substances that one may use to remain eternally young.

The persistence of these themes suggests that throughout history and up to the present it has been difficult to distinguish between myth and history, between magic and science. The development of the systematic study of aging can be seen in this light, for it is these very distinctions that it attempts to make clear.

WHY STUDY AGING?

Why study aging? At first, the question may seem odd, but that is because individuals are so rarely asked to explain why they chose to work in a particular substantive area or why they chose one discipline over another (e.g., gerontology instead of demography). The answer comes in five parts.

1. Despite what has been written about the long history of aging, aging itself is a relatively new phenomenon. Never before have so many people lived to be old. Historian Ronald Blythe (1979) suggests that if a Renaissance or Georgian man could return, he would be just as astonished by the sight of so many elderly people as he would be by a television set. In his world, it was the exception to go gray, to retire, to grow old. Today, this process is ordinary, but that does not make it any less novel. This is a real-life experiment of sorts. As Blythe points out, these "are the first generations of the full-timers and thus the first generations of old people for whom the state . . . is having to make special supportive conditions." The novelty, the experimentation, and the uncertainty all make gerontology an exciting field today, and that excitement has drawn many people to the study of aging.

2. Students of gerontology have come to view aging as a lifelong process in which humans and all other living things participate. From this perspective, aging is seen as ongoing, starting at conception and ending with death. Aging is not reserved for senior citizens or Golden Agers; it is shared by infants, children, teenagers, and young adults, as well as the more mature. It occupies the total life span, not merely the final stage of life. Without knowledge and understanding of the entire life span, it is difficult to understand the events of any one life phase. In this sense, one studies the aged to learn not only about the final phase of life but also about youth and the middle years.

3. Maddox (1979) indicates that many sociologists, psychologists, and others have begun to study aging because they see the later years as a strategic site for examining a wide range of scientific issues of fundamental importance in their disciplines. Examples of these issues include status maintenance (Henratta & Campbell, 1976), role multiplicity (Moen, Dempster-McClain & Williams, 1992), and social support (Hogan & Eggebeen, 1995).

4. Another reason to study aging simply has to do with the dramatic increase in interest in the problems of old people in the United States. Although it has been said sardonically that people admire aging only in bottles, in recent decades, as more people have encountered old age, many elaborate programs have been promoted and financed on behalf of elderly citizens. One reason for the promotion of these governmental and nongovernmental programs is that the situation of the elderly has come to be defined by many as the responsibility of society as a whole. The burden of this responsibility is reason enough for studying the aged. Only by knowing more about elderly people and the difficulties and changes they face can society really come to grips with its problems.

5. Different matters hold intrinsic fascination for different scientists. This may explain, in part, why some choose the field of gerontology. I find the study of aging intrinsically exciting and interesting. For me, as for many others, one answer to the question "Why study aging?" is "Because the study of aging can become an end in itself."

DEFINING THE FIELD

Gerontology is the term used to describe "the study of aging from the broadest perspective" (National Institute on Aging, 1986). Though gerontology may include the study of aging in plants and animals below humans on the evolutionary scale, the term generally refers to the study of later adulthood among humans.

Gerontology is an interdisciplinary study. Its major elements are drawn from the physical and social sciences, although the humanities and arts, business, and education are also represented in the content of gerontology. In 1954, Clark Tibbitts, a pioneer in the modern scientific era of gerontology, introduced the term *social gerontology* to describe the study of the impact of social and sociocultural factors on the aging process. Tibbitts and others recognized that aging does not occur in a vacuum. Rather, the aging process occurs in some social context—a social context that helps determine the meaning of aging as both an individual and a societal experience. Gerontology is not only an academic discipline, it is also a field of practice that involves aspects of public policy and human service. In 1909, a Vienna-born physician, I. L. Nascher, coined the term *geriatrics* to describe one subfield of gerontological practice: the medical care of the aging.

The student of aging faces three main tasks: theoretical, methodological, and applied (Bromley, 1974). The *theoretical* task involves confirming and extending the conceptual frameworks that explain the observed facts of aging. The *methodological* task involves developing suitable methods of research for examining the nature of aging. The *applied* task involves attempts to prevent or reduce the adverse effects of aging. Some gerontologists specialize in one or another task area; others find it difficult to separate theory, research, and practice. Gerontology is not a disinterested science. For many gerontologists, apparently, understanding the aging process is not enough. They must also address the practical and immediate problems of old people.

Gerontology is a complex field, encompassing a wide variety of substantive areas of study—health, family life, political economy, and retirement, among others. Yet, there are no dominant paradigms in the broader field; and standardization of measurement, a common conceptualization of issues, and systematic testing of hypotheses derived from theory are often lacking (Maddox & Wiley, 1976). As Maddox and Wiley point out, applied, problem-oriented studies of the societal consequences of aging have dominated the field. This book reflects these facts. It attempts to introduce undergraduate and beginning graduate students to the major concepts and issues in the field of gerontology. In doing so, however, this text recognizes the current state of affairs in gerontology. It recognizes, first, the importance of making the connection between basic and applied research without downplaying the role applied research has played in the development of gerontology or the need for additional research at a basic level. Second, it recognizes the need to bring diverse disciplinary and interdisciplinary approaches to the study of aging.

THE HISTORY OF AGING

The study of aging is now considered to be scientific. As has been seen, however, particular nonscientific themes in concepts of human aging have persisted with some consistency through the prescientific and into the scientific era. This is especially clear when one looks at the imagery in discussions of the causes of aging. Bromley (1974) summarizes this imagery in three categories. In the first, the body is a container full of some essential substance or spirit. This substance is gradually depleted or destroyed, leading to diminished capacities and increased vulnerability to disease and death. In the second image, aging represents a conflict within each person between positive and negative forces. Eventually, the negative forces of evil, disease, corruption, and the like prevail. Finally, aging is seen as symbolizing a process of renewal of life. Like the seed within the dry decaying shell, or the reptile that sheds its outer skin, aging represents the casting off of one's "mortal coil" in preparation for life after death.

The astute reader of this brief history will recognize these images in theories of aging from Greco-Roman medicine to modern times. The similarity of imagery employed by different theorists at different times reflects the enormous difficulty involved in conceptualizing human aging—for example, in distinguishing between aging as a cause and aging as an effect (Bromley, 1974). The careful reader may also conclude that much of what passes for new knowledge in gerontology today is not new at all but rather is the result of a systematizing and "scientizing" of ideas that have been in circulation for a long time.

Greece and Rome

In the Western world, the first full explicit theory of the causation of aging is found in Greco-Roman medicine and the Hippocratic theory (about the fourth century B.C.) (Grant, 1963). According to the Hippocratic theory, the essential factor in life is heat. At that time, the common belief was that individuals have a fixed quantity of some life force. This material, characterized by Hippocrates as "innate heat," is used up during the course of a lifetime, although the rate of utilization varies with the individual. In general, old age was equated with a continuous diminishing of innate heat, and aging was seen as a consequence of a natural course of events. The latter point in itself constitutes a remarkable breakthrough, because many writers of the time confused the aging process with diseases in the old.

About a century after Hippocrates, Aristotle expanded on the "innate heat" theory of aging in his book *On Youth and Old Age, On Life and Death and On Respiration.* Aristotle likened the heat to a fire that had to be maintained and provided with fuel. Just as a fire could run out of fuel or be put out, innate heat could also be exhausted (as in the case of a natural death due to aging) or extinguished (as in a death due to violence or disease). The contributions of Greek philosophers reached their peak with Galen (circa A.D. 130–200), who clearly differentiated between aging and dying and who was perhaps the first to characterize aging as a process beginning with conception (Grant, 1963). To Aristotle's innate heat, Galen added the elements of blood and semen. Blood and semen were sources of generation; drying in the form of heat produced the tissues.

> By this means, then, the embryo is first formed and takes on a little firmness; and after this, drying more, acquires the outlines and faint patterns of each of its parts. Then, drying even more, it assumes not merely their outlines and patterns, but their exact appearance. And now, having been brought forth, it keeps growing larger and drier and stronger, until it reaches full development. Then all growth ceases, the bones elongating no more on account of their dryness, and every vessel increases in width, and thus all the parts become strong and attain their maximum power.
>
> But in ensuing time, as all the organs become even drier, not only are their functions performed less well but their vitality becomes more feeble and restricted. And drying more, the creature becomes not only thinner but also wrinkled, and the limbs weak and unsteady in their movements. This condition is called old age.... This, then, is one innate destiny of destruction for every mortal creature....
>
> These processes, then, it is permitted no mortal body to escape; but others, which ensure, it is possible for the forethoughtful to avoid. Moreover, the source of these is from attempting to correct the aforesaid inevitable processes. (Grant, 1963)

It is interesting that, for Galen, the very element that appears to bring life (drying) leads quite naturally (and unequivocally) to its end.

The attitude of the Greeks expressed their ambivalence toward aging. They emphasized family love and the wisdom of age, but they also recognized the weaknesses and eccentricities of the aged (Bromley, 1974). Aristotle condemned old age and presented youth and old age as opposites. He characterized youth as a time of excess and later life as a time of conservativeness and small-mindedness (Hendricks & Hendricks, 1977). Plato had a somewhat positive view of old age. In *The Republic,* he referred to two important features of late life: the persistence of characteristics from earlier life and the relief of having outgrown some of life's difficulties (including frustrated ambition and unfulfilled sexual desire).

Cicero (106–43 B.C.), in his *De Senectute,* has become a favorite source for contemporary writers on aging. Nevertheless, as Bromley points out, he was typical of his day. Although Cicero recognized that advanced age brought biological degeneration, he emphasized the relationship between aging and development, including the continuing capacity for psychological growth, and placed great value on experience accumulated over time. In fact, Cicero recommended intellectual activity as part of a regimen to resist premature aging.

The Greek influence persisted. Freeman, a noted historian of aging, writes of the physician Villanova and the Franciscan friar Roger Bacon, thirteenth-century experts on aging, who essentially "followed the Galenic thought that aging was due to the loss of innate heat" (1965). In many respects, however, Bacon was a precursor of the scientific era to come. He argued that three factors tended to hasten the diminution of heat: infection, negligence, and ignorance of matters related to health. He proposed a method of hygiene that would allow men and women to achieve their rightful term of years in good health.

The Early Scientific Era

The scientific method, born during the sixteenth and seventeenth centuries, involved a radical break from earlier modes of thought. Magic, faith, and speculation no longer sufficed; observation, experimentation, and verification were the order of the day. One of the chief proponents of this new way of thinking, Francis Bacon, also wrote about aging. He attempted to dispel prior theories of aging because he believed them "corrupt with false opinion." Bacon wrote that "for both these things, which the vulgar physicians talk(e), of radical moisture, and natural heat, are but meer [sic] fictions." Unfortunately, Bacon himself was unable to escape completely the old ways of thinking. He simply replaced the Greek notion of innate heat with that of "spirit" or "pneuma" and argued that every body part (bones, blood, and so on) has such a spirit enclosed within it. With use, these spirits were consumed or dissolved—hence, old age. As might be expected, Bacon was unable to verify this idea; yet, he believed that with the proper method, the "secrets of nature" could be discovered (Grant, 1963).

Despite the new scientific approach, many people's basic ambivalence toward old age did not change. Bacon reflected this ambivalence in his discussion of the qualities intrinsic to youth and age:

Men of age object too much, consult too long, adventure too little, repent too soon, and seldom drive business home to the full period, but content themselves with a mediocrity of success . . . [yet] age doth profit rather in the powers of understanding, than in the virtues of the will and affections. (quoted in Hendricks & Hendricks, 1977)

THE CAUSES OF CERTAIN ACCIDENTAL ACCOMPANIMENTS OF OLD AGE, ESPECIALLY OF GRAY HAIRS, WRINKLES, AND BALDNESS

The Italian physician, Gabriele Zerbi (1445–1505), published *The Gerontocomia* in 1489. Arguably the first practical manual on the problems of old age, the word comes from the Greek *gerontokomeion,* an alms house or hospital for the aged, or *gerontokomos,* the warden of such a hospital.

Zerbi argues that there are two kinds of causes of old age, extrinsic and intrinsic. The extrinsic causes include the influence of the planets, "of Jupiter in the first period of old age upon the animate body and of Saturn in the last period, bringing the individual finally to about the age of ninety-eight . . . from the beginning of his exit from the mother's womb to the end of his life" (p. 34). For these extrinsic causes of old age, astrologers were deemed expert practitioners to the aged. "The best astrologer will be able to prevent most adverse events which are to occur according to the stars for when he knows the figure of the region of the city and of the horoscope constructed suitable to the individual he will be able to foretell expertly the events which happen to the person" (p. 35).

The intrinsic causes of old age are those sought out and identified by physicians. These causes include sluggishness, indigestion, and accidents. According to Zerbi, indigestion creates gray hairs as a result of certain putrefying vapors being trapped in the hair. Supporting evidence for this view is provided by observation "that hairs covered with hats . . . grow gray more quickly because the covering prevents the wind from blowing the hair and thus preventing putrefaction" (p. 48). Consumption of certain foods, fruits and vegetables, for example, also were believed to produce gray hair.

Wrinkles were thought to result from the combination of dry skin and contact with the cold. "Dryness causes laxity and coldness causes corrugation because coldness by stretching a fold of the skin over another folds them together and thus creates wrinkles" (pp. 49–50).

Baldness was identified by Zerbi as occurring more in old age than in any other age period of the life course. And he attributed baldness to "superabundant dryness in . . . the aged body" (p. 50). Also, baldness is more likely to occur in the front of the head along the hair line because "in the anterior part the skin is closer to the skull and more free from flesh by which it must be humidified. Thus when the brain is diminished and along that part of the skull the skin dries out and . . . the hairs fall" (p. 50). Zerbi advises that those who have a "moister brain do not grow bald easily or swiftly" (p. 50).

In summary, according to 15th century physician, Gabriele Zerbi, watch your horoscope, avoid indigestion, keep warm and stay moist, do not wear hats and, presumably, you may be able to avoid or slow what are otherwise "accidental accompaniments" of old age.

Source: Gabriele Zerbi, *Gerontocomia: On the Care of the Aged,* translated by L. R. Lind (Philadelphia: American Philosophical Society, 1988). Reprinted by permission.

A more positive sixteenth-century view was put forth by Paleotti, who, in terms reminiscent of Cicero 16 centuries before, concluded that "wisdom, maturity, and a cooling down of certain emotional currents give old age its peculiar form of creativeness unobtainable at other life periods" (quoted in Hendricks & Hendricks, 1977).

In Europe and America, many books were written on and advances made in physiology, anatomy, pathology, and chemistry during the seventeenth and eighteenth centuries, although pre-Enlightenment ideas were still around in abundance. One of the first Americans to write about aging was Cotton Mather (1663–1728). His orientation was theological: Illness was conceived as punishment for original sin, and only through temperance could longevity be achieved. Longevity was also the issue in what, perhaps, was the first complete American work on aging. William Barton, in his *Observations on the Progress of Population and the Probabilities of the Duration of Human Life in the United States of America* (1791), attempted to show that people in the United States lived longer and were healthier than people in Europe. He deduced that the likelihood of a person living past age 80 was greater in America than abroad (Achenbaum, 1978).

The first American work in geriatrics, *Account of the State of the Body and Mind in Old Age,* was published in 1793 by the physician Benjamin Rush. Perhaps more accurately than anyone before him, Rush described the changes in the body and the mind that accompany old age. A historian of aging describes Rush as striking one of the last blows at the idea that old age is itself a disease: "Few persons appear to die of old age. Some of the diseases which have been mentioned generally cuts [sic] the last thread of life" (Rush, quoted in Grant, 1963). Rush and his contemporaries—Hufeland in Germany and Bichat in France, for example—represent the beginning of a more modern period. Science flowered, and writers of the time believed the principles of life would be discovered by scientific observation and experimentation.

The nineteenth century experienced an increase in the capacity for scientific research and some outstanding technological innovations, including advances in microscopy and thermometry. Lister, Pasteur, and Metchnikoff revolutionized public health by their discoveries of methods to control epidemic diseases and infection. Medical specialization was increasing, and one could begin to envision the outlines of a fledgling branch dealing with old age. The French physician Charcot attended particularly to the clinical aspects of old age; he believed that management of diseases of aging and the aged should be based on an established clinical regimen. According to Freeman (1965), Charcot was responsible for dividing the study of aging into two permanent lines of inquiry. One investigates the facts of aging, describes its effects, and measures its changes in capacities. The other looks for principles of aging, for a central theme or cause.

This distinction may have been anticipated by the Belgian mathematician Quetelet, considered by some to be the first gerontologist. Quetelet, one of the earliest statisticians, helped discover the concept of the normal distribution. The *normal distribution* indicates that there is an average or central tendency around which are distributed higher and lower measurements. Quetelet applied this notion to various traits such as hand strength and weight, records of birth and death rates, and the relationship between age and productivity (Birren & Clayton, 1975).

Sir Francis Galton, an English statistician responsible for developing the index of correlation, was influenced by Quetelet's work. Galton's fundamental contribution to the study of aging is the data gathered by his Anthropometric Laboratory at the International Health Exhibition in London in 1884 (Freeman, 1965). Over 9,000 males and females ranging in age from 5 to 80 were measured on 17 different characteristics, including hearing, vision, and reaction time. Galton used these data to show how human characteristics change with age. This was the first large survey related to aging, and the data were still being analyzed in the 1920s.

The Twentieth Century

In the early part of the twentieth century, interest in aging involved including old age in a developmental psychology framework (Birren & Clayton, 1975). G. Stanley Hall, president of Clark University and founder of the Psychology Department of Johns Hopkins University, had specialized in childhood and adolescence, but concern with his own retirement led him to write *Senescence, the Last Half of Life,* published in 1922. Although he may have been tempted to characterize the second half of life as a regression occurring among the same lines as development, Hall struck a new note:

> As a psychologist I am convinced that the psychic states of old people have great significance. Senescence, like adolescence, has its own feeling, thought, and will, as well as its own psychology, and their regimen is important, as well as that of the body. Individual differences here are probably greater than in youth. (Hall, 1922, p. 100)

Hall used questionnaire data to investigate the relationship between religious belief and fear of death. The conventional wisdom at the time was that, with age, fear of death increased and people became more religious in an attempt to reconcile themselves to an uncertain future. Hall argued that religious fervor did not increase with age, nor were old people more fearful of death than were the young. In fact, he said, fear of death seemed to be a young person's concern (Freeman, 1965).

During the early part of the twentieth century, biologists such as Child, Metchnikoff, Minot, Pearl, and Weismann were writing prolifically on aging. An internist at Johns Hopkins University, William Osler, while considering the high frequency of cases of arteriosclerosis among the elderly, discovered that aging was closely related to the state of the blood vessels, and he saw the impact hardening of the arteries had on brain functioning. Clearly, the locus of aging study was shifting to the United States during this period, although important research was being carried out by Pavlov in Russia and Tachibana in Japan.

By the 1930s, a new attitude toward old age had emerged, one that has had enormous impact on the growth of gerontology as a scientific discipline. Stimulated by the changing demographics of modern societies, by an increased life expectancy, and by a growing older population, and perhaps by an economic depression, people began to see old age as a social problem (Maddox & Wiley, 1976). Recognizing the prevalence of incapacity, isolation, and poverty among aged citizens, Western society's concern turned toward social action on behalf of the aged (Burgess, 1960). Interestingly, this concern and the accompanying perceived need for collective social action were reflected not only in legislation (such as the passage of the Social Security Act in 1935) in the United States but also in a new institutional approach to aging as a social scientific problem.

In the late 1930s and early 1940s, conferences on aging were sponsored by professional and governmental organizations such as the American Orthopsychiatric Association and the National Institutes of Health. Private foundations, including the Josiah Macy Foundation, also provided assistance in conducting conferences on aging. Many of the issues raised at these early conferences anticipated some of the current concerns in gerontology: mental health and aging, aging and intellectual functioning, and aging and worker productivity. One of the earliest reports on the implications of the changing demographic structure of U.S. society was initiated by the Social Science Research Council (Pollak, 1948).

World War II interrupted the continuing development of gerontology. When the war ended in 1945, however, gerontologists resumed activity and founded the Gerontological Society (now The Gerontological Society of America). The Society publishes two influential journals in the field of aging: the *Journal of Gerontology* and *The Gerontologist*. Other professional associations soon appeared. The American Psychological Association established a division on maturity and old age in 1946; the American Geriatric Society was founded in 1950. The American Society on Aging, organized initially as the Western Gerontological Society, was founded in 1954.

The founding of a gerontological unit of the National Institutes of Health in 1946 led to the creation of the National Institute of Aging in 1974. Robert Butler, a psychiatrist and gerontologist, became its first director. The International Association of Gerontology was organized in 1948 and had its first meeting in Liege, Belgium. Today, many other professional societies, including the American Sociological Association and the American Public Health Association, maintain sections for those members with a specific interest in aging.

By the 1950s, the volume of gerontological literature had increased dramatically, and it continues to increase unabated. The major journals of gerontology were started between 1946 and the early 1970s. In addition to those mentioned previously, these include *Geriatrics* (1946), *Gerontologia* (1956), *Experimental Gerontology* (1966), *Journal of Geriatric Psychiatry* (1967), *Aging and Human Development* (1971), *Ageing and Society* (1981), *Journal of Aging and Health* (1989), and the *Journal of Applied Gerontology* (1982). An attempt to create a definitive bibliography of biomedical and social science research in aging for the years 1954 to 1974 yielded

50,000 titles (Woodruff & Birren, 1975). Many gerontologists express both joy and dismay at this explosive increase in gerontological research. The joy comes with being able to participate in an exciting and growing scientific enterprise; the dismay comes with trying to keep pace with the growth of gerontological knowledge.

Several attempts have been made to synthesize this growing body of literature. Landmarks in this regard are Birren's *Handbook of Aging and the Individual: Psychological and Biological Aspects* (1959), Tibbitts's *Handbook of Social Gerontology: Societal Aspects of Aging* (1960) and Burgess's *Aging in Western Societies* (1960). This effort was later matched in three volumes edited by Matilda W. Riley and colleagues and supported by the Russell Sage Foundation: *Aging and Society: An Inventory of Research Findings* (Riley & Foner, 1968), *Aging and the Professions* (Riley, Riley, & Johnson, 1969), and *A Sociology of Age Stratification* (Riley, Johnson, & Foner, 1972). More recent reviews of the field are provided in the recent editions of the Handbook of Aging Series: *Handbook of the Biology of Aging* (Schneider & Rowe, 1990), *Handbook of the Psychology of Aging* (Birren & Schaie, 1990), and *Handbook of the Aging and the Social Sciences* (Binstock & George, 1990).

Almost every discipline involved in gerontology has had its pioneer through this modern period, and clearly all cannot be listed here. E. V. Cowdry, considered by some the father of modern gerontology, led the way with his seminal volume *Problems of Aging,* published in 1939. Early on, he recognized the interdisciplinary nature of gerontology, synthesized a variety of materials in his field, and contributed significantly to the establishment of the International Association of Gerontology (Kaplan, in Schwartz & Peterson, 1979). The social psychologist Bernice Neugarten began teaching the psychology of aging at the University of Chicago in the early 1930s. She and her students have contributed immeasurably to the development of gerontology, as well as to the broader study of human development. Other outstanding work was produced in psychology by Birren and Schaie, in sociology by Shanas and Rosow, in anthropology by Simmons and Clark, in economics by Kreps, and in history (more recently) by Fischer and Achenbaum. These people and others not named here have also contributed to the development of strong university centers at Brandeis, Chicago, Duke, Southern California, and elsewhere.

The study of aging continues to grow, in part fueled by funding from federal government sources. The National Institutes of Health, including the National Institute of Mental Health and the newer National Institute on Aging, and the Administration on Aging, through state and area offices on aging, provide the primary funding for interdisciplinary research and training in gerontology. Other governmental agencies (e.g., the Department of Labor), as well as private organizations such as the American Association of Retired Persons, also fund research and training programs related to aging.

If one were to write a more detailed history of the last three or four decades in gerontology, an important point to develop would be the extent to which it has been institutionalized on the U.S. academic scene. Courses on aging are taught on almost every college and university campus; students major in gerontology and professors identify themselves as gerontologists. The Association for Gerontology in Higher Education (AGHE) was established in 1974 for the purpose of advancing gerontology as a field of study within institutions of higher learning. The 1994 AGHE Directory lists over 1,000 formal gerontology programs at member colleges and universities. A *formal gerontology program* is defined as one offering a degree, certificate, concentration, specialization, emphasis, or minor in gerontology, or is identified as a research and/or clinical training center in gerontology/geriatrics.

Still, there remains much debate over whether gerontology ought to be recognized as a discipline in its own right, as are psychology, physics, and philosophy. Some argue that gerontologists have not really succeeded in creating a body of theory all their own, that gerontology is just a consumer of theories from other sciences, and that gerontologists should be satisfied to have the field function as an applied social science. One contributing factor in this argument involves the lack of consensus over what constitutes the common core of knowledge in gerontology. A joint committee of the AGHE and the Gerontological Society has addressed this issue. According to this committee, insufficient consensus exists about the common core of knowledge in gerontology. Defining *consensus* as 90 percent agreement, this committee found that gerontological educators and practitioners could agree on only three topics—the psychology of aging, health and aging, and the biology of aging—for inclusion in an essential content of gerontology (Jacobson, 1980). Other topics that came close included the demography of aging, sensory change, the sociology of aging, and the environment and aging.

Thomas Jefferson and many of the American Founding Fathers argued for a style of agrarian democracy which, in Jefferson's picturesque phrase, was based on no man living so close to his neighbor that he could hear his dog bark. Unfortunately, the way gerontology is sometimes practiced in colleges and universities in the United States allows the appropriate paraphrase to be that "no gerontologist lives so close to his academic neighbor that he reads his work" (Kart, 1987, p. 86).

The future of gerontology continues to be dependent on the willingness of traditional academic departments (e.g., psychology, sociology, and biology, among others) to cooperate in the gerontological enterprise. If academic competition becomes the order of the day, the field will surely suffer. If these traditional disciplines make a commitment to interdisciplinary activity, the field will surely flourish. Some in the field are optimistic, for they (and I) understand that no discipline by itself is capable of providing adequate education in gerontology.

METHODOLOGICAL ISSUES IN AGING RESEARCH

Earlier, *gerontology* was defined as the study of aging from the broadest perspective. In addition, gerontology was described as an interdisciplinary study with *major* elements drawn from the physical and social sciences. In this regard, active researchers in gerontology have relied and continue to rely on scientific methods of investigation. Actually, as Popenoe (1991) points out, scientists can take one of three pathways in the pursuit of knowledge. One path, involving reasoning from the general to the specific or from certain premises to a logically valid conclusion, is referred to as the use of *deductive logic.* A second path, involving the direct perception of truth apart from any reasoning process or logic, can be referred to as *intuition.* Gerontologists do not reject deductive logic and intuition as pathways to knowledge, but they do rely more heavily on a third path—the empirical method. The *empirical method* involves the use of human senses (e.g., sight and hearing) to observe the world (Popenoe, 1991). This method is public; the observations of one researcher can be checked for accuracy by others using the same process. Gerontological "truths" cannot be accepted on the basis of logic and/or intuition. They must be subjected to empirical investigation.

Most students reading this text have limited experience with empirical research (and, likely, even less experience with such research carried out by gerontologists). Moreover, much of this experience comes from reading research reports required for fulfilling course assignments. Typically, what the student sees is a finished product, which includes a statement of the problem to be investigated, some theoretical justification, discussion of the research methods employed, presentation of the data, and discussion of the findings. Rarely does the student get a chance to observe firsthand the problems involved in carrying out the research process. These include how the project may have changed in the course of the research process and the judgments that the researcher was forced to make as difficulties were encountered (Williamson, Karp, & Dalphin, 1977).

The research problems gerontologists encounter are much like those encountered by scientists working in a wide array of scientific disciplines. Common concerns include the appropriateness of research technique and design, the validity and reliability of measurement devices, and problems of sampling and data analysis. The following brief description of the most frequently used methods in gerontological research provides examples from the social sciences (with particular emphasis on sociology and psychology) to show how research is currently carried out in the field of aging.

Field Research

Field research is generally observation centered. It is most useful in the study of relatively small groups of individuals or well-defined social settings and may allow the researcher to establish and maintain close, firsthand contact with subjects and their actions (Williamson, Karp, & Dalphin, 1977). Zelditch (1962) distinguishes among three types of strategies for field research: (1) participant observation, (2) informant interviewing, and (3) enumeration and samples.

Participant observation includes observing and participating in events, interviewing other participants during the events, and maintaining stable relationships in the group. *Informant interviewing* involves interviewing an informant about others in the group and about events that have happened in the past. *Enumerations and samples* include small surveys and structured observations that require a low level of participation in group events.

Field work requires what Smith (1975) describes as "distinctive methodological attitudes." In general, this means that the researcher must be comfortable with the lack of standardization and the unstructured nature of the field research process. Field research must be quite flexible and adaptable to changing environmental conditions as well as to emerging theoretical concerns. In this regard, field methods are much more conducive to description than inferential analysis and more conducive to hypothesis generation than to hypothesis testing (Smith, 1975). As Keith (1986, p. 1) argues, with regard to the use of participant observation for old-age research, so little is known about the quality of older people's lives that many other research approaches simply cannot be used before some preliminary field work identifies the relevant questions.

A significant problem the field researcher faces has to do with the possible influence or effect the research itself may have on the field setting. For example, Smith (1975) indicates that the more the researcher finds it necessary to participate in the field setting, the more the research role will depend on the ability to establish successful relationships of trust with individuals in the field setting. The fact that informant contacts are established with some subjects and not others may affect the relationships among these subjects. Also, such relationships with informants may bias data collection toward one point of view and away from others.

A number of gerontological researchers have employed field research methods, principally participant observation, with considerable success in the study of retirement communities (Keith, 1977/1982; Jacobs, 1974; Hochschild, 1973; Johnson, 1971), nursing homes (Gubrium, 1975), and single-room-occupancy (SRO) hotels (Stephens, 1976). Keith (1977/1982) and her husband took an apartment at Les Floralies, a high-rise retirement residence with a planned capacity of 150, which was built by the French national retirement fund for construction workers and is located in a suburb outside of Paris. Residents included those who had worked in the construction trades and their spouses. The average age of residents was 75 years old, almost two-thirds were female, and 90 percent received some form of government assistance to meet the costs of living in the residence. Keith immersed herself in the activities of the retirement community, as she attempted to outline a map of social relations within the residence:

> I participated in every possible aspect of community life.... Access to organized activities was easy: committee meetings once a week, a weekly sewing and knitting group, daily work with volunteer residents in the kitchen, the laundry or the research office, and the afternoon *belote* game. These activities ... led to invitations to ... people's apartments. Neighbors invited us too, and the head of the Communist faction became my knitting teacher. (1977/1982, pp. 29–30)

Les Floralies is not just an apartment house for elderly retirees. Rather, as Keith states, it is inhabited by people who are engaged together in the process of creating community. This work identifies a number of factors that contribute to the creation of community among these people. First, residents shared many characteristics in common in addition to age, such as occupation, educational level, income, ethnicity, and social class. Second, these old people believed that their alternatives were few. Thus, they made considerable financial and emotional investment in the move. Being "here for the rest of our lives" was certainly an important source of identification with the community. Third, they entered this setting in small enough numbers to get to know each other personally; the physical arrangements, in particular those in the dining room, helped promote a greater sense of participation in the residence. The dining facility employed small round tables as opposed to the long, institutional tables (familiar to university student cafeterias) often used in nursing homes and other residences. This allowed the "possibility for immediate, primary ties which consistently appear in studies of human groups as essential for linking the individual to a larger community" (Keith, 1977/1982, p. 157).

Keith believes that these factors allowed residents to turn to each other for the fulfillment of their social needs. They supported each other in illness and emergency, just as they laughed and danced together at parties. Further, they were able to evaluate each other in terms of the life they shared in the residence, rather than according to the status system of the outside world. In this regard, they identified themselves as members of a community of age-mates sharing refuge from an outside world fraught with physical, financial, social, and psychological dangers for them.

Although Keith's insightful work involves the study of only one specific retirement community—a fact that makes generalization to other communities problematic—it can be added to a body of field research on retirement communities (e.g., Hochschild, 1973; Jacobs, 1974; Johnson, 1971) that suggests that the factors important for community formation among old people in the suburbs of Paris may be the same for communities of old people in the United States.

Use of Existing Records

Examination of existing records of individual behavior or social conditions can serve as a useful method of research for the gerontologist. Such records include personal written accounts, such as diaries or letters; public documents, such as birth, death, marriage, and probate records; and print media, film records, and sound recordings. Another kind of existing record that can be very useful to a researcher is the statistical compilation (Palmer, 1978). Although the best and most widely used statistical compilations are the official publications of the U.S. Bureau of the Census, other organizations provide additional sources of statistical information.

In recent years, there has been considerable growth in the number of machine-readable data files available for statistical analysis. Archival organizations have become important in making these data files available to researchers. The two largest machine-readable data archives in the United States serving the general social science community are the Inter-University Consortium for Political and Social Research (ICPSR) at the University of Michigan and the Roper Center (Sinott et al., 1983).

Many universities and research institutes serve their social science researchers by providing facilities for ordering data from these two repositories. Such data can be used for *secondary analysis,* a term that describes a reanalysis of data produced by someone else, and often for other purposes. One problem with secondary analysis is that the current researcher is at the mercy of the original researcher in terms of what questions were asked to collect the data. Nevertheless, secondary analysis can be quite fruitful and, given the prohibitive costs of doing research, is likely to become even more popular in the future.

Researchers who use existing records not provided in some statistical format are likely to engage in some kind of *content analysis.* Here, the researcher establishes a number of categories, each of which refers to some repeated or patterned occurrence in the content of the record. Tabulations made of the frequency of each element or combination of elements may constitute the basic data in the research (Palmer, 1978). It is important in content analysis that the categories used are precisely defined and well tailored to the research problem at hand.

Engler-Bowles and Kart (1983) engaged in a content analysis of 60 wills sampled from Wood County, Ohio, probate records filed between 1820 and 1967. They were interested in the extent to which inheritance practices reflected changes in the family relationships of older people in a largely rural area of northwest Ohio during this time period. Testamentary documents commend themselves for such use because of their public and permanent accessibility as well as the demands for legal accuracy (Bryant & Snizek, 1975). In addition, the will represents a particularly candid and forthright form of communication. Nevertheless, testamentary records do have some limitations. Systematic bias may be introduced as a result of the number of people who die intestate (without a will). Also, the wills themselves often do not contain relevant demographic, social, and economic information that is important for addressing certain research questions.

In order to categorize the way elderly testators disposed of their estates, Engler-Bowles and Kart (1983) used a typology of inheritance patterns adapted from Rosenfeld (1979) to identify the presence or absence of family obligation. This typology was used to measure the relative degree of that obligation, as indicated by the following three categories of inheritance patterns: familistic inheritance, articulated inheritance, and disinheritance.

Familistic inheritance represents the strongest degree of obligation by the testator to family ties. Wills in this category generally distribute the estate among family members only. *Articulated inheritance* is the dual recognition of kin and nonkin, with priority placed on nonkin heirs in testamentary disposition. *Disinheritance* is the total exclusion of family members from testamentary disposition and, therefore, the apparent absence of family obligation as perceived by the testator.

The familistic inheritance pattern dominated the time period explored by Engler-Bowles and Kart (1983). Articulated wills appeared rarely; several wills seemed equally divided between familistic and articulated bequests, and no examples of total family disinheritance were evident in this population of wills. Across this lengthy time span, married testators emphasized their conjugal relations, showing the strong emphasis placed on the nuclear family throughout the period. In the early part of this time period, direct bequests to children were usually unequal, sometimes reflecting differences in sex and individual circumstances such as advancements made to certain children. Starting in the latter part of the nineteenth century, sons and daughters were equally likely to receive testamentary bequest.

Misconceptions about the family lives of elderly Americans past and present abound. Stereotypical images of alienated families and the isolated elderly are popular topics for research and mass media reports. The study by Engler-Bowles and Kart (1983) presents a different picture. Their analysis suggests that elderly Wood County, Ohio, testators were active participants in family life and maintained strong ties to their children from the early nineteenth century until the mid-twentieth century. Still, additional historical research is necessary to determine whether the results of this study are idiosyncratic to a small sample of will writers in rural northwest Ohio.

Survey Research

Survey research differs from other methods of data collection in two important ways. First, the focus is generally on a representative sample of a relatively large population. Second, data are collected from respondents directly, often at their homes, through the use of either interviews or questionnaires or both. The major elements that combine to make up the survey research process include sampling procedures, questionnaire or interview schedule construction and testing, interviews carried out by trained interviewers, and data preparation and analysis (Palmer, 1978).

Studies that employ a survey research approach may follow a cross-sectional or a longitudinal design. A *cross-sectional* study is carried out at one time and examines the relationships among a set of variables as they occur at that time. A *longitudinal* study involves repeated contacts with the same respondents over a period of time and is particularly attentive to changes that occur with time. This type of research design is frequently referred to as a *panel study.*

Panel studies are found increasingly preferable by gerontological researchers, but they pose special methodological problems, not the least of which is referred to as the *age/period/cohort (APC) problem.* Interest in this problem first developed among psychologists attempting to understand what happens to intellectual functioning in old age (Schaie, 1976) and among political scientists interested in voting behavior across the life cycle (Hudson & Binstock, 1976). Both groups of researchers came to realize the importance of distinguishing, both conceptually and empirically, among changes in individuals that were a function of individual maturation (aging), those that were a function of biographical factors (cohort), and those that resulted from environmental and/or historical factors (period).

Older people should be able to pursue opportunities for the full development of their potential.

Identifying the relative importance of age, period, and cohort effects is no easy task. Maddox and Campbell (1985) offer as example the introduction of vitamin D into milk supplies. This innovation was made instantaneously and thus can be thought of as a period effect that cut across all age groups. Yet, certain cohorts of newborns received the benefits of vitamin D supplements in their milk almost immediately from birth, whereas preceding cohorts received the benefits no earlier than the date of introduction. Thus, the period effect had potentially different consequences for different cohorts. Some received the vitamin supplements throughout their childhood years; others received the supplements for a smaller proportion of those years. Is this nutritional innovation a period or a cohort effect, or both?

Important differences exist between questionnaires and interviews as data-collecting tools in survey research. Questionnaires, delivered to respondents at work or school or mailed to them at home, are filled out by the respondents themselves. This permits access to many people who are spread over a large geographical area while saving time and money. Disadvantages include the need for a literate population and the low response rate that can be expected (30 percent is not uncommon). Also, questionnaires must be relatively brief, as respondents may lose interest quickly. Thus, questionnaires often cannot provide for an in-depth probing of respondents' attitudes.

Interviews can be carried out either face to face or over the telephone. The latter are less expensive, as interviewer travel time is virtually eliminated. A serious obstacle to the personal interview is the initial resistance to being interviewed. Nevertheless, as Blalock and Blalock (1982) point out, refusals to be interviewed once a contact has been made are relatively rare, and most respondents are cooperative, seem to enjoy the experience, and appear to take it seriously. Among older people, the response rate does appear to be lower for telephone surveys than for face-to-face interviews. Also, people seem more willing to respond "I don't know" on the telephone than in face-to-face interviews (Herzog & Rodgers, 1988). Still, Herzog, Rodgers, and Kulka (1983) conclude that telephone interviews are about as effective for older adults as are personal interviews, which are prohibitively expensive for most studies.

With funding from the AARP Andrus Foundation, Kart and Engler (1994) attempted to identify and describe self-health care practices and attitudes within a national sample of older people. In particular, these authors sought to specify characteristics of older people that may predispose them to provide health care to themselves. In the fall of 1991, trained interviewers completed over 700 extensive telephone interviews with a national probability sample of noninstitutionalized adults aged 55 years and older. By the definition offered earlier, this study represents a cross-sectional research design.

According to these authors, self-health care is a multifaceted concept that includes self-evaluation and treatment of illness symptoms, as well as overall assessment of the capacity to take care of one's own health. Although elements of this study are too numerous to identify here, among other methods employed to assess self-health care, respondents were presented with a list of 20 illness symptoms ranging from minor to potentially serious in consequence. They were asked if they had experienced the symptom in the past six months and, if yes, what they did about the symptom. For example, 6 in 10 (60.4 percent) had experienced pain or stiffness in a joint; at the other extreme, only 12.3 percent experienced frequent constipation during the past six months.

For each symptom experienced, respondents were categorized as using professional care (e.g., physician care, prescription medicine) only for treatment, some combination of self-care plus professional care, or self-care only to deal with the symptom (e.g., home remedy, over-the-counter medication, doing nothing). More than five of six respondents (86.3 percent) indicated experiencing at least one of the 20 symptoms within the past six months for which they employed self-care only. An index of actual self-care revealed that, on average, across these 20 symptoms, study respondents employed self-health care responses 14.3 percent of the time.

Being female, white, perceiving an inability to maintain control over one's own health, having vision and/or hearing problems, and having one or more serious chronic illnesses (e.g., heart disease, cancer) were characteristics of respondents most likely to respond to illness symptoms with self-care. Kart and Engler (1994) conclude that researchers and health care policymakers can no longer ignore the phenomenon of self-health care among the elderly and how it interfaces with patterns of utilization of the formal health care system.

> Self-health care is an often overlooked component of the total health care received by older individuals in the United States.... Still, too little is known about this.... The question remains, do different illness symptoms lend themselves to self-care more than others, or is it that certain groups of individuals, more than others, are predisposed to undertake self-health care, regardless of illness symptoms and comorbidities? (Kart & Engler, 1994, pp. S305-S307)

Laboratory Experimentation

Laboratory experimentation, used primarily by psychologists, involves the systematic observation of phenomenon under controlled conditions. In the simplest experiment, there is a single independent variable (I) and a single dependent variable (D). The research hypothesis is that I leads to D. As Abrahamson (1983) suggests, the effect of the independent variable on the dependent variable need not be viewed as causal, although it ordinarily is in experiments. The primary objective of the experimental procedure is to eliminate the possibility that any variable other than the independent variable will affect the dependent variable.

The operationalization of the independent variable acts to define experimental and control groups in the simple laboratory experiment. These groups are composed of subjects who are alike in every way except that those in the experimental group are exposed to I, whereas those in the control group are not. Assuming initial equality, any observed differences between the two groups on the dependent variable can be attributed to the influence of the experimentally introduced independent variable (Palmer, 1978). A variation on this model is that subjects in the experimental and control groups are alike in every way except one—age, for example. The two groups are exposed to the same stimuli; differences in their responses (the dependent variable) are assumed to result from age (the independent variable). Other variations on this uncomplicated model have been developed and are represented in the gerontological literature. An example follows.

Everybody experiences memory failures. How these failures are evaluated and what causal attributions are made can have important implications. A memory failure in a young adult may be ignored or joked about, but the same failure in an aged person may be taken as a sign of mental decline or onset of dementia. Erber, Zsuchman, and Rothberg (1990) refer to this difference in appraisal of memory failure as a "double standard." More recently, Erber and Rothberg (1991) speculate that judgments of the attractiveness of the person experiencing the failure might have consequences for the causal attribution made. Further, the researchers devised an experiment to test whether the memory failures of elderly adults and unattractive adults would be evaluated differently from those same failures in young adults and attractive adults.

Of the 72 women who were subjects for the experiment, 36 were young adults, aged 19 to 32, recruited from a local university; 36 were elderly adults, aged 64 to 81, recruited from the community. The women were asked to read vignettes describing short-term (e.g., immediately forgetting material), long-term (e.g., forgetting material learned 30 minutes to several hours ago), and very long-term memory failures (e.g., forgetting very familiar and overlearned information).

Each vignette was accompanied by a photograph of an attractive or unattractive young or elderly female target person. These photos were selected from a large pool of magazine and yearbook photos on the basis of evaluations by young and old female raters. There was a high level of agreement about the photographs among the raters. Subjects judged each vignette for possible reasons for the memory failure, including target's effort, motivation, attention, and ability. Subjects also rated whether they believed the failure was a sign of mental difficulty and whether medical and/or psychological intervention was indicated.

Erber and Rothberg (1991) report an unequivocal demonstration of the double standard. The memory failures of elderly targets were attributed more to lack of ability, whereas the failures of young targets were attributed to lack of effort. Also, the memory failures of older targets were seen as indicating greater mental difficulty and a more urgent need for medical/psychological evaluation than were the identical failures of younger targets. Similar findings were reported on the attractiveness dimension. Generally, attractive targets were evaluated in a more positive light than unattractive targets. Target age, however, was more important than target attractiveness in evaluating the memory failures. Young subjects, in particular, considered very long-term memory failures to be more indicative of mental difficulty and need for evaluation than short-term or long-term failures. Clearly, more research is needed to understand the different criteria for judgment used by younger and older people in order to identify the basis for leniency in the evaluations made by older adults.

SUMMARY

There are several reasons for studying aging, not the least of which is the intrinsic fascination of the field. There have been students of aging for several thousand years. In the past, perhaps the most prominent concern was the quest to prolong life, as reflected in the antediluvian, hyperborean, and fountain themes, all still represented today.

The scientific study of the aging process is a recent phenomenon, which arose out of a need to make clear distinctions between myth and history, magic and science. The first full and explicit theory of the causation of aging is found in Greco-Roman medicine and the Hippocratic theory. The Greek influence persisted, and a radical break with earlier modes of thought did not occur until the scientific method was born during the sixteenth and seventeenth centuries.

By the nineteenth century, capacity for scientific research increased; by the latter part of the century, a fledgling science of old age could be envisioned. During the early part of the twentieth century, the locus of aging study shifted toward the United States. By the 1930s, a new attitude toward old age emerged—a perception of old age as a social problem. Recognition of the prevalence of incapacity, isolation, and poverty among elderly people had enormous impact on the growth of gerontology as both a scientific and applied discipline.

In the 1970s, gerontology was institutionalized on the U.S. academic scene. There is still much debate over whether gerontology can be recognized as a discipline in its own right. Some argue that gerontologists have not created a body of theory of their own and should be satisfied to see gerontol-

ogy function as an applied social science. Nevertheless, gerontologists today show a strong research orientation and employ a variety of research procedures in their efforts, including field research, use of existing records, survey research, and laboratory experimentation. Gerontologists are also concerned with a number of special methodological issues in aging research, including issues of design and, in particular, the age/period/cohort problem, as well as the common concerns shared by scientists in a wide array of scientific disciplines.

STUDY QUESTIONS

1. Describe the antediluvian, hyperborean, and fountain themes of aging. How are these themes reflected in modern society?

2. What does it mean to say that gerontology is an interdisciplinary study?

3. Identify the three main tasks confronting the student of aging.

4. The Hippocratic theory of "innate heat" was the first explicit theory of aging in the Western world. Describe this theory, and explain why it is considered a breakthrough in the study of aging.

5. With the advent of the scientific era, thinking about aging both changes as well as remains the same. How is this the case?

6. Changing attitudes in the 1930s resulted in a major growth of the field of gerontology. Old age was increasingly recognized as a social problem. Discuss

some social and demographic factors that influenced this change in attitude.

7. Discuss the application of field research in the study of gerontology. Distinguish between (a) participant observation, (b) informant interviewing, and (c) enumeration and samples.

8. Explain how survey research differs from other methods of data collection. What are the major elements of the survey research process?

9. Why is it important to distinguish age, period, and cohort effects in gerontological research?

10. Identify the following:
    a. secondary analysis
    b. content analysis
    c. cross-sectional study design
    d. longitudinal study design
    e. experimental group
    f. control group

REFERENCES

Abrahamson, M. (1983). *Social research methods*. Englewood Cliffs, NJ: Prentice-Hall.

Achenbaum, W. A. (1978). *Old age in the new land*. Baltimore, MD: Johns Hopkins University Press.

Binstock, R., & George, L. K. (1990). *Handbook of aging and the social sciences* (3rd ed.). San Diego, CA: Academic Press.

Birren, J. (1959). *Handbook of aging and the individual: Psychological and biological aspects.* Chicago: University of Chicago Press.

Birren, J., & Clayton, V. (1975). History of gerontology. In D. Woodruff & J. Birren (Eds.), *Aging: Scientific perspectives and social issues.* New York: Van Nostrand.

Birren, J., & Schaie, W. (1990). *Handbook of the psychology of aging* (3rd ed.). San Diego, CA: Academic Press.

Blalock, A. B., & Blalock, H. M., Jr. (1982). *Introduction to social research* (2d ed.). Englewood Cliffs, NJ: Prentice-Hall.

Blythe, R. (1979). *The view in winter: Reflections on old age.* New York: Harcourt Brace Jovanovich.

Bromley, D. B. (1974). *The psychology of human aging* (2nd ed.). Middlesex, England: Penguin Books.

Bryant, C., & Snizek, W. (1975). The last will and testament: A neglected document in sociological research. *Sociology and Social Research, 59,* 219–230.

Burgess, E. (1960). *Aging in Western societies.* Chicago: University of Chicago Press.

Engler-Bowles, C. A., & Kart, C. S. (1983). Intergenerational relations and testamentary patterns: An exploration. *Gerontologist, 23* (2), 167–173.

Erber, J. T., & Rothberg, S. T. (1991). Here's looking at you: The relative effect of age and attractiveness on judgements about memory failure. *Journal of Gerontology, 46* (3), P116–123.

Erber, J. T., Zsuchman, L. T., & Rothberg, S. T. (1990). Everyday memory failures: Age differences in appraisal and attribution. *Psychology and Aging, 5,* 236–241.

Freeman, J. (1965). Medical perspectives in aging (12–19th century). *Gerontologist, 5,* 1–24.

Grant, R. L. (1963). Concepts of aging: An historical review. *Perspectives in Biology and Medicine, 6,* 443–478.

Gruman, G. (1966). *A history of ideas about the prolongation of life.* Philadelphia: American Philosophical Society.

Gubrium, J. F. (1975). *Living and dying at Murray Manor.* New York: St. Martin's.

Hall, G. S. (1922). *Senescence, the last half of life.* New York: Appleton.

Hendricks, J., & Hendricks, C. D. (1977). *Aging in mass society: Myths and realities.* Cambridge, MA: Winthrop Publishers.

Henratta, J., & Campbell, R. (1976). Status attainment and status maintenance: A study of satisfaction in old age. *American Sociological Review, 41,* 981–992.

Herzog, A. R., & Rodgers, W. L. (1988). Interviewing older adults: Mode comparison using data from a face-to-face survey and a telephone survey. *Public Opinion Quarterly, 52,* 84–99.

Herzog, A. R., Rodgers, W. L., & Kulka, R. A. (1983). Interviewing older adults: Comparison of telephone and face-to-face modalities. *Public Opinion Quarterly, 47,* 405–418.

Hochschild, A. R. (1973). *The unexpected community.* Englewood Cliffs, NJ: Prentice-Hall.

Hogan, D. P., & Eggebeen, D. J. (1995). Sources of emergency help and routine assistance in old age. *Social Forces, 73* (3), 917–936.

Hudson, R., & Binstock, R. (1976). Political systems and aging. In R. Binstock & E. Shanas (Eds.), *Aging and the social sciences.* New York: Van Nostrand Reinhold.

Jacobs, J. (1974). *Fun City: An ethnographic study of a retirement community.* New York: Holt, Rinehart and Winston.

Jacobson, R. L. (1980). Gerontology said to lack identity as an academic discipline. *The Chronicle of Higher Education, March 17,* 4.

Johnson, S. K. (1971). *Idle Haven: Community building among the working class retired.* Berkeley: University of California Press.

Kart, C. S. (1987). The end of conventional gerontology? *Sociology of Health and Illness, 9* (1), 77–87.

Kart, C. S., & Engler, C. A. (1994). Predisposition to self-health care: Who does what for themselves and why? *Journal of Gerontology, 49* (6), S301–S308.

Keith, J. (1977/1982). *Old people, new lives.* Chicago: University of Chicago Press.

Keith, J. (1986). Participant observation. In C. L. Fry, J. Keith, & contributors (Eds.), *New methods for old age research.* South Hadley, MA: Bergin & Garvey.

Maddox, G. (1979). Sociology of later life. *Annual Review of Sociology, 5,* 113–135.

Maddox, G., & Campbell, R. T. (1985). Scope, concepts and methods in the study of aging. In R. Binstock & E. Shanas (Eds.), *Aging and the social sciences* (2nd ed.). New York: Van Nostrand Reinhold.

Maddox, G., & Wiley, J. (1976). Scope, concepts and methods in the study of aging. In R. Binstock & E. Shanas (Eds.), *Aging and the social sciences.* New York: Van Nostrand Reinhold.

Moen, P., Dempster-McClain, D., & Williams, R. M. (1992). Successful aging: A life-course perspective on women's multiple roles and health. *American Journal of Sociology, 97* (6), 1612–1638.

National Institute on Aging. (1986). *Age words: A glossary on health and aging.* NIH Publication No. 86-1849. Washington, DC: U.S. Government Printing Office.

Palmer, N. (1978). Measurement procedures. In C. Kart (Ed.), *Exploring social problems.* Sherman Oaks, CA: Alfred.

Pollak, O. (1948). *Social adjustment in old age: A research planning report.* New York: Social Science Research Council.

Popenoe, D. (1991). *Sociology* (8th ed.). Englewood Cliffs, NJ: Prentice-Hall.

Riley, M. W., & Foner, A. (1968). *Aging and society: An inventory of research findings.* New York: Russell Sage Foundation.

Riley, M. W., Johnson, M., & Foner, A. (1972). *A sociology of age stratification.* New York: Russell Sage Foundation.

Riley, M. W., Riley, J., & Johnson, M. (1969). *Aging and the professions.* New York: Russell Sage Foundation.

Rosenfeld, J. (1979). *The legacy of aging: Inheritance and disinheritance in social perspective.* Norwood, NJ: Ablex.

Schaie, W. (1976). Quasi-experimental research design in the psychology of aging. In J. Birren & W. Schaie (Eds.), *The psychology of aging.* New York: Van Nostrand Reinhold.

Schneider, E. L., & Rowe, J. W. (1990). *Handbook of the biology of aging* (3rd ed.). San Diego, CA: Academic Press.

Schwartz, A., & Peterson, J. (1979). *Introduction to gerontology.* New York: Holt, Rinehart and Winston.

Sinnott, J. D., Harris, C. S., Block, M. R., Collesano, S., & Jacobson, S. G. (1983). *Applied research in aging: A guide to methods and resources.* Boston: Little, Brown.

Smith, H. W. (1975). *Strategies of social research: The methodological imagination.* Englewood Cliffs, NJ: Prentice-Hall.

Stephens, J. (1976). *Loners, losers, and lovers: Elderly tenants in a slum hotel.* Seattle: University of Washington Press.

Tibbitts, C. (1960). *Handbook of social gerontology: Societal aspects of aging.* Chicago: University of Chicago Press.

Williamson, J. B., Karp, D. A., & Dalphin, J. R. (1977). *The research craft: An introduction to social science methods.* Boston: Little, Brown.

Woodruff, D., & Birren, J. (1975). *Aging: Scientific perspectives and social issues.* New York: Van Nostrand Company.

Zelditch, M., Jr. (1962). Some methodological problems of field studies. *American Journal of Sociology, 67,* 566–576.

CHAPTER 3

THE DEMOGRAPHY OF AGING

More than 33 million people in the United States are aged 65 years and older. This group represents the fastest-growing age group in the nation's population: If the U.S. population of those 65 years and over were all grouped together, they would make up the most populous state in the nation, exceeding the population of California. Actually, there are more people aged 65 and older in the United States than the combined total resident populations of New England (Maine, New Hampshire, Vermont, Massachusetts, Rhode Island, and Connecticut) and the Mountain States (Montana, Idaho, Wyoming, Colorado, New Mexico, Arizona, Utah, and Nevada).

Assessing the circumstances of old people in the United States requires an understanding of how this group is currently constituted, how the elderly population has changed from the past, and how it may change in the future. Population attributes—fertility, mortality, and migration—influence and are influenced by social and economic conditions. High birthrates in the first decades of the twentieth century have yielded large numbers of elderly people 65 to 75 years later. Progress in public health and medicine has reduced the rates of illness and mortality in the population, especially among the young, allowing more of the population to live to be old. Immigration to the United States has also had an impact on the growth of the elderly population in recent years. Migrants who were young adults at the time of their immigration in the first two or three decades of the twentieth century increased the numbers of persons in their respective age groups, leading to large numbers of older people decades later.

This chapter presents a systematic study of aged population trends and phenomena in relation to their social setting. Much of the available data in the United States define the elderly as those 65 years of age and older. Although 65+ is an imprecise identifier of the older population, it is a useful designation for gerontologists, and it is followed in this chapter. This definition, however, is not universal. Most everyone can recognize the differences between 20-year-olds and 40-year-olds, but that same 20-year difference between 55-year-olds and 75-year-olds is often overlooked. Neugarten (1974) makes the distinction between the *young-old* (55 to 74 years of age) and the *old-old* (75 years of age and older). Recently, the National Institute on Aging has sought research proposals to study those individuals 85 years of age and older. This activity suggests the usefulness of further subdividing the old-old into those 75 to 84 years (*the elderly*) and those 85 years and over (*the very old* or *the oldest-old*). The young-old are healthier, wealthier, and better educated than the old-old, and their family and career experiences and expectations are quite different.

NUMBER AND PROPORTION
OF THE ELDERLY

The elderly population of the United States has grown consistently since the turn of the century, when about 3.1 million men and women were age 65 and over. By 1990, this population had increased tenfold to 31.1 million (see Table 3–1). This is much greater than the rate of increase for the total U.S. population, which increased only a little more than threefold (from 76 million to 250 million) in the same period.

As Table 3–1 shows, the absolute and proportional increases in the aged population are expected to continue into the twenty-first century, though at a slowed pace until the 2010–2020 decade. Between 1990 and 2000, the projected increase in the aged population is about 4.24 million, or a 13.6 percent decennial increase. This compares with the 5.6 million, or 21.6 percent decennial, increase between 1980 and 1990. This slowed growth rate in the elderly population is a reflection of the small cohorts caused by the low birthrate during the Great Depression and up to World War II.[1] The earliest of these small cohorts reach age 65 during the 1990s. When the post–World War II babies, sometimes referred to as Baby Boomers, begin to reach age 65 shortly after the year 2010, the growth rate in the elderly population will again increase. Table 3–1 shows this; the projected increase in the elderly population between 2010 and 2020 is 33.0 percent. Later, this growth rate will likely fall, reflecting a decline in birth rates that began in the 1960s.

Demographers have considerable confidence in these projections, because all those who will be elderly by 2050 have already been born. The accuracy of these projections will be determined ultimately by how accurately demographers predict mortality among these maturing individuals. This is not an easy task. For a time, demographers employed a single assumption of regular small declines in

---

[1]All persons born during the same year who are analyzed as a unit throughout their lifetime constitute a cohort (Petersen, 1975).

TABLE 3–1   Total Aged Population and Percentage of Total Population That Is Aged, 1970–2050

	1970	1980	1990	2000	2010	2020	2030	2040	2050
					Projections				
65 years and older (thousands)	19,973	25,550	31,080	35,322	40,104	53,349	70,175	77,014	80,109
Percentage of total population (%)	9.8	11.3	12.5	12.9	13.3	16.4	20.1	20.7	20.4
Increase in preceding decade (%)	—	27.9	21.6	13.6	13.5	33.0	31.5	9.7	4.0

Source: U.S. Bureau of the Census, *Statistical Abstract of the United States: 1995* (Washington, DC, 1995), Tables 14 and 17.

Note: Based on middle series Census Bureau. These projections are based on the following assumptions: (1) 2.15 lifetime births per woman; (2) life expectancy in 2050 of 82.6 years; and (3) net immigration of 880,000.

mortality rates among older adults. Siegel (1979) argues that this is no longer a safe course to follow. Death rates may decline at different rates in successive periods, or may even rise occasionally as they have in the last several decades. Crimmins (1980) suggests that the nation has entered a new era of mortality decline due primarily to reduced death rates from cardiovascular diseases and reduced death rates generally at older ages. If this is so, there will be a substantial increase in the number of people over age 65 in the population.

How accurate have past projections of the older population been? U.S. Census Bureau projections of the population 65 years of age and over for 1975 were published at various dates from August 1953 to December 1972 and varied from 20.7 million to 22.2 million. The current figure used is 22.4 million, 7.9 percent above the low estimate and 1.1 percent above the high estimate. As Siegel (1979) points out, the percentage deviation from the current figure declined as the publication date approached 1975. This is what might have been expected. After all, the first projections were made about a future that was 22 years away; but in December 1972, this future was only 3 years ahead.

This phenomenon has already appeared in projections for the year 2000. Until 1975, estimates for the older population of 2000 were in the range of 28 to 29 million. In 1975, the Census Bureau increased the estimate to about 30.5 million. The latest projection is 15.7 percent greater, or almost 35.3 million people aged 65 and over in the year 2000. These newly revised estimates reflect lower-than-anticipated mortality in the 1970s and 1980s and the use of more favorable mortality rates in making future estimates.

The first year in which over two million Americans died was 1983. It is likely that there will never again be a year in which there is fewer than two million deaths in the United States (Spencer, 1989). By 2020, when Baby Boomers begin to reach age 65, the numbers of deaths should rise quickly and exceed three million.

The aged are a diverse population.

Generally, however, death rates are expected to continue to decline, though at a less rapid rate than in the past two decades (Siegel & Davidson, 1984). There is also the possibility of marked future reductions in death rates at the older ages, at the same time that increases are seen in the proportion of deaths in the United States that come in old age. By 2020, the Census Bureau estimates that 76.4 percent of all deaths will be of individuals 65 years of age or older.

Such changes in the trends of death rates could bring a somewhat larger elderly population and greater increases than are shown by the Census Bureau's middle series of population projections used in this book. As Table 3–1 indicates, the middle series of population projections used by the Census Bureau assumes mortality rates consistent with achieving an *average life expectancy at birth* of 82.6 years in the year 2050. Using the highest series of population projections, including the assumption that life expectancy in 2050 will be 87.5 years, the Census Bureau projects 35.8 million elderly in the year 2000 and 57.4 million by the year 2020. The highest series projects an aged population that is 500,000, or 1.4 percent larger than that projected by the middle series for 2000, and 4.1 million, or 7.7 percent larger for 2020.

The proportion of the total population that older people will make up in the future will be determined, in great part, by fertility (birthrate) levels. The middle series of population projections used by the Census Bureau includes an assumption of 2.15 lifetime births per woman. As Table 3–1 indicates, under this assumption, the elderly are expected to constitute about 16.4 percent of the total U.S. population by the year 2020. Using a lowest series projection, which assumes a fertility rate of 1.89, the Census Bureau estimates that the elderly will constitute 16.3 percent of the total U.S. population in 2020. With the highest series projection, which assumes a rate of 2.62 lifetime births per woman, the elderly would constitute 15.8 percent of the total population in the United States in 2020.

AGING OF THE OLDER POPULATION

Not only has the older population of the United States grown in absolute size and in its proportion of the total population during this century but it has also aged. The median age of the 65-and-over population in the United States was 73.3 years in 1990, up from 71.9 in 1960. Table 3–2 shows that since 1950, the proportion of the aged who are 65 to 74 years of age has been getting smaller and that it will continue to do so until 2010. The proportion aged 75 or over has been getting larger, and this trend is also expected to continue until 2010. By 2010, the percentage of persons aged 65 and over who are 65 to 74 years of age will be about 52.3 percent. After 2010, the aging trend of the population 65 years and over should reverse itself, as larger cohorts born in the post–World War II period enter the younger segment (65 to 74 years) of the elderly population.

A pervasive trend throughout the latter part of the twentieth century—one that is expected to continue virtually throughout the next century—is the overall aging of the population. The median age of the U.S. population was 32.8 years in 1990 and is expected to rise to 35.5 years by 2000 (middle series projections). This figure is projected to rise to 39.0 years by 2050.

The aging of the older population that is expected to occur over the next two decades or so has important policy implications for local, state, and federal agencies. One example involves the likelihood of an increased need for extended care among the growing number of the very old (Siegel & Davidson, 1984).

TABLE 3–2   Percentage Distribution of the Population 65 Years and Over, by Age, 1950–2020

	1950	1960	1970	1980	1990	2000	2010	2020
65 years and over	100.0	100.0	100.0	100.0	100.0	100.0	100.0	100.0
65–74	68.5	66.3	62.2	60.8	58.1	52.5	52.3	57.9
75–84	26.7	28.1	30.7	30.4	32.2	35.2	32.8	29.0
85 years and over	4.8	5.6	7.1	8.8	9.7	12.3	14.9	13.1

Source: U.S. Bureau of the Census, *Statistical Abstract of the United States: 1995* (Washington, DC, 1995), Tables 14 and 17.

Note: Based on middle series Census Bureau Projections. See Table 3–1 for explanation of assumptions.

THE DEMOGRAPHIC TRANSITION

The pattern of an increasing number and proportion of elderly persons in the U.S. population is no surprise to students of demography. In fact, it is predictable from a theory of population change used by many demographers to explain the growth in a society's population. This theory is concerned with the relationship between birthrates and death rates (as well as migration rates) and the resulting effects on the age composition of populations. It allows one to understand and predict changes in the age composition of a society. The theory, which describes a three-stage process whereby a population moves from high fertility and high mortality to low fertility and low mortality, is often called the *demographic transition.*[2]

The first stage of the demographic transition, characterized by high birthrates and high death rates, has been called the *high growth potential* stage because a decline in mortality, in the absence of other changes, implies very high rates of population growth (Matras, 1973, p. 25). Preindustrial societies, with their very high death rates, are examples of populations in the first stage. They were extremely vulnerable to crop failure and famine, possessed very limited environmental health controls, and had no health technologies for caring for the sick and disabled. Individuals in such societies usually had a life expectancy of no more than 35 or 40 years, on average. Fertility was also necessarily high, as mortality took such a substantial toll that the continued existence of the society required high birthrates.

The second stage, sometimes called the stage of *transitional growth,* is characterized by continued high birthrates but a declining mortality. In this second stage of demographic transition, the population grows very rapidly and also undergoes changes in age composition. Typically, the declining death rates are due to technological changes: increased food production, distribution, and availability, and reduced vulnerability to crop failures and famine. The age composition changes accompanying the technological changes usually involve a slightly increased proportion of the elderly (increased longevity being the likely cause) and a marked increase in the proportion of the population that is young (resulting from a significant decline in infant and child mortality).

The third stage, characterized by *low mortality and low or controlled fertility,* is most often descriptive of modern Western societies. Populations experiencing this stage are capable of controlling birthrates so that very low or no population growth may eventually occur. No population has yet shown the long-term low fertility rates expected in the third stage. As the demographer Matras (1973) points out, during World War II, France and Belgium had depressed fertility and an excess of deaths over births and thus experienced a decline in population size. Ireland may offer the best historical example of absolute decline in population. In 1851, Ireland had a population of 5.1 million; by 1951, it had declined to just under 3 million, a reduction of 42 percent. In the 1980 census, the number was back up to

---

[2]Zopf (1984), among others, offers a version of the demographic transition that allows for identifying more refined variation among societies and includes seven stages. For purposes of simplicity, a three-stage version of the demographic transition is offered here.

3.3 million, equal to what the population had been in 1905. Demographer Kingsley Davis (1963) suggests that this case represents the result of a wide range of demographic responses that people made to the realities in their lives and their country. These included efforts to reduce family size as a way to minimize costs of child rearing and to maximize other opportunities, and migration out of the country in search of economic opportunities in large urban centers such as Boston, London, and New York.

Several nations are approaching what some would consider the completion of the third stage. Donald Bogue developed an index to measure the extent to which a nation has completed the demographic transition. Applying his index to 1960 data, Bogue (1969) found that the European nations were the furthest along, with a median percentage of demographic transition completed of 91.4. The former Soviet Union was next, with a percentage between 80.0 and 90.0, and the nations of North America had a median percentage of 79.0. In contrast, the African nations had a median percentage of demographic transition completed of 19.9. Many nations, including the United States, have made substantial moves toward completing the transition since 1960. By 1980, the former East and West Germany and Switzerland were showing absolute decline in population of 0.1 percent per year (Zopf, 1984).

Some demographers believe that demographic transition theory is a useful tool only for analyzing population change in the West. William Petersen (1975), for example, argues that today's so-called underdeveloped nations and totalitarian societies exhibit patterns of fertility, mortality, and migration that make them difficult to analyze in terms of a three-stage transition process. Typically, underdeveloped countries interested in rapid development have imported Western health programs and medical technology on a wholesale basis. This has resulted in significant declines in their death rates. Unfortunately, efforts to cut fertility have been less successful, with enormous population growth as a result. Some nation-states have attempted intervention in an effort to achieve specific demographic goals. Policies such as family subsidies, creation of state-controlled abortion centers, forced migration, and immigration or emigration restrictions have been employed to affect population dynamics.

The Population Pyramid

One graphic technique that is often employed to depict the demographic transition process is the population pyramid. The *population pyramid* is a special type of bar graph, with the various bars representing successive age categories, from the lowest at the bottom to the highest at the top. The population represented in this graphic device is usually broken down into 5- or 10-year intervals, with each bar divided between males at the left and females at the right. The length of the bars represents the population either in absolute figures or as a percentage.

Figure 3–1 shows population pyramids for the United States in 1995, 2010, and 2030. The reason for the basic shape of the pyramid is that among those born in a given year—1940, for example—some have died in each year since then, thus reducing the length of the bars representing successively higher ages. However,

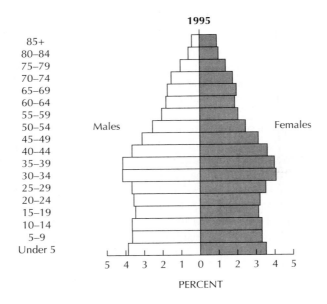

1995

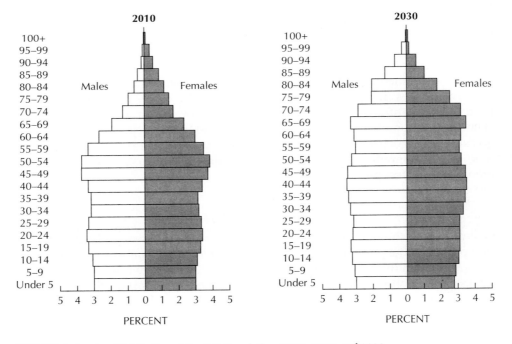

2010

2030

FIGURE 3–1   Age Distribution of the U.S. Population: 1995, 2010, and 2030

Source: U.S. Senate Special Committee on Aging, *Aging America: Trends and Projections,* 1991 ed. (Washington, DC: U.S. Department of Health and Human Services, 1991), Figure 1; Current Population Reports p. 25–1104 (Washington, DC: Government Printing Office, 1993), Table 2.

the shape is not ordinarily pyramidal because birthrates, death rates, and rates of migration all vary from year to year. The 1995 pyramid is somewhat bottom heavy, with the largest age groups being 30 to 34 and 35 to 39 years of age and birthrates somewhat lower since 1967 or thereabout (Spencer, 1989). The narrowness of the top of the 1995 pyramid (from 65 to 69 years and up) is a result of (1) lower birthrates during the Depression and up to World War II and (2) deaths that have already occurred within the early twentieth-century birth cohorts.

By the year 2000, the large Baby Boom cohorts will all be over age 35, increasing the median age of the population, as was already indicated. The pyramid for 2010 reflects continuing expectation of lower birthrates throughout the remainder of the twentieth century and into the first decade of the twenty-first century. After 2010, the Baby Boom cohorts no longer have such disproportionate influence on the shape of the pyramid; the median age of the population will begin to rise at a much slower rate. If it is possible to maintain the consistently low birth and death rates required in stage three of the demographic transition, the pyramid would come to look like a rectangle turned on its end (e.g., see the pyramid for the year 2030), with relatively no population growth over the long term. Under such hypothetical conditions, the proportion of the population that was aged would rise steadily and become stationary toward the end of the twenty-first century. By 2080, almost 25 percent of the population could be expected to achieve age 65 years; the Census Bureau projects 5 to 7 percent of the total population at age 85 years and over in the year 2080, and 0.5 percent of the population at 100 years of age or over (Spencer, 1989).

THE DEPENDENCY RATIO

The growth of the elderly population has led gerontologists to look to the demographic relationship between it and the rest of the population. To the degree that the old are to be supported by the society to which they have contributed, this relationship may suggest the extent of social, economic, and political effort a society may be asked to make in support of its elderly.

One measure used to crudely summarize this relationship is known as the *dependency ratio.* Arithmetically, the ratio represents the number or proportion of individuals in the dependent segment of the population divided by the number or proportion of individuals in the supportive or working population. Although the dependent population has two components, the young and the old, students of gerontology have especially concerned themselves with the old-age dependency ratio. Definitions of *old* and *working* are "65 and over" and "18 to 64" years of age, respectively. Thus, the old-age dependency ratio is, in simple demographic terms, 65+/18–64.[3] This does not mean that every person aged 65 and over is dependent

---

[3]Actually, in order to ensure the presentation of the old-age dependency ratio in whole numbers, compute as follows: (those 65+ years of age/those 18 to 64 years of age) × 100.

or that every person in the 18 to 64 range is working. However, these basic census categories are used to depict the relationship between these two segments of the society's population.

Table 3–3 shows old-age dependency ratios for the United States from 1970 to 2050. The ratio has increased slowly since 1970 and is expected to continue to do so until the year 2020, when a dramatic increase is projected. During the decade between 2010 and 2020, the Baby Boomers of the late 1940s and 1950s will begin reaching retirement age, thus increasing the numerator; and a relatively low birth-rate (such as now exists) means a relatively smaller work force population (18 to 64), reducing the denominator (Cutler & Harootyan, 1975). Another dramatic increase is projected between 2020 and 2030. The projected old-age dependency ratio of 35.7 in 2030 indicates that every 36 individuals 65 years of age or over will hypothetically be supported by 100 working persons between the ages of 18 and 64. This constitutes a ratio of less than 1 to 3. In 1930, this ratio was about 1 to 11, and in 1960, it was about 1 to 6.

Some demographers have begun to distinguish between a *societal* old-age dependency ratio (discussed previously) and a *familial* old-age dependency ratio. The familial old-age dependency ratio can be used to illustrate the shifts in the ratio of elderly parents to children who would support them. This ratio is also defined in simple demographic terms: population aged 65 to 79/population aged 45 to 49. This does not mean that all persons aged 65 to 79 need support or even have children, or that every person in the 45 to 49 age range is willing or able to provide. Yet, these age categories are used to depict the ratio of the number of elderly persons to the number of younger persons of the next generation.

Table 3–4 shows familial old-age dependency ratios for the United States from 1960 to 2050. The ratios increased from 1960 to 1980 and then are projected to decline until 2020, when a dramatic increase is expected. In 1960, there were 129

TABLE 3–3   Societal Old-Age Dependency Ratios, 1970–2050

Year	Ratio
1970	17.6
1980	18.6
1990	20.2
Projections	
2000	20.9
2010	21.5
2020	27.4
2030	35.7
2040	37.1
2050	36.2

Source: U.S. Bureau of the Census, *Statistical Abstract of the United States: 1995* (Washington, DC, 1995), Tables 14 and 17.

TABLE 3–4   **Familial Old-Age Dependency Ratios, 1960–2050**

Year	Ratio
1960	129
1970	135
1980	185
1994	152
Projections	
2000	128
2010	130
2020	225
2030	254
2040	237
2050	243

Source: G. Spencer, *Projections of the Population of the United States, by Age, Sex, and Race: 1988 to 2080,* Current Population Reports, Population Estimates and Projections Series P-25, No. 1018 (Washington, DC: U.S. Department of Commerce, Bureau of the Census, 1989), Table 4; U.S. Bureau of the Census, *Statistical Abstract of the United States: 1995* (Washington, DC, 1995), Table 16.

Note: The familial old-age dependency ratio is computed as follows: Population aged 65 to 79 years/Population aged 45 to 49 years × 100.

persons aged 65 to 79 for every 100 persons 45 to 49. This figure reached 185 in 1980. A higher figure of 225 is projected for 2020. Changes in the familial old-age dependency ratio result mainly from past trends in fertility. For example, the relatively high ratio in 1980 reflects the combination of high fertility (and in-migration) in the early part of this century (population aged 65 to 79 years) and reduced birthrates during the 1930s (population aged 45 to 49 years). The higher ratio expected in 2020 results from high fertility during the post–World War II Baby Boom years and the lower birthrates of the early 1970s.

Shifts in the societal and familial old-age dependency ratios suggest that support of the aged will become increasingly problematic through the remainder of this century and especially serious after 2010. It would seem that unless the elderly of the future are better able to support themselves than are current cohorts of elderly, an increasing burden will fall on the working population, requiring government to play a larger part in providing health and other services to the aged. Further, low fertility, low or no population growth, and aging of the population may predict no or slow economic growth. Such a scenario would increase the burden on the working population and make it more difficult to support rising public retirement and health care expenditures (Palmer & Gould, 1986).

Some would disagree, however. It may be argued that the dependency burden of the elderly should not be measured in a vacuum and that the level of the child- or "young-age" dependency ratio should be taken into account, because the share of society's support available for the elderly is affected by the level of young-age dependency (Siegel & Davidson, 1984). Table 3–5 presents the young- and old-age

TABLE 3–5   Old- and Young-Age Dependency Ratios, 1970–2050

Year	Total Dependents	Young-Age Ratio	Old-Age Ratio
1970	79.0	61.4	17.6
1980	65.1	46.5	18.6
1990	61.8	41.6	20.2
Projections			
2000	63.3	42.4	20.9
2010	60.9	39.4	21.5
2020	67.3	39.9	27.4
2030	77.9	42.2	35.7
2040	78.9	41.8	37.1
2050	78.1	41.7	36.4

Source: U.S. Bureau of the Census, *Statistical Abstract of the United States: 1995* (Washington, DC, 1995), Tables 14 and 17.

Note: Based on middle series Census Bureau projections. See Table 3–1 for an explanation of assumptions.

dependency ratios for the United States for 1970 through 1990 and projected through the year 2050. The child- or young-age dependency ratio,[4] which is the number of children under age 18 per 100 persons 18 to 64 years, is expected to decline from 61.4 in 1970 to 42.2 in 2030. This results from a continued expectation of reduced fertility and implies a generally decreasing burden on the working population. The combination of old- and young-age dependency ratios, representing an overall dependency burden on the working-age population, declined sharply between 1970 and 1980 and is expected to be relatively stable through the year 2020. The total dependency burden in 2020, projected to be 67.3, is very close to the figure (65.1) used to describe the total burden in 1980. Between 1980 and 2020, the projected proportion of the total dependency burden accounted for by those under 18 years of age declines from 71.4 to 59.3 percent. By 2030, when the total dependency ratio is projected to increase to 77.9 (it was 79.0 in 1970), those under 18 years of age will account for only 54.2 percent of the total dependency burden.

Presumably, this decline would permit the conversion of some funds and other support resources from use by children to use by the elderly. Support costs for the elderly are generally thought to be greater than for the young and historically more likely to become a public responsibility; in the United States, support for children tends to be a private family responsibility (Clark & Spengler, 1978). As a result, despite the expected shift in dependency burden between 1980 and 2030 from the young to the old, government may be expected to play a larger part in providing health and other support services to the aged.

Richard Easterlin (1991), a noted demographer, has attempted to place concern about the total dependency burden in the United States and other advanced industrial countries in some historical context. Using data from the Organization

---

[4]The child- or young-age dependency ratio is computed as follows: (those less than 18 years of age/ those between 18 and 64 years) × 100.

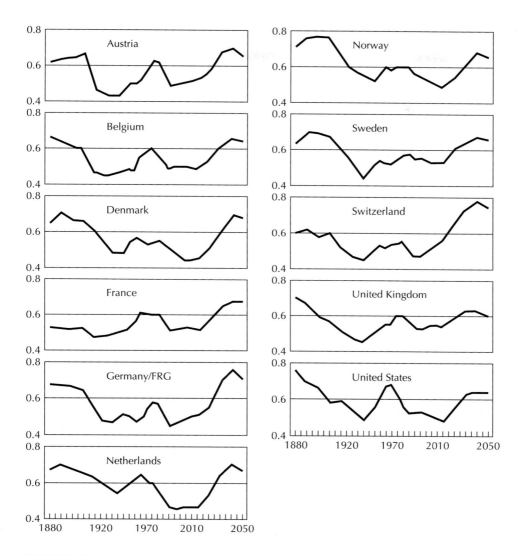

FIGURE 3–2   Total Dependency Ratio, Actual and Projected, Specified Country, 1880–2050 (Ratio of Persons Aged 0–14 and 65+ to Those Aged 15–64)

Source: R. A. Easterlin (1991), The economic impact of prospective population changes in advanced industrial countries: An historical perspective, *Journal of Gerontology,* 46(6). Copyright © The Gerontological Society of America.

for Economic Cooperation and Development (OECD) and the United Nations, Easterlin plotted separately the total dependency burden, actual and projected, from 1880 to 2050 for the United States and 10 other western industrial nations. Two questions emerge from the projections: Will the process of technological invention and innovation slow as a result? and Will the working population be able to support rising public retirement and health care expenditures?

Over the long term, from 1870 to 1986, population growth has shown a downward trend in Austria, Belgium, Denmark, Germany, the Netherlands, Norway, Sweden, Switzerland, United Kingdom, and the United States. Only France shows a higher rate of population growth in the period from 1973 to 1986 than the period from 1870 to 1913. At the same time, the rate of real per capita income growth in these nation-states has trended upward. Only Sweden and Switzerland show real per capita income growth rates in 1973 to 1986 that are lower than the rates in 1870 to 1913. According to Easterlin (1991), any future negative effects of an aging labor force will likely be offset by a more educated work force (and older population) and by continued increases in female labor force participation.

When viewed in historical perspective, projections for the total dependency burden are not unique either. Figure 3–2 shows total and projected dependency ratios, actual and projected, for 11 different nations (including the United States) for 1880 to 2050. Ratios are calculated as the total number of persons aged 14 and under and aged 65 and over to those aged 15 to 64. On average, projected total dependency rates in 2050 are about the same as in 1880. In part, this results from a rising old-age dependency that is offset by a declining youth dependency. Only France and Switzerland show significantly higher dependency ratios projected for 2050 than experienced in 1880. Several nations—the United States, the United Kingdom, and Norway—show projections for 2050 to be noticeably lower than was actually experienced in 1880. Thus, working populations should be able to handle the tax burdens related to programs for older dependents because there will be reduced need to support younger dependents.

Two caveats are in order, however. First, more research is needed on the issue of how private funds are used to support younger and older dependents. After all, tax burdens are about public monies, and public funds only represent a portion of the total available funds to support dependent populations. Second, shifting public expenditures from support of younger dependents to older dependents is a political problem. Projecting the feasibility of such a transfer is considerably more problematic than projecting the dependency rates!

SEX, RACE, AND ETHNIC COMPOSITION

Elderly women outnumber elderly men in virtually all settings within which aging takes place (Cowgill, 1972), despite the fact that the number of male births in a population always exceeds the number of female births (Matras, 1973, pp. 145–146). Typically, after the earliest ages, the male excess is reduced by higher male mortality; at the most advanced ages, the number of females exceeds the number of males.

In the United States, the number of males for every 100 females—the *sex ratio*—in the over 65 population has been declining throughout the twentieth century. In 1900, the sex ratio was 102; by 1930, it had declined to 100.4. The sex ratio in these years, however, was still heavily influenced by the predominantly male immigration prior to World War I. As Table 3–6 shows, the 1990 sex ratio in the older population was 68.7 (it was 95.4 for the total population) and is projected to increase slowly until about 2030. Principally, the sex ratio of the aged population is explained in terms of the higher mortality of males, particularly at ages below 65. This higher mortality among males reduces the relative number of survivors at the older ages.

Until recently, the female population aged 65 and over has been growing much more rapidly than the male population in this age stratum. Between 1960 and 1970, the female population 65 years old and over increased 28 percent, whereas the comparable male population increased by only about 12 percent; between 1980 and 1990, the increase in the aged female population was about 22 percent, for the aged male population about 24 percent. This marginal differential in growth rates, significant for the change in pattern it represents, added to the continued excess of males among the newborns, continues to yield a proportion of those aged 65 and over among females that is considerably above that for males. For 1990, aged females constitute about 14.6 percent of the total female population, and aged males constitute about 10.5 percent of the total male population. The sex ratio of the elderly population in 1990 corresponds to almost 6 million more women than men, or about 18.5 percent of the total aged population. Thirty years earlier, in 1960, the excess was about 1.6 million women (accounting for about 9.5 percent of the aged population). The latest Census Bureau estimates for the year 2000 project about 6.3 million more women than men, or about 18.2 percent of the total population 65 years old and over (Spencer, 1989).

TABLE 3–6 Males per 100 Females by Age and Race, 1960–2050

Age	1960	1970	1980	1990	Projections 2000	2010	2020	2030	2040	2050
All Races										
All ages	97.0	94.8	94.8	95.4	95.7	95.9	95.8	95.1	94.3	94.0
65+	82.6	72.0	67.5	68.7	69.3	71.2	75.7	77.3	75.2	74.7
Whites										
All ages	98.1	96.3	95.2	96.0	96.5	96.8	96.7	96.0	95.1	94.9
65+	82.0	71.3	67.2	68.7	69.5	71.6	76.5	78.1	75.9	75.3
Blacks										
All ages	93.8	91.8	89.6	90.9	91.5	91.9	92.0	91.7	91.2	91.0
65+	86.5	76.3	68.0	67.4	69.0	70.6	74.0	76.2	75.6	75.9

Sources: G. Spencer, *Projections of the Population of the United States, by Age, Sex, and Race: 1988 to 2080,* Current Population Reports, Population Estimates and Projections Series P-25, No. 1018 (Washington, DC: U.S. Department of Commerce, Bureau of the Census, 1989), Table 4; J. S. Siegel & M. Davidson, *Demographic and Socioeconomic Aspects of Aging in the United States,* Current Population Reports, Special Studies Series P-23, No. 138 (Washington, DC: U.S. Department of Commerce, Bureau of the Census, 1984), Table 3.1.

Because of enumeration problems, statistics on *minority elderly* should be viewed with some caution. African American elderly make up about 8.3 percent of the total elderly population, whereas 12.4 percent of the total U.S. population is black. In general, the African American population in the United States is younger than the population of whites. The proportion of the black population that is 65 years of age and over is considerably smaller than that of the white population, for both males and females. Smaller proportions of blacks than whites survive to old age, although survival rate differences between the races narrow somewhat in old age. For example, according to *life tables* for 1992, 77 percent of white males survive from birth to age 65, as compared with 58 percent for African American males; for survival from age 65 to age 85, these percentages converge to 31 and 24 percent, respectively.

The key factor in the relative youthfulness of the African American population is the higher fertility among blacks. On average, black women have 2.3 children, compared to the 1.8 recorded for white women. Approximately 44.3 percent of all African Americans are under age 25, but only about 34.5 percent of all whites are in this age grouping. The median age of blacks is roughly 5.7 years less than that of whites. In 1990, for example, African Americans had a median age of 27.5 years; the comparable figure for whites was 33.2 years.

EDUCATIONAL ATTAINMENT IN THE UNITED STATES BY AGE AND RACE/ETHNICITY, 1994

Americans aged 65 to 74 years may be the best educated generation of older people the United States has ever seen (Treas, 1995). More than two of three finished high school, compared with 55 percent of those 75 years of age and over. The honor of being the best educated older generation will not last very long, however. As the table below shows, future generations of elderly will have even higher levels of educational success. Already three of four (76 percent) Americans 55 to 64 years of age have completed four years of high school or higher, whereas more than five of six (87 percent) individuals aged 25 to 54 report similar educational accomplishment.

Still, many older people in the United States remain disadvantaged by a lack of sufficient education to read the daily newspaper or directions for preparing a holiday dinner. In 1990, 5.7 percent of those 65 years of age and older had completed fewer than five years of formal schooling, and 16.1 percent had fewer than eight years of formal schooling.

Basic literacy remains a problem for a substantial proportion of minority elderly. While 45 percent of African Americans 65 to 74 years of age have reported completing four years of high school or higher (see table), as many as 12 percent of African American elderly in the U.S. had fewer than five years of formal education. Elderly Hispanics are even more educationally disadvantaged. Only about one-third (32 percent) of those 65 to 74 years have completed high school (see table), and more than one in four (27 percent) elderly Hispanics have completed fewer than five years of formal schooling.

Education is an important resource in later life. Older people with more education typically have greater employment potential, higher income, more assets, fewer disabilities, and better overall health. Education also affects access to information, including knowledge about benefits and services available, consumption patterns, and quality of life.

In the future, educational differences within the older population will become smaller yet remain substantial. For example, as seen in the table, 87 percent of Americans aged 25 to 54 years completed four years of high school or higher, and only 25 percent of this group had graduated from college. The table also suggests that African Americans are closing the educational gap with the U.S. population as a whole at a faster pace than is the case for Hispanics. For instance, 82 percent of African Americans aged 25 to 54 years completed four years of high school or higher, but only 58 percent of comparably aged Hispanics had done similarly.

Total, African American, and Hispanic Educational Attainment in the U.S. by Age, 1994

	Age			
	25–54 yrs	**55–64 yrs**	**65–74 yrs**	**75+**
Total				
4 yrs of HS or higher	87%	76%	68%	55%
1 or more yrs of college	53	38	31	24
4 or more yrs of college	25	19	14	11
African Americans				
4 yrs of HS or higher	82%	57%	45%	25%
1 or more yrs of college	42	28	17	10
4 or more yrs of college	15	11	7	4
Hispanics				
4 yrs of HS or higher	58%	39%	32%	26%
1 or more yrs of college	30	19	14	9
4 or more yrs of college	10	7	7	3

Source: Current Population Survey, March 1994.

Note: Hispanics may be of any race.

Next to African Americans, Hispanic Americans make up the largest minority in the United States, and this population is fast growing. In 1990, Hispanic Americans constituted about 7.9 percent of the U.S. population, or about 20 million people. Officially, this population increased by 34.5 percent between 1980 and 1990. The actual rate of growth, however, has probably been higher as a result of illegal immigration. The Census Bureau forecasts another 26.8 percent increase in the Hispanic population between 1990 and 2000, with Hispanics approaching about 72 percent of the size of the African American population in the United States.

The Hispanic population is a heterogeneous group. About 60 percent are of Mexican origin. One in seven Hispanics is of Puerto Rican background (14 percent), 6 percent are Cuban, and 21 percent are of other Spanish heritage. About half of the Hispanic American elderly were not born in the United States. Cubans and Puerto Ricans are more recent immigrants than Mexican Americans, many of whom are descendants of original settlers of territories annexed by the United States in the Mexican-American War. The Hispanic American population is an even younger population than that of African Americans (43 percent under 20 years of age versus 39 percent, respectively). High fertility and large family size, in addition to immigration of the young and repatriation of the middle-aged, contribute to the youthfulness of this group.

Many *ancestry groups* are represented within the U.S. population. Table 3–7 presents some data on single and multiple ancestry groups collected through surveys conducted by the Census Bureau in 1990. German, Irish, and English ancestry groups are the largest in the United States. Ancestry groups, large and small, are likely to have substantial proportions of elderly. For example, groups of Polish, Russian, and Italian ancestry are likely to have high proportions of elderly, resulting from the considerable migration to the United States that occurred early in the twentieth century, mostly before the mid-1920s. English and Irish migration largely took place in the nineteenth century. Thus, the high proportion of elderly in these groups is likely a result of declining fertility in the early years of the twentieth century. Recent immigrants, most of whom are relatively young, are most likely to have come from Mexico, the Caribbean (e.g., Dominican Republic), and Asia (e.g., China, the Philippines, and Vietnam).

Migration has had great impact on the age distribution of the foreign-born population in the United States. Before World War I, immigration was relatively unrestricted. After that war, changes in policy brought a sharp curtailment to immigration. In 1970, a relatively high proportion of the elderly were themselves

TABLE 3–7   Population by Selected Ancestry Groups, and Persons 65 Years and Over Speaking a Language Other than English at Home: 1990

Ancestry	Total (1,000)	Ancestry	Total (1,000)
German	57,947	Dutch	6,227
Irish	38,736	Asian[1]	5,904
English	32,652	Scotch-Irish	5,618
African American	23,777	Scottish	5,394
Italian	14,665	Swedish	4,681
Mexican	11,587	Norweigian	3,869
Polish	9,366	Russian	2,953
American Indian	8,708	Spanish	2,024

Persons 65 years old and over	31,195,000
Speak only English	27,381,000
Speak other language (total)	3,814,000
Speak Asian or Pacific Island language	355,000
Speak Spanish or Spanish Creole	1,057,000
Speak some other language	2,402,000

Source: U.S. Bureau of the Census, *Statistical Abstract of the United States: 1995* (Washington, DC, 1995), Tables 56 and 57.

[1]Includes Asian Indian, Chinese, Filipino, Japanese, Korean, and Vietnamese.

foreign-born—among those 65 years of age and older, 15.3 percent were born outside the United States. The proportion of the elderly population that is foreign-born will likely continue to decline in the near future.

GEOGRAPHIC DISTRIBUTION

The elderly population, like the total population, is not distributed equally across the United States. Generally, the elderly are most numerous in the states with the largest populations. Florida, California, and New York have the largest elderly populations, with more than two million each. New Jersey, Pennsylvania, Illinois, Ohio, Michigan, and Texas each have over one million aged residents. Together, these nine states account for 52.7 percent of the entire 1990 aged population in the United States. Table 3–8 lists the states by percentage of population age 65 and over for 1990.

In all states, the aged population increased between 1980 and 1990, though at widely differing rates. By 1990, Florida showed the highest proportion of its population 65 years of age and older (18.3 percent), with almost 2.4 million elderly residing in the state. On the other end of the continuum, Alaska showed the smallest proportion of its population 65 years of age and older (4.1 percent), or about 22,500 elderly residing in the state.

TABLE 3–8   States by Percentage of Population Aged 65 Years and Over, 1990

Percentage		State
18.3	1	Florida
14.7–15.4	6	Arkansas, Iowa, Pennsylvania, Rhode Island, South Dakota, West Virginia
13.8–14.3	5	Kansas, Missouri, Nebraska, North Dakota, Oregon
13.0–13.6	10	Arizona, Connecticut, Maine, Massachusetts, Montana, New Jersey, New York, Ohio, Oklahoma, Wisconsin
12.0–12.9	11	Alabama, Delaware, District of Columbia, Idaho, Kentucky, Illinois, Indiana, Minnesota, Mississippi, North Carolina, Tennessee
11.1–11.9	7	Louisiana, Michigan, Hawaii, New Hampshire, South Carolina, Vermont, Washington
10.0–10.8	9	California, Colorado, Georgia, Maryland, Nevada, New Mexico, Texas, Virginia, Wyoming
8.7	1	Utah
4.1	1	Alaska
	51	

Residential Mobility

Some of the growth in state elderly populations is due to natural increase, but some is the result of interstate migration. Compared to younger persons, the elderly are much less likely to be residentially mobile. During 1992 and 1993, only 6 percent of the elderly were residentially mobile, while the figure for the total U.S. population was 16 percent (U.S. Bureau of the Census, 1995). In general, most residentially mobile individuals and families move within the same county. Between 1992 and 1993, movers age 65 years and older were only half as likely as the total U.S. population to move to a different county (3 percent vs. 6 percent) and only a third as likely to move to a different state (1 percent vs. 3 percent). This is somewhat similar to a pattern described by Biggar (1984), for the period between 1975 and 1980, when fewer than 5 percent of the U.S. elderly population made an interstate move, compared with 10 percent of the total U.S. population (Biggar, 1984).

Biggar (1984) points out that 12 states drew more than half of the nation's elderly migrants. Five *Sunbelt states* ranked among the top 10 most popular destinations; Florida, California, Arizona, and Texas were ranked first through fourth, respectively. Florida alone attracted more than one-fourth of the entire nation's elderly migrants (Biggar, 1984). Elderly Sunbelt migrants seem to be younger, better educated, more financially secure, and more likely to be married than migrants to other states. This seems especially the case for Arizona and Florida. California appears to receive the greatest number of poorer migrants. According to Biggar, in states such as Arizona and Florida, the graying of the Sunbelt brings increased demands for consumer goods as well as housing, recreational, health, and protective services. For California, the elderly migration increases the demands placed on state and local social and welfare service agencies for the aged.

Where do migrants to the Sunbelt come from? Several major streams from noncontiguous states provide a source of migrants to the Sunbelt. Between 1975 and 1980, major streams into Florida came from Connecticut, Indiana, Massachusetts, Michigan, New Jersey, New York, Ohio, and Pennsylvania. From this list, only Michigan also provided a major stream of migrants to Arizona, which also drew from Illinois, Iowa, Minnesota, Washington, and Wisconsin. Migrants to California were drawn from Illinois and Washington. In the central Sunbelt, Texas has become a destination for streams of elderly migrants from Kansas and Missouri. Another newly emerging Sunbelt destination is North Carolina, drawing migrants from Maryland and New Jersey (Biggar, 1984).

Often, states with high in-migration rates also have high out-migration rates. This seems especially the case for California and Florida. Between 1975 and 1980, major streams of elderly migrants left Florida for Michigan, New York, Ohio, and Pennsylvania. Longino (1979) reports that one-third of the national interstate migrating older population residing outside their state of birth in 1965 returned by 1970. Given that the states identified here all provide major streams of elderly migrants to Florida, Biggar (1984) hypothesizes that much of this out-migration involves returning home to be near family after a spouse dies or with the onset of health and/or financial problems.

California may represent a different case of "returning home." States receiving streams of out-migrants from California include Arkansas, Colorado, Idaho, Missouri, Oklahoma, Utah, and Washington. Only Washington provided a sizable stream into California. Others on this list may represent states of birth for individuals who migrated to California in early adulthood. Remember that during the first half of the twentieth century California was an important destination for migrants of all ages seeking a "land of opportunity."

Residential Concentration

Increasingly, the elderly have become an urbanized population, locating in central cities or in places that structurally and functionally are parts of larger metropolitan areas (Golant, 1975). In 1988, only 14.1 percent of the elderly were on farms. According to Golant (1972), the growth in the urban elderly population is largely the result of younger cohorts aging "in place" and of residential relocations made earlier in the life span, rather than of relocation made after retirement. Still, it is important to remember that 21 states have at least 40 percent of their older population in rural areas; and in 9 states (Alaska, Arkansas, Mississippi, North Carolina, North Dakota, South Carolina, South Dakota, Vermont, and West Virginia), more than half of the older population is rural. Also, 13 states have more than 10 percent of their older populations living on farms (here, for the moment, the elderly is defined as those 60 years of age and over). This has important policy implications given that so many government programs are designed to serve an urban population.

In 1990, 79 percent of the U.S. population resided within a metropolitan area; the comparable figure was probably somewhat lower for the population age 65 years and over. Metropolitan population growth in the United States has been a function of the growth of suburbs, however, and these have been the fastest growing sites for the elderly population in recent decades. In 1960, only about 17 percent of all elderly citizens were living in the urban fringe around central city areas; by 1980, this proportion exceeded 28 percent and is still higher today. This reflects less the migration of those age 65 and over than the aging of suburban populations.

SUMMARY

The elderly population of the United States has been increasing since 1900. Changes in fertility, mortality, and migration have all contributed to this growth. The absolute number of the elderly and the proportion of the population they constitute are expected to increase further in this century, though at a slowed pace. In addition, the aged population is itself aging. By 2010, approximately

half (48.3 percent) of the aged will be 75 years of age or over.

The old-age dependency ratio is a measure often used to summarize the demographic relationship between the elderly and the rest of the population. It is expected to increase slowly in the coming years, with dramatic increases by 2020 and again by 2030. Continued expectations for reduced fertility during this same period should allow for a projected decline in the young-age dependency ratio. Thus, the total dependency burden over the next 30 to 40 years should be relatively stable, with the projected dependency ratio in 2030 lower than the figure for 1970.

Elderly women outnumber elderly men, a difference that has been increasing for the past several decades. Because of enumeration problems, data on minority elderly must be evaluated cautiously. African Americans constitute the largest group of nonwhite elderly, although they represent a smaller proportion of the total elderly population than of the total general population. The Hispanic elderly population has undergone dramatic increase in recent decades, a trend that is expected to continue. This population, however, is even more youthful than the black population.

In general, the elderly population is concentrated in the largest states. Some growth in state populations of elderly is due to interstate migration. Sunbelt states rank among the most popular destinations for elderly migrants. Streams of elderly migrants seem to come to the Sunbelt principally from the Northeast and Midwest. Recently, gerontologists have identified streams of out-migrants returning home from the Sunbelt states. For individual elderly persons, this may be a consequence of widowhood or of the onset of health and/or financial problems.

Like the rest of the U.S. population, the elderly have become increasingly urbanized. Still, in nine states, more than half of the older population is rural. These patterns reflect the aging in place of populations that may have relocated earlier in life more than they do migration of those over 60 years of age.

STUDY QUESTIONS

1. Discuss the roles fertility, mortality, and migration have played in the growth of the elderly population in the United States during the twentieth century.

2. Should people have confidence in U.S. Census Bureau projections of the growth in numbers and proportion of the elderly population in the United States in the future? Why or why not?

3. What is a dependency ratio? Distinguish between the *societal* old-age dependency ratio and the *familial* old-age dependency ratio. How is the mix of old-age and young-age dependency ratios expected to change in the United States in the future?

4. Can you put dependency ratios in some historical and cross-national perspective? How does what is projected to occur in the United States compare with the projections for other nations? Assume these projections about the future

are accurate and discuss their consequences. What, if any, are the caveats about dependency ratios in the future?

5. Define *sex ratio*. Applying the concept to the elderly population, how has the sex ratio changed since the beginning of the twentieth century? Why has it changed?

6. Why is recognition of minority elderly issues likely to increase in the future? Why may the importance of ancestry groups diminish among the elderly in this same future?

7. Describe the residential mobility patterns of the elderly in the contemporary United States. What role do the Sunbelt states play in elderly migration? In this context, what is meant by "returning home"?

8. How has the residential concentration of the elderly population changed in recent decades? Why?

REFERENCES

Biggar, J. C. (1984). *The graying of the sunbelt.* Washington, DC: Population Reference Bureau.

Bogue, D. J. (1969). *Principles of demography.* New York: Wiley.

Clark, R. L., & Spengler, J. J. (1978). Changing dependency and dependency costs: The implications of future dependency ratios and their composition. In B. Herzog (Ed.), *Aging and income: Programs and prospects for the elderly.* New York: Human Sciences Press.

Cowgill, D. (1972). A theory of aging in cross-cultural perspective. In D. Cowgill & L. Holmes (Eds.), *Aging and modernization.* New York: Appleton-Century-Crofts.

Crimmins, E. M. (1980). *Implications of recent mortality trends for the size and composition of the population over 65.* Paper presented at the annual meeting of the Gerontological Society of America, November.

Cutler, N., & Harootyan, R. (1975). Demography of the aged. In D. Woodruff & J. Birren (Eds.), *Aging: Scientific perspectives and social issues.* New York: Van Nostrand.

Davis, K. (1963). The theory of change and response in modern demographic history. *Population Index, 29,* 362–366.

Easterlin, R. A. (1991). The economic impact of prospective population changes in advanced industrial countries: An historical perspective. *Journal of Gerontology, 46* (6), S299–309.

Golant, S. M. (1972). *The residential location and spatial behavior of the elderly.* Research Paper 143, University of Chicago, Department of Geography.

Golant, S. M. (1975). Residential concentrations of the future elderly. *Gerontologist, 15,* 16–23.

Longino, C. F. (1979). Going home: Aged return migration in the United States 1965–70. *Journal of Gerontology, 34* (5), 736–745.

Matras, J. (1973). *Populations and societies.* Englewood Cliffs, NJ: Prentice-Hall.

Neugarten, B. (1974). Age groups in American society and the rise of the young-old. *Annals of the American Academy,* September, 187–198.

Palmer, J. L., & Gould, S. G. (1986). Economic consequences of population aging. In A. Pifer & L. Bronte (Eds.), *Our aging society: Paradox and promise.* New York: Norton.

Petersen, W. (1975). *Population* (3rd ed.). New York: Macmillan.

Siegel, J. S. (1979). *Prospective trends in the size and structure of the elderly population, impact of mortality trends and some implications.* Current Population Reports, Special Studies Series P-23, No. 78. Washington, DC: U.S. Department of Commerce, Bureau of the Census.

Siegel, J. S., & Davidson, M. (1984). *Demographic and socioeconomic aspects of aging in the United States.* Current Population Reports, Special Studies Series P-23, No. 138. Washington, DC: U.S. Department of Commerce, Bureau of the Census.

Spencer, G. (1989). *Projections of the population of the United States, by age, sex, and race: 1988 to 2080.* Current Population Reports, Population Estimates and Projections Series P-25, No. 1018. Washington, DC: U.S. Department of Commerce, Bureau of the Census.

Treas, J. 1995. Older Americans in the 1990s and beyond. *Population Bulletin, 50* (2), 2–46.

U.S. Bureau of the Census. (1995). *Statistical abstract of the United States: 1995* (115th ed.). Washington, DC: U.S. Government Printing Office.

Zopf, Paul, Jr. (1984). *Population: An introduction to social demography.* Palo Alto, CA: Mayfield.

CHAPTER 4

WHAT ARE THE RESULTS OF AGING?

Cary S. Kart, Eileen S. Metress, and Seamus P. Metress

The physician Alexander Leaf (1973) quotes Frederic Verzar, the Swiss gerontologist, as saying, "Old age is not an illness. It is a continuation of life with decreasing capacities for adaptation." Some students of aging would disagree. It has been a popular view that if old age is not an illness in and of itself, there is at least a strong relationship between biological aging and pathology. This view posits that biological deterioration creates a state of susceptibility to disease, and susceptibility to particular diseases leads to death.

One way to resolve this disagreement may be to distinguish between biological and pathological aging. It is difficult to say at what point in life a person is old, but it is clear that everyone becomes so. Everyone ages. Genetic and other prenatal influences set the stage for the aging sequence, and factors in the postnatal environment (demographic, economic, psychological, and social) act to modify this sequence. The changes that accompany aging occur in different people at different chronological ages and progress at different rates. Changes in physical appearance are the most easily recognized; it is also well known that some physical capabilities diminish. These changes may be placed in the category of *biological aging.*

Disease is another matter. As individuals grow older, they are more likely to become afflicted with certain diseases, many of which prove fatal. Changes that occur as a result of disease processes may be categorized as *pathological aging.* Kohn (1985) offers three ways to define disease:

1. Some diseases are universal, progressive, and inevitable with age. Atherosclerosis, a chronic disease of the blood vessels, exemplifies this type of disease. It increases a person's vulnerability to other diseases, but in many respects is indistinguishable from normal aging.

2. Some diseases are age related, but are neither universal or inevitable. For example, the risks of contracting many forms of cancer increase with age, but not all elderly people contract cancer.

3. Some diseases are not age related, but their impact is greater as the individual ages. Death rates from respiratory diseases, for example, are dramatically higher in older age groups than in younger and middle-aged groups.

We begin this chapter by discussing recent progress in mortality and life expectancy among the elderly. This is followed by a description of the results of biological aging—those important bodily changes that occur as age increases. Current theories or explanations of biological aging are evaluated in Chapter 5. Disease processes related to pathological aging are reserved for discussion in Chapter 6.

For those who wonder why a social gerontologist needs to know so much about biology, the gerontologist Robert Atchley has an answer: Understanding the physiological changes that accompany aging is important for the social gerontologist "because they represent the concrete physiological limits around which social arrangements are built" (Atchley, 1972, p. 47). Broadly interpreted, Atchley's statement means that changes fundamental to aging do not occur in isolation. Psychological and social changes both affect and are affected by the physiological changes taking place. The social gerontologist who is ignorant about the biological aspects of aging cannot hope to comprehend the important relationships among the physical, psychological, and social changes that accompany aging.

MORTALITY

Gerontologists use the term *senescence* to describe all postmaturational changes and the increasing vulnerability individuals face as a result of these changes. Senescence describes the group of effects that lead to a decreasing expectation of life with increasing age (Comfort, 1979). Strehler (1962) distinguishes senescence from other biological processes in four ways: (1) Its characteristics are universal, (2) the changes that constitute it come from within the individual, (3) the processes associated with senescence occur gradually, and (4) the changes that appear in senescence have a deleterious effect on the individual.

Is senescence a fundamental, or inherent, biological process? Comfort (1979) is doubtful. He believes that attempts to identify a single underlying property that explains all instances of senescent change are misplaced. Yet, there does appear to be some pattern to one's increased vulnerability through the life course. Roughly speaking, it appears that the probability of dying doubles every eight years.

This phenomenon has been recognized since 1825, when Benjamin Gompertz observed that an exponential increase in the death rate occurred between the ages of 10 and 60. After plotting age-specific death rates on a logarithmic scale and finding an increase that was nearly linear, Gompertz suggested that human mortality was governed by an equation with two terms. The first accounted for chance deaths that would occur at any age; the second, characteristic of the species, represented the exponential increase with time. These observations, sometimes referred to as *Gompertz's law,* reasonably seem to describe human mortality in many human societies (Fries & Crapo, 1981). However, although one can accept the principle that the probability of dying increases with age, it is important to emphasize that the probabilities themselves differ for males and females, vary by race, and change through time.

During 1992, an estimated 2.2 million deaths occurred in the United States. The preliminary death rate for that year was 8.5 deaths per 1,000 population. The majority of these deaths involved elderly people. Over 1.57 million (or about 72 percent) of the deaths occurred among individuals who had passed their 65th birthday.

The leading cause of death among the elderly is heart disease, which accounts for almost 38 percent of all deaths in old age. Malignant neoplasms (cancer) account for 23 percent of the deaths (26 percent for men, 20 percent for women) and cerebrovascular diseases account for another 8 percent of deaths among the elderly. Together, these three categories accounted for about 69 percent of all deaths of elderly people and approximately 64 percent of all deaths in the United States in 1992. Obviously, the high proportion of the deaths of elderly people due to these three causes is an expression of vulnerability to these afflictions that begins earlier in the life cycle.

Table 4–1 shows the pattern of death rates for these three leading causes of death among the elderly between 1950 and 1990. Death rates for the elderly have declined overall since 1950; between 1970 and 1990, death rates for males aged 65 to 74 years declined by 28 percent, and the decline for comparably aged females was 23 percent. The death rate for elderly men is considerably higher than that of elderly women, continuing a long-term trend. Among whites aged 65 to 74 years of age, for example, the death rate from all causes was 95 percent higher for males than females in 1970, and 77 percent higher in 1990.

As Table 4–1 indicates, the death rates for two of the three leading causes of death, heart disease and stroke (cerebrovascular disease), declined significantly between 1950 and 1990. The death rate for cancer, the second leading cause of death in 1990, has increased over the years (25.9 percent for individuals 65 to 74 years of age in the 1950–1990 period). Sex differences in death (not shown in this table) are pronounced for different forms of cancer; in 1990, among individuals aged 65 to 74 years, males had a death rate for respiratory cancer approximately 2.5 times higher than that for females. Since 1970, however, there have been large annual increases in respiratory cancer mortality for older women associated with cigarette smoking. The increase from 1970 to 1990 in mortality rates from respiratory cancer among women aged 65 to 74 was 307 percent. This compares with a 15.8 percent increase in mortality rates from breast cancer for comparably aged women over the same time period. In 1990, for women aged 65 to 74 years and 75 to 84 years, the death rates from respiratory cancer were higher than those from breast cancer.

TABLE 4–1 U.S. Death Rates for Diseases of the Heart, Cerebrovascular Diseases (Including Stroke), and Malignant Neoplasms (Cancer), by Age, 1950–1990

Age	1950[a]	1960[a]	1970	1980	1990
		Diseases of the Heart			
55–64 years	808.1	737.9	652.3	494.1	357.0
65–74 years	1,839.8	1,740.5	1,558.2	1,218.6	872.0
75–84 years	4,310.1	4,089.4	3,683.8	2,993.1	2,219.1
85+ years	9,150.6	9,317.8	8,468.0	7,777.1	6,618.4
		Cerebrovascular Diseases			
55–64 years	195.3	147.3	115.8	65.2	46.4
65–74 years	549.7	469.2	384.1	219.5	139.6
75–84 years	1,449.6	1,491.3	1,254.2	788.6	479.4
85+ years	2,990.1	3,680.5	3,234.6	2,288.9	1,587.7
		Malignant Neoplasms			
55–64 years	392.9	396.8	423.0	436.1	448.4
65–74 years	692.5	713.9	754.2	817.9	871.6
75–84 years	1,153.3	1,127.4	1,168.0	1,232.3	1,351.6
85+ years	1,451.0	1,450.0	1,417.3	1,594.6	1,773.9

Sources: National Center for Health Statistics, *Health, United States, 1988,* DHHS Publication No. (PHS) 89-1232, Public Health Service (Washington, DC: U.S. Government Printing Office, 1989); U.S. Bureau of the Census, 1994, Table 128.

Note: Deaths per 100,000 population in specified group.

[a]Includes deaths of nonresidents of the United States.

Most elderly people die as a result of some long-standing chronic condition, which is sometimes related to personal habits (e.g., smoking, drinking, poor eating habits) or environmental conditions (e.g., harsh work settings, air pollution) that go back many years. Preventing illness and death from these conditions must begin before old age. Some deaths, such as those from accidents, have declined significantly. The death rate from accidents and violence, for example, for white males aged 65 years and over in 1990 was 8 percent lower than that in 1980; the comparable decline for elderly African American males during this period was 18.7 percent.

Sex Differences in Mortality

As can be seen from Table 4–2, comparisons by race show that men have higher death rates than women in every age category. Some of this difference is almost certainly attributable to biological factors. For example, the larger proportion of males who die in infancy is apparently not explainable by any systematic variation in physical and/or social environmental factors. For most adults, however, it may be difficult to distinguish between biological and environmental contributors to death. Male/female differences in mortality may be due, in part, to sex differences in the use of physician services. Typically, women report using health ser-

TABLE 4–2   Age-Specific Death Rates, by Race and Sex, 1990

Age	Whites		African Americans	
	Male	Female	Male	Female
All ages	9.3	8.5	10.0	7.5
Age adjusted	6.4	3.7	10.6	5.8
Under 1	9.0	6.9	21.1	17.4
1–4	0.5	0.4	0.9	0.7
5–14	0.3	0.2	0.4	0.3
15–24	1.3	0.5	2.5	0.7
25–34	1.8	0.6	4.3	1.6
35–44	2.7	1.2	7.0	3.0
45–54	5.5	3.1	12.6	6.4
55–64	14.7	8.2	26.2	14.5
65–74	34.0	19.2	49.5	28.7
75–84	78.5	48.4	91.3	56.9
85+	182.7	144.0	169.6	133.1

Source: U.S. Bureau of the Census, 1994, Tables 117 and 118.

Note: Deaths per 1,000 people.

vices more frequently than men do. This may result in earlier and more effective treatment of their illnesses and may contribute to lower death rates relative to men (Marcus & Siegel, 1982). The childbearing experience of females and the overrepresentation of males in dangerous occupations are two additional factors that make it difficult to determine the relative effect on mortality of biological and environmental or sociocultural factors.

Francis Madigan (1957) attempted to differentiate between biological and environmental factors in mortality. His classic study compared the mortality experience of Catholic brothers and nuns who were members of teaching communities. Madigan argued that the life patterns of these two groups are quite similar and that, over time, brothers and nuns are subjected to the same sociocultural stresses. Of particular importance here is the absence of sex-linked activities that are relevant to mortality—namely, childbearing for females and participation in dangerous occupations for males. Madigan found that the difference in death rates between brothers and nuns was greater than between males and females in the population as a whole and that this difference had been increasing during the decades under study. From this, he argued that biological factors are more important than sociocultural ones. Further, Madigan hypothesized that the death rate advantage enjoyed by women was bound up in their greater constitutional resistance to degenerative diseases.

Such a hypothesis is difficult to test empirically. Table 4–3 presents ratios of male to female death rates for the population 65 years of age and over, by age and race, for 1990. In general, the table shows a decline in male/female death ratios by age for whites and African Americans. Among people aged 55 to 64, the male death rate is about 80 percent higher than that of females, whereas the death rate

TABLE 4–3   Male/Female Death Ratios among the Elderly, by Age and Race, 1990

Age	Whites	African Americans
55–64	1.78	1.80
65–74	1.77	1.73
75–84	1.62	1.61
85+	1.27	1.27

Note: Ratios computed from data in U.S. Bureau of the Census, 1994, Table 118.

of men in the group 85 years and older is only 27 percent higher than that of women.

The general increase in mortality differences between the sexes very likely reflects a major shift in the cause pattern of mortality. During the twentieth century, the contribution of infectious and parasitic diseases and maternal mortality to overall mortality rates has diminished relative to that of chronic degenerative diseases such as diseases of the heart, malignant neoplasms, and cerebrovascular diseases (Siegel, 1979). However, changes in recent decades in the male/female mortality ratio appear to be more closely associated with social and environmental factors than with biological ones. For example, according to Petersen (1975), the age-adjusted death rate from cancers was 65 percent higher for females than males in 1900, about equal between the sexes in 1947, and 20 percent higher for males by 1963. This changing pattern would seem to have more to do with technological advancements than with innate biological factors. The diagnosis and cure of the cancers most frequently occurring among females (i.e., breast and uterine) have improved at a more rapid rate than those for cancers most frequently occurring among males (i.e., lung and digestive system).

Can the pattern of increasing male/female death rate ratios among the elderly continue? Among those of all races and of whites aged 65 to 69, ratios actually fell between 1970 and 1980, and again between 1980 and 1990. This deceleration suggests that the death rate differential between older men and women will not increase in the future as it has in the past (Zopf, 1986). This is especially the case for the young-old.

Race Differentials in Mortality

The large racial differential in mortality rates often does not receive the attention it deserves because it is a hidden factor. Return to Table 4–2 and look across the first row ("All ages"). Note that the death rate for African American males is slightly higher than that for white males (10.0 versus 9.3), whereas the death rate for African American females is slightly lower than that for white females (7.5 versus 8.5). Nevertheless, because of higher birthrates, African Americans have a younger age structure, and this tends to mask true mortality. By examining mortality across the second row ("Age adjusted") and in individual age groups, the full impact of race emerges. For example, infant mortality in the United States in 1990 was 152 percent higher among African American than white females (17.4 versus 6.9) and 134 percent higher among African American than white males (21.1 versus 9.0). Death rates among young adults 25 to 34 years of age are 139 percent greater for African American males and 167 percent greater for African American females than for whites. Only at age 85 does the racial differential in death rates tend to disappear. According to the demographer Donald Bogue, "Throughout almost all of the ages when great progress in death control has been accomplished, death rates for Blacks are about double those of whites" (1969, pp. 595–596).

Although there has been some longer-term progress in reducing the racial differential in mortality, most recently this trend has reversed itself. In 1970, the age-adjusted death rate for African Americans was 35 percent higher than the comparable figure for whites. For 1980, this differential was 33 percent, and by 1990, it was 38 percent.

The race differential in mortality is greater for males than for females. As Table 4–2 shows, in 1990, African American males had an age-adjusted death rate that was 66 percent higher than the rate for white males in 1980 (10.6 versus 6.4); this differential for females was 57 percent (5.8 versus 3.7). Also, the sex differential in mortality is smaller for African Americans on a proportional basis than for the white population. Among whites, males have an age-adjusted death rate that is 73 percent higher than that among females; among African Americans, this difference is 83 percent. It appears that African American women have not been able to achieve as large a share of the available advancements in death control as have African American men (Bogue, 1969, pp. 596–597).

Two additional points need to be stressed when dealing with racial differentials in mortality. First, there is no reason to believe that African Americans, in particular, or nonwhites, in general, are biologically less fit than whites in their capacity to survive. What this point emphasizes is that racial differentials in mortality reflect unnecessarily high mortality among nonwhites. Second, other factors, not the least of which is socioeconomic status, confound mortality data. Kitagawa and Hauser (1973) show the age-adjusted mortality rates for Japanese Americans to be about one-third the corresponding rates for whites and one-half the rate for African Americans. Their analysis of median family income among these groups suggests that socioeconomic status may account for a considerable proportion of the race differentials in mortality.

How does low socioeconomic status contribute to higher mortality rates among African Americans? Their lack of access to high-quality medical care is one reason. According to the U.S. Office of Health Resources Opportunity (1979), African Americans receive considerably fewer preventive health services, on average, than do white people. Also, medical treatment of African Americans is often delayed until the onset of later stages of disease (Gonnella, Louis, & McCord, 1976). A recent report in the *International Journal of Epidemiology* examined the number of Americans between the ages of 15 and 54 who died between 1980 and 1986 from a dozen disorders that normally are not lethal if treated early. Among the illnesses examined were appendicitis, pneumonia, gall bladder infection,

asthma, influenza, and hernia. Of the more than 120,000 premature deaths, 80 percent were African Americans. According to one coauthor, "If detected early and
quality treatment is provided, nobody should be dying of these things.... Either
[the patients] are not seeking the care or they are being blocked from the care"
(*Toledo Blade*, 1990, p. 1).

It is impossible to say precisely whether biological or social factors are more
important contributors to mortality differentials among different population
groups in U.S. society. However, it is apparent that aging, even biological aging,
does not occur in a social vacuum. Age-adjusted death rates in the U.S. total population are, for example, only about one-third what they were at the beginning of
this century. Additionally, even when considering those who, as a group, are already chronologically old, there has been a significant decline in death rates since
1960. For males aged 65 to 74 years, for example, the reduction from 1960 to 1990
is about 27 percent; for comparably aged females, the reduction is 23 percent.
These reductions in the death rates of the population reflect at least four factors, all
of which involve attempts begun in the nineteenth century to increase control over
the environment (Dorn, 1959): (1) increased food supply, (2) development of commerce and transportation, (3) changes in technology and industry, and (4) increased control over infectious disease.

LIFE EXPECTANCY

Progress in the reduction of mortality is also reflected in figures for average life
expectancy at birth. *Average life expectancy at birth,* defined as the average number
of years a person born today can expect to live under current mortality conditions,
has shown great improvement since 1900. It rose from 49.2 years in 1900–02 to 75.4
years in 1990 (see Table 4–4). This change constitutes a 53 percent increase in life
expectancy at birth, or an average annual gain of 0.3 year in this period. Still, just
as there are significant sex and racial differentials in mortality, there are similar
differentials in life expectancy. Table 4–4 shows that the population group with the
highest life expectancy at birth in 1990 is white female (79.4 years); nonwhite
males have the lowest life expectancy (67.0 years). All groups have substantially
increased life expectancies since 1900. Better sanitary conditions, the development
of effective public health programs, and rises in the standard of living are three
factors often cited to explain increased life expectancy in the twentieth century.

Life expectancy at birth is a function of death rates at all ages. Thus, the statistic does not show at what specific ages improvement has occurred. Gerontologists
are particularly interested in judging progress in "survivorship" for those aged 65
and over. One technique for judging such progress is to look at actual survivorship rates. For example, in 1900–02, 40.9 percent of newborn babies could be
expected to reach age 65; by 1990, 85 percent of the female birth cohort and 74 percent of the male birth cohort could be expected to experience age 65.

A second technique for measuring changes in survivorship involves looking at changes in age-specific life expectancy. Table 4–5 presents life expectancies at various elderly ages by sex and race in the United States for 1900–02, 1980, and 1990. In particular, gains in life expectancies for aged males (both whites and Afri-

TABLE 4–4   Years of Life Expectancy at Birth, by Race and Sex, 1900–1902 to 1990

Years	All Groups	White		Other Races	
		Male	Female	Male	Female
1900–1902	49.2	48.2	51.1	32.5	35.0
1909–1911[a]	51.6	50.3	53.7	34.2	37.7
1919–1921[a]	56.6	56.6	58.6	47.2	47.0
1929–1931	59.3	59.2	62.8	47.5	49.5
1939–1941	63.8	63.3	67.2	52.4	55.4
1949–1951	68.2	66.4	72.2	59.1	63.0
1959–1961	68.9	67.6	74.2	61.5	66.5
1969–1971	70.7	67.9	75.5	61.0	69.1
1980–1981	73.9	70.8	78.4	65.7	74.8
1990	75.4	72.7	79.4	67.0	75.2

Sources: National Center for Health Statistics, *Vital Statistics of the United States, 1978,* Vol. 2, Sec. 5, *Life Tables* (1980), Tables 5-A and 5-5; Annual Summary of Births, Deaths, Marriages, and Divorces: United States, 1981, *Monthly Vital Statistics Report,* Vol. 30, No. 13 (1982), pp. 3–4, 15. Data for 1990 taken from U.S. Bureau of the Census, 1994, Table 114.
[a]Death registration states only.

TABLE 4–5   Years of Life Expectancy at Various Elderly Ages, 1900–02, 1980, and 1990

Year and Age	Whites		African Americans	
	Male	Female	Male	Female
1900–1902[a]				
65 years	11.5	12.2	10.4	11.4
75	6.8	7.3	6.6	7.9
85	3.8	4.1	4.0	5.1
1980				
65 years	14.2	18.5	13.5	17.3
75	8.8	11.5	8.9	11.4
85	5.0	6.3	5.3	7.0
1990				
65 years	15.2	19.1	13.7	17.8
75	9.4	12.0	8.6	11.2
85	5.2	6.4	5.0	6.3

Sources: National Center for Health Statistics, *Vital Statistics of the United States,* 1978, Vol. 2, Sec. 5 *Life Tables* (1980), Table 5–4; Advance Report of the Final Mortality Statistics, 1980, *Monthly Vital Statistics Report,* Vol. 32, No. 4 (1983), Table 2. Data for 1990 taken from U.S. Bureau of the Census, 1994, Table 116.
[a]Death registration states only.

can Americans) have not kept pace with those for aged females. Overall, life expectancy at age 65 has moved ahead more slowly than has life expectancy at birth since 1900. The small increase of "expectation" values for those age 65 and over between 1900–02 and 1990 is, in part, a function of the relative lack of success the health sciences have had in reducing adult deaths caused by heart disease, cancer, and cerebrovascular diseases. These have been the leading causes of death among persons 65 years and over since 1950. Although some modest progress in reducing death rates due to heart disease and cerebrovascular diseases has been made in the last 40 years, the death rate from malignant neoplasms (cancer) has increased by more than 20 percent since 1950.

AGE-RELATED PHYSIOLOGICAL CHANGES[1]

It is important to recall that all people age, but not at the same rate. Some individuals show symptoms of aging before they are chronologically old. Others, who are chronologically old, do not yet show all of the results of senescence. According to Leaf (1973, p. 52), the average person at age 75, compared with the same person at age 30, will have 92 percent of his or her former brain weight, 84 percent basal metabolism, 70 percent kidney filtration rate, and 43 percent maximum breathing capacity. Still, the loss of function reflected in these figures does not occur at the same rate in every individual. More important, these changes do not, in and of themselves, bring dysfunction. Yet, these figures do provide empirical support for something many of us (even those under age 75) have long suspected: We are not the people we once were!

What happens physiologically as people age? What are the specific results of senescence?

The Skin

To most people, the condition of the skin, hair, and connective tissue collectively represents the ultimate indicator of age. People are often judged to be of a certain age on the basis of visible wrinkles or the degree of graying of the hair. Many older people (as well as younger people) invest in so-called miracle creams and hair dyes in an attempt to disguise these signs of age. Although perceptions of age, like those of beauty, are in the eyes of the beholder, one's outward appearance does change as one ages.

The speed and degree of some age-associated skin changes are related to a number of factors such as heredity, hormone balances, and life-style, including

[1]Materials presented in this section are adapted from Kart, Metress, and Metress, 1992.

smoking, nutrition, and exposure to sun, wind, or chemicals. Long-term exposure to sunlight accelerates time's metamorphosis of the skin. It is the major environmental/modifiable factor contributing to cosmetic alteration and cancer of the skin. Thus, recreational and occupational pursuits can hasten age-associated skin changes. Likewise, the rate of melanoma, the most serious form of skin cancer, differs geographically on the basis of sun exposure.

Most of these skin changes are not life threatening. However, they are those that many in this highly youth-oriented society equate with dreaded old age. Such changes, cosmetic and benign (as they are described here), may affect an individual's self-concept. Older people have pride in their appearance, and such concerns should not be dismissed because of their age.

The skin is a marvelous organ that generally serves its owner well throughout life, including old age. Its elasticity, suppleness, and musculature allow freedom of movement and expression. It also protects one against various physical and chemical injuries while serving as an important heat regulator and sensory device. As a protective sheath, skin limits water loss and prohibits the entrance of countless numbers of disease-causing microorganisms. These various functions of the human skin are aided by the presence of subcutaneous fat tissue, sweat- and oil-secreting glands, pigment cells, and blood vessels. Changes in these structures lead to various age-associated changes in the form and function of the skin.

Certainly the most obvious age-associated skin change is wrinkling, which begins during one's twenties and continues throughout life. Wrinkling is influenced by several factors. The human face, because of its musculature, is capable of tremendous movement and expression of emotions. Indeed, facial expressions represent an extremely important component of human communication. Smiles, laughter, frowns, disappointment, anger, rage, and surprise are all recorded. The hand of time captures these expressions and outlines them on the face. The lines that begin to form in areas of greatest movement proliferate and become deeper as the years pass. By the age of 40, most people bear the typical lines of their expressions.

Wrinkling is also caused by a loss of subcutaneous fat tissue as well as skin elasticity. The latter is significantly affected by chronic exposure to ultraviolet radiation. The loss of fat tissue is generalized but is usually most obvious in the face and the upper and lower extremities. The entire body becomes wrinkled and thus changed in appearance. Diminished subcutaneous fat tissue is also largely responsible for the characteristic emaciated look of old age. A once filled-out form gives way to a frame that seems to exhibit many of the constituents of which it is made. The hands prominently display the bones, tendons, and blood vessels that make them up. Likewise, bony prominences and vessels of the face, trunk, and extremities become more apparent.

A loss of padding, normally provided by subcutaneous fat tissue, predisposes many older persons to the development of pressure sores. These sores develop in areas between bony prominences and overlying skin areas when pressure is unrelieved. These serious lesions represent an important problem in the health care of older persons.

The skin is a marvelous organ that often is the first indicator of age-associated changes in one's appearance.

The loss of subcutaneous fat tissue alters certain normal functions of the skin. Subcutaneous fat serves as an important insulator of the body; as it diminishes, greater amounts of body heat escape, often leaving an individual feeling chilly. Older people often complain of being cold when others around them are comfortable. Complaints of being cold are caused largely by a loss of body insulation and, in part, by a diminished blood flow to the skin and extremities.

Older people are also more likely to suffer from heat exhaustion because of changes in their capacity to perspire as a result of atrophy of the sweat glands. Thus, elderly individuals should avoid being in hot, stuffy rooms, spending too much time in the sun on a warm day, or overexerting themselves. Furthermore, atrophic changes in the sweat glands make the use of deodorants and antiperspirants unnecessary for many older people.

As has already been noted, aging is accompanied by a reduction of blood flow to the skin. The diminished blood supply contributes to the coolness of the surface of the aged skin as well as to thickened fingernails and toenails and a generalized loss of body hair, including a reduction of head hair.

The hair also grays with age—one of the most noted age-associated physical changes. Loss of hair color as well as loss of one's previously characteristic skin color occurs as a result of a decrease in the number of functioning pigment-producing cells. As if to compensate for their loss, some pigment cells of the skin enlarge. These enlarged areas are responsible for many of the pigmented blotches seen on aged skin.

Various factors contribute to increased skin infections in the elderly—for example, blood vessel changes, an altered immune response, and atrophy of the sebaceous or oil-secreting glands. Blood vessels supply the body with the nutrients and chemicals that help to repair tissue and combat foreign invaders such as infectious microorganisms. If blood flow is decreased, so is the important supply of these substances. Furthermore, skin may dry and crack because of the atrophy of the oil-secreting glands. Cracks and breaks in the skin not only lead to discomfort but also can serve as portals of entry for bacteria, viruses, and fungi.

The elderly are susceptible to the same skin disorders as are persons in younger age groups. Still, certain skin disorders are more common among older persons, such as senile pruritus (itching), keratosis (a localized thickening of the skin), skin cancer, and pressure sores.

The Skeletomuscular System

One's bones and muscles provide support, stability, and shape to the body; protect vital organs; and allow freedom of movement and locomotion. These provisions of the skeletomuscular system are ones that we take very much for granted. As one ages, however, many of these functions become limited and, on occasion, denied. Joint changes, along with diminished bone and muscle mass, can give way to increased falls and fractures, stooped posture and shortened stature, loss of muscle power, misshapen joints, pain, stiffness, and limited mobility.

Arthritis and allied bone and muscular conditions are among the most common of all disorders affecting people 65 years of age and over. In fact, joint and muscular aches and pains, as well as stiffness, are often expected in old age. Frequently, all such symptoms are lumped together as discomforts of arthritis or rheumatism. Such a practice can be dangerous. The stiff limbs of Parkinson's disease and the bone pain of osteomalacia may be dismissed, thereby causing a delay in needed medical attention. Chronic, recurrent muscular and joint pain is *not* natural; in response to such symptoms, people of all ages should seek prompt medical attention.

Bone and muscle changes are significant in that they can greatly alter an individual's life-style by making certain tasks of daily living much more difficult. It should be emphasized that even though certain degenerative changes occur, they need not necessarily be disabling if proper diagnosis, treatment, and maintenance are given. Changes or disease states of the skeletomuscular system rarely serve directly to shorten the life span. Nevertheless, if a person is bedridden and immobilized as a result of pain, stiffness, falls, or fractures, complications can result that lead to death.

Arthritis is a generic term that refers to an inflammation or a degenerative change of a joint. It occurs worldwide and has occurred throughout time; it is one of the oldest known diseases. Indeed, the cartoon image of Neanderthal man as a stooped brute with a bent-knee gait represents a caricature of an arthritic relative who lived over 40,000 years ago. This condition is still very prevalent today; it represents the number one crippler of all age groups in the United States.

Osteoarthritis, the most common joint disease, is a degenerative joint change that takes place with aging. Its cause is not definitely known. It is also referred to as "wear-and-tear arthritis" and "degenerative joint disease." With this condition, there is a gradual wearing away of joint cartilage. The resultant exposure of rough underlying bone ends can cause pain and stiffness. Bony outgrowths known as osteophytes may appear at the margin of the affected bone. Long-standing osteoarthritis can also do damage to the internal ligaments, resulting in abnormal movements of the bones and joint instability or disorganization. The joints reflecting such involvement are most generally those associated with weight bearing.

Although osteoarthritis affects more people (perhaps as many as 40 million in the United States), *rheumatoid arthritis* is the more serious disease and carries the greatest potential for pain, disfigurement, and crippling. It may commence at any age, but persons most commonly develop initial symptoms somewhere between the ages of 20 and 50 years. The disease is not typically a condition of old age per se; most people carry it into old age.

Rheumatoid arthritis is a chronic, systemic, inflammatory disease of connective tissue that is two to three times more common among women than men. This condition is most commonly characterized by persistent and progressive joint involvement leading to disorganized joints and great pain and discomfort. Symptoms include malaise, fatigue, weight loss, fever, joint pain, redness, swelling, and stiffness and deformity. Many joints are affected. Extra-articulated tissue—especially that of the heart, lungs, eyes, and blood vessels—is also involved. The disease is characterized by acute episodes or flares alternating with remissions or periods of relative inactivity. Within 10 to 15 years, most rheumatoid arthritis victims will develop moderate to marked decline in functional capacity.

The cause of rheumatoid arthritis is not fully understood. It is now viewed as an autoimmune disease—that is, one that results from the production of antibodies that work against the body's own tissues. The autoantibody known as rheumatoid factor (RF) is present in 85 percent of rheumatoid arthritis patients. Multiple factors that probably lead to the development of this condition include possible previous exposure to an infectious agent and genetic factors that program a given immune response.

Associated with the aging process is a gradual loss of bone that reduces skeletal mass without disrupting the proportions of minerals and organic materials. This general loss of bone is known as *osteopenia.* When the condition advances to undermine the actual structural integrity of bone, *osteoporosis* is said to occur. Osteoporosis has been recognized for many years since it was first described by German anatomists. The quantitative decrease in bone mass can result in diminished height, slumped posture, backache, and a reduction in the structural strength of bones that makes them more susceptible to fracture. For many persons, however, bone loss is asymptomatic.

Osteoporosis can involve most bones of the body; those most critically involved, however, include the vertebra, wrist, and hip. Some diminution in the density of the vertebral column eventually occurs in most individuals beyond a certain age, resulting in vertebral compression and an age-associated shortening of the trunk and loss of stature. Osteoporosis of the spine is a common cause of backache in the elderly, with symptoms of vertebral involvement ranging from minor to severe back pain. A more severe consequence of osteoporosis is a femoral neck fracture. The neck of the femur is forced to bear much weight, and osteoporosis can so diminish its mechanical integrity that a fracture results. It is now believed that many of the falls and associated hip fractures of old age actually represent an osteoporotic femoral neck that broke under its weight-bearing task. In fact, radiographic evidence indicates that approximately three out of four of those elderly individuals who suffer from a broken hip express evidence of osteoporotic involvement of the femoral neck. So significant is the mortality associated with a hip fracture among the elderly that osteoporosis is listed as the twelfth leading cause of death in the United States.

The Neurosensory System

The nervous system is important in controlling the functioning of the body—including activities such as smooth and skeletal muscle contractions—and in receiving, processing, and storing information. The special senses of vision, hearing, taste, smell, and touch provide an individual with a link to the outside world. Neurosensory changes that can influence an individual's functioning, activities, response to stimuli, and perception of the world do occur with age. It is also true that the world's perception of an individual may be unduly influenced by neurosensory changes that he or she has undergone. For example, the older person with impaired hearing or vision may be labeled as stubborn, eccentric, or even senile.

Nerve cells, or neurons, are lost during the process of aging. The number of the basic functioning units begins to decline around the age of 25. Associated with this decline is a decreased capacity for sending nerve impulses to and from the brain. Conduction velocity decreases, voluntary motor movements slow down, and the reflex time for skeletal muscles is increased. Degenerative changes and disease states involving the sense organs can alter vision, hearing, taste, smell, and touch.

The Gastrointestinal System

The gastrointestinal tract is the product of millions of years of biocultural evolution. The human species evolved from primate ancestors who were primarily vegetarians but capable of omnivorous alimentation. The omnivorous nature of the species helped it expand and evolve to fit a wide variety of ecological conditions. Judging from the development of a great variety of cultural traditions with dissimilar eating customs, it seems that the gastrointestinal system has served the species well.

Like other body systems, the gastrointestinal system is subject to the aging process. Age-associated changes include atrophy of the secretion mechanisms, decreasing motility of the gut, loss of strength and tone of the muscular tissue and its supporting structures, changes in neurosensory feedback on such things as enzyme and hormone release, innervation of the tract, and diminished response to pain and internal sensations. Although the indisputable evidence for the relationship between these changes and aging is still not overwhelming, there is certainly enough circumstantial evidence to warrant a consideration of the possibilities.

Gastrointestinal symptoms such as indigestion, heartburn, and epigastric discomfort increase with age, although identifying and evaluating these symptoms is difficult. Many symptoms are caused by normal functional changes in the tract. With increasing age, however, they often are associated with serious pathological conditions such as cancer. The threat or fear of cancer can exert a great deal of psychological pressure on individuals. Stress of this type not only affects mental health but can also affect other body systems to cause or exacerbate problems such as hypertension and chronic respiratory disease.

The signs and symptoms often associated with one part of the gastrointestinal tract may actually be associated with another part of the tract. This is caused by the phenomenon of *referral*, as well as by the fact that the organs are part of an integrated system and thus are interrelated. The tract includes the mouth, esophagus, stomach, small intestine, gall bladder, liver, pancreas, and large intestine. Discomfort perceived as originating in the stomach may actually be coming from the lower gastrointestinal tract. An organ-based survey of the gastrointestinal system and its age-related problems is beyond the scope of this chapter. Still, several caveats are in order. Health professionals who deal with gastrointestinal disorders of the aged must be flexible in their approach. Disorders should be carefully evaluated before being dismissed as functional manifestations. If evaluation indicates a functional disorder, an effort should be made to explain the problem to the patient in clear, jargon-free terms. A sympathetic attitude and a face-to-face discussion of the situation can sometimes do more for people than medical intervention.

The Cardiopulmonary System

Generally, the anatomical and physiological changes that take place in the aging heart still allow it to function adequately if the coronary artery system is not greatly damaged by disease. Because coronary artery disease is prevalent among older Americans, however, it is difficult to determine the extent to which the heart ages independently of the disease. In the absence of disease, the heart tends to maintain its size; in some individuals, it may become smaller with age. In particular, the left ventricular cavity, that chamber of the heart that sends oxygenated blood to the body, may decrease in size because of a reduction in activity and physical demands in old age. Older people who are malnourished, confined to bed, or experiencing extended illness may show additional atrophy of the heart. Accompanying this reduction in heart size is a reduction in heart muscle strength and cardiac output. Still, without disease or additional alteration in heart function, cardiac output should be quite adequate as the body's requirements are reduced because of the atrophy of other body tissues and a decreased basal metabolism rate.

The heart valves tend to increase in thickness with age, and certain valves may be the sites of calcium salt deposits. These changes are not clinically significant unless there is a modification in the normal closing of a heart valve, which may stimulate more serious heart disease. Blood pressure also tends to increase with age. Systolic pressure—associated with the phase of the cardiac cycle in which the heart contracts, expelling blood—tends to stabilize at approximately 75 years of age. Diastolic pressure—involving the phase of the cardiac cycle during which the heart relaxes and its chambers fill with blood—tends to stabilize at age 65 and then may gradually decline.

Coronary artery disease increases in incidence with age and represents the major cause of heart disease and death in older Americans. In this condition, there is a deficiency of blood to the heart tissue because of the narrowing or constricting of the cardiac vessels that supply it. Tissue denied an adequate blood supply is called *ischemic;* hence, coronary artery disease is also known as *ischemic heart disease.*

The factors responsible for the narrowed and constricted arteries are not definitely known. What is known is that an overwhelming number of persons living in industrialized nations develop a condition known as *atherosclerosis.* In atherosclerosis, the large arteries, in particular, undergo a narrowing of their passageways as a result of the development of plaques on their interior walls. These plaques—which contain an accumulation of smooth muscle cells and fat and cholesterol crystals in combination with calcium salts, connective tissue, and scar tissue—serve to reduce the size of the passageway in such a manner that the vessel may eventually become totally closed off. The closing of an artery can cause ischemic heart tissue.

Arteriosclerosis, a generic term referring to the loss of elasticity of the arterial walls, is sometimes called "hardening of the arteries." This condition, which occurs in all populations, is progressive and age related. Ultimately, this age-associated loss of elasticity of arteries can contribute to reduced blood flow to an area. Unfortunately, the terms *arteriosclerosis* and *atherosclerosis* are often confused or used interchangeably. Arteriosclerosis is a general aging phenomenon, whereas atherosclerosis is variable in individuals and populations.

A number of aging changes collectively exert an effect on the respiratory system. These changes, which serve to reduce maximum breathing capacity, cause elderly people to become fatigued more easily than younger persons. Nevertheless, these changes are not sufficient to cause apparent symptoms at a resting state. In the absence of disease, they do not significantly affect the life-style of an older individual. Changes do occur, but they are not necessarily incapacitating.

The airways and tissues of the respiratory tract, including the air sacs, become less elastic and more rigid with age. Osteoporosis may alter the size of the chest cavity as a result of the downward and forward movement of the ribs. Also, the power of the respiratory muscles becomes reduced along with that of the abdominal muscles, which can hinder the movement of the diaphragm.

Respiratory diseases are more prevalent in older individuals than in the general population. The threat of serious respiratory infection increases with age, as does the threat of the obstructive conditions of chronic bronchitis, emphysema, and lung cancer. Some researchers believe the threat of respiratory infection is related to age-associated reductions in resistance to infectious microorganisms. Nevertheless, obstructive pulmonary conditions and lung cancer are not solely the results of inherent age factors. Environmental conditions such as exposure to secondhand cigarette smoke and polluted air play an important role in their development. Recently, data from the Department of Health and Human Services show that death rates from lung cancer increase fourfold throughout the adult life of a nonsmoker. Nevertheless, the risk of developing lung cancer in an elderly moderate smoker (one-half to one full pack of cigarettes a day) is ten times as great as in a nonsmoker. With additional increase in the degree of exposure to tobacco, the risk increases still further.

The Urinary System

The bladder of an elderly person has a capacity of less than half (250 milliliters) that of a young adult (600 ml) and often contains as much as 100 ml of residual urine. Moreover, the onset of the desire to urinate, often referred to as the *micturition reflex*, is delayed in older persons. Normally, this reflex is activated when the bladder is half full, but in the elderly, it often does not occur until the bladder is near capacity. The origin of this alteration of the micturition reflex is unclear, but it may be related to age changes in the frontal area of the cerebral cortex or to damage associated with a cerebral infarction or tumor. Reduced bladder capacity, coupled with a delayed micturition reflex, can lead to problems of frequent urination and extreme urgency of urination. These conditions, even if they do not render an individual incontinent, are an annoyance to older persons.

There appears to be a decrease in average renal function with age. This may result from a loss of nephrons, the basic cell unit in the kidneys. With increasing age, the kidneys themselves are found to be smaller, and the nephrons are smaller in size and fewer in number. Despite these apparently dramatic changes, loss of renal tissue is probably secondary in importance to the structural vascular changes that occur in the kidney with age. In general, the arterial tree atrophies, and blood flow to the kidneys is reduced, decreasing the functional efficiency of the system. These vascular changes likely contribute to the loss of nephrons, and this is especially significant when the kidney is seriously malfunctioning or when severe atherosclerosis is superimposed on the aging process.

SEXUALITY AND AGING
Late-Life Sexuality: Myths and Reality

The reputedly "long-lived" Abkhasians attribute their longevity to their practices in sex, work, and diet (Benet, 1971). They normally do not begin regular sexual relations before the age of 30, the traditional age of marriage. They believe such self-discipline is necessary to conserve energy, including sexual energy, in order to enjoy prolonged life. The anthropologist Sula Benet (1971) reports that one medical team investigating the sex life of the Abkhasians concluded that many men retain their sexual potency long after the age of 70 and almost 14 percent of the women continue to menstruate after the age of 55.

Although there is no hard evidence to link Abkhasian sexual practices with longevity, it is fair to say that the relationship between sexuality and age expressed in Abkhasian society is quite different from the norm in U.S. society. In the latter, sex and aging are often linked to negative humor that is filled with disdain and an apprehensiveness about growing older. Popular themes for such humor often include the impotence of older men and the unquestioned unattractiveness of older women. Examples abound:

> An eighty-five-year-old man was complaining to his friend, "My stenographer is suing me for breach of promise." His friend answered, "At eighty-five, what could you promise her?" (Adams, 1968)

> It may be that life begins at forty but everything else starts to wear out, fall out, or spread out. (*Reader's Digest*, 1972)

Such jokes may reflect basic attitudes, thoughts, and feelings that are not commonly stated, which makes one wonder why most attitudes are so negative about sex in later life. Certainly some of this reflects negative feelings about old people and aging in general—what has been referred to in this book as *ageism*. Among the stereotypes of ageism is the myth of desexualization: If a person is old (or getting old), he or she is alleged to be finished with sex. This myth is part of what Butler and Lewis (1976) refer to as the "aesthetic narrowness" about sex that prevails in U.S. society. Stated simply, there is a widespread assumption in the United States (and in most of the Western world) that sex is only for the young and beautiful. Unfortunately, it is not just the young who believe this but many older people as well.

Misinformation surrounds the issue of late-life sexuality. For example, there is a common presumption that sexual desire diminishes with age, but this is not necessarily the case. Verwoerdt, Pfeiffer, and Wang (1969a, 1969b) found the following:

1. The incidence of sexual interest does not show an age-related decline—interest may persist into the eighties.
2. The incidence of sexual activity declines from a level of more than 50 percent in the early sixties to a level between 10 and 20 percent for people in their eighties.

3. The sexual behavior patterns of the later years correlate with those of the younger years. If there was interest and satisfying activity in the early years, there is likely to be interest and satisfying activity in the later years as well.

Sexual interest, capacities, and functions change with age. For the most part, like many biological and psychological functions discussed in this book, these dimensions of sexuality decline with increasing age. This decline can be seen as part of the normal aging process, but it does *not* mean that older men and women in reasonably good health should not be able to have an active and satisfying sex life.

Age-Related Changes in the Genital System[2]

The genital system is characterized by a number of age-related changes in physiology and anatomy. On the whole, very few age-specific disorders are associated with this body system. Most of the problems of sexuality and aging are sociogenic or psychogenic.

The Male Genital System. The male reproductive system continues to produce germ cells (*sperm*) and sex hormones (*testosterone*) well into old age. Production of both declines with advancing age, although testosterone production is maintained at a higher level longer than is estrogen production in women. The decrease of testosterone has definite effects on older men, including a possible waning of sexual desire, although other physiological changes such as decreased sensitivity of the penis may be even more responsible for the decline.

A number of major physical changes occur in the genital system. The size and the firmness of the testes decrease. Sperm production takes place within the testes in seminiferous or sperm-bearing tubules, which thicken and decrease in diameter with age. This reduces sperm production, although abundant spermatozoa are found even in old age. The production of sex hormones also takes place in the testes but is independent of the sperm-producing structures. The cells responsible for hormone production, located between the seminiferous tubules in proximity to blood vessels, are called *interstitial cells.* Age-related fibrosis, involving an increase in the amount of fibrous connective tissue in the testes, constricts the blood supply and reduces production capacities of the sperm and hormone-producing structures.

Fibrosis may also affect the penis, the male organ for sexual intercourse and for the delivery of semen for reproductive purposes. The penis has no bone and no intrinsic muscles; its components are sheathed in fibrous coats and enclosed within a loose skin. Erection is a purely vascular phenomenon, and age-related increase in fibrous tissue can affect blood supply.

---

[2]This part relies heavily on Katchadourian (1972) and Fulton (1992).

A SEXUAL REVOLUTION FOR THE ELDERLY
At Nursing Homes, Intimacy Is Becoming a Matter of Policy
Matthew Purdy

They met last New Year's Eve. He was tall with an easy manner. She was petite with a girlish smile. He asked her to dance and held her close. "I didn't push him away," she said. "I've been around awhile. I've pushed a lot of men away."

It was a modern romance, at once pure and complicated. First, there was his wife. He was still married, although separated. Then, there was his walker.

Fritzie Heilbron's prince came to her not astride a white horse, but in black orthopedic shoes, shuffling along with the help of a walker. He is 76 years old, impaired by Parkinson's disease, and with enough fear of his wife to want his name kept private. But Mrs. Heilbron is smitten. She's 85 and has waited 45 years since her husband died to fall in love again.

This is not a case of geriatrics going clubbing. It is a scene from a nursing home, where those who care for the elderly and infirm report a kind of sexual revolution. The revolution is not among the elderly, who experts say have always demonstrated an enduring urge for intimacy, but in the attitude of those who provide care. They are beginning to recognize that sexual activity is normal and beneficial for patients—even for those with Alzheimer's disease.

At the Hebrew Home for the Aged, a 1,200-bed nursing home and Alzheimer's research center in the Riverdale section of the Bronx where Mrs. Heilbron and her companion found each other, a new policy gives patients the right to privacy so they can carry on intimate relationships. In confronting the issue directly, the Hebrew Home is in the vanguard of the shift away from seeing sex in nursing homes as a behavior problem.

The home is training its staff to recognize and respect intimate relationships, and

officials there say they will try to assist budding romances by moving one member of a couple to a single room to provide privacy. . . .

"A couple of years ago, when there were people who were sexually involved, we thought we had to separate them," said Robin Bouru, a social worker at the Hebrew Home.

Because most nursing home residents share rooms, some homes around the country have set aside rooms that couples can use for privacy, and others have formalized policies for addressing sexual activity, like the one at the Hebrew Home. But Meredith Wallace, a geriatric nurse at the Hospital of Saint Raphael in New Haven who has written about sexuality of the aged, said many homes are moving slowly, if at all, to break down "the old stereotypes."

Antonette Zeiss, a clinical psychologist at the Veterans Administration Health Care system in Palo Alto, California, who has instructed nursing home administrators in California on sexual relations among patients, said the subject is difficult to confront because "it's the conjunction of two taboos about sex." "The first," she said, "is that sex is for the young. The second is that sex is for the cognitively intact."

She said that in her experience most people who run nursing homes agree that residents have a right to sexual expression, but it is difficult for staff members to support "because they feel uncomfortable with it."

Others have raised more straightforward objections, from the danger of patients physically hurting themselves to the violation of moral laws at homes that are run by religious organizations.

Janet Lowe, a nurse's aide at the Hebrew Home, said that the first time she realized two unwed residents were having a relationship, "I was shocked. You don't think of your grandparents having sex." Ms. Lowe said other members of the staff had stronger objections. "Some people thought it should be stopped because they weren't married."

Jacob Reingold, the vice chairman of the Hebrew Home, which is run according to Orthodox Jewish law, acknowledges that the home would face a quandary if two unwed patients wanted to live together as a couple.

For many at the Hebrew Home, romance is a welcome relief from the unbroken landscape of aches and pains and dwindling days. "I think it's beautiful, seeing a man and a woman walking together holding hands," said Ethel Hoberman, who is 81, healthy, spry and available. "It sort of gives the place the feeling of being alive, rather than waiting to die."

Some staff members and residents find the sexual relationships between unwed, elderly people immoral or distasteful, or both. "There are some women who say: 'Yuck, that's disgusting. They're going to give them rooms so they can do things there?'" said Grace Meltzer, a resident of the Hebrew Home.

Sonya Kantor, who is 86 and president of the residents council at the home, discreetly, said, "I have a gentleman friend here" and explained the negative comments this way: "The disapproval of some of the women may come from the fact that they don't have male friends."

Officials at the Hebrew Home said intimate relationships return some dignity to residents who give up privacy and freedom in exchange for assistance and security. "Can't we allow them to have some vestige of normalcy in this critical area?" said Douglas Holmes, a psychologist who heads the home's research division. "I'm totally pro-sex as long as no one is victimized."

The thorniest issue of sexual conduct at nursing homes involves relations between patients with dementia.

Psychologists and doctors say aberrant behavior like public masturbation and unwanted kissing and touching of others is common with Alzheimer's patients, who often lose the ability to make social judgments. But, said Dr. Philip D. Sloane, a professor at the University of North Carolina medical school who advises the Manor Health Care chain of 170 nursing homes on Alzheimer's care, "a lot of time, the activity we think of as sexually deviant behavior is just reaching out for intimacy."

Like the Hebrew Home, the Manor Health Care homes have a protocol for evaluating instances where patients with dementia exhibit a strong attraction. He said it is not unusual for the staff, in conjunction with a resident's family, to allow casual intimacy—holding hands, hugging—but that sex is rarely if ever allowed, out of concern for the patients' safety and the difficulty of determining whether they consent.

At the Hebrew Home, Mrs. Meltzer, who lives on a different floor than her husband because he suffers from dementia, said even in his confused state his need for closeness emerges.

"I think intimate sex is the farthest thing from his mind," she said. "He reaches for my hand and kisses me. And he says why don't you just get undressed and get into bed. I think he just wants intimacy."

Mrs. Meltzer said the need for companionship doesn't fade with age. She said that when she first moved to the home she was told about a man who was found naked and dead in the bed of a woman who lives there. Mrs. Meltzer said she still remembered her reaction: "I said, 'Well, anyway, he died happy.'"

Source: New York Times, November 6, 1995, p. A14. Copyright © 1995 by The New York Times Co. Reprinted by Permission.

Secretions of the prostate gland account for much of the volume of semen as well as its characteristic odor. The prostate gland often enlarges in older men. The ejaculatory duct, which empties into the urethra (the tube that leads out of the bladder), and the urethra itself traverse the prostate gland. Thus prostatic enlargement often has the dual effect of making ejaculatory contractions less forceful and urination more difficult. Cancer of the prostate is a frequent neoplasm among older men. All older men should have regular physical examinations to monitor the condition of the prostate.

Masters and Johnson (1970) have translated these physical changes into their impact on the sexual functioning of the older male. Summarized, these impacts include the following:

1. It takes an older man longer to achieve a full erection, which may not be as full or as firm as for a younger man.

2. It usually takes an older man longer to achieve a orgasm. There is a reduction in the force and amount of the ejaculation and fewer genital spasms are experienced.

3. In an older man, erection subsides more rapidly after ejaculation.

4. It takes an older man longer than a younger man to have a second erection and orgasm.

The Female Genital System. The female reproductive system becomes less efficient with age, with a reduction in secretion of sex hormones (estrogen and progesterone), in ovulation, and in the ability of the uterine tube (where fertilization occurs) and the uterus (womb) to support a young embryo.

Many physical changes occur in the female genital tract. The external genitalia of the female, known as the *vulva,* include the major and minor lips, the clitoris, and the vaginal orifice. With age, the folds of the major and minor lips become less pronounced, and the skin becomes thinner. Vascularity and elasticity decrease, and the area becomes more susceptible to tissue trauma and the development of pruritus (itching). Glands decrease in number, as does the level of secretion, leading to shrinking and drying of the area.

Among the internal female reproductive organs, the uterus decreases in size, becomes more fibrous, and has fewer endometrial glands. The cervix, or lower portion of the uterus, is reduced in size, and the cervical canal (which is surrounded by the upper end of the vagina) decreases in diameter. The uterine tubes (where ova pass and are fertilized) become thinner, and the ovaries take on an irregular shape. Ovulation becomes irregular and finally stops, and there is a drastic reduction in the production of female hormones.

The latter changes, along with irregular or absent menstruation, often characterize *menopause,* a term used to describe the conclusion of a 20- to 30-year period of change in the female genital system that progresses differently in each individual. Approximately 50 percent of all women go through menopause between ages 45 and 50, about 25 percent before age 45, and about 25 percent after age 50 (Hafez,

1976). The age of onset can be accelerated by debilitating disease, endocrine disorder, or both.

A number of symptoms are associated with menopause, although they appear to be less common than is popularly thought. These include irritability, anxiety, depression, loss of appetite, insomnia, and headache. Some of these symptoms are more psychologically than physiologically based. It has been observed that these symptoms are found more often in women with a history of psychotic behavior. Hot flashes, patchy redness on the face and chest, and sweating are associated with vasomotor instability, which causes irregularity in blood vessel diameter and thus irregularity of blood flow to the surface. There is a tendency to deposit fat in the abdominal and pelvic areas. Pubic hair becomes abundant, and breasts may atrophy. The nipples become smaller and less erectile. Still, postmenopausal women can continue to be interested and active sexually.

How do these changes affect female functioning in sexual relations? According to Masters and Johnson (1970):

1. Older women take a longer time to respond to sexual stimuli.
2. Lubrication takes longer and is generally less effective than in younger women.
3. The vagina has reduced elasticity and expansive qualities. The tissues lining the vagina are more easily irritated.
4. In the older women, the clitoris is reduced in size, though still responsive to stimulation.
5. Orgasms are generally less intense and of shorter duration.

The changes described here are a normal part of aging, but individual variations should be recognized. Individuals should understand these age-related changes and not be alarmed when they occur. With proper education, the aging person may be assured that competent sexual function and fulfillment can continue into the later years.

Sexual dysfunction is certainly not an inevitable result of the aging process. The same factors that lead to sexual problems in the younger years are also important in the elderly, especially when superimposed on the changing genital system. These factors include drug abuse, fatigue, emotional problems, disease, urogenital surgery, alcoholism, overeating, and sociocultural pressures. In the elderly, these factors are compounded by fear of failure and society's expectations concerning sexual behavior and the older adult.

A special note is in order about disorders of the female genital system. The uterus and breast are frequent sites of cancer. Breast cancer is the leading cause of death among women between the ages of 40 and 60. Cervical cancer peaks during these same ages, whereas uterine cancer does so at about 65 years of age. Cancer of the vulva is more a disease of older women; over 50 percent of all cases occur in those over age 60. These are all good reasons that sex organs should not be cloaked in myth and mystery. All these disorders give early warnings that should be taken seriously. Not every swelling of the breast indicates breast cancer, and not every vaginal discharge is evidence of carcinoma. These are some of the early signs of cancer, however, and are *not* normal age-related changes. Women can be alert to them without becoming preoccupied. Often, the difference between alertness and ignorance may be one of life and death.

SUMMARY

Senescence describes the effects that lead to the increasing vulnerability individuals face with increasing age. Is senescence an inherent biological process? That may be difficult to say, yet as long ago as 1825 Gompertz identified a pattern to increased vulnerability through the life course.

A variety of factors influence the point at which people become old and, in particular, the time when they show the kind of vulnerability to aging processes that result in mortality. These include not only differences in biological potential but also in social and environment factors that may limit the expression of biological potential. The leading cause of death among the elderly is heart disease, followed by cancer and stroke. Death rates differ significantly by sex and race. Average life expectancy at birth has increased about 50 percent since the turn of the century, and survivorship rates to old

age have improved even more dramatically. In 1990, the proportion of newborn babies expected to reach age 65 was 74 percent for males and 85 percent for females, almost twice the proportion in 1900–02. Age-specific life expectancy at 65 years has moved ahead more slowly than has life expectancy at birth during the twentieth century.

What are the specific results of senescence? Age-related physiological changes affect the skin and the skeletomuscular, neurosensory, gastrointestinal, cardiopulmonary, and urinary systems.

Misinformation surrounds the issue of sexuality and aging. Some people may experience declines in sexual desire and activity with advancing age. Such a decline can be seen as part of the normal aging process. Nevertheless, older people in reasonably good health should be able to have active and satisfying sex lives.

STUDY QUESTIONS

1. Distinguish between *biological aging* and *pathological aging*. Define *senescence*. How can it be distinguished from other biological processes?

2. Taking biological and socioenvironmental factors into consideration, explain the impact of sex on mortality rates. What role do socioeconomic factors play in the racial differences in mortality rates observed in the United States today?

3. Explain (a) increased life expectancy at birth in the twentieth century and (b) the small increase in life expectancy from age 65 in the twentieth century.

4. Discuss those changes in the form and function of the skin that are associated with the aging process.

5. Define and distinguish *osteoarthritis*, *rheumatoid arthritis*, *osteopenia*, and *osteoporosis*. Describe the resulting com-

plications for those afflicted with these conditions.

6. How is the neurosensory system subject to aging? The gastrointestinal system?

7. Discuss coronary heart disease, making the distinction between *atherosclerosis* and *arteriosclerosis*.

8. Why are attitudes generally so negative about sex in later life? Discuss the impact on the sexual functioning of older males of physical changes associated with the aging process. Do the same for older females.

REFERENCES

Adams, J. (1968). *Joey Adams' encyclopedia of humor.* New York: Bonanza Books.

Atchley, R. (1972). *Social forces in later life.* Belmont, CA: Wadsworth.

Benet, S. (1971). Why they live to be 100, or even older in Abkhasia. *New York Times Magazine,* December 26.

Bogue, D. J. (1969). *Principles of demograp hy.* New York: Wiley.

Butler, R., & Lewis, M. (1976). *Love and sex after sixty.* New York: Harper and Row.

Comfort, A. (1979). *The biology of senescence* (3rd ed.). New York: New American Library.

Dorn, H. (1959). Mortality. In P. Hauser & O. Duncan (Eds.), *The study of population.* Chicago: University of Chicago Press.

Fries, J. F., & Crapo, L. M. (1981). *Vitality and aging.* San Francisco: W. H. Freeman.

Fulton, G. B. (1992). Sexuality and aging. In C. Kart, E. Metress, & S. Metress (Eds.), *Human aging and chronic disease.* Boston: Jones and Bartlett.

Gonnella, J. S., Louis, D. Z., & McCord, J. J. (1976). The staging concept: An approach to the assessment of outcome of ambulatory care. *Medical Care, 14,* 13–21.

Hafez, E. (1976). *Aging and reproductive physiology.* Ann Arbor, MI: Ann Arbor Science.

Kart, C., Metress, E., & Metress, J. (1992). *Human aging and chronic disease.* Boston: Jones and Bartlett.

Katchadourian, H. (1972). *Human sexuality: Sense and nonsense.* New York: Norton.

Kitagawa, E. M., & Hauser, P. M. (1973). *Differential mortality in the United States: A study in socioeconomic epidemiology.* Cambridge, MA: Harvard University Press.

Kohn, R. R. (1985). Aging and age-related diseases: Normal aging. In H. A. Johnson (Ed.), *Relations between normal aging and disease.* New York: Raven Press.

Leaf, A. (1973). Getting old. *Scientific American, 299* (3), 44–52.

Madigan, F. C. (1957). Are sex mortality differentials biologically caused? *Milbank Memorial Fund Quarterly, 35* (2), 202–223.

Marcus, A. C., & Siegel, J. M. (1982). Sex differences in the use of physician services: A preliminary test of the fixed role hypothesis. *Journal of Health and Social Behavior, 23,* 186–196.

Masters, W., & Johnson, V. (1970). *Human sexual response.* Boston: Little, Brown.

Petersen, W. (1975). *Population* (3rd ed.). New York: Macmillan.

Reader's Digest. (1972). *Treasury of American humor.* New York: American Heritage.

Siegel, J. S. (1979). *Prospective trends in the size and structure of the elderly population, impact of mortality trends, and some implications.* Current Population Reports, Special Studies Series P-23, No. 78. Washington, DC: U.S. Department of Commerce, Bureau of the Census.

Strehler, B. (1962). *Time, cells and aging.* New York: Academic Press.

Toledo Blade. (1990). Report: Blacks die needlessly because of lack of routine care. November 29, pp. 1, 6.

U.S. Office of Health Resources Opportunity. (1979). *Health status of minorities and low-income groups.* DHEW Publication No. (HRA) 79-627. Health Resources Administration. Washington, DC: U.S. Government Printing Office.

Verwoerdt, A., Pfeiffer, E., & Wang, H. S. (1969a). Sexual behavior in senescence. I. Changes in sexual activity and interest of aging men and women. *Journal of Geriatric Psychiatry, 2,* 163–180.

Verwoerdt, A., Pfeiffer, E., & Wang, H. S. (1969b). Sexual behavior in senescence. II. Patterns of change in sexual activity and interest. *Geriatrics, 24,* 137–154.

Zopf, P. E., Jr. (1986). *America's older population.* Houston, TX: Cap and Gown.

CHAPTER 5

WHY DO PEOPLE BECOME OLD?

Cary S. Kart and Eileen S. Metress

Why do people become old? Potential answers to this question are being researched at both the cellular and physiological levels. According to Comfort (1979), there are four classical hypotheses that attempt to explain the mechanism of aging. These include the beliefs that vigor declines as a result of the following: (1) changes in the properties of multiplying cells, (2) loss of or injury to nonmultiplying cells (e.g., neurons), and (3) primary changes in the noncellular materials of the body (e.g., collagen). A fourth hypothesis locates the mechanism of aging in the so-called software of the body—"in the overall program of regulation by which other aspects of the life cycle are governed" (Comfort, 1979, p. 17). These hypotheses are not mutually exclusive. After all, aging is a complex phenomenon. Different explanations may be required for different aspects of the aging process; diverse phenomena may act together to account for biological aging. Comfort points out that although some of these hypotheses have been around for 200 years, none has yet been eliminated by convincing experimental data. The alert reader may recognize these classic hypotheses in the brief summaries of research in biological aging that follow.

Differentiating between normal aging and superimposed disease is vital to understanding why people become old. The ultimate cause of the majority of deaths in older adults is physiological decline that increases the risk of disease. Mortality results when the ability to withstand the challenge of disease is overwhelmed. For instance, the increased risk of death from pneumonia among older persons is associated with age-related declines in the body's immune defense and reduced pulmonary reserve and function (Rothschild, 1984).

Unlocking the mystery of aging and extending the human life span has been the dream of many. As noted in Chapter 2, efforts at prolonging life have been described in the written and oral records of societies dating back many thousands of years. Research efforts in biogerontology continue. There are no magic potions to cure or prevent aging, despite the fact that books on longevity and its promotion have appeared on best-seller lists in recent years.

What follows is an overview of some of the important research in the biology of aging. We distinguish cellular theories of aging from physiological theories of aging. The goal of this research, regardless of whether it is aimed at understanding aging from the cellular or organismic level, is not to grant immortality but to understand the aging process and improve the quality of life for the growing numbers of people who are being added to the ranks of the aged.

CELLULAR THEORIES OF AGING

In the early twentieth century, it was widely believed that if some cells were not immortal, at the very least they could grow and multiply for an extended time. Child (1915) "showed" that senescence in planarians (small flatworms that move by means of cilia) is reversible; Carrel (1912) "demonstrated" that tissue cells taken from adult animals could be propagated indefinitely *in vitro* (in a test tube or other artificial environment). In the same vein, Bidder (1925, 1932) "identified" a number of instances in fish where the life span was not believed to be fixed—that is, general vigor appeared to persist indefinitely.

Recent experiments, particularly those observing cell growth and development in tissue culture, suggest that this earlier research was inaccurate. Still, this work had a significant impact on the field of gerontology. During most of the first half of the twentieth century, aging was not considered a characteristic of cells (Cristofalo, 1985).

Since the late 1950s, Leonard Hayflick has shown that fibroblast cells (which give rise to connective tissue) from human fetal tissues cultured *in vitro* undergo a finite number of divisions and then die. Across several experiments, Hayflick and Moorhead (1961) observed that such cells undergo an average of 50 divisions *in vitro*, with a range from about 40 to about 60, before losing the ability to replicate themselves. In 1965, Hayflick reported that fibroblasts isolated from human adult tissue undergo only about 20 divisions *in vitro*. On the basis of these and other studies, he argued that (1) the limited replicative capacity of cultured normal human cells is an expression of programmed genetic events and (2) the limit on normal cell division *in vitro* is a function of the age of the donor. It is now generally believed that there is an inverse relationship between the age of a human donor and the *in vitro* cell division capacity of fibroblasts derived from the skin, lung, and liver (Hayflick, 1977).

Although it appears that normal cells have a finite lifetime, this is not the case for abnormal cells. Such cells, which are distinguishable from normal cells in structure, by genetic makeup, or by both factors, are capable of unlimited division. Cancer cells, for example, are able to divide indefinitely in tissue culture. A famous line of human cancer cells named HeLa (after Henrietta Lacks, the woman from whom they were taken after her death in 1951) is still being cultured for use in standardized cancer cell studies (Gold, 1981). Whatever causes noncancerous cells gradually to lose the ability to divide appears to be lacking in cancer cells. The study of cancer may yet reveal what limits the ability of normal cells to divide indefinitely.

Tissue culture studies have limitations, and these experiments almost certainly do not literally replicate the aging process. Yet, the experiments have been analyzed by many investigators, and all confirm the findings. Fries and Crapo (1981) report that in 1962, Hayflick froze many vials of embryo cells that had completed several divisions. Each year since that time, some vials have been thawed and cultured; they always go on to complete their natural growth to the same roughly 50 divisions.

Do humans age solely because their cells have an intrinsically limited capacity to reproduce? This seems unlikely. Nerve and muscle cells do not divide at all in adult life, although they do show deterioration with age.

Researchers continue to suggest that aging may be genetically programmed into cells. Bernard Strehler has hypothesized that programmed loss of genetic material could cause aging. As Strehler (1973) points out, most cells contain hundreds of repetitions of the same DNA (the molecule of heredity in nearly all organisms—*deoxyribonucleic acid*) for the known genes they contain. This simply means that the cell does not have to rely on a single copy of its genetic blueprint for any one trait. In experiments done on beagles, Strehler found that, as cells age, a considerable number of these repetitions are lost (Johnson, Crisp, & Strehler, 1972). This is especially true for brain, heart, and skeletal muscle cells. How the loss occurs is not specifically known, although there is some speculation that it results from age-related changes in cell metabolism. Strehler suspects that cells may be programmed, at a fixed point in life, to start manufacturing a substance that inhibits protein synthesis.

Another school of thought claims that senescence is largely a result of the accumulation of accidental changes that occur to cells over a period of time. Sinex (1977) thinks that random mutations may produce aging by causing damage to DNA molecules. Although the cell has DNA repair mechanisms, it is likely that either some mutational changes are too subtle for the repair process to detect or that mutations occur too rapidly for all of them all to be repaired. It is theorized that as cellular mutations accumulate, cells begin to lose their ability to function, including even a loss of the ability to divide.

Orgel (1963, 1973) has also hypothesized that random errors or mutations could show up in the transcriptions of DNA into RNA (*ribonucleic acid,* which carries instructions from the DNA) or through errors in the translation of RNA into proteins. He suggests that random errors in the synthesizing of information-carrying proteins would lead to a cascade of other errors. This *error cascade* (sometimes referred to as an *error catastrophe*) results in cell deterioration. This hypothesis has not been confirmed experimentally. No one has yet been able to detect errors at the protein level, although efforts continue to be made (Fries & Crapo, 1981). This error or mutation theory may not be incompatible with the theory of genetic programming. It is certainly possible that a shutoff of cellular repair mechanisms is a programmed genetic event. Cell mutations may also be the result of extrinsic factors—air or water pollutants, as well as toxins in food.

Another explanation of aging involves the belief that *free radicals,* highly unstable molecules containing an unpaired electron), reduce cellular efficiency and cause an accumulation of cellular waste. Free radicals may be produced by radiation, extreme heat, or oxidation reactions. They are created in small quantities as part of the normal oxidant cell metabolism. According to Sanadi (1977), the hypothesis that excessive amounts of free radicals, regardless of their source, may damage cellular membranes and other cellular components merits further consideration. Such damage could accelerate aging and bring about the premature death of an organism. Some believe that the fatty "age pigment" lipofuscin, which accumulates to an appreciable extent in neurons and cardiac and skeletal muscle cells, may be an end product of cellular membrane damage caused by free radicals (Cristofalo, 1990). It should be emphasized, however, that current thinking holds that lipofuscin is an indicator rather than a cause of aging.

Harman (1961, 1968), among others, has done work attempting to reduce the source of free radicals. Certain chemicals, called *antioxidants* (a common one is the food preservative BHT), have been used to combine with and disarm free radicals. Harman reported that the inclusion of antioxidants in the diet increased the average life span of experimental animals by 15 to 30 percent. The animals receiving the antioxidants showed lower weight, suggesting the possibility that dietary restriction itself may prolong the average life span. Another effect of adding antioxidants to the diet of experimental animals was a reduction in tumor production (Harman, 1968).

A well-known antioxidant is vitamin E. Although there is some evidence that vitamin E deficiency reduces the life expectancy of experimental animals, no experimental evidence is available to show that supplementing the diet with vitamin E extends average life expectancy (Tapple, 1968). In addition, there is no current evidence to support the idea that dietary supplementation of other vitamins (A and C) and minerals (e.g., silenium) with antioxidant properties can extend human life (Ames, 1983; Schneider & Reed, 1985; Willet & MacMahon, 1984). There is evidence, however, that eating foods rich in vitamin C and beta carotene, or taking antioxidant supplements, is linked with decreased risk of various cancers. The role of free radical reactions in aging and human disease and the avoidance of their excess formation remains an area of significant interest. Free radicals have been suggested to play a role in at least 50 diseases, including atherosclerosis, cancer, stroke, and Parkinson's disease (Aruoma, Kaur, & Halliwell, 1991).

Higher organisms do possess sophisticated biochemical systems for scavenging free radicals. The enzyme *superoxide dismutase* is a part of such a system. A relationship has been noted between superoxide dismutase activity and life span in varying species and species strains (Bartosz, Leyko, & Fried, 1979; Kellogg &

Fridovich, 1976; Munkres, Rana, & Goldstein, 1984; Tolmasoff, Ono, & Cutler, 1980). It is possible that the regulation of superoxide dismutase is under the control of the same genes that dictate the life span of a particular species (Schneider & Reed, 1985). Superoxide dismutase tablets have been touted for their so-called antiaging effect. Nevertheless, there is no evidence that oral administration of the enzyme prolongs life. In fact, one report demonstrates that blood and tissue levels of this enzyme are not affected by its ingestion (Zidenburg-Cherr et al., 1983).

The aforementioned theories are concerned with aging at the cellular (and molecular) level; it is a long leap from cell biology to studying aging in the total organism. Several physiological theories attempt to relate aging to the performance of the total organism and these deserve attention.

PHYSIOLOGICAL THEORIES OF AGING

One physiological theory of aging involves the autoimmune mechanism. This theory postulates that many age-related changes can be accounted for by changes in the immune response. Normally, the immune system, through the action of special immune cells and the production of antibodies, protects the body from material that it reads as foreign, including cancer cells. With age, immune cell function declines, and increased levels of autoantibodies are found in the blood (Goidl, Thorbecke, & Weksler, 1980; Walford, 1982; Weksler, 1982). *Autoantibodies* are substances that are produced against host tissues. In usual circumstances, the body's immune system is able to distinguish between host body cells and foreign substances subject to attack.

The significance of age-associated increases in autoantibodies is not well understood, but they are believed to contribute to inefficiencies in physiological functioning. Why these antibodies are produced against one's own tissue is not known. Perhaps, once-normal body cells begin to look different as a result of accumulated changes resulting from mutation or free-radical damage. If immune cells undergo similar changes, this might cause production of aberrant antibodies. Also, body constituents may break down from disease or other damage and present as new substances that the body's defense mechanism will not tolerate. Potentially, all of these factors may interact to produce autoimmunity.

Diminished immunocompetence has been established as an age-related change. Schneider and Reed (1985) suggest that the decline in immune function may have evolved as a protective mechanism against the ravages of autoimmunity. Presumably, a vigorous immune reaction might allow for an even greater production of autoantibodies.

The immune system is not organ specific. It is in constant contact with all body cells, tissues, and organs. Any alteration in the immune system could be expected to exert an effect on all body systems (Kay & Baker, 1979; Kay & Makinodan, 1982). Thus, as immune competence decreases, the incidence of autoimmunity, infection, and cancer can be expected to increase (Good & Yunis, 1974; MacKay, Whittington, & Mathews, 1977).

In humans, the immune system begins to decline shortly after puberty. This decline includes beginning atrophy of the thymus, the gland thought by many to be the structure central to the aging of the immune system. Thymic hormone influences immune functioning. Its progressive age-related loss is associated with declines in the reactivity of certain immune cells. The percentage of immature immune cells increases in association with the lack of thymic hormone. Other substances, called *lymphokines,* are also important in activating and maintaining the immune response. One lymphokine, interleukin-2(IL-2), undergoes limited production with age (Thoman, 1985).

Thompson and associates (1984) report on the immune status of a group of healthy centenarians. This study population withstood the risk of cancer and an assortment of other diseases for at least 100 years. Their immune systems appeared to function in a fashion similar to the immune systems of much younger individuals. The researchers were left asking (1) when changes in the immune cells of these centenarians began, (2) whether these changes represent irreversible programmed aging that simply began later in this group, and (3) whether other outside factors are responsible for immune decline.

This last question is particularly important, given that recent work in the area of *psychoneuroimmunology* has shown that stressful social situations—such as being in a troubled marriage (Kiecolt-Glaser, Fisher, et al., 1987) or caring for someone with Alzheimer's disease (Kiecolt-Glaser, Glaser, et al., 1987)—can cause suppression of the immune system. Interestingly, immune system function may be increased as a result of positive social situations (Kennedy, Kiecolt-Glaser, & Glaser, 1990).

Another theory with a long history is the *wear and tear theory* of aging. In effect, this theory posits an inverse relationship between rate of living and length of life—that is, those who live too hard and fast cannot expect to live very long. In the early part of this century, Rubner (described in Comfort, 1979) carried out calorimetric experiments to determine the energy requirements necessary for the maintenance of body metabolism. He suggested that senescence might reflect the expenditure of fixed amounts of energy used to complete particular chemical reactions. An important question then arises: Can an individual live a life that causes a speedup or slowdown in the expenditure of such energy?

Many theorists using this model employ machine analogies to exemplify the theory's underlying assumption that an organism wears out with use. Nevertheless, these analogies often fail to take into account two important characteristics of living organisms: (1) living organisms have mechanisms for self-repair that are not available to machines and (2) functions in a living organism may actually become more efficient with use.

Hans Selye's work on stress has been used by some to support the wear and tear theory. Selye (1966), on the basis of his experiments with animals, identified three stages of responses to continued stress. Each stage of response parallels a phase of aging. Stage 1 is characterized by an alarm reaction in which the body's adaptive forces are being activated but are not yet fully operational. This stage is reminiscent of childhood, in which adaptability to stress is growing but in which adaptability is still limited. Stage 2 is the stage of resistance—mobilization of the defensive reactions to stress is completed. This phase parallels adulthood, during which the body has acquired resistance to most stress agents likely to affect it. Stage 3, the stage of exhaustion, results eventually in a breakdown of resistance and, at last, in death. This final stage parallels the process of senescence in human beings.

Although it makes intuitive sense that an old animal is less able to withstand the same stress that can be tolerated by a young animal, there is little empirical evidence that accumulated stress is the cause of aging. Selye's work remains important in showing the relationship between stress and disease, but it has not yet been helpful in attempts to specify the mechanisms of aging.

Collagen, an extracellular component of connective tissue, has also been implicated in age-related changes in physiological functions. Widely scattered throughout the body, collagen is included in the skin, blood vessels, bone, cartilage, tendons, and other body organs. With age, collagen shows a reduction in its elastic properties as well as an increase in cross-linkages. *Cross-linkage* is a process whereby proteins in the body bind to each other.

According to the cross-linkage theory of aging, alteration in collagen plays an important role in impairing functional capacities. For example, the reduced efficiency of cardiac muscle may be the result of increasing stiffness. Connective tissue changes in small blood vessels may lead to the development of hypertension. Less elastic vessels may alter permeability, affecting nutrient transport and waste removal. Such changes could have far-reaching effects on all body organs.

Diabetics may be susceptible to excessive cross-linking. They undergo many complications that are similar to age-related changes, such as cataract formation and atherosclerosis. Diabetes is often referred to as a model for studying the aging process. Elevated blood sugar levels promote cross-linkage formation (Cerami, 1985). It is now believed that many of the long-term complications of diabetes are related to glucose-induced cross-linkage, especially the cross-linkage of collagen. Future work will likely provide greater insight into the possible role of glucose as a mediator of aging. Researchers at Rockefeller University are studying a drug that prevents blood sugar from promoting protein cross-linkage. It is hoped that this drug can be used in the future treatment of diabetic complications. Perhaps its most provocative use in the distant future might be the treatment of aging disorders in nondiabetic persons (Wechsler, 1986).

Nathan Shock, a noted gerontologist, suggests that there is sufficient evidence to entertain the possibility that aging results from some breakdown or impairment in the performance of endocrine and neural control mechanisms (Shock, 1961, 1962, 1974). Studies carried out by the Gerontology Research Center of the National Institutes of Health show that age-related declines in humans are greater for functions that are complex and require the coordinated activity of whole organ systems. Measurements of functions related to a single physiological system, like nerve conduction velocity, show considerably less age decrement than do functions such as maximum breathing capacity, which involve coordination between systems (in this case, between the nervous and muscular systems).

The relationship between age and task performance also shows greater age-related decline that is most likely associated with task complexity. For example, simple motor performance, as demonstrated by the time it takes an individual to push a button in response to a signal of light, increases only modestly across the human life span. Complex motor performance, on the other hand, does show significant decrement with age. Complex motor performance can involve having an individual select one of several possible responses after the presentation of a complex stimulus. Although simple motor performance involves the transmission of nerve impulses over short distances and through relatively few synapses, complex motor performance requires transmission through many synapses and is influenced by other factors in the central nervous system. Interestingly, however, elderly people often show significantly improved motor performance with practice (Botwinick, 1973).

PROLONGEVITY

Some information presented in this and previous chapters may lead readers to believe that length of life has been increased and will continue to increase almost automatically as a by-product of technological and social changes. Whether this is really so is unclear and points up the necessity of distinguishing between the concepts of life expectancy and life span. Whereas *life expectancy* refers to the average length of life of persons, *life span* refers to the longevity of long-lived persons. Life span is the extreme limit of human longevity, the age beyond which no one can expect to live (Gruman, 1977, p. 7). Gerontologists estimate the life span at about 110 years; some have argued that it has not increased notably in the course of history.

Is the human life span an absolute standard? Or should people expect a significant extension of the length of life? Those who have always believed that human life should be lengthened indefinitely are proponents of *prolongevity,* the significant extension of the length of life by human action (Gruman, 1977, p. 6). Others believe that new treatments and technology, as well as improved health habits, may continue to increase life expectancy but that the human life span is unlikely to increase. In attempting to estimate the upper limits of human longevity, Olshansky, Carnes, and Cassel (1990) suggest that it is highly unlikely that life expectancy at birth would ever exceed the age of 85. They argue that to achieve an average life expectancy at birth of 85 years in the U.S. population, mortality from all causes of death would need to decline at all ages by 55 percent and at ages 50 and over by 60 percent.

Older people often show significantly improved physical performance with practice and exercise.

Prolongevitists often point to the peoples in mountain regions of Ecuador (the Andean village of Vilacabamba), Pakistan (the Hunza people of Kashmir), and the former Soviet Union (the Abkhasians in the Russian Caucasus) as examples of populations that have already extended the human life span (Leaf, 1973). Each of these groups purportedly shows a statistically higher proportion of centenarians in the population, with many individuals reaching 120, 130, or even 150 and 160 years. Unfortunately, there are many reasons for doubting the validity of these claims (Kyncharyants, 1974; Mazess & Forman, 1979; Medvedev, 1974, 1975). Russian gerontologist Medvedev says that none of these cases of superlongevity is scientifically valid. He offers the following case as explanation of why many in the Caucasus claim superlongevity:

> The famous man from Yakutia, who was found during the 1959 census to be 130 years old, received especially great publicity because he lived in the place with the most terrible climate.... When ... a picture of this outstanding man was published in the central government newspaper, *Isvestia,* the puzzle was quickly solved. A letter was received from a group of Ukrainian villagers who recognized this centenarian as a fellow villager who deserted from the army during the First World War and forged documents or used his father's.... It was found that this man was really only 78 years old. (Medvedev, 1974, p. 387)

There continues to be interest—even mass interest—in increasing human longevity. A good part of this interest originates in the antediluvian theme found in tradition and folklore that people lived much longer in the distant past. Noah, after all, supposedly lived to be 950 years old.

What are the prospects for continued reduction in death rates and life extension? As already seen, death rates have declined and are likely to continue to do so. Nevertheless, some research suggests that there is little room for improvement, unless some significant breakthrough eliminates cardiovascular diseases. In any case, small improvements would seem to be attainable. According to Siegel (1975), if the lowest death rates for females in the countries of Europe are combined into a single table, the values for life expectancy at birth and at age 65 exceed those same values for the United States by 4.3 and 1.4 years, respectively. Table 5–1 shows the projected average life expectancy at birth in selected countries for the years 1994 and 2000. Although the United States has experienced gains in life expectancy during the twentieth century, it is clear that Canada, France, Italy, the Netherlands, Hong Kong, Japan, Australia, and Israel have life expectancies at birth that exceed those of the United States in 1994 and are projected to continue to do so into the beginning of the twenty-first century.

Most elderly people die as a result of some long-standing chronic condition that is sometimes related to personal habits (e.g., smoking, drinking alcohol, eating an unhealthy diet) or environmental conditions (e.g., harsh work environments, air pollution) that go back many years. Attempts to prevent illness and

TABLE 5–1   Projected Life Expectancy at Birth for Selected Countries, 1994 and 2000

Country	1994	2000	Country	1994	2000
North America			*Asia (continued)*		
Canada	78.1	79.1 years	Japan	79.3	80.0 years
Mexico	72.9	75.0	Vietnam	65.4	67.1
United States	75.9	76.4	*South America*		
Europe			Brazil	62.3	60.9
Denmark	75.8	77.4	Colombia	72.1	74.2
Finland	75.9	77.5	Paraguay	73.3	74.9
France	78.2	79.2	Peru	65.6	68.1
Italy	77.6	78.7	*Africa*		
Netherlands	77.8	78.8	Algeria	67.7	69.6
Poland	72.7	75.0	Burundi	40.3	39.1
Romania	71.7	74.4	Ethiopia	52.7	55.4
Russia	68.9	70.5	Nigeria	55.3	59.1
United Kingdom	76.8	78.1	South Africa	65.1	67.0
Asia			*Other Areas*		
China	67.9	70.2	Australia	77.6	78.7
Hong Kong	80.1	80.6	Israel	78.0	78.9
India	58.6	61.4	Saudi Arabia	67.9	71.1

Source: U.S. Bureau of the Census, 1994, Table 1353.

ACTIVE LIFE EXPECTANCY

Active life expectancy (ALE) is operationally defined by Katz, Branch, and Banson (1983) as that period of life free of limitations in activities of daily living (ADLs—see Chapter 6). A basic tenet of ALE as a measure is that simple longevity (as reflected in average life expectancy at birth or age-specific life expectancy) is not a sufficient criteria for assessing the quality of life of older people; freedom to pursue their daily activities, or independence, may be more important in defining health and quality of life. This begs the question of whether it should matter that other countries have higher life expectancies at birth than does the United States (see Table 5–1). What would seem to matters more is: Is there variation in the United States in ALE? By gender? By geography? How does active life expectancy in the United States compare with other industrialized nations?

With data from 10,000 Caucasian men and women from three disparate geographic areas (East Boston, MA; New Haven, CT; and two largely rural Iowa counties), Branch and colleagues (1991) calculated ALEs using life table techniques developed by the U.S. Bureau of Labor Statistics. For example, at age 65, men in the three sites who were ADL independent had ALEs ranging from 11.3 to 12.9 years; similarly, ADL-independent women had ALEs ranging from 15.4 to 17.0 years. For both men and women, the low values were from East Boston, Massachusetts, and the high values were from rural Iowa.

Average life expectancy may also be presented as a percent of remaining life, which is independent in ADLs. This calculation may be expressed by dividing the ALE by age-specific life expectancy (and multiplying by 100 to yield a percent). Interestingly, despite the fact that it is well known that women have greater life expectancy than do men at every age, the data provided by Branch and colleagues (1991) show women to have approximately equal percentages of ALE in comparison with men at age 65 years. For example, men and women in East Boston who were 65 years of age showed ALEs of 85.6 percent and 83.2 percent, respectively; for New Haven, these values were 77.2 percent and 79.9 percent, respectively.

However, given that, on average, women have a greater life expectancy than men, these comparable percentages point to the fact that women can expect a greater number of years of dependency than men. In rural Iowa, at age 65, the average woman can expect 17.1 years of ALE and 4.3 years of dependency, whereas the average man can expect 12.9 years of ALE and 3.8 years of dependency. In addition, the data suggest that, all other things being equal, a pattern of increasing life expectancy in the United States will likely create additional dependency and, thus, impose additional pressure for an adequate supply of long-term care services (Branch et al., 1991).

Recently, Tsuji and associates (1995) calculated ALEs for elderly residents of Sendai City, Japan, the eleventh largest city in Japan with a population of approximately 900,000. The ALE for those aged 65 in Sendai City was longer than among comparably aged Americans in the three U.S. sites reported above. Japanese men had an ALE of 14.7 years, or 91.3 percent of age-specific life expectancy, whereas Japanese women had an ALE of 17.7 years, or 86.8 percent of age-specific life expectancy. These data suggest that the Japanese live longer than Americans (see Table 5–1), with a longer duration of ADL-independent functioning. Why would this be the case? Are differences between the United States and Japan real or artifacts of differences in study methods? At least two reasons exist for exerting caution in the interpretation of these differences.

First, there are slight differences in the studies related to the criteria for ADL independence. In the U.S. study, people were asked if they needed help to perform one or more of the following ADLs: bathing, dressing, transferring from a bed or a chair, and eating. In the Japan study, ADLs included toileting instead of transferring from a bed to a chair because the use of a bed is less common among elderly Japanese (Tsuji et al., 1995, p. M175). Different criteria would cause different estimates of ADL independence or dependence, and perhaps this accounts for at least a portion of the differences in ALE between the U.S. and Japanese samples.

Second, the data do not allow one to determine whether the differences between the U.S. and Japanese samples of elderly reflect true differences in ADL independence or merely reflect the difference in willingness in the populations to report their problems. After all, ADLs are measured by self-report. Tsuji and colleagues (1995) suggest the possibility that Japanese elderly may be *less* likely than U.S. elderly to admit their own functional limitations at age 65, although they do not explain why this might be so.

Extending active life expectancy is now considered a major goal for the future in the United States (U.S. Department of Health and Human Services, 1990). As a measure of the health and quality of life of elderly Americans, it may be a more important measure than average life expectancy at birth or even age-specific life expectancy. Standardized measures of ALE need to be established and international comparisons made in order to evaluate and promote improvements in the quality of life of older people in the United States and around the world.

death from these conditions must begin before old age. But what if death from these conditions could be prevented? Table 5–2 gives a partial answer to this question. Using available life table data, notice that the elimination of all deaths in the United States caused by accidents, influenza and pneumonia, infective and parasitic diseases, diabetes mellitus, and tuberculosis would increase life expectancy at birth by 1.6 years and at age 65 by 0.6 year. Even the elimination of cancer as a cause of death would result in only a 2.5-year gain in life expectancy at birth and little more than half that (1.4 years) at age 65. This is because cancer affects indi-

TABLE 5–2   Gain in Life Expectancy If Various Causes of Death Were Eliminated

Various Causes of Death	Gain in Years	
	At Birth	At Age 65
1. Major cardiovascular-renal disease	11.8	11.4
2. Malignant neoplasms	2.5	1.4
3. Motor vehicle accidents	0.7	0.1
4. Influenza and pneumonia	0.5	0.2
5. Diabetes and mellitus	0.2	0.2
6. Infective and parasitic diseases	0.2	0.1

Source: U.S. Public Health Service data of life tables by cause of death for 1969–1971, U.S. Bureau of the Census, *Current Population Reports,* Series P-23, No. 59, January 1978 (revised).

viduals in all age groups, although the risk of developing cancer increases with age. If the major cardiovascular-renal diseases were eliminated, there would be a 11.8-year gain in life expectancy at birth, and even an 11.4-year gain in life expectancy at age 65.

Recent work by Olshansky, Carnes, and Cassel (1990) supports these data. These researchers estimate that if all mortality attributable to the combination of all circulatory diseases, diabetes, and cancer were eliminated, life expectancy at birth would increase by 15.8 years for females and 15.3 years for males. Such a decline in mortality from these diseases would represent approximately three-fourths of all deaths in the United States. These diseases are not likely to be eliminated in the near future, although death rates as a result of them may be reduced. There remains substantial room for improvement in death rates and life expectancies in the United States among men and nonwhites. As has already been pointed out in Chapter 4, the death rate for aged men is considerably higher than the rates for aged women. Controlling for sex, the death rates for elderly African Americans are higher than those for their white counterparts.

Much more discussion of biogerontological research on prolongevity is needed. Improving death rates and life expectancies in the United States along the lines suggested herein still would not achieve an extension of the life span. On the other hand, if major advances in genetic engineering and new life-extending technologies are forthcoming, as some believe (Olshansky, Carnes, & Cassel, 1990), then significant declines in mortality and extensions of longevity will likely follow. Should people live to be 120 or 130 years of age? Before the reader answers, assume first that this would involve more than a simple increase in time at the end of life. Imagine that researchers could alter the rate of aging in such a way as to add extra years to all the healthy and productive stages of life. Under these conditions, extra years might be difficult to turn down. But what if a longer life meant a longer "old age"? Many readers, while considering whether the human life span should be extended, will think about pollution, overpopulation, dwindling energy resources, retirement policies, Social Security benefits, and the like. The long list of negative implications may simply reflect one's negative characterization of old age. Those readers who think of old age in terms of the continuation of productive possibilities may very well accept those extra years, however and whenever they come.

SUMMARY

Answers abound to the question, "Why do people become old?" They reflect the commitment of biogerontologists to aging research at both the cellular and the organismic level. Clearly, more research is needed to understand biological aging and to improve the quality of life for increasing numbers of the aged. Attempts should be made to test the relative merits of genetic programmed theory, mutation theory, autoimmune theory, cross-linkage theory, and stress theory, among others. Perhaps the expectation that there is one overall theory of biological aging should be discarded. Aging is a complex phenomenon, and it may well be that different explanations are required for different aspects of the aging process.

What would be the effect of a solution to the riddle of biological aging? Should prolongevity be welcomed? Have people thought sufficiently about its potential impact on themselves, others, and society as a whole?

STUDY QUESTIONS

1. List the four classical hypotheses, identified by Comfort, that attempt to explain the mechanisms of aging. Can you link any of the theories of biological aging discussed in this chapter with these classical hypotheses? How?

2. Which cellular theories suggest that aging may be genetically programmed into cells? Which cellular theories of aging appear to implicate diet or nutrition in the aging process?

3. Identify the following physiological theories of aging: (a) autoimmune theory, (b) wear and tear theory, and (c) collagen theory. How may a breakdown in endocrine or neural mechanisms influence the aging process?

4. Define *prolongevity*. Distinguish between *life expectancy* and *life span*. Do the Abkhasians of the Russian Cauca-

sus really live as long as they claim? Explain your answer.

5. Compare the life expectancy at birth of people in the United States with that of citizens of other industrialized nations. Which groups in the United States show the greatest potential for improvement in the values of life expectancy and death rates?

6. How much gain in life expectancy in the United States could be realized through the elimination of certain diseases? Where would the greatest gain come from?

7. Eliminating certain diseases and thereby extending life expectancy would seem to be an inherently positive thing. Is the idea of extending the human life span equally positive? Explain your answer.

REFERENCES

Ames, B. (1983). Dietary carcinogens and anticarcinogens: Oxygen radicals and degenerative disease. *Science, 221,* 1256–1264.

Aruoma, O. I., Kaur, H., & Halliwell, B. (1991). Oxygen free radicals and human diseases. *Journal of the Royal Society of Health, 111* (5), 172–177.

Bartosz, G., Leyko, W., & Fried, R. (1979). Superoxide dismutase and life span of Drosophila melanogaster. *Experientia, 35,* 1193.

Bidder, G. P. (1925). The mortality of Plaice. *Nature, 115,* 495.

Bidder, G. P. (1932). Senescence. *British Medical Journal, 115,* 5831.

Botwinick, J. (1973). *Aging and behavior.* New York: Springer.

Branch, L. G., Guiralnik, J. M., Foley, D. J., Kohout, F. J., Wetle, T. T., Ostfeld, A., & Katz, S. (1991). Active life expectancy for 10,000 Caucasian men and women in three communities. *Journal of Gerontology: Medical Sciences, 46* (4), M145–150.

Calle, E. E., Martin, L. M., & Thun, M. J. (1993). Family history, age, and risk of fatal breast cancer. *American Journal of Epidemiology, 138* (9), 675–681.

Carrel, A. (1912). On the permanent life of tissues. *Journal of Experimental Medicine, 15,* 516.

Cerami, A. (1985). Hypothesis: Glucose as a mediator of aging. *Journal of American Geriatrics Society, 33,* 626–634.

Child, C. M. (1915). *Senescence and rejuvenescence.* Chicago: University of Chicago Press.

Comfort, A. (1979). *The biology of senescence* (3rd ed.). New York: New American Library.

Cristofalo V. (1985). The destiny of cells: Mechanisms and implications of senescence. *Gerontologist, 25,* 577–583.

Cristofalo, V. (1990). Biological mechanisms of aging: An overview. In W. Hazzard, R. Andres, E. Bierman, & J. Blass (Eds.), *Principles of geriatric medicine and gerontology.* New York: McGraw-Hill.

Fries, J. F., & Crapo, L. M. (1981). *Vitality and aging.* San Francisco: W. H. Freeman.

Garfinkel, L. (1995). Probability of developing or dying of cancer, United States, 1991. *Statistical Bulletin, 76* (4), 31–37.

Goidl, E., Thorbecke, G., & Weksler, M. (1980). Production of auto-anti-idiotypic antibody during the normal immune response. *Proceedings of National Academy of Science, 77,* 6788.

Gold, M. (1981). The cells that would not die. *Science 81, 2* (3), 28–35.

Good, R., & Yunis, E. (1974). Association of autoimmunity, immunodeficiency and aging in man, rabbits and mice. *Federal Proceedings, 33,* 2040–2050.

Gruman, G. (1977). *A history of ideas about the prolongation of life.* New York: Arno Press.

Harman, D. (1961). Prolongation of the normal lifespan and inhibition of spontaneous cancer by antioxidants. *Journal of Gerontology, 16,* 247–254.

Harman, D. (1968). Free radical theory of aging. *Journal of Gerontology, 23,* 476–482.

Hayflick, L. (1965). The limited *in vitro* lifetime of human diploid cell strains. *Experimental Cell Research, 37,* 614–636.

Hayflick, L. (1977). The cellular basis for biological aging. In C. Finch & L. Hayflick (Eds.), *Handbook of the biology of aging.* New York: Van Nostrand Reinhold.

Hayflick, L., & Moorhead, P. S. (1961). The serial cultivation of human diploid cell strains. Experimental Cell Research, 25, 585–621.

Johnson, R., Crisp, C., & Strehler, B. (1972). Selective loss of ribosomal RNA genes during the aging of post-mitotic tissues. *Mechanisms of Aging and Development, 1.*

Katz, S., Branch, L. G., & Banson, M. H. (1983). Active life expectancy. *New England Journal of Medicine, 309,* 1218–1224.

Kay, M., & Baker, L. (1979). Cell changes associated with declining immune function: Physiology and cell biology of aging. In A. Cherkin et al. (Eds.), *Aging* (Vol. 8). New York: Raven Press.

Kay, M., & Makinodan, T. (1982). The aging immune system. In A. Viidik (Ed.), *Lectures on gerontology, Vol. 1: On biology of aging, Part A.* London: Academic Press.

Kellogg, E., & Fridovich, I. (1976). Superoxide dismutase in the rat and mouse as a function of age and longevity. *Journal of Gerontology, 31,* 405–408.

Kennedy, S., Kiecolt-Glaser, J. K., & Glaser, R. (1990). Social support, stress, and the immune system. In B. R. Sarason, I. G. Sarason, & G. R. Pierce (Eds.), *Social support: An interactional view.* New York: Wiley.

Kiecolt-Glaser, J. K., Fisher, L. D., Ogrocki, P., Stout, J. C., Speicher, C. E., & Glaser, R. (1987). Marital quality, marital disruption, and immune function. *Psychosomatic Medicine, 49,* 13–34.

Kiecolt-Glaser, J. K., Glaser, R., Shuttleworth, E. C., Dyer, C. S., Ogrocki, P., & Speicher, C. E. (1987). Chronic stress and immunity in family caregivers of Alzheimer's disease victims. *Psychosomatic Medicine, 49,* 523–535.

Kyncharyants, V. (1974). Will the human life-span reach one hundred. *Gerontologist, 14,* 377–380.

Leaf, A. 1973. Getting old. *Scientific American, 299* (3), 44–52.

MacKay, I., Whittington, S., & Mathews, J. (1977). The immunoepidemiology of aging. In T. Makinodan & E. Yunis (Eds.), *Immunity and aging.* New York: Plenum Press.

Mazess, R., & Forman, S. (1979). Longevity and age exaggeration in Vilacabamba, Ecuador. *Journal of Gerontology, 34,* 94–98.

Medvedev, Z. A. (1974). Caucasus and Altay Longevity: A biological or social problem? *Gerontologist, 14,* 381–387.

Medvedev, Z. A. (1975). Aging and longevity: New approaches and new perspectives. *Gerontologist, 15,* 196–210.

Munkres, K., Rana, R., & Goldstein, E. (1984). Genetically determined conidial longevity is positively correlated with superoxide dismutase, catalase, gluthathione peroxidase, cytochrome peroxidase and ascorbate free radical reductase activities in Neurospora crass. *Mechanisms of Aging and Development, 24,* 83–100.

Olshansky, S. J., Carnes, B. A., & Cassel, C. (1990). In search of methuselah: Estimating the upper limits to human longevity. *Science, 250* (November 2), 634–640.

Orgel, L. E. (1963). The maintenance of the accuracy of protein synthesis and its relevance to aging. *Proceedings of the National Academy of Sciences, 49,* 517.

Orgel, L. E. (1973). The maintenance of the accuracy of protein synthesis and its relevance to aging. *Proceedings of the National Academy of Sciences, 67,* 496.

Rothschild, H. (1984). The biology of aging. In H. Rothschild (Ed.), *Risk factors for senility.* New York: Oxford University Press.

Sanadi, D. R. (1977). Metabolic changes and their significance in aging. In C. Finch & L. Hayflick (Eds.), *Handbook of the biology of aging.* New York: Van Nostrand Reinhold.

Schneider, E., & Reed, J. (1985). Life extension. *New England Journal of Medicine, 312,* 1159–1168.

Selye, H. (1966). *The stress of life* (2nd ed.). New York: McGraw-Hill.

Shock, N. (1961). Physiological aspects of aging in man. *Annual Review of Physiology, 23,* 97–122.

Shock, N. (1962). The physiology of aging. *Scientific American, 206* (1), 100–111.

Shock, N. (1974). Physiological theories of aging. In M. Rockstein (Ed.), *Theoretical aspects of aging.* New York: Academic Press.

Siegel, J. S. (1975). Some demographic aspects of aging in the United States. In A. Ostfeld and D. Gibson (Eds.), *Epidemiology of aging.* Bethesda, MD: National Institutes of Health.

Sinex, F. M. (1977). The molecular genetics of aging. In C. Finch & L. Hayflick (Eds.), *Handbook of the biology of aging.* New York: Van Nostrand Reinhold.

Strehler, B. (1973). A new age for aging. *Natural History,* February.

Tapple, A. L. (1968). Will antioxidant nutrients slow aging processes? *Geriatrics, 23,* 97.

Thoman, M. (1985). Role of interleukin-2 in the age-related impairment of immune function. Journal of American Geriatrics Society, 33, 781–787.

Thompson, J., Wekstein, D., Rhoades, J., Kirkpatrick, C., Brown, S., Rozman, T., Straus, R., & Tietz, N. (1984). The immune status of healthy centenarians. *Journal of American Geriatrics Society, 32,* 274–281.

Tolmasoff, J., Ono, T., & Cutler, R. (1980). Superoxide dismutase: Correlation with life span and specific metabolic rate in primate species. *Proceedings of the National Academy of Sciences, 77,* 2777–2781.

Tsuji, I., Minami, Y., Fukao, A., Hisamichi, S., Asano, H., & Sato, M. (1995). Active life expectancy among elderly Japanese. *Journal of Gerontology: Medical Services, 50A* (3), M173–176.

U.S. Department of Health and Human Services. (1990). *Healthy people 2000: National health promotion and disease prevention objectives.* Washington, DC: Author.

Walford, R. (1982). Studies in immunogerontology. *Journal of American Geriatrics Society, 30,* 617.

Wechsler, R. (1986). Unshackled from diabetes. *Discover, 7,* 77–85.

Weksler, M. (1982). Age-associated changes in the immune response. *Journal of American Geriatrics Society, 30,* 718.

Willet, W., & MacMahon, B. (1984). Diet and cancer—An overview. *New England Journal of Medicine, 310,* 633–638, 697–703.

Zidenberg-Cherr, S., Keen, C., Lonnerdal, B., & Hurley, L. (1983). Dietary superoxide dismutase does not affect tissue levels. *American Journal of Clinical Nutrition, 37,* 5–7.

CHAPTER 6

HEALTH STATUS
OF THE ELDERLY

Human organs gradually diminish in function over time, although not at the same rate in every individual. By itself, this gradual diminution of function is not a real threat to the health of most older people. Diseases are another matter. Diseases represent the chief barriers to extended health and longevity. And when they accompany normal changes associated with biological aging, maintaining health and securing appropriate health care becomes especially problematic for older people.

This chapter begins with a discussion of the physical health status of older people. Of particular interest are the patterns of chronic illness among the elderly, the variation in their self-assessments of health, and the functional decrements they experience. The text will also focus on the mental health status of the elderly, as well as whether or not patterns of morbidity among the elderly are changing such that there is compression of the length of illness before death. Finally, the chapter concludes by identifying two additional factors that may contribute to the difficulty older persons face in maintaining their health status: (1) the medical model and (2) expectations held by older people and others about what aging means.

Efforts at maintaining health and functioning in old age include the formidable task of assessing health status. This assessment task is described as formidable for three related reasons (Kane & Kane, 1981). First, the elderly are often subject to multiple illnesses and, thus, to multiple diagnoses. Second, the physical, mental, and social health of elderly individuals are closely interrelated; as a result, assessment must be multidimensional. Finally, measures of functioning that allow for assessment of an individual's ability to carry on independently, despite disease or disability, are probably the most useful indicators for practitioners.

The concept of *physical health* can be divided into at least three subcategories: (1) general physical health, or the absence of illness; (2) the ability to perform basic self-care activities, including what are known as activities of daily living (ADLs); and (3) the ability to perform more complex self-care activities that allow for greater independence, including what are known as instrumental activities of daily living (IADLs). These subcategories are thought to reflect a hierarchical order in that each level generally requires a higher order of functioning than the preceding one.

Most health survey data show a pattern in which vigorous old age predominates, but there is a clear association of advancing age with poorer functioning (Manton, 1989). Manton (1989) suggests that function can be maintained well into advanced old age and that people vary greatly in the rate at which functional loss occurs. The potential for rehabilitation exists even where a decline in functioning is the result of a currently untreatable disease (Besdine, 1988). An active approach to preserving function with increasing age includes changing medical and institutional responses to disabilities and chronic diseases among the elderly. It also includes altering negative attitudes about normal aging, even though these attitudes are accepted by many elderly persons themselves.

The great majority of older Americans live in the community and are cognitively intact and fully independent in their activities of daily living. Those who remain active may be individuals who exercise, eat nutritiously, and have a positive psychological view of life. Still, many older Americans have had or currently have a serious illness. Today, chronic illnesses are the key health problems affecting middle-aged and older adults. In fact, when compared with younger age groups, middle-aged and older adults generally present lower rates of acute conditions, including infective and parasitic conditions, respiratory conditions, conditions of the digestive system, and injuries (U.S. Bureau of the Census, 1994, Table 207).

Not only are chronic conditions long lasting but their progress most often causes irreversible pathology. Generally, the prevalence of chronic conditions among the elderly is higher than among younger persons. The reported prevalence rates among the elderly for a wide array of chronic conditions—including heart conditions, hypertension (high blood pressure), arthritis, diabetes, and visual and hearing impairments—show the most substantial differences for both females and males when compared with the prevalence rates of chronic conditions among those in the younger age groups (see Table 6–1).

In the Supplement on Aging (SOA) to the 1984 National Health Interview Survey (NHIS), over 16,000 respondents aged 55 years and older were asked if they ever had one or more of a list of 13 illnesses, including heart disease, cancer, stroke, and Alzheimer's disease, among others. About 4 in 10 (43.3 percent) reported never having had one of these illnesses; 21.2 percent reported having two or more of these illnesses. Table 6–2 shows the number of illnesses by different demographic characteristics of the SOA respondents. Those aged 55 to 64 years are the only demographic group represented in the table that shows a majority (53.2 percent) of individuals never having one of these serious illnesses. Those aged 75 to 84 years are twice as likely as the youngest group (27.6 percent versus 13.2 percent) to have two or more of these illnesses; 34.9 percent of the old-old (those aged 85 years or more) report having two or more illnesses.

Modest differences in number of reported illnesses also exist by gender, family income, race, and residence. In general, females, people with incomes below $15,000, nonwhites, and rural residents reported the greatest number of illnesses.

TABLE 6–1 Prevalence of Selected Chronic Conditions, by Age and Sex, 1992

Chronic Condition	Conditions (1,000)	Male				Female			
		Under 45 years old	45–64 years old	65–74 years old	75 years and over	Under 45 years old	45–64 years old	65–74 years old	75 years and over
Arthritis	33,317	26.1	199.2	364.8	417.2	42.2	315.9	508.7	611.2
Dermatitis	10,146	32.6	32.1	33.5	37.9	48.6	50.1	49.1	24.8
Visual Impairments	8,976	31.1	66.1	96.6	131.9	14.5	33.1	49.6	98.4
Hearing Impairments	23,777	44.3	216.2	322.3	452.7	30.4	96.9	204.3	392.9
Orthopedic Impairments	31,605	102.1	181.8	154.9	185.8	100.5	167.4	167.1	242.9
Ulcer	4,408	11.1	23.2	38.4	31.8	13.4	29.5	34.1	26.9
Diabetes	7,417	6.1	52.5	119.6	96.8	9.1	59.2	109.2	110.2
Heart conditions	21,584	25.7	150.8	334.7	408.5	32.9	120.3	220.6	401.2
Hypertension	27,816	37.5	231.1	341.4	314.7	30.2	222.1	377.7	374.3
Varicose veins	7,281	5.3	26.7	34.3	56.3	24.2	76.9	84.4	101.1
Hemorrhoids	9,562	19.1	77.3	63.9	56.7	30.5	65.6	51.6	68.9
Chronic bronchitis	13,494	40.9	43.6	76.6	40.1	57.9	71.9	79.9	65.9
Asthma	12,375	50.7	32.4	28.9	35.7	53.6	56.6	55.9	32.8
Hay fever	26,698	102.4	98.2	61.5	63.7	109.2	104.8	102.9	90.5
Chronic sinusitis	36,659	108.5	152.7	123.9	120.2	154.9	219.3	185.4	183.6

Source: U.S. Bureau of the Census, 1994, Table 208.

Note: Rate per 1,000 persons.

TABLE 6–2   Number of Illnesses and Average Number of Bed Days by Selected Characteristics

	Number of Illnesses			Bed Days	
	None	1	2+	(1)	(2)
Age					
55–64 years	53.2%	33.5%	13.2%	9.4	32.4
65–74	42.2	36.0	21.8	10.7	40.2
75–84	34.9	37.5	27.6	14.9	52.2
85+	30.7	34.3	34.9	20.9	67.8
Gender					
Male	47.5%	31.9%	20.5%	10.9	40.5
Female	40.2	38.2	21.6	12.4	43.4
Family Income					
Under $15,000	38.0%	37.6%	24.5%	15.1	50.8
$15,000 or more	47.3	33.8	19.0	8.4	29.3
Race					
White	43.8%	34.8%	21.4%	11.4	39.9
Nonwhite	38.4	43.5	18.1	16.2	63.7
Residence					
Central city	42.7%	36.8%	20.5%	13.1	45.2
Suburban	46.2	34.1	19.8	10.6	38.1
Rural	40.7	36.2	23.1	12.0	44.3

Source: 1984 Supplement on Aging, National Health Interview Survey.

Note: (1) Average number of days per last 12 months, all cases.
(2) Average number of days per last 12 months, *excluding* all cases with zero days.

Table 6–2 also shows the average number of days spent inactive in bed in the past 12 months as reported by SOA respondents. There seems to be a linear relationship between age and "bed days"; with advancing age, the average number of bed days increases, so that those 85 years and older spend twice as many days in bed as those aged 55 to 64 years. Females, people with lower income, nonwhites, and nonsuburbanites spend the most time, on average, inactive in bed.

Table 6–3 reports on the self-assessment of health status made by SOA respondents. About 70 percent of SOA respondents reported their health status in positive terms (excellent, very good, or good). It is important to note that a positive correlation exists between subjective health status and measures of functional status in aged adults (Ferraro, 1980, 1985) and between self-assessment of health by older adults and health ratings by physicians (LaRue, Bank, Jarvik, & Hetland, 1979; Maddox & Douglas, 1973). Whereas almost three out of four (74.9 percent) persons aged 55 to 64 years assessed their health in positive terms, fewer than two of three (63.6 percent) of those 85 years and older did similarly. Even among those aged 85 and older living in the community, however, only about one-third (36.4 percent) assessed their health as fair or poor.

There is variable correlation between other demographic measures and self-assessment of health among the aged. For example, less affluent elderly persons were almost twice as likely as were more affluent elderly (39.3 percent versus 21.3

TABLE 6–3   Self-Assessed Health Status by Selected Characteristics

	Excellent or Very Good	Good	Fair	Poor
Age				
55–64 years	44.1%	30.8%	16.6%	8.4%
65–74	36.5	32.0	21.1	10.3
75–84	36.0	31.1	20.7	12.2
85+	35.0	28.6	23.2	13.2
Gender				
Male	39.4	30.3	19.1	11.2
Female	37.9	32.0	20.4	9.7
Family Income				
Under $15,000	30.2	30.5	24.7	14.6
$15,000 or more	46.9	31.8	15.2	6.1
Race				
White	39.5	31.8	19.1	9.6
Nonwhite	28.7	25.6	27.1	18.5
Residence				
Central city	38.0	31.1	20.6	10.3
Suburban	42.0	32.3	17.5	8.2
Rural	35.3	30.3	21.7	12.7

Source: 1984 Supplement on Aging, National Health Interview Survey.

percent, respectively) to assess their health as fair or poor. Whites are more likely than nonwhites to assess their health positively; 45.6 percent of nonwhites and 28.7 percent of whites assess their health as fair or poor. This differential is consistent with prior research (Schlesinger, 1987). Most nonwhites in the SOA are black (86 percent). Black/white differences in self-assessment of health status reflect real differences in health status and health service utilization (Gibson & Jackson, 1987). Geographic locale is also an important consideration. Elderly suburbanites have more positive assessments of their health than do elderly residents of central city and rural areas. Gender differences in self-assessments of health status among the aged are quite modest. This is particularly interesting in light of the significant female advantage over males in mortality rates and life expectancy (Zopf, 1986).

CHRONIC ILLNESS

A *chronic illness* is a long-lasting illness or disease. Three chronic illnesses—already identified as causing the great proportion of mortality among the elderly, and that contribute as well to functional deficits and activity limitations—are heart disease, cancer, and cerebrovascular disease (stroke). These conditions are briefly discussed in this section.

Heart Disease

Heart disease is the principal cause of death among the elderly; it also accounts for a great deal of morbidity, disablement, and inactivity in older people. The dominant factor associated with the incidence of heart disease is *atherosclerosis*—a condition characterized by a buildup of fatty deposits within the arterial walls. With this buildup, arteries supplying heart tissue become narrowed, reducing blood flow to the heart. Tissue that is denied an adequate blood supply is described as *ischemic*. Heart disease is also known as *ischemic heart disease*, coronary heart disease (CHD), and coronary artery disease.

A common form of ischemic heart disease is *myocardial infarction*, or heart attack. In time, if a deficient blood supply to the heart persists, heart tissue will die. The dead area is known as an *infarct*. The extent of heart tissue involved determines the severity of the heart attack. Most often, only a small portion of heart muscle is affected, and cardiac reserves allow the work of the heart to be continued. In some older persons, there may not be sufficient heart reserve to withstand the attack. Heart attack may also result from a cardiac arrest, resulting from some interruption in the normal pattern of cardiac contractions.

In an older adult, a heart attack may be triggered by an array of different mechanisms. A coronary artery may be suddenly blocked by a blood clot (*coronary thrombosis*) or other fibrous debris released into an arterial channel. Hemorrhaging near the site of already obstructive arterial plaque may further constrict blood flow and cause the death of heart tissue and heart attack. Finally, strenuous exercise or activity, such as snow shoveling, can suddenly increase the oxygen needs of the heart, resulting in severe ischemia and heart attack.

Mortality associated with myocardial infarction for persons over 70 years of age is twice that of those under age 70. With advanced age, there may be insufficient cardiac reserve to withstand the attack. Still, the direct effect of age itself is not clearly understood. Poor prognosis following a heart attack is predicted by dysfunction in the left ventricular chamber of the heart and multivessel coronary artery disease. These predictors are more likely to be present in the elderly than in younger heart attack victims (Morley & Reese, 1989).

Brocklehurst and Hanley (1981) point out that, in many respects, heart disease is no different in old age than in youth. The symptoms and presentation of myocardial infarction, however, may be an exception. These authors indicate, for example, that whereas complete absence of chest pain is very rare in acute myocardial infarction up to middle age, it is a "mundane occurrence" in old people. In fact, only about one-third of elderly patients present with a classical prolonged episode of chest pain. Other atypical presentations (representing about another one-third of the cases) include (1) development of acute brain failure, (2) severe breathing difficulty, (3) severe fall in blood pressure, (4) formation of an arterial embolism or clot in the area of the infarction, and (5) vomiting and weakness.

Some myocardial infarcts in the aged are completely "silent" and may be discovered only with an electrocardiograph (EKG) (Brocklehurst & Hanley, 1981). It is not precisely clear why this occurs, although it is speculated that age-associated desensitivity to ischemic pain is involved. This desensitivity may also result from reduced blood flow to the brain, which is secondary to the related reduction in cardiac output.

Prevention of morbidity and mortality associated with heart disease must take into account certain modifiable risk factors. For example, cigarette smokers have twice the rate of heart attack of nonsmokers and are most at risk for sudden death from heart attack (American Heart Association, 1990). High blood pressure is also associated with increased risk of CHD mortality, as are high serum cholesterol levels. Both are modifiable with proper diet, exercise, and medication, if necessary. Diabetes, obesity, sedentary life-style, and excessive stress are also contributing factors to heart disease that may be modified. Heredity, gender (male), race (black), and age are additional risk factors that cannot be changed. The more risk factors present, the greater the chance of development of serious atherosclerotic lesions and heart disease.

Recently, the U.S. Department of Health and Human Services (1992) issued a report entitled *Healthy People 2000,* which spells out health promotion and disease prevention objectives for the U.S. population for the year 2000. Risk-reduction objectives related to heart disease and stroke include:

1. Increase the proportion of people whose high blood pressure is under control.
2. Reduce the mean serum cholesterol level among adults, in part, by increasing the proportion of adults with high blood cholesterol who are aware of their condition.
3. Reduce dietary fat intake and average unsaturated fat intake among children and adults.
4. Reduce the prevalence rates of adults for obesity and overweight.
5. Increase the proportion of children and adults who engage in regular, preferably daily, light to moderate physical activity for at least 30 minutes a day.
6. Reduce cigarette smoking among people aged 20 and older.

None of these risk-reduction objectives is specific to older people. They all suggest that reducing deaths in old age from coronary heart disease, stroke, and end-stage renal disease requires health promotion and illness-prevention behaviors that begin much earlier in the life course.

Cancer

Cancer is the second-leading cause of death in the United States. Over 530,000 Americans died of cancer in 1993. The incidence of cancer increases with age such that the death rate in 1992 among males 75 to 84 years of age was 49 times that among those aged 25 to 34 and more than 12 times that among males aged 45 to 54 years of age. In part, these facts reflect two important understandings that have been developed about the etiology of cancer: (1) Most forms of cancer have a long latent period, and initiating factors start during youth; and (2) increasing age and the accompanying physiologic changes make the patient more susceptible to the actions of carcinogens.

The death rate from cancer for women 75 years of age and older was about 50 percent that for aged men in 1992. Table 6–4 shows the differences in death rates from cancer for persons 65 years and older by sex and the site of cancer in that year. Cancer of the lungs (respiratory), digestive organs, and genital and urinary organs are primary sites for men. Digestive, breast, respiratory, and genital (cervical) cancers are primary sites among women.

The onset and management of many cancers do not vary greatly in the old and young (Brocklehurst & Hanley, 1981). Prevention is still the order of the day regarding cancer. Where possible, known causes of cancer should be avoided and removed from the environment. This includes (1) avoiding unnecessary exposure to ionizing and ultraviolet radiation, (2) implementing hygienic measures in occu-

TABLE 6–4   Death Rates from Cancer, by Sex, Age, and Selected Type, for Persons 65 Years and Over, 1992

	Male	Female
Total U.S. rate	220.8	188.2
AGE AT DEATH AND SELECTED TYPE OF CANCER		
Persons 65–74 Years Old		
Respiratory, intrathoracic	439.8	195.3
Digestive organs, peritoneum	263.5	148.4
Breast	1.1	109.3
Genital organs	122.0	70.5
Lymphatic and hematopoietic tissues (excl. leukemia)	58.7	41.0
Urinary organs	51.2	19.8
Lip, oral cavity, pharynx	20.3	7.8
Leukemia	36.0	19.0
Persons 75–84 Years Old		
Respiratory, intrathoracic	587.5	216.0
Digestive organs, peritoneum	444.0	288.7
Breast	2.0	140.8
Genital organs	355.7	97.2
Lymphatic and hematopoietic tissues (excl. leukemia)	106.5	74.8
Urinary organs	104.5	40.0
Lip, oral cavity, pharynx	23.3	10.9
Leukemia	72.3	38.0
Persons 85 Years Old and Over		
Respiratory, intrathoracic	545.4	160.8
Digestive organs, peritoneum	683.7	495.1
Breast	4.4	195.5
Genital organs	808.1	115.8
Lymphatic and hematopoietic tissues (excl. leukemia)	138.8	92.5
Urinary organs	192.8	69.8
Lip, oral cavity, pharynx	32.8	16.9
Leukemia	116.8	67.7

Source: U.S. Bureau of the Census, 1995, Table 132.

Note: Deaths per 100,000 population in specified age groups.

pations involving exposure to cancer-producing chemicals and dusts, and (3) avoiding exposure to tobacco and cigarette smoke.

Older people should be encouraged to have periodic preventive medical examinations. Physicians should take corrective and preventive measures with regard to any predisposing factors or premalignant conditions. Older persons and health care personnel must not misattribute such factors or conditions to old age. Even in the oldest patients, cancer can be cured if it is detected early and diagnosed at a localized stage.

Lung cancer, among a number of diseases related to cigarette smoking, is probably the most preventable health problem in the United States. Lung cancer is principally a disease of older persons who have smoked cigarettes (Tockman & Ball, 1990). Risk of the disease increases with the intensity and duration of cigarette smoking, the depth of inhalation, and the tar and nicotine content of the cigarettes. Lung cancer risk decreases with smoking cessation. The reduced risk will approach that of a nonsmoker 10 to 15 years after smoking has ceased (Doll & Peto, 1976).

Risk-reduction objectives for cancer specified in the *Healthy People 2000* report by the U.S. Department of Health and Human Services include:

1. Reduce cigarette smoking among people aged 20 and older. (Special population targets are offered for high-risk populations—the less well educated, blue-collar workers, military personnel, blacks, Hispanics, American Indians, Southeast Asian men, women of reproductive age, pregnant women, and women who use oral contraceptives.)

2. Reduce dietary fat and average unsaturated fat intake among children and adults.

3. Increase complex carbohydrates and fiber-containing foods in the diets of children and adults.

4. Increase the proportion of people of all ages who limit sun exposure, use sunscreens and protective clothing when exposed to sunlight, and avoid artificial sources of ultraviolet light.

Stroke

Just as heart tissue can be denied adequate blood supply, changes in blood vessels that serve brain tissue, cerebral infarction, or cerebral hemorrhage can reduce nourishment carried to the brain and result in a malfunction or death of brain cells. Such impaired brain tissue circulation is referred to as *cerebrovascular disease.*

When a portion of the brain is completely denied blood, a *cerebrovascular accident (CVA),* or stroke, results. The severity of the accident is determined by the particular area affected as well as by the total amount of brain tissue involved. A stroke may affect such a small area of the brain that it goes unnoticed or such a large area that it causes death. After diseases of the heart, malignant neoplasms (cancers), and accidents, cerebrovascular disease is the fourth-leading cause of death in the United States today.

Cerebral thrombosis, a main cause of stroke in the elderly, occurs when a formed clot becomes lodged in an already narrowed artery. There may be no transient symptoms before the stroke occurs, or there may be what Brocklehurst and Hanley (1981) describe as a *stroke-in-evolution*. In the latter case, the stroke may develop over hours or even days. Symptoms may appear within minutes or hours after the onset of a stroke. Mini-strokes, referred to as *transient ischemic attacks (TIAs)*, may also precede a CVA. TIAs are warning signs of an impending stroke. Sudden motor weakness, speech dysfunction, dizziness, sudden changes in vision (especially in one eye), and sudden falls are possible transitory symptoms that may accompany TIAs and precede a major stroke.

A cerebral embolism may also be responsible for a CVA. In this instance, the thrombus does not form locally but is derived from elsewhere in the body and travels to obstruct a vessel supplying the brain. In such cases, the stroke and its damage appear almost instantly.

When a stroke does occur, varying degrees of damage may result. Exton-Smith and Overstall (1979) list disorders of motor function, including weakness or paralysis on one side of the body, sensory disturbances, aphasia (speech disorders), and mental symptoms, among others as possible clinical features of a CVA. Rehabilitation efforts should begin immediately. Success in these efforts is a function of area and degree of brain damage as well as support of a rehabilitative team of family, friends, and medical professionals.

Aphasia, which refers to impaired ability to comprehend or express verbal language, is a clinical feature of stroke in many elderly victims. The condition is emotionally disturbing to the victim, especially to those persons who were very verbal before a stroke, as well as to family members and friends. In *receptive aphasia*, a person has difficulty processing external stimuli. Because of damage within the speech center of the brain, the individual may not understand others' speech or what is read; also, familiar objects may become unrecognizable. When a person understands what is said but cannot form the words or gestures to respond to stimuli, *expressive aphasia* has resulted. Frequently, an aphasiac suffers from a mixed condition.

Tragically, aphasia may be incorrectly associated with mental deterioration. In such cases, people may assume that comprehension is impaired when it is not, and the patient may be infantilized (treated as a child) while being fully aware of the situation. Patients should be encouraged to speak, and those around them should listen patiently and should not rush the patient or cut him or her off in the middle of an attempt. Such behavior on the part of a listener can cause the patient to feel awkward and self-conscious, and it may foster depression and withdrawal.

The extent of the damage and the degree of deficit that has taken place determine to what extent functional language skills can be regained. Unless the aphasia lasts only a few days, it may be difficult for geriatric patients ever to regain their former level of articulation. This is not to say that they cannot reestablish functional language patterns, but they and their families should not set goals too high. Every attempt should be made at language rehabilitation, and every gain should be recognized. The success of small forward steps should not be discounted because of failure to meet great expectations. A paternalistic or overly helpful attitude toward the stroke victim, although well intended, may slow recovery and make the patient feel helpless or even useless. Any gain in independent living can only enhance a person's sense of self-worth and dignity.

ACTIVITIES OF DAILY LIVING

General physical health measures have limits, especially for assessing the degree of independence and functioning an individual possesses, even in the face of a serious illness such as cancer or heart disease. Self-ratings are subject to variation over time and distortion based on psychological and environmental mechanisms. Because of these two facts, practitioners and researchers have sought to develop measures that reflect the practical aspects of physical functioning. Activities of daily living (ADLs) scales have developed as the ultimate indicators of the elderly individual's capacity to deal with basic self-care.

With some variation across different instruments, items included to measure basic self-care or activities of daily living include bathing, dressing, going to the bathroom, getting into or out of a bed or chair, walking, getting outside the house or apartment, and feeding. These are ordered in terms of decreasing dependency and are thought to form a Guttman scale (Katz et al., 1963). That is, it is generally found that bathing is the least restrictive and most common problem, whereas lack of the ability to feed oneself is indicative of the most severe restriction of function. Difficulty in feeding oneself is highly associated with the presence of other problems and is the least common ADL difficulty. Kane and Kane (1981) point out that the actual choice of ADL scale may influence results, with different indicators being more or less sensitive to change in physical functioning over time.

Being able to complete household chores may be a more appropriate measure of assessing independence and functioning in an elderly individual than the presence of a serious illness.

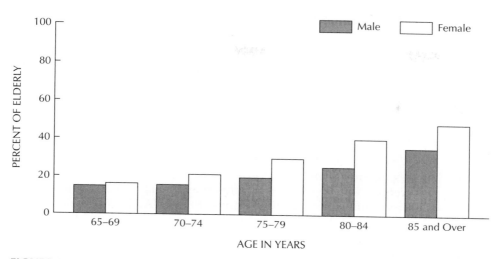

FIGURE 6–1   Percent of Persons 65 Years of Age and Over Who Reported Difficulty with at Least One Activity of Daily Living, by Sex, for All Respondent-Assessed Health Statuses: United States, 1986

Notes: Data are based on household interviews of the civilian noninstitutionalized population. ADL is activity of daily living. Excludes unknown respondent-assessed health statuses. Excludes those for whom information was missing on all ADLs. Persons reported as not performing an ADL were classified with those reported as having difficulty with that ADL. ADLs include eating, toileting, dressing, bathing, walking, getting in and out of a bed or chair, and getting outside.

Source: National Center for Health Statistics: Data from the National Health Interview Survey 1986 Functional Limitations Supplement.

Generally, as Figure 6–1 shows, problems with ADLs increase with advancing age. In the age 65 to 69 category, 15 percent of males and 16 percent of females report difficulty performing at least one ADL. By age 85 and over, 35 percent of the males and 48 percent of the females report difficulty performing at least one ADL. Data from the Supplement on Aging, referred to above, confirms this pattern. In that data set, the oldest-old, women, those elderly with a family income under $15,000, nonwhites, and those residing in rural areas report the most limitations in ADLs. For example, SOA respondents with family income under $15,000 were about twice as likely as more well-to-do respondents (income greater than $15,000) to report imitations in ADLs (25.5 percent versus 13.1 percent, respectively).

INSTRUMENTAL ACTIVITIES OF DAILY LIVING

Instrumental activities of daily living (IADLs) include both the personal self-care reflected in the ADL measures and more complex activities. For example, going shopping, a commonly used IADL indicator, requires being able to get out of bed, dress, walk, and leave the house. Because the IADL tasks are more complicated and multifaceted, functional decrements are expected to show up first in the IADL items, and more older people are expected to report limitations in carrying out these instrumental activities than in performing the more basic activities of daily living. IADLs include six home-management activities: preparing meals, shopping, managing money, using the telephone, doing light housework, and doing heavy housework.

Difficulties in performing IADLs are related to age and sex, as is revealed in Figure 6–2. For both males and females, the percent reporting difficulty with IADLs increased with advancing age. And, at every age subgroup, a greater percent of women than men reported difficulty in performing IADLs. According to Furner (1992), these sex differences may not, however, be the result of true functional differences between men and women, but rather may be the result of differences in role socialization (with men typically performing fewer IADLs than women, thus causing men's reports of difficulty to be underestimated). Conceivably, these sex differences may also be the result of age bias within each subgroup (on average, within any given age subgroup, women had higher mean ages than men).

Nathanson (1975) offers three categories of explanation for why women report more illness and limitation and use more medical service than do men:

1. It is culturally more acceptable for women to be ill.

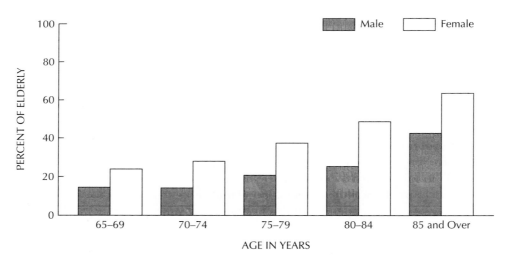

FIGURE 6–2   **Percent of Persons 65 Years of Age and Over Who Reported Difficulty with at Least One Instrumental Activity of Daily Living, by Sex, for All Respondent-Assessed Health Statuses: United States, 1986**

Note: Data are based on household interviews of the civilian noninstutionalized population. IADL is instrumental activity of daily living. Excludes unknown respondent-assessed health status. Excludes those for whom information was missing on all IADLs. Persons reported as not performing and IADL were not classified with those reported as having difficulty with that IADL. IADLs include meal preparation, shopping, managing money, using the telephone, light housework, and heavy housework.

Source: National Center for Health Statistics: Data from the National Health Interview Survey 1986 Functional Limitations Supplement.

2. Women's social roles are more compatible with reports of illness and use of medical services than is the case for men.

3. Women's social roles are, in fact, more stressful than those of men; consequently, they have more real illness and need more assistance and care.

The merits of these explanations continue to be debated (Verbrugge & Madans, 1985).

Kane and Kane (1981) suggest that, because of the complexity and multifaceted nature of IADLs, the way respondents report on the individual items may be biased by variations in motivation, mood, and overall emotional health. For instance, a depressed older person might be more likely to neglect IADLs such as managing money or doing the housework than basic aspects of personal self-care such as dressing or using the toilet.

It can also be argued that social structural and environmental factors contribute to IADL limitations. A widower who never performed certain IADL tasks when his spouse was alive and fit may report limitations because he never learned the skills, not because he is unable to perform the function. Similarly, an older woman may report limitations in shopping because markets are scarce in her inner-city neighborhood and she lacks transportation to area stores.

As Lawton and Nahemow (1973) reported in the early 1970s, when the fit between an individual's competence and the environment in which the individual resides is good, adaptation is positive. This may be the case for the great majority of older people. When environmental demands are too great, adaptation is poor and the outcome (including self-care capacity) is likely to be negative.

MENTAL HEALTH

Estimates vary as to the proportion of the elderly population with mental health problems. According to Pfeiffer (1977), approximately 15 percent of the elderly population in the United States suffer from significant, substantial, or moderate psychopathological conditions. Gurland and Toner (1982) argue that 15 percent may represent only that proportion of the elderly with clinically significant depression. Roybal (1984) states that as many as 25 percent of the elderly have significant mental health problems. Presumably, this percentage includes both long-term care facility and community residents.

Blazer (1980) reports that the rate of severe impairment of subjects in various studies ranges from 4 to 18 percent of community-dwelling elders and from 32 to 47 percent of those elderly persons residing in long-term care institutions. Among the specified diagnoses, organic brain syndromes, depressive disorders, schizophrenia, and alcohol disorders account for high rates of patient care episodes in outpatient psychiatric services for old people in the United States. The same list obtains for inpatient facilities. According to Blazer (1980), 15 to 70 percent of those found in various sorts of long-term care institutions showed symptoms of dementia.

Figures on the mental health status of the elderly must be viewed with some caution. The epidemiology of psychopathological conditions is beset by conceptual and methodological difficulties. Even under careful conditions of assessment, diagnosing schizophrenia or depression is often difficult. Different doctors, using different definitions and criteria, and varying widely in their competence as well as in their understanding of aging processes, should make one suspicious of the adequacy of their diagnoses. For example, there has been a tendency to overestimate the incidence of dementia among the old, while underestimating that of depression. The symptoms of these disorders are similar, and correct diagnosis can also be confounded by attitudes toward the elderly (Butler & Lewis, 1982; Eisdorfer & Cohen, 1982). In addition, as Libow (1973) states, much of the early mental change shown by elderly persons can be explained by changes in the environment.

A National Institute of Mental Health study of healthy male volunteers, whose average age was 70 at the start of the study and who were followed for 11 years, found a strong relationship between survival and the organization of a subject's daily behavior (Bartko & Patterson, 1971). The greater the complexity and variability of a day's behavior, the greater the likelihood of survival.

Sampling error also contributes to the generation of inaccurate estimates of the incidence of mental health problems among the aged. If samples are drawn from lists of present users of mental health services, then older people will be underrepresented. According to Kermis (1986), because older people do not use mental health services, the belief is that they do not need them. If samples are drawn from a community at large, older people with mental health problems are also underrepresented because many of them reside in group or institutional settings (Kermis, 1986).

Despite the conceptual and methodological difficulties involved in determining the degree and extent to which psychopathological conditions are distributed among the elderly, it is quite clear that some older people do have mental health problems. These problems are often categorized according to the degree of actual impairment in brain functioning.

Depression appears to be the most common of the functional psychiatric disorders in the later years, yet it is not often recognized in older people (Kermis, 1986). A recent National Institutes of Health (NIH) Development Conference concluded that depression in the aging and the aged is a major public health problem (NIH, 1991). Depression can vary in duration and degree; it may be triggered by loss of a loved one or by the onset of a physical disease. A depressed individual may show any combination of psychological and physiological manifestations. Criteria for the diagnosis of depression include: (1) changes in appetite and weight; (2) disturbed sleep; (3) motor agitation or retardation; (4) fatigue and loss of energy; (5) depressed or irritable mood; (6) loss of interest or pleasure in usual activities; (7) feelings of worthlessness, self-reproach, or excessive guilt; (8) suicidal thinking or attempts; and (9) difficulty with thinking or concentration (American Psychiatric Association, 1987). Kermis (1986) lists some atypical clinical features that further confuse diagnosis, including pseudodementia (apathy and slowness of cognition resembling dementia) and somatic complaints without obvious mood changes.

Depression in older persons is a treatable syndrome. If untreated, it may become chronic and lead to social dysfunction, drug use, and/or physical morbidity (Gurland & Toner, 1982). Drug therapies are popular and effective. According to NIH, there is now evidence from at least 25 randomized double-blind trials that antidepressants are more effective than placebo in the treatment of acute depression (NIH, 1991). Other available treatment modalities include electroconvulsive therapy (ECT) and psychosocial treatments such as cognitive behavior therapy, behavior therapy, interpersonal therapy, and short-term psychodynamic therapy. Many professionals view the elderly as poor candidates for the psychosocial treatments, and there is no clear consensus on the efficacy of these interventions.

Suicidal thoughts often accompany depression. Gardner, Bahn, and Mack (1964) found in their research that the majority of older persons committing suicide have been depressed. According to the U.S. Center for Health Statistics, the suicide rate among the elderly in 1992 was about 180 percent that among the total population. This statistic may present a conservative picture. Many doctors do not report suicides because they think it stigmatizes the surviving family members; family members themselves often hide or destroy suicide notes—usually unnecessarily—to try to ensure payments by life insurance companies.

Table 6–5 presents suicide rates by sex, race, and age group for 1992. Elderly white males show the highest suicide rate of any group. Among males aged 65 to 74 years their rate is almost 3 times that of aged African American males, more than 5 times that of aged white females, and almost 12 times that of aged African American females. Aged females in the United States have among the lowest suicide rates in the world. Aged U.S. males fall in the middle of the range represented by selected countries. Male elderly have higher suicide rates in Austria, Denmark, France, and West Germany; countries in which the elderly have lower suicide rates than in the United States include England and Wales, Australia, Canada, Italy, Poland, and the Netherlands (U.S. Bureau of the Census, 1994, Table 1360).

TABLE 6–5   Suicide Rates by Sex, Race, and Age Groups, 1992

	Male		Female	
	White	Black	White	Black
All ages	21.2	12.0	5.1	2.0
10–14 years	2.6	2.0	0.9	—
15–19 years	18.4	14.8	3.7	1.9
20–24 years	26.6	21.2	4.0	2.6
25–34 years	25.1	20.7	5.4	3.7
35–44 years	25.2	16.9	7.2	4.0
45–54 years	24.0	12.4	7.9	3.2
55–64 years	26.0	10.1	7.2	2.6
65–74 years	32.0	11.8	6.3	2.6
75–84 years	53.0	18.5	6.6	—
85 years and over	67.6	—	6.3	—

Source: U.S. Bureau of the Census, 1995, Table 136.

Two additional common functional psychiatric disorders in the later years are paranoia and hypochondriasis. *Paranoia* is a delusional state that is usually persecutory in nature. It often involves attributing motivations to other people that they simply do not have. Paranoia is more common in individuals suffering from sensory deficits such as hearing loss (Post, 1980). Some paranoia may be caused by changes in life situation, such as relocation or other stresses. Kermis (1986) describes a 72-year-old woman, hospitalized while recovering from major heart surgery, who had a persistent delusion that agents of the Central Intelligence Agency were spying on her. She recorded these occurrences and reported them to the staff, who discovered that her CIA visits corresponded to security guards' checks of the floor.

Characteristically, the initial premise of the paranoid is irrational, although the rest of the delusional system often follows logically. Kermis (1986) notes that if the paranoid person's basic premise is accepted, the rest of the delusion often makes sense. Most paranoid individuals have a fairly focused problem and are not impaired in their daily functioning. If the disorder remains chronic, however, social and marital function may be negatively affected.

Hypochondriasis is an overconcern for one's health, usually accompanied by delusions about physical dysfunction and/or disease. The conventional wisdom is that hypochondriacs displace their psychological distress onto the body. A number of observers have emphasized the utility of the condition—after all, it is far more acceptable in this society to be physically ill than it is to be emotionally or mentally disabled (Pfeiffer & Busse, 1973). Hypochondriacs will diligently seek medical help, yet treatment of the disorder is difficult because they are not predisposed to psychological explanations of their condition.

The 1987 revised edition of the *Diagnostic and Statistical Manual of Mental Disorders (DSM-III-R)* of the American Psychiatric Association (APA) makes the distinction between organic mental syndromes and organic mental disorders. *Organic mental syndrome (OMS)* is used to refer to a group of psychological or behavioral signs and symptoms without reference to etiology; *organic mental disorder (OMD)* designates a particular OMS in which the etiology is known or presumed (APA, 1987). OMS can be grouped into six categories:

1. Delirium and Dementia, in which cognitive impairment is global
2. Amnestic Syndrome and Organic Hallucinosis, in which there is selective cognitive impairment
3. Organic Delusional Syndrome, Organic Mood Syndrome, and Organic Anxiety Syndrome, with features resembling schizophrenia, mood, and anxiety disorders, respectively
4. Organic Personality Syndrome, where personality is affected
5. Intoxication and Withdrawal, associated with the ingestion of or reduction in use of a psychoactive substance
6. Organic Mental Syndrome Not Otherwise Specified, a residual category

According to the *DSM-III-R* (APA, 1987, p. 98), the most common forms of OMS are delirium, dementia, intoxication, and withdrawal. These syndromes display great variability in the same individuals over time, as well as across different individuals, and may be present in the same individual simultaneously. Dementia is most common in the elderly and, most often, takes the form of Primary Degenerative Dementia of the Alzheimer's Type.

The *DSM-III-R* identifies Primary Degenerative Dementia of the Alzheimer's Type as an organic mental disorder arising in the senium and presenium. What this means is that the disease is believed to be a physical disorder and that it is subtyped according to age of onset. Senile onset (after age 65) is much more common than presenile onset, with few cases developing before the age of 50. Between 2 and 4 percent of the entire population over the age of 65 may have this dementia, with the proportion increasing in those over 75 years of age. The disorder is slightly more common in females than in males, and in rare cases, it is thought to be inherited as a dominant trait. Down's syndrome is a predisposing factor to Alzheimer's disease.

Dementia of the Alzheimer's Type has an insidious onset and gradually progressive course (APA, 1987). It brings a multifaceted loss of intellectual abilities— including memory, judgment, and abstract thought—as well as changes in personality and behavior. Initially, the Alzheimer's victim experiences minor symptoms that may be attributed to stress or physical illness. With time, however, the person becomes more forgetful. Things get misplaced, routine chores take longer, and already answered questions are repeated. As the disease progresses, memory loss as well as confusion, irritability, restlessness, and agitation are likely to appear. Judgment, concentration, orientation, writing, reading, speech, motor behavior, and naming of objects may also be affected. Even when a loving and supportive family is available, the Alzheimer's victim may ultimately require institutional care (U.S. Department of Health and Human Services, 1984).

At present, the conventional view is that the only way to diagnose Alzheimer's disease is by brain autopsy. Brain-imaging techniques have been used to diagnose other forms of dementia such as multi-infarct. With careful screening and the use of an extensive battery of tests, the disease may be diagnosed prior to autopsy. Typically, complete diagnostic examinations for dementia consist of thorough medical workups, blood tests, brain imaging, and neuropsychological tests consisting of those for intelligence, memory, and language used by clinicians to identify specific cognitive problems. Table 6–6 summarizes the criteria for the diagnosis of probable Alzheimer's disease.

There is no cure at present for Alzheimer's disease. What are the possible causes of this debilitating disease? Since the 1970s, research scientists have been studying the evidence of a significant and progressive decrease in the activity of the enzyme choline acetyltransferase (ChAT) in the brain tissue of Alzheimer's patients. ChAT is an important ingredient in neurotransmissions involved with learning and memory. There appears to be a link between changes in this neurochemical activity and changes in cognition and the physical appearance of the brains of Alzheimer's patients (U.S. Department of Health and Human Services, 1984). Additional research is needed to determine whether accumulations of trace metals in the brain (such as aluminum) are a primary cause of Alzheimer's disease or if other factors (such as slow-acting transmissible viruses) might combine with

TABLE 6–6 Criteria for the Diagnosis of Probable Alzheimer's Disease

1. Criteria for clinical diagnosis of *probable* Alzheimer's disease include:
   a. Dementia established by clinical examination and documented by the Mini Mental State Test, Blessed Dementia Scale, or some similar examination and confirmed by neuropsychological tests
   b. Deficits in two or more areas of cognition
   c. Progressive worsening of memory and other cognitive functions
   d. No disturbance of consciousness
   e. Onset between ages 40 and 90, most often after age 65
   f. Absence of systemic disorders or other brain diseases that in and of themselves could account for progressive deficits in memory and cognition

2. Diagnosis of probable Alzheimer's disease is supported by:
   a. Progressive deterioration of specific cognitive functions, such as language (asphasia), motor skills (apraxia), and perception (agnosia)
   b. Impaired activities of daily living and altered patterns of behavior
   c. Family history of similar disorders, particularly if confirmed neuropathologically
   d. Laboratory results of normal lumbar puncture as evaluated by standard techniques; normal pattern or nonspecific changes in EEG, such as increased slow-wave activity; and evidence of cerebral atrophy on CT with progression documented by serial observation

3. Other clinical features consistent with diagnosis of probable Alzheimer's disease, after exclusion of causes of dementia other than Alzheimer's disease, include:
   a. Plateaus in the course of progression of illness
   b. Associated symptoms of depression; insomnia; incontinence; delusions; illusions; hallucinations; catastrophic verbal, emotional, or physical outbursts; sexual disorders; and weight loss
   c. Other neurological abnormalities in some patients, especially with more advanced disease and including motor signs, such as increased muscle tone, myoclonus, or gait disorder
   d. Seizures in advanced disease
   e. CT normal for age

4. Features that make the diagnosis of probable Alzheimer's disease uncertain or unlikely include:
   a. Sudden, apoplectic onset
   b. Focal neurological findings such as hemiparesis, sensory loss, visual field deficits, and uncoordination early in the course of the illness
   c. Seizures or gait disturbance at onset or very early in the course of the illness

5. Clinical diagnosis of probable Alzheimer's disease:
   a. May be made on the basis of dementia syndrome, in the absence of other neurological, psychiatric, or systemic disorders sufficient to cause dementia and in the presence of variations in onset, in presentation, or in the clinical course.
   b. May be made in the presence of a second systemic or brain disorder sufficient to produce dementia, which is not considered to be the cause of dementia.
   c. Should be used in research studies when single, gradually progressive severe cognitive deficit is identified in the absence of other identifiable cause.

6. Criteria for diagnosis of definite Alzheimer's diseases are:
   a. Clinical criteria for probable Alzheimer's disease
   b. Histopathological evidence obtained from biopsy or autopsy

7. Classification of Alzheimer's disease for research purposes should specify features that may differentiate subtypes of the disorder, such as:
   a. Familial occurrence
   b. Onset before age 65
   c. Presence of trisomy-21
   d. Coexistence of other relevant conditions, such as Parkinson's disease

Source: National Institute of Neurological, Communication Disorders and Stroke, undated.

environmental factors to trigger the onset of the disease (U.S. Department of Health and Human Services, 1984).

Some scientists see an inherited predisposition or genetic marker to Alzheimer's disease. Zubenko and colleagues at the University of Pittsburgh have discovered an abnormality in the blood that may predict the later onset of Alzheimer's. This abnormality was found in blood platelets, particles vital to the process of blood clotting. The blood platelets of Alzheimer's patients show less rigidity in their structural membranes, although this abnormality does not impair blood platelet functioning.

Such an alternation would not likely have any direct causal effect bearing on Alzheimer's, but scientists speculate that the gene that does cause this change may have different, as yet unidentified, effects on brain cells (Schmeck, 1987). The platelet abnormality was not found in people with depression or mania, conditions sometimes confused with Alzheimer's disease. Interestingly, when the platelet was found in an Alzheimer's patient, it was 3.5 to 11 times more likely to appear in close relatives of the patient than in the general population at large. Family studies have already found that first-degree relatives of Alzheimer's patients are at a significantly higher lifetime risk of developing dementia, especially if the affected family member is a parent and if onset occurs before age 70 (Schmeck, 1987).

Do social or psychological experiences contribute to the cause or development of Alzheimer's disease? Too little research has been aimed at this question. For the most part, social and behavioral scientists have focused on the development of diagnostic tests, the changes in language use that results from brain dysfunction, and the need for special support for the families of disease victims (U.S. Department of Health and Human Services, 1984).

The descriptions of the organic brain syndromes presented in the *DSM-III-R* are clear and straightforward and give the impression that their recognition and diagnosis are equally so. However, there is some reliable evidence to demonstrate that OBS is overdiagnosed (Clark, 1980; Fox, Topel, & Huckman, 1975; Glassman, 1980; Kaercher, 1980; Marsden & Harrison, 1972; Seltzer & Sherwin, 1978; Wells, 1978). For example, Duckworth and Ross (1975) compared psychiatric diagnoses given to patients over age 65 in Toronto, New York, and London. They found that organic brain disorders were diagnosed with more than 50 percent greater frequency in New York than in either Toronto or London. Although variation in patient populations may account for some of this difference, Wells (1978) suggests that in Toronto and London, a greater emphasis is placed on recognizing functional disorders in the aged; therefore, elderly patients are more likely to be labeled correctly.

Libow (1973) uses the term *pseudosenility* to refer to conditions that may manifest themselves as senility and thus cause misdiagnosis or mislabeling of OMS or OMD. Causes of pseudosenility include drug interactions, malnutrition, and fever. When these conditions are treated, the senility often goes away. While admittedly there are no definitive studies identifying the frequency of pseudosenility, a task force sponsored by the National Institute on Aging suggests that 10 to 20 percent of all older people diagnosed with mental impairments have these reversible conditions (NIA, 1980).

The importance of OMS and OMD, in both numerical and personal terms, is being recognized increasingly. This recognition is reflected in gerontological and popular literature that points out that many curable physical and psychological disorders in the elderly produce intellectual impairments that may be difficult to distinguish from OMS or OMD. More important, this growing body of literature states clearly, if not emphatically, that normal aging does not include the symptoms of OMS or OMD; these are diseases, not inevitable accompaniments of aging.

IS THERE COMPRESSION OF MORBIDITY?

What if the time spent in chronic mental or physical illness or with functional limitations in the ADLs or IADLs before death could be reduced from current levels? Presumably, this would mean more years of a higher quality old age, even in an absence of further improvements in life expectancy. Fries (1980, 1987) argues that this "compression of morbidity" may already be occurring. According to Fries (1987), a compression of morbidity may be considered to occur if the length of time between onset of disease and death is shortened.

This compression of morbidity hypothesis has generated some considerable debate in the gerontological literature. Some have argued that there simply is no evidence to support it. Kaplan (1991), employing data over the last 25 years from the Alameda County, California, studies of two cohorts of adults living in the community, points out that although there have been significant declines in age-specific mortality rates, these declines have been accompanied by an increase in the age-specific prevalence of chronic conditions and symptoms. From Kaplan's view, the overall picture is one of increased survival accompanied by increased morbidity and disability. This view is supported by others. Guralnik (1991) projects that the distribution of age at death will change such that more deaths will be taking place at the oldest ages. He argues that this is likely to lead to an increased number of years spent disabled prior to death for the total population aged 65 and older. Using 1986 data on disability among older Americans as baseline, Kunkel and Applebaum (1992) estimate that by 2040, when the Baby Boomers reach their eighties and nineties, the numbers of disabled elderly will have increased by between 190 and 343 percent.

Olshansky and associates (1991) also suggest the possibility of an expansion of morbidity through two hypothetical mechanisms. First, medical technology may continue to improve survival from disabling conditions associated with fatal diseases, but the progress of the diseases themselves may remain unchanged. Second, as mortality from fatal diseases at older ages is reduced, the morbidity and disability resulting from nonfatal diseases could continue unabated. Thus, the trade-off becomes reduced mortality in middle and older ages for a redistribution of causes of disability and an expansion of morbidity (Olshansky et al., 1991). Much work remains to determine whether reductions in risk factors such as smoking and improvements in medical treatments lead to a compression of morbidity

AGE, SOCIOECONOMIC STATUS, AND HEALTH

House, Kessler, Herzog, and colleagues (1990) argue that people need to move beyond the dispute over whether compression of morbidity is occurring in the total population and determine whether certain subgroups of the population are experiencing greater postponement of morbidity and functional limitations than others. They express surprise at the extent to which socioeconomic differentials in the relation of aging and health have been neglected in the compression of morbidity debate. The researchers point out how, even as average life expectancy has advanced, socioeconomic differences in mortality and health have persisted in the United States and elsewhere. They hypothesize that the higher socioeconomic strata in U.S. society already approximate the compression of morbidity scenario (i.e., low levels of morbidity and functional limitations until quite late in life), whereas levels of morbidity and functional limitations increase steadily throughout middle-age and early-old age for those in the lower socioeconomic strata.

Data from the Americans' Changing Lives (ACL) survey, including 3,617 respondents aged 25 and over interviewed in 1986, was used to test the hypothesis. The key dependent variables were three self-reported indicators of physical health. Four different levels of socioeconomic status (SES), defined in terms of education and income, were identified for purposes of the analyses. Respondents in the lowest level of SES had both 0 to 11 years of education *and* income below $20,000; those in the highest level of SES had 16+ years of education *and* income of $20,000 or more.

The results of the analyses show a particularly striking pattern of differences in the relation of age to health for all three indica-

tors across four levels of socioeconomic status defined by education and income. Only the specific pattern for one indicator of physical health—number of chronic conditions experienced in the past year—is described here.

Among survey respondents aged 25 to 34, there are no socioeconomic differences in prevalence of chronic conditions. Marked differences become evident for those in early middle-age (35 to 44 years), and these differences become larger still among those 45 to 54 years and those in early-old age (55 to 64 years and 65 to 74 years). The differences are much smaller among persons 75 years and older. More importantly, the lowest socioeconomic stratum shows a prevalence of chronic conditions at ages 35 to 44 that is not seen in the highest stratum until after age 75. The prevalence of chronic conditions peaks at ages 55 to 64 in the lowest SES group, at ages 65 to 74 in the next group, but not until age 75 and over for the two highest SES groups.

In sum, considerable postponement of morbidity seems to be occurring in the highest socioeconomic group, where the mean number of chronic conditions remains below 1.0 until age 75. In contrast, the mean number of chronic conditions in the lowest socioeconomic group rises sharply between ages 25 and 54 and exceeds 2.0 by age 55. On the basis of this research, these authors identify the vast amount of "excess" or preventable morbidity and functional limitations as being located in the lowest SES groups in U.S. society. Clearly, efforts to postpone morbidity, disability, and even mortality in U.S. society must include serious efforts to reduce socioeconomic differentials in health in middle and early old age.

or whether causes of disability are redistributed with a resulting longer life with worsening health.

Two additional factors contribute to the difficulty older people face in maintaining both physical and mental health, and these deserve a brief mention here. One has to do with the basic orientation of modern medicine, the so-called medical model. The other pertains to the attitudes and expectations that older people, their family and friends, and health care providers have about what aging means.

THE MEDICAL MODEL

The concept of the *medical model* describes the basic paradigm that rules medical practice. Eliot Freidson employs the term *medical-intervention pattern* to describe what is meant here:

> The medical man is prone to see the patient's difficulty as a transitory technical problem that can be overcome by some physical or biochemical intervention which only the physician is qualified to perform. The assumption is that the patient can be cured and discharged. (1988, pp. 132–133)

In this model, attention is aimed at obtaining a diagnosis of a condition and developing a treatment regimen for its cure. Efforts are almost always geared at identifying just one condition or dysfunction. Among the elderly in ill health, however, a single condition is unusual. More often, elderly patients have multiple conditions, including degenerative changes associated with biological aging and diseases associated with pathological aging. In addition, specific disease states may manifest themselves differently among the elderly than is the case among the young. These multiple changes, along with age-based differences in symptom manifestation, can lead to confusion in trying to diagnose accurately and to further difficulty in generating an appropriate treatment plan.

This confusion would occur even if the presence of disease, its diagnosis, and its treatment could be defined objectively. There is considerable evidence, however, that such objectivity is a questionable assumption underlying the medical model (Wolinsky, 1988). Zola (1962, 1966) has demonstrated that the differing world views of patients and differences in their cultural backgrounds affected how they presented symptoms to attending physicians. For example, Zola found that Irish patients tended to understate their symptoms, whereas Italians were more likely to generalize and even embellish their symptoms. Wolinsky summarizes the sociological principle in effect here:

> The selection, salience, and presentation of symptoms are at least partially determined by sociocultural factors and conditioning. . . . If the symptoms of disease are socioculturally relative, then disease itself must be in part defined relative to sociocultural phenomena. (1988, p. 77)

Even if symptoms of illness were presented in some objective fashion, there is a serious question about whether all physicians would or could identify the signs and presence of disease. As Wolinsky (1988) points out, although physicians are comparably trained, there is no uniform mechanical procedure for examining all patients or even all elderly patients. Some physicians routinely check blood pressure, pulse, and respiration during an examination or office visit; others do not. Also, diseases linked to sociocultural traits (e.g., obesity and hypertension among older black women or osteoporosis among elderly white women) may cue physician attention toward or away from particular diagnoses.

Kovar addresses the fact that the medical model treats all older people as if they were representatives of a homogeneous grouping.

> The range in health status is just as great in this age group as in any other, even though the proportion of persons who have health problems increases with age and a minor health problem that might be quickly alleviated at younger ages tends to linger. Aging is a process that continues over the entire lifespan at differing rates among different persons. The rate of aging varies among populations and among individuals in the same population. It varies even within an individual because different body systems do not age at the same rate. (1977, p. 9)

ATTRIBUTION OF ILLNESS

Health is as much a subjective as an objective phenomenon. Individuals assess their health on the basis of various factors, including their own expectations about how people like themselves should feel. People experiencing changes in usual body functioning try to make sense of their experiences, often by hypothesizing about the possible causes of symptoms. A central issue in most perceptions of causality is whether to attribute a given experience to internal or external states (Freedman, Sears, & Carlsmith, 1978). *External* attribution ascribes causality to anything external to the individual, such as the general environment, role constraints or role losses, stressful tasks being worked on, and so on. *Internal* causes include such factors as disease states, biological aging, personality, mood, and motivation (Freedman, Sears, & Carlsmith, 1978).

Potentially, the development of illness attribution and misattribution can be affected by many factors both internal and external to the individual. These include the perceived seriousness of symptoms, the extent of disruption of normal activities involved, the frequency and persistence of the symptoms, the amount of pain and discomfort to which a person is accustomed, the extent of the person's medical knowledge, the need to deny the illness, the nature of competing needs, the availability of alternative explanations, and the accessibility of treatment (Mechanic, 1978).

According to Jones and Nisbitt (1971), actors and observers tend to make different causal attributions. *Actors* usually see their behavior as a response to an external situation in which they find themselves; typically, *observers* attribute the same response to factors internal to the actor. This difference between an actor's and an observer's attributions can lead to misunderstanding, perhaps especially so in a health care context. Patients and their physicians may see the same event from different perspectives. The patient attributes his response to environmental factors (e.g., stress at home) that are out of the purview of the physician, but the physician attributes the patient's response to internal physical processes—disease states or biological aging. These internal processes are, for the most part, the only causal explanations available to the physician, who may be handicapped by a lack of information about those factors to which the patient is responding in the environment.

This is the basis for problems in the doctor/patient relationship. The noncompliant patient may be deemed uncooperative or recalcitrant by the physician ("The patient has a personality problem"), whereas the patient may attribute noncompliance to situational factors ("The medication made me sick") (Janis & Rodin, 1979).

The elderly themselves seem overly ready to make attributions to internal physical processes rather than to the environment (Janis & Rodin, 1979). Their perceptions often include grossly exaggerated notions of what happens during normal aging. Too many associate pain and discomfort, debilitation, or decline in intellectual function with aging in itself. These are not normal accompaniments of aging. Unfortunately, such associations are supported by significant others (e.g., "What do you expect at your age?") as well as by physicians. In fact, the aged patient/doctor relationship may be a *special* case of actor/observer interaction, when both agree that events are attributable to internal physical processes (e.g., biological aging).

This consensus may reinforce a set of consequences that are essentially negative. First, elderly individuals may assume that aging has had a greater impact on them than it really has. For example, Kahn and associates (1975) found that only a small amount of memory loss was evident in an elderly sample; yet patients perceived a high degree of loss. These perceptions were highly correlated with depression. Second, the elderly may attribute all negative changes in health and mood to aging in itself. Chest pain as a warning signal of heart disease may be considered another attack of heartburn; bone pain, which may herald a fracture or bone cancer, may be ascribed to age-related rheumatism. A change in bowel habits is a well-known danger signal of cancer but such an alteration may easily be ignored by an older person who seems to be plagued by bowel problems. Even rectal bleeding may be attributed to hemorrhoids.

Attributing illness or biological changes to so-called normal aging may incorrectly focus an elderly person (and his or her physician) away from situational and social factors that are stress inducing and that affect health. Much of the remainder of this book is concerned with the impact on health and other aspects of the lives of older people of events and processes, including retirement, widowhood, and changing living environments, among others.

SUMMARY

Disease is the chief barrier to extended health and longevity in older people. Today, chronic illnesses—including heart disease, cancer, and stroke—represent the key health problems affecting middle-aged and older adults. The prevalence of chronic conditions varies by age, sex, race, income, and residence. Chronic illness can be burdensome in terms of days spent in bed and deficits in the elderly individual's capacity to engage in activities of daily living (ADLs) and instrumental activities of daily living (IADLs). The oldest-old, women, those elderly with family income under $15,000, nonwhites, and those residing in rural areas report the most limitation in ADL score. The pattern is similar for IADLs.

Estimates vary as to the proportion of the elderly population with mental health problems. Perhaps as many as 25 percent of the elderly have some mental health problems, with the percentage being lower for those residing in the community and higher for those in long-term care institutions. According to the NIH, depression among the aging and aged is a major public health problem. Depression, paranoia, and hypochondriasis are common functional psychiatric disorders in the later years. Suicidal thoughts often accompany depression. In 1991, the suicide rate among the elderly was almost 200 percent higher than that among the total population, although much of this difference is attributable to the very high suicide rate among aged white males.

Alzheimer's disease is an organic mental disorder. Between 2 and 4 percent of the elderly population may have this dementia, with the proportion increasing in the population aged 75 and over. Females are somewhat more likely to have the disease, and in rare cases, the disease is thought to be inherited as a dominant trait. At present, there is no known cure for Alzheimer's disease, and little is known about the extent to which social and psychological experiences may contribute to the onset of the disease.

Fries (1987) offers a hypothesis of "compression of morbidity," suggesting the likelihood that people can expect to live longer and healthier with a shorter duration of illness and disability in old age before death. House and colleagues (1990) suggest that considerable postponement of morbidity seems already to be occurring in the highest socioeconomic groups. However, at this point, evidence in support of the compression of morbidity hypothesis is mixed and some projections into the twenty-first century suggest increases in the numbers of elderly who are disabled.

Two additional factors that affect the health status of older people are the orientation of modern medicine and the attitudes and expectations of old and young alike toward the difficulty of maintaining health in the later years. The elderly, along with health care professionals, may be too ready to attribute illness or biological changes to supposedly normal aging.

STUDY QUESTIONS

1. What does the concept of *physical health* encompass? Distinguish among the absence of illness, basic self-care activities, and more complex indicators of functioning.

2. What is the relationship between sociodemographic characteristics of the elderly (such as age, sex, race, family income) and residence and self-assessment of health, ADLs, and IADLs?

3. What is the relationship between the high prevalence of chronic conditions among the elderly and the way this population assesses its health? How does self-assessment of health by the elderly vary by sex, race, and income?

4. Discuss the dominant causes or forms of heart disease and their impacts on the elderly.

5. What understandings have developed about the etiology of cancer? Describe the death rate differences from cancer between older men and women. Which are primary sites of cancer for men? For women?

6. What social and psychological problems does aphasia create for the stroke victim?

7. Identify and describe the common functional psychiatric disorders in the later years. How do suicide rates vary by sex and race among the elderly?

8. Distinguish between *organic mental syndrome* and *organic mental disorder*. What are the diagnostic problems in determining the prevalence rate of these and other mental disorders afflicting the elderly?

9. What is Alzheimer's disease? Describe its symptoms. What is known about the causes and cures for Alzheimer's?

10. What does the concept of *compression of morbidity* describe? Is there evidence for this phenomenon? If so, what is it?

11. Explain the medical model as it is applied to the elderly. What are its primary limitations?

12. How does the attribution (or misattribution) of illness to the normal aging process pose serious health and social problems for older individuals?

REFERENCES

American Heart Association. (1990). *Heart facts—1990*. Dallas, TX: National Office.

American Psychiatric Association. (1987). *Diagnostic and statistical manual of mental disorders* (3rd ed., revised). Washington, DC: Author.

Bartko, J., & Patterson, R. (1971). Survival among healthy old men: A multivariate analysis. In S. Granick & R. Patterson (Eds.), *Human aging II. An 11-year follow-up*. Washington, DC: U.S. Government Printing Office.

Besdine, R. (1988). Dementia and delirium. In J. W. Rowe & J. W. Besdine (Eds.), *Geriatric medicine*. Boston: Little Brown.

Blazer, D. (1980). The epidemiology of mental illness in late life. In E. Busse & D. Blazer (Eds.), *Handbook of geriatric psychiatry*. New York: Van Nostrand Reinhold.

Brocklehurst, J. C., & Hanley, T. (1981). *Geriatric medicine for students*. Edinburgh: Churchill Livingstone.

Butler, R., & Lewis, M. (1982). *Aging and mental health* (2nd ed.). St. Louis: C. V. Mosby.

Clark, M. (1980). The scourge of senility. *Newsweek*, September 15, pp. 85–86.

Doll, R., & Peto, R. (1976). Mortality in relation to smoking: Twenty years observation on male British doctors. *British Medical Journal, 2,* 1525–1536.

Duckworth, G. S., & Ross, H. (1975). Diagnostic differences in psychogeriatric patients in Toronto, New York and London, England. *Canadian Medical Association Journal, 112,* 847–851.

Eisdorfer, C., & Cohen, D. (1982). *Mental health care of the aging: A multidisciplinary curriculum for professional training*. New York: Springer.

Exton-Smith, A. N., & Overstall, P. W. (1979). *Geriatrics*. Baltimore: University Park Press.

Ferraro, K. F. (1980). Self-ratings of health among the old and old-old. *Journal of Health and Social Behavior, 21,* 377–383.

Ferraro, K. F. (1985). The effect of widowhood on the health status of older persons. *International Journal of Aging and Human Development, 21,* 9–25.

Fox, J. H., Topel, J. L., & Huckman, M. S. (1975). Dementia in the elderly—A search for treatable illnesses. *Journal of Gerontology, 10,* 557–574.

Freedman, J., Sears., D., & Carlsmith, J. (1978). *Social psychology* (3rd ed.). Englewood Cliffs, NJ: Prentice-Hall.

Freidson, E. (1988). *Profession of medicine.* Chicago: University of Chicago Press.

Fries, J. F. (1980). Aging, natural death and the compression of morbidity. *New England Journal of Medicine, 303,* 130–135.

Fries, J. F. (1987). An introduction to the compression of morbidity. *Gerontologica Perspecta, 1,* 5–7.

Furner, S. E. (1992). Health status. In R. A. Cohen, J. F. Van Nostrand, & S. E. Furner (Eds.), *Chartbook on health data on older Americans: United States, 1992.* Washington, D.C.: National Center on Health Statistics.

Gardner, E., Bahn, A., & Mack, M. (1964). Suicide and psychiatric care in the aging. *Archives of General Psychiatry, 10,* 547–553.

Gibson, R., & Jackson, J. (1987). The health, physical functioning, and informal supports of the black elderly. *Milbank Memorial Fund Quarterly, 65* (Suppl.), 421–454.

Glassman, M. (1980). Misdiagnosis of senile dementia: Denial of care to the elderly. *Social Work, 25,* 288–292.

Guralnik, J. M. (1991). Prospects for the compression of morbidity: The challenge posed by increasing disability in the years prior to death. *Journal of Aging and Health, 3* (2), 138–154.

Gurland, B. J., & Toner, J. A. (1982). Depression in the elderly: A review of recently published studies. In C. Eisdorfer (Ed.), *Annual review of geriatrics and gerontology.* New York: Springer.

House, J. S., Kessler, R. C., Herzog, A. R., et al. (1990). Age, socioeconomic status and health. *The Milbank Quarterly, 68* (3), 383–311.

Janis, I., & Rodin, J. (1979). Attribution, control and decision making: Social psychology and health care. In C. G. Stone et al. (Eds.), *Health psychology—A handbook.* San Francisco: Jossey-Bass.

Jones, E., & Nisbett, R. (1971). *The actor and the observer: Divergent perceptions of the causes of behavior.* Morristown, NJ: General Learning Press.

Kaercher, D. (1980). Senility: A misdiagnosis. *Better Homes and Gardens,* November, pp. 27–32, 34–37.

Kahn, R., Zarit, S., Hilbert, N., & Niederehe, G. (1975). Memory complaint and impairment in the aged. *Archives of General Psychiatry, 32,* 1569–1573.

Kane, R. A. & Kane, R. L. (1981). *Assessing the elderly: A practical guide to measurement.* Lexington, MA: D.C. Heath.

Kaplan, G. A. (1991). Epidemiologic observations on the compression of morbidity: Evidence from the Alameda County study. *Journal of Aging and Health, 3* (2), 155–171.

Katz, S., Ford, A., Moskowitz, R., Jackson, B., & Jaffee, M. (1963). Studies of illness in the aged. The index of ADL: A standardized measure of biological and psychosocial function. *Journal of the American Medical Association, 185,* 914–919.

Kermis, M. D. (1986). *Mental health in late life: The adaptive process.* Boston: Jones and Bartlett.

Kovar, M. G. (1977). Health of the elderly and use of health services. *Public Health Reports, 92,* 9–19.

Kunkel, S. R., & Applebaum, R. A. (1992). Estimating the prevalence of long-term disability for an aging society. *Journal of Gerontology, 47* (5), S253–S260.

LaRue, A., Bank, L., Jarvik, L., & Hetland, M. (1979). Health in old age: How do physicians' ratings and self-ratings compare? *Journal of Gerontology, 8,* 108–115.

Lawton, M., & Nahemow, L. (1973). Ecology and the aging process. In C. Eisdorfer & M. P. Lawton (Eds.), *Psychology of adult development and aging.* Washington, DC: American Psychological Association.

Libow, L. (1973). Pseudo-senility: Acute and reversible organic brain syndrome. *Journal of the American Geriatrics Society, 21,* 112–120.

Maddox, G., & Douglas E. (1973). Self-assessment of health, a longitudinal study of elderly subjects. *Journal of Health and Social Behavior, 14,* 87–92.

Manton, K. (1989). Epidemiological, demographic, and social correlates of disability among the elderly. *The Milbank Quarterly,* *67,* 13–57.

Marsden, C. D., & Harrison, M. J. G. (1972). Outcome of investigation of patients with presenile dementia. *British Medical Journal, 2,* 249–252.

Mechanic, D. (1978). *Medical sociology* (2nd ed.). New York: Free Press.

Morley, J., & Reese, S. (1989). Clinical implications of the aging heart. *American Journal of Medicine, 86,* 77–86.

Nathanson, C. (1975). Illness and the feminine role: A theoretical review. *Social Science and Medicine, 9,* 57–62.

National Institute on Aging. (1980). Treatment possibilities for mental impairment in the elderly. *Journal of the American Medical Association, 244,* 259–263.

National Institutes of Health. (1991). *Diagnosis and treatment of depression in late life: Consensus statement.* Bethesda, MD: U.S. Department of Health and Human Services.

Olshansky, S. J., Rudberg, M. A., Carnes, B. A., Cassel, C. K., & Brody, J. A. (1991). Trading off longer life for worsening health: The expansion of morbidity hypothesis. *Journal of Aging and Health, 3* (2), 194–216.

Pfeiffer, E. (1977). Psychopathy and social pathology. In J. Birren & K. Schaie (Eds.), *Handbook of the psychology of aging.* New York: Van Nostrand Reinhold.

Pfeiffer, E., & Busse, E. (1973). Mental disorders in later life: Affective disorder, paranoid, neurotic and situational reactions. In E. Busse & E. Pfeiffer (Eds.), *Mental illness in later life.* Washington, DC: American Psychiatric Association.

Post, F. (1980). Paranoid, schizophrenia-like and schizophrenia states in the aged. In J. E. Birren & R. B. Sloane (Eds.), *Handbook of mental health and aging.* Englewood Cliffs, NJ: Prentice-Hall.

Roybal, E. R. (1984). Federal involvement in mental health care for the aged. *American Psychologist, 39,* 163–166.

Schlesinger, M. (1987). Paying the price: Medical care, minorities, and the newly

competitive health care system. *Milbank Memorial Fund Quarterly, 65* (Suppl.), 270–296.

Schmeck, H. M. (1987). Blood abnormality may predict the onset of alzheimer's disease. *New York Times,* October 29, p. 12.

Seltzer, B., & Sherwin, I. (1978). Organic brain syndromes: An empirical study and critical review. *The American Journal of Psychiatry, 135,* 13–21.

Tockman, M., & Ball, W., Jr. (1990). Lung cancer. In W. Hazzard, R. Andres, E. Bierman, & J. Blass (Eds.), *Principles of geriatric medicine and gerontology.* New York: McGraw-Hill.

U.S. Bureau of the Census. (1994). *Statistical abstract of the United States, 1994.* Washington, DC: U.S. Government Printing Office.

U.S. Department of Health and Human Services. (1984). *Progress report on Alzheimer's disease* (Vol. II). National Institutes of Health Publication No. 84-2500. Washington, DC: U.S. Government Printing Office.

U.S. Department of Health and Human Services. (1992). *Healthy people 2000: Summary report of national health promotion and disease prevention objectives.* Boston: Jones and Bartlett.

Verbrugge, L., & Madans, J. (1985). Social roles and health trends of American women. *Milbank Memorial Fund Quarterly, 63* (4), 691–735.

Wells, C. E. (1978). Chronic brain disease: An overview. The American *Journal of Psychiatry, 135,* 1–12.

Wolinsky, F. D. (1988). *The sociology of health.* Belmont, CA: Wadsworth.

Zola, I. K. (1962). *Sociocultural factors in the seeking of medical care.* Unpublished Ph.D. dissertation. Harvard University.

Zola, I. K. (1966). Culture and symptoms: An analysis of patients presenting complaints. *American Sociological Review, 31,* 615–630.

Zopf, P. E. (1986). *America's older population.* Houston, TX: Cap and Gown Press.

CHAPTER 7

PSYCHOLOGICAL ASPECTS OF AGING

In perhaps the first book on aging written by a psychologist, G. Stanley Hall (1922) divided life into five stages: (1) childhood; (2) adolescence; (3) middle life (or "the prime," ranging from age 25 to age 40 or 45 and comprising the "best" years); (4) senescence (beginning in the early 40s "or before in woman"); and (5) senectitude (constituted by "old age proper"). Hall was 78 years old when the book was published and, according to his biographer (Ross, 1972), he resented every moment that moved him further from youth. One might have guessed as much; after all, Hall placed the onset of senescence at age 45. Apparently, the noted psychologist associated growing older with declining physical and mental vitality. His concern for the latter, however, was clearly related more to others than to himself.

The physical changes that accompany aging have already been discussed in some detail. This chapter deals with the study of aging with respect to mental vitality—the psychology of aging. The psychology of aging is a broad field, including, among other substantive areas, personality development, intelligence functioning, and sensory and motor processes.

In some contexts, it is difficult to distinguish between biological and psychological aspects of aging. Biological changes do affect an individual's psychological state of being, and psychological and psychosocial changes may affect biological functioning. Almost 60 years ago, the philosopher-educator John Dewey addressed the problems of aging and made this very point.

> Biological processes are at the root of the problem and of the methods of solving them, but the biological processes take place in economic, political, and cultural contexts. They are inextricably interwoven with these contexts so that one reacts upon the other in all sorts of intricate ways. We need to know the ways in which social contexts react back into biological processes as well as to know the ways in which the biological processes condition social life. (1939)

A former president of the American Psychological Association suggests that since the time Dewey wrote these words, "We have made little progress in coming to know the ways in which psychosocial and biological processes interact in the production of age-correlated changes" (Jarvik, 1975). Some would disagree. This chapter provides a perspective on some psychological aspects of aging that lends support to the view that the psychology of aging has matured markedly in recent years.

HUMAN DEVELOPMENT ACROSS THE LIFE SPAN

Social scientists have accumulated enormous amounts of data on specific features of adult life. This book is filled with statistics on health and illness, life expectancy and death rates, and income and occupation. Curiously, however, the extensive information known about adult life has provided relatively little toward identifying some basic developmental principles of adulthood. In fact, only recently have mature adulthood and old age been placed within a developmental framework. This differs markedly from the cases of childhood and adolescence for which the developmental perspective has helped identify principles that affect all people as they pass through these life periods.

The different rates of development of child psychology and the psychology of adulthood are a function of several factors. First, there are enormous conceptual and methodological difficulties involved in studying whole lives, one of which involves the fact that concepts and measures used by a researcher in a longitudinal study may be relevant at one age but not at a later age.[1] This has resulted, until quite recently, in a scarcity of empirical research on the psychology of middle and later adulthood. Second, the work of Sigmund Freud has influenced and continues to influence the development of a psychology of adulthood.

Freud had a theory of the origins of personality that emphasized how development in the early years significantly influenced one's later life (Lidz, 1976). For Freud, personality problems of the adult years could be understood largely in terms of what had happened in infancy and early childhood. Infants and children could be expected to pass through a series of stages of psychosexual development—oral, anal, and genital—each involving the experience of bodily pleasure through these erogenous zones of the body, assuming all went well. If things did not go well, if parents were overly anxious, or if there was a failure to achieve gratification through other channels, the child could become fixated on securing pleasure through oral or anal modes. Such fixations could activate personality attributes. Thus, some persons would become *oral types,* overeating and otherwise

---

[1]Methodology itself becomes an issue in understanding the relationship between intelligence and aging. This is discussed later in this chapter and, at that time, the longitudinal study is further defined.

gaining satisfaction through the mouth. Others would become *anal types,* hoarding and behaving in a constricted, constipated way (Clausen, 1986).

Freud was perhaps the first theorist to recognize important processes of early emotional development. Yet, he regarded adulthood as a theater in which the dramas of unconscious childhood conflicts are acted out and reenacted. Adulthood, then, is not for further development, according to Freud. Several prominent theories of life-cycle development have used Freud's psychosexual stages as a point of departure. A number of these theories include a personality dimension. It may be useful to consider these theories briefly in order to see how they conceptualize the relationships among life-cycle development, personality, and aging.

Conceptions of the Life Cycle

An early pioneer of developmental psychology was Charlotte Buhler. As head of the Vienna Research Center in Child Psychology, Buhler was interested mainly in the psychology of childhood and adolescence. In the early 1930s, she began to extend this work to include the rest of the life span. Buhler's (1933) early work, *Der Menschliche Lebenslauf als Psychologisches Problem,* is as interesting for its methodology as it is for its conceptualization of the course of the life span. It is based on analyses of 250 individual life spans; 50 of these case histories were gathered in retrospective fashion from aged people, and the rest were taken from biographies and autobiographies.

Buhler did not confine herself to the analyses of diverse life histories; she tried to detect similarities and regularities in the structure of behavior and thought across the diverse life histories of different individuals (Filipp & Olbrich, 1986). She suggested that five major phases or periods in the life course can be identified, and that the psychological curve of life parallels the biological curve of ascent and decline, although these curves do not necessarily proceed synchronously. The phases are as follows (Frenkel-Brunswick, 1963):

1. During the first phase, the child lives at home and his or her life centers around family and school.

2. The second phase begins at about age 15 and is characterized by entrance into independent activity. This period lasts until the latter half of the third decade. Often, the turning point for this phase can be placed at the time the young person leaves the home of his or her family. Preparation for career and the acquisition of personal relations also mark this phase.

3. The third phase begins between the 26th and 30th years of life. It is representative of the most fruitful and creative aspects of life. Definitive career choices are made; marriage and the establishment of home and family are other likely accomplishments.

4. A decrease in the amount of one's activities as well as "negative dimensions" characterize the fourth and fifth phases, the former beginning at about age 50. Illness, loss of associates, death of relatives and friends, and reduction in

social activities are noteworthy in the fourth phase. Psychological crises, discontent, and unrest are often evident in this phase.

5. The fifth period is often introduced by complete retirement from work (at about age 65). There is an obvious further decrease in social activities; retrospection and life review are very characteristic of this period. Sickness and death are preeminent in these years.

Although Buhler has attempted to identify and determine the regularity with which the various phases of life succeed one another, not all the experiences mentioned here are expected to be present in every individual. For example, some people may not experience as negative the reduction in physical and social activities that accompanies movement from the third to the fourth phase. They may not seek their measure in physical efficiency but rather in a continued mental vitality that brings new interests and attitudes.

The psychoanalytic theorists have dealt most explicitly with the personality dimension as it relates to age. Yet, as has been indicated, much of this work involves developmental theories of childhood and adolescence. Stated tersely, the psychoanalytic theories regard adult personality as stable (Neugarten, 1977). Jung (1933) is an exception. He begins his discussion of the stages of life with youth—a period extending from after puberty to about age 35. In general, this period involves giving up childhood and widening the scope of one's life. The next stage begins at about age 35 and continues to old age. He characterizes this stage as follows:

> At first it is not a conscious and striking change; it is rather a matter of indirect signs of a change which seems to take its rise in the unconscious. Often it is something like a slow change in a person's character; in another case certain traits may come to light which had disappeared since childhood; or again, one's previous inclinations and interests begin to weaken and others take their place. Conversely—and this happens very frequently—one's cherished convictions and principles, especially the moral ones, begin to harden and to grow increasingly rigid until, somewhere around the age of fifty, a period of intolerance and fanaticism is reached. It is as if the existence of these principles were endangered and it were therefore necessary to emphasize them all the more. (Jung, 1971)

Jung sees significant personality changes in old age. The individual's attention may turn inward in an attempt to find meaning in life. Often, he says, individuals will change into their opposites. He argues, "We cannot live the afternoon of life according to the programme of life's morning; for what was great in the morning will be little at evening and what in the morning was true will at evening have become a lie" (Jung, 1971).

The most important exception to the general thrust of psychoanalytic theory has been the theories of Erik Erikson (1950, 1963, 1968). Erikson outlines eight ages of humanity stretching from birth to death, each representing a choice or a crisis. Intrinsically social or *psychosocial*, these crises occur within the context of relationships with other people. If decisions are made well during one age, then successful adaptation can be made in the subsequent age. Whereas Freud believed a person became fixated at a particular stage, Erikson sees each stage as reworking elements of the prior stage. Thus, people could act as their own therapists and rework difficult areas of their personalities (Kermis, 1986). Each age leads to further differentiation of the personality, and each new accomplishment is integrated into experiences and may be drawn upon in later years (Clausen, 1986).

Erikson's first five ages rely heavily on the work of Freud and deal largely with childhood development, whereas the last three ages focus on adult development. The eight ages are:

1. In early infancy, the development of a sense of basic *trust* versus a sense of mistrust
2. In later infancy, when some anal muscular maturation has occurred, a growing sense of *autonomy* versus a sense of shame and doubt
3. In early childhood, a developing sense of *initiative* versus a sense of guilt
4. In the middle years of childhood, a sense of *industry* versus a sense of inferiority
5. In adolescence, a sense of *ego identity* (involving certainty about self, career, sex role, and values) versus role confusion
6. In early adulthood, the development of *intimacy* (including more than simply sexual intimacy) versus a sense of ego isolation
7. In middle adulthood, the development of *generativity* (the desire to become a caring and productive member of society) versus ego stagnation
8. In late adulthood, a sense of *ego integrity* (including a basic acceptance of one's life as having been appropriate and meaningful) versus a sense of despair

McAdams, de St. Aubin, and Logan (1993) examined age differences in generativity among young, midlife, and older adults, in an effort to test for differences in generativity. According to Erikson, generativity should peak in middle-age and progressively decline throughout old age. Data were collected on four dimensions of generativity:

1. *Generative concern* described the extent to which an individual expresses concern about the future generation.
2. *Generative strivings* described the specific actions an individual would like to take to help nurture the next generation.
3. A listing of specific actions that an individual has already carried out would describe *generative action.*
4. The degree to which past memories reflect the theme of generativity is described in the concept of *generative narration.*

Results were partially supportive of Erikson's theory. Younger adults (22 to 27 years) showed the lowest levels of generativity. Middle-aged adults (37 to 42 years) scored higher than younger adults but *not* higher than older adults. Thus, generativity would seem to be more characteristic of middle-age and older adulthood than younger adulthood. Although, interestingly, McAdams, de St. Aubin, and Logan (1993) report that, within each age group, study participants showed a strong positive relationship between generativity and life satisfaction and happiness.

The sense of ego integration generated in late adulthood is very much a function of what has taken place in the previous ages. Erikson contends that good adjustment in this age comes only when important matters have been placed in proper perspective and when the successes and failures of life have been seen as inevitable. According to Erikson,

> Only in him who in some way has taken care of things and people and has adapted himself to the triumphs and disappointments adherent to being the originator of others or the generator of products and ideas—only in him may gradually ripen the fruit of these seven stages. (1963)

A deficit in this accumulated ego integration is often characterized by a failure to accept one's life and ultimately by fear of death.

Not all agree with Erikson. Butler (1975), for one, finds the idea that people are, in old age, a function of what they were before to be potentially regressive. He argues that, although it is important to recognize the basic foundation of one's identity, it is equally important to recognize the existence of continuing possibilities. Butler quotes the art historian Bernard Berenson, who, at age 83, stated, "I for one have never touched bottom in self, nor even struck against the surface, the outlines, the boundaries of this self. On the contrary, I feel the self as an energy which expands and contracts" (Berenson, in Butler, 1975, p. 401).

Still, Butler (1963) has provided a concept, *life review,* that seems integral to carrying out the tasks of Erikson's eighth age. All people reminisce. Yet, according to Butler, this is not an idle process. Rather, life review occurs naturally so that unresolved conflicts may be given attention and resolved. Old age and, perhaps, impending death highlight this process. If conflicts are not resolved, there may be a failure in adjustment, resulting in what Erikson describes as "despair."

Peck (1968) attempted to refine Erikson's theory, paying special attention to the crucial issues of middle and old age. He describes four developmental tasks of middle age:

1. Valuing wisdom over physical powers
2. Socializing versus sexualizing in human relations
3. Emotional flexibility versus emotional impoverishment
4. Mental flexibility versus mental rigidity

Peck sees three issues as central to old age. First, the individual must establish a wide range of activities so that adjustment to loss of accustomed roles such as those of worker or parent is minimized (ego differentiation versus work-role preoccupation). Second, because nearly all elderly individuals suffer physical decline and/or illness, activities in the later years should allow them to transcend their physical limitations (body transcendence versus body preoccupation). Finally, although death is inevitable, individuals may, in various ways, make contributions that extend beyond their own lifetimes; this may provide meaning for life and overcome despair that one's life was meaningless or should have been other than it was (ego transcendence versus ego preoccupation).

THE OLD ALCHEMIST (FROM BURMA)

Once upon a time, there lived an old man with his beautiful daughter. She fell in love with a handsome lad, and the two married with the old man's blessing. The young couple led a happy life, except for one problem: The husband spent his time working on alchemy, dreaming of a way to turn base elements into gold. Soon enough, he ran through his patrimony, and the young wife struggled to buy food each day. She finally asked her husband to find a job, but he protested. "I am on the verge of a breakthrough!" he insisted. "When I succeed, we will be rich beyond our dreams!"

Finally, the young wife told her father about the problem. He was surprised to learn that his son-in-law was an alchemist, but, promising to help his daughter, he asked to see him the next day. The young man went reluctantly, expecting a reprimand. To his surprise, his father-in-law confided in him, "I, too, was an alchemist when I was young!" The father-in-law inquired about the young man's work, and the two spent the afternoon talking. Finally, the old man stirred with excitement. "You have done everything I did!" he exclaimed. "You are surely on the verge of a breakthrough. But you need one more ingredient to change base elements into gold, and I have only recently discovered this secret." The old man paused and sighed. "But I am too old to undertake the task. It requires much work."

"I can do it, dear father!" the young man volunteered. The old man brightened. "Yes, perhaps you can." Then he leaned over and whispered, "The ingredient you need is the silver powder that grows on banana leaves. This powder becomes magic when you plant the bananas yourself, and it casts certain spells."

"How much powder do we need?" the young man asked.

"Two pounds," the old man replied.

The son-in-law thought out loud, "That requires hundreds of banana plants!"

"Yes," the old man sighed, "and that is why I cannot complete the work myself."

"Do not fear!" the young man said, "I will!" And so the old man taught his son-in-law the incantations and loaned him money for the project.

The next day, the young man bought some land and cleared it. He dug the ground himself, just as the old man had instructed him, planted the bananas, and murmured the magic spells over them. Each day, he examined his plants, keeping weeds and pests away, and when the plants bore fruit, he collected the silver powder from the leaves. There was scarcely any on each plant, and so the young man bought more land, and cultivated more bananas. After several years, the young man collected two pounds of the magic dust. He rushed to his father-in-law's house.

"I have the magic powder!" the young man exclaimed.

"Wonderful!" the old man rejoiced. "Now I can show you how to turn base elements into gold! But first you must bring your wife here. We need her help." The young man was puzzled, but obeyed. When she appeared, the old man asked his daughter, "While your husband was collecting the banana powder, what did you do with the fruits?"

"Why, I sold them" the daughter said, "and that is how we earned a living."

"Did you save any money?" the father asked.

"Yes," she replied.

"May I see it?" the old man asked. So his daughter hurried home and returned with several bags. The old man opened them, saw they were full of gold, and poured the coins on the floor. Then he took a handful of dirt, and put it next to the gold.

"See," he said as he turned to his son-in-law, "you have changed base elements into gold!"

For a tense moment, the young man was silent. Then he laughed, seeing the wisdom in the old man's trick. And from that day on, the young man and his wife prospered greatly. He tended the plants while she went to the market to sell the bananas. And they both honored the old man as the wisest of alchemists.

Source: Summarized from " The Old Alchemist" from *In the Ever After: Fairy Tales and the Second Half of Life* by Allan B. Chinen. Copyright © 1989 by Chiron Publications. Reprinted by permission.

Levinson and colleagues (1978), based on their research on men aged 35 to 45 years, view the life cycle as evolving through a sequence of eras, each lasting approximately 20 to 25 years. In the broadest sense, each era is a "time of life" with its own distinctive qualities. As in Erikson's psychosocial theory, personal crises and developmental tasks characterize each era. In contrast to Erikson, however, Levinson believes that relationships and personal commitments through which tasks of one period are accomplished may *not* serve the needs of the individual beyond that period. Figure 7–1 shows Levinson's developmental periods in early and middle adulthood. A primary developmental task of late adulthood (which begins at about age 60) is to find a new balance between involvement with society and with the self. This new balance is necessary because individuals begin to see a physical decline in self and age-mates and because they are now viewed as "old" in the eyes of society. It is during this era, according to Levinson, that Erikson's final age (ego integrity versus despair) occurs.

Employing the same extensive biographical interviewing used to study men, Levinson turned his attention to women aged 35 to 45 (Brown, 1987). Studying homemakers, businesswomen, and women from academia, Levinson found that women go through the same sequence of periods at the same ages as men. One substantial difference between men and women, and between groups of women, concerns the life plans envisioned between the ages of 22 and 28. Typically, young men organize a "tentative life structure" around occupation. Young women have more difficulty forming their plans for the life course. According to Levinson, "Everything in society supports men having an occupational dream, but for a woman, there is still a quality of going into forbidden territory" (Brown, 1987, p. 23). For many women, the themes of career and family are viewed as two mutually exclusive choices. As Levinson points out, there is no preponderance of cul-

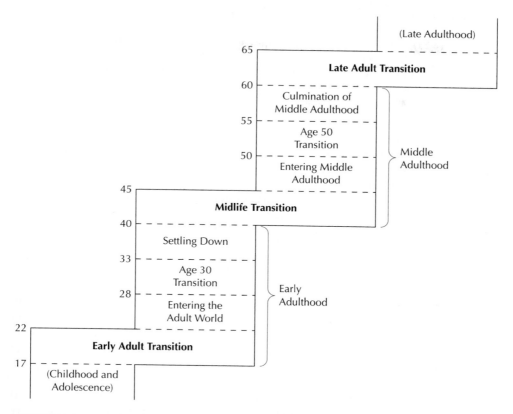

FIGURE 7–1   Levinson's Developmental Periods in Early and Middle Adulthood
Source: From *The Seasons of a Man's Life* by Daniel J. Levinson et al. Copyright © 1978 by Daniel J. Levinson. Reprinted by permission of Alfred A. Knopf, Inc.

tural wisdom to aid women with these choices. In many respects, they are pioneers.

A careful reading of the conceptual schemas of development and aging offered by Erikson and Levinson reveals some considerable agreement between the two, despite the fact that the labels for stages and transitions are different. Both seem to characterize adulthood as reflecting the change from career considerations to generativity, with older adulthood marked by a shift toward the search for meaning and final integration.

These stage theories have strong intuitive appeal, yet they have at least three general limitations. First, stage theories are difficult to verify. Reported data are typically rich in anecdotal material, characteristic of a clinical tradition, but without quantifiable results. Second, these stage theories have a tendency to focus too extensively on developmental crises, such as the classic midlife crisis. Vaillant argues that such crises are rare.

The term *midlife crisis* brings to mind some variation of the renegade minister who leaves behind four children and the congregation that loved him in order to drive off in a magenta Porsche with a twenty-five-year-old striptease artist. Like all tabloid fables, these is much to be learned from such stories, but such aberrations are rare, albeit memorable, caricatures of more mundane issues of development. As with adolescent turmoil, midlife crises are much rarer in community samples than in clinical samples. (1977, pp. 222–223)

Third, more recently researchers of adult development and aging have given recognition to the potential importance of cohort and period effects on behavior and attitude. For example, Rossi (1984) argues that most of the individuals originally studied by Levinson were born around the time of the Great Depression and, thus, were in formative adolescence during World War II. What were the pressures faced by members of those birth cohorts in light of the historical period in which they grew up? And, is what was true for these individuals when they reached age 40 true for, say, college students today when they reach age 40?

Personality Theory

Although most psychologists of the life cycle have dealt more or less implicitly with the relationship between personality and aging, there is no theory useful to gerontologists that conceptualizes this relationship specifically. Scientific methods for studying personality have not been very successful and are still in somewhat of an elementary state (Neugarten, 1977). Havighurst (1968) suggests that what is needed is a theory of the relationship between personality and successful aging.

Thomae (1980) offers a cognitive theory of personality that can also be viewed as a cognitive theory of aging. Three postulates are offered to explain personality development and adjustment to aging. First, perception of change may be just as important, or more so, as objective change. Personality change is dependent, to a degree, on whether the individual perceives the change as normative. For example, experiencing the death of a spouse when one is 75 years of age may produce less change because the event occurs at a time perceived as normative for the cohort. Experiencing the death of a spouse at age 25 will likely produce more change because the event is not perceived as being a normative one.

Second, people evaluate changes in their lives in terms of their dominant concerns and expectations at the time. Individuals have different motives and concerns at different stages of life, leading them to perceive situations differently. Finally, the adjustment to aging is determined by the balance between people's cognitive and motivational structures.

Whitbourne's (1987) life story approach to personality and aging is also very much reliant on the subjective perceptions of individuals. She argues that people build their own conceptions of how their lives should proceed, and this is part of a *life-span construct*—a person's unified sense of the past, the present, and the future. There are two important components of this construct. The *scenario* consists of the expectations a person has for the future. It is the game plan of how one

Individuals may, in various ways, make contributions that extend beyond their own lifetimes.

expects and wants one's life to be in the future. The *life story* is a personal narrative history that organizes past events into a coherent sequence, giving them meaning and continuity. The life story, what a person tells others when he or she is asked about the past, can become overrehearsed and stylized. Distortions occur with time and retelling (Neisser & Winograd, 1988). Life-story distortions are actually ways of coping, which allow a person to feel that he or she was "on time" rather than "off time" in past events. Such distortions may allow people to feel better about their plans and goals, and make them less likely to feel a sense of failure.

Personality changes during adulthood are not easily reduced to simple yes/ no dichotomies or to a simple score on a personality test. Thomae (1980) identifies a series of methodological issues important to the study of personality and aging. Not the least of these issues has to do with the selectivity of study samples. For example, studies of elite population groups such as centenarians or the survivors in longitudinal studies, are much more likely to show homogeneity of personality characteristics than are samples from normal aging or even institutionalized aging population groups. Thomae suggests that the particular personality pattern an individual shows may depend on a complex interaction of 10 factors influential for longevity and survivorship. These factors are as follows:

1. The person at the beginning of the process
2. Recent changes in the individual's biological systems
3. Recent changes in the social system in which the person lives
4. The individual's socioeconomic status and ecologic situation

5. Consistency or change in the individual's cognitive functioning
6. Consistency or change in the individual's personality (including measurable change in activity, interest, mood, creativity, adjustment, or ego control)
7. The individual life space of the person
8. The individual's life satisfaction
9. The person's capacity for restoring balance to his or her life by coping actively
10. The person's social competence

Unfortunately, most researchers have not taken these factors into account in their research designs. It may be useful for the reader to remember the complexity of factors that may influence personality patterns across the life course.

Reichard, Livson, and Peterson (1962) studied 87 elderly working men in the San Francisco area, 42 retired and 45 not retired. They rated these respondents on 115 personality variables and, after a cluster analysis, identified five types of "agers." Three of these types were judged on the basis of additional analysis to be well adjusted to the aging process; two types were rated as low on adjustment-to-aging measures. Those elderly men judged as successful in aging were labeled the "mature," "rocking chair," and "armored," respectively; those judged unsuccessful were the "angry" and "self-haters." The *mature* group took a constructive view of life; the *rocking-chair* group was more dependent. The *armored* men did not accept dependency; many of them protected themselves from it by avoiding retirement. The *angry* men directed hostility at the world, which they blamed for all that was wrong in their lives. Finally, the *self-haters* blamed themselves for their difficulties.

These men were making quite different behavioral adjustments to aging. As Reichard, Livson, and Peterson point out, however, these personality patterns did not likely emerge for the first time in old age. For most men, they were carryovers of adjustment and coping styles from the younger years. Some achieved successful aging through activity; others achieved it through disengagement. In general, those whose personal adjustment was high were effective in overcoming frustrations; they were able to resolve conflicts and remain socially active and accepted. The poorly adjusted, however, were unhappy, fearful of contact with others, withdrawn, and incompetent.

The Kansas City Study of Adult Life took place over a 10-year period and was one of the first longitudinal studies of personality in adulthood. Carried out on a large sample of adults aged 40 to 80, measures included projective tests, self-administered questionnaires, and interviews. From this research, Neugarten (1973, 1977) concludes that, in most respects, personality is relatively stable across the years, while at the same time age-related changes do occur as well.

Coping styles, methods of attaining life satisfaction, and goal directedness were among the most stable characteristics. Age-related changes included feelings about the extent to which the social environment could be controlled. For example, 40-year-olds expressed considerable active control over the environment and were willing to take risks; 60-year-olds were more likely to perceive the environment as threatening and thus avoided risk taking. Neugarten describes this personality change as moving from *active* to *passive mastery*. Gutmann (1977) noted a similar pattern among Navajo Indians, isolated groups in Israel, and the Mayans of Mexico. Passive mastery seems to reflect a greater orientation toward introspection and self-reflection, sometimes referred to as *interiority* (Rosen & Neugarten, 1964).

Patterns for coping, finding life satisfaction, and goal direction are probably established in youth. It should be remembered, however, that an individual's personality often develops along the lines of the demand for adaptation he or she receives from the social environment. Changes in the social environment may require changes in personality. In this regard, personality should not be seen as a fixed system that is completed in early childhood. Personality and personality changes in adults should be looked at in terms of long-range developmental changes in, among other things, motivation, intellectual functioning, and the social environment.

One personality study, carried out by Douglas and Arenberg (1978), attempted to measure such changes with longitudinal and cross-sectional research designs. Over 300 males ($N = 336$) from the highly select group of participants in the Baltimore Longitudinal Study (Stone & Norris, 1966), ranging in age from 20 to 81, were tested with the Guilford-Zimmerman Temperament Survey (GZTS), then retested an average of seven years later. The GZTS provides an assessment of 10 personality traits. Half (5) of the scales showed significant change between the first and second testing, but only 2 scales were interpreted as showing age effects:

1. Beginning at age 50, preference for rapidly paced activity declined.
2. At all ages, men declined in masculine interests.

The three other scales showing declines attributed to sociocultural changes include friendliness, thoughtfulness, and personal relations.

Schaie and Parham (1976) also carried out a test-retest study of 19 personality traits over a seven-year period. They concluded that stability of personality traits is the rule rather than the exception. Still, they point out that such stability cannot be equated with lack of change after adolescence, as many personality theorists believe. Rather, it is likely that much change does, in fact, take place. The direction it takes may be a function of early socialization experiences, cohort differences, and social change (Schaie & Parham, 1976).

Does personality continue to develop through middle-age into old-old age? There are few longitudinal studies of personality into mature adulthood, and those that continue into old age are rare indeed. One such study is the Berkeley Older Generation Study, a longitudinal study of adults begun in 1928. Using this data set, Field and Millsap (1991) recently reported on personality development from young-old age into old-old or oldest-old age.

The Berkeley Older Generation Study is a longitudinal study of approximately 420 men and women first interviewed in 1928–1929, when they were young-adult residents of Berkeley, California, who have been reinterviewed at periodic intervals since. Most recent reinterviews took place in 1969 and 1983. These open-ended and intensive interviews were carried out by a psychologist or clinical social worker with no prior knowledge of the interviewee. Complete data from both these interviews are available for 51 women and 21 men, with mean ages of 69.0 in 1969 and 82.7 in 1983. Each interview was "blindly" read and rated independently on 21 personality characteristics by two well-trained raters. Differences in ratings were discussed by the raters, and agreement was reached in each in conference.

Five personality components were identified from the analysis: intellect, agreeableness, satisfaction, energetic, and extraversion. Four of these resemble those found in other, earlier studies; energetic is quite different from outcomes in previous work. *Intellect* is made up of five indicators of cognitive functioning plus one indicator of open-mindedness. *Agreeableness* describes a person who is cheerful, agreeable, not critical of offspring, open and frank. *Satisfaction* is a measure of self-esteem. *Energetic* reflects a dimension of activity and health. *Extraversion* is composed of three items: talkativeness, frankness, and excitability (it could have been called "emotionality").

Satisfaction was the most stable trait. More than half the participants showed no reliable change, although one-fifth of the study members increased reliably on this dimension. Field and Millsap (1991) relate this dimension of personality to Butler's (1963) concept of life review, which emphasizes the importance of coming to terms with one's life in old age.

More than one-third of the participants increased significantly over time in *agreeableness.* The researchers relate this dimension of personality to Erikson's final stage of life, ego integrity versus despair. They found a substantial number of study participants reflecting generativity, caring about offspring, and being less critical and less inclined to worry in old age.

Although *intellect* ratings were strongly correlated with formal tests of intelligence, the researchers believe the dimension may be more a reflection of what could be described as social intelligence. A number of previous studies have suggested that this type of intelligence is more salient than psychometric intelligence in old age. Stability scores are high on this dimension; 79 percent of the Berkeley group did not decline in intellect from 1969 to 1983.

Extraversion showed reliable decline for about one-third of the study members, including both sexes. This decline in extraversion suggests that many in the study group may have "settled in" during their later years.

Energetic showed the least stability of all the dimensions; mean scores declined as well. The authors speculate that this dimension of personality in old age may be the most affected by environmental circumstances and health factors.

In sum, while *agreeableness* seems to show a developmental increase in old age, the pattern for *extraversion* is one of decline. *Satisfaction* and *intellect* show relative stability, even into advanced old age. Do people become rigid, cranky, and conservative as they age? Hardly. Based on this research, stability or continuity in personality in the final years of life seems to be the pattern.

Life-Span Developmental Psychology

Recent years have seen dramatic growth in developmental psychology. In particular, after an extended gestation period, there has been increasing recognition of the value of a life-span developmental perspective (Baltes, 1983). Life-span developmental psychology claims the entire life course as its unit of analysis (Fillip & Olbrich, 1986). From this perspective, emphasis on a particular age group or life phase, such as old age, is misplaced. Changes experienced by individuals during adulthood may not show the same characteristics as changes experienced during childhood.

Interestingly, the life-span developmental perspective has emphasized the importance of biological, social, and psychological factors contributing to development and has diminished the importance of chronological age itself as an explanatory variable. The life-span perspective places explicit emphasis on the temporal interrelatedness of earlier and later components of the human life course. Thus, at any time, an individual's behavior is conceptualized not only as the result of interactions between present biological, social, and psychological factors but also as a result of their interactions with earlier (and perhaps later) experiences and processes (Fillip & Olbrich, 1986).

Because the entire life span is the unit of analysis for this perspective, developmental psychology has had to be open to the contributions of other disciplines and scientific approaches, including biology and sociology, among others. Developmental psychology has also had an impact on these other disciplines. As developmental psychology becomes truly developmental, the life-span perspective will gain in scientific status and make a greater contribution to understanding the varieties of human development.

AGE-RELATED PSYCHOLOGICAL CHANGES

This section deals with age-related changes in sensory processes and psychomotor responses, the relationship between age and intelligence, and the topics of memory and learning. The more common forms of intrapersonal and interpersonal psychopathology observed in later life were discussed in Chapter 6.

In traditional preindustrial societies, old people have often been found to be held in high esteem. In many cases, however, this lasted only as long as they were able to retain their faculties and a semblance of their previous strength. Old people who lost their sight or hearing, their speed of hand or foot—who became less able to pull their own weight and contribute to the group—were more likely to be neglected, abandoned, or even killed outright. Barash (1983) points out that although such treatment seems harsh, even vicious, it reflects the hard realities of primitive life, not the hardness of the hearts of primitive people.

Anthropologist John Moffat once found an old Hottentot woman left by herself in the South African desert. She spoke as follows:

> Yes, my children, three sons and two daughters, are gone to yonder blue mountain and have left me to die. I am very old you see, and am not able to serve them. When they kill game, I am too feeble to help in carrying home the flesh. I am not able to gather wood and make a fire and I cannot carry their children on my back as I used to. (Barash, 1983, p. 178)

Why was this old woman abandoned by her children? It was, as Barash indicates, for the same reason a resident of this country might discard any possession that was worn out and no longer worked. Many will recognize this attitude in themselves when it comes to old things. But what about attitudes toward old people who do not work quite as well as they once did?

Sensory Processes[2]

The nervous system is important in controlling body functioning—especially in controlling smooth and skeletal muscle contractions—and in receiving, processing, and storing information. The senses of vision, hearing, taste, smell, and touch provide links with the outside world. Neurosensory changes that influence an individual's functioning, activities, response to stimuli, and perception of the world do occur with age. Similarly, the world's perception of an individual may be influenced by age-related neurosensory changes that he or she has undergone. Witness, for example, the older person with impaired hearing or vision who may be labeled as stubborn, eccentric, or senile.

Nerve cells, or neurons, are lost during the process of aging. The number of the basic functioning units begins to decline around the age of 25. This decline brings a decreased capacity for sending nerve impulses to and from the brain, a decrease in conduction velocity, a slowing down of voluntary motor movements, and an increase in reflex time for skeletal muscles. In addition, degenerative changes and disease states (for the most part involving the sense organs) may alter the sensory processes.

Vision. Many persons maintain near-normal sight well into old age. Still, surveys of the incidence of blindness and problems of visual acuity in different age groups show that these problems of vision are associated with older age. The incidence of visual impairment increases more than fourfold per 1,000 persons when comparing those less than 45 years of age and those 75 years and over (U.S. Bureau of the Census, 1994, Table 208). The incidence of poorer visual acuity, as defined by conventional clinical standards, also increases with age (Anderson & Palmore, 1974).

---

[2]Materials on sensory processes were adapted from Chapter 8 in Kart, Metress, and Metress (1988) and Chapter 7 in Kart, Metress, and Metress (1992).

According to a recent National Health Survey report, about 40 percent of those 60 years of age who were surveyed had visual acuity of 20/20 or better; however, this declined to about 25 percent at 70 years of age and to only 10 percent of those 80 years old. Degenerative changes and eye disorders that become more frequent with age contribute to the poorer visual acuity incurred by older people.

Presbyopia is not a disease but a degenerative change that occurs in the aging eye. With this condition, the lens loses its ability to focus on near objects. Visual accommodation or focusing is normally permitted by the ability of the lens to change shape or to accommodate for distant and near vision. This ability is at a maximum around the age of 10 and is almost nonexistent in most persons by the age of 55. Because of presbyopia, the majority of individuals need reading glasses or bifocals by the time they are in their 40s or 50s. The glasses mechanically compensate for the loss of accommodation and allow the individual to focus on objects both near and far.

Changes in the lens of the eye lead to farsightedness. Thus, there is a marked tendency for older persons to hold things at a distance in order to see them. The newspaper or letter from a loved one may be held at arm's length because the print cannot be discriminated at closer range. Reading glasses allow the individual to discern objects that are in the field of near vision.

With presbyopia, there is a tendency for the lens of the eye to undergo a yellowing effect. This change is significant in that it becomes more difficult for the person to discern certain color intensities, especially the cool colors (blue, green, and violet), which are filtered out. Warm colors (yellow, red, and orange) are generally seen more easily; thus, it is advisable to mark objects such as steps and handrails with these colors, which tend to stand out.

Cataracts are the most common disability of the aged eye. It has been said that *all* people would develop them, even if only to a mild degree, if everyone lived long enough. Cataracts represent an opacity and frequently a yellowing of the normally transparent lens of the eye. The opaqueness of the lens interferes with the passage of light to the retina. Depending on the degree of cataract development, an individual will suffer dimmed and blurred or misty vision. A person may need brighter light to read and may need to hold objects extremely close in order to be able to see them. As the cataract advances, useful sight is lost. Surgical removal of the opaque lens provides safe and effective treatment for cataracts. Eyeglasses, contact lenses, or intraocular lens implants are used to compensate for the loss of the lens. The latter consists of a plastic lens permanently implanted in the eye. It has become the most common means of compensating for the loss of the natural lens.

Glaucoma is the second-leading cause of blindness in adults in the United States and the first cause among African Americans (Leske, 1983). The disease generally develops somewhere between the ages of 40 and 65 years in response to increased pressure within the eyeball. The increase in pressure is caused by a buildup of aqueous humor, a nutrient fluid that circulates in the anterior chamber of the eye. If this fluid is formed faster than it can be eliminated, an increase in eye pressure results. This pressure can lead to irreparable damage to the optic nerve and to total blindness.

A gradual loss of peripheral vision is one of the earliest indications of glaucoma. This loss of side vision may cause its victim to bump into things or fail to see passing cars in the next highway lane. In time, so much of the normal range of vision becomes eliminated that the victim is said to suffer from "tunnel vision." Left untreated, this limited field of sight will also disappear, leaving the person totally blind.

Primary disease may be designated as either *angle-closure* or *open-angle* glaucoma. Angle closure accounts for less than 5 percent of glaucoma cases (Jindra, 1984). Primary angle-closure glaucoma is an acute form of the disease; it appears suddenly and runs a short course. Symptoms include nausea, vomiting, eye pain, and redness along with clouded vision. Prompt medical attention is imperative if severe vision loss or blindness is to be prevented.

Approximately 90 percent of all primary glaucoma is of the open-angle type (Jindra, 1983). This chronic form of the disease develops slowly and is often referred to as the "sneak thief of vision." The initial symptoms are so subtle that much damage may be done before medical attention is sought.

Persons over 40 years of age should probably have periodic eye examinations that include glaucoma testing. The irreparable damage the disease causes makes its prompt diagnosis and management imperative. There is no cure for glaucoma, but there are techniques for reducing the intraocular pressure and keeping it at a safe level. Drugs and eye drops may be used to indirectly control the pressure within the eye. Surgery is also an option in the most severe cases.

Age-related macular degeneration (AMD), formerly known as *senile macular degeneration,* is the leading cause of registered blindness among older adults in the United States, but it remains a poorly understood disease. As the name implies, the condition involves damage to the macula, the key focusing area of the retina. Peripheral vision is retained, but with this disease, there is typically a decline in central visual acuity, making tasks dependent on discrimination of detail (such as driving or reading) difficult to impossible.

Some individuals manifest a "dry" or atrophic AMD, a slow version of the disorder. The majority of those legally blind due to AMD have a neovascular or exudative form of the disease. In the latter condition, abnormal blood vessels form within the retina, with resultant hemorrhaging and distortion of vision (Ferris, Fine, & Hyman, 1984). Patients with the disease are at risk of continued development of these abnormal blood vessels in both the affected and the uninvolved eye (Farber & Farber, 1990).

Increasing age has the strongest association with AMD of all risk factors examined to date. However, age is not believed to be a causal factor in the disease. Rather, research suggests that it is familial/genetic and environmental factors active with the passage of time that make this an age-related condition. Solar radiation, for example, is likely responsible for some of the deteriorative changes that lead to AMD (Young, 1988).

Diabetic retinopathy is a complication of diabetes that affects the capillaries and arterioles of the retina. A ballooning of these tiny vessels can eventually give way to hemorrhaging, neovascular growth, scarring, and blindness. Vascular changes of diabetic retinopathy occur in and around the macula, leading to macula edema. The retina swells, absorbing the fluid from leaking vessels, and eventually loses its shape so that the image it receives is distorted.

This disease increases with the duration of diabetes. The prevalence of diabetic retinopathy is 7 percent in those who have had diabetes for less than 10 years, whereas it is 63 percent in those who have had diabetes for over 15 years (Stefansson, 1990). Laser therapy, used to seal off hemorrhaging vessels, has proved beneficial in the treatment of diabetic retinopathy (Early Treatment Diabetic Retinopathy Study Group, 1985).

Age-related visual impairment may produce alterations in behavior as well as in feelings of self-esteem. The older person who is visually impaired may suffer from serious communication problems. Vision represents one of the most important links with the outside world. During a lifetime, an individual becomes dependent on vision for receiving and processing information about the world and for functioning in his or her surroundings. Information about the local and world scene is offered through newspapers, magazines, books, and television. Carrying out activities of daily living involves the ability to master various chores that characteristically depend on visual acuity: sewing on a button, turning on the stove, stirring the sauce until it is bubbly, getting dressed in the morning, matching socks of the same color, and so on. A person may be hesitant to perform tasks, especially new ones, because of self-consciousness about the situation.

Special efforts can and should be carried out to help make independent living possible among older adults who are visually impaired. Coding schemes can be employed in the home setting to help make independent living possible. Fluorescent tape around electric outlets, light switches, door handles, and keyholes can make things much easier for someone who suffers some visual impairment.

An older person who is sent home from a hospital or a neighborhood pharmacy with a vial of medicine may not be able to read the dosage instructions printed on the bottle. All too often, such a situation and its possible consequences are not comprehended. Large-print instructions can sometimes help solve the problem. Many older persons take a number of different drugs, and impaired vision may make it difficult to differentiate one bottle of pills from another. Taping different-colored pieces of paper to the various medicine vials might help alleviate the problem. For persons not able to discriminate the colors, other coding methods can be employed. The medicine with the piece of sandpaper on the cap can be identified as the pain reliever; the one with the felt-cap top might be the antihypertensive medication.

A final point that is useful for family members, friends, and health care workers to remember is that persons who have been blind since birth have had a lifetime to adjust to living in a world that assumes everyone can see. For those who suffer visual impairments after having depended on their sight for many years, the adjustments may be quite difficult.

Hearing. Although most persons past 65 years of age retain hearing sufficient for normal living, the elderly individual is 6 times more likely to display a significant loss of hearing than is a young or middle-aged adult. Data from the National Center for Health Statistics indicate that the ratio of hearing impairments for women under age 45 is 30.4 per 1,000 persons; this ratio increases 13 times to 392.9 per 1,000 persons for women 75 years and over (U.S. Bureau of the Census, 1994, Table 208). The figures for men are comparable. Some of this loss is due to age-related physiological change in the auditory system and some is due to disease and superimposed environmental insults.

There are three major types of hearing loss: conductive, sensorineural, and mixed. *Conductive* losses involve the outer and middle ear; *sensorineural* losses involve the inner ear. An elderly person may manifest both conductive and sensorineural changes resulting in a mixed loss.

The most common cause of conductive hearing loss in older adults occurs when excessive ear wax, or *cerumen,* blocks the external ear canal. This condition is reversible. Older persons should be checked for a buildup of cerumen, which can be removed by irrigating the canal with a wax-dissolving solution.

Hardening of the middle ear bone can also impede the transmission of sound waves. This condition, known as *otosclerosis,* actually begins during youth but may not become evident until later life. Although its cause is not fully understood, it can sometimes be corrected surgically and with a special hearing aid.

Sensorineural hearing loss encompasses disorders of the inner ear where conducted sound vibrations are transformed into electrical impulses by the *cochlea.* This auditory receptor organ has been dubbed the most complex mechanical apparatus in the human body (Hudspeth, 1985). Sound waves transferred to the inner ear generate fluid movement in the cochlea and the undulation of hair cells. Hair-cell stimulation produces nerve impulses that are carried by the auditory nerve to the hearing center of the brain where they are perceived as sound. Sensorineural hearing loss in older adults may be due to presbycusis, environmental/ occupational noise, drug toxicity, or disease.

Presbycusis is the most common cause of bilateral, sensorineural hearing deficit in older adults (Olsen, 1984). It may involve permanent loss of the ability to detect high-frequency tones and is due to senescent changes that occur within the structures of the ear.

Presbycusis influences the ability to hear high-pitched tones, while varying in their effects on other aspects of hearing. At first, the loss of the ability to perceive higher frequencies does not involve the perception of normal speech patterns; but as the condition progresses, the capacity to engage in conversation becomes affected. Because consonant sounds are typically in the higher frequencies and vowel sounds in the lower frequencies, speech discrimination becomes poor. Speech can be heard but words cannot be detected. The victim may hear an unintelligible collection of vowel sounds. As the condition advances, middle and lower tones may also be lost. There is variability in the progression of presbycusis and it can coexist with other factors that impede hearing acuity.

Noise-induced hearing loss, known as *acoustic trauma,* is recognized as the second-most common cause of irreversible hearing decline in older persons (Darbyshire, 1984; Surjan, Devald, & Palfalvi, 1973). Exposure to excessive noise induces hair-cell loss and sensorineural hearing deficit. The fact that older men have tended to exhibit slightly more hearing loss than older women may be related to workplace noise. Perhaps, as noise exposure becomes more uniform, fewer gender-based differences in hearing decline will be seen.

Medications toxic to the ear can compromise hearing; these are known as *ototoxic drugs.* Because elderly people often take several different drugs, their hearing should be monitored. Likewise, because elderly patients may already have some degree of hearing loss, known ototoxic drugs should be used with caution. It is sometimes possible to reverse the toxic effects of certain medications if early intervention takes place.

Hearing impairment can lead to social isolation, fear, frustration, embarrassment, low self-esteem, and anxiety for its elderly victim. A study of elderly men in a Veteran's Administration facility suggested that hearing impairment can have significant adverse effects on the quality of life (Mulrow, Aguilar, Endicott, et al., 1990). Depression has a twofold greater incidence in the hearing-impaired elderly (Herbst & Humphrey, 1980).

An elderly individual with a permanent hearing loss should be evaluated for amplification via a hearing aid and should have the benefit of aural rehabilitation. Hearing aids are not a perfect substitute for normal hearing, however. They cannot restore the full frequency range of more severe losses. Sounds are made louder, but not necessarily clearer. Hearing aids also pose adjustment problems. Many new users claim that the devices seem unnatural. For many persons who have insidiously lost their hearing over a long period of time, the new sounds delivered by the hearing aid are surely "unnatural" to them. Hearing aids amplify all sounds, not just those of speech. Thus, the new hearing aid user may have a difficult time separating restaurant noises, car horns, or television sounds from conversational patterns. Hearing aid users and their families need to be counseled appropriately.

There are various helpful principles and common courtesies for communicating with people who are hearing impaired. In general, shouting should be avoided. Shouting does nothing to aid in the delivery of lost frequencies and results in a booming and distortion of intelligible sounds. One should speak in a normal tone of voice—a little louder, perhaps, but without shouting. Shouting often conveys a speaker's apparent annoyance and can lead to defensive or withdrawn behavior. A speaker should also talk slowly. A message is much easier to understand if it is delivered at a slower pace. Besides, talking rapidly can create an impression of being in a hurry. This situation may cause the person who is hard of hearing to feel as if he or she is a burden and taking too much of the speaker's time.

If a message is not understood the first time, finding other words to say the same thing may also be helpful. It not only gives the person who is hearing impaired an additional set of sounds from which to understand a message but it also gives more context from which meaning can be derived. Often, hearing one word can make the meaning of a whole sentence clear. Additionally, a speaker should be aware of the powers of nonverbal communication. Facial expressions serve to convey moods, feelings, negatives, positives, excitement, and disapproval. They serve to enhance the comprehension of the spoken words and to assist the hearing impaired in sharing in the lives of those around them.

With or without a hearing aid, lip reading can help with communication. A complicating factor is that some persons do not form words normally when speaking to the those who are hard of hearing. Exaggeration can serve to confuse the lip reader. The lip reader can be helped by facing him or her directly, by letting the light fall on the speaker's face, and by not exaggerating lip movements. For some with impaired vision, the lip-reading task may be more difficult.

Patient compliance can be greatly affected by a person's hearing loss. Health care institutions are complex facilities. A stay in one of them brings an individual into contact with a number of workers, many of whom have directions to give and important information to impart. Unfortunately, such information may not be heard or understood by the patient who is hard of hearing.

Health workers may perceive a patient's limited reaction as apparent disinterest. In the early stages of progressive hearing loss, an individual may appear preoccupied, inattentive, irritable, unsociable, and absentminded (Voeks et al., 1990). Health workers may not be aware of a patient's hearing loss, not having known the person before admission to the health care facility. Too often, confusion associated with hearing loss may be falsely attributed to senility in the older patient.

When planning for discharge from an institution, hearing loss must be acknowledged so that instructions about the use of mechanical devices or drug therapy are understood. Failure to hear such instructions may mean delayed recovery and even tragedy in the home situation. Written instructions can be provided to the patient. The person may have also suffered visual losses, however, so the writing should be in large print. Also, a health worker or family member can ask the patient to repeat instructions to make certain that they were properly heard and understood.

Hearing aids are most useful when background noise is at a minimum, as in a quiet theater or a lecture hall, or in private conversation in person or over the telephone. In noisy gatherings, the wearer may be better assisted by switching off the aid. Individual adjustments, however, dictate the most appropriate behavior. Some persons, though initially annoyed by background noise, may learn to tune it out.

Problems associated with a new hearing aid may be caused by an improperly fitted earmold. In order to serve the wearer, the earmold must closely fit the anatomic structure of the individual's ear canal. Prolonged complaints about a hearing aid should be investigated. Difficulty may be due to more than just a long adjustment period—perhaps the earmold does not fit!

Not all of the elderly who need hearing aids actually have them. This situation may be related to a number of factors. The older person may perceive that a hearing loss is an irreparable and normal part of getting old. Some researchers suggest that physicians, too, regard hearing loss as normal aging and intervention as futile (Humphrey, Herbst, & Faurqui, 1981). The individual may not want to admit that a hearing loss exists. Likewise, a hearing aid may be rejected for cosmetic purposes and the social stigma associated with it. Also, hearing aids are expensive. Neither routine hearing exams nor hearing aids are reimbursed under Medicare. A recent study indicates that the potential need for hearing aids exceeds their actual use (Gates et al., 1990).

As losses advance, hearing aid amplification may become less useful. *Cochlear implants* are being tested and refined in order to bypass the cochlea and its faulty hair cells so that the auditory nerve can be directly stimulated. A cochlear implant is an electronic prosthetic device that utilizes electrodes that are microsurgically implanted into or near the cochlea to stimulate the nerve. They are intended for those with profound sensorineural hearing loss (Harrison, 1987).

Taste, Smell, and Touch. Loss of taste is a common complaint among the elderly. This can be caused by atrophy of the taste buds, which comes with age (Arey, Tremaine, & Monzingo, 1936), as well as by lesions of the facial nerve and the medulla, thalamus, and temporal lobe of the brain. There are small but clearly measurable increases in both detection thresholds (concentration at which subjects can first detect a difference between a stimulus and water) and recognition thresholds (concentration at which subjects can first recognize a quality such as sweet).

A general decline is experienced in olfactory functioning with age (Schiffman, 1979, 1987). Diminished smell perception among the elderly can result from a variety of anatomic and physiological losses that are a consequence of normal aging (Schiffman, Orlandi, & Erickson, 1979). Medical conditions such as cancer, diabetes mellitus, hypertension, and multiple sclerosis, as well as pharmacological agents, smoking habits, and changes in salivary flow may also play a role in the alteration of taste and smell among the elderly (Schiffman, 1983).

Loss of touch sensitivity has been reported to occur in a small proportion of the aged population. Birren, in reviewing this scarce literature, concludes that "Touch sensitivity remains unchanged from early adulthood through about age fifty to fifty-five, with a rise in threshold thereafter" (1964). In an often cited study, Thompson, Axelrod, and Cohen (1965) had young adult (18 to 34 years) and older adult (60 to 77 years) subjects touch a variety of objects without looking at them. The task was to identify the objects with those represented on a visual display. The older adults did less well than the younger group did, although the researchers attributed this as much to decline in visual acuity as to a decline in touch sensitivity.

There is some clinical evidence that old people do not feel pain as intensely as do younger people. Yet, subjective sensory complaints are very common in old age (Botwinick, 1973). Part of the inconsistency in the literature lies in the fact that a subject's response to noxious stimuli has cognitive, motivational, personality, and cultural components as well as a sensory component (Melzack, 1973). Thus, as Gelfand (1964) points out, the way a subject views an experimental situation, the experimenter, and even the instructions given may affect the outcome of laboratory experiments on pain threshold and pain tolerance.

Psychomotor Responses

Psychomotor response is more complex than simple sensation and/or perception. If the concept of psychomotor response could be presented diagrammatically, it would show the organism taking in sensory input (or information), giving meaning to this new information through perceptual and integrative processes, determining whether or not this new information calls for any action, sending instructions to the appropriate activity center (e.g., a muscle), and activating the appropriate response. Psychomotor performance may be limited by a weakness at any point in this chain of events. It may be limited by changes in the sensory threshold, in the processes dealing with perception, in the translation from perception to action, in the strength of the sensory signal, and in muscular output.

Psychomotor performance changes as an individual ages. Evidence of the slowing of behavioral responses with age has been accumulating for decades (Birren, Woods, & Williams, 1980). This relationship is complicated by a number of factors, including sensation, perception, attention, short-term memory, intelligence, and personality. The nature of the stimulus and the complexity of the response also appear to affect reaction time.[3]

Researchers investigating age differentials in reaction time have employed three types of tasks in their experiments. *Simple reaction time* involves responding to one stimulus, such as pressing a button as fast as possible when a light comes on. Simple reaction time has two component parts: decision time (the time from the onset of the stimulus until the response is initiated) and motor time (the time needed to complete the physical part of the response). Salthouse (1985) reports that the most noticeable age difference is in the decision-time component.

Choice reaction time tasks involve presenting people with more than one stimulus and requiring that they respond differently to each. Older adults are much slower on these tasks than are younger adults (Fozard, Thomas, & Waugh, 1976). *Complex reaction time* tasks are the most difficult and involve making numerous decisions about when and how to respond. Cerella, Poon, and Williams (1980) report the greatest age differences on these tasks, with older adults being disadvantaged relative to younger adults when rapid response is required for complex and difficult tasks.

Botwinick (1973) points out that practice at a task and exercise may reduce the effects of a slowing reaction time. However, practice alone rarely eliminates age differences between young and older adults entirely. Some response slowing does appear to be an inevitable part of growing old (Spirduso & MacRae, 1990).

---

[3]*Reaction time* is a measure of how rapidly a person can respond to a stimulus, such as how quickly one steps on the brake of a car to avoid hitting a dog that has run out into the road.

Age decrements in performance may also be related to cerebral cortex functioning. Thus, circulatory deterioration, reduced cerebral metabolism, or suppressed brain rhythms will produce slower reaction times (Hendricks & Hendricks, 1977). Botwinick and Storandt (1974) point out that cardiovascular problems may also serve to depress reaction time in a way that cannot be overcome by exercise or practice.

The impact of an age-related decline in psychomotor performance on social functioning should be obvious. In general, such decline—especially in combination with sensory and perceptual decline—reduces the aged individual's ability to exert control over his or her environment. Tasks that were formerly nonproblematic, such as driving a car or using a sewing machine, may become hazardous with advancing age. Some work activities may also suffer, mainly in jobs relying on exceptionally speedy reactions or responses to incoming information. Activities directly related to health maintenance and care may also become more difficult to carry out. Also, as Atchley indicates (1977, p. 49), the nature of the decline in psychomotor performance is such that it is difficult to offset mechanically in the way glasses or hearing aids can be used to offset declines in sensory processes.

Intellectual Development

Adult intelligence has been studied from two different perspectives. One, organized around the work of Jean Piaget, is concerned with the development and evolution of thought processes underlying performance. The other, sometimes referred to as a *psychometric approach,* is concerned with measurement issues and views intelligence in terms of performance on standardized tests. Both perspectives are worthy lines of research.

According to the Swiss psychologist, Jean Piaget (1970), the critical question in human development is how people intellectually adjust to the world. Piaget argues that all people are in continuing interaction with the environment and, as a result, they develop or construct a series of schemes (concepts or models) for coping with the world. Piaget employs this term, *schemes,* to describe cognitive structures that people develop for dealing with specific situations in their environment. Further, Piaget believes that the development of intelligence involves the evolution of increasingly complex cognitive structures.

Piaget conceptualizes intelligence in terms of two principles: adaptation to the environment and organization of thought. *Adaptation* occurs through two processes: assimilation and accommodation. *Assimilation* describes the process by which people make sense out of incoming information and integrate it into what they already know. The schemes one constructs are stretched as far as possible to fit new information, but frequently new observations are confronted that do not fit the current scheme, and so a new scheme must be invented to encompass the new information. *Accommodation* is the process of changing one's knowledge or schemes to make a better match with the real world. If assimilation is the fitting of new experiences to old ones; accommodation is the fitting of old experiences to new ones.

The principle of *organization* refers to how people put their thoughts together. The organization of thought is reflected in cognitive structures that change over the life span. Changes in cognitive structures involve fundamental changes in how people think. Piaget's research, which began with careful and systematic observation of his own three children, led him to set forth a four-stage theory of cognitive development: sensorimotor, preoperational, concrete operational, and formal operational. Presumably, all individuals pass through the same stages. Each stage, though more complex than its predecessor, is based on the preceding one, and prepares the person for the succeeding one.

During the *sensorimotor* stage, intelligence is reflected in action, the use of sensory and motor skills. The major feature of this stage is mastery of the principle of object permanence, exemplified by the infant who grasps that an object (e.g., a toy or mother's smiling face) still exists when it is out of view. The *preoperational* stage is characterized by two processes. First, because children develop a capacity to employ symbolic language, they are no longer limited to dealing with stimuli that are immediately present in the here and now. Second, they are oriented toward egocentric thought. Thus, children believe that everyone experiences the world exactly as they do.

Logical reasoning—including arithmetic, class and set relationships, measurement, and conceptions of hierarchy—emerge in the stage of *concrete operations*. Children come to realize that a ball of clay can be changed in shape and still remain the same in amount. But in this stage, abstract concepts are understood only in concrete terms. The *formal operations* stage represents adult thought, as children acquire the ability to deal with abstractions and hypothetical situations, and solve problems in a systematic way.

Researchers employing Piaget's framework are only beginning to focus on older adults. One study has shown that older adults do not perform as well as younger adults on formal operational tasks (Clayton & Overton, 1973). However, this may not be due to differences in ability, but rather to lack of interest on the part of older adults in doing tasks that are perceived as abstract or as childish (Chandler, 1980).

Cavanaugh and colleagues (1985) interpret age differences in formal operational tasks as indicative of a fifth stage of intellectual development, which they refer to as postformal thought. *Postformal thought* is characterized by an increased tolerance of ambiguity, acceptance of more than one correct answer to problems, and the understanding that reality constraints are important. Blanchard-Fields (1986) reports that nearly all adults can recognize a conflict between two opposing viewpoints and decide on a position to adopt. Labouvie-Vief and Lawrence (1985) suggest, however, that adults make this decision because they believe it to be more or less valid for the context in question, not because it is viewed as absolutely right or wrong.

Piaget's work is not without critics. Flavell (1978) argues that human cognitive and intellectual growth may be too varied and heterogeneous to fit into any stage theory of the Piagetian kind. Others have challenged Piaget's view that special training or practice can have no or little effect on accelerating progress through the stages (Zimmerman, 1978). Finally, there is some question about whether's Piaget's stage theory is culture bound or universal. Some aspects of development among children in other societies seem to conflict with assumptions of Piagetian theory (Ashton, 1975; Dasen, 1977).

Intellectual Functioning

The conventional view today is that aging brings with it a decline in intelligence functioning, but most researchers agree that there are a great many problems associated with this assumption. Botwinick (1977) identifies five areas of concern that must be dealt with in evaluating the conventional view that age brings intellectual decline:

1. What age period is being looked at?
2. What tests are used?
3. How is *intelligence* defined?
4. What sampling techniques are employed?
5. What are the problems associated with specific research methods?

According to the psychometric approach, intelligence can be surmised only from performance scores; therefore, problems of measurement and testing affect outcomes. The most popular tool used to study age-related changes in intelligence has been the Wechsler Adult Intelligence Scale (WAIS). Results of studies with the WAIS often describe a "classic aging pattern" that shows a plateau reached in the 20s, maintenance of performance on verbal subtests, such as Vocabulary and Comprehension, until the 60s, but early adult decline on performance tests such as block design and object assembly (Botwinick, 1977).

Critics of the WAIS argue that the test measures mental skills and abilities that are currently being emphasized by the educational system. This makes it a more appropriate tool for determining the intelligence of younger people. These critics and others argue that testing procedures that reflect the intellectual functioning required in everyday life should be used to test the relationship between age and intelligence. After all, they maintain, intelligence is only one of the important ingredients necessary in carrying out successful behavior. This has been done to a limited extent. Demming and Pressey (1957) measured intellectual functioning in three task-related ways. They asked if respondents could (1) use the telephone directory, (2) understand some common legal terms, and (3) secure social services that they might require. Middle-aged and older adults, as a group, scored higher on these performance measures than younger respondents. Fisher (1973) suggests that the concepts of social competence and effectiveness be used in place of intellectual functioning when evaluating the aged.

Baltes and Labouvie (1973) argue that intelligence is not a single factor but consists of many abilities. In an extensive literature review, they report on many studies that conceptualize intelligence as a complex of mental abilities. The relationship between age and intelligence presented in these studies varies depending on which mental abilities are stressed. Cunningham (1987) represents the structure of intelligence as a hierarchy consisting of a general intelligence factor, third-order factors, second-order factors, primary factors, individual tests, and test items. Most research on adult development has focused on primary and second-order factors.

Research design appears to influence strongly the results of studies of age and intelligence. By and large, cross-sectional studies show early intelligence decrements, whereas longitudinal studies show stability of intelligence into late adulthood. Cross-sectional research is conducted at one point in time; the effect of age is determined by comparing people of different ages at the time the research is carried out. However, cross-sectional studies do not provide information about age change because the effects of age and cohort membership are confounded.

Longitudinal research involves observing the same people over an extended period of time, thereby producing information about continuity and change for a particular group of individuals. Subject attrition, lack of generalizability to other cohorts, and changing theories and measures are disadvantages of longitudinal designs. Because cross-sectional studies sample respondents from different age cohorts or generations and longitudinal studies sample respondents from a single cohort or generation, comparable outcomes should not be expected. Generations differ as to their genetic potential and historical experiences (Baltes & Labouvie, 1973). Many people who are old today did not have the advantage of long years of formal education. This intellectual underdevelopment is sometimes confused with a lack of intelligence. Schaie (1965) and Baltes (1968) propose the use of both cross-sectional and longitudinal studies to attempt to disentangle these genetic and experiential components. Another alternative is a sequential design, which combines elements of longitudinal and cross-sectional designs. Such designs allow for examination of age differences and age changes in order to tease out the effects of birth cohort.

In 1956, Schaie began a series of comprehensive longitudinal and cohort-sequential studies of intelligence across adulthood in Seattle, Washington, with a primary focus on five *primary mental abilities (PMAs):* number, word fluency, verbal meaning, inductive reasoning, and space. The first cross-sectional study revealed age differences in all abilities by age 60. Over time, it became clear that cohort effects heavily influence adult intellectual development. Still, data from the Seattle Longitudinal Study (Schaie, 1983, 1984) show that, over a seven-year period, about 67 percent of the young-old and 50 percent of the old-old were able to maintain their functional level of intelligence. Data from the 14-year longitudinal sequences show only slight decrements during the decade of age 50 to 59 years, but noticeable decline in all PMAs across the group being followed after age 60.

Two secondary mental abilities have received considerable attention in the research literature: fluid intelligence and crystallized intelligence. *Fluid intelligence* is a person's innate information-processing skills, independent of acquired experience and formal education—for example, reasoning and problem solving. *Crystallized intelligence* represents intelligence as cultural knowledge acquired through experience and formal education. Standardized intelligence tests typically measure elements of both fluid and crystallized intelligence.

Figure 7–2 shows graphically how fluid and crystallized intelligence develop differently across adulthood. Fluid intelligence declines as a person ages; in contrast, crystallized intelligence increases with continued learning (Horn, 1982). This may explain why older people have problems learning new tasks, but experience few problems with familiar tasks.

A mediating factor that must be considered in the relationship between age and intelligence is health status. Birren (1968) argues that the average person growing older should not expect to show a typical deterioration of mental functioning in the later years. Rather, "limitation of mental functioning occurs precipitously in individuals over the age of 65 or 70 and is closely related to health status." Particularly problematic are vascular diseases, which affect the cerebral

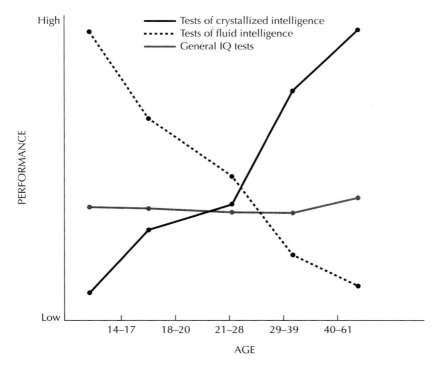

FIGURE 7–2   Performances on Tests Used to Define Fluid, Crystallized, and General Intelligence, as a Function of Age

Source: "Organization of Data on Life-Span Development of Human Abilities" by J. L. Horn, 1970, in L. R. Goulet and P. B. Baltes (Eds.), *Life-Span Developmental Psychology: Research and Theory,* p. 463. New York: Academic Press. Copyright © 1970 by Academic Press, Inc. Reprinted by permission.

cortex and probably influence the brain's capacity to store information. Related to this are the results of several studies that show a relationship between intelligence decline and survival among elderly subjects. Five years after an initial survey of elderly subjects in good health, Birren (1968) compared survivors and nonsurvivors with respect to their WAIS scores. It was primarily the verbal skills tests that distinguished them; nonsurvivors had significantly lower verbal scores at the time of initial survey. Eleven years after the initial survey, Granick (1971) reported both low verbal *and* low performance scores to be associated with early death.

Health practitioners and others should be aware that intelligence differences among individuals are great enough so that use of conventional ideas in this area is problematic. Although aging influences intellectual functioning to some extent, careful observation and evaluation of each elderly person is in order before conclusions can be drawn. An individual should not be underestimated in these matters simply because he or she is old. Intellectual decline before the late 50s is probably pathological rather than normal. And, as has already been indicated, from the early 60s on, there is decline in some but not all abilities, for some but not all individuals.

As we point out again in later chapters on old age institutions and alternatives to institutionalization, the impact of the environment (psychosocial and physical) in which the elderly person resides also deserves careful evaluation. The possibility that environmental considerations are constraining intellectual functioning in some of the aged should not be ignored. Finally, the pace of sociocultural change has been rapid. As a result, many older people (including the young-old) suffer from what can only be described as obsolescence effects, and compare poorly with younger peers, even though they may function as well as they ever have (Schaie, 1980).

Memory

Three aspects of memory are of particular interest to researchers focusing on the relationship between memory and aging. *Primary memory* is extremely short-lived and includes information that is "in mind" only while it is being used—for example, a person remembering a zip code he or she looked up long enough to write it on the letter being addressed. There are relatively few changes in primary memory with age (Poon, 1985). *Secondary memory* is the ability to remember more extensive amounts of information over longer periods of time. An example is performing on a course examination. Generally, older adults do worse than younger adults on tests of recall, but differences between the two groups are virtually nonexistent on recognition tasks (Poon, 1985).[4] Also, age differences for remembering the gist of prose may be more a function of education and personal ability than age itself (Hultsch & Dixon, 1990).

---

[4]Recognition is often tested by asking a person to pick out the items that were learned from a longer list that includes both target and distractor items.

Tertiary memory describes very long-term storage of information and includes facts presumably learned earlier in life. Research in this area is difficult. It is not clear how to measure performance on tertiary memory tasks because it is not known whether failure to remember a fact from the long-ago past is due to an inability to retrieve the information or to a failure to have initially learned the information. Tertiary memory may also be related to crystallized intelligence, suggesting the likelihood of small to no decrement with age.

Some research has compared the performance of older adults on everyday-life tasks versus traditional laboratory-learning tasks used in experimental research. Overall, age decrements in performance are less visible on the everyday-life tasks than they are in the laboratory (West, 1986). Further, older adults consistently perform better when they are presented with information that is familiar, although Perlmutter and Monty (1989) suggest that this is because older people are more motivated to perform familiar tasks.

Does learning ability decline with advancing age? The research literature indicates that, as a group, older adults tend to be slower at learning new material than they were when younger and in comparison with younger cohorts. However, some of their decline is explainable by learning-related and individual difference-related variables other than chronological age (Poon, 1987). Attitudes toward learning may change with age as well. The older individual may be less ready to learn than was the case in youth. Aged individuals may be more likely to attempt to solve problems on the basis of what they already know, rather than learn new solutions (Poon, 1985).

SUMMARY

Psychological aspects of aging are tied up with biological and social processes—and these are often difficult to tease out. Social scientists have collected a great deal of data on adult life. Little of it has been useful for developing a psychology of the life cycle. A number of different conceptions of life-cycle development have been put forth in the last 50 years or so—including those of Buhler, Jung, Erikson, and Levinson and his colleagues. More research is needed, and methodological difficulties involved in studying adult development must be overcome. Personality theory remains an underdeveloped area for psychologists of aging. Yet, much research suggests that styles of coping and adjustment carry over from the younger to the later adult years.

Age-related sensory changes in individuals affect the quality and quantity of their interaction with the world at large. Degenerative changes and eye disorders that increase with age are contributing factors in the poorer visual acuity experienced by many older people. Cataracts, glaucoma, and senile macular degeneration are the most common eye disorders among the elderly. Impaired hearing is also associated with aging. Additionally, there is a small diminishment of the perception of taste and smell among the elderly that is a consequence of normal aging. Loss of touch sensitivity has also been reported to occur in some elderly individuals.

Psychomotor response changes as an individual ages but the relationship is complicated by a number of other factors. Age-based differences in reaction time are present in a wide array of tasks.

Adult intelligence has been studied from two different perspectives. The work of Piaget represents the effort to specify the stages of development and evolution of thought processes underlying performance. The psychometric approach is concerned with measurement issues and views intelligence in terms of performance on standardized tests.

The relationship between intelligence and aging is a complex one. Primary mental abilities (PMAs) begin to show decrement in the 60s. The pattern for secondary mental abilities (SMAs) is mixed. Fluid intelligence declines with age, while crystallized intelligence increases with continued learning. Health status is an important intervening variable. Still, whether health status affects intelligence functioning or whether intellectual decline is a precursor of ill health or even mortality is subject to some debate.

Short-lived memory shows little age-related change. Older adults do worse than younger adults on tests of recall, but differences in recognition are minimal to nonexistent. Older people do better on tasks of everyday life than they do on laboratory-based memory tasks. This is especially the case for information with which elders are familiar.

STUDY QUESTIONS

1. Explain why the development of a psychology of adulthood has been slowed. How is Freud's theory of the origins of personality implicated?

2. Describe Erikson's conception of the life cycle. List the eight ages. In attempting to refine Erikson's theory, Peck pointed out three issues as central to old age. Briefly describe each issue.

3. Describe any similarities or differences between the conceptual schemas of development and aging offered by Erikson and Levinson? What are the general limitations of stage theories?

4. How have methodological issues contributed to the way the relationship between personality and aging has been conceptualized to date? List the 10 factors identified by Thomae as influential for longevity and survivorship.

5. Thomae identifies 10 factors that may influence the particular personality pattern an individual shows in old age. Does any 1 or 2 of these seem particu-

larly important to you? Which? And why? In reading the brief descriptions on different studies of personality and aging carried out in Baltimore, Berkeley, Kansas City, and Seattle, do any of Thomae's 10 factors seem particularly influential? Why or why not?

6. Discuss the sensory deprivations that occur with the aging process. What are the social-psychological implications for elderly individuals experiencing visual and hearing impairments?

7. Distinguish between the cognitive stage theory of intellectual development and the psychometric approach. What is the relationship between aging and intelligence functioning? Discuss the weaknesses and/or strengths of intelligence testing with the elderly. What factors should be considered when administering and evaluating intelligence tests to this age group?

8. To what extent does the aging process influence memory? Learning?

REFERENCES

Anderson, B., & Palmore, E. (1974). Longitudinal evaluation of ocular function. In E. Palmore (Ed.), *Normal aging*. Durham, NC: Duke University Press.

Arey, L., Tremaine, M. J., & Monzingo, F. L. (1936). The numerical and topographical relations of taste buds to human circumvillate papillae throughout the life span. *Anatomical Record, 64* (1), 9–25.

Ashton, P. T. (1975). Cross-cultural Piagetian research: An experimental perspective. *Harvard Educational Review, 45,* 475–506.

Atchley, R. C. (1977). *Social forces in later life* (2nd ed). Belmont, CA: Wadsworth.

Baltes, P. B. (1968). Longitudinal and cross-sectional sequences in the study of age and generation effects. *Human Development, 11,* 145–171.

Baltes, P. B. (1983). Life-span developmental psychology: Observations on history and theory revisited. In R. M. Lerner (Ed.), *Developmental psychology: Historical and philosophical perspectives*. Hillsdale, NJ: Lawrence Erlbaum.

Baltes, P. B., & Labouvie, G. (1973). Adult development of intellectual performance: Description, explanation and modification. In C. Eisdorfer & M. P. Lawton (Eds.), *The psychology of adult development and aging*. Washington, DC: American Psychological Association.

Barash, D. (1983). *Aging: An exploration*. Seattle: University of Washington Press.

Birren, J. (1964). *The psychology of aging*. Englewood Cliffs, NJ: Prentice-Hall.

Birren, J. (1968). Psychological aspects of aging: Intellectual functioning. *Gerontologist, 8* (1, Part II), 16–19.

Birren, J., Woods, A., & Williams, M. V. (1980). Behavioral slowing with age. In L. W. Poon (Ed.), *Aging in the 1980s*. Washington, DC: American Psychological Association.

Blanchard-Fields, F. (1986). Reasoning on social dilemmas varying in emotional saliency: An adult developmental study. *Psychology and Aging, 1,* 325–333.

Botwinick, J. (1973). *Aging and behavior*. New York: Springer.

Botwinick, J. (1977). Intellectual abilities. In J. Birren & K. Schaie (Eds.), *Handbook of the psychology of aging*. New York: Van Nostrand Reinhold.

Botwinick, J., & Storandt, M. (1974). Cardiovascular status, depressive effect and other factors in reaction time. *Journal of Gerontology, 29* (5), 543–548.

Brown, P. L. (1987). Studying seasons of a woman's life. *New York Times,* September 14, p. 23.

Buhler, C. (1933). *Der menschliche lebenslauf als psychologisches problem*. Leipzig: Hirzel.

Butler, R. (1963). The life review: An interpretation of reminiscence in the aged. *Psychiatry, 26,* 65–76.

Butler, R. (1975). *Why survive? Being old in America*. New York: Harper and Row.

Cavanaugh, J. C., Kramer, D. A., Sinnott, J. D., Camp, C. J., & Markley, R. P. (1985). On missing links and such: Interfaces between cognitive research and everyday problem solving. *Human Development, 28,* 146–168.

Cerella, J., Poon, L. W., & Williams, D. M. (1980). Age and the complexity hypothesis. In L. W. Poon (Ed.), *Aging in the 1980s*. Washington, DC: American Psychological Association.

Chandler, M. J. (1980). Life-span intervention as a symptom of conversion hysteria. In R. R. Turner & W. Reese (Eds.), *Life-span developmental psychology: Intervention*. New York: Academic Press.

Clausen, J. (1986). *The life course: A sociological perspective*. Englewood Cliffs, NJ: Prentice-Hall.

Clayton, V. P., & Overton, W. F. (1973). *The role of formal operational thought in the aging process*. Paper presented at the meeting of the Gerontological Society of America, Miami.

Cunningham, W. R. 1987. Intellectual abilities and age. In K. W. Schaie (Ed.), *Annual review of gerontology and geriatrics.* New York: Springer.

Darbyshire, J. (1984). The hearing loss epidemic: A challenge to gerontology. *Research on Aging, 6,* 384–394.

Dasen, P. R. (Ed.) 1977. *Piagetian psychology: Cross-cultural contributions.* New York: Gardner Press.

Demming, J., & Pressey, S. (1957). Tests "indigenous" to the adult and older years. *Journal of Counseling Psychology, 2,* 144–148.

Dewey, J. (1939). Introduction. In E. V. Cowdry (Ed.), *Problems of aging.* Baltimore, MD: Williams and Wilkins.

Douglas, K., & Arenberg, D. (1978). Age changes, cohort differences, and cultural change on the Guilford-Zimmerman Temperament Survey. *Journal of Gerontology, 33* (5), 737–747.

Early Treatment Diabetic Retinopathy Study Research Group. (1985). Photocoagulation for diabetic macular edema: Early treatment diabetic retinopathy study report, No. 1. *Archives of Ophthalmology, 103,* 1796–1806.

Erikson, E. (1950). *Childhood and society.* New York: W. W. Norton.

Erikson, E. (1963). *Childhood and society* (2nd ed.). New York: W. W. Norton.

Erikson, E. (1968). *Identity: Youth and crisis.* New York: W. W. Norton.

Farber, M., & Farber, A. (1990). Macular degeneration. *Postgraduate Medicine, 88,* 181–183.

Ferris, F., Fine, S., & Hyman, L. (1984). Age-related macular degeneration and blindness due to neovascular maculopathy. *Archives of Ophthalmology, 102,* 1640–1642.

Field, D., & Millsap, R. E. (1991). Personality in advanced old age: Continuity or change? *Journal of Gerontology, 46* (6), 229–308.

Fillip, S., & Olbrich, E. (1986). Human development across the life-span: Overview and highlights of the psychological perspective. In A. Sorensen, F. E. Weinert, & L. R. Sherrod (Eds.), *Human development*

and the life course: Multidisciplinary perspectives. Hillsdale, NJ: Lawrence Erlbaum.

Fisher, J. (1973). Competence, effectiveness, intellectual functioning and aging. *Gerontologist, 13,* 62–68.

Flavell, J. H. (1978). Developmental stage: Explanans or explanandum? *Behavioral and Brain Sciences, 1,* 187.

Fozard, J. L., Thomas, J. C., & Waugh, N. C. (1976). Effects of age and frequency of stimulus repetitions on two-choice reaction time. *Journal of Gerontology, 31,* 556–563.

Frenkel-Brunswick, E. (1963). Adjustments and reorientation in the course of the life-span. In R. Kuhler & G. Thompson (Eds.), *Psychological studies of human development* (rev. ed.). New York: Appleton-Century-Crofts.

Gates, G., Cooper, J., Kannel, W., & Miller, N. (1990). Hearing in the elderly: The Framingham cohort, 1983–1985. Part I. Basic audiometric test results. *Ear and Hearing, 11,* 247–256.

Gelfand, S. (1964). The relationship of experimental pain tolerance to pain threshold. *Canadian Journal of Psychology, 18,* 36–42.

Granick, S. (1971). Psychological test functioning. In S. Granick & R. Patterson (Eds.), *Human aging II: An eleven-year follow-up biomedical and behavioral study.* Washington, DC: U.S. Government Printing Office.

Gutmann, D. L. (1977). The cross-cultural perspective: Notes toward a comparative psychology of aging. In J. E. Birren & K. W. Schaie (Eds.), *Handbook of the psychology of aging.* New York: Van Nostrand Reinhold.

Hall, G. S. (1922). *Senescence, the last half of life.* New York: Appleton.

Harrison, R. (1987). Cochlear implants: A review of the principles and important physiological factors. *Journal of Otolaringology, 16,* 268–275.

Havighurst, R. (1968). Personality and patterns of aging. *Gerontologist, 8,* 20–23.

Hendricks, J., & Hendricks, C. (1977). *Aging in a mass society.* Cambridge, MA: Winthrop.

Herbst, K., & Humphrey, C. (1980). Hearing impairment and mental state in the elderly living at home. *British Medical Journal, 281*, 903.

Horn, J. L. (1982). The aging of human abilities. In B. B. Wolman (Ed.), *Handbook of developmental psychology.* Englewood Cliffs, NJ: Prentice-Hall.

Hudspeth, A. (1985). The cellular basis of hearing: The biophysics of hair cells. *Science, 230*, 745–752.

Hultsch, D. F., & Dixon, R. A. (1990). Learning and memory in aging. In J. E. Birren & K. W. Schaie (Eds.), *Handbook of the psychology of aging* (3rd ed.). San Diego, CA: Academic Press.

Humphrey, C., Herbst, K., & Faurqui, S. (1981). Some characteristics of the hearing-impaired elderly who do not present themselves for rehabilitation. *British Journal of Audiology, 15*, 25–30.

Jarvik, L. F. (1975, May). Thoughts on the psychobiology of aging. *American Psychologist*, pp. 576–583.

Jindra, L. (1983). Open-angle glaucoma: Diagnosis and management. *Hospital Practice, 18*, 114c–114p.

Jindra, L. (1984). Closed-angle glaucoma: Diagnosis and management. *Hospital Practice, 19*, 114–119.

Jung, C. (1933). *Modern man in search of a soul.* New York: Harcourt, Brace & World.

Jung, C. (1971). The stages of life. In J. Campbell (Ed.), *The portable Jung.* New York: Viking Press.

Kart, C., Metress, E., & Metress, J. (1988). *Aging, health and society.* Boston: Jones and Bartlett.

Kart, C. S., Metress, E. K., & Metress, S. P. (1992). *Human aging and chronic disease.* Boston: Jones and Bartlett.

Kermis, M. D. (1986). *Mental health in late life: The adaptive process.* Boston: Jones and Bartlett.

Labouvie-Vief, G., & Lawrence, R. (1985). Object knowledge, personal knowledge, and process of equilibration in adult cognition. *Human Development, 28*, 25–39.

Leske, M. C. (1983). The epidemiology of open-angle glaucoma: A review. *American Journal of Epidemiology, 118*, 166–191.

Levinson, D. J., Darrow, C. N., Klein, E. B., Levinson, M. H., & Mckee, B. (1978). *The seasons of a man's choice.* New York: Alfred A. Knopf.

Lidz, T. (1976). *The person: His or her development throughout the life cycle* (2nd ed.). New York: Basic Books.

McAdams, D. P., de St. Aubin, E. & Logan, R. L. (1993). Generativity among young, midlife and older adults. *Psychology and Aging, 8*, 221–230.

Melzack, R. (1973). *The puzzle of pain.* New York: Basic Books.

Mulrow, C., Auilar, C., Endicott, J., and others. (1990). Association between hearing impairment and the quality of life in elderly individuals. *Journal of the American Geriatrics Society, 38*, 45–50.

Neisser, U., & Winograd, E. (Eds.). (1988). *Remembering reconsidered.* New York: Cambridge University Press.

Neugarten, B. (1973). Personality change in late life: A developmental perspective. In C. Eisdorfer & M. P. Lawton (Eds.), *The psychology of adult development and aging.* Washington, DC: American Psychological Association

Neugarten, B. (1977). Personality and aging. In J. Birren & K. Schaie (Eds.), *Handbook of the psychology of aging.* New York: Van Nostrand Reinhold.

Olsen, W. (1984). When hearing wanes, is amplification the answer? *Postgraduate Medicine, 76*, 189–198.

Peck, R. (1968). Psychological developments in the second half of life. In B. Neugarten (Ed.), *Middle age and aging: A reader in social psychology.* Chicago: University of Chicago Press.

Perlmutter, L. C., & Monty, R. A. (1989). Motivation and aging. In L. W. Poon, D. C. Rubin, & B. A. Wilson (Eds.), *Everyday cog-*

nition in adulthood and late life. New York: Cambridge University Press.

Piaget, J. (1970). Piaget's theory. In P. H. Mussen (Ed.), *Carmichael's manual of child psychology* (3rd ed.). New York: Wiley.

Poon, L. W. (1985). Differences in human memory with aging: Nature, causes and clinical implications. In J. Birren & K. Schaie (Eds.), *Handbook of the psychology of aging* (2nd ed.). New York: Van Nostrand Reinhold.

Poon, L. W. (1987). Learning. In G. L. Maddox (Ed.), *The encyclopedia of aging*. New York: Springer.

Reichard, S., Livson, F., & Peterson, P. G. (1962). *Aging and personality*. New York: John Wiley & Sons.

Rosen, J. L., & Neugarten, B. (1964). Ego functions in the middle and later years: A thematic apperception study. In B. L. Neugarten (Ed.), *Personality in middle and late life*. New York: Atherton.

Ross, D. (1972). *G. Stanley Hall: The psychologist as prophet?* Chicago: University of Chicago Press.

Rossi, A. (1984). Gender and parenthood. *American Sociological Review, 49*, 1–19.

Salthouse, T. A. (1985). Speed of behavior and its implications for cognition. In J. E. Birren & K. W. Schaie (Eds.), *Handbook of the psychology of aging* (2nd ed.). New York: Academic Press.

Schaie, K. W. (1965). A general model for the study of developmental problems. *Psychological Bulletin, 64*, 92–107.

Schaie, K. W. (1980). Intelligence and problem solving. In J. E. Birren & R. B. Sloane (Eds.), *Handbook of mental health and aging*. Englewood Cliffs, NJ: Prentice-Hall.

Schaie, K. W. (1983). *Longitudinal studies of adult psychological development*. New York: Guilford Press.

Schaie, K. W. (1984). Midlife influences upon intellectual functioning in old age. *International Journal of Behavioral Development, 7*, 463–478.

Schaie, K. W., & Parham, I. A. (1976). Stability of adult personality traits: Fact or fable? *Journal of Personality and Social Psychology, 34* (1), 146–158.

Schiffman, S. S. (1979). Changes in taste and smell with age: Psychological aspects. In J. M. Ordy & K. Brizzee (Eds.), *Sensory systems and communication in the elderly: Volume 10. Aging*. New York: Raven Press.

Schiffman, S. S. (1983). Taste and smell in disease. *New England Journal of Medicine, 308*, 1275–1279, 1337–1343.

Schiffman, S. S. (1987). Smell. In G. L. Maddox (Ed.), *The encyclopedia of aging*. New York: Springer.

Schiffman, S. S., Orlandi, M., & Erickson, R. P. (1979). Changes in taste and smell with age: Biological aspects. In J. M. Ordy & K. Brizzee (Eds.), *Sensory systems and communication in the elderly: Volume 10. Aging*. New York: Raven Press.

Spirduso, W. W., & MacRae, P. G. (1990). Motor performance and aging. In J. E. Birren & K. W. Schaie (Eds.), *Handbook of the psychology of aging* (3rd ed.). San Diego, CA: Academic Press.

Stefansson, E. (1990). The eye. In W. Hazzard, R. Andres, E. Bierman, & J. Blass (Eds.), *Principles of geriatric medicine and gerontology*. New York: McGraw-Hill.

Stone, J. L., & Norris, A. H. (1966). Activities and attitudes of participants in the Baltimore Longitudinal Study. *Journal of Gerontology, 21*, 575–580.

Surjan, L., Devald, J., & Palfalvi, J. (1973). Epidemiology of hearing loss. *Audiology, 12*, 396–410.

Thomae, H. (1980). Personality and adjustment to aging. In J. E. Birren & R. B. Sloane (Eds.), *Handbook of mental health and aging*. Englewood Cliffs, NJ: Prentice-Hall.

Thompson, L. W., Axelrod, S., & Cohen, L. D. (1965). Senescence and visual identification of tactual-kinesthetic forms. *Journal of Gerontology, 20* (2), 244–249.

U.S. Bureau of the Census. (1994). *Statistical abstract of the United States, 1994*. Washington, DC: U.S. Government Printing Office.

Vaillant, G. (1977). *Adaptation to life.* Boston: Little, Brown.

Voeks, S., Gallagher, C., Langer, E., & Drinka, P. (1990). Hearing loss in the nursing home: An institutional issue. *Journal of the American Geriatrics Society, 38,* 141–145.

Welford, A. (1980). Sensory, perceptual, and motor processes in older adults. In J. E. Birren & R. B. Sloane (Eds.), *Handbook of mental health and aging.* Englewood Cliffs, NJ: Prentice-Hall.

West, R. L. (1986). Everyday memory and aging. *Developmental Neuropsychology, 2,* 323–344.

Whitbourne, S. K. (1987). Personality development in adulthood and old age: Relationships among identity style, health, and well-being. In K. W. Schaie (Ed.), *Annual review of gerontology and geriatrics* (Vol. 7). New York: Springer.

Young, R. (1988). Solar radiation and age-related macular degeneration. *Survey of Ophthalmology, 32,* 252–269.

Zimmerman, B. J. (1978). A social learning explanation for age-related changes in children's conceptual behavior. *Contemporary Educational Psychology, 3,* 11–19.

CHAPTER 8

SOCIAL ASPECTS OF AGING

This chapter introduces the concept of the *life course* and contrasts it with the life-stage and life-span developmental approaches identified in the previous chapter. The life course—that is, a schedule or sequence of roles and group memberships that individuals are expected to follow as they move through life—is socially prescribed. Thus, basic anthropological and sociological concepts are useful for describing and understanding its structure. In a second section, concepts such as *social role* and *role transition* are used to help explain the sequencing of the life course. Finally, although the life course may include predictable, socially recognized transitions, most people experience events and circumstances over which they have little or no control. Coping with change or stress and developing successful strategies for adaptation are important elements of the life course. The chapter ends with a review of some work on life stress and adaptation. Chapter 9 deals in specific terms with sociological theories of aging.

THE LIFE-COURSE PERSPECTIVE

In Chapter 7, the reader was introduced to life-stage and life-span developmental approaches to understanding the changes people experience as they age. The work of Erikson and that of Levinson represent examples of the *life-stage* approach. These frameworks appear to contend that development proceeds through a set pattern of sequential stages that most individuals experience. Levinson and colleagues summarize this approach: "We are interested in generating...hypotheses concerning *relatively universal, genotypic, age-linked, adult developmental periods* within which variations occur" (1974, p. 244; emphasis in original).

A second perspective is found in the growing body of work on *life-span* developmental psychology. This approach was originally developed as a counterpoint to life-stage or life-cycle theories that posited irreversible, unidirectional, age-determined change through the lifetime (Bush & Simmons, 1981). Life-span developmental psychology is devoted to "the description and explication of ontogenetic (age-related) behavioral changes from birth to death" (Baltes & Goulet, 1970, p. 12). Although proponents of the life-span approach can be accused of focusing a good deal of attention on intrapsychic phenomena, it is fair to say that in recent years researchers have shifted some focus to environmental determinants of behavior. Thus, as Bush and Simmons (1981) point out, many life-span researchers now emphasize the interaction of individual and social characteristics in explanations of behavioral change.

The life-course perspective "concentrates on age-related transitions that are *socially created, socially recognized,* and *shared*" (Hagestad & Neugarten, 1985, p. 35; emphasis in original). Life-course researchers focus on the ways in which social norms and definitions influence the pattern or sequence of role changes and role transitions in the life course. Generally speaking, intraindividual or biological phenomena are excluded from analysis. This is especially the case after the individual reaches adulthood or biological maturation. Table 8–1 compares the life-stage, life-span, and life-course perspectives.

All societies divide the lifetime into recognized seasons of life—what Zerubavel (1981) describes as a *sociotemporal order*—that regulate the structure and dynamics of social life. Passing from one "season" to another often marks multiple changes in social identity. The way lifetime is divided or segmented differs in different cultures. Typically, periods of life are identified and defined; age criteria are used to channel people into positions and roles. Rights, responsibilities, privileges, and obligations are assigned on the basis on these culturally specific definitions (Hagestad & Neugarten, 1985). The St. Lawrence Island Eskimos exemplify a culturally defined life-course typology. Among these people, age is used simply to separate boys from men, and girls from women; as men and women mature, they "continue doing what [they have] always done as long as possible," then finally enter old age (Hughes, 1961).

Linton (1942) suggested that the minimal number of age groupings in a society must be four: infancy, childhood, adulthood, and old age. Keith (1982) reports studying 60 traditional societies and finding a range of two to eight categories or age-grades used to "slice" up the life course. Cowgill (1986) identifies at least 10 age-grades in the contemporary United States: infancy, preschool age, kindergarten age, elementary school age, intermediate school age, high school age, young adult, middle-aged, young-old, and old-old.

Early in the seventeenth century, Shakespeare's character Jaques in *As You Like It* limited life's script to seven acts or ages:

> All the world's a stage,
> And all the men and women merely players;
> They have their exits and their entrances,

TABLE 8–1 Conceptualizations of Change and Individual Development through the Lifetime According to Life-Stage, Life-Span, and Life-Course Perspectives

Change Issues	Amount of Change Possible	Abruptness of Change	Direction of Change	Universality of Change	Origin of Change
Perspectives:					
Life stage	Change between stages; little change within.	Abrupt between stages	Unidirectional	Universal	Largely internal
Life span	Change throughout life, but amount varies depending on individual characteristics, life experiences, history.	Varies	Reversible	Relative	Internal and external, emphasis on latter
Life course	Change throughout life, but amount varies depending on individual experiences, age norms, cohort effects, and history.	Varies	Reversible	Relative	Internal and external, much emphasis on latter

Source: From "Socialization Processes over the Life Course" by D. M. Bush and R. G. Simmons, in *Social Psychology: Sociological Perspectives*, edited by Morris Rosenberg and Ralph H. Turner. Copyright © 1981 by The American Sociological Association. Reprinted by permission of Basic Books, Inc., Publishers.

And one man in his time plays many parts,
His acts being seven ages.

(act 2, scene 7, lines 139–143)

The seven acts or ages (applicable to a woman's life script as well) constitute the sequence of roles that make up a life course, each role symbolizing age-appropriate behaviors.

At first the infant,

Mewling and puking in the nurse's arms.
Then the whining schoolboy, with his satchel
And shining morning face, creeping like snail
Unwillingly to school. And then the lover,
Sighing like furnace, with a woeful ballad
Made to his mistress' eyebrow. Then a soldier,
Full of strange oaths and bearded like the pard,
Jealous in honor, sudden and quick in quarrel,
Seeking the bubble reputation
Even in the cannon's mouth. And then the justice,
In fair round belly with good capon lined,
With eyes severe and beard of formal cut,
Full of wise saws and modern instances;
And so he plays his part. The sixth age shifts
Into the lean and slippered pantaloon,
With spectacles on nose and pouch on side;
His youthful hose, well saved, a world too wide
For his shrunk shank; and his big manly voice,
Turning again toward childish treble, pipes
And whistles in his sound. Last scene of all,
That ends this strange eventful history,
Is second childishness and mere oblivion,
Sans teeth, sans eyes, sans taste, sans everything.

(act 2, scene 7, lines 143–166)

For Shakespeare, life begins with a helpless dependency and ends absent sensory capabilities that make it worth living. The course between these end points is described in terms of social roles. But understanding how the "mewling, puking infant" becomes the lover, the soldier, the justice, and finally enters "second childishness" and "mere oblivion" requires some familiarity with the process of socialization.

Researchers often assume that the layperson views the world as they do. Just how do ordinary people visualize the life course? Do they set age boundaries for different stages or age-grades? And how do they characterize the behaviors assigned to these different stages? Recently a team of anthropologists (Ikels et al., 1992), using cross-cultural studies in Hong Kong, the United States, Ireland, and Botswana, sought to identify how different people perceive old age and its place in the life course.

The research strategy used to elicit people's perceptions of the life course involved use of the *Age Game*. In this game, informants were provided a deck of cards containing descriptive material on individuals in terms of sex, marital status, participation in various activities, and the like. Materials on the cards were culture specific, based on extensive pretesting. Informants read the cards themselves or, in the cases of nonliterate participants primarily in Hong Kong and Botswana, had card descriptions read to them aloud by the researcher. Informants were asked to group cards that described people who were in the same stage of life and to order the groupings by age.

The great majority of informants across all research sites recognized between three and six age groupings. Most Hong Kong Chinese used a simple three-stage age scheme—youth, the middle years, and old age—and then modified these categories to make further accommodations. Many informants simply divided the middle years and old age into two stages each. Informants could usually assign an age range to an age category, but age was not really the most salient issue that defined membership in a particular category. For example, for Hong Kong Chinese, grandparenthood, reduced responsibilities, increased leisure, and retirement were all seen as markers of becoming old.

In Blessington, Ireland, just south of Dublin, residents perceived a four-stage life course. The first stage, 18 to 30 years of age, was characterized by freedom from responsibility for finances and family. In the second stage, 30 to 50 years of age, people settle down and accept responsibilities for employment and family. Stage three, including those from age 50 to 65, was characterized by a reaping of the fruits of labor and family rearing. Grandparenthood is a marker for this stage. The last stage of life (70 years of age or more) is viewed by many in Blessington as a return to a youthlike carefree state.

Common to Hong Kong and Blessington, Ireland, is the extent to which responsibility is viewed by residents as a central theme in the life course. Although the aged are characterized in different terms in the two societies (physically weak and out of touch in Hong Kong and fearful of ill health and the consequences of living alone in Blessington), the life stage of old age is actually described in similar terms in these two societies—relief from the burdens and struggle of middle-age.

SOCIALIZATION AND SOCIAL ROLES

The human animal is distinguished by its capacity to learn, and this capacity underlies the efforts in human society to develop and institutionalize modes of instruction designed to prepare individuals to function as members of society. Stated more succinctly, human behavior is primarily learned. The learning process, called *socialization,* involves the transmission, by language and gesture, of the culture into which people are born. As Clausen reminds us, socialization is a lifelong process: "the process of transmitting the skills and knowledge needed to perform roles that one will (or may) occupy as one moves along the life course" (1986, p. 17).

Much socialization effort is directed toward the developing child. The function of early socialization is to present a single world of meaning as the only possible way to organize perceptions (Berger & Luckman, 1986). But socialization goes on long after physical maturity has been achieved. Early socialization is insufficient to prepare a person for the many different roles of adulthood in a modern industrial society. When focused on the adult life course, socialization stresses the importance of the demands that institutions and other members of the society make on the individual (Brim, 1968). These demands shape attitudes, interests, and opinions. They require *desocialization* (learning to give up a role) and *resocialization* (learning new ways to deal with the old role partners). Such changes carry with them the potential for major reorganization of the self (Hess, Markson, & Stein, 1988).

The concept of *social role* describes society's expectations for individuals who occupy a given social position or status. Each distinctive social status has a set of role, or behavioral, expectations attached to it. It is the concept of social role that leads one to expect that college students submit their assignments on time, that accountants be familiar with current tax law, and that police officers respond to a citizen in distress. It is also the concept that helps one understand how the same individual can juggle the different expectations associated with being a mother, professor, community volunteer, friend, spouse, and theater patron all in the same day.

Roles are not acted out in a social vacuum. They are usually defined in the context of interacting social roles performed by others. Thus, the expectations I fulfill in my role as a professor are often carried out in association with someone else fulfilling the role of student. Only with the cooperation of two individuals fulfilling their roles of daughter and son, respectively, have I been able to carry out the expectations associated with being a father. Many social roles come in pairs or sets such as these (professor-student; father-child). Such role pairs or sets are known as *complementary roles* because they require that the behavior of two or more persons interact in specific ways.

Social roles, including complementary roles, are not defined in specific or uniform terms throughout a society. Some of this lack of uniformity comes from variation in actual performance across individuals. One professor may befriend students and provide advice and counsel on personal matters, whereas another may focus strictly on duties related to the coursework at hand. In one family, the father may play a strong role as decision maker, whereas in another, the mother may take responsibility for most decisions. Generally speaking, to operate effectively, the roles people assume must complement the roles of those with whom they interact most of the time.

Social roles are a significant component of the social structure. They allow people to anticipate the behavior of others and to respond or pattern their own actions accordingly. The individual acquisition of social roles is a key element in the socialization process. Although Freud presumably never used the concept of role, the end product of psychosexual development appears to be male and female sex roles (Sales, 1978).

Piaget's concern with the development of cognitive and interpretive capabilities seems to stem from the presumption that social roles require such capabilities (Bush & Simmons, 1981). Piaget (1970; Piaget & Inhelder, 1969) posits three broad stages of cognitive development: sensorimotor, concrete operations, and formal operations. Movement through these stages represents, in part, the shift from being self- or ego-centered to being decentered, and from understanding concrete objects or pairs of objects to comprehending complex relationships. As a result, by about age 13 or 14, the adolescent is presumed to be capable of grasping social and physical changes without ever seeing the relevant material reality. This ability is crucial because, among other things, "it enables the individual to have affective relationships in which she/he not only realizes that others may have different perspectives from her/his own, but she or he is able to coordinate other's perspectives with her or his own as well" (Bush & Simmons, 1981, p. 139).

George Herbert Mead's (1934) theory of the development of the self also highlights the importance of social roles. According to Mead, the self is composed of two parts: the *I* and the *me*. The *I* is the spontaneous part of self, the active responder; the *me* is the person's conception of self. How does this differentiated self become a whole? Basically, Mead argues that the self evolves as a function of social interaction with others—social interaction in which the individual takes the role of the other and comes to understand how the social roles encountered are related to one another. For Mead, understanding social roles and being able to assume the role of the other are basic components of socialization.

While social interaction with others represents external stimuli, internal stimuli may also affect how we learn or acquire social roles. According to Brim, the internal demands of self may be as important as the demands of others and society:

> There may be small but incremental shifts from time to time in what an individual asks of himself, and the resultant day-to-day alterations in his behavior, rewarded by himself, lead to a cumulative change which over the years makes him much different from what he was when he was younger... until one day he finds himself a person quite different from that of a decade earlier, without knowing how the change occurred. (1968, pp. 191–192)

OLD AGE AND SOCIAL ROLES

Is old age a social role? Do people have behavioral expectations for those who achieve old age? These are difficult questions to answer. Some have suggested that old age is a formal status or position in society and that expectations for behavior are attached to that position. Others, arguing that the problems of older people in society center around the absence of expectations others have for them, have characterized old age as the "roleless role." Clearly, when people become old, when they achieve some chronological or even functional definition of old age, they continue to occupy many of the social roles they occupied during the life course. They continue to be family members, community members, and volunteers, and some continue to be employed. Perhaps a more appropriate strategy, then, is to ask, "How does age affect the social roles one occupies?" As Keith (1982) points out, in many societies, when people can no longer work, they are defined as old, but in the United States, the situation is reversed—when people are defined as old, they can no longer work. Thus, in the United States, chronological age is used to mark the border between work and retirement. Age is employed as an eligibility criterion for social roles. At the same time, it makes one ineligible to work but eligible to occupy the status of retiree.

Age also influences people's ideas about the appropriateness of certain behaviors. Neugarten, for example, has argued that perceptions in the United States about behaviors appropriate at given ages have relaxed considerably:

> There is no longer a particular year—or even a particular decade—in which one marries or enters the labor market, or goes to school or has children.... It no longer surprises us to hear of a 22-year old mayor or a 29-year old university president—or a 35-year old grandmother or a retiree of 50. No one blinks at a 70-year old college student or at the 55-year old man who becomes a father for the first time—or who starts a second family. I can remember when the late Justice William Douglas, in old age, married a young wife. The press was shocked and hostile. That hostility would be gone today. People might smirk a little, but the outrage has vanished. (1980, p. 66)

Still, a relaxation of age norms should not be equated with the absence of age norms. As Karp and Yoels (1982) indicate, Americans have fairly rigid ideas concerning who may have intimate sexual relationships with whom. Discrepancies in age between sexual partners are frequently a premise for ridicule. And Justice Douglas notwithstanding, if Grandpa Joe came home one evening and announced his intention to marry a 25-year-old woman he met at the local dance club, he might be facing an institutional commitment hearing by morning!

The age norms that develop in age-homogeneous communities can be quite distinctive. Keith (1977, 1982) lived for one year in Les Floralies, a French retirement residence. An amusing moment in her fieldwork came when she overheard several French men and women commenting on a patronizing article in the daily newspaper about the benefits of sex for the elderly. This idea was not considered to be revolutionary among the residents of Les Floralies. Not only was sex an acceptable topic for discussion but it was also considered an appropriate *activity* for those who wanted it. Further, men and women who shared an apartment, appeared together in public, and were presumed to have a sexual relationship were "married" in the eyes of other residents, even if not in the eyes of French law.

ROLE TRANSITIONS

The Mesakin of the Sudan are obsessed with witchcraft (Nadel, 1952). An older man is almost always the alleged witch accused of attempting to harm a younger man. The Mesakin explain this in terms of older men's resentments of the young. One important reason that "old" Mesakin men may be resentful of the young is that they are not chronologically old. In fact, the Mesakin have only three age-grades, and men enter the oldest one in their late 20s. The change in expected behavior when the new grade is entered is quite abrupt. The privileges of youthful vigor—wrestling, spear fighting, and living in cattle camps—are given up absolutely while the men are still very young, both physically and chronologically. The abruptness with which men are expected to make the behavioral changes would seem another reason why there is conflict between Mesakin old and young.

In theory, at least, anticipatory socialization could cushion the shock associated with a role or status change such as the one that just described. _Anticipatory socialization_ describes a socialization prior to or preparation for successfully taking on a new role. The concept has been applied to the transition to occupational and professional careers. Medical sociologists, for example, have used the concept to speak to the "training for uncertainty" (Fox, 1957) and "loss of idealism" (Becker et al, 1961) experienced by those preparing for entry into the medical profession.

But what good is anticipatory socialization if the behavioral expectations associated with the future role are not visible or clear? Rosow (1974) argues that

Different societies maintain different behavioral expectations for those who achieve old age.

many of the problems faced by the old in adjusting to their new roles are caused by the lack of clarity in these roles. Whereas there is much prescribed activity associated with other life transitions, there is little prescribed activity that attends to old age.

Some literature suggests that negative effects of role or status transitions such as those experienced by Mesakin men can be offset by *rites of passage,* rituals that help individuals move from one known social position to another and provide signals to the rest of society that new expectations are appropriate. Ceremonial rituals can be used to mark losses or gains in privilege, responsibility, influence, or power. Typical status passages marked by ceremonial ritual in U.S. society include that from child to adult (confirmation or bar or bas mitzvah), from high school to college student (graduation), from single to married person (marriage), from worker to retiree (retirement party), and from living person to ancestor (funeral).

Are status changes in society (such as those itemized here) made easier by rites of passage? Foner and Kertzer (1978) offer that most of the evidence for the advantage of such rites of passage comes from studies of non-Western cultures. Some of their own work with African societies, however, shows that the absence of firm rules of transition encourages conflict over the timing of such transitions. Thus, those in powerful positions may attempt to delay ceremonial rites of passage because they do not want to give up their privileges, whereas those who will gain from the transition make an effort to hasten the rites of passage.

Keith argues that the most distinctive characteristics of rites of passage for old people in the United States is in their absence or incompleteness: "At most, an older person and the others who have social ties to him or her are offered *exit* signs. The separation phase of a rite of passage may be there in retirement parties or gold watches, but there is no clear pathway back to social reincorporation" (1982, p. 30). The lack of public ceremonial ritual to mark transitions experienced by the old may be further evidence of their roleless roles. Older people themselves, however, may be creating transition rituals. This is exemplified by the extended retirement trip, which makes it easier to change expectations on return, or the change in residence, which also makes it easier for some people to face changed expectations.

The Timing of Role Transitions

Most societies appear to have a timetable for the ordering of life events and (almost by definition) role transitions. Describing empirical studies begun by Neugarten and colleagues in the 1950s, Neugarten and Hagestad (1976) report that interviewees were easily able to respond to questions such as "What is the best age for a man to marry?" or "What is the best age for a woman to become a grandmother?" There was greatest agreement in response to questions dealing with the timing of major role transitions. For example, most middle-class men and women agreed that the best age for a man to marry was from 20 to 25; most men should be settled in a career by age 24 to 26; they should hold their top jobs by age 40; and they should be ready to retire by age 60 or 65 (Neugarten & Hagestad, 1976).

The timing of role transitions is not static. Cohort differences and historical period effects have contributed to changes in the timing of role transitions. Table 8–2 shows the average age of selected critical life events in the early stages of the family life cycle of ever-married white mothers in five birth cohorts between 1900 and 1949. The mean age at marriage of the 1900 to 1909 cohort is 1.5 years higher than that of the 1940 to 1949 cohort. The average age of a mother at the time of the birth of a first child declined by 2.4 years across these five birth cohorts. These cohorts also completed their childbearing at very different ages. In part, this is explained by differences in the number of children born, on average, to women in these cohorts. Nevertheless, the fact that these cohorts completed their childbearing in different historical periods cannot be overlooked. Women born between 1940 and 1949 finished childbearing in the 1970s and had, on average, 2.4 children; women born between 1900 and 1909 finished their childbearing in the Depression years and averaged 3.0 children.

Schoen and colleagues (cited in Siegel & Davidson, 1984) have developed some measures of important events occurring in later segments of the family life cycle (see Table 8–3). Comparing cohorts born in the years from 1908 to 1912 to those born between 1938 to 1942, they observed a decline in the average duration of a first marriage that is slightly greater for men (28.7 years versus 26.1 years) than for women (29.5 years versus 27.4 years). This decline for men and women is clearly a function of an increase in the proportion of first marriages ending in divorce. While 25 percent of men born between 1908 and 1912 had their first marriage end in divorce, almost 40 percent of those born between 1938 and 1942 had a first marriage end in that fashion.

The mean age at widowhood has increased more dramatically for men (64.5 versus 68.4 years) than for women (64.7 versus 66.1 years), but the average duration of widowhood has remained about the same (6.6 years for men and 14.3 years for women). Much smaller proportions of husbands outlive their wives than is the case for wives who outlive their husbands. Increases in the mean age at widowhood just described are likely a function of the greater increase in longevity of women over men experienced in the period in question. In addition, to date, the

TABLE 8–2   Average Age at Which Selected Critical Life Events Occurred for Ever-Married White Mothers Born between 1900 and 1949

Life Cycle Event	Birth Cohort				
	1940–1949	1930–1939	1920–1929	1910–1919	1900–1909
Age at first marriage	20.2	20.6	21.4	22.2	21.7
Age at birth of first child	21.8	22.3	23.6	24.6	24.2
Age at birth of last child	25.4	29.1	31.2	32.5	30.8
Mean number of children	2.4	3.4	3.3	3.0	3.0

Source: Data from C. B. Spanier & R. C. Glick, "The Life Cycles of American Families: An Expanded Analysis," *Journal of Family History,* 5(1), 1980, pp. 98–111, and from June 1975 Marital History Supplement of the Current Population Survey.

TABLE 8–3 Measures of the Marital Life Cycle of Men and Women, for Selected Birth Cohorts: 1908–1912 to 1938–1942

Item (Years)	Males Cohort (Year of Birth)				Females Cohort (Year of Birth)			
	1908–1912	1918–1922	1928–1932	1938–1942	1908–1912	1918–1922	1928–1932	1938–1942
Average age at first marriage	26.2	25.0	23.8	23.3	23.3	22.3	21.1	21.2
Average duration of first marriage	28.7	28.9	28.5	26.1	29.5	29.2	29.7	27.4
Outcome of first marriage (%)								
Divorce	25.1	29.3	33.2	39.4	23.8	27.3	31.5	36.7
Widowhood	22.8	21.1	19.6	17.6	53.0	50.3	48.5	45.1
Death	52.0	49.6	47.3	43.0	23.2	21.2	19.9	18.3
Mean age at								
Widowhood	64.5	66.7	67.8	68.4	64.7	65.6	66.0	66.1
Divorce	40.7	39.7	40.1	38.7	37.4	36.5	37.1	36.5
Mean duration of								
Widowhood	6.6	6.7	6.7	6.6	14.4	14.3	14.4	14.3
Divorce	4.4	4.4	4.5	4.2	8.9	8.7	9.7	9.6

Source: T. Siegel & M. Davidson, *Demographic and Socioeconomic Aspects of Aging in the United States*, U.S. Bureau of the Census, *Current Population Reports*, Series P-23, No. 138, Table 7–8 (1984), p. 97.

percentage of first marriages ending in widowhood has declined. Whereas 53 percent of women born from 1908 to 1912 had their first marriages end in widowhood, 45.1 percent of women born in 1938 to 1942 had their marriages end in a similar fashion.

Changes in the timing of role transitions make it more difficult to assess the importance of being "on time" or "off time" in taking on new roles or disengaging from old ones. This assessment is further exacerbated by the problem of what Roth (1963) describes as "an interacting bundle of career timetables." This may best be observed in early adulthood, where a veritable traffic jam of transitions takes place. Around college campuses in May or June of any year, this compression is highly visible. In a matter of a few short weeks, any number of individuals can be found who are completing an education, marrying, embarking on career paths, settling into new communities, and becoming active in volunteer or civic roles. Presumably, such people use the remainder of the life course to rest up from this whirlwind of personal change!

Some authors have suggested that being off time (early or late) in taking on new roles or exiting old ones may create additional stresses. The source of such stresses may be *internal*, emanating from the individual's internalization of age norms, or *external*, from the reactions of peers and/or friends (Sales, 1978). Blau (1961) found that women who were widowed relatively early and men who retired earlier than their colleagues had greater disruptions in their social relationships than did those women and men for whom the events occurred on time. Unanticipated role displacement also complicates the transition process. Postretirement adjustment is generally more problematic when the withdrawal from work is unexpected (e.g., see Streib & Schneider, 1971).

In opposition to the hypothesis that being off time is stressful, several authors have offered evidence of the benefits of being off time. Nydegger (1973), for example, showed that men who were fathers relatively late in life were more effective and more comfortable in the role than those who entered the role early or on time. One explanation for the greater comfort and effectiveness of these "late" fathers is that the demands of parenthood did not compete with the demands of early career building. Along similar lines, Neugarten and Hagestad (1976) cite interviews carried out by Likert with women returning to school in their middle years. These women saw themselves as having an advantage over younger women because they were taking one thing at a time and had fewer role changes to negotiate.

LIFE STRESS AND ADAPTATION

Much of the discussion about the social aspects of aging highlights the stresses associated with role transitions and changing behavioral expectations. The age-linked role transitions that are of particular interest are major life transitions: changes in parent roles as children leave home, grandparenthood, retirement, and widowhood, among others. Coping with the stresses of such transitions and adapting more or less successfully to them is an important element in the life course generally, as well as in achieving successful aging. There are various modes of defending against stressors and various modes of coping. *Coping* describes the behaviors individuals use to prevent, alleviate, or respond to stressful situations (George, 1980).

COPING WITH CHANGE

Immigrating to a new country, voluntarily or not, is an atypical life transition, regardless of age. Howard Litwin (1995) believes that older immigrants face a double jeopardy, however. They must overcome the stresses of geographical displacement experienced by all immigrants, young and old alike. In addition, older immigrants must cope with the loss of resources and opportunities that so frequently characterize the aging process, without the familiarity of social supports available to them at home. How common is the older immigrant experience anyway? Although it is difficult to identify the number of older immigrants in any one year, it is clear that political and economic upheavals around the world, so visible on TV news broadcasts, continue to force dislocations of older people. This is the case in Bosnia, in the reunified Germany, and in the republics of the former Soviet Union, among other places in the world.

In a recent study, Litwin (1995) has written of the experiences of elderly Soviet Jews who immigrated to Israel between 1989 and 1991. In particular, he was interested in the social networks of older immigrants—in the networks they leave as well as the ones they are able to create in the new host society in which they find themselves. *Social networks* may be defined "as the range of social ties that people maintain and that provide them with a sense of identify, feelings of belongingness, guidance, orientation to action, and practical assistance of various kinds" (Litwin, 1995, p. 2). Thus, social networks are thought to include the interpersonal environment in which

people live and work—family, friends, neighbors, fellow employees, as well as other significant individuals with whom people interact on a regular basis. Litwin clearly believes that successful organization (or reorganization) of a social network in the new host country has important positive consequences for the lives of elderly immigrants. In particular, he asks, How do Soviet Jewish immigrants to Israel cope with the stresses of being uprooted in old age? and What role, if any, do network shifts from the country of origin to the host play in reducing stress and maintaining a sense of personal well-being?

Approximately 350,000 Soviet Jews migrated to Israel in the period from 1989 to 1991. To put this number in some perspective, only about 6,000 Soviet immigrants reached Israel in the seven preceding years (1981 to 1988). Litwin attributes the significant increase to three factors: (1) a loosening of restrictive Soviet policies regarding exit visas, (2) a tightening of U.S. policies with regard to Soviet emigrants, and (3) a changing of Israeli policies vis-à-vis absorption of new immigrants, which provided faster processing at the point of entry into the country and more immigrant choice in place of residence. Approximately 13 percent of those arriving in Israel between 1989 and 1991 were 65 years of age or over; 19 percent were 60 years or older. Most were European—that is, they were from the western republics of the Soviet Union—and over one-half were women (among the elderly, women made up closer to two-thirds of the group).

Litwin sampled 260 Soviet immigrants to Israel (1989 to 1991), between the ages of 62 and 92 years, from three disparate locations in the country: 100 from Jerusalem, and 80 each from Tel Aviv and two smaller municipalities in the southern region. Preimmigration and postimmigration networks were assessed in terms of size, number of intimates, duration of ties, frequency of contacts, and the content of support received from each network member, among a host of other measures. In general, immigrants reported that their social networks in Israel were smaller and showed reduced potential for support when compared to their networks in the Soviet Union, although "network changes were less predictive of well-being among elderly immigrants than were factors related to current network structure and support" (Litwin, 1995, p. 174).

Two measures of personal well-being—mental health and immigration satisfaction—could be predicted, in part, by different aspects of social networks. For example, the relationships between network variables and mental health (measured by a score on a depression screening scale) could be stated as follows: (1) The higher respondents' satisfaction with their current network, the less likely they were to report depressive symptoms; (2) the smaller the loss of available emotional support when compared with such support in the Soviet Union, the less likely respondents were to report depressive symptoms; and (3) the larger the size of the social network in Israel, the less likely respondents were to report depressive symptoms.

Litwin's study provides support for the influence of social networks in enhancing the well-being of older immigrants. Clearly, the content of network ties, and not just the existence of ties, is important in the lives of elderly immigrants. Exactly how does a social network enhance the well-being of an individual immigrant? Generally, as the literature has now established, social networks can serve to mitigate stress in a range of situations or to buffer the individual against relocation stress. In fact, Litwin suggests that *network mediation* may be especially useful in the early stages of adaptation to the new society. One example of this would involve community-based social workers reaching out to elderly immigrants and helping them to do *network construction*. In effect, through outreach and recruitment, social workers would be helping elderly immigrants find others with similar interests and concerns to form associations similar to self-help groups. One place in which such network construction could take place is in neighborhood-based senior centers.

Coping strategies generally take one of two forms: behavioral strategies and cognitive/emotional strategies. *Behavioral coping strategies* include a wide array of actions that individuals can employ to change or alleviate stress. Personal resources—including finances, health, education, and social supports—provide reserves or aids that individuals may draw on in a stressful situation. *Cognitive/emotional strategies* refer to ways in which individuals may employ social/psychological mechanisms to deal with stress. Clausen (1986) points out that, although coming to grips with a problem and finding ways of overcoming it tend to have more favorable consequences for the individual, researchers are beginning to learn that defensive maneuvers such as denial may be quite useful. Thus, Clausen suggests that denial of some deficits brought on by old age may be less problematic for the person than dwelling on those deficits about which nothing can be done.

Pearlin and Schooler (1978) have analyzed the coping strategies individuals employ when they face problems in four areas of life: marriage, parenthood, household economics, and occupational goals and activities. Three broad categories of coping responses were identified: (1) responses that modify situations, (2) responses that are used to reappraise the meaning of problems, and (3) responses that help individuals to manage tension. The researchers found that coping responses employed were often specific to an area of life. Reappraisal was the response of choice in the area of household economics, where changes in values or goals were required. In the areas of marriage or parenthood, direct action responses were seen as more valuable and effective.

Are specific coping skills or responses associated with old age? It is generally believed that, throughout adulthood, "individuals develop and refine a repertoire of workable coping strategies that are compatible with their personal dispositions and lifestyles" (George, 1980, p. 34). A number of researchers have put forth specific models of adjustment or adaptation in later life. Several of these are worthy of attention.

Lieberman and Tobin (Lieberman, 1975; Tobin & Lieberman, 1976) have examined adaptation to changes in living arrangements among older, impaired people. They suggest that change in residence causes *subjective* stress, experienced as a sense of loss, and *objective* stress, experienced as a disruption of customary behavior patterns. The elements of this conceptual model are depicted in Figure 8–1. The model begins with an assessment of personal resources and current functioning. Three adaptive outcomes are possible: (1) enhanced competence, in which functioning is improved after a crisis; (2) homeostasis, in which functioning is at the same level before and after a crisis; or (3) adaptive failure, in which functioning is impaired as a result of the crisis. The basic model was applied in four residential relocation studies. Across all the studies, 48 to 56 percent of the subjects experienced adaptive failure. The authors found the degree of environmental change generated by the relocation to be the most important predictor of adaptive outcome: The greater the change, the greater the decline in health or social or psychological functioning among the residents. Perceptions of stress, personal resources, and coping skills seem relatively irrelevant to the adjustment or adaptation process.

Residential relocation is only one event an individual experiences that requires adaptation to change. What if someone experiences other losses or events requiring change in addition to a necessary relocation? According to the *life events model of adaptation*, "The normal state of the individual is one of homeostasis and ... life events that require change are crises to the extent that they require time and energy to return to a steady state of functioning" (Whitbourne, 1985, p. 597). From this perspective, stress is a mediator between an event and adaptation to the event and therefore causes physical and psychological damage in direct proportion to the disruption of an individual's usual life routine. The life events scales have been used to research variation in the impact of events—including having children move out, death of a spouse, and illness—typically experienced by older adults. Age, sex, and socioeconomic status, as well as other personal and social

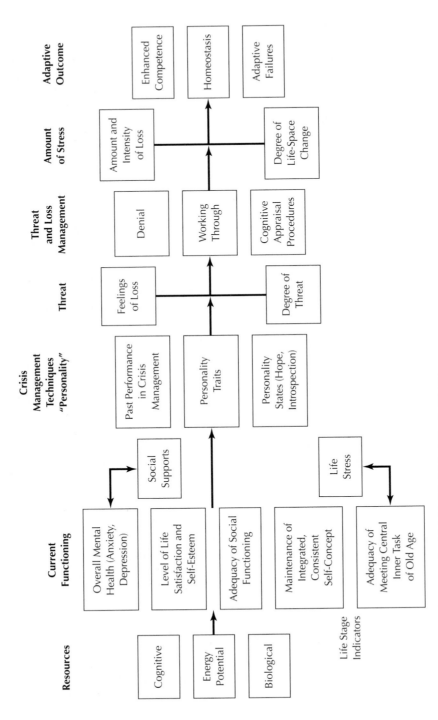

FIGURE 8–1 Lieberman and Tobin's Model of Adaptation to Life Crises

Source: "Adaptive Processes in Late Life" by M. Lieberman, 1975, in N. Datan & L. H. Ginsberg (Eds.), *Life-Span Development Psychology: Normative Life Crises.* New York: Academic Press. Copyright © 1975 by Academic Press, Inc. Reprinted by permission.

resources, have had a mediating role between such life changes and illness (e.g., Pearlin, 1980).

The Social Readjustment Rating Scale (SRRS) has become the basic tool for measuring stress of life events (Holmes & Rahe, 1967). It is a checklist of 43 events that have been rated with regard to their intensity and the length of time needed to accommodate them. Scores on the SRRS have generally correlated at a low to moderate level with physical illness and emotional disturbance. Whitbourne (1985) has itemized a series of criticisms of the life events approach, not the least of which has to do with whether life events have differing significance to individuals as they move through the life course.

According to Clausen (1986), the nearest approach to a theoretical statement of the importance of adaptation across the life course is given by Vaillant (1977). Vaillant's essential argument is, "If we are to master conflict gracefully and to harness instinctual striving creatively, our adaptive styles must mature." The devices people employ to protect themselves as children from painful experiences will not serve them well in adulthood. Mature ways of coping with unacceptable or painful feelings must be developed. Thus, each person can be expected to create a unique set of coping strategies to maximize personal happiness and effective functioning. Too little is known about the cumulative effects of stress and the costs and benefits of particular coping strategies employed across the life course.

SUMMARY

The life-course perspective is introduced and compared with life-stage and life-span developmental approaches. The life-course perspective concentrates on age-related transitions that are socially created, socially recognized, and shared. Life-course researchers emphasize the ways in which social norms and definitions influence the sequence of role changes in the life course.

All societies divide the lifetime into different periods. Typically, age criteria are used to place people into positions and roles. How many periods or age grades there are in a society may depend on its level of modernization.

Human behavior is primarily learned through a process of socialization. This is a lifelong process that involves transmitting skills and knowledge needed to perform social roles across the life course. The concept of social role describes the expectations society has for individuals who occupy a given social position or status. Is old age a social role in the United States? Some disagreement seems to exist on this point. Age is employed as a criterion for certain social roles, including employment and retirement. Age also influences the ideas people have about the appropriateness of certain behaviors.

In most societies, social role transitions are ordered along a timetable. The timing of these transitions changes as a function of cohort or historical effects. Role transitions can be stressful, although stresses may be reduced by anticipatory socialization and rites of passage. Keith argues that the most distinctive characteristics of rites of passage for older people in the United States is in their absence or incompleteness.

Being off time in taking on new roles or disengaging from old ones may create additional stresses. The source of such stress may be internal or external, personal or social. Several authors, however, offer evidence of the benefits of being off time.

Coping with transitions and adapting to them are important elements of the life course. There are various modes of defending against stressors and various strategies for coping, although generally these take one of two forms: behavioral or cognitive/emotional. Some coping strategies are problem specific.

Models of adaptation seem relatively primitive to date. Lieberman and Tobin emphasize the detriment associated with a single significant environmental change. The life-events approach emphasizes the aggregate effect of life changes. Vaillant argues for the need for coping strategies to develop or mature as one moves through the life course.

STUDY QUESTIONS

1. Distinguish the *life-course perspective* from the life-stage and life-span developmental approaches.

2. Define *socialization*. Why is early life-course socialization insufficient to prepare a person for the role and transitions of adulthood?

3. Freud and Piaget almost certainly did not use the concept of *social role*. Mead certainly did. Nevertheless, the three major theorists likely would have agreed on the importance of the concept. Why? What is the importance of the concept of social role?

4. Is old age a social role? How does age affect the social roles people occupy?

5. How are status changes in U.S. society made easier by *anticipatory socialization* and *rites of passage?* What does Keith argue is the most distinctive characteristic of rites of passage for old people in the United States. Why?

6. Provide several examples to show that the timing of role transitions is not static in the United States. How do such timing changes make it more difficult to assess the importance of being "on time" or "off time" in assuming new roles or exiting old ones?

7. Are specific coping skills associated with old age? What is the importance of environmental change in the Lieberman and Tobin work on adaptation during residential relocation?

8. What is the life-events model of adaptation? Do specific life events have the same importance whenever they occur in the life course? Explain your answer. What is Vaillant's view of change in adaptive styles through the life course?

REFERENCES

Baltes, P. B., & Goulet, L. R. (1970). Status and issues of a life-span developmental psychology. In L. R. Goulet & P. B. Baltes (Eds.), *Life-span developmental psychology.* New York: Academic Press.

Becker, H., Greer, B., Hughes, E. C., & Strauss, A. (1961). *Boys in white: Student culture in medical school.* Chicago: University of Chicago Press.

Berger, J., & Luckman, T. (1966). *The social construction of reality.* Garden City, NY: Doubleday.

Blau, Z. (1961). Structural constraints on friendships in old age. *American Sociological Review, 26,* 429–439.

Brim, O. G. (1968). Adult socialization. In J. A. Clausen (Ed.), *Socialization and society.* Boston: Little, Brown.

Bush, D. M., & Simmons, R. G. (1981). Socialization processes over the life course. In M. Rosenberg & R. H. Turner (Eds.), *Social psychology: Sociological perspectives.* New York: Basic Books.

Clausen, J. A. (1986). *The life course: A sociological perspective.* Englewood Cliffs, NJ: Prentice Hall.

Cowgill, D. O. (1986). *Aging around the world.* Belmont, CA: Wadsworth.

Foner, A., & Kertzer, D. (1978). Transitions over the life course. *American Journal of Sociology, 83,* 1081–1104.

Fox, R. C. (1957). Training for uncertainty. In R. K. Merton, G. Reader, & P. L. Kendall (Eds.), *The student-physician.* Cambridge, MA: Harvard University Press.

George, L. K. (1980). *Role transitions in later life.* Monterey, CA: Brooks/Cole.

Hagestad, G. D., & Neugarten, B. L. (1985). Age and the life course. In R. H. Binstock & E. Shanas (Eds.), *Handbook of aging and the social science* (2nd ed.). New York: Van Nostrand Reinhold.

Hess, B., Markson, E., & Stein, P. (1988). *Sociology* (3rd ed.). New York: Macmillan.

Holmes, T. H., & Rahe, R. H. (1967). The Social Readjustment Rating Scale. *Journal of Psychosomatic Research, 11,* 213–218.

Hughes, C. (1961). The concept and use of time in the middle years: The St. Lawrence Island Eskimo. In R. W. Kleemeier (Ed.), *Aging and leisure.* New York: Oxford University Press.

Ikels, C., Keith, J., Dickerson-Putnam, J., Draper, P., Fry, C., Glascock, A., & Harpending, H. (1992). Perceptions of the adult life course: A cross-cultural analysis. *Ageing and Society, 12* (1), 49–84.

Karp, D. A., & Yoels, W. C. (1982). *Experiencing the life cycle: A social psychology of aging.* Springfield, IL: Charles C. Thomas.

Keith, J. (1977). *Old people, new lives: Community creation in a retirement residence.* Chicago: University of Chicago Press.

Keith, J. (1982). *Old people as people: Social and cultural influences on aging and old age.* Boston: Little, Brown.

Levinson, D. J., Darro, C. M., Klein, E. B., Levinson, M. H. & McKee, B. (1974). The psychosocial development of men in early adulthood and the mid-life transition. In D. F. Ricks, A. Thomas, & M. Roth (Eds.), *Life history research in psychotherapy.* Minneapolis: University of Minnesota Press.

Lieberman, M. A. (1975). Adaptive processes in late life. In N. Datan & L. H. Ginsberg (Eds.), *Life-span developmental psychology: Normative life crises.* New York: Academic Press.

Linton, R. (1942). Age and sex categories. *American Sociological Review, 7,* 589–603.

Litwin, H. (1995). *Uprooted in old age: Soviet Jews and their social networks in Israel.* Westport, CT: Greenwood.

Mead, G. H. (1934). *Mind, self, and society.* Chicago: University of Chicago Press.

Nadel, S. F. (1952). Witchcraft in four African societies. *American Anthropologist, 54,* 18–29.

Neugarten, B. (1980, April). Acting one's age: New rules for the old. *Psychology Today,* pp. 66–74, 77–80.

Neugarten, B., & Hagestad, G. (1976). Age and the life course. In R. H. Binstock & E. Shanas (Eds.), *Handbook of aging and the social sciences.* New York: Van Nostrand Reinhold.

Nydegger, C. (1973, October). *Late and early fathers.* Paper presented at the annual meeting of the Gerontological Society, Miami Beach.

Pearlin, L. (1980). Life strains and psychological distress among adults. In N. J. Smelser & E. H. Erikson (Eds.), *Themes of work and love in adulthood.* Cambridge, MA: Harvard University Press.

Pearlin, L., & Schooler, C. (1978). The structure of coping. *Journal of Health and Social Behavior, 19,* 2–21.

Piaget, J. (1970). *Structuralism.* New York: Basic Books.

Piaget, J., & Inhelder, B. (1969). *The psychology of the child.* New York: Basic Books.

Rosow, I. (1974). *Socialization to old age.* Berkeley: University of California Press.

Roth, J. (1963). *Timetables.* Indianapolis: Bobbs-Merrill.

Sales, E. (1978). Women's adult development. In I. H. Frieze, J. E. Parsons, P. B. Johnson, D. N. Ruble, & G. L. Zellman (Eds.), *Women and sex-roles: A social psychological perspective.* New York: Norton.

Siegel, J., & Davidson, M. (1984). *Demographic and socioeconomic aspects of aging in the United States.* Current Population Reports, Special Studies Series P-23, No. 138. Washington, DC: U.S. Department of Commerce, Bureau of the Census.

Spanier, G. B., & Glick, P. C. (1980). The life cycles of American families: An expanded analysis. *Journal of Family History, 5* (1), 98–111.

Streib, G., & Schneider, C. J. (1971). *Retirement in American society: Impact and process.* Ithaca, NY: Cornell University Press.

Tobin, S., & Lieberman, M. A. (1976). *Last home for the aged.* San Francisco: Jossey-Bass.

Vaillant, G. (1977). *Adaptation to life.* Boston: Little, Brown.

Whitbourne, S. K. (1985). The psychological construction of the life span. In J. E. Birren & K. W. Schaie (Eds.), *Handbook of the psychology of aging* (2nd ed.) New York: Van Nostrand Reinhold.

Zerubavel, E. (1981). *Hidden rhythms: Schedules and calendars in social life.* Chicago: University of Chicago Press.

CHAPTER 9

SOCIOLOGICAL THEORIES OF AGING

The field of social gerontology has been criticized for its emphasis on practical issues and problems confronting the elderly. Many scholars believe that this concern, admirable as it may be, has grown at the expense of the development of statements of a theoretical orientation. As a result, these scholar-critics contend, no current comprehensive theoretical framework exists within which to address the question: What happens to human beings socially as they grow old?

This is not to say, however, that there have been no attempts to answer this important question. This chapter presents some answers—theoretical statements that have been placed in two broad categories: (1) theories that attempt to conceptualize the adjustment of individuals to their own aging and (2) theories that deal with the relationship between a society's social system and its older members. Some of these approaches show considerable overlap and often differ only in emphasis.

Readers may have difficulty identifying with the overconcern for theory expressed by gerontologists, perhaps because of a misunderstanding of theory. Most students think of theory as boring and not down to earth. But in fact, just the opposite is true. Theory is the way people accumulate knowledge and make sense of the world. It allows people to see more clearly and logically what they sometimes perceive only vaguely. Strictly speaking, theory differs from vague perception in that it is presented in the form of a generalized statement (or set of systematically organized statements) that can be tested through empirical research.

Theories are created to be rejected. A theory that, in principle, cannot be rejected is of little use because its acceptance must be on faith. However, a theory that is rejected advances the state of the art by reducing the number of possible answers by one. Those theories that survive the rejection process provide, for the present at least, the best answer to a question. In this regard, a theory is never really proven; the next empirical test might always disprove it.

Theorizing in social gerontology has a long way to go. Some of the theories examined in this chapter are not theories in the strictest sense. Few, for example, are presented in the form of a set of systematically organized statements. Some are more descriptive than explanatory and might more accurately be referred to as orientations or perspectives rather than theories. None has been sufficiently tested so as to be completely rejected. Each suggests some important factor or set of factors that may be related to aging. In doing so, the theories act as continuing guides to further research. The continuation of such research increases the potential for theory building in social gerontology.

AGING AND THE INDIVIDUAL

Role Theory

The earliest attempt in social gerontology to understand the adjustment of the aged individual was placed within a role-theory framework (Cottrell, 1942). Generally speaking, research done within this framework was concerned with the consequences of role change among older people. The changes individuals undergo in the aging process fall into two categories: (1) the relinquishment of social relationships and roles typical of adulthood and (2) their replacement by retirement and the acceptance of social relationships typical of the later years, such as dependency on offspring (Cavan et al., 1949). The special dilemma of role change for older people is that they are more likely to lose roles than to acquire new ones. Further, these losses, such as the loss of the worker role with retirement, are largely irreversible and may lead to erosion of social identity and decline in self-esteem (Rosow, 1985).

In an example of empirical research carried out within the role-theory framework, Phillips (1957) has shown the relationship between role loss and adjustment to old age. In his study of almost 1,000 individuals aged 60 and over, he found significantly more maladjustment to old age in the retired when compared with the employed, in the widowed when compared with the married, and in people over age 70 when compared with those aged 60 to 69. Maladjustment is measured by self-reports on the amount of time spent daydreaming about the past, thinking about death, and being absentminded.

Another important variable used by Phillips is labeled *identification as old*. This item, a measure of self-image, simply asks, "How do you think of yourself as far as age goes—middle-aged, elderly, old?" Individuals who perceive themselves as elderly or old are significantly more maladjusted than are those who perceive themselves as middle-aged. In addition, age identification appears to reverse the relationship between role loss and maladjustment. Thus, for example, those who are employed but identify themselves as old are more likely to be maladjusted than are those who are retired but identify with middle age. The means by which some elderly individuals, even those who have suffered role loss, identify with middle age are still open to empirical investigation.

Recently, several researchers have looked at the relationship between sex roles and life satisfaction in old age. Sex-role differentiation has traditionally been quite strong in U.S. society. Men are expected to be aggressive and independent, whereas women are expected to be passive-dependent and nurturant. Sinnott (1977), after reviewing many studies on middle and old age, came to the conclusion that survival and satisfaction in old age often accompany flexibility in sex roles.

Reichard, Livson, and Peterson (1962) studied how 87 men between the ages of 55 and 84 adjusted to aging. The best adjusted exhibited personalities *not* dominated by male traits. Reichard and colleagues concluded that growing old may make it possible for a man to integrate formerly unacceptable feminine traits (e.g., nurturance) into his personality. Their research shows that those best able to make the integration are rewarded by a more successful old age. Similarly, Neugarten and associates (Neugarten, Crotty, & Tobin, 1964) found older men and women who were the most satisfied with life to be those who had best achieved an integration of traits culturally defined as masculine with traits culturally defined as feminine.

While studying the structure of self-concept, Monge (1975) found certain continuities as well as discontinuities across the life cycle. Over 4,000 male and female subjects, aged 9 to 89 and recruited from diverse sources, rated the concept "My Characteristic Self" on 21 polar adjective pairs (e.g., leader/follower or strong/weak). Four factors emerged for all age groups: (1) achievement/leadership; (2) congeniality/sociability; (3) adjustment (the self-perception of health and energy); and (4) masculinity/femininity. Figure 9–1 shows the mean component scores for these four factors by age group and sex. Monge's results suggest that as men and women become older they become more *androgynous*—more alike and, perhaps, more accepting of traits of the opposite sex in themselves.

For example, as Figure 9–1b depicts, congeniality/sociability is higher at all points in the life span for women than for men, although both show a decrease at midlife and a subsequent increase in later adulthood. Importantly, men and women are most alike in terms of mean scores on this factor (and all others) in old age. The increase in late adulthood, steeper in men, may reflect the lifting of certain burdens of concern in the area of work responsibilities, which may allow more time for social interaction.

Clearly, more research on sex-role change across the life course needs to be carried out. In particular, we need to learn more about the blurring of sex roles in old age. Some of the aforementioned research suggests that certain aspects of sex-role identification may be less integral to adult personality in later life than in early adulthood.

Activity Theory

One theory of aging related to role theory has appeared implicitly in much gerontological research. This theory, referred to here as *activity theory* but often called the

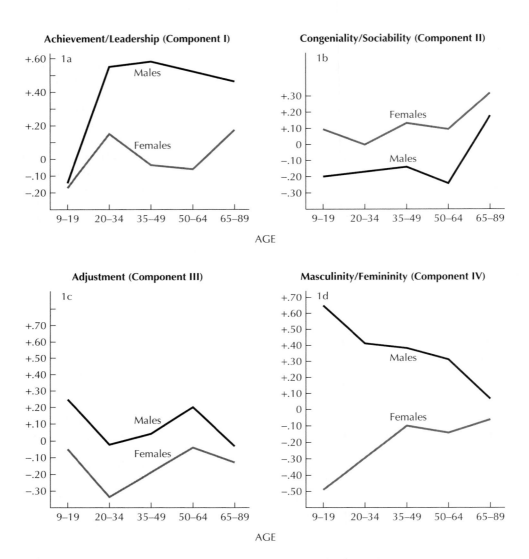

FIGURE 9–1   Factors of Self-Concept across the Adult Life Span: Mean Component Scores on Four Components by Age Group and Sex

Source: Monge, R. H. (1975). "Structure of the Self-Concept from Adolescence through Old Age." *Experimental Aging Research, 1*(2), 281–291. © Beech Hill Publishing Company (formerly EAR, Inc.).

implicit theory of aging, states that there is a positive relationship between activity and life satisfaction. The theory holds that, although aging individuals face inevitable changes related to physiology, anatomy, and health status, their psychological and social needs remain essentially the same. Those who adopt this view recognize that the social world may withdraw from older people, making it more difficult for them to fulfill these needs. Yet, the person who ages optimally is the one who stays active and manages to resist the withdrawal of the social world (Havighurst, 1968). According to activity theory, the individual who is able to maintain the activities of the middle years for as long as possible will be well adjusted and satisfied with life in the later years. This person will find an avocation to substitute for work and will replace the old friends and loved ones who have died with new ones.

Lemon, Bengtson, and Peterson (1972) attempted a formal and explicit test of the activity theory. Using a sample of 411 potential in-movers to a southern California retirement community, and distinguishing among informal activity (with friends, relatives, and neighbors), formal activity (participation in voluntary organizations), and solitary activity (maintenance of household), they found that only social activity with friends was significantly related to life satisfaction. Knapp's (1977) study of 51 elderly people residing in the south of England lends support to these findings. Within this sample, there was a strong positive relationship between "the number of hours spent in a typical week with friends and relatives (informal activity)" and life satisfaction. In addition, several measures of formal activity were also found to be strongly related to life satisfaction.

Longino and Kart (1982) report on the results of a formal replication of the work on activity theory carried out by Lemon and colleagues. Using probability samples from three distinct types of retirement communities ($N = 1,209$), they found support for the positive contribution made by informal activity to the life satisfaction of respondents. Interestingly, they observed formal activity to have a *negative* effect on life satisfaction. Longino and Kart speculate that participation in formal activities may damage self-concept and lower morale through the development of status systems that tend to emerge in formal activity settings. Invidious comparisons that can lead to dissatisfaction are less likely to operate in primary relationships with family and friends than in secondary ones limited to formal organizational settings.

Activity theory is often presented in juxtaposition with the disengagement theory of aging (which will be discussed later). Such a presentation leads to comparison of the theories and often causes students to overlook problems that may be internal to the theory. There are several theoretical problems inherent in the activity approach that deserve some mention here.

First, the activity perspective assumes that individuals have a great deal of control over their social situations. It assumes that people have the capacity to construct—or, more appropriately, reconstruct—their lives by substituting new roles for lost ones. Clearly, this may be the case for the upper-middle-class individual whose locus of control has always been internal and whose social and economic resources allow for such reconstruction. But the retired individual who suffers a dramatic decline in income, or the widow who faces an equally dramatic decline in her social relationships, may find it difficult, even with sufficient motivation, to substitute an avocation for work or to replace old friends and loved ones who have died. In this regard, the theory may be revealing more about the relationships among socioeconomic status, life-style, health, and well-being, than about the relationship between activity and life satisfaction.

Second, the activity perspective emphasizes the stability of psychological and social needs through the adult phases of the life cycle. This makes considerable sense if one thinks about these needs developing in a stable social and physical environment. But what about the person whose environment changes at a particular age—for example, when he or she retires, is deprived of status, or is widowed? Might this individual's social and psychological needs change in the face of the substantial change in environment? Many would answer yes. A no answer smacks of a biological and/or psychological determinism, which many social scientists (including gerontologists) find unacceptable. And what of the fate of older people who cannot maintain the standards of middle age or cannot adjust to substantial changes in the environment? Activity theory offers little about what happens to these people.

Finally, an important problem in activity theory is the expectation that activities *of any kind* can substitute for lost involvement in work, marriage, and parenting. Weiss (1969), in his study of the Parents Without Partners (PWP) organization, dubbed this the "fund of sociability" hypothesis. According to this idea, people require a certain *quantity* of interaction with others and may achieve this in a variety of ways—through one or two intense relationships or perhaps through a larger number of lesser relationships. Weiss was not able to substantiate this hypothesis. He found that the "sociability" that accrued to a person through participation in the PWP organization did not necessarily compensate for the marital loss. This suggests that substitutability for different losses may be governed by different considerations. Filling a particular role may not do. Fulfillment of those particular needs may be accomplished only through specific role substitution or, perhaps, through the alteration of a person's entire configuration of roles. Whichever is the case, the emphasis here is on the quality rather than the quantity of such interaction.

Disengagement Theory

Disengagement theory, put forth by Cumming and Henry (1961), stands in contrast to role theory and activity theory. The authors used data based on 275 respondents ranging in age from 50 to 90, all of whom resided in Kansas City and were physically and financially self-sufficient. The authors characterized the decreasing social interaction they observed to come with old age as a *mutual withdrawal* between the aging individual and others in the social system to which he or she belongs. Under the terms of the disengagement theory, the aging individual accepts—perhaps even desires—the decrease in interaction. In addition, proponents of this theory argue that gradual disengagement is functional for society, which would otherwise be faced with disruption by the sudden withdrawal of its members. As Cumming has stated it:

The disengagement theory postulates that society withdraws from the aging person to the same extent as the person withdraws from society. This is, of course, just another way of saying that the process is normatively governed and in a sense agreed upon by all concerned. (1963)

In its original form, the disengagement theory was concerned with the modal case in the United States. Important disengagements included the departure of children from families and retirement for men or widowhood for women. It was not concerned with nonmodal cases—early widowhood or late retirement—nor was it concerned with the special effects of poverty or illness. In 1963, Elaine Cumming, one of the originators of disengagement theory, published a paper in which she discussed the relationship between personality (or what she called "temperament") and disengagement. She wrote that all people have a style of adaptation to the environment, and went on to identify two different modes of interacting with the environment: the impinging mode and the selecting mode. The *impinger* is an activist, willing to try out his or her style of adaptation on others, whereas the *selector* is more measured in his or her ways. Each may react differently to disengagement. As Cumming describes it, the impinger's judgment may not be as good as it was, but he is likely to be viewed as an unusual person for his age.

Ultimately, as he becomes less able to control the situations he provokes, he may suffer anxiety and panic through failure both to arouse and to interpret appropriate reactions. His problem in old age will be to avoid confusion. (1963)

The selector can be expected to be more measured in his or her ways. As a youth, this individual may have appeared to others as withdrawn. With age, this style seems more appropriate. "In old-age, because of his reluctance to generate interaction, he may, like a neglected infant, develop a kind of marasmus. His foe will be apathy rather than confusion" (Cumming, 1963).

Finally, in summarizing the disengagement theory, it is useful to point out that, in the initial presentation of the theory, Cumming and Henry (1961) argued that the process of disengagement was both *inevitable* and *universal*. All social systems, if they were to maintain successful equilibrium, would necessarily disengage from the elderly. Disengagement was seen as a prerequisite to social stability. Older people could be released from societal expectations that they work and be productive. Presumably, they would adapt by participating in satisfying family relationships and friendships. "When a middle-aged, fully engaged person dies, he leaves many broken ties, and disrupted situations. Disengagement thus frees the old to die without disrupting vital affairs" (Cumming, 1963, pp. 384–385).

The disengagement theory has generated much critical discussion. Many have found the theory wanting and indefensible, whereas others defend it quite strenuously. Through the 1960s and 1970s, most research efforts were unable to offer empirical support to the theory. Youmans (1967) found that a sample of the rural elderly did not, in general, experience disengagement. Palmore (1968) interviewed 127 individuals whose average age was 78. He found little to support the notion that disengagement necessarily increases with age. Others' research has suggested possible modifications on the disengagement theme. For example, Tallmer and Kutner (1970) found that physical and social stress, rather than aging per se, often produces disengagement. Atchley's (1971) study of emeritus professors showed that individuals could disengage socially without psychological disengagement. This suggests that the extent to which a person disengages may be a function of that individual's occupation or position in the community. Thus, a retired college professor may continue to be involved in the intellectual issues in his or her field of study, while a retired construction worker may not have similar opportunities to remain professionally involved.

The controversy surrounding disengagement continues. Hochschild (1975) has examined the theory and found three problems that she believes continue to fire the controversy. First, Hochschild argues that the disengagement theory allows no possibility for counterevidence. She points out that in their original work, entitled *Growing Old*, Cumming and Henry (1961) offered four types of "back-door" explanations to handle cases that did not fit the theory. These types included "unsuccessful" disengagers, those whose disengagement was "off schedule," exceptional individuals who had reengaged, and those who were offered as examples of "variation in the form" of disengagement.

Second, the major variables in the theory—age and disengagement—turn out to be "umbrella" variables, which are divisible into numerous other promising variables. Earlier, reference was made to one study that distinguished between social and psychological disengagement. Carp (1969) distinguishes among types of social disengagement, including disengagement from family, friends, social activities, and material possessions. Similarly, in discussing psychological disengagement, one could differentiate among personal adjustment, ego energy, affect intensity, mastery, and so on. As Hochschild points out, one consequence of this continual fission is that theoretical propositions that once appeared quite simple grow into something much more complex.

Third, the disengagement theory essentially ignores the aging person's own view of aging and disengagement. Behavior that looks like disengagement to the observer may have a completely different meaning for the aging person. Based on his exploratory study of retirement among 99 English couples, Crawford (1971) advances three types of meaning that men attribute to retirement: retiring *back to* something, retiring *from* something, and retiring *for* something. In the first and third types, men view their retirement in terms of continued engagement with new involvements—in the latter case, discarding past obligations to work and building a new social life outside of work; in the former, giving up work and returning to the family. Despite the objective disengagement (retirement), the men attribute different meanings to the event.

One assumption inherent in disengagement has not come under much scrutiny, perhaps because it is supportive of stereotypes about the productive capacities of older people. This assumption is that older people's withdrawal from productive roles is necessarily good for society. How can it be good for society to deprive the workplace of the skills, knowledge, and experience held by older workers? How can it be better for society to encourage people to retire early and begin collecting their pensions than to encourage people to stay in the workplace and continue paying into the Social Security Trust Fund and other public and private pensions systems?

Until the last decade or so, the activity and disengagement perspectives dominated the theoretical discussion in social gerontology, but several alternative perspectives have recently been put forth. Four somewhat related theories that deserve mention are the continuity theory, socioenvironmental theory, exchange theory of aging, and symbolic interactionism. None of the four has as yet received the research attention required for determining its explanatory power.

Continuity Theory

Continuity theory holds that middle-aged and older adults make adaptive choices in an effort to preserve ties with their own past experiences (Atchley, 1989). Continuity is a subjective phenomenon and can be internal, external, or both. *Internal continuity* requires memory and is tied to "a remembered inner structure, such as the persistence of a psychic structure of ideas, temperament, affect, experiences, preferences, dispositions, and skills" (Atchley, 1989, p. 184). Pressures and attractions that move people toward internal continuity include the importance of cognitive continuity for maintaining mastery and competence, a sense of ego integrity, and self-esteem. Also, people can be motivated toward internal continuity as an appropriate means of meeting basic human needs for food, shelter, clothing, and social interaction with others.

External continuity involves memory of the physical and social environments of one's past, including role relationships and activities. Older people may be motivated toward external continuity by the expectations of others; the desire for predictable social support; or the need to cope with physical and mental health changes as well as changes in social roles involving the empty nest, widowhood, or retirement (Atchley, 1989).

According to Atchley (1989), individuals classify the degree of continuity in their lives into three general categories: too little, optimum, and too much. When individuals perceive that life is unpredictable or discontinuous, too little continuity can be said to be present. Presumably, too little continuity leads to low satisfaction with life and difficulty in adapting to changing conditions. Change may be so severe and unpredictable that previous skills, personal strategies, and social experiences are of little use in adapting.

The older adult assumes optimum continuity when the pace of change is consistent with personal preferences and societal demands, and is in line with a person's capacity to cope with the change. In such a case, an individual's personality, prior preferences, role relationships, and social experiences serve them well in adjusting to change.

The older adult who characterizes his or her life as having too much continuity is describing a life that is uncomfortably predictable. Previously used strategies are adequate, but life is perceived as having a sameness of quality absent new and enriching experiences.

Continuity theory has intuitive appeal. Clearly, however, additional work must be carried out to validate all or parts of the theory. Some limitations of the theory seem evident, even in advance of needed empirical research. For example, are earlier stages of development in the life course the standard for old age? Can life-styles observed in old age ever be an appropriate response to growing old, or must they always reflect continuity of lifelong patterns? As was already described in discussing the role theory of aging, some studies suggest that satisfaction in old age comes from flexibility in sex roles and being able to integrate formally unacceptable traits into personality. What about previous life-style patterns that were maladaptive? Does continuity theory require their continuation? Can people free themselves from social roles and behaviors they disliked (Fox, 1981–82)? Also, continuity theory, as presented by Atchley, focuses almost uniformly on the individual and his or her social relationships with others. Are there structural factors that may constrain or prevent continuity, or even enhance it?

Socioenvironmental Theory

Socioenvironmental theory directs itself at understanding the effects of the immediate social and physical environment on the activity patterns of aged individuals. The chief proponent of this theory is Jaber Gubrium (1973, 1975). Although other gerontologists have clearly concerned themselves with the environments of old people, Gubrium concerns himself with the meaning old people place on life and with the effect different physical and social contexts may have on that meaning. This approach is based on the understanding that people respond to the social meaning of events rather than to some absolute aspect of these events. Moreover, the responses of persons to the same event might easily be different if the social meaning placed on the event by one varies from the meaning placed on that event by the other.

According to Gubrium (1973), two factors that affect the meaning old people place on events—and thus their interaction patterns—are the physical proximity of other persons and the age homogeneity of an environment. A substantial body of literature supports the importance of these two variables in affecting social interaction among both young and old. For example, Rosow's (1967) seminal work on elderly people in Cleveland shows that old people residing in apartment buildings with a high concentration of aged people were more likely to develop friendships with neighbors than was the case for old people residing in buildings with a low concentration of elderly.

A number of studies show the relationship between age homogeneity and friendship patterns. Bultena and Wood (1969) found that with a population of elderly retired males, friendships occurred primarily among persons of the same age.

Messer (1967) found that elderly people in age-homogeneous public housing projects in Chicago interacted more frequently than did elderly persons living in age-heterogeneous settings.

On the basis of the possible contributions of the two variables, physical proximity and age homogeneity, Gubrium (1973) developed a typology of social contexts, each of which, he suggests, has differential impact on social interaction. The four types of social context are as follows:

Type I: Age *homogeneous, close* physical proximity
Type II: Age *heterogeneous, close* physical proximity
Type III: Age *homogeneous, distant* physical proximity
Type IV: Age *heterogeneous, distant* physical proximity

Socioenvironmental theory posits that Type I social contexts have the highest degree of age concentration and are thus quite conducive to social interaction. Residential apartment buildings for the elderly are the Type I variety. Individuals living in such environments hold age-linked behavior expectations for each other. Type IV social contexts are the least age concentrated and offer reduced opportunity for initiating interaction. These social contexts include age-heterogeneous neighborhoods of single homes. Type II contexts, represented by age-heterogeneous apartment buildings, and Type III contexts, represented by retirement communities commonly found in Florida and California, fall between Types I and IV in terms of their conduciveness to social interaction.

Of utmost importance to the socioenvironmental theory is the recognition that different social contexts generate different sets of activity norms for aged people. To the extent such norms place behavioral demands on individuals, it becomes clear that different social contexts place different demands on the elderly. Gubrium suggests that individuals who have the resources (health, financial solvency, and social support) to meet the demands of the environment will show high morale and self-satisfaction. Incongruence between environmental expectations and activity resources leads to low morale and diminished life satisfaction.

Exchange Theory

An abundance of gerontological literature has consistently shown that older Americans receive regular support from family, friends, and neighbors in carrying out activities of daily living (Shanas, 1979; Stoller & Earl, 1983; Sussman, 1976). This support may be task oriented, meaning help with housework, shopping, transportation, and the like. Support may also take the form of social or emotional assistance provided in times of stress or illness. This literature also reminds the reader that older people may themselves be support providers, helping family members or neighbors deal with instrumental or emotional problems (Riley & Foner, 1968; Sussman, 1976).

Informal helping or social support networks, especially those that involve a "reciprocal flow of valued behavior between the participants" (Emerson, 1976), may easily be placed within an exchange approach to social interaction. Such an approach views social interaction as governed by rules of fairness or justice. Gouldner (1960) identified one rule of exchange as the "norm of reciprocity." According to him, this norm establishes a set of reciprocal demands and obligations that lend stability to social systems. One component of the norm of reciprocity is that "people should help those who have helped them" (Gouldner, 1960, p. 171).

Gouldner recognized that the norm of reciprocity requiring an exchange of good for good is not the only rule regulating social interaction. In fact, he proposed what could be described as a norm of beneficence, which requires that individuals help others as necessary without thought to what the others have done or can do in return. Gouldner is not alone in recognizing that such nonrational impulses are important components of the broader social intercourse. Almost by definition, there are groups in society who are identified by their incapacity to engage in strict exchange. The mentally disabled may represent one such group. For many of them, beneficence supersedes reciprocity as the prevailing norm.

Dowd (1984) has suggested that in one's relations with the very old, the requirements of reciprocity may have been superseded by those of beneficence. This shift, he argues, results from a redefinition of age strata that itself has emerged from a need to reallocate scarce policy resources in the society at large. In effect, Dowd believes that the norm of reciprocity will still apply to young-old people who receive in social policy terms what is perceived to be something in balance with the value of their current social worth. Policy treatment of the very old, Dowd expects, will be regulated by a principle of beneficence—every person or household will receive as much as is needed, to a limit, regardless of the value attached to their current social worth.

Homans (1958, 1974) suggests another rule of exchange. He argues that social exchange is governed by a *rule of distributive justice.* This rule is defined in terms of the relationship between actors' rewards and costs: The greater the costs, the greater the rewards. Actors are seen as trying to strike a balance, or achieve proportionality, in social exchange. Homans indicates, "Persons that give much to others try to get much from them, and persons that get much from others are under pressure to give much to them. This process of influence tends to work out at equilibrium to balance in the exchanges." According to Homans, when individuals experience imbalance or distributive injustice, when they give more than they get (or get more than they give), they are offended and experience dissatisfaction.

Dowd (1975, 1978, 1980) attempts to place aging within an exchange framework. He believes that the problems of the aged in twentieth-century industrial societies are in reality problems of decreasing power. Dowd argues that in social exchanges between the aged and society, the aged gradually lose power until all that is left is the capacity to comply. The shift in balance of power between the aged and society reflects the economic and social dependency of the elderly. More than any other event, the phenomenon of retirement seems to exemplify this decline in power. The worker who once exchanged his or her skill for wages must comply with retirement in exchange for pension and health care benefits.

Kart and Longino (1987) carried out what they believe to be a definitive test of distributive justice within the context of aged social exchange networks. In 1977, 1,346 persons residing in diverse settings were interviewed in the Social Security Administration's Midwestern Retirement Community Study (Longino, 1980). Respondents were asked to list all the people who were important in their lives, up to as many as 15 persons. The respondents were then asked what each of these persons did on a more or less regular basis that the respondent really appreciated. Next, the relationship was reversed, and the respondents were asked what they themselves did for each person on the list, on an ongoing basis, that was important to the latter.

Students of social support research have suggested that many researchers emphasize the *amount* of support at the expense of the *types* of support being received and given (Thoits, 1982). Thus, supportive activities, given and received, were coded into one of three possible categories: emotional, social, and instrumental. In addition, each individual was assigned a score based on responses to 13 items drawn from the Life Satisfaction Scale B (Neugarten, Havighurst, & Tobin, 1961). Finally, each respondent was asked to summarize his or her relationships in terms of how obligated the respondent felt generally toward others.

Initially, Kart and Longino (1987) examined the amount of support given and received as they separately predicted life satisfaction and feelings of obligation. The amount of support the respondent *received,* as well as the support *given,* regardless of type, had little apparent effect on feelings of obligation to others. Correlations between the support measures and life satisfaction showed a different pattern. Low inverse correlations were present between all types of support given, emotional and social support received, and life satisfaction. Thus, the more support given *or* received, the lower the life satisfaction.

The reciprocal supportive relationship between the respondent and each primary relation was also examined. Within each support type, a ratio of support given to support received was calculated. The retirement community residents, as a whole, had a ratio above 1.0 for each type of support, indicating that they tended to receive more support than they gave. The associations between support ratios and feelings of obligation, however, were weak to nonexistent, nor did the reciprocal imbalance seem to affect the level of life satisfaction.

Kart and Longino (1987) conclude that, when actual reciprocal exchange relationships are examined, the exchange paradigm does not operate as straightforwardly between older people and those significant to them as other exchange theorists might have predicted (e.g., see Dowd, 1978). Only the support *given* by older respondents in their primary relationships seems to be systematically and inversely related to life satisfaction. Even here, the correlations were quite modest by any standard. One conclusion to draw from these empirical results is quite simply that the exchange theory fails to explain the relationship between support systems and the well-being or life satisfaction of older persons. Of course, leaping to such a conclusion may be similar to throwing out the baby with the bath water. Ward (1985) points out that the literature on the contributions of support systems to well-being in later life is equivocal. For example, Conner, Powers, and Bultena (1979) found that both the number and frequency of social ties were unrelated to life satisfaction among the elderly. Ward, Sherman, and Lagory (1984) reported only a weak relationship between access to instrumental and expressive supports (through involvement with kin, friends, and neighbors) and overall morale.

When attempting to explain the contributions of social support systems to the life satisfaction of older people, the exchange theory makes good sociological as well as intuitive sense. In part, this is because it dovetails nicely with at least two other long-standing sociological traditions that address the relationship between social support and feelings of well-being. Both symbolic interactionism (to be discussed) and Durkheimian anomie theory posit that social interaction with others can provide a basis for psychological good feeling (Thoits, 1982). One advantage of formalizing theory is that it facilitates replication and reformulation by other researchers. More seems to be gained at this point by encouraging additional replications and reformulations of exchange theory in a gerontological context than by premature rejection of the theory.

Symbolic Interactionism

According to Herbert Blumer (1969), the theoretical framework known as *symbolic interactionism* is based on the premise that people behave toward objects (including other people) according to perceptions and meanings developed through social interaction. From this perspective, individuals are seen as conscious actors in the world who adapt to situations and events on the basis of the perceptions and meanings they have constructed for these situations and events. It is important to note that perceptions and meanings are not constructed in a vacuum. Rather, as Blumer points out, they arise out of social interaction with others:

> Human beings in interacting with one another have to take account of what each is doing or is about to do; they are forced to direct their own conduct or handle their situations in terms of what they take into account. Thus, the activities of others enter as positive factors in the formation of their own conduct; in the face of actions of others one may abandon an intention or purpose, revise it, check or suspend it, intensify it, or replace it. The actions of others enter to set what one plans to do, may oppose or prevent such plans, may require a revision of such plans, and may demand a very different set of such plans. One has to *fit* one's own line of activity in some manner to the actions of others. (1969, p. 8)

The importance of social interaction cannot be exaggerated for the symbolic interactionist. The emphasis in this theoretical perspective is on the human capacity for *socially* constructing reality.

In recent years, symbolic interactionism has been seen as having important implications for the study of aging. At one level, it may provide a basis for understanding how older people perceive and assign meaning to the experience of old age in U.S. society (or in any other society, for that matter). Ward (1984), for example, sees symbolic interactionism as essential to recognizing the importance of change in the social and symbolic worlds of the aging. He argues that role losses, residential mobility, health problems, and other age-related changes pull the elderly from familiar groups and situations. Thus, they may become alienated from past worlds and identities and, at the same time, be granted the potential for new worlds and new identities. This creates the possibility of satisfying personal change and growth, but also may result in stress, marginality, and unhappiness (Ward, 1984, p. 360).

Spence (1986) has explored the implications of the symbolic interactionist perspective for understanding developmental issues of later life. From his view, this perspective is unique because it emphasizes the subjective and focuses on process and change in identity as one develops. Where one is going is secondary to the processes of getting there (Spence, 1986). Marshall (1979) has applied the symbolic interactionist perspective to aging through his use of the concept of *status passage*. To speak of aging as a status passage is to suggest the image of an individual negotiating a passage from one age-based status to another (and, perhaps, to others), finally coming to the end of the passage through life, at death.

A status passage may have both an objective as well as a subjective reality. Objectively, any status passage can be defined in terms of a series of dimensions, including physical or social time and space; duration; and the extent to which it is desirable or undesirable, inevitable or optional, voluntary or involuntary. Subjectively, as Marshall indicates, awareness of any of these properties of the passage may vary. Thus, people may differ in their degree of awareness that they are even undergoing a passage. For the symbolic interactionist, the objective and subjective dimensions of the status passage set the parameters within which the lives of individuals (in this context, aging individuals) will be shaped by themselves. The degree of control over the passage becomes of central importance for aging persons. This is particularly true for this status passage because, unlike others, it offers no exit from the passage except through death. Other passages in life involve preparation for something to come. Here, however, the passage is all there is. As Marshall indicates, "No future lies beyond the passage, only the passage and its termination become relevant" (1979).

One theme of this status passage, according to Marshall, is that preparation for death involves the attempt to make sense of death itself and to make sense of one's life. This theme appears in psychoanalytic theory and in Butler's concept of *life review* (see Chapter 7). An important difference for symbolic interactionists is their recognition that control over one's own biography involves reconstruction of the past through reminiscence. Marshall (1979) argues that this process is most successful when it is conducted socially. Unfortunately, as Marshall sees it, socializing agents—such as institutional settings (including hospitals, nursing homes, retirement communities)—may severely threaten an aged person's ability to maintain control of the status passage. Too often, status passage control becomes a dilemma for the aging individual who must choose between allowing others to shape his or her passage, on the one hand, and isolation on the other. This decision is most obvious in cases where others employ criteria for desired behavior that contradict the attempts of the aging person to maintain personal control (Marshall, 1979).

Much more empirical research must be done to determine fully the utility of the symbolic interactionist paradigm in social gerontology. Still, one can be optimistic about any framework that suggests that older people retain the human capacity to construct and share meanings and the human tendency to attempt to maintain control over their own lives.

AGING AND SOCIETY
The Subculture of the Aging

In an attempt to clarify the nature of relations between older persons and the rest of society, Rose (1965) offers the concept of an *aged subculture.* A subculture may develop when particular members of a society interact with each other significantly more than they do with others in the society. This pattern of interaction develops when group members have common backgrounds and interests and/or are excluded from interaction with other population groups in the society. Rose believes that both circumstances exist for the large proportion of older people in U.S. society.

In addition, Rose outlines a variety of demographic, ecological, and social organizational trends that contribute to the development of an aged subculture. These include the growing number and proportion of persons who live beyond the age of 65; the self-segregation of older persons in inner cities and rural areas (caused by migration patterns of the young); the decline in employment of older people; and the development of social services designed to assist older people. Each of these trends either improves the opportunities for older people to identify with each other or separates them from the rest of society.

Rose recognizes that not all the distinctive behavior of the elderly can be attributed to the aged subculture. Biological changes, society's expectations for the elderly, and generational differences in socialization all contribute to making the elderly more segregated from other age categories than is true for the rest of society.

What of the content of this aged subculture? According to Rose, the status system among the elderly is only partially a carryover from that of the general society. Wealth carries over from the general culture, as do occupational prestige, achievement, and education, although with some lessening in importance. Physical and mental health and social activity, usually accepted as a given by younger people, have special value in conferring status among the elderly.

What are the consequences of the development of an aged subculture? Rose discusses two areas: aging self-conception and aging group consciousness. Rose argues that many Americans suffer a change in self-conception as they grow older, largely as a consequence of the negative evaluation of old age in U.S. culture. Unfortunately, the development of an aged subculture does not necessarily combat this negative evaluation. Rather, it may simply facilitate identification as old. This is a negative consequence of the development of an aged subculture. On the positive side, development of an aged subculture may stimulate a group identification and consciousness, with potential for social action. Rose envisioned older people becoming a voting bloc that exerts political power either within the existing political party structures or on its own.

Despite some debate in the gerontological literature about whether or not the elderly fit a traditional definition of a subculture (Streib, 1965), the notion of an aged subculture has served as a useful descriptive guide to the relationship between older persons and U.S. society. Nevertheless, its predictive power generally has been found wanting (Hendricks & Hendricks, 1986). However, one research team has attempted to test Rose's aged subculture hypothesis. Longino, McClelland, and Peterson (1980) compared elderly residents of eight midwestern retirement communities (five age-segregated residential settings and three age-concentrated neighborhoods) with a shadow sample of elderly respondents drawn from a national survey of public attitudes toward older Americans (National Council on Aging, 1976). The shadow sample involved a random selection of older people in such a way as to replicate or shadow the characteristics of residents of the retirement communities. For example, for every widowed African American woman over age 75 with an elementary school education and living on less than $2,000 a year in a retirement community, a person with the same profile was placed in the shadow sample. Comparisons were made using measures of social participation, preferences for age-based interaction, general perceptions of elders, and self-conception.

The study provided partial support for Rose's subculture of aging theory. On the whole, residents of the retirement communities show a distinctive pattern of responses to the measures of comparison employed. In matters of social participation, differences show up more in quality than quantity. The social life of retirement community residents appears no more strenuous than elsewhere, but residents find this level of activity more satisfying. Problems of feeling lonely and bored and not feeling needed seem easier to avoid in retirement communities than in more age-integrated settings. The self-conceptions of retirement community residents are mixed. Although the residents tend to have significantly greater self-regard than do their shadow samples in judging their own characteristics, they do not surpass shadow sample respondents in judging themselves as useful members of their communities. Community residents are also significantly more likely to say that older people get just the right amount of respect, or even too much. In effect, this suggests that retirement community residents see themselves in less positive terms than they think society sees them. Finally, according to the authors of this study, evidence for the development of an aging group political consciousness, at least as Rose envisioned it, was nowhere to be found.

Although Longino, McClelland, and Peterson (1980) admit that aging group consciousness exists in some local settings among the elderly, they point out that it may not necessarily arise in response to age-segregated residence. Further, they suggest that as applied to retirement communities, aged subculture theory may need modification to take account of this essentially retreatist phenomenon.

Modernization Theory

In their book, *Aging and Modernization*, Cowgill and Holmes (1972) developed a theory of aging in cross-cultural perspective. As the theory emerged, and was subsequently revised (Cowgill, 1974), it described the relationship between modernization and the changes in role and status of older people. The theory was originally expressed in 22 propositions. Stated tersely, however, it held that with increasing modernization, the status of older people declines. This declining status is reflected in reduced leadership roles, power, and influence, as well as increased disengagement of older people from community life.

In the initial presentation of the theory, the definition of *modernization* was somewhat elusive. Later, Cowgill put forth an explicit definition of the concept:

> Modernization is the transformation of a total society from a relatively rural way of life based on animate power, limited technology, relatively undifferentiated institutions, parochial and traditional outlook and values, toward a predominantly urban way of life based on inanimate sources of power, highly developed scientific technology, highly differentiated institutions matched by segmented individual roles, and a cosmopolitan outlook which emphasizes efficiency and progress. (1974, p. 127)

In addition, Cowgill argued that no part of the society is left untouched, and that all change, although not uniform, is unidirectional (i.e., it always moves from the rural form to the urban form).

Four subsidiary aspects of modernization were identified as salient to the conditions of older people in a society: (1) scientific technology as applied in economic production and distribution, (2) urbanization, (3) literacy and mass education, and (4) health technology. Each of these aspects of modernization helps produce the lower status of older people in society (Cowgill, 1974).

Figure 9–2 presents, in schematic form, the modernization theory as revised by Cowgill. Briefly, the causal sequences depicted in the figure can be described as follows:

1. The application of health technology—including public health measures, nutrition, and all aspects of curative and surgical medicine—dramatically affects the age structure of a society so that there is an aging of the population. This comes about through a prolongation of adult life as well as a decline in the birthrate. The theory argues that within the context of an industrialized society with emphasis on youth and new occupations, the extension of adult life leads to an intergenerational competition for jobs. Therefore, older people are forced out of

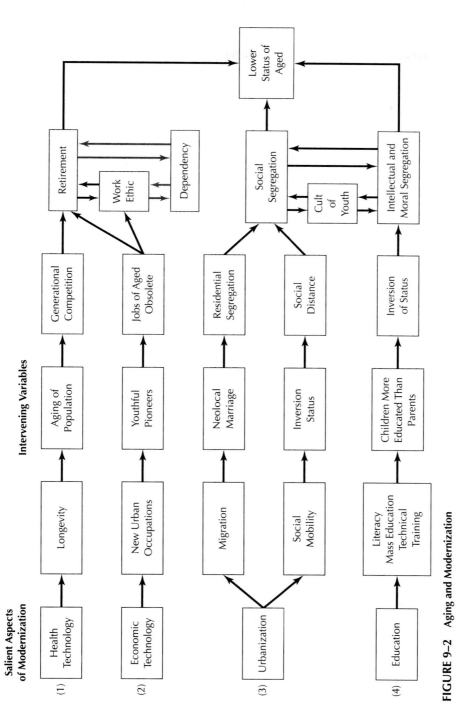

Salient Aspects of Modernization

Intervening Variables

FIGURE 9–2 Aging and Modernization

Source: From D. Cowgill, "Aging and Modernization: A Revision of the Theory," in J. Gubrium (Ed.), *Late Life: Communities and Environmental Policies,* 1974. Courtesy of Charles C Thomas, Publisher, Springfield, Illinois.

the labor market; they retire. Because they are denied participation in the work ethic, the elderly experience reductions in monetary income, prestige, and honor, and thus decrement in status.

2. The application of economic and industrial technology leads to new occupations located increasingly in an urban setting. Geographically and socially mobile youth migrate to these jobs, while older people are left in positions that are less prestigious and often obsolete. The lack of opportunities for retraining (especially in rural areas) leads to early retirement. This retirement, accompanied by loss of income, may also bring a reversal of traditional family and community roles. Formerly, the young were dependent on the old; now the old suffer dependency.

3. Urbanization, including the separation of work from home and the geographical separation of youthful urban migrants from their parental homes, profoundly changes the nature of intergenerational relations. Residential segregation of the generations changes the bonds of familial association, increases social distance between generations, and—with upward mobility among the young—leads to a reduced status of the aged. This effect is compounded by retirement and dependency.

4. Promoting literacy and education (almost always targeted at the young in modernization efforts) generates a situation in which children are more literate and have greater skill than their parents do. This imbalance has the effect of inverting roles in the traditional society: The child's generation has higher status than the parents', and children occupy positions in the community formerly held by their parents. The increasing social change brought by that modernization widens the gap between the generations, thus causing an intellectual and moral separation or segregation of the generations. Youth comes to symbolize progress, and society directs its resources toward the young and away from the old, accentuating the decline in status of the aged.

The Coast Salish Indians of western Washington state and British Columbia represent a challenge to the view that modernization is detrimental to the old (Amoss, 1981). They live on the same wooded coasts and valleys inhabited by their forebears, although their social, economic, and cultural world has changed dramatically. Still, contemporary Coast Salish elders enjoy rank comparable to that of the old people in times before contact with white society. The prestige accorded modern elders, as for their forebears, is based on a recognition of their contribution to the group; the contribution, however, has changed.

In the precontact era, elders were held in high esteem for their special skills in food procurement and processing as well as in canoe building. They made important contributions to group solidarity by maintaining the extended-family household. Modern old people do little of this. The nuclear household is the unit of production and consumption, and the skills of the elderly are of no economic importance. Yet, old men and women are held in high standing because of their knowledge of old religious ritual practices and because the people believe that elders control a special spiritual power.

In some societies, elders are accorded prestige based on a recognition of their contributions to the group.

In particular, tribal elders play a central role in aboriginal-style spirit-dancing rituals carried out in winter, when the individual spirit guardians return, and inspire tribal members to song and dance. The elders are essential to these ritualistic gatherings in three ways (Amoss, 1981). First, because the old-style rituals were not performed for many years, the elders are the only ones who know how things should be done. Second, old people, though generally poor, contribute directly to the ritual occasions by giving goods and money. Third, elders control the initiation process that is the only route to full participation in the winter-dancing ceremonial system. Old people also have status in the group as a function of the monopoly they hold over ritual roles that control the welfare of others. Shamans, who have the power to inflict fatal illness, and mediums, who see ghosts and officiate at funerals, are all old men or women.

The work of Erdman Palmore has generally supported the modernization theory. Palmore and Whittington (1971) found that the status of the aged was lower than that of the younger population on a series of socioeconomic measures and had declined significantly from 1940 to 1969. Palmore and Manton (1974) explored the relationship between modernization and the economic status of the aged in 31 countries. Indicators of modernization included the gross national product (GNP) per capita, the percentage of the labor force engaged in agriculture, the change in the proportion of the labor force engaged in agriculture, the percentage of literate adults, the percentage of people aged 5 to 19 in schools, and the percentage of the population in higher education. The relative status of the aged was measured by indexes that compared the differences in employment and occupation of the older population (age 65 and over) with those age 25 through 64. In general, correlation between the indicators of modernization and measures of the status of the aged demonstrated the theory. The relative status of older people was lower in the more modernized nations. Interestingly, Palmore and Manton discovered some patterns within their data that imply that the status of the aged decreases in the early stages of modernization (exemplified by nations such as Iran, El Salvador, and the Philippines) but that, after a period of modernization, status may level off and even rise somewhat (exemplified by New Zealand, Canada, and the United States).

Finally, Palmore (1975) has used the case of Japan to show how culture may mitigate the impact of modernization on the status of the aged. According to Palmore, the social and ethnic homogeneity of the Japanese population, the attitude of the Japanese toward time, the tradition of respect for the aged reflected in filial piety, and the prominence of ancestor worship have all helped maintain the relatively high status and integration of older Japanese. Palmore quotes from Japan's 1963 National Law for the Welfare of the Elders, a law comparable in the United States to The Older Americans Act of 1965: "The elders shall be loved and respected as those who have for many years contributed toward the development of society, and a wholesome and peaceful life shall be guaranteed to them." The Older Americans Act of 1965 makes no mention of love and respect for the aged, nor does it *guarantee* a wholesome and peaceful life.

After a return to Japan, Palmore and Maeda (1985) point out that the status and integration of Japanese elderly have declined from a peak when Japan was an agricultural society. Still, they argue that even after this decline, there are large differences between the situations of Japanese elderly and those in the United States and other countries. And, importantly, in their view, these trends are likely to continue into the foreseeable future, even as Japan undergoes a westernization.

The modernization theory, however, has its critics. A number of these point out how often the term *modernization* is used as synonym for development, change, progress, and westernization—suggesting that the concept is often used because of its vagueness. Two historians, Achenbaum and Stearns (1978), who have written on old age in historical perspective, believe the concept of modernization is worth pursuing in gerontology only with the following stipulations:

1. There should be clear agreement on when the modernization process began. For example, David Hacket Fischer, author of *Growing Old in America* (1977), believes that America's shift from a gerontophilic to a gerontophobic society took place between 1770 and 1820. These dates precede the beginning of the fundamental aspects of modernization Cowgill finds so salient for influencing the status of older people.

2. Modernization is not necessarily a linear process. It may proceed in stages, some of which are protracted. Each stage may have a different impact on the status of the elderly.

3. The elderly in preindustrial society demonstrated great diversity of situation. Some owned property and wielded considerable power; others suffered severe

MODERNITY IN SOUTH KOREA

Premodern Korea was a traditional agricultural society in which the elderly occupied positions of status and power. Aged men were heads of households and highly respected, with important decision-making power inside and outside of the family. The position of the elderly also received support from Confucianism, the emphasis on filial piety, and the accompanying norm of obedience to parents. With modernization, the old have experienced loss of status. The familial roles of the elderly have become ambiguous, even in circumstances of joint living arrangements.

Although Cowgill's theory of the effects of modernization employs society as the unit of analysis, Hong and Keith (1992) were interested in the extent to which individual modernity and the modern circumstances of the family affected the status of the elderly within the family. They hypothesized that (1) the more modern the family environment, the less power the elderly have in family decision-making; and (2) the greater the individual modernity of the elderly, the less power they have in family decision making.

Face-to-face interviews were carried out with 252 Korean men and women aged 60 years or older in Seoul, Korea. All sample members were living with one of their married children and other relatives. Key indicators of modern family circumstances included urban residence and high educational attainment of the children. The measure of individual modernity was an index

of 13 items assessing attitudes toward different areas of Korean life. For example, respondents were asked to give their opinions about equal education opportunities for both daughters and sons. Family decisions were divided into four dimensions and respondents were asked who made the final decision in each of 13 different family matters.

Having highly educated children and living in rural areas significantly affected the decision-making power of the aged in the hypothesized direction. Contrary to what was hypothesized, however, individual modernity among the elderly was found to be positively related to decision-making power in the family. Young-old married men with modern attitudes and highly educated children had the most power in decision-making. Hong and Keith speculate that individual modernity is a resource that aids the elderly in negotiating with the younger generation to gain more involvement in decision making within the family. It also may be the case that the children, especially those with higher levels of education, find these modern attitudes supportive and of value in contemporary Korean life. These data from Korea suggest that older people can protect themselves from the ravages of modernization by becoming modern themselves, even if only in attitude. Being young-old, having good health, and having a higher education were predictive of individual modernity among these Korean aged.

degradation. Inevitably, the situation for some improved with modernization as it deteriorated for others.

4. The process of modernization has affected different age groups in different ways. This is particularly interesting in light of societal transformations that necessitated the invention of "adolescence" and redefined childhood. Today, distinctions are made among young-old and old-old. Each may modernize in a different way, with different degrees of success.

Age Stratification

Age stratification is less a formal theory than a conceptual framework for viewing societal processes and changes that affect aging and the state of being old. Matilda White Riley (1971, 1976; Riley, Johnson, & Foner, 1972) and Anne Foner (1975) are the architects of this conceptual framework.

Society is divided into strata not only by social class but by age as well. Members of the age strata differ in the social roles they are expected to play and in the rights and privileges accorded them by society. This is similarly the case for members of different social classes, who also have different societal expectations for behavior and differential access to rewards granted by society. Age stratification and class stratification approaches have much in common. In fact, Riley (1971) argues that two concepts central to class stratification theory, *social class* and *social mobility,* are analogous to two concepts central to age stratification, *age strata* and *aging.* She suggests that sociologists of age stratification use those questions that are important to class stratification theorists to stimulate thinking about age strata and aging. Four sets of these questions are reproduced here:

> *First,* how does an individual's location in the class structure channel his attitudes and the way he behaves? Here there is much evidence that, for example, a person's health, his desire to achieve, his sense of mastery over his own fate, or the way he relates to his family and to his job depend to a considerable extent upon his social class.
>
> *Second,* how do individuals relate to one another within and between classes? Within class lines, many friendships are formed, marriages often take place, and feelings of solidarity tend to be widespread. Between classes, relationships, even if not solidary, are often symbiotic, as people of unlike status live harmoniously in the same society. However, there seems to be greater opportunity between, than within, classes, for cleavage or conflict, as in struggles over economic advantages or clashes in political loyalties.
>
> *Third,* what difficulties beset the upwardly (or downwardly) mobile individual, and what strains does his mobility impose upon the group (such as his parents of one class) whom he leaves behind and upon the new group (such as his wife's parents of a different class) who must now absorb him?
>
> *Fourth,* to the extent that answers can be found to these three sets of questions, what is the impact of the observed findings upon the society as a whole? If there are inequalities between classes, for example, what do these portend for the prosperity, the morality, or the stability of the overall structure of classes? What pressures for societal change are generated by differences, conflicts, or mobility between classes?[1]

---

[1]*Source:* "Social Gerontology and the Age Stratification of Society" by M. W. Riley, 1971, *The Gerontologist,* Vol. II, Part 1, Spring, 1971, p. 80. Copyright © The Gerontological Society of America.

In age stratification terms, the first question becomes: How does an individual's location within the age structure of a society influence his or her behavior and attitudes? I have already discussed in Chapters 4 through 7 the fact that age strata differ in physical and sensory capabilities, psychomotor performance, and probabilities of death. Psychologists of the life cycle often describe age strata in terms of their involvement in different developmental tasks. In addition, research shows that age strata differ in political and social attitudes, world outlook, style of life, organizational attachments, happiness, and so on (Riley & Foner, 1968). How do age stratification theorists explain these differences in behavior and attitudes among people of different age strata and the similarities among people within a stratum?

Riley (1971) suggests that two coordinates or dimensions useful for locating an individual in the age structure of a society are the *life-course dimension* and the *historical dimension.* The first of these reflects chronological age, itself a rough indicator of biological, psychological, and social experience. This is only to say that individuals of the same age have much in common. They are alike in biological development as well as in the kinds of social roles they have experienced (worker, spouse, parent). The second dimension refers to the period of history in which a person lives. People born at the same time (a cohort) share a common history. Those born at different times have lived through a different historical period. Even when people born at different times share an historical event, they are likely to experience it differently. For example, persons born in 1920 and 1950, respectively, were likely to experience the Vietnam War quite differently. Riley uses the term *cohort-centric* to describe the view of the world (i.e., the behavior and attitudes) that develops from a particular intersection of the life-course and historical dimensions. People in the same place on the life-course dimension (in the same age stratum) experience historical events similarly and, as a result, may come to see the world in a like fashion. The cohort-centricity of different age strata explains the different behaviors and attitudes associated with those age strata. More recently, Riley (1985) has described the *fallacy of cohort-centrism*—that is, the erroneous assumption that members of all cohorts will age in exactly the same fashion as members of our own cohort.

The second question becomes: How do individuals relate to one another within and between age strata? This question stimulates thinking about the nature of social relationships within age strata and the nature of intergenerational relations. From the age-stratification perspective, within-age stratum solidarity and consciousness are predictable. People's similarity in age and cohort membership often signals mutuality of experiences, perceptions, and interests that may lead to integration or even to age-based groups and collective movements (Riley, 1985). Yet, the continuous flow of cohorts in and out of an age stratum weakens identification with a particular stratum. As Foner (1975) points out, this is quite different from class strata, members of which share common experiences and often have a lifetime to reinforce identification with the group.

Relations among age strata reflect many factors, not the least of which is the distribution of power and wealth in a society. What about intergenerational relations within the family? Are they sequential or reciprocal? Foner (1969, cited in Riley, 1971) asked parents of high school students what they would do with money unexpectedly received. Only 2 percent said they would use it to help their aged parents; most indicated a willingness to use the money to help the children get started in life. Furthermore, she reports that the aged generation concurs with this decision. This suggests agreement among generations about the flow of material support—sequential, not reciprocal, with each generation attempting to aid the younger generation.

The third set of questions asks about age mobility. When aging is viewed as mobility through the age strata, it is revealed as a process that brings many of the same strains and stresses as does class mobility. Still, age mobility is different. Whereas social mobility affects only a few, age mobility affects everyone. Although individuals age in different ways and at different rates, no one can achieve downward age mobility. As Mannheim wrote, the "sociological phenomenon of generations is ultimately based on the biological rhythm of birth and death" (1952, p. 290). Over time, a succession of waves of new individuals reach adulthood. Each wave, or cohort, is changed by *and* changes the prevailing culture. Mannheim described this as "fresh contact" (Kertzer, 1983). Second, each cohort, because of its special relationship to historical events, experiences age mobility differently. For example, successive cohorts in U.S. society in this century have had increased longevity and formal education. Both these facts have dramatically changed how successive cohorts have aged.

Finally, the fourth set of questions reminds one that age stratification cannot be viewed in isolation. The system of age stratification in society influences and is influenced by the changing social-political-economic fabric of society. Sometimes, social changes may directly reflect "innovations" that emanate from one or more cohorts (Riley, 1971). Thus, for example, the large proportion of "early" retirements from the labor force in recent cohorts of those aged 55 to 65 has already had enormous impact throughout the society—for example, on the financing of Social Security and other pension plans, on housing, and on leisure—and will continue to do so in the future. On the other hand, when many individuals in the same cohort are affected by social change in similar ways, the change in their collective lives can in turn produce further social change. That is, new patterns of aging are not only caused by social change; they also contribute to it (Riley, 1985).

In Maoist China (1949–1976), three policies were implemented that are repeatedly cited as evidence for a decline in the status of older people in that country. First, a new marriage law, enacted in 1950, replaced absolute parental authority with reciprocity between parents and children. Second, the elimination of private property removed the parental control of family wealth as a power resource. Third, the state emphasized patriotism over filial piety; children were encouraged to expose family members who were ideologically against the state. In the 1970s, with the death of Mao, modernization in the form of economic development was emphasized in earnest. Although research on the impact on the aged of this intensive modernization is still ongoing, application of the modernization theory would seem to predict a further decline in the status of old people.

Peter Yin and Kwok Humg Lai (1983) have attempted to understand the changes in status experienced by the elderly in Maoist China within the context of the age stratification theory. In effect they ask: Did the aged lose status because they were old (*age effect*) or because of their life experiences (*cohort effect*)? Yin and Lai argue for an explanation of the status of older people in China based on cohort effects. Their position is that older age groups suffered diminished status in Maoist China mainly because of their life experience in the prerevolutionary era, when the previous government advocated capitalism and communists were in the role of revolutionaries. When the communists came to power, they feared that older adults could provide a major impetus to a revival of capitalism. In sum, these authors suggest that the position of the aged was diminished in Maoist China not as a function of their old age but, rather, as a result of generational conflict based on different life experiences.

The age stratification approach suggests a new way of viewing an increasing body of information on growing old and being old. The research literature on age stratification is still relatively scarce. Yet, it is clear the approach raises interesting and important questions. Only additional research efforts will determine its viability.

Political Economy of Aging

The political economy perspective on aging requires that the problems of aging be viewed in social structure rather than individual terms. According to Estes, Swan, and Gerard, this perspective "starts with the proposition that the status and resources of the elderly and even the trajectory of the aging process itself are conditioned by one's location in the social structure and the economic and social factors that affect it" (1984, p. 28). Clearly, the political economy perspective is not concerned with old age as a biological or psychological problem but, rather, as a problem for societies characterized by major inequalities in the distribution of power, income, and property. Implicit in this approach is the question of whether the logic of capitalism as a productive social system is reconcilable with the needs of elderly people.

Radical political economists of aging answer that capitalism is irreconcilable with meeting the needs of the elderly. Phillipson (1982) offers four arguments:

1. Whenever capitalism is in crisis—as in the 1930s and in the early 1980s—it attempts to solve its problems through cuts in the living standards of working people.

2. Capitalism has a distinct set of priorities, which almost always subordinates social and individual needs to the search for profits.

3. Because of the cyclical nature of the capitalist economies, elderly people often find themselves caught between their own need for better services and the steady decline of facilities within their neighborhood.

4. In capitalist economies, a ruling class still appropriates and controls the wealth produced by the working class.

Navarro (1984) has analyzed the health care problems of older Americans, using a political economy approach. He concludes that the misery and impoverishment many elderly suffer today is a function of the dominance of the capitalist class over U.S. political, economic, and social institutions. From his view, support of capitalist class interests has required shifting government resources from social and health expenditures, which benefit the majority of the U.S. population, to military and defense expenditures, which benefit the few. Interestingly, Navarro remains optimistic enough to suggest that the interest-group mentality prevalent in the United States be replaced by an appreciation among the majority of Americans (whites, blacks, Latinos, females, young and old people) for their shared working-class status and hence for their collective power.

Others are not so sanguine. Estes and Binney (1991) use the concept of the *biomedicalization of aging* to describe the overdevelopment of a geriatric medical industrial complex based on the social construction of aging as a medical problem. The social construction of aging as a medical problem equates aging with illness and disease. Thus, despite increasing evidence of the importance of social and behavioral factors in the relationship between health and aging, the elements of the medical model—with its emphasis on objectivity in diagnosis and treatment of disease, concern solely for matters of physiological functioning, and evaluation solely in the domain of physicians—define the basic processes and problems of aging. As a result, viewpoints on aging emphasize more sophisticated diagnosis, therapeutic intervention or prevention, and identification of modifiable biological markers of aging (Adelman, 1988).

From this perspective, aging is considered an undesirable pathological condition, rather than a phase or stage in the life cycle that brings new risks but also opportunities. Aging is equated with reduced activity, disengagement from social life, an exchange of independence for dependency, and a general loss of personal control and self-esteem (Rodin & Langner, 1980). As Estes, Gerard, Zones, and Swan (1984) note, all this places social control of the elderly in the hands of physicians who medically define, manage, and treat them.

Political economy of aging is not a theory in the strictest sense. It is not presented in the form of a set of systematically organized statements. Rather, political economy is an orientation or perspective, that, at this relatively early stage in its development, may provide a useful guide for aging policy and research. Estes, Gerard, and Minkler (1984) employ the perspective to frame four important questions about aging policy. They believe that the answers to these questions speak to the heart of the relationship between this society and its aged constituents:

1. To what extent will aging interest groups ally themselves with a broader base and expand their concerns to encompass generic issues rather than those identified as aging issues only?

2. To what extent will state and local officials continue to accept the federal retrenchment and shift of governmental responsibility to state and local government?

3. Will the interests of the wealthy and the middle class continue to dominate public policy for the aging?

4. To what extent will the organizations serving the aging, as well as professionals and individuals, involve themselves in attempting to set the agenda for future public policy?

SUMMARY

The theories in social gerontology reviewed in this chapter were divided into two broad categories. One group of theories attempts to conceptualize the adjustment of individuals to their own aging, while other theories deal with societal change and aging. Theories in the first category include the role, activity, disengagement, continuity, socioenvironmental, exchange, and symbolic interactionist theories. Those in the latter category include the subcultural, modernization, and age stratification theories, as well as the political economy perspective. None of the theories has been sufficiently tested to be completely rejected. Each acts as a guide to further research.

The earliest theory in social gerontology concentrated on adjustments to role change among the elderly. In general, this approach pointed out that role loss led to maladjustment. The activity theory states a positive relationship between activity and life satisfaction. Activity theorists argue that, although aging individuals face inevitable changes, many psychosocial needs remain the same. Thus, individuals able to maintain the activities of the middle years will be well satisfied with life in the later years. Several empirical tests of the theory show only social activity with friends to be related to life satisfaction in later life.

Standing in some contrast to these approaches, disengagement theory characterizes old age as a time of mutual withdrawal between the aging individual and society. This mutual withdrawal is seen as functional for and desired by both aging individuals and the social system. Much critical discussion still surrounds the theory, although most research efforts are unable to provide empirical support for it.

Continuity theory argues that people make adaptive choices in old age that involve applying familiar strategies in familiar arenas of life. Thus, the elderly attempt to preserve and maintain inner psychological continuity as well as external continuity of social behavior and circumstances.

Socioenvironmental theory is directed at acknowledging the effects of the social and physical environment on the activity patterns of aged individuals. Exchange theory attempts to explain the interaction patterns of the old in terms of the relationship between support given and received. When these are out of balance, injustice is experienced and life satisfaction declines. Symbolic interactionism emphasizes the power of aged individuals to socially construct their reality.

Rose offered the concept of an aged subculture to explain the impact of trends promoting the segregation of the old from the rest of society. The development of an aged subculture has both negative and positive consequences. The most positive of these includes the potential for the elderly to form a social action group.

Modernization theory describes the relationship between modernization and the changes in role and status of older people. Stated briefly, the theory holds that increasing modernization brings a decline in the status of the aged. Riley proposes an age-stratification approach to understanding the aging process and old age. She advises that an approach similar to that used in the analysis of class stratification would be useful for shedding light on problems of growing old and being old.

Political economy is a new perspective that sees the aged and the aging process as conditioned by location in the social structure. The perspective questions whether the logic of the U.S. economic system is reconcilable with the needs of older people.

STUDY QUESTIONS

1. Discuss the role theory in relation to adjustment in old age. What are the major role changes individuals experience during the aging process according to this theory? What happens to sex-role differentiation with aging?

2. Compare and contrast disengagement and activity theories. Are there similarities, or continuities, between the activity and continuity theories? Explain your answer.

3. Explain how Gubrium integrates the concepts of physical proximity and age homogeneity into the socioenvironmental theory of aging. List the elements of his resulting typology of social contexts and describe them.

4. Discuss exchange theory and explain how it can be applied to understand the support networks of older people.

5. Explain how the theory of symbolic interactionism can be used to provide a basis for understanding how older people perceive and assign meaning to things, events, and people in their lives.

6. Discuss the positive and negative consequences of development of an aged subculture.

7. Four aspects of modernization have been identified as salient to the conditions of older people in a society. List them and explain how each affects the status of the elderly.

8. Explain how questions of social stratification can be adapted to a conceptual framework of age stratification.

9. According to radical political economists of aging, capitalism is not reconcilable with meeting the needs of the elderly. Do you agree or disagree? Why? How may the political economy perspective help frame future policy and research questions?

REFERENCES

Achenbaum, A., & Stearns, P. (1978). Old age and modernization. *Gerontologist, 18* (3), 307–312.

Adelman, R. (1988). The importance of basic biological science to gerontology. *Journal of Gerontology, 43* (1), B1–2.

Amoss, P. T. (1981). Coastal Salish elders. In P. T. Amoss & S. Harrell (Eds.), *Other ways of growing old*. Stanford, CA: Stanford University Press.

Atchley, R. (1971). Disengagement among professors. *Journal of Gerontology, 26,* 476–480.

Atchley, R. (1989). A continuity theory of normal aging. *The Gerontologist, 29* (2), 183–190.

Blumer, H. (1969). *Symbolic interactionism.* Englewood Cliffs, NJ: Prentice-Hall.

Bultena, G., & Wood, V. (1969). The American retirement community: Bane or blessing? *Journal of Gerontology, 24,* 209–217.

Carp, F. (1969). Compound criteria in gerontological research. *Journal of Gerontology, 24,* 341–347.

Cavan, R., Burgess, E., Havighurst, R., & Goldhammer, H. (1949). *Personal adjustment in old age.* Chicago: Science Research Associates.

Conner, K., Powers, E., & Bultena, G. (1979). Social interaction and life satisfaction: An empirical assessment of late-life patterns. *Journal of Gerontology, 34,* 116–121.

Cottrell, L. (1942). The adjustment of the individual to his age and sex roles. *American Sociological Review, 7,* 617–620.

Cowgill, D. (1974). Aging and modernization: A revision of the theory. In J. Gubrium (Ed.), *Late life: Communities and environmental policy.* Springfield, IL: Charles C. Thomas.

Cowgill, D., & Holmes, L. (1972). *Aging and modernization.* New York: Appleton-Century-Crofts.

Crawford, M. P. (1971). Retirement and disengagement. *Human Relations, 24,* 255–278.

Cumming, E. (1963). Further thoughts on the theory of disengagement. *International Social Science Journal, 15* (3), 377–393.

Cumming, E., & Henry, W. (1961). *Growing old: The process of disengagement.* New York: Basic Books.

Dowd, J. (1975, September). Aging as exchange: A preface to theory. *Journal of Gerontology, 30,* 584–594.

Dowd, J. (1978). Aging as exchange: A test of the distributive justice proposition. *Pacific Sociological Review, 21,* 351–375.

Dowd, J. (1980). *Stratification among the aged: An analysis of power and dependence.* Monterey, CA: Brooks-Cole.

Dowd, J. (1984). Beneficence and the aged. *Journal of Gerontology, 39* (1), 102–108.

Emerson, R. M. (1976). Social exchange theory. In A. Inkeles, J. Coleman, & N. Smelser (Eds.), *Annual review of sociology* (Vol. 2). Palo Alto, CA: Annual Reviews.

Estes, C. L., & Binney, A. A. (1991). The biomedicalization of aging: Dangers and dilemmas. In M. Minkler & C. L. Estes (Eds.), *Critical perspectives on aging.* Amityville, NY: Baywood.

Estes, C. L., Gerard, L. E., & Minkler, M. (1984). Reassessing the future of aging policy and politics. In M. Minkler & C. L. Estes (Eds.), *Readings in the political economy of aging.* Farmingdale, NY: Baywood.

Estes, C. L., Gerard, L. E., Zones, J. S., & Swan, J. H. (1984). *Political economy, health and aging.* Boston: Little, Brown.

Estes, C. L. Swan, J. H., & Gerard, L. E. (1984). Dominant and competing paradigms in gerontology: Towards a political economy of aging. In M. Minkler & C. L. Estes (Eds.), *Readings in the political economy of aging.* Farmingdale, NY: Baywood.

Fischer, D. (1977). *Growing old in America.* New York: Oxford University Press.

Foner, A. (1975). Age in society: Structures and change. *American Behavioral Scientist, 19* (2), 289–312.

Fox, J. H. (1981–82). Perspectives on the continuity perspective. *International Journal of Aging and Human Development, 14,* 97–115.

Gouldner, A. W. (1960, April). The norm of reciprocity. *American Sociological Review, 25,* 161–178.

Gubrium, J. (1973). *The myth of the golden years: A social-environmental theory of aging.* Springfield, IL: Charles C. Thomas.

Gubrium, J. (1975). *Living and dying at Murray Manor.* New York: St. Martin's Press.

Havighurst, R. (1968). Personality and patterns of aging. *Gerontologist, 8,* 20–23.

Hendricks, J., & Hendricks, C. D. (1986). *Aging in mass society: Myths and realities* (3rd ed.). Boston: Little, Brown.

Hochschild, A. (1975). Disengagement theory: A critique and proposal. *American Sociological Review, 40,* 553–569.

Homans, G. (1958, May). Social behavior as exchange. *American Journal of Sociology, 63,* 597–606.

Homans, G. (1974). *Social behavior: Its elementary forms* (rev. ed.). New York: Harcourt, Brace & World.

Hong, S. M. H., & Keith, P. M. (1992). The status of the aged in Korea: Are the modern more advantaged? *The Gerontologist, 32* (2), 197–202.

Kart, C. S., & Longino, C. F. (1987). The support systems of older people: A test of the exchange paradigm. *Journal of Aging Studies, 1* (3), 239–251.

Kertzer, D. I. (1983). Generation as a sociological problem. *Annual Review of Sociology, 9,* 125–149.

Knapp, M. (1977). The activity theory of aging: An examination in the English context. *Gerontologist, 17* (6), 553–559.

Lemon, B., Bengtson, V., & Peterson, J. (1972). Activity types and life satisfaction in a retirement community. *Journal of Gerontology, 27,* 511–523.

Longino, C. F. (1980). The retirement community. In F. Berghorn & D. Schafer (Eds.), *Dynamics of aging: Original essays on the experience and process of growing old.* Boulder, CO: Westview Press.

Longino, C. F., & Kart, C. S. (1982). Explicating activity theory: A formal replication. *Journal of Gerontology, 17* (6), 713–722.

Longino, C. F., McClelland, K. A., & Peterson, W. A. (1980). The aged subculture hypothesis: Social integration, gerontophilia and self-conception. *Journal of Gerontology, 35* (5), 758–767.

Mannheim, K. (1952). The problem of generations. In *Essays on the sociology of knowledge.* New York: Oxford University Press.

Marshall, V. (1979). No exit: A symbolic interactionist perspective on aging. *International Journal of Aging and Human Development, 9,* 345–358.

Messer, M. (1967). The possibility of an age-concentrated environment becoming a normative system. *Gerontologist, 7,* 247–250.

Monge, R. H. (1975). Structure of the self-concept from adolescence through old age. *Experimental Aging Research, 1* (2), 281–291.

National Council on the Aging. (1976). *The myth and reality of Aging in America.* Washington, DC: Author.

Navarro, V. (1984). The political economy of government cuts for the elderly. In M. Minkler & C. L. Estes (Eds.), *Readings in the political economy of aging.* Farmingdale, NY: Baywood.

Neugarten, B., Crotty, W., & Tobin, S. (1964). Personality types in an aged population. In B. Neugarten et al. (Eds.), *Personality in middle and late life.* New York: Atherton Press.

Neugarten, B., Havighurst, R., & Tobin, S. (1961). The measurement of life satisfaction. *Journal of Gerontology, 16,* 134–143.

Palmore, E. (1968). The effects of aging on activities and attitudes. *Gerontologist, 8,* 259–263.

Palmore, E. (1975). *The honorable elders: A cross-cultural analysis of aging in Japan.* Durham, NC: Duke University Press.

Palmore, E., & Maeda, D. (1985). *The honorable elders revisited: A revised cross-cultural analysis of aging in Japan.* Durham, NC: Duke University Press.

Palmore, E., & Manton, K. (1974). Modernization and status of the aged. *Journal of Gerontology, 29* (2), 205–210.

Palmore, E., & Whittington, F. (1971). Trends in the relative status of the aged. *Social Forces, 50,* 84–90.

Phillips, B. (1957). A role theory approach to adjustment in old age. *American Sociological Review, 22,* 212–217.

Phillipson, C. (1982). *Capitalism and the construction of old age.* London: Macmillan.

Reichard, S., Livson, F., & Peterson, P. (1962). *Aging and personality.* New York: John Wiley & Sons.

Riley, M. W. (1971). Social gerontology and the age stratification of society. *Gerontologist, 11,* 79–87.

Riley, M. W. (1976). Age strata in social systems. In R. Binstock & E. Shanas (Eds.), *Handbook of aging and the social sciences.* New York: Van Nostrand Reinhold.

Riley, M. W. (1985). Age strata in social systems. In R. Binstock & E. Shanas (Eds.),

Handbook of aging and the social sciences (2nd ed.). New York: Van Nostrand Reinhold.

Riley, M. W., & Foner, A. (1968). *Aging and society: An inventory of research findings.* New York: Russell Sage Foundation.

Riley, M. W., Johnson, M., & Foner, A. (1972). *Aging and society: A sociology of age stratification.* New York: Russell Sage Foundation.

Rodin, J., & Langer, E. (1980). Aging labels: The decline of control and the fall of self-esteem. *Journal of Social Issues, 36* (2), 12–29.

Rose, A. (1965). The subculture of the aging: A framework in social gerontology. In A. M. Rose & W. A. Peterson (Eds.), *Older people and their social worlds.* Philadelphia: F. A. Davis.

Rosow, I. (1967). *Social integration of the aged.* New York: The Free Press.

Rosow, I. (1985). Status and role change through the life cycle. In R. H. Binstock & E. Shanas (Eds.), *Handbook of aging and the social sciences* (2d ed.). New York: Van Nostrand Reinhold.

Shanas, E. (1979). The family as a social support system in old age. *Gerontologist, 19,* 169–174.

Sinnott, J. D. (1977). Sex-role inconstancy, biology, and successful aging: A dialectical model. *Gerontologist, 17* (5), 459–463.

Spence, D. L. (1986). Some contributions of symbolic interaction to the study of growing old. In V. W. Marshall (Ed.), *Later life: The social psychology of aging.* Beverly Hills: Sage Publications.

Stoller, E. P., & Earl, L. L. (1983). Help with activities of everyday life: Sources of support for the noninstitutionalized elderly. *Gerontologist, 23* (1), 64–70.

Streib, G. (1965). Are the aged a minority group? In A. Gouldner & S. M. Miller (Eds.), *Applied sociology.* New York: The Free Press.

Sussman, M. (1976). The family life of old people. In R. Binstock & E. Shanas (Eds.), *Handbook of aging and the social sciences.* New York: Van Nostrand Reinhold.

Tallmer, M., & Kutner, B. (1970, Winter). Disengagement and morale. *Gerontologist, 10,* 317–320.

Thoits, P. (1982). Conceptual, methodological, and theoretical problems in studying social support as a buffer against life stress. *Journal of Health and Social Behavior, 23,* 145–159.

Ward, R. A. (1984). *The aging experience* (2nd ed.). New York: Harper and Row.

Ward, R. A. (1985). Informal networks and well-being in later life: A research agenda. *Gerontologist, 25,* 55–61.

Ward, R. A., Sherman, S., & Lagory, M. (1984). Subjective network assessments and subjective well being. *Journal of Gerontology, 39,* 93–101.

Weiss, R. (1969). The fund of sociability. *Transaction, 6,* 26–43.

Yin, P., & Lai, K. H. (1983). A reconceptualization of age stratification in China. *Journal of Gerontology, 38* (5), 608–613.

Youmans, E. G. (1967). Disengagement among older rural and urban men. In E. G. Youmans (Ed.), *Older rural Americans.* Lexington: University of Kentucky Press.

CHAPTER 10

AGING AND FAMILY LIFE

The institution of the family is one that is best known and that affects most people. The effects of other institutions—political, educational, and economic—are felt, but it is the family that touches people more deeply and continuously than any other. Families help regulate sexual activity and provide a context within which children are conceived and raised. Families afford individuals protection, affection, intimacy, and social identity.

Among social scientists, there is greater consensus about the functions of the family than about its form or structure. For example, anthropologists have largely been unable to agree on a common definition of a family. This should not be surprising, since much of the literature of anthropology and family sociology highlights the wide variety of forms families can take. This becomes especially clear in comparing different cultures—their mate-selection procedures, child-rearing practices, and degree of interaction allowed among family members. Variation in family structure exists within societies as well. Although most Americans today live in some form of nuclear family (husband/wife couple with children living in a common household), there is a wide array of family types in the United States. In fact, Bengtson, Rosenthal, and Burton (1990) suggest that today's elderly are participants in a "quiet revolution" that is changing family structure, roles, and relationships. For example, Shanas (1980) estimates that about 50 percent of people over age 65 are members of four-generation families, and Hagested (1988) reports that 20 percent of women who died after the age of 80 were members of five-generation families.

There has been much discussion about the relationship between family structure and the role and status of aged people in a society. One form of family structure is often considered advantageous for the aged—the extended family. The term *extended family* is conventionally used to describe all those individuals one is related to through blood and marriage; yet, the term is also used to characterize three or more generations who share living arrangements. Premodern, or preindustrial, societies, generally believed to be organized around the extended family, are often offered as evidence of the favored status of older people in extended family settings. In such societies, the aged are thought to be well integrated into family life, with family members living and working together harmoniously. This view is most likely an overly simplistic one: The premodern family should not be seen as a monolithic entity. First, by reflecting on the patterns of longevity in such societies, it is clear at once that too few older people survived for families including three or more generations to be universal. Also, preindustrial societies evinced a wide variation in family organization; many, even those in which the extended family was evident, treated old people quite poorly. Sieroshevski (1901) has written of the Yakuts of Siberia as follows:

> The Yakuts treat their old relatives, who have grown stupid, very badly. Usually they try to take from them the remains of their property, if they have any; then constantly, in measure, as they become unprotected they treat them worse and worse. Even in houses relatively self-sufficient, I found such living skeletons, wrinkled, half-naked, or even entirely naked, hiding in corners, from where they crept out only when no strangers were present, to get warm by the fire, to pick up together with children bits of food thrown away, or to quarrel with them over the licking of the dish emptied of food. (quoted in Simmons, 1945, p. 197)

Simmons (1945, 1960), a student of aging in many different societies, argues that throughout human history, the family has been the safest haven for the aged, even though the condition of the Yakut elderly shows otherwise. Simmons studied the position of the aged among 71 different premodern societies, and his data reveal that it was the organization of kinship relationships that primarily determined the destiny of aged people. In particular, opportunities for the aged to remain effective participants in society seemed to be related to their opportunities to (1) marry younger mates, (2) exercise managerial roles in the family, (3) rely on family care and support, and (4) rely on the support of their sons-in-law. Important as kinship relationships were, however, they were not the only determinants of the position of the aged in these societies. Also included were the climate and physical environment, as well as cultural factors, including the principal means of economy, the permanency of residence, the constancy of food supply, the nature of the political system, and the establishment of property rights in land, crops, herds, and other goods.

What about the relationship between family structure and the position of aged people in modern societies such as that in the United States?

OLD AGE AND THE U.S. FAMILY: A LOOK BACKWARD

In the United States, the past—that is, the preindustrial and early industrial period from the country's beginnings up to the turn of the twentieth century—is often characterized as an idyllic time during which three or more generations of relatives lived harmoniously together on the family farm. Such extended families were thought to be led by the elders, those respected members of the family and community. As we shall see, however, this respect, along with the obligation to care for elders, often was based on their control of resources, reinforced by religious tradition and normative sanction.

This picture of family life in an earlier time is often contrasted with that of contemporary family life, involving nuclear family units composed of husband/wife couples and their children. Conventional wisdom says that these nuclear family units live apart from one another and that bureaucratic institutions perform many of the functions once fulfilled by the family, including care of the elderly sick. Moreover, younger people no longer give the parental generation the love and respect that traditionally has been its due. In fact, as Treas (1977) points out, many blame this family indifference for the social isolation and economic insecurity that confront many older people.

The major cause of this shift in family organization from the extended to the nuclear family is thought to be industrialization. Advocates of this view argue that extended families are advantageous in agrarian societies because all family members (including children and the elderly) contribute economically to the family. This is not the case in an industrial society, where children and the elderly are largely unemployable. Moreover, because they consume at a high rate, these dependent relatives are a burden rather than an advantage.

This unemployability of dependent relatives is seen as only one cause of the transformation of the extended family into the nuclear family in industrialized societies. With industrialization, the location of work shifted away from the home. Workers migrated to places where job opportunities existed. This geographical mobility strained kinship bonds and decreased the frequency and intimacy of contact among family members. In addition, some have argued that industrialization opened up opportunities for women to participate in work activities outside the home, thus diminishing the importance of some extended family functions.

With the passing of the extended family, it is believed that older people lost their economic role and became isolated from their children and relatives. Even the most noted sociologist adopted this view: Over 50 years ago, Talcott Parsons wrote that with marriage and occupational independence of children comes "the depletion of [the] family until the older couple is finally left alone" (1942). Parsons contrasted this situation with that of other kinship systems (e.g., extended families) "in which membership in a kinship unit is continuous throughout the life cycle."

Although the position of the aged in the family in the United States certainly has undergone some historical change, not all share the perspective that a change in family structure from extended to nuclear is associated with loss of status and isolation for the elderly. For example, historical demographers now argue that the nuclear family has been viable throughout history and probably was the dominant type of family structure during the American colonial period.

It is not at all likely that the family evolved from an extended to a nuclear form. Rather, it has probably remained much the same. Gerontologist Clark Tibbitts has written that "it is now clear that the nuclear parent-child family has always been the modal family type in the United States and three-generation families have always been relatively rare" (1968).

Many family sociologists today have come to use the notion of a *modified extended family structure* to describe the interchange of visits and help between older parents and their children, which they believe to be more the rule than the exception. From this view, they argue that the family—far from being irrelevant, as some contend—is becoming increasingly important as a place where older people can find support and interpersonal warmth as society becomes more bureaucratic and impersonal.

How does one account for the fictionalized (some would say idealized) version of the U.S. extended family of the past? This is a difficult question. While arguing that this idealization of the past obscures its real character, Goode points out that "in each generation people write of a period still more remote, their grandparents' generation, when things really were much better" (1963). Perhaps, then, the answer lies in some universal belief that things were better in the past.

The general view in sociology has been that the nuclear family was founded in western Europe and the United States and is a result of the urban-industrial revolution. As already indicated, the extended family is the form thought to have been prevalent prior to the urban-industrial revolution. This view has come into question, however, as much evidence now suggests that the nuclear family was the dominant form of family organization in Europe during the preindustrial period as well.

Greenfield argues that the "small nuclear family was brought to the United States and Great Britain by its earliest settlers" (1967) and even suggests that the nuclear family helped produce the industrial revolution. Laslett and Harrison, in their study of two seventeenth-century English counties, Clayworth and Cogenhoe, found that the family was not extended; the "household did not ordinarily contain more generations than two. . . . Living with in-laws or relatives was on the whole not to be expected" (1963).

Two additional studies deserve mention. Back (1974) examined census records in England from 1574 to 1821 and found that only 6 percent of households contained three or more generations of family members. It is interesting that these extended households appeared to result almost always from a family tragedy of some sort, such as widowhood. Back concluded that there is no evidence that three-generation households were the preferred family pattern during the preindustrial period. Given the low percentage of extended families to begin with (6 percent), one would be hard pressed to argue that industrialization caused a decline in multigenerational households.

Apparently, England was not the only western society in which the nuclear family was the predominant form. Examining census records from 1847 to 1866 for a small community in Belgium, Van de Walle (1976) found that about two-thirds of the households were nuclear families; approximately 10 percent consisted of extended families, and 11 percent consisted of households in which more than one nuclear family lived together. Van de Walle observed nuclear families to be more lasting, and suggested (in support of Back) that extended households were transitional patterns that resulted from family disruption.

What about the United States? Were extended families indigenous to this country? A number of studies of the American colonial family conclude that the extended structure was the exception rather than the rule. Using family wills as a source, Demos observed of the Plymouth colony that "there was not extended families at all in the sense of 'under the same roof,'... married brothers and sisters never lived together in the same house," and "as soon as a man becomes betrothed, plans were made for the building, or purchase, of his own house...and it was most unusual for married fathers with married sons to live together in an extended family group" (1965, p. 279).

In describing the family structure in seventeenth-century Andover, Massachusetts, Greven (1966) distinguishes between the family of residence, which is nuclear, and the family of interaction or obligation, which he terms *modified extended*. Greven defines the *modified extended family* as a kinship group of two or more generations living within a single community in which the children continue to depend on their parents after they have married and are no longer living under the same roof. Demos supports this distinction in more recent studies of family structure in colonial New England. In Bristol, Rhode Island, "married adults normally lived with their own children and apart from all other relatives" (1968, p. 44). Yet, grown children, established in their own households, were still very much a part of a family's social environment. As Demos (1978) points out, the details of intrafamilial relationships in colonial times remains somewhat obscure; however, the simple fact of the children's presence within the same community was important in its own right.

Has this revised picture of the early U.S. family altered the view gerontologists have of the elderly during this period? Remember, it is generally believed that in early America, the elderly were in a more favorable position vis-à-vis family and society than they are today. Many associate this historically favorable position with the extended family and the subsequent loss of status and prestige with the change in family structure. The change in family structure (from extended to nuclear) appears to be more fiction than fact, but the change in the way Americans view the elderly is not.

Historian David H. Fischer has written about this changing disposition toward the elderly in the United States. In the following summary of his writing, notice that Fischer does not associate the historical decline in the status of older people with a change in family structure. Rather, he associates it with the kinds of cultural, demographic, and technological changes often associated with the modernization theory (discussed in Chapter 9).

Fischer (1977) lends support to the positive characterization of the position of the elderly in families of bygone days. At least, he argues, through its colonial phase, America was a gerontophilic place where being old conferred power and prestige. As Cotton Mather wrote in 1726, "the two qualities together, the ancient and the honorable." Seating arrangements in Massachusetts meetinghouses were determined by age rather than by wealth or status. Elders ran the churches. The aged occupied positions of community leadership; "grey champions" were turned to in crucial times. Names for persons in authority, such as senator and alderman, were derived from words meaning old. Men tended to overstate rather than understate their age, and powdered wigs and long coats were used to give an older appearance.

Fischer believes that between 1770 and 1820, a revolution in age relations took place in the United States. This revolution, fueled by the ideology of liberty and equality, had the effect of dissolving the authority formerly vested in age. Fischer offers numerous manifestations of this revolution in age relations. By the later part of the eighteenth century, most New England town meetings had abandoned the practice of seating members on the basis of age. Northampton, Massachusetts, sold seats at auction rather than assigning them on the basis of age. Thus, the best seats went to the highest bidder, and rank and status in the meetinghouse thereafter rested on wealth, without regard to age.

Mandatory retirement for public officials first appeared in the United States at the end of the eighteenth century. In 1777, the state of New York introduced compulsory retirement at age 70 for judges. New Hampshire followed suit in 1792, as did Connecticut in 1818. New York reduced the retirement age to 60 years old in 1821. These statutes angered former President John Adams, who wrote to Thomas Jefferson of his indignation: "I can never forgive New York, Connecticut, or Maine for turning out venerable men of sixty or seventy, when their judgment is often the best." Jefferson later responded, "It is reasonable we should drop off, and make room for another growth. When we have lived our generation out, we should not wish to encroach upon another" (Fischer, 1977, p. 77). Jefferson, it seems, shared the revolutionary spirit in a way Adams could not.

Further evidence of a revolution in age relations between 1770 and 1820 in America included a shift in age preference (people began to pretend to be younger than they actually were); a shift in the age bias of dress (fashion flattered the young rather than the old); and a reduction in the frequency with which children were given the same names as their grandparents. What caused this revolution? Fischer suggests that one key factor was the changing age composition of society. The number of aged was increasing, partly because more people were surviving to old age. Perhaps more important, however, is the fact that in the decade from 1800 to 1810, birthrates began to fall (and continued to do so for about 150 years). The aged became a slowly increasing proportion of the population. At the same time that old age became more common, it also became more contemptible: "Where the Puritans had made a cult of age, their posterity made a cult of youth instead" (Fischer, 1977, p. 114). By 1847, Henry David Thoreau could write:

> Age is no better, hardly so well, qualified for an instructor as youth, for it has not profited so much as it has lost.... Practically, the old have no very important advice to give the young, their experience has been so partial, and their lives have been such miserable failures, for private reasons, as they must believe; and it may

be that they have some faith left which belies that experience, and they are only less young than they were. (quoted in Fischer 1977, pp. 115–116)

The developing urbanization and industrialization of U.S. society accompanied demographic changes. The young, instead of waiting to inherit the family land, could move to the city and find work. Through the nineteenth and into the twentieth centuries, moving to the city became a strategy for leaving farming and parental control alike. Industrialization and urbanization contributed to changes in the character of generational relations. The young were no longer captive to a parental generation that controlled the family property and other economic resources.

THE FAMILY
IN CONTEMPORARY SOCIETY

As has already been described, Bengtson, Rosenthal, and Burton (1990) argue that a demographic revolution in family structure, roles, and relationships is underway. They attribute this revolution to at least two demographic trends. First, there has been significant decline in mortality during the twentieth century, and life expectancy has increased more than 50 percent since 1900. Second, the number of children born per female has decreased dramatically from 3.7 children in 1900 to 2.1 in 1990.[1] Other factors contributing to this demographic revolution include the rise of teenage childbearing at the same time that many couples were delaying childbearing (Connidis, 1989).

Social roles have changed as a function of these demographic trends. For example, Watkins, Menken, and Bongaarts (1987) show that because of the dramatic increase in survival of aging parents over time, women in 1980, compared to their peers in 1800, spent four times the number of years as a daughter with both parents alive. By 1980, the time spent by a woman as an adult child of one or more parents over the age of 65 was 18 years.

Sussman (1976) examined the structure of contemporary U.S. families and created a resulting taxonomy. His categories and data are best "guesstimates" based on data collected in the mid-1970s from a wide array of largely governmental sources, but provide guidelines for estimating the proportion of the adult population living in various family arrangements.

Approximately 6 in 10 of all adults live in a nuclear family. This includes 37 percent living in the traditional "intact" U.S. family (nuclear family living with children), 11 percent of couples who have no children (or whose children no longer live at home), and 11 percent of couples who have remarried. Single-parent families represent about 12 percent of all adults, and approximately 19 percent of

---

[1]1990 showed the highest fertility rate since 1971, when the figure was 2.3. By 1976, the fertility rate had declined to 1.7 and has generally trended up since that time.

the U.S. adult population is single, widowed, separated, or divorced and living alone. Only 4 percent of adults live in an extended family household in which three or more generations share living arrangements.

Although some scholars view such data as evidence that the U.S. family is not only nuclear but isolated as well, contrary arguments abound. Many contemporary family sociologists and gerontologists simply do not agree that the U.S. nuclear family lives in isolation from its extended kin network.

Eugene Litwak (1965) was one of the first to question the isolation of the U.S. nuclear family. In his studies, he found that most Americans function in *modified extended families* made up of nuclear families that exhibit partial dependence on each other and exchange services. Lillian Troll (1971) supports this view and has made special reference to the position of the "postparental" couple in this modified extended kin structure. In her view, the aged conjugal unit is not isolated.

Marvin Sussman has argued that the isolated nuclear family is a myth, and that there exists in modern urban-industrial societies "an extended kin system, highly integrated within a network of social relations and mutual assistance, that operates along historical kin lines and vertically over several generations" (1965, p. 179). According to Sussman, this extended kin network is the basic social system in U.S. urban society. More recently, he has argued that the proliferation of services for the elderly has created new roles for kin as mediators between institutional bureaucracies and elderly relations. Children and relatives act as resources for the elderly, informing them about housing, pensions, medical care, and other available options and entitlements. They also assist the aged in dealing with housing authorities, pension trustees, insurance companies, and hospitals (Sussman, 1985).

PARENTS AND THEIR ADULT CHILDREN

How does one know whether an old person is isolated or well integrated into an extended kin network? To answer this question, many researchers have studied relationships between older people and their relatives. In particular, research has focused on relationships between older parents and their adult children. In a 1975 nationwide poll, Louis Harris and associates found that 81 percent of those aged 65 and over reported having children (NCOA, 1976). According to Troll, Miller, and Atchley (1979), most older people who have no living children have never married. This section reviews some of the available research on aged parent/adult child relationships.

Residential Proximity

Almost all studies show that older people prefer to live near, but not with, their children. In a study of old people in three industrial societies, Shanas and associates (1968) found that 84 percent of those over 65 years old lived less than one hour away from one of their children. Most elderly wish to retain their independence as long as possible, sharing "intimacy from a distance" (Hareven, 1994). Reasons usually cited for preferring separate households include the desire to preserve independence and privacy and to avoid interference and potential conflict with children (Connidis, 1983; Lopata, 1980a).

Using data from nationwide surveys of the adult noninstitutionalized population of the United States, Okraku (1987) has offered evidence that since 1973, attitudes toward multigenerational residence has become more positive. The relationship between age and level of approval is inverse, however. Younger cohorts expressed more unconditional support for coresidence, whereas older cohorts expressed more conditional approval. Situations that include poor health or inadequate finances most often seem to necessitate living with a child.

Figure 10–1 shows the percentages of elderly (60 years of age and over) whites and blacks actually residing with adult children in each available census year from 1900 to 1980 (Ruggles & Goeken, 1992). At the turn of the century, more than 55 percent of whites aged 60 years or older resided with adult children. The propor-

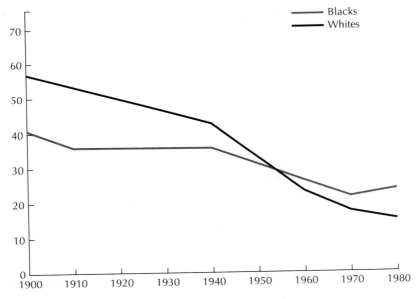

FIGURE 10–1   **Percentage of Persons Aged 60 and Over Residing with Adult Children Controlling for Age, Sex, Marital Status, Presence of Spouse, Metropolitan Residence, and Farm Residence by Race and Census Year**

Source: Reprinted from "Race and Multigenerational Family Structure, 1900–1980," by S. Ruggles and R. Goeken, in *The Changing American Family: Sociological and Demographic Perspectives,* edited by S. J. South and S. E. Tolnay, 1992, Figure 2.3b, p. 24. Copyright © 1992 by WestviewPress. Reprinted by permission of WestviewPress.

tion of elderly blacks with such living arrangements was about 40 percent. By 1980, the situation had changed dramatically. Only about 15 percent of elderly whites resided with adult children, whereas about 25 percent of elderly blacks did so.

According to Ruggles and Goeken (1992), the decline in coresidence among whites came in the category of elderly persons residing with their never-married children. These researchers argue that it became socially acceptable for unmarried women to live on their own and, at the same time, obligations for caring for elderly parents declined. Also, in the years since the end of World War II, increasing income among the elderly allows a greater proportion to reside independently. For African Americans, changes in population composition and improved income, especially since 1960, explain the more modest decline in coresidence.

Why is the decline in coresidence with adult children so much more modest among elderly African Americans? Some have argued that the African American extended family is more instrumental, as elderly kin help the younger generations deal with single parenthood and poverty. Ruggles and Goeken conclude, "Multigenerational families among blacks have served the needs of the younger generation as much as the needs of the older, and this may have helped the survival of this family type into the late twentieth century" (1992, p. 33).

More elderly women than elderly men live in a household headed by one of their children. Of these elderly, more are likely to live with an unmarried child than with a married one, and more with a daughter (65 percent) than with a son (35 percent) (Troll, Miller, & Atchley, 1979). These joint households usually consist of two, not three, generations; only about 4 percent of U.S. households are true three-generation families.

Interaction with Children

Most older parents and their adult children see each other quite often. The Harris Poll (NCOA, 1976) referred to earlier found that 55 percent of those surveyed who were age 65 and over had seen one of their children within the last day or so; 26 percent had seen one of their children within the last week or two. These findings are consistent with those of other studies. In Shanas's study of older people in Denmark, England, and the United States, she reports that 84 percent of the U.S. elderly with living children had seen at least one of their children within the previous week (Shanas et al., 1968). Still, much evidence exists for the considerable and growing diversity in older parent/adult child relations among contemporary families. Researchers have concentrated on several specific factors of social differentiation, including ethnic and racial differences, proximity, urban/rural differences, and gender.

A study of aged ethnics in Washington, DC, and Baltimore revealed that 90.5 percent of the respondents had frequent to almost daily contact with their children (Gutman et al., 1979). There was some variation in contact with children among the ethnic groups: Greeks had the most frequent contact—almost twice as much as did aged Estonians. The nature of the contact was also different among ethnic groups. Hungarians had the highest percentage of those who had face-to-face contact with children, whereas the Lithuanians had the highest amount of phone contact with their children.

Distance may also be a strong determinant of frequency of contact with family for older people. In their study of elderly black residents of Cleveland, Ohio, Wolf and colleagues (1983) report that those who had adult children in the neighborhood had contact with them daily. Those whose children lived an hour away reported significantly less contact.

Conventional wisdom supports an expectation of greater kinship ties and more frequent interaction across the generations in rural areas. Krout (1988) interviewed 600 individuals aged 65 and over residing in a continuum of community settings from farm areas to the central city of a large metropolis in western New York State. His findings suggest that the impact of rurality on the elderly person's in-person contact with children has been overstated. Proximity was a far stronger predictor of in-person contact between elderly parents and their children. Krout concludes that "people in rural areas do not have especially strong family ties or at least they are not evidenced by greater frequency of in-person contact nor are urban areas characterized by a lower level of intergenerational contact" (1988, p. 202).

There appears to be some truth to the maxim that "a son is a son until he gets a wife, and a daughter is a daughter all her life." Research does show visitation to be more frequent along the female line. Husbands are more likely to be in touch with the wives' parents than their own, unless the wife mediates contact with the husband's parents. According to Atkinson, Kivett and Campbell (1986), familial linkages between generations that are female based are predictive of greater exchange of help. From the point of view of these researchers, women are indeed the keepers of kin.

The order of frequency of interaction among New York Jewish families is with wife's mother, husband's mother, wife's father, and husband's father (Leichter & Mitchell, 1967). In a study of three-generation Mexican American families in San Antonio, Texas, respondents were asked how often they engaged in certain activities (e.g., recreation outside the home, religious activities, telephone conversation) with each of their family members in the other two generations. All-female dyads showed higher levels of association than all-male and cross-sex dyads (Markides, Boldt, & Ray, 1986).

Quality of Interaction

Many people believe that as parents age, the parent/child relationship undergoes a role reversal. The parent assumes the role of dependent, while the child takes on the supportive role of the parent. Certainly, this should not be expected; in fact, many gerontologists argue that it cannot work. Clark and Anderson write:

> In our culture there simply cannot be any happy role reversals between the generations.... The mores do not sanction it and children and parents resent it. The parent must remain strong and independent.... The child, on the other hand,

CHINA SEEKS WAYS TO PROTECT ELDERLY
Support Agreements Replacing Traditional Respect for the Aged
Lena H. Sun

Zhao Chunlan, a 73-year-old widow, knows she can count on her son to look after her in her old age. It is not just the notion of filial piety that is putting Zhao's mind at ease; her 51-year-old son and daughter-in-law have signed a support agreement to provide for her material and mental well-being.

In the agreement, the couple has promised to cook her special meals and take her for regular medical checkups. They also agree to give her the largest room in the house, put the family's color television in her room and "never make her angry." Zhao acknowledges that her son took good care of her even before the agreement, "but now that he's signed it, he will be more conscious of his commitment," she said with a smile.

Such support agreements between children and their elderly parents . . . are a new phenomenon in a country that for thousands of years prided itself on reverence for age. Together with rising incidences of abuse and neglect of the aged in recent years, the agreements reflect the growing social problem posed by the country's rapidly increasingly elderly population.

Because of a longer life expectancy and the implementation more than a decade ago of a birth control policy that permitted families to have only one child, China's over-60 population has increased much faster than the overall population. . . . About 65 million people, or 6 percent of China's population, are over 65 . . . the figure is likely to mushroom to 41 to 45 percent of the overall population by the middle of the 21st century. . . .

"The trend of the future will be what we call the ratio of 4:2:1," said Song Yuhua, an official of China's National Committee on Aging, which oversees affairs of the elderly. "That means one child will have to take care of two parents and four grandparents,

and this could result in a series of problems." Western demographers note that no country has yet had more than 18 percent of its population in the 65-and-older category. . . . Some Chinese planners, partly as a result of the aging problem, are now suggesting that the controversial one-child policy be modified to allow families to have two children by the end of the century.

The economic reforms of the past decade have also contributed to new social problems for the elderly. Communes, which carried out important welfare functions, were dismantled in the late 1970s, and the return of private initiative has left local authorities with far less power than before to become involved in the affairs of families. Those trends, together with the lack of a national social security system, have made the elderly even more dependent on family financial support. . . . In some cases, the burden has led to severe mistreatment of the elderly. . . . Some elderly have had their money misappropriated, been denied food and medicine, and been beaten. Some have committed suicide.

In one case in Zhejiang province, an 81-year-old woman was scolded and beaten by her son and daughter-in-law, driven out of their home and forced to become a beggar, according to a report this summer in the official *Legal Daily* newspaper.

She sued her son, and a court ordered that 45 yuan, or about $9, be deducted from his factory wages each month to support his mother. But her son and daughter-in-law assaulted her for refusing to return the benefits, and the woman died within a few months. Police detained the son but released him a few days later.

"What requires our attention is that these cases have not aroused enough attention from the local legal authorities, and this situation has encouraged the bad trend of mistreating the elderly," the newspaper said.

Moreover, the newspaper said, the incident was not an isolated case. In a partial survey of 37 cities and counties in Zhejiang province alone, 187 elderly Chinese have died "abnormal deaths" since 1988 as a result of being denied medical treatment, being coerced into turning over property and being bullied and tortured. These deaths included suicide by poisoning, hanging, jumping from tall buildings and drowning.

"China has a long tradition of respect for the elderly, but as a result of the economic development, we are beginning to see individual instances of neglect of the elderly," said Yuan Xinli, an official with China's National Committee on Aging.... The loosening of controls that came with the economic reforms "made it easy for people to think of their private ends," he said, "so it was easy for the elderly to become neglected."

China's marriage law includes provisions for the care of the elderly, but authorities say the elderly need more protection. Authorities are currently drafting a national law that would include specific measures such as guaranteeing the elderly the right to enjoy the same standard of living as their children, Yuan said.

Financial support for China's elderly depends almost completely on their families, except for a pension program that benefits part of the urban population. The retirement system applies only to employees of the state, workers in state-owned enterprises and workers in large urban collective enterprises.

Western and Chinese experts on aging say it is unlikely that China will develop a national pension or social security system in the near future. According to the latest figures, only about 22 million people received some sort of retirement benefits in 1988... most rural workers have no retirement system, and the government expects sons and their spouses and children to provide financial support and all necessary care for their aged parents.

To help protect the rights of the elderly, particularly in rural areas, some localities have begun requiring contracts of support between elderly parents and their children. A case in point is the village of Tiezu, or Iron Mouth in English, located in Qindu county on the outskirts of Xianyang, a former ancient capital of China in central Shaanxi province.

Starting this year, newlyweds in Qindu district have been required to sign contracts pledging to support their parents after age 60. Older, more-established married couples have been required to sign such more detailed agreements.

"The aim of the agreements is to prevent the rejecting of old parents, to prevent children from cutting off their responsibility of support [to] their parents," said Shi Quanji, vice chairman of the county's committee on aging. With an elderly population of 27,200, an estimated 4,000 couples have so far signed some kind of support agreement, he said.

Although cases of abuse have been rare here in Tiezu, he said, it is very common for children, particularly sons, who are the traditional care-providers, to quarrel among themselves about who will take care of the parent.

The agreements, enforced by the aging committee, try to prevent such quarrels by laying out each child's responsibilities as clearly as possible. In the case of Zhao Jianfang and his wife, for example, their eldest son, Zhao Xiaobao, has agreed to provide the material for his parents' clothes, shoes, and socks, while their younger son, Zhao Erbao, will be responsible for making the clothes.

Source: © 1996, The Washington Post. Reprinted with permission.

must not threaten the security of the parent with request for monetary aid or other care when parental income has shrunk through retirement. The ideal situation is when both parent and child are functioning well. (1967, pp. 275–276)

One measure of the quality of intergenerational family relationships that has interested researchers involves the patterns of assistance that exist between parents and their adult children. In general, it appears that assistance flows both from adult children to their parents, and from the parents to their children. However, Rossi and Rossi (1990) find that parental help to children declines over time, but children's help to parents continues at the same level.

Assistance takes many forms. It may involve carrying out nonessential, informal services that people often perform for each other when they live nearby—occasional shopping, carrying packages, or helping with household maintenance, for instance. Or it may involve providing highly organized, essential assistance such as regular babysitting or continued financial aid. Most studies of aging families focus on the elderly as stressors rather than as resources. Greenberg and Becker (1988) found that aging parents become an important resource when their adult children experience major life changes, most notably in coping with divorce or chemical dependency. Bankoff (1983) reports that supportive elderly parents play a crucial role for their widowed daughters. In fact, her analysis of questionnaire data from a nationwide sample of widows indicates that parents are the single-most important source of support for still grieving widows and that such support is strongly related with the psychological well-being of recently widowed women.

The type of assistance offered (and received) varies by the sex of the parents and the children, as well as by social class. Older men are more likely to assist their children with household maintenance and repairs, whereas elderly women help with child rearing and domestic functions. According to Harris and Cole (1980), adult male children are likely to receive monetary aid from parents, and daughters are likely to receive services. Mutual aid in lower-class families usually involves exchanges of services and shared living arrangements; the middle classes are more likely to provide direct financial assistance. Because of anecdotal evidence of involvement in mutual support activities, it is often assumed that minorities (African Americans, Mexican Americans, and other Hispanic groups) have stronger kin networks than do whites. However, several recent studies have not shown this to be the case (Eggebeen, 1992; Eggebeen & Hogan, 1990).

The two-way flow of support may persist until the onset of extreme frailty in the elderly parent or relative. Even then, rarely are the elderly dumped into institutions. The formal system of government and community agency programs plays only a minor role in providing for the elderly and is viewed by caregivers to the elderly as a last resort when the responsibilities become too complex to handle even with assistance (Stone, Cafferata, & Sangl, 1987). Families act as "case managers," facilitating contact between the elderly individual and the bureaucracy (Seltzer, Ivry, & Litchfield 1987), and provide between 80 and 90 percent of medically related care, home nursing, personal care, household maintenance, transportation, and shopping (Day, 1985).

There is a tendency to overestimate the extent to which parents and their adult children are engaged in some exchange of support services. Using data from the 1987–88 National Survey of Families and Households, Hogan, Eggebeen and Clogg (1993) report only 11.3 percent of the U.S. adult population to be "high exchangers"—that is, parents and their adult children highly involved in exchanges, giving and receiving support on several different dimensions (e.g., giving and/or receiving money, advice, transportation or other assistance, and direct care).

Estimates from the 1982 National Long-Term Survey and Informal Caregivers Survey indicate that in the United States, approximately 2.2 million caregivers were providing unpaid assistance to 1.6 million noninstitutionalized adults with disabilities. Almost three out of four (73 percent) caregivers were either a spouse or a child. The majority (72 percent) were women, with adult daughters comprising 29 percent of all caregivers and wives constituting 23 percent of this population; husbands comprise 13 percent of caregivers and 9 percent were sons. The average age of the caregiver population was 57 years; 36 percent were 65 years or older.

Mathews (1987) reports that when older families include more than one living adult child, filial responsibility is shared. Interestingly, however, her study of 50 pairs of sisters who had at least one parent over the age of 75 found that members of the same family may not share perceptions of how responsibility is being divided. For example, only 52 percent of the pairs of sisters agreed on the way responsibility was divided in the family for giving emotional or moral support to an elderly parent. Data from this same study highlight the impact of employment status on the division of responsibility between sisters. Nonemployed sisters contributed relatively more tangible services than their employed sisters, especially when parents' health status was poorer. Such services included taking a parent to a medical appointment or handling daytime emergencies and care (Mathews, Werkner, & Delaney, 1989).

According to Hareven (1994), life-course antecedents were crucial determinants of whether an individual was cast in the role of "parent keeper." For the most part, children who took on care-giving responsibilities evolved into this role over the life course. Before World War II, among many ethnic groups, the expectation was for the youngest daughter to remain at home and to postpone or give up marriage in order to ensure supports for parents into old age. Even among those care-giving daughters who married, researchers have identified care giving as disruptive to one's work career, a stressor in marriage, and an extra hurdle to overcome in preparing for her own and spouse's retirement (Hareven & Adams, 1994). A number of studies have questioned the focus on women as caregivers for aging parents. Several studies identify a division of labor in which males (sons as well as sons-in-law) perform managerial and maintenance tasks while women provide the daily hands-on care giving (Dwyer & Coward, 1991; Dwyer & Seccombe, 1991).

Does the mutual assistance that appears to characterize intergenerational relations in U.S. families simply reflect feelings of obligation or a sense of duty, or do older parents and their adult children really like each other? In a wide array of studies across geographically disparate areas, older parents and their adult children report positive feelings for each other as well as considerable satisfaction with their relationships. Among aged ethnics living in the Washington, DC, and Baltimore metropolitan areas, over 80 percent of each ethnic group indicated satisfaction with their family relationships. The highest proportion of "very satisfactory" relationships (85.8 percent) was reported by Polish in Baltimore, the lowest (65 percent) was reported by Latvians (Gutman et al., 1979).

Lowenthal, Thurnher, and Chiriboga (1975), reporting on a San Francisco sample, found that middle-aged parents felt good about their children. Bengtson and Black (1973) discovered high levels of regard reported by both older parents and their middle-aged children, although higher levels of sentiment are reported by the older parents. Older parents in a Boston study also rated their relationships with their adult children higher than their children did (Johnson & Bursk, 1977). These studies support the *generational stake theory* (Bengtson & Kuypers, 1971), meaning that the older generation is more invested in the parent/child relationship than are the young.

Many studies about the feelings parents and children have for each other suffer methodologically. Often, they rely on self-reports and they rarely involve both parents and children in the research (Mangen, Bengtson, & Landry, 1988). Nevertheless, researchers' reports show remarkable consistency in the positive feelings older parents and their adult children have for one another. Perhaps this should not be surprising. Similar findings are reported in studies of parent/child relationships across the life cycle (e.g., of high school students and their parents). And why not? After all, Troll and Bengtson (1978) call attention to the high degree of intergenerational continuity there is within the family. Reviewing the available literature on generations in the family, they found parent/child similarity strongest in religious and political affiliations, but important also in sex roles and personality. Although social and historical forces affect people of different ages in different ways, there appears to be great similarity in values within families. These similarities may help explain why aged parents and adult children like each other—although not entirely. As studies seem to indicate, even when aged parents and their adult children disagree, they continue to see each other.

THE FAMILY LIFE CYCLE

Families change with time. The functions the family fulfills shift in importance, just as family structure and patterns of interrelationships change. Where Duvall (1977) speaks of the "generational spiral" and Hess and Handel (1959) of "family themes," some family sociologists now use the notion of the *family life cycle* to characterize the changes families undergo. A well-known and frequently adopted staging of the family life cycle has been put forth by Duvall (1977):

Stage 1:   Establishment (newly married, childless)

Stage 2:   New parents (infant to age 3)

Stage 3:   Preschool family (child aged 3 to 6, possibly younger siblings)

Stage 4:   School-age family (oldest child aged 6 to 12, possibly younger siblings)

Stage 5:   Family with adolescent (oldest child 13 to 19, possibly younger siblings)

Stage 6:   Family with young adult (oldest child aged 20, until first child leaves home)

Stage 7:   Family as launching center (from departure of first child to that of last child)

Stage 8:   Postparental family (after all children have left home)

It is important to recognize that this sequence of stages is an ideal representation of the life of a couple that marries, has children, and stays together through the course of the life cycle. Obviously, some people never marry, others marry and do not have children, and many marry and later divorce. Furthermore, any sequencing of stages downplays the variation in family life that can be produced by differences in the earlier life experiences of family members and by changing historical conditions (Cherlin, 1983).

Family life cycles can overlap, and, as a result, a family chain may go on. Children born into a family (sometimes referred to as their *family of orientation*) may later marry and begin their own families (their *family of procreation*). It is the adult child's family of procreation that produces the role of grandparent for the older parent.

Although this chapter especially focuses on the last stage of the family life cycle, it should be understood that the stages themselves are not stagnant: Within each stage, significant changes in family structure and relationships may take place. For example, one might assume, and much literature suggests, that the quality of the marriage relationship changes significantly in stage 2 with the onset of parenthood. In addition, as will be seen shortly, events that occur during the last stage—birth of a grandchild, retirement, death of a spouse, remarriage—may clearly change the character of the older person's family life.

The Postparental Family

Marital status is a simple, obvious criterion for distinguishing older people who are in families from those who are not. Table 10–1 shows the marital status distribution of older males and females in 1993. The marital distribution of men differs sharply from that of women in the three age groupings shown. In 1993, four of five men aged 65 to 74 years (80.1 percent) were married; only about one of eleven (9.4 percent) was widowed. Women, especially those aged 75 years and over, are much more likely to be widowed than married. In 1993, 54.0 percent of women aged 65

TABLE 10–1   Marital Status of the Elderly by Sex and Age, 1993

	Single	Married	Widowed	Divorced	Total
Male					
55–64 years	6.6%	80.9%	3.7%	8.9%	100.0%
65–74 years	4.8	80.1	9.4	5.6	100.0
75 years and older	3.8	71.0	22.6	2.6	100.0
Female					
55–64 years	4.2%	69.1%	14.4%	12.2%	100.0%
65–74 years	3.7	54.0	35.2	7.1	100.0
75 years and older	5.4	26.6	63.8	4.2	100.0

Source: U.S. Bureau of the Census, *Statistical Abstract of the United States: 1994* (114th edition). Washington, DC: U.S. Government Printing Office, Table 60.

to 74 and 26.6 percent of women aged 75 and over were married; about one-half of all women 65 years of age and older were widowed (63.8 percent among those aged 75 and over). The changes in marital status since the end of World War II have been quite substantial, especially for men. The proportion of elderly men who are married has increased, and the proportions of single and widowed men have fallen significantly.

Two important factors contribute to the sharply different marital distributions of men and women. The first is the much higher mortality rates of married men than for married women. As discussed earlier, men have higher mortality rates than women. In addition, husbands are typically older than their wives by a few years. Siegel (1976) indicates that the expectation of life at age 65 for married women exceeds that of their husbands at age 70 by about nine years. Thus, not only do most married women outlive their husbands, but they tend to do so by many years.

A second factor accounting for the significantly higher proportion of widows than widowers is the higher remarriage rate of widowers. The marriage rate of elderly men is about seven times that of elderly women, and the vast majority of these are remarriages. Societal norms are much more supportive of an elderly man marrying a younger woman than of the opposite. Men also have a demographic advantage in the marriage market. As Table 10–1 shows, in each age group, the proportion of older women who are unmarried is more than twice as great as the proportion of unmarried men (19.9 versus 46.0 percent among those 65 to 74 years, for example).

The Older Couple

Most elderly couples today have grown old together. The average couple has launched a family and can expect about 15 years of living together after the departure of the last child. At the turn of the century, more than half of all marriages were interrupted by the death of one spouse, usually the husband, before the last child left home (Harris & Cole, 1980). The increase in these postparental years, sometimes referred to as the *empty-nest period*, is due to increased life expectancies as well as to more closely spaced and smaller families.

Researchers have examined closely what happens after the launching of the children, yet consensus is difficult to achieve. Some studies show that marital satisfaction is as high or higher among older couples as it is among child-rearing couples, and that older couples report fewer marital problems. Several researchers have suggested that this pattern represents a supposedly typical marital life cycle in which satisfaction is high right after marriage, lower during the child-rearing years, and higher again during the postparental period (Rollins & Cannon, 1974; Stinnett, Carter, & Montgomery, 1972). Lowenthal, Thurnher, and Chiriboga (1975) found that most married couples look forward to the postparenting years. Many see the possibility for increased closeness and companionship. Stinnett, Collins, and Montgomery (1970) found elderly couples to be happier, less lonely, and financially more stable than elderly single persons. However, if many unhappy or financially unstable marriages have previously ended in divorce, there may be a survivor effect in long-lived marriages.

The *marital relationship* may not be a blessing for all older people, however. Marital disenchantment may surface during the latter stages of the family life cycle, resulting in reduced satisfaction with the relationship, loss of intimacy, and less sharing of activities. Care-giving responsibilities may place a special strain on some elderly marriages (Barusch, 1988). For many couples, the marital relationship becomes subordinate during the child-rearing years and remains so after the children leave home. Atchley (1980) reports that every year nearly 10,000 older Americans are divorced. Divorce among older people has more than doubled since 1960 and divorce rates are currently higher among younger cohorts of adults (Uhlenberg & Myers, 1981). Table 10–1 provides data to suggest that divorce is inclined to be more prevalent among future cohorts of older people; in 1993, men and women aged 55 to 64 report being currently divorced at a rate higher than that for men and women aged 65 to 74. What the table does not show is that men and women aged 45 to 54 already show higher rates of divorce than those 55 to 64 years old. Also, because many elderly view being divorced as a stigma, there is reason to believe that the elderly actually underreport their current marital status as divorced.

Chiriboga (1982) points out that older persons appear particularly vulnerable to the divorce process. From a study of separated men and women living in the San Francisco-Oakland metropolitan area, he concludes that, relative to the young, older respondents were unhappier and reported fewer positive emotional experiences. Further, he notes that "their dealings with the social world appeared more tortured, there were more signs of personal discomfort, and their perceptions of the past and future reflected both greater pessimism and long-term dissatisfaction" (p. 113).

Cain argues that divorce among the elderly has been a hidden social phenomenon undistinguished from divorce among the young. She quotes one aged divorceé as follows:

They lump us all together.... My daughter divorced at 33, and it was the pits for her, I well remember. But divorce for her was in no way the same as divorce for me.... She was heartbroken to be sure...but it was not the end of the world for her. She still had her children, a good job and a ton of divorced friends who "celebrated" the end of her marriage. When I was left at 64, the children were grown and scattered. I had no job, less than no confidence, and I did not know one woman my age who was similarly dumped. (1982, pp. 89–90)

Although the majority of older couples define the empty-nest period favorably, some do experience serious problems. Women especially may find this to be a crucial time. A larger percentage of wives evaluated the postparental period both more favorably and more unfavorably than did husbands. The difficulties appear to center on three areas: (1) the advent of menopause and other disabilities associated with the aging process, (2) the final recognition and definition in retrospect of oneself as a "failure" either in terms of the work career or the child-raising process, and (3) the inability to fill the gap left in the family by the departure of the children (Deutscher, 1964).

Most elderly couples seem to adjust to retirement quite well. Research in this area focuses primarily on the changes in family role differentiation that occur when a male retiree enters the wife's domain—the household. Some studies suggest that a large proportion of wives do not look forward to their husbands' retirements. Many wives resent the intrusion into the household of husbands who are home all day. They also express concern about having to live on a reduced income. Heyman and Jeffers (1968) found a positive relationship between the length of husbands' retirements and the proportion of wives expressing negative attitudes toward their husbands' retirements.

Kerckhoff (1966) observed social class differences in the effect of retirement on the redefinition of roles in the elderly household. Husbands' participation in domestic chores was welcomed by wives and seen as desirable by both spouses in upper- and middle-class households. Among working-class couples, however, both husbands and wives viewed increased participation in household chores by the husband as undesirable. Ballweg (1967) suggests that although sharing domestic duties, in general, contributes to marital harmony among retirement couples, it does so especially when traditional sex-role task differentiation is continued. Thus, men may assume responsibility for so-called masculine household tasks involving physical and mechanical skills, whereas women retain the more so-called feminine tasks such as laundry and dusting. One study of couples married for 50 or more years seems to substantiate this finding (Sporakowski & Hughston, 1978).

Widowhood

About one-half of all women aged 65 years and older are widows, and they outnumber widowers by a ratio of about five to one. Thus, it is not surprising that most of the research literature on widowhood deals with aged women. The few studies of widowers indicate that their main problems include loneliness, social isolation, fewer contacts with family and friends, and discomfort over self-maintenance. These studies have been principally concerned with the question of whether widowhood is harder on men or on women. Although widowers may be confronted with unfamiliar domestic and self-maintenance tasks, widowers also are more likely to drive a car and to have a higher income than widows. Adjustment to widowhood is especially problematic for men when they suffer several role losses within a short time span. As one would expect, the combination of loss of job, reduction of income, declining health, and loss of spouse can be traumatic. Still, some research suggests that the similarities between widows and widowers is more striking than the differences (Feinson, 1986).

In the United States, the role of older widow is ambiguous. Although the term *widow* is useful for describing a marital status, it is not at all useful for understanding how someone who occupies this status is expected to behave. In fact, there are no clear expectations for behavior in this role. Given the anomic situation in which older widows find themselves, it is no wonder that the great bulk of the research on widowhood highlights the negative personal consequences that accompany the change from spouse to widow. Statistics indicate that the widowed have higher rates of mortality, mental disorders, and suicide. It has generally been assumed that widowhood brings low morale. Shulman (1975) has reported that widows are more likely than single or married elders to describe the past as the happiest time of life, and twice as likely to be depressed or lonely.

Helena Lopata, perhaps the foremost student of widowhood, believes that the modern urban United States presents a unique cultural context for widowhood. Three factors appear to contribute to this uniqueness relative both to the historical past and to some other parts of the contemporary world:

1. The modern nuclear family in the United States is expected to be socially and economically independent. Ties to the broader kinship network are there, but they are loose. In particular, ties to the male family line are weak.

2. Although the situation is beginning to change in the United States, it is still clearly the case that wives are economically dependent on their husbands' sources of income.

3. U.S. society places extremely high importance on the marital relationship and on the development of strong mutual dependence between marital partners (Lopata, 1980b).

Lopata (1973) has attempted to divide the widowhood experience into four stages: (1) official recognition of the event, (2) temporary disengagement or withdrawal from established lines of communication, (3) limbo, and (4) reengagement. The first stage typically begins with the funeral and includes the initial mourning period. *Grief work* is a term that describes the confrontation that must be made with the death of a spouse. This takes time and may involve a temporary withdrawal from previous social activities and responsibilities. Reengagement may begin with the question, How and where do I go from here?

Reengagement does not bring with it an end to the problems associated with widowhood—it may only be the beginning. The most serious problems widows must face are loneliness and a severe drop in income. Lopata (1978) has written of the failure of community resources to provide supports for widows who are trying to rebuild their lives and who have difficulty dealing with their problems. Children are key figures in the support systems of the widowed elderly, but relations between adult children and their widowed parents may be less likely to be reciprocal than is the case between adult children and their married parents (Heinemann, 1983). Because of the difficulties associated with being dependent on children, there is some indication that widows in support networks of friends or neighbors show higher morale (Balkwell, 1985). This finding is particularly interesting in light of the *principle of substitution* (Shanas, 1979b), which argues that elderly in need of support are likely to receive it in serial order, depending on availability, from a spouse, then a child, and then from siblings, other relatives, and friends and neighbors.

Despite one's understanding of the trauma of widowhood and of the adjustments it necessitates for many aged women, one must be careful not to overstate its impact. Some women downgrade the wife role, have less satisfying relationships with their husbands, and are in marriages that are less couple oriented than more successful marriages are. This configuration of attitudes may reduce the impact of widowhood.

It is also the case that the lower morale experienced by widows may come not from widowhood but from changes brought about as a result of widowhood. Morgan (1976) has looked at the relationship between widowhood and morale while controlling for some accompaniments of widowhood, such as loss of income and loss of self-image. He found that, when these things were held constant, the morale scores of widowed women were not different from those of their nonwidowed counterparts.

Remarriage

Remarriage may be a desirable alternative for many elderly divorced or widowed people. Whether it is a realistic alternative is another matter. In 1988, only 1 percent of all the brides and 1.9 percent of the all grooms in the United States were 65 years old and over. However, in the same year, women aged 65 and older accounted for 2.8 percent of all remarriages among women, whereas men in this age group accounted for 5.2 percent of all remarriages among men. For those aged 35 years and older, remarriage rates among men and women, divorced and widowed, have increased somewhat since 1980. Still, the great majority of these remarriages occur among those aged 35 to 55 years. Society offers little impetus to marry in the later years. The reasons for marriage in the United States today are not pertinent to the single aged: premarital pregnancy or the desire for children, escape from parental domination, social validation of adult heterosexuality, and pressure for conformity.

Aged marriages appear to be successful. Treas and VanHilst (1976) found that remarriages of the aged were most successful when based on mutual affection and financial security. Children's approval seemed to contribute to the success of the marriages. Vinick (1978) studied remarriage in a small sample of Massachusetts elderly. Most remarriages were formed on the basis of companionship. Many in the sample used the statement "It just turned into something" to describe the courtship. The desire for care was also important to the men; the personal qualities of the mate were important to the women. Those who were unhappy with their remarriages felt forced into the marriage because of external circumstances, such as financial need. For men, marital satisfaction was positively correlated with their past attitudes toward remarriage and their mental and physical health. For women, marital satisfaction was associated with the attitudes of peers, the quality of housing, and financial position.

Grandparenting

Grandparenting has become an event of middle age. Early marriage, earlier child-bearing, and longer life expectancy are producing grandparents in their 40s (Troll, Miller, & Atchley, 1979). The rocking-chair image of grandparents is disappearing. Grandparents still work and remain quite active. Moreover, as Troll and associates point out, many find their loyalties split between helping to care for their grandchildren and helping to care for their aged parents.

About 75 percent of the elderly in the United States have living grandchildren (Troll, Miller, & Atchley, 1979). The Harris poll referred to earlier in this chapter reports that nearly one-half of all U.S. grandparents see a grandchild every day or so, although it is generally believed that only a small fraction of households headed by older people include a grandchild.

The high rates of divorce and remarriage in the United States have provided dramatic changes in the kinship networks of grandparents. Expanding networks are more common among paternal grandmothers, who are much more likely to retain relationships with former daughters-in-law than are maternal grandmothers with former sons-in-law (Johnson & Barer, 1987). But the expansion may be considerably broader. From the grandmothers' perspective, the relatives of children's divorces include former children-in-law, their parents and children, and even their new spouses and their relatives. With the remarriage of children, potential relatives include new children-in-law, their parents and children, and even their former spouses and relatives (Johnson & Barer, 1987). This "stretching out" of kinship networks can force role changes for many grandparents; some may even have to employ several different styles of grandparenting.

The grandparent role has different meanings for different people, and often the meaning of the role is reflected in the style of grandparenting. Neugarten and Weinstein (1964) have classified the different styles of grandparenting into five categories:

Most elderly in the United States having living grandchildren, and many elderly grandparents see a grandchild every day.

1. The *formal* grandparent likes to provide special treats and indulgences for the grandchild but maintains clearly demarcated lines between parenting and grandparenting. This grandparent leaves parenting strictly to the parents, maintaining constant interest in the grandchild but offering no advice.

2. The *fun seeker* maintains a playful and informal relationship with the grandchild, with the emphasis on mutual satisfaction.

3. The *surrogate parent* role is played by grandmothers whose daughters work and who assume responsibility for taking care of the child during the day.

4. The *reservoir of family wisdom* refers mainly to grandparents who possess special skills or resources and who expect young parents to maintain a subordinate position.

5. The *distant figure* is the grandparent who has contact with the grandchildren only on holidays and special occasions but otherwise remains distant and remote from the grandchild's life.

The styles of grandparenting are related to age. *Fun seekers* and *distant figures* are usually younger, whereas *formal* grandparents are more typically older.

McCready (1985) has used national survey data to determine whether ethnicity can usefully explain variation in the styles of grandparenting that are adopted. Although not every older person in these national surveys is an actual grandparent, the respondents represent a "grandparent cohort" of people of like age and experience. The ethnic groups represented were English, Scandinavian, German, Irish, Italian, and Polish. Characteristics of children were grouped in a fashion that approximated the five styles of grandparenting described here, though the *formal* and *distant* styles were combined because there was no measure of contact frequency upon which to base distance (McCready, 1985).

Generally, males were more likely to exhibit attitudes and responses linked to the formal/distant style of grandparenting, whereas the women emphasized the more informal and affect-oriented styles of behavior (McCready, 1985). Scandinavians, Irish, and Italians (grandmothers and grandfathers alike) were above the mean on scores of the formal/distant and surrogate styles; English and Italian grandmothers were the only groups to score above the mean on measures representing the reservoir-of-wisdom style of grandparenting. German grandfathers scored high on the formal/distant and surrogate styles though German grandmothers only scored positively on the latter. Almost uniformly, representatives of the ethnic groups in this study scored low or negative on indicators of the fun-seeking style. McCready suggests that "the affective dimensions of the grandparent-grandchild relationship are not as prized by these respondents as the more behavioral and 'correct' dimensions of childrens' behavior" (1985, p. 57). Clearly, the cultural diversity that exists within grandparent populations in the United States reveals itself in diverse styles of grandparent/grandchild interaction.

Some attention has begun to focus on the growing number of great-grandparents in the United States. Employing data from a small sample, Doka and Mertz (1988) identify two basic styles of grandparenting: remote and close. In the *remote* style, great-grandparents had limited and ritualistic contact with their greatgrandchildren. Typically, this occurred on family and holiday occasions. Those who adopted a *close* style had frequent and regular contact with their great-grandchildren, often babysat for them, and took them on trips or shopping. As Doka and Mertz conclude, there are many similarities between grandparenthood and great-grandparenthood, but clearly more research is needed to gain a fuller perspective on the dynamics of four- or five-generation families.

What do grandchildren think of their grandparents? Children often develop attitudes toward their grandparents (and perhaps to the aged in general) that are consistent with the attitudes of their parents. Some research suggests that children observe how their parents treat their grandparents and then treat their parents similarly when they become old.

The type of grandparent a child prefers appears strongly related to the age of the child. Kahana and Kahana (1970) found that younger children (preschool age) favored indulgent grandparents who gave them gifts; older children wanted grandparents to be active and fun. Robertson (1976) found that grandchildren between the ages of 16 and 26 had extremely favorable attitudes toward their grandparents; 92 percent of them indicated that they would miss having grandparents if they did not have them. For these grandchildren, the most desirable qualities that these grandchildren wanted in a grandparent were intelligence, love, gentleness, understanding, sense of humor, ability to communicate, and industriousness. It appears that although the role of grandparent is not meaningful to all older people, most grandchildren seem to have strong affection toward their grandparents.

Friendship: Quasi-Familial Relations?

Much gerontological research focuses on marriage and parental status. As Schneider (1980) articulates it, U.S. culture is still strongly pronatalist and marriage is normative. Yet, more than 20 percent of older adults in the United States have no children and some 5 to 6 percent have never married. As Table 10–1 shows for 1993, among those 65 to 75 years of age, 19.9 percent of males and 46 percent of females report being unmarried; while for those 75 years of age and older, 29 percent of males and 73.4 percent of females similarly report being unmarried.

Friendships are particularly important in later life, and especially so for elderly people who are unmarried, lack close family nearby, and have lost the social contacts of work. For those who live alone, friends may be the main, even the sole, source of emotional support. They offer protection from a hostile society, yet also provide a context within which new roles can be developed. According to Kahn and Antonucci (1980), the value of friends in late life consists of three elements: aid, affect, and affirmation. Friends may provide aid through practical assistance with the daily tasks of living. They also are valuable in affirming a person's identity and self-worth through expressions of liking, respect, and agreement.

A number of researchers report that life satisfaction among older adults is positively related to the quantity and quality of contacts with friends (Antonucci, 1985; Essex & Nam, 1987), and this relationship appears to cut across gender and ethnicity. The support of close friends has been found to buffer the effects of stress on mental and physical health (Bankoff, 1983), to maintain morale (Schafer, Coyne, & Lazarus, 1981), and to encourage preventive health behaviors (Abella & Heslin, 1984). One explanation for these effects is that friendships develop voluntarily, and are based on companionship and mutual gratification. Family relationships are often sustained through prescribed norms and formal obligations; they are not always positive. Older adults are especially concerned that they not become burdens to their families.

Although friendships are generally chosen, Arber and Ginn (1991) point out that opportunities for friendships may be structured by material and social circumstances—employment, social class position, health, marital status, and even gender all have impact on friendship patterns. As Allan describes, adult men and women "occupy separate spheres...have different demands made of them, and consequently...develop different skills and abilities...[and] different friend-ship patterns" (1989, p. 66). Men, especially among the working and lower middle-classes, often develop work-based friendships that are weakened at retirement.

Women, on the other hand, may also lose daily contact with workmates, but, more importantly, as they age, women experience greater freedom from demands of children and extra time for existing and new friends. They are also more likely than men to replace lost friends with new ones (Wright, 1989). Older women typi-cally have more friends, on average, than do older men (Fischer & Oliker, 1983). Also, the quality of their friendships appears to differ from those of men. Women's friends are more likely to be close confidantes who share the ups and downs of emotional life, whereas elderly men are thought to rely on their spouses to fulfill this function.

Rubinstein and associates (1991) used extensive interviews to explore the important relationships of never-married, childless older women. They identify six types of key personal relationships, including two based on blood ties, three types of "constructed" relationships, and friendship. *Blood ties* included the cores-ident daughter role (living with one or both parents until their deaths) and collat-eral ties based on the aunt role (involvement in the life of a sibling's family). *Constructed ties* included (1) affiliation with nonkin families (being "adopted" into a family to which they are not biologically related), (2) development of quasi-parental relations with younger nonrelatives to whom they acted like parents, and (3) sometimes coresidential, same-generation, same-gender companionate rela-tions that often resemble extended family.

Although *friendships* were very significant in the lives of almost all the women interviewed, they were distinguishable from companionate relations by the absence of a feeling of certain and secure care if the need arose. In fact, typically, the women did not desire that their friendships be sources of care, "fearing the change of voluntary mutuality into dependency" (Allen, 1989, p. S275). Still, enduringness was a characteristic of these friendships:

> You understand each other better if you know each other for fifty years or seventy years or whatever it is. And complete trust of course. You trust them with deci-sions, they trust you with decisions. You understand each other without talking. After all, seventy years is older than most married couples. (Allen, 1989, p. S275)

Antonucci (1985) does report that there is an age-related decline in friends and acquaintances that presumably has consequences for women as well as men, regardless of marital status. Reasons for this decline include:

1. Movement from the relatively age-segregated environments of youth (high school and college) into age-integrated work settings and neighborhoods makes friendships more difficult to establish.

2. Geographic mobility during middle and later adulthood makes long-term friendships difficult to maintain.

3. Focus on development of family and career (and often two careers) reduces the size of friendship networks.

4. The likelihood that members of one's friendship network will die increases with age.

Will the differentials observed in patterns of friendship between current cohorts of older women and men hold up in future cohorts of aged? One view is that as young women are more involved in careers and workplaces, their future friendship patterns may more resemble those of men. Arber and Ginn (1991) suggest that this is likely only if men also change in the future, being more equally involved in child care and other domestic tasks.

SUMMARY

The common perspective that family structure has changed in the United States from the extended to the nuclear type has come under serious question. Historical demographers now argue that the nuclear family probably was the dominant type of family structure during the American colonial period and has since been the modal family type in the United States.

In its colonial phase, this country was a gerontophilic society, where being old conferred power and prestige. Cultural, demographic, and technological changes have brought a loss of status to older people.

Family sociologists and gerontologists use the notion of a modified extended family to describe the place of the elderly in the contemporary U.S. kin network. There is little evidence that older people are isolated from their families. Most older people live near, but not with, their children and interact with them frequently. Assistance in the form of goods, services, and financial aid flows both from adult children to their parents, and from the parents to their children, although there is great diversity in patterns of association and exchange.

The marital distribution of elderly men differs sharply from that of elderly women. Most elderly men are married, whereas about one-half of all elderly women are widowed. Most older couples are satisfied with their marriages and have adjusted to retirement.

Widowhood is a more difficult adjustment. The widowed have high rates of mortality, mental disorders, and suicide. The most serious problems that widows face are loneliness and a decline in income. Few elderly get the opportunity to remarry, although there is a demographic advantage to men, who are a relatively scarce resource. Aged marriages do seem to be successful.

Many, but not all, grandparents find grandparenting a significant role to play. There is significant diversity in grandparenting styles in the United States today. Most grandchildren seem to have strong affection for their grandparents.

Some older people have never married; a sizable percentage of those who have married have no children. Friendships are particularly important for those who are unmarried, or have no children, or lack close family nearby. Friends provide practical assistance as well as affect and affirmation. Opportunities for friendships may differ as a function of health and gender, among other factors. There does appear to be an age-related decline in friendships experienced by both men and women.

STUDY QUESTIONS

1. Discuss the contrasting views social historians have of the U.S. family of bygone days.

2. Define *modified extended family*. How does such a family differ from the extended and nuclear families?

3. Discuss Fischer's notion of a "revolution in age relations" that occurred in the United States between 1770 and 1820. What are its implications for the position of the elderly in families?

4. In relation to frequency and quality of interaction, discuss the relationship between aging parents and adult children in the contemporary U.S. family.

5. Explain what is meant by the *empty-nest period*. What are the positive and negative implications for the older couple experiencing this period of the family life cycle?

6. Helena Lopata divided widowhood into four stages. List and explain each of these stages.

7. Neugarten and Weinstein have classified the different stages of grandparenting into five categories. List and explain each of these stages.

8. Why are friendships viewed as so important for the aged? How do friendships differ from family relationships? How would you explain different friendship patterns among men and women?

REFERENCES

Abella, R., & Heslin, R. (1984). Health, locus of control, values, and the behavior of family and friends: An integrated approach to understanding health behavior. *Basic and Applied Social Psychology, 5*, 283–293.

Adams, B. (1971). Isolation, function and beyond: American kinship in the 1960's. In C. Broderick (Ed.), *A decade of family research and action*. Minneapolis: Council on Family Relations.

Allan, G. (1989). *Friendship: Developing a sociological perspective*. Hemel Hempstead: Harvester Wheatsheaf.

Antonucci, T. (1985). Personal characteristics, social support, and social behavior. In R. H. Binstock & E. Shanas (Eds.), *Handbook of aging and the social sciences* (2nd ed.). New York: Van Nostrand Reinhold.

Arber, S., & Ginn, J. (1991). *Gender and later life: A sociological analysis of resources and constraints*. London, England: Sage.

Atchley, R. (1980). *Social forces in later life* (3rd ed.). Belmont, CA: Wadsworth.

Atkinson, M. P., Kivett, V. R., & Campbell, R. T. (1986). Intergenerational solidarity: An examination of a theoretical model. *Journal of Gerontology, 41* (3), 408–416.

Back, K. (1974). *The three-generation household in pre-industrial society: Norm or expedient*. Paper presented at the meeting of the Gerontological Society, Portland, OR.

Balkwell, C. (1985). An attitudinal correlate of the timing of a major life event: The case of morale in widowhood. *Family Relations, 34* (4), 577–581.

Ballweg, J. (1967). Resolution of conjugal role adjustment after retirement. *Journal of Marriage and the Family, 299*, 277–281.

Bankoff, E. (1983). Aged parents and their widowed daughters: A support relationship. *Journal of Gerontology, 38* (2), 226–230.

Barusch, A. S. (1988). Problems and coping strategies of elderly spouse caregivers. *The Gerontologist, 28*, 667–685.

Bengtson, V., & Black, K. (1973). Intergenerational relations and continuities in socialization. In P. Baltes & K. Schaie (Eds.), *Life-span developmental psychology*. New York: Academic Press.

Bengtson, V., & Kuypers, J. A. (1971). Generational differences and the "developmental stake." *Aging and Human Development, 2* (1), 249–260.

Bengtson, V., Rosenthal, C., & Burton, L. (1990). Families and aging: Diversity and heterogeneity, In R. H. Binstock & L. K. George (Eds.), *Handbook of aging and the social sciences* (3rd ed.). San Diego, CA: Academic Press.

Cain, B. (1982). Plight of the gray divorcé. *New York Times Magazine, December 19*, pp. 89–90, 92, 94.

Cherlin, A. (1983). A sense of history: Recent research on aging and the family. In M. W. Riley, B. B. Hess, & K. Bond (Eds.), *Aging in society: Selected reviews of recent research*. Hillsdale, NJ: Lawrence Erlbaum.

Chiriboga, D. (1982). Adaptation to marital separation in later and earlier life. *Journal of Gerontology, 37* (1), 109–114.

Clark, M., & Anderson, B. (1967). *Culture and aging*. Springfield, IL: Charles C. Thomas.

Connidis, I. (1983). Living arrangement choices of older residents. *Canadian Journal of Sociology, 8*, 359–375.

Connidis, I. (1989). *Family ties and aging*. Toronto: Butterworths.

Day, A. T. (1985). *Who cares? Demographic trends challenge family care for the elderly.* Number 9: Population Trends and Public Policy. Washington, DC: Population Reference Bureau.

Demos, J. (1965). Notes on life in Plymouth Colony. *William and Mary Quarterly (Third Series), 22*, 264–286.

Demos, J. (1968). Families in colonial Bristol, Rhode Island: An exercise in historical demography. *William and Mary Quarterly (Third Series), 25*, 40–57.

Demos, J. (1978). Old age in early New England. *American Journal of Sociology, 84* (Supplement), S248–287.

Deutscher, I. (1964). The quality of postparental life. *Journal of Marriage and the Family, 26* (1), 52–59.

Doka, K. J., & Mertz, M. E. (1988). The meaning and significance of great-grandparenthood. *The Gerontologist, 28* (2), 192–197.

Duvall, E. M. (1977). *Family development* (5th ed.). Philadelphia: J. B. Lippincott.

Dwyer, J. W., & Coward, R. T. (1991). A multivariate comparison of the involvement of adult sons and daughters in the care of impaired parents. *Journal of Gerontology, 46* (5), S259–S269.

Dwyer, J. W., & Seccombe, K. (1991). Elder care as family labor: The influence of gender and family position. *Journal of Family Issues, 12*, 229–247.

Eggebeen, D. J. (1992). Family structure and intergenerational exchanges. *Research on Aging, 14*, 427–447.

Eggebeen, D. J., & Hogan, D. P. (1990). Giving between generations in American families. *Human Nature, 1*, 211–232.

Essex, M. J., & Nam, S. (1987). Marital status and loneliness among older women. *Journal of Marriage and the Family, 49*, 93–106.

Feinson, M. J. (1986). Aging widows and widowers: Are there mental health differences? *International Journal of Aging and Human Development, 23* (4), 241–255.

Fischer, D. (1977). *Growing old in America*. New York: Oxford University Press.

Fischer, C., & Oliker, S. (1983). A research note on friendship, gender, and the life cycle. *Social Forces, 62*, 124–133.

Goode, W. (1963). *World revolution and family patterns*. New York: The Free Press.

Greenberg, J. S., & Becker, M. (1988). Aging parents as family resources. *The Gerontologist, 28* (6), 786–791.

Greenfield, S. (1967). Industrialization and the family in sociological theory. *American Journal of Sociology, 67*, 312–322.

Greven, P. (1966). Family structure in seventeenth century Andover, Mass. *William and Mary Quarterly (Third Series), 23*, 234–356.

Gutman, D., Kolm, R., Mostwin, D., & Associates (1979). *Informal and formal support systems and their effect on the lives of the elderly in selected ethnic groups*. Washington, DC: The Catholic University of America.

Hagested, G. O. (1988). Demographic change and the life course: Some emerging trends in the family realm. *Family Relations, 37,* 405–410.

Hareven, T. (1994). Aging and generational relations: A historical and life course perspective. In J. Hagan & K. S. Cook (Eds.), *Annual review of sociology, Volume 20, 1994.* Palo Alto, CA: Annual Reviews.

Hareven, T., & Adams, K. (1994). The generation in the middle: Cohort comparisons in assistance to aging parents in an American community. In T. Hareven (Ed.), *Aging and generational relations over the life course: A historical and cross-cultural perspective.* Berlin: Walter de Gruyter.

Harris, T., & Cole, W. (1980). *Sociology of aging.* Boston: Houghton Mifflin.

Heinemann, G. D. (1983). Family involvement and support for widowed persons. In T. H. Brubaker (Ed.), *Family relationships in later life.* Beverly Hills: Sage.

Heyman, D., & Jeffers, F. (1968). Wives and retirement: A pilot study. *Journal of Gerontology, 23,* 488–496.

Hogan, D. P., Eggebeen, D. J., & Clogg, C. C. (1993). The structure of intergenerational exchanges in American families. *American Journal of Sociology, 98* (6), 1428–1458.

Johnson, C. L., & Barer, B. M. (1987). Marital instability and the changing kinship networks of grandparents. *The Gerontologist, 17,* 90–96.

Johnson, E., & Bursk, B. (1977). Relationships between the elderly and their adult children. *The Gerontologist, 17,* 90–96.

Kahana, B., & Kahana, E. (1970). Grandparenthood from the perspective of the developing grandchild. *Developmental Psychology, 3* (1), 98-l05.

Kahn, R., & Antonucci, T. (1980). Convoys over the life course: Attachment, roles and social support. In P. Baltes & O. Brim (Eds.), *Life-span development and behavior* (Vol. 3). New York: Academic Press.

Kart, C., & Engler, C. (1985). Family relations of aged colonial Jews: A testamentary analysis. *Ageing and Society, 5,* 289–304.

Kerckhoff, A. (1966). Family patterns and morale in retirement. In I. Simpson & J. McKinney (Eds.), *Social aspects of aging.* Durham, NC: Duke University Press.

Krout, J. (1988). Rural versus urban differences in elderly parents' contact with their children. *The Gerontologist, 28* (2), 190–203.

Laslett, P., & Harrison, W. (1963). Clayworth and Cogenhoe. In H. Bell & R. Ollard (Eds.), *Historical essays, 1660–1750.* London: Adam and Charles Black.

Leichter, H., & Mitchell, W. (1967). *Kinship and casework.* New York: Russell Sage Foundation.

Litwak, E. (1965). Extended kin relations in an industrial democratic society. In E. Shanas & G. F. Streib (Eds.), *Social structure and the family.* Englewood Cliffs, NJ: Prentice-Hall.

Lopata, H. (1973). *Widowhood in an American city.* Cambridge, MA: Schenkman.

Lopata, H. (1978). The absence of community resources in support systems of urban widows. *Family Coordinator, 27* (4), 383–388.

Lopata, H. (1980a). The widowed family member. In N. Datan & N. Lohmann (Eds.), *Transitions of aging.* New York: Academic Press.

Lopata, H. (1980b). Widows and widowers. In H. Cox (Ed.), *Aging* (2nd ed.). Guilford, CT: Dushkin.

Lowenthal, M., Thurnher, M., & Chiriboga, D. (1975). *Four stages of life.* San Francisco: Jossey-Bass.

Mangen, D., Bengtson, V. L., & Landry, P. H. (1988). *Measurement of intergenerational relations.* Beverly Hills: Sage.

Manton, K. G., & Liu, K. (1984). *The future growth of the long-term care population.* Projections based on the 1977 National Nursing Home Survey and the 1982 Long-Term Care Survey.

Markides, K. S., Boldt, J. S., & Ray, L. A. (1986). Sources of helping and intergenerational solidarity: A three-generations study of Mexican Americans. *Journal of Gerontology, 41* (4), 506–511.

McCready, W. C. (1985). Styles of grandparenting among white ethnics. In V. L. Bengtson & J. F. Robertson (Eds.), *Grandparenthood*. Beverly Hills: Sage.

Morgan, L. (1976). A reexamination of widowhood and morale. *Journal of Gerontology, 31* (6), 687–695.

National Council on the Aging. (1976). *The myth and reality of aging in America*. Washington, DC: Author.

Neugarten, B., & Weinstein, K. (1964). The changing American grandparent. *Journal of Marriage and Family, 26* (2), 199–204.

Okraku, I. O. (1987). Age and attitudes toward multigenerational residence, 1973 and 1983. *Journal of Gerontology, 42* (3), 280–287.

Parsons, T. (1942). Age and sex in the social structure of the U.S. *American Sociological Review, 7*, 604–616.

Pineo, P. (1961). Disenchantment in the later years of marriage. *Marriage and Family Living, 23* (1), 3–11.

Reiss, P. (1962). Extended kinship system: Correlates of and attitudes on frequency of interaction. *Marriage and Family Living, 24*, 333–339.

Riley, M. W., & Foner, A. (1968). *Aging and society* (Vol. I). New York: Russell Sage Foundation.

Robertson, J. (1976). Significance of grandparents: Perception of young adult children. *The Gerontologist, 16* (2), 137–140.

Rollins, B., & Cannon, K. (1974). Marital satisfaction over the family life cycle. *Journal of Marriage and Family, 36*, 271–282.

Rollins, B., & Feldman, H. (1970). Marital satisfaction over the family life cycle. *Journal of Marriage and the Family, 32* (1), 20–28.

Rossi, A. S., & Rossi, P. H. (1990). *Of human bonding: Parent-child relations across the life course*. New York: Aldine.

Rubinstein, R. L., Alexander, B. B., Goodman, M., & Luborsky, M. (1991). Key relationships of never married, childless older women: A cultural analysis. *Journal of Gerontology: Social Sciences, 46* (3), S270-S277.

Ruggles, S., & Goeken, R. (1992). Race and multigenerational family structure, 1900–

1980. In S. J. South & S. E. Tolnay (Eds.), *The changing American family: Sociological and demographic perspectives*. Boulder, CO: Westview Press.

Schafer, C., Coyne, J., & Lazarus, R. (1981). The health related functions of social support. *Journal of Behavioral Medicine, 4*, 381–406.

Schneider, D. M. (1980). *American kinship: A cultural account*. Chicago: University of Chicago Press.

Seltzer, M. M., Ivry, J., & Litchfield, L. C. (1987). Family members as case managers: Partnership between the formal and informal support networks. *The Gerontologist, 27* (6), 722–728.

Shanas, E. (1979a). Social myth as hypothesis: The case of the family relations of old people. *The Gerontologist, 19* (1), 3–9.

Shanas, E. (1979b). The family as a social support system in old age. *The Gerontologist, 19*, 169–174.

Shanas, E. (1980). Older people and their families: The new pioneers. *Journal of Marriage and the Family, 42*, 9–15.

Shanas, E., Townsend, P., Wedderburn, D., Friis, H., Milhhoj, P., & Stehouver, J. (1968). *Old people in three industrial societies*. New York: Atherton Press.

Shulman, N. (1975). Life-cycle variations in patterns of close relationships. *Journal of Marriage and Family, 37* (4), 813–821.

Siegel, J. (1976). *Demographic aspects of aging and the older population in the United States*. Current Population Reports, Special Studies Series P-23, No. 59. Washington, DC: U.S. Department of Commerce, Bureau of the Census.

Simmons, L. (1945). *The role of the aged in primitive society*. New Haven, CT: Yale University Press.

Simmons, L. (1960). Aging in preindustrial societies. In C. Tibbitts (Ed.), *Handbook of social gerontology*. Chicago: University of Chicago Press.

Sporakowski, M., & Hughston, G. (1978). Prescriptions for happy marriages: Adjustment and satisfaction of couples married for 50 years or more. *Family Coordinator, 27* (4), 321–327.

Stinnett, N., Carter, L., & Montgomery, J. (1972). Older persons' perceptions of their marriages. *Journal of Marriage and Family, 34,* 665–670.

Stinnett, N., Collins, J., & Montgomery, J. (1970). Marital need satisfaction of older husbands and wives. *Journal of Marriage and Family, 32,* 428–434.

Stone, R., Cafferata, G. L., & Sangl, J. (1987). Caregivers of the frail elderly: A national profile. *The Gerontologist, 27* (5), 616–626.

Sussman, M. (1965). Relationships of adult children with their parents in the U.S. In E. Shanas & G. F. Streib (Eds.), *Social structure and the family.* Englewood Cliffs, NJ: Prentice-Hall.

Sussman, M. (1976). The family life of old people. In R. Binstock & E. Shanas (Eds.), *Handbook of aging and the social sciences.* New York: Van Nostrand Reinhold.

Sussman, M. (1985). The family life of old people. In R. Binstock & E. Shanas (Eds.), *Handbook of aging and the social sciences* (2nd ed.). New York: Van Nostrand Reinhold.

Tibbitts, C. (1968). Some social aspects of gerontology. *The Gerontologist, 8* (2), 131–133.

Treas, J. (1977). Family support systems for the aged: Some social and demographic considerations. *The Gerontologist, 17* (6), 486–491.

Treas, J., & VanHilst, A. (1976). Marriage and remarriage rates among older Americans. *The Gerontologist, 16,* 132–136.

Troll, L. (1971). The family of later life: A decade review. *Journal of Marriage and the Family, 33,* 263–290.

Troll, L., & Bengtson, V. (1978). Generations in the family. In W. Burr et al. (Eds.), *Contemporary theories about the family.* New York: The Free Press.

Troll, L., Miller, S., & Atchley, R. (1979). *Families in later life.* Belmont, CA: Wadsworth.

Uhlenberg, P., & Myers, M. A. (1981). Divorce and the elderly. *The Gerontologist, 21,* 276–282.

Van de Walle, E. (1976). Household dynamics in a Belgian village, 1874–1866. *Family History, 1* (1), 80–94.

Vinick, B. (1978). Remarriage in old age. *Family Coordinator, 27* (4), 359–364.

Watkins, S. C., Menken, J. A., & Bongaarts, J. (1987). Demographic foundations of family change. *American Sociological Review, 52,* 346–358.

Wolf, J. H., Breslau, N., Ford, A., Ziegler, H., & Ward, A. (1983). Distance and contacts: Interactions of Black urban elderly adults with family and friends. *Journal of Gerontology, 38* (4), 465–471.

Wright, F. (1989). Gender differences in adults' same and cross-gender friendships. In R. Adams, & R. Blieszner (Eds.), *Older adult friendship.* London: Sage.

CHAPTER 11

THE ECONOMICS OF AGING

Mrs. Mary Fremont is a 77-year-old African American woman who has lived alone for 20 years. She rents an apartment in the inner city of a major metropolitan area in the upper Midwest. Her yearly income as of December 1993, provided from the federally administered Supplemental Security Income (SSI) Program, was $3,826, or about the average for all aged recipients of SSI in December 1993. The actual poverty threshold for an aged individual in 1993 was $6,930.

The Evanses are recent migrants to a retirement community in the Southwest. They are white, middle class, and college educated. Mr. Evans worked in an executive capacity for a large corporation in the East. His approximate current retirement income is $35,000 and includes income from Social Security, a private pension, and other assets. The Evans's income is approximately four times the 1993 poverty threshold level for an aged couple ($8,741).

Mrs. Fremont fits the stereotype of an aged person living on what appears to be inadequate income. Certainly, most readers must be wondering how anybody in the United States today (or even in 1993) could get by on $3,826 in yearly income. What about the Evanses? It is difficult to think of them as being disadvantaged. Which case example best represents the economic situation of the elderly? A nationwide survey of adults between the ages of 18 and 64 found almost two-thirds of them (63 percent) expressing the view that not having enough money to live on was a "very serious" problem for most people over 65 years of age (NCOA, 1976). Interestingly, however, this same survey found only 15 percent of those over age 65 indicated that lack of money was a very serious problem.

How does one account for this discrepancy? Is economic deprivation among the elderly a myth? Or are the elderly just kidding themselves about their financial situation? This chapter attempts to answer these and other important questions. The economic status of the elderly is discussed first, followed by an investigation of the adequacy of their financial resources in relation to their needs.

THE ECONOMIC STATUS
OF THE ELDERLY

The importance of one's economic status in old age cannot be exaggerated. The presence or absence of financial resources will have considerable impact on an individual's capacity to adjust to aging. Income will affect whether a retiree's values and preferences can be realized. The older person with adequate financial resources can maintain some degree of control over his or her life, including making decisions about which leisure activities to pursue, how much to travel, what kind of diet to maintain, and how much preventive medical care to seek. Older people without money can do none of these things.

Money Income of the Aged

Older Americans receive direct money income from a variety of sources. Some have earnings, either salaries or wages or self-employment income; most have a retirement pension (including Social Security) of one kind or another. Direct money income can also come from welfare payments, dividends, interest, rents, alimony, unemployment, veterans' and workers' compensation payments, and gifts from others.

Figure 11–1 shows the sources of money income for the elderly. Clearly, Social Security is the major source (39 percent), although earnings (17 percent) and asset income (21 percent) contribute to the income position of many elderly persons. Not all elderly individuals receive income from all the sources identified in the figure. Table 11–1 describes the proportion of the elderly (combining married couples and nonmarried men and women) receiving income from a diverse list of income sources. In 1990, over 90 percent of the elderly, including 96 percent of aged couples and 91 percent of the unmarried elderly, received some income from Social Security. Married elderly people were more likely to receive income from wages, assets, private pensions, and government pensions than were the single aged. A higher proportion of unmarried elderly people received income from public assistance than of the married elderly.

The accessibility of some income sources for the elderly has changed since the early 1960s as a result of broadened coverage of Social Security benefits and the

TABLE 11–1   Percentage of Aged Units with Income from Various Sources, 1962, 1984, 1990

Source	1962	1984	1990
Earnings	36	21	22
Social Security	69	91	92
Government employee pensions	5	14	15
Private pensions or annuities	9	24	30
Income from assets	54	68	69

Source: S. Grad, *Income of the Population 55 and Over, 1990* (Washington, DC: U.S. Department of Health and Human Services, Social Security Administration, 1992), Table I.1.

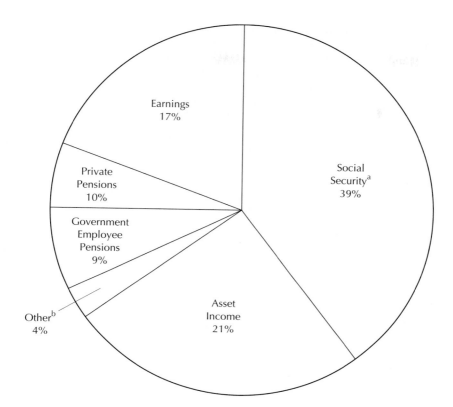

FIGURE 11–1   **1992 Sources of Aged Income**

Source: S. Grad, *Income of the Population 55 and Over: 1992* (Washington, DC: U.S. Department of Health and Human Services, Social Security Administration, 1994).
[a]Includes railroad retirement (1%).
[b]Includes public assistance (1%).

rising impact of private pensions. For example, in 1962, only 65 percent of unmarried elderly persons (compared to 91 percent in 1990) were receiving income from Social Security. In addition, the proportion of elderly couples with private pension income rose from 16 percent in 1962 to 41 percent in 1990; for the single elderly, the increase was from 5 to 22 percent (Grad, 1992).

The accessibility of income sources for the elderly is likely to continue to change in the future. In particular, the impact of private pensions, and especially that of individual retirement accounts (IRAs) and tax-sheltered annuities, is expected to alter the configuration of sources from which the elderly derive income. In 1981, the great majority of Americans became eligible to open IRAs, to invest up to $2,000 annually on a tax-deductible basis even if covered by a qualified pension plan. According to the Internal Revenue Service, almost 12 million tax returns for 1982 listed this deduction. However, the Tax Reform Act of 1986 placed significant limitations on the use of IRAs, although individuals not covered by company retirement plans remain eligible to take a tax deduction of up to $2,000 annually for a deposit in an individual retirement account. Also, couples earning less than $40,000 per year and single persons earning less than $25,000 per year remain eligible to make a $2,000 tax-deductible contribution to an IRA. Even workers with earnings in excess of these amounts or those covered by a qualified pension plan may establish nondeductible individual retirement accounts. All IRAs—those established with nondeductible as well as deductible contributions—accumulate interest and capital gains on a tax-free basis until the withdrawal of funds. Individuals can begin withdrawing on these funds when they reach the age of 59½ years or older, when their incomes are expected to be lower than during their peak working years. An estimated $857 billion was in IRA accounts by 1993.

Just how much income do the elderly have? Table 11–2 shows the total money income of persons age 65 and over with earnings and without, by marital status, in 1992. Most elderly couples had incomes under $25,000; the median income for all aged people with earnings was $26,717, whereas those without earnings was $11,915. The differential between those with earnings (i.e., those who are still working) and those without earnings (i.e., those who are retired) was $14,802. Thus, in 1992, individuals aged 65 years and older without earnings had a median income that was 45 percent of those aged with earnings. This differential was somewhat higher both among married couples 65 years of age and older (62 percent) and the nonmarried elderly (45 percent).

Since 1965, the median income of aged families has increased almost 7 times, from $3,514 to $23,352. The relative income position of the aged also has improved over this time period. For example, as depicted in Figure 11–2, the ratio of median income of aged families to the median income of all families (in constant 1989 dollars) rose from 44.7 percent in 1966 to 52.2 percent in 1989. This improvement in relative income status suggests that elderly families have enjoyed growth rates in income above the national average. In fact, median income for aged families

TABLE 11–2 Money Income of Persons Age 65 or Older, with Earnings and without, by Marital Status, 1992

Aged Units	Median Income
Age 65 or older	
Earnings, yes	$26,717
Earnings, no	11,915
Married Couples	
Earnings, yes	32,850
Earnings, no	20,530
Nonmarried Persons	
Earnings, yes	17,569
Earnings, no	8,838

Source: S. Grad, *Income of the Population 55 and Over, 1992* (Washington, DC: U.S. Department of Health and Human Services, Social Security Administration, 1994), Table III.6.

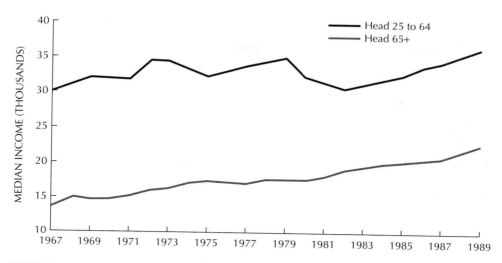

FIGURE 11–2   Median Income of Elderly and Nonelderly Families in 1989 dollars, 1967–1989

Source: U.S. Bureau of the Census, *Current Population Reports,* various reports in Series P-60.

increased about 26 percent during this period, while comparable growth for families with a head between 25 and 64 years of age was about 14 percent.

In describing the characteristics of an entire population, summary statistics (like those presented here) are frequently used. These measures represent statistical generalizations. It is important to recognize that the aged are a heterogeneous group, and there is wide variation in income among them. The reader has already seen how income varies along the lines of employment and marital status. Obvious other factors associated with income variation among the elderly are age of the elderly and race.

The elderly are not age homogeneous. Chapter 3 distinguished between the young-old and the very old or old-old. Although most data on the income of the aged groups all persons together, Table 11–3 disaggregates the data by age and shows the decline in median income of households with old-age members. Those household units that include one or more members 85 years of age or older have a median income that is about 67 percent of that for households with one or more members aged 55 to 61 years and 80 percent of that for households with one or more members aged 65 to 69. Some of this income differential may be a function of current work experience, with the youngest elderly more likely to be participating in the labor force (even if only part time). In addition, many of the old-old began their work careers before Social Security and private pension plans became commonplace. The data in Table 11–3 should not necessarily be read as indicating that the economic status of older individuals declines as they grow older. Ross, Danziger, and Smolensky (1987) show that the average income of cohorts of older persons, when controlling for retirement and marital status, did not decline between

TABLE 11–3   Money Income of Older Age Units (Married and Nonmarried), Age 55 and Over, 1992

Age	Median Income	Less than $10,000	$10,000–$40,000	$40,000 or more	Total Percent
55–61	$15,177	35%	47%	18%	100
62–64	14,905	35	53	12	100
65–69	12,727	39	51	11	100
70–74	11,787	41	52	7	100
75–79	12,361	40	55	5	100
80–84	11,435	40	57	4	100
85+	10,126	50	47	4	100

Source: S. Grad, *Income of the Population 55 and Over, 1992* (Washington, DC: U.S. Department of Health and Human Services, Social Security Administration, 1994), Table III.1.

1950 and 1980. Rather, incomes were found to decline with status changes such as movement into retirement and/or widowhood.

Differences in median income by gender and race for 1992 are presented in Table 11–4. Regardless of gender or marital status, the median income of African Americans and Hispanics approximates about 60 percent of that for whites. Grad (1994) reports that aged African Americans are more likely than aged whites to receive income from public assistance (22 percent vs. 5 percent, respectively) and less likely to receive income from assets (26 percent vs. 72 percent, respectively). Literature summarized in Chapter 15 describes the double jeopardy or multiple hazards of being aged and of minority status in the United States. This may be especially the case with regard to income and health status (Dowd & Bengtson, 1978).

Assets and In-Kind Income

Approximately 21 percent of all income to the elderly in this country comes from financial assets. These assets—sometimes referred to as *liquid assets* because of their easy conversion to goods, services, or money—generally take the form of bank deposits and corporate stocks and bonds. Typically, liquid assets are accu-

TABLE 11–4   Median Income of Persons Age 65 and Older, by Race and Gender, 1992

Race	Married Couples	Males	Females
White	$24,616	$12,601	$9,632
African American	14,545	7,262	5,962
Hispanic[1]	14,988	7,758	5,693
All	23,817	11,740	9,042

Source: S. Grad, *Income of the Population 55 and Over, 1992* (Washington, DC: U.S. Department of Health and Human Services, Social Security Administration, 1994), Table III.1 and III.3.

[1]Hispanic persons may be of any race.

mulated through the course of life. Individuals may save for different reasons, often as a precaution against unexpected need in the future or to smooth out irregularities in the flow of income during the lifetime. As Schulz (1992) points out, however, assets put aside as precaution against unexpected needs—medical or nursing home bills, for example—are not available for immediate needs. Accumulation of assets does not necessarily stop with old age. Inflation, increasing property taxes, or the desire to take a retirement cruise may all be appropriate reasons to continue to save during old age. There is disagreement among economists about the evidence on continued saving among the elderly. Some suggest that the elderly, as a group, continue to accumulate assets; only the old-old do not (Torrey & Taeuber, 1986). Others argue that the elderly are significant dissavers, using their savings for current expenditures (Radner, 1989).

Asset income is not distributed equitably across the elderly population. In fact, about 14 percent of all elderly couples and about 25 percent of unrelated individuals had no financial assets in 1984 (Schulz, 1992). The concept of *net worth* is used to aggregate all the assets of a household, including financial assets, real estate (e.g., own home, rental property, etc.) and business holdings, and even the value of motor vehicles. U.S. Bureau of the Census data for 1991 identify 35 percent of aged household units in the lowest quintile of net worth with a median of $32,172. However, net worth minus the equity in an owned home for this group is reduced to a median of $3,577; 63 percent of aged units in the lowest two quintiles had median net worth minus home equity of less than $30,000. Even $30,000 in assets hardly constitutes a significant income supplement. Depending on the form of investment, given the relatively low interest rates prevalent in the mid-1990s, even $30,000 will likely yield no more than about $2,000 per year in income. Assets tend to be correlated with income: Those families with the highest incomes are most likely to have substantial assets; those with the lowest incomes are least likely to have any assets.

Some assets have less liquidity because they require more time to convert to money. These *nonliquid assets* include equity in housing or a business and possessions such as automobiles. Homes are the most common asset (liquid or nonliquid) of older people. About 77 percent of elderly households reside in an owned home. Four-fifths of these homeowners own their homes free of any mortgage. This might suggest to some that older people need less income because they have no mortgage payments and have considerable equity tied up in a home. This may not be the case, however. Elderly households residing in mortgage-free homes are typically in older homes—homes they purchased 30 or more years ago but that were built 40 or 50 years ago. Monthly maintenance bills on such older housing stock may make up for the absence of an older low-interest mortgage payment.

Just how much equity do the elderly have in their homes? U.S. Bureau of the Census data from 1991 suggest that approximately 65 percent of aged household units have $30,000 or more in equity in their homes; 36 percent have $80,000 or more in home equity, and almost one-in-five aged household units (19 percent) have home equity in excess of $100,000. Until very recently, however, this equity

IF THE HAIR IS GRAY, CON ARTISTS SEE GREEN
Constance L. Hays

Betty Norman was no match for the telephone con men who emptied her pockets of more than $40,000. A plain-talking widow who runs a small motel in Ionia, Michigan, a town of state prisons and apple orchards, Mrs. Norman, born and raised here, was taught to believe that people are essentially honest. So she trusted salespeople who picked up details about her life in seemingly casual telephone chat while pitching her pens, costume jewelry and other trinkets. And after being swindled out of thousands of dollars, she lost even more to people promising to recover her original investments.

"It makes you feel like taking your life, to think you've been skinned," said Mrs. Norman, 68, who for months was too mortified to reveal it to her grown children. "I've been struggling along. People here have lent me money, and I'm trying to get it paid back."

Few have been hurt as badly as Mrs. Norman, but millions of older Americans know what it is to be hounded by marketers—some legitimate, some not—who consider the elderly easy marks. With plenty of assets, ranging from life-insurance payouts to mortgage-free homes, they are seen as lonely and more trusting than cynical baby boomers. They tend to worry about interest rates: high rates signal inflation eating away their nest eggs, while low ones mean certificates of deposit will yield less.

All this makes them prime targets for people trying to sell, sell, sell—everything from interests in wireless cable, obscure metals and "dirt piles" said to conceal nuggets of gold to mutual fund shares and limited partnerships that promise the moon.

Not that the elderly are the only victims. It's just that they don't often see themselves as pigeons. In a recent survey sponsored by AT&T, 18 percent of Americans, up from 14 percent two years ago, admitted to being scam victims. And even though fewer respondents over 65 said they knew a victim, younger respondents said they thought the elderly were the most likely to be preyed upon. Law-enforcement officials agree; indeed, F.B.I. agents working a telephone-marketing sting in 1993 got many salespeople to admit they targeted the elderly.

What's more, it is harder for the elderly to bounce back after being swindled—either by taking legal action, earning enough to repair their finances, or turning for help to their children who might see the mishap as proof of a loss in judgment or sign of frailty.

"It's often very, very difficult for them to admit they've been exploited because it's so humiliating," said Herbert Rosedale, a Manhattan lawyer who helps elder victims of fraud. "It's not like a kid who can say, 'So, I bought into a scam. I'll grow out of it.'"

Finding victims is simple. Older people are fairly easy to contact, either through zip codes or mailing lists of retirees. Sometimes they're taken for a ride by apparent friends, whether it's young people who turn up on doorsteps offering to carry groceries or middle-aged people who ease into church groups.

Even trusted local business people can turn into predators. The elderly "just like the Marcus Welby view of the world, that people in business are basically honest," said Philip A. Feigin, Colorado's securities commissioner and president of the North American Securities Administrators Association, which tracks investment fraud. "So many times when we crack a scam, the investors who call us are absolutely furious that we broke it up."

Of course, any investment made at any age, can go sour. But "if you blow it when you're 30, you've got 35 years to make it up before you retire," says Barbara Roper, director of investment protection for the Consumer Federation of America. "If you blow it at 65, you may have to go back to work for the rest of your life."

Fraud that reaches the elderly by mail or telephone has been refined to a high art. Telemarketing fraud alone is believed to be a $40 billion business. Sometimes the scam starts with a puzzle or a contest, promising prizes; other times a breathless broker, complete with ticker-tape sound effects, pushes a trendy commodity or a stock too hot to resist.

"I had a lot of time to waste," said Bea Johnson a 77-year-old retired beautician who lives alone in Roseville, Minn., and became addicted to puzzles she got in the mail. The puzzles, mostly word or number games, were supposed to qualify her for prizes like new cars or $10,000 in cash; she merely had to return them a check for $10 or $50 or more.

Mrs. Johnson lost $11,000 over two years by the time she quit in 1993. The case wound up with the Minnesota Attorney General and Mrs. Johnson became something of a celebrity, as the widow who learned to say, "No." "I still work on those puzzles they send me, but I don't send them in."

Bill Duryea, a retired Sears service representative who lives in Casa Grande, Arizona, got taken in several years ago by a salesman who called and urged him to invest in wireless cable. Mr. Duryea sent a check for $6,400. "He was blabbering and jabbering, and I don't listen to them too good," said Mr. Duryea, 80. But the same salesman had once urged him to buy shares in a cellular phone company, and Mr. Duryea regretted ignoring that pitch.

He sent off his money in 1991—a cashier's check, fetched by a courier (two clear warning signs of a fraud in progress). He has received nothing but a telemarketing barrage since then. Now, he says with a chuckle, he has an answering machine that says, "If you're trying to sell me something, forget it."

Investigators say telemarketers sell one another "mooch lists" of people like Mr. Duryea, people who once took the bait, and are thus considered likely to do so again. Such lists sell for $5 to $10 a name, compared with 50 cents a name for typical mail-order lists, Mr. Barker said.

Mrs. Norman described being called repeatedly, at all hours, by a man claiming to be with an outfit called the National Recovery Service. "He would tell me to go to Western Union and send him $300, or $1,500, and he'd send me my money," she said. "One time he called and I was on the phone, and he had the operator butt in and say it was an emergency and he was my grandson. Another time he said he was driving to Michigan to bring me my money. He said he was driving a little Ford Pinto, and told me the color." He and the Pinto never arrived, and neither did her money. She ended up spending $32,000, just for the supposed recovery, between September and December of last year. She had lost perhaps $10,00 on various contests before that, she said.

People who suspect they may have been victims of an investment fraud can contact their state Attorney General's office. The National Fraud Information Center operates a special telephone line weekdays from 9 A.M. to 5:30 P.M.: 800–876–7060.

was not available to aged homeowners for day-to-day living expenses. Since January 1, 1979, the Federal Home Loan Bank Board (FHLBB) has allowed federally chartered savings and loan associations to offer *reverse annuity mortgages.* Under this mortgage, a homeowner may sell some equity in the house and, in turn, receive a fixed monthly sum based on a percentage of the current market value of the house (Schulz, 1995). Each federal savings institution must have its reverse annuity program approved by the FHLBB, but these mortgages are not commonly employed at this time. Recently, Congress gave authority to the Federal Housing Administration to insure up to 25,000 reverse mortgages for homeowners 62 years of age and older over a five-year period. Such insurance, which protects both lenders and borrowers in the event of bankruptcy or takeover, may unlock some of the vast equity held by elderly homeowners. The October 1992 issue of *Consumer Reports* magazine estimated that only about 3,000 FHA applications for reverse annuity mortgages had been processed by mid-1992.

The elderly receive indirect or in-kind income in the form of goods and services that they obtain free or at reduced cost from a wide array of federal, state, and local programs benefiting the elderly over and above those providing direct income. The largest of these federal programs, Medicare and Medicaid, provide older people with health care services. There are numerous programs aimed at providing housing to older people that is below the cost for similar housing on the open market. Under its various assistance programs, the federal government houses nearly 1.5 million older persons in 1.25 million units (Lawton, 1985). These programs are discussed in detail in Chapter 16. The food-stamp program is another visible source of indirect income to those elderly who are eligible to participate.

It is difficult to say how much in terms of income these programs are worth today to the aged. Information on the value of comparable services available in the marketplace is sometimes difficult to obtain. In addition, the value recipients may place on in-kind services may differ sharply from their market value. Total social welfare expenditures for aged and nonaged persons in the United States under public programs approximated $1,050 billion dollars in 1990; the federal share was $617 billion, or 59 percent of the total. Still, the great majority of aged people receive no federal in-kind benefits. According to the U.S. Bureau of the Census, only about one in five (19 percent) U.S. households (aged and nonaged) in 1992 received any means-tested noncash benefits such as food stamps, school lunches, public housing subsidies, or health care through Medicaid. In fact, more than one in three (37 percent) U.S. households with income below the poverty level did not receive any means-tested noncash benefits in 1992.

Taxes and Inflation

When I reported previously that the median income of aged couples in the United States in 1990 was $23,352, I was giving a pretax figure. Almost all income data, especially figures published by the Social Security Administration and U.S. Census Bureau, represent gross income or income before taxes. The scarcity of after-tax data makes it difficult to analyze the impact of taxation on the elderly and to determine whether, relative to other age groups, they are advantaged or disadvantaged by tax laws. Gist and Mulvey (1990) have analyzed returns filed in 1990 and, using computer simulations, estimate that average federal income tax rates are about two and one-half times as great for the single population under age 65 as for the single elderly, and nearly twice as great for married persons under age 65 as for married elderly persons.

Congressional action in 1984 imposed federal income taxes on up to one-half of Social Security benefits received by taxpayers whose adjusted gross incomes exceed certain base amounts. The base amount was $25,000 for a single taxpayer, $32,000 for a married couple filing a joint return, and zero for married persons filing separate returns. Beginning in 1994, the law was changed to increase the tax burden on higher-income Social Security beneficiaries. Initially, this 1994 increase was estimated to affect only about 20 percent of Social Security beneficiaries (Pattison & Harrington, 1993). Schulz (1995) argues that eventually inflation and increases in real income will push a greater proportion of the aged into the taxable range. The Tax Reform Act of 1986 increased the personal tax exemption to $1,900 for all individuals, and, in 1993, allowed an additional deduction of $1,400 for an aged couple and $900 for a single person who is 65 years or older. This additional deduction increases periodically to reflect increases in the Consumer Price Index (CPI). Once in their lives, persons age 55 years and over are permitted to exclude from federal taxation up to $125,000 resulting from the sale of a personal residence. Property tax reductions are now granted to the elderly in every state. The latter points would seem to be of more help to the higher-income elderly—those who are more likely to itemize deductions on federal income tax returns and who are more likely to be property owners.

Inflation has been called a hidden tax, one that can have a disastrous impact on the economic situation of people of all ages. Generally, the term is used to describe increases in the level of prices measured by the Consumer Price Index. The CPI, a product of the Bureau of Labor Statistics, is a weighted index of the annual consumption patterns of Americans. It covers the expenditures of approximately 80 percent of the noninstitutional population, including retirees and the unemployed. A majority of workers under contract in the United States have their earnings pegged to the CPI as well.

Schulz (1995) lists five principal ways older people can be affected adversely by unanticipated inflation:

1. Assets that do not adjust with inflation depreciate in value.
2. Income sources may not adjust to inflation, reducing real income.
3. For employed people, adjustments in earnings may lag behind inflation, reducing real wages.
4. The tax burden may rise because the tax brackets are defined in money rather than real terms.

5. Elderly persons may allocate their budgets differently from others (e.g., more for food, housing maintenance, and health care). Because indexes used to measure and adjust various sources of income may not correctly reflect aged buying patterns, the elderly may not be fully compensated for increased prices.

The last two points deserve additional discussion. Many aged persons will not pay income taxes because their incomes are low. All but the highest income recipients of Social Security will be exempt from federal taxes as well. In the past, those who paid federal income taxes faced a problem. Some compensation received as protection from inflation was taxed away, at progressively higher rates (Schulz, 1992). Starting in 1985, tax brackets were indexed to take inflation into account. The Tax Reform Act of 1986 simultaneously reduced the number of tax brackets and the progressivity in the federal tax structure. These actions have eliminated the problem. Unfortunately, the income exemption ceiling below which Social Security benefits are not taxed is not indexed to take inflation into account. Thus, as inflation pushes the income of Social Security beneficiaries higher, in the future more of these people will find their Social Security benefits subject to the federal income tax (Schulz, 1995).

Clearly, persons living primarily on fixed incomes or pensions are hurt the most by the rising prices that accompany inflation. Historically, this has been the case for the elderly, but recent developments have changed this situation. The Social Security program, the major source of retirement income, now adjusts benefits automatically on the basis of the rate of inflation. The Social Security Amendments of 1983 have affected cost-of-living adjustments (COLA) to Social Security benefits in two ways. First, the July 1983 COLA was delayed until January 1984, with all future automatic adjustments being effective on a calendar-year basis. Second, if Social Security trust fund assets decline relative to the outflow of funds, then future automatic COLAs will be pegged to the lesser of increases in prices (measured by the CPI) or to increases in wages.

Several in-kind income sources, such as the food-stamp program, also peg their benefits to the rate of inflation. Some private pension benefits are also adjusted automatically as the cost of living increases. All this suggests that many elderly people are in an advantaged position relative to other age groups in that a major portion of their direct and indirect money income keeps pace with the rate of inflation.

THE ADEQUACY OF AGED INCOME

It is one thing to describe how much income the elderly have; it is quite another to say what they do with their income and whether it is adequate for their needs.

Like Americans of all ages, the elderly are consumers of a vast array of goods and services. In 1970, older persons spent about $60 billion, or over 10 percent of the national total. This figure was consistent with the proportion of the U.S. population made up by older people in 1970, also 10 percent. It is likely that as the elderly population increases (and their incomes increase), so will the proportion of all goods and services they account for in purchases. On this basis, one would estimate personal expenditures of the aged in 1990 at about $436 billion, or about 12 percent of total personal consumption expenditures in the United States in 1990.

How do older Americans spend their income? Table 11–5 compares the average annual out-of-pocket expenditures of households with a head 65 years of age or older with those of all household units. Older household units spend proportionately more of their income on transportation, food, health care, utilities, and cash contributions, and less on housing, clothing, personal insurance and pensions, and entertainment. Interestingly, older households spend proportionately less on shelter but more on upkeep of their households than do all consumers.

The pattern of expenditures among the elderly is similar to the pattern of expenditures among lower-income groups in general. Still, one must ask, Is low income an adequate income? The most frequently used measure of income adequacy is the poverty index developed in the early 1960s by the Social Security Administration, based on the amount of money needed to purchase a *minimum adequate diet* as determined by the Department of Agriculture. The index has been described as follows:

TABLE 11–5   Average Annual Expenditures of Consumer Units by Type of Expenditure, 1992

Type of Expenditure	Amount Expended			Percentage Distribution		
	All Units	55–64 Yrs	65+ Yrs	All Units	55–64 Yrs	65+ Yrs
Total	$28,846	$31,704	$20,616	100.00	100.00	100.00
Housing	7,493	7,181	4,917	25.1	22.7	23.9
Shelter	5,411	5,105	3,241	18.1	16.1	15.7
Operations, supplies, and furnishings	2,082	2,076	1,676	7.0	6.6	8.2
Transportation	5,228	5,684	3,290	17.5	17.9	18.0
Food	4,273	4,354	3,198	14.4	13.7	15.5
At home	2,643	2,833	2,211	8.9	8.9	10.7
Away from home	1,631	1,521	987	5.5	4.8	4.8
Health care	1,634	1,993	2,474	5.5	6.3	12.0
Utilities	1,984	2,255	1,816	6.6	7.1	8.8
Cash contributions	958	1,620	1,227	3.2	5.1	5.9
Clothing	1,710	1,631	882	5.7	5.1	4.3
Personal insurance and pensions	2,750	3,103	724	9.2	9.8	3.5
Entertainment	1,500	1,587	754	5.0	6.0	3.7
Other	2,316	2,296	1,334	7.8	7.2	6.5

Source: Statistical Abstract of the United States, 1994 (Washington, DC: U.S. Bureau of the Census, 1994) Table 703.

The food budget is the lowest that could be devised to supply all essential nutrients using food readily purchasable in the U.S. market (with customary regional
variations). The poverty line is then calculated at three times the food budget
(slightly smaller proportions for one- and two-person families) on the assumption—derived from studies of consumers—that a family that has spent a larger
proportion of its income on food will be living at a very inadequate level. The food
budgets and the derivative poverty income cutoff points are estimated in detail for
families of differing size and composition (62 separate family types) with a farm/
nonfarm differential for each type. This variation of the poverty measure in relation to family size and age of members is its most important distinguishing characteristic. (U.S. House Committee on Ways and Means, 1967)

In 1993, the poverty index level for a two-person family with an aged head was
$8,741; the comparable level for a single person was about $6,930.

Figure 11–3 shows that, in general, poverty has been declining among older
people during the period 1966–1989, although most of the relative gains in income
for the elderly were accomplished between 1966 and about 1975. As depicted in
Figure 11–4, poverty varies among subgroups of the elderly. Aged whites are less
likely to live in poverty than is anyone in the total U.S. population, with 9.6 percent living below the poverty level; however, 30.8 percent of aged blacks are living
in poverty.

Critics of the poverty index argue that it is set too low. Remember that the
index is calculated at three times the minimum adequate food budget, with differ-

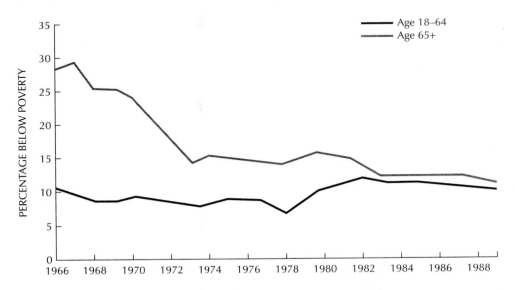

FIGURE 11–3   Poverty Rates of Elderly and Nonelderly Adults, 1966–1989
Source: U.S. Bureau of the Census, "Money Income and Poverty Status in the United States: 1989."
Current Population Reports, Series P-60, No. 168 (September 1990).

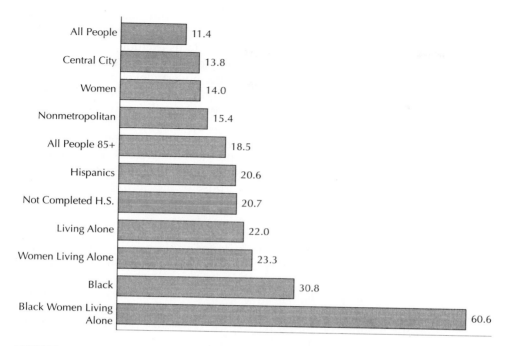

FIGURE 11–4   Percentage of Elderly below the Poverty Level, by Selected Characteristics, 1989

Source: U.S. Bureau of the Census, "Money Income and Poverty Status in the United States: 1989." *Current Population Reports,* Series P-60, No. 168 (September 1990) and unpublished data from the March 1990 *Current Population Survey.*

Note: Unless otherwise noted, data are for age 65+.

ent food budgets constructed for different types of families. The following characteristics are used in combination to develop indices for family units:

1. Age of head over or under 65 years
2. Size of family (two to nine or more)
3. Number of related children under age 18
4. "Unrelated" family units

The 3:1 ratio was set as a result of surveys made in 1955 and 1960–61 of the ratio of food consumption to other expenditures for *all* families in the United States. A congressional report indicates that based on Consumer Expenditure Surveys of 1972 to 1973, the current ratio likely exceeds 5:1 (Poverty Studies Task Force, 1976). In testimony before the U.S. House Select Committee on Aging, one student of aging in the United States suggested that shifting to more realistic levels of what constitutes poverty would more than double the number of aged poor, so that the number of either poor or near poor would include approximately 40 percent of the aged (Orshansky, 1978). Orshansky (1978) also points out that the index is not applied to the "hidden poor" (those who are institutionalized or living with relatives). Thus, even the current figures on poverty status exclude millions of aged who are unable to live independently. According to Chen (1985), one in four of the aged had incomes at or below 125 percent of the poverty level measure in 1981. Had this near-poverty benchmark been employed, the number of aged persons defined as impoverished would have risen from 3.9 million to 6.4 million, an increase of 64 percent.

Another criticism of the poverty index argues that poverty statistics are artificially high because the value of in-kind or noncash transfers is not included as income. Should government expenditures for food stamps, housing subsidies, or Medicaid be included as income for the purpose of measuring poverty? If the answer is yes, then, by definition, many people will have additional income and the poverty rate will decline.

Table 11–6 shows the poverty rates for all persons and for those 65 years of age and older employing three different methods for valuing in-kind and noncash transfers developed by the census bureau (U.S. Bureau of the Census, 1985): market value, recipient value, and poverty budget share value. *Market value* is equal to the purchase price in the private market of the goods and services received by the recipient. *Recipient value* is the amount of cash that would make the recipient just as well off as the in-kind transfer; it reflects the recipient's own valuation of the benefit. *Poverty budget share value* limits the value of food, housing, or medical benefit transfers to the proportions spent on these items by persons at or near the poverty line in 1960 to 1961, when in-kind transfers were minimal. Remember also that the household consumption surveys of 1960 to 1961 are the continuing basis for the assumption in the poverty index that food represents one-third of household expenditures for the poor. According to the table, the market value approach has the effect of reducing poverty the most. Under the market valuation approach for food, housing, and medical benefits, the poverty rate for all persons in the United States would be under 10 percent (9.7 percent), and poverty would be near nonexistent for the aged (2.6 percent).

A second measure of the adequacy of aged income is the *Retired Couple's Budget* developed by the Bureau of Labor Statistics but no longer published. The

TABLE 11–6   Poverty Rate by Age, Using Alternative Methods of Valuing Noncash Benefits, 1984

	Current Poverty Definition (%)	Valuing Food and Housing Only			Valuing Food, Housing, and All Medical Benefits		
		Market Value (%)	Recipient Value (%)	Poverty Budget Share Value (%)	Market Value (%)	Recipient Value (%)	Poverty Budget Share Value (%)
All persons	14.4	12.9	13.2	13.0	9.7	12.2	12.1
65 years and over	12.4	10.5	10.8	10.5	2.6	7.3	7.6

Source: Statistical Abstract of the United States, 1986 (Washington, DC: U.S. Bureau of the Census, 1985), Table 774.

retired couple is defined as a husband age 65 or over and his wife. They live independently and are assumed to be in good health. Actually, the Bureau of Labor Statistics provides three different budgets for aged couples, reflecting different standards of living: lower, intermediate, and higher. Table 11–7 presents the monthly budget for a retired couple for the three different levels as it was set in the autumn of 1981. Budget items pertain to urban families only and have been updated on the basis of changes in the Consumer Price Index. For the fall of 1981 (the last year for which the index is available), the budget for a retired couple living in an urban area was set at approximately $7,226 (lower level), $10,226 (intermediate level), and $15,078 (higher level).

One problem with the Retired Couple's Budget is that little explanation is given for why one of the three standards should be used over the other two. All those who are officially poor in terms of the poverty index are still so under terms of the Retired Couple's Budget. But what about those who have incomes above the poverty level but below the budget level? Chen (1985) has calculated that in 1985, 18 percent of retired couples had incomes below the lower budget and 35 percent had incomes below the intermediate budget. Whether such persons are officially deemed poor or not may be moot. Clearly, many of these elderly have substantial economic difficulties, which are likely to manifest themselves in poor nutrition, neglect of medical needs, inadequate housing, and the like.

THE SOCIAL SECURITY SYSTEM

Nine out of ten U.S. workers are covered and over 90 percent of the elderly receive some income support through a public retirement pension system administered by the federal government and colloquially referred to as *Social Security*. Despite recent public attention to the problems involved in financing this system, few people are really familiar with its principles and provisions. This section discusses

TABLE 11–7   Monthly Budget for a Retired Couple, Urban United States, Autumn 1981

	Lower		Intermediate		Higher	
	$	%	$	%	$	%
Food	182	30	242	28	304	24
Housing	198	33	283	33	442	35
Transportation	46	8	89	10	163	13
Clothing and personal care	37	6	58	7	88	7
Medical care	90	15	91	11	92	7
Other family consumption	23	4	38	4	75	6
Other cost	26	4	51	6	93	7
Totals	602	100	852	99	1257	99

Source: Statistical Abstract of the United States, 1982–83 (Washington, DC: U.S. Bureau of the Census, 1982), Table 763, p. 465.

Social Security, focusing primarily on pension benefits and selected special issues such as the needed reform of provisions related to women. Several related programs, including Supplemental Security Income (SSI), will be reviewed.

Background

The notion of an old-age pension received as a right by a person who had led a productive life was not seriously discussed until the end of the nineteenth century (Bromley, 1974). Even then, the prevailing opinion was that an individual was solely responsible for making financial provision for himself or herself in old age. Such provision would come out of a lifetime's earnings, through either savings or insurance. Individuals unable to provide for themselves were subject to "poor laws" and the scarce resources of private charities.

By 1889, a system of social insurance had been created in Germany that included a pension scheme. For the first time, the aged were given a measure of economic security as a right rather than a charity. In Denmark, state support for needy old people was introduced in 1891. Pension rights were introduced in Great Britain in 1908 for people over the age of 70 who had been in regular employment but had little or no income.

During the early part of the twentieth century and into the 1920s continuing attempts were made in the United States to define pensions as a right of aged Americans. These attempts met with limited success. Several states enacted old-age pension legislation, and reform groups such as the American Association of Old Age Security began to appear. The Great Depression, with its devastating economic impact on the lives of many Americans, helped create conditions that would ultimately allow the enactment of federal legislation promoting the pension rights of the aged and guaranteeing unemployment insurance.

Unemployment during the Great Depression was more than 25 percent among the elderly. Bank failures and the declining value of estates exhausted the financial resources of millions, including even those among the more prosperous middle and upper-middle classes. In 1932, the American Federation of Labor reversed its previous position and endorsed unemployment insurance and old-age assistance at the state and federal levels.

During this period, utopian schemes were prevalent. In 1933, Upton Sinclair put forth his 12-point EPIC ("end poverty in California") plan to make people self-supporting and to grant a $50-a-month old-age pension to all needy persons who had resided in California for at least three years. Sinclair won the Democratic nomination for governor but was soundly defeated, with his opponents insisting EPIC actually meant "end property, introduce communism" in California (Fischer, 1977).

The so-called ham and eggs movement, also based in California, proposed a weekly pension be given to everyone who was 50 years of age or over and out of work. The pension, initially proposed to be "twenty-five dollars every Tuesday" and later improved to "thirty dollars every Thursday," would be in the form of stamped scrip, which would expire at a given date. Not only would the economic situation of the older unemployed be enhanced by this scheme, but also the economy would be invigorated by increased circulation of money (Fischer, 1977).

Perhaps the most popular of these utopian schemes was that put forth by Dr. Francis Townsend of Long Beach, California. The essence of the Townsend plan was that all Americans over age 60 receive a monthly sum of $200 on the condition that they spent their pension within 30 days; a 2 percent tax on all business transactions was to pay for the plan (Achenbaum, 1978). By 1936, Townsend claimed a national following of over 5 million and at least 60 U.S. representatives sympathetic to his measure (Putnam, 1970).

Clearly, the idea of an old-age pension had achieved legitimacy. The institutional structure needed to implement this idea was the Social Security Act of 1935. With its passage, the United States became one of the last industrial nations to establish a federal old-age pension program.

Principles

The influence of this piece of legislation on the whole question of retirement and pension in the United States would be difficult to overestimate. As one historian of old age in the United States has pointed out, the Social Security Act of 1935 (1) established the principle of a guaranteed "floor" income as a right bought by contributions over the course of a working life, (2) gave added impetus to demands for the extension of private pension coverage, (3) provided a standard age by which retirement could be defined, and (4) signaled a new era in financial arrangements for life after retirement (Calhoun, 1978).

Still, it is important to remember that this legislation was very much a political document, reflecting divergent views prominent at the time. Should a program be aimed at preventing or relieving economic destitution? Should a straight government pension be provided, or a contributing insurance system for wage earners? What about England's plan, which included both insurance *and* old-age assistance? Should there be a single federal system or an aggregate of state plans? Should the plan be voluntary or compulsory, universal or selective (Achenbaum, 1978)?

Schulz (1992) outlines seven principles inherent in the Social Security legislation accepted by President Roosevelt and the Congress. Some of these principles clearly reflect a consensus or compromise position on the questions raised here.

1. For the designated groups, *participation was compulsory.*
2. Social Security was set up as an *earnings-related system.*
3. *Social adequacy* was taken into account in the determination of benefits for recipients. Weighted benefits favored workers with lower earnings.
4. Social Security was not intended to be the sole means of economic protection; it was only to provide *a floor of protection.*

5. Funds for operating the program were to come from earmarked payroll taxes called *contributions*.
6. Workers were to earn their benefits through participation in the program; there was to be *no means test*.
7. A *retirement test* was established; pension benefits were withheld if an eligible person worked and earned more than a specified amount.

Pension Benefits

The Social Security Act of 1935 established a federal old-age insurance (OAI) (pension) program and a federal-state system of unemployment insurance. The original legislation, weak by comparison with other Western nations, has been strengthened and expanded since 1939, when survivors' and dependents' benefits were added (OASI). Disability insurance (OASDI) was added in 1956, Medicare (OASDHI) in 1965. Changes legislated in 1972 included the automatic adjustment of benefits for inflation (begun in 1975) and the establishment of Supplemental Security Income (SSI) to replace aid to the indigent, blind, and disabled. Important changes were made again in the Social Security Amendments of 1983.

In 1948, only 13 percent of all persons age 65 years and over were receiving Social Security payments. Since 1950, however, additional groups of workers have been brought into the system: certain farm and domestic workers (1950), the self-employed (1954), members of the uniformed services (1956), Americans employed by foreign governments (1960), physicians (1965), and ministers (1967). In 1974, the railroad retirement program was integrated into the Social Security system. Starting in January 1984, the following new groups have been covered under Social Security: (1) newly hired federal employees, including executive, legislative, and judicial branch employees; (2) current employees of the legislative branch who are not participating in the Civil Service Retirement System; (3) all members of Congress, the president, the vice president, federal judges, and most executive-level political appointees; and (4) current and future employees of private, tax-exempt nonprofit organizations. Currently, about 95 percent of all jobs in the United States are covered by Social Security.

Social Security eligibility is related to work rather than to need. An individual (and his or her dependents and survivors) is eligible if he or she has worked in employment that is covered and has worked long enough to have acquired "insured status." Most workers in jobs not covered are aware of this and are often covered by another retirement system. Insured status is acquired by earning a minimum amount during a specified number of calendar quarters in jobs covered by Social Security. In 1994, a person was credited with a quarter of coverage for each $620 earned during the year, with a maximum of four quarters of coverage in a given year. A person who reached age 62 in 1991 or later needed 10 years of work, or 40 quarters, in covered employment to achieve minimum eligibility for retirement benefits.

Benefits are financed by payroll taxes paid by both employees and employers on income up to a certain level. In 1994, this tax was 15.30 percent (7.65 percent withheld from employees; 7.65 percent withheld from employers) applied to a base level of earnings, which (since 1974) rises automatically as average earnings rise. The self-employed paid this same rate of 15.30 percent in 1994. Actually, the 1994 tax rate of 7.65 percent on employee wages represents the total of three different tax rates: (1) a rate of 5.6 percent, applied to wages (a maximum of $60,600 in 1994), that is deposited to the Old Age and Survivors Insurance (OASI) Trust Fund, the fund out of which retirement benefits are paid; (2) a rate of 0.6 percent, also applied to wages up to $60,600, that is deposited to the Disability Insurance (DI) Trust Fund, the fund out of which workers' disability benefits are paid; and (3) a rate of 1.45 percent, applied to all wages with no upper limit, that is deposited to the Health Insurance (HI) Trust Fund, the fund out of which Medicare benefits are funded.

Some have argued that this payroll tax is regressive. That is, because only income up to a certain level is subject to taxation, those with higher incomes pay a lower proportion of their income into the Social Security tax fund. For example, an individual earning $25,000 a year pays 7.65 percent, or $1,912.50, to Social Security, but someone earning $100,000 a year pays approximately $5,207 (6.2 percent (5.6 + 0.6) of the first $60,600 plus 1.45 percent of $100,000), or about 5.2 percent of his or her total income. Thus, the tax contribution is a heavier proportional burden for the lower-income worker, although such workers do receive proportionately higher benefits when they retire (see the discussion of pension replacement rates later in this chapter). It is also likely (perhaps even *more* likely for the lower-income worker) that the employer's share of tax contributions is actually borne by employees in lower wages and reduced benefits.

Benefits are paid to persons who have worked for a minimum period of time on a covered job. The *minimum benefit* (eliminated by 1981 legislation for workers who attained age 62 after 1982) of approximately $3,000 per year is provided to beneficiaries who reach age 62 before 1982. The *basic benefit,* applicable with retirement at age 65, is based on a worker's average indexed monthly earnings (AIME) in covered employment. It is derived from a benefit formula weighted to provide low-wage workers with a relatively greater percentage of earnings replacement than workers with higher wages. The primary insurance amount (PIA), or Social Security benefit, provided to a retired worker on a monthly basis is computed by applying a formula to the AIME. The formula consists of brackets in which 3 percentages are applied to amounts of AIME. The dollar amounts defining the brackets are called *bend points* and are different for each calendar year of attainment of age 62.

For retired workers who attained age 62 in 1994, the bend points are $422 and $2,545. The formula is 90 percent of the first $422 of AIME; plus 32 percent of the next $2,123 of AIME; plus 15 percent of AIME above $2,545. The following are examples of monthly PIA computations for such workers with different AIME amounts.

1. If a retired worker has an AIME of $300, the PIA is $270 per month (90 percent of $300).
2. If the AIME is $952, the monthly PIA is $549.40 (90 percent of $422 plus 32 percent of $530).
3. If the AIME is $2,845, the monthly PIA is $1,104.10 (90 percent of $422 plus 32 percent of $2,123 plus 15 percent of $300).

The average monthly benefit actually paid to a retired worker in December 1993 was $8,088 a year, or $674 a month.

This relatively low average benefit level reflects the fact that over half of current Social Security recipients *do not* receive full benefits. This is due, in part, to the popularity of the early retirement option. Early retirement benefits may be paid to people who retire at ages 62 to 64. These benefits are reduced to take into account the longer period over which they will be paid. Benefits are actually reduced by 1/180 for each month before age 65, with a maximum reduction of 20 percent. Thus, if the full PIA amount for a worker who retired at age 63 was $1,000, the actual monthly benefit would be reduced by 13.33 percent, or 1/180, of $1000 multiplied by 24 months. The resulting reduction, $133.33, is subtracted from $1,000 to obtain $866.67, which is rounded to $867.

Delayed benefit credits (sometimes referred to as the *delayed retirement credit* [DRC]) are also available. The DRC increases the Social Security benefit payable to workers who postpone retirement past age 65 and up to age 70. The annual rate of increase under the DRC is 5 percent for workers who reach age 62 in 1993 or 1994. DRCs will increase an additional 0.5 percent every other year until reaching 8 percent per year for workers aged 62 after 2004.

The Retirement Test

The Social Security Administration employs a retirement test to determine whether a person otherwise eligible for retirement benefits is considered retired. Unless a person can be considered substantially retired, benefits are not payable. Essentially, the retirement test acts to reduce benefits paid to persons under age 70 who earn more than a certain amount. For example, a 67-year-old woman could earn up to $11,160 in 1994 ($930 monthly) *without* any reduction in her Social Security benefits. Benefits are reduced $1 for every $3 earned above the exempt amount. The retirement test also applies to Social Security recipients who are 62 to 64 years of age. A 63-year-old woman could earn up to $8,040 ($670 monthly) in 1994 without any reduction in her Social Security benefits. For beneficiaries in this age group, however, the retirement test "tax" is $1 for each $2 of earnings above the exempt amount.

One estimate is that 1.2 million individuals had their Social Security benefits reduced by the retirement test in 1989 (Bondar, 1993). Much controversy surrounds discussion of the test, as evidenced by persistent congressional attempts to repeal or drastically modify it. Critics argue that the retirement test acts as a work-disincentive plan in that earnings above the exempt amount are, in effect, taxed at a 50 percent rate for early retirees and a 33⅓ percent rate for retirees aged 65 and over. These critics posit that eliminating the retirement test will cause some of those no longer affected by the test to increase their work effort and thus their earnings. Others suggest that the test itself is a form of age discrimination because persons age 70 and older are not required to meet it. Proponents of the test point out that liberalization or even elimination of the retirement test would be very costly and would ultimately help only a small number of aged who are least in need.

Packard (1990) simulated the elimination of the retirement test for the 1986 population of persons aged 65 to 69. He concluded that 8.1 million of the 9.7 million persons in this age group (84 percent) would not likely be affected by such a change; 600,000 persons in this age group could increase their earnings with elimination of the retirement test, but an equal number would be likely to decrease their earnings. What about tax revenues? The National Commission on Social Security (1981) estimated that complete elimination of the test would cost $6 or $7 billion in the first year. Packard's (1990) simulation suggests that changes in total tax revenue (payroll taxes plus taxation of benefits plus income taxation of earnings), though difficult to predict in advance, are likely to be quite small, especially because only a small proportion of those aged 65 to 69 are likely to change their work effort and earnings.

Responding to intense political pressure to abolish the retirement test, Congress has liberalized provisions over the past 15 years or so in three different ways:

1. It reduced the maximum age for the retirement test from age 72 to 70, effective in 1983.
2. It increased the annual exempt amount and wage-indexed the amount.
3. It changed the reduction in the "take-back" rate after age 65 from 50 to 33⅓ percent, effective in 1990.

Social Security Replacement Rates

Social Security has had an enormous impact on the extent of poverty among the aged. In 1966, 60 percent of Social Security benefits went to people whose incomes otherwise would have been below the poverty line, and 90 percent of these were lifted from poverty by virtue of the Social Security payments (Hollister, 1974). This has led at least one economist to characterize Social Security as the most successful social program in the history of the country (Hollister, 1974). Still, many are uncomfortable with the program and especially with what is perceived to be an inadequate replacement of preretirement income. Is this perception accurate? An answer requires evaluation of Social Security replacement rates.

In 1967, a U.S. House Ways and Means Committee report specified that the retirement benefit of a man aged 65 and his wife should represent at least 50 percent of his average wages under the Social Security system. Some have argued that, even assuming reduced expenses and lower taxes, 50 percent of wages is not enough. Palmer (1989) estimates that a hypothetical couple retiring in 1988 with preretirement gross earnings of $25,000 would have $4,769 less in taxes, elimination of $738 in work-related expenses, and $1,622 less in savings. Thus, $17,871, or 71 percent of gross preretirement earnings, would be required by this couple to maintain their style of living into retirement. Palmer estimates that replacement rates vary between 82 and 66 percent for couples earning $15,000 to $80,000.

How can that much income be generated in the retirement years, with people no longer working? And, how much of preretirement earnings can be (or should be) replaced by Social Security alone? One must remember that Social Security is only one source of income for most of the elderly; many supplement this income. Private pensions, wages, asset income, intrafamily transfers and aid, and even welfare and SSI benefits for the poorest of the elderly all provide help to individuals attempting to maintain a preretirement standard of living.

Munnell (1977) has evaluated the replacement rate structure of Social Security benefits in 1975 and finds it to be quite progressive: As the earnings record of a worker rises, the Social Security replacement rate falls. The proportion of income replaced for the worker with a history of low earnings ranged from 99.4 percent for the worker who retires at age 65 and whose spouse was also 65 or over, to 53 percent for a worker who retired at age 62 without a spouse or whose spouse was under age 62.

One important problem involved in assessing the replacement rate structure of Social Security has to do with how earnings are actually calculated. One common technique calculates the ratio of benefits derived from Social Security to earnings in the last year before claiming benefits. Grad (1990) assesses replacement rates in two different ways for persons first receiving Social Security retired-worker benefits in the early 1980s. First, she calculates the ratio of benefits received to the average of the five years of highest earnings over a career (hereafter referred to as "highest earnings"). Second, she calculates the ratio of benefits received to the average earnings received during the five years immediately before benefit receipt (hereafter referred to as "last earnings"). Table 11–8 shows the median replacement rates from Social Security based on highest and last earnings, for those with and without private employer pensions, by sex. The table also shows the median total replacement rates for those workers with private employer pensions. Median Social Security replacement rates for workers with no employer pensions ranged from 27 to 30 percent based on highest earnings and from 43 to 48 percent based on last earnings. Median total replacement rates for workers with employer pensions ranged from 42 to 48 based on highest earnings and from 56 to 59 percent based on last earnings. As can be seen in Table 11–8, employer pensions increased replacement rates, on average, by 70 to 75 percent for men and by 48 to 50 percent for women. Still, even when pension income is taken into account, replacement rates fall well below a level necessary for many to maintain living standards in retirement.

Several authors have examined the adequacy of replacement rates in the United States in relation to those that exist in other countries. Horlick (1970) found

TABLE 11–8   Median Social Security and Total Replacement Rates Based on Highest and Last Earnings for Those with and without Employer Pensions, by Sex

Replacement Rates	Men		Women	
	With Employer Pensions	No Employer Pensions	With Employer Pensions	No Employer Pensions
Highest Earnings:				
Social Security rate	24%	27%	32%	30%
Total rate	42	27	48	30
Increase in rate as a percent	175	100	150	100
Last Earnings:				
Social Security rate	33	43	40	48
Total rate	56	43	59	48
Increase in rate as a percent	170	100	148	100

Source: S. Grad, *Income of the Population 55 and Over, 1990* (Washington, DC: U.S. Department of Health and Human Services, Social Security Administration, 1992), Table 9.

that the average retired couple in the United States enjoys an intermediate replacement rate among the 13 industrialized nations he studied. Five were significantly higher, three were about the same, two were slightly lower and two were significantly lower. For example, Austria has a pension formula based on average earnings over the last 7 years of coverage (changing to 10 years from 1987). It is also time related, providing about 57 percent of earnings after 30 years of labor and increasing to 79.5 percent after 45 years (U.S. Department of Health and Human Services, 1986). In practice, a man who retired in 1986 after 35 years of working received about 65 percent of his average earnings in the 7 years before retirement, aside from other benefits.

One difficulty involved in making these international comparisons has to do with the varied systems that exist among nations. Many nations (e.g., Australia, Finland, Ireland, Israel, the Netherlands, and New Zealand) have flat-rate systems, whereas others (e.g., Sweden, Canada, and Great Britain) have double-decker systems. Such systems include a flat pension benefit supplemented by an earnings-related pension program and provide higher replacement for low-wage workers and increased benefits for middle and high-wage workers (Schulz et al., 1974). For example, aged Canadians receive a universal pension earned at a rate of one-fortieth of the maximum pension for each year of residence in Canada after age 18, up to a maximum of 40 years and with a minimum of 10. In addition, earnings-related pensions are provided replacing approximately 25 percent of average earnings (U.S. Department of Health and Human Services, 1986).

Women and Social Security

In recent years, a question has emerged about the equity of Social Security coverage for certain groups, especially women. It is generally believed that women are disadvantaged by the Social Security system. Flowers (1977), pointing out that most of the provisions of the law pertaining to women have been in effect for about 40 years, asks "why significant controversy has developed only fairly recently." In answer, she notes that the feminist movement has heightened interest in all aspects of the treatment of women in U.S. society and that the Social Security benefit structure reflects a pattern of family life that is no longer typical in the United States.

In 1939, the Social Security Act was amended to provide additional protection for spouses, widows (and widowers), and children of workers covered by the program. These amendments were based on two important presumptions generally accepted in the 1930s: First, a man is solely responsible for the support of his wife and children, and second, the overwhelming majority of married women *do not* work. Several important social trends have played havoc with these presumptions—not the least of these is the dramatic increase of women (particularly married women) in the labor force. In 1990, almost 58 percent of all women were working, and most of these women make a significant economic contribution to the standard of living of the family.

Just how are women disadvantaged by the Social Security system? Benefits tend to be lower for women than for men. The average monthly benefit for a female retiree was 74 percent of that of a retired man in June 1995 ($570 versus $769). Social Security benefits depend, to a great extent, on average earnings and length of participation in the labor force. Many women have marginal work careers with low earnings; in addition, many women earn substantially less than their equally skilled male counterparts. Finally, increasing numbers of married women divide their lives so as to spend a part as homemakers and another part in the paid labor force. This reduces their length of participation in covered employment.

Because homemaking yields no credit as work, a homemaker is fully dependent on her husband's benefits. It is generally recognized that work performed in the home by homemakers accounts for a very large amount of all unpaid work. Unfortunately, there is little consensus on an approach to placing a value on household work. One approach, the *market cost approach,* assumes that the wage rate for tasks performed in the marketplace can be applied to the same work performed *outside* the marketplace. Application of this approach placed the average 1972 value of a housewife at $4,705, with wide variation by age (U.S. Senate Special Committee on Aging, 1975). Treating household work as covered employment would give women Social Security work credit, leave them no longer fully dependent on a husband's benefits, and increase the average monthly benefit for women. Homemaker credits are now used in several countries. In the United Kingdom, Germany, and Japan, voluntary contributions to the Social Security system are permitted by all the nonemployed, including homemakers. In Japan, 80 percent of eligible homemakers are reported to participate (Lapkoff, 1981; U.S. Department of Health and Human Services, 1986).

Women who are divorced before 10 years of marriage are not entitled to any of their husband's benefits. Retired female workers remain at a slight benefit disadvantage relative to widows with survivors' benefits. The average monthly benefit for a retired woman is 91 percent of that for a woman receiving survivors' benefits in June 1995 ($603 versus $660).

The Social Security Amendments of 1983 improved the benefit status of women in the Social Security system in several important ways. Two are identified here. First, Social Security benefits will no longer be terminated for surviving divorced spouses and disabled widows and widowers who remarry after entitlement to benefits. Previously, remarriage would result in termination. Second, effective January 1, 1985, a divorced spouse aged 62 or over who has been divorced for at least two years may receive benefits based on the earnings of a former spouse who is eligible for retirement benefits, regardless of whether the former spouse has applied for benefits or has benefits withheld under the earnings test. In the past, the divorced spouse could not qualify until the former spouse had filed an application.

As mentioned before, homemaker credits are not available in the Social Security system in the United States, and, over the years, little political support for reform has developed. However, an alternative reform approach—to divide the Social Security earnings credits of married couples equally between spouses—has received considerably more attention. Although *earnings sharing* is a relatively new idea for Social Security, the concept has been in use in community property states, especially in divorce settlements (Schulz, 1992). The Technical Committee on Earnings Sharing, a private group seeking to improve the position of women in the Social Security system, has endorsed a proposal designed to be implemented over several decades that would result in benefit increases for women with lower benefits under current law; some decreases would be experienced by women with high benefits (Fierst & Duff, 1988). To date, the Congress has not acted on this proposal. One problem is that cost estimates for the proposal vary widely. Another problem is that benefits will decline for some retirees.

The Social Security Retirement Age

The term *age,* as used by the Social Security Administration, is the age when workers can retire and receive an unreduced retirement benefit. Over the years, there has been support for raising the age. Numerous reasons have been given, including the increased longevity and health experienced by so many older Americans, future predictions of a need for additional labor, and rising pension costs resulting in part from the trend toward earlier retirement. It seems clear that this latter point was most salient for the Congress when it voted in 1983 to amend Social Security and raise the "normal" retirement age. Under the new provisions, workers starting in 2027 will have to be age 67 before receiving a full retirement benefit. Individuals will still be able to retire as early as age 62 but will suffer a 30 percent reduction in their benefit. These changes are scheduled to occur gradually, beginning in 2003 and achieving full implementation in 2027. Because the changes are not to occur for many years, the intervening period provides an opportunity for study of the consequences of the change. Already, some members of Congress have filed bills to repeal the provisions; others have suggested that the schedule to full implementation be speeded up. Congressional hearings on the matter are a certainty!

Supplementary Security Income

The Social Security Act of 1935 included a mandate for the establishment of a separate program of old-age assistance under which benefits (coming mostly from federal funds) would be distributed to needy aged people and administered by the states. Similar programs for the blind and disabled were established in the 1935 act and subsequent amendments. Under the Social Security Amendments of 1972, a new federal program of Supplemental Security Income (SSI) for the aged, blind, and disabled replaced the former state-operated welfare programs. When the SSI program began making payments in January 1974, 3.2 million recipients were on the rolls. By 1992, this figure had increased to 5.6 million, less than 30 percent of whom were 65 years or older.

The SSI program was envisioned as a basic national income maintenance system for the aged, blind, and disabled (U.S. Senate Committee on Finance, 1977). It was intended to present minimal barriers to eligibility by having few requirements other than lack of income. Yet, as its title indicates, the program was

Maintaining health and having access to medical care are important quality-of-life issues for older people.

expected to supplement the Social Security program primarily by providing income support to those not covered by Social Security.

Because SSI is an assistance program, applicants must prove need by meeting an assets test. As of January 1, 1989, assets may not exceed $2,000 for an individual and $3,000 for a couple. Excluded from the assets test are the value of a home (up to a certain market value), household goods, personal effects, an automobile used for essential transportation, a life insurance policy with a face value of $1,500 or less, and burial funds not exceeding $1,500. SSI benefits are reduced, dollar for dollar, by *any* income (earned or unearned) above $20 per month and also by 50 percent of *earned* income above $65 per month. In 1994, federal SSI payments were $446 a month for an individual and $669 a month for a couple (if both members are eligible). Many states provide an additional supplement to the federal benefit. In June 1995, Iowa provided the largest supplement to an aged person ($165.55); Utah provided the lowest supplement ($2.54). Cost-of-living increases in SSI are based on change in the Consumer Price Index.

Critics of SSI argue that although the program is targeted at the right population, eligibility requirements limit people's ability to lift themselves from poverty status. For example, an eligible individual working part time whose gross income was $500 in gross monthly earnings would receive only $238.50 in federal SSI payments:

$$\$446 - ((\$500 - \$85) / 2) = \$446 - \$207.50 = \$238.50$$

Another major concern has arisen because of the low participation level of eligible persons in the SSI program. The Social Security Administration estimates that about one in three eligible aged persons do not participate in the program. Drazaga, Upp, and Reno (1982) offer two reasons for the relatively low levels of participation in SSI: lack of knowledge about the program and stigma. Their study found that 45 percent of nonparticipants had never heard of the SSI program. Even among the many who did know of SSI, some indicated a reluctance to become involved in a means-tested program.

The Future of Social Security

The most crucial questions about the future of the Social Security system concern its financial status. Current and future retirees (current contributors) want to know if the system is solvent or whether it will go bankrupt and deprive millions of a retirement pension they have counted on. The latter appears highly unlikely. As Dorcas R. Hardy, former Commissioner of Social Security, has written, "Social Security and justice are inextricably linked" (1987, p. 5). According to Hardy, the system is sound, has a trust fund reserve that is expected to grow significantly into the next century (to be discussed), and is not likely to face another financial crisis until well into the next century.

During the early years of Social Security, more revenue was taken in from contributions than was paid out in benefits, and a trust fund was developed. By 1975, this situation had changed. Between 1975 and 1981, the trust fund paid out $16 billion more than was taken in. At that rate, the trust fund would likely have run out during the mid-1980s. In 1977, however, significant amendments were made in the Social Security system. Many, including then President Carter, believed these changes provided a long-term financial solution for the system's problems. By 1982, economic conditions again made the financial status of the system appear vulnerable. On January 20, 1983, the National Commission on Social Security Reform (NCSSR) presented its recommendations. Passed with almost unprecedented speed after bipartisan effort, Public Law 98–21 was signed by President Reagan on April 20, 1983. This law represents the Social Security Amendments of 1983 and is substantially in line with the NCSSR recommendations. A number of the changes brought about by these amendments have already been noted in the previous discussion. In signing the bill into law, President Reagan stated:

> This bill demonstrates for all times our Nation's ironclad commitment to Social Security. It assures the elderly that America will always keep the promises made in troubled times a half a century ago. It assures those who are still working that they, too, have a pact with the future. From this day forward, they have our pledge that they will get their fair share of benefits when they retire. Our elderly need no longer fear that the checks they depend on will be stopped or reduced. These amendments protect them. Americans of middle age need no longer worry whether their career-long investment will pay off. These amendments guarantee it. And younger people can feel confident that Social Security will still be around when they need it to cushion their retirement.

For approximately the next 25 years or so, under current economic forecasts, the Social Security Trust Fund is expected continually to have excesses of income over outgo, creating a buildup that will peak in 2020 at about $1.7 trillion in 1993 dollars. The 1993 excess of receipts over expenditures was estimated at $50.2 billion and increased the total in the trust fund to $369.3 billion. Reserves are expected to decline as the Baby Boom generation retires (the first Baby Boomers turned 50 years of age on January 1, 1996), and further increases in payroll taxes will likely be needed before 2036 to meet future obligations. Could sour economic conditions again place the Social Security system in jeopardy? Perhaps, but Social Security is a vital program and, most important, it is guaranteed by the taxing power of the federal government of the United States of America. It is also useful to remember that the federal government has the capacity to reduce benefit levels, in which case future payroll tax increases could be deferred.

PRIVATE PENSIONS

By 1990, about 43 million wage and salary workers in private industry (45 percent) were covered by private pension plans of one sort or another. This represents sig-

---

nificant growth over the last 50 years or so. In 1940, only about 12 percent of the labor force was covered by private pensions. In 1982, only 23 percent of all those age 65 and over received money income from private pensions or annuities. Table 11–9 shows which U.S. workers were *not* covered by pension plans in 1988 (Woods, 1989). Almost 40 million workers did not participate in a private pension plan in 1988. According to Schulz (1992), the two key factors are union status and firm size: Almost all workers without pension coverage are nonunion and work for firms with a relatively small number of employees.

Private pensions were first introduced into U.S. industry by the railroad and express companies. The first plan, established by the American Express Company in 1875, was financed solely by the employer. The first plan supported jointly by

TABLE 11–9   Full-Time Workers[1] *NOT* Pension Covered in May 1988

Selected Worker Characteristics	Percent Not Covered
Under age 21	84%
Age 25–29	57
Age 45–49	42
Age 60+	52
Race:	
White	52%
Black	57
Other	51
Size of firm:	
Less than 10 workers	89%
50–99 workers	59
250 or more workers	31
Union	24%
Nonunion	56
Men	50%
Women	57
Job tenure:	
Less than 1 year	81%
1–4 years	62
15–19 years	26
Industry:	
Construction	68%
Manufacturing—Durable goods	34
Manufacturing—Nondurables	39
Trade—Wholesale	51
Trade—Retail	68
Services—Professional	54
Services—Other	74

Source: J. R. Woods, Pension coverage among private wage and salary workers: Preliminary findings from the 1988 Survey of Employee Benefits. *Social Security Bulletin, 52* (October, 1989), 2–19.
[1] Private wage and salary workers.

employee and employer contributions was inaugurated by the Baltimore and Ohio Railroad Company in 1880. The railroad industry was the first to adopt pension plans rather widely; by the time of World War I, over half of all railroad employees were covered by such plans, and by the late 1920s, the proportion covered had risen to four-fifths (Institute of Life Insurance, 1975).

Labor unions played an important part in the expansion of pension coverage. Many unions developed their own plans in industries that provided no company coverage. The first trade union plan was that of the Granite Cutters in 1905. Two years later, the first of the larger international unions, the International Typographical Union, adopted a formal pension plan for its members. By 1930, about 20 percent of all trade union members in the United States and Canada were covered by a union pension plan (Institute of Life Insurance, 1975).

Economic conditions during the 1930s reduced the growth of the private pension movement. The passage of the Social Security Act of 1935 did help create a climate in which the idea of pension planning would continue to flower. Schulz (1992) attributes the tremendous growth in private pension coverage since 1940 to a variety of reasons. These include:

1. The continued industrialization of the U.S. economy
2. Wage freezes during World War II and the Korean War that encouraged fringe benefit growth in lieu of wages
3. Inducements offered by the federal government, such as the Revenue Act of 1942, which made employer contributions to qualified pension plans tax deductible
4. A favorable decision by the Supreme Court in 1949 that pensions were a proper issue for collective bargaining
5. The development of multiemployer pension plans

In 1974, Congress passed the Employee Retirement Income Security Act (ERISA). This legislation established minimum standards for pension programs and strengthened the regulation and supervision of such programs. Prior to this, the policing function was left primarily in the hands of participants. Unfortunately, this had tragic consequences in many cases. Workers lost pension benefits as a result of company bankruptcies, plant closures, and unemployment. In addition, financial irregularities, including mismanagement of funds, left many new retirees with nothing despite a lifetime of paying into the company's pension fund.

The major provisions of ERISA as passed in 1974 are as follows (Skolnick, 1974):

1. A company must permit an employee to participate in a pension plan if he or she has reached the age of 25 and has worked for the employer for one year.

2. Vesting is the nonforfeitable right of an individual to receive a future pension based on his or her earned credits even if the person leaves the job before retirement age. All private pension plans must now vest benefits according to one of the

three ways: (a) 25 percent of pension benefits would be vested after 5 years with the company, increasing to 100 percent after 15 years of service; (b) 100 percent pension benefits would be vested after 10 years of service; or (c) 50 percent of pension benefits would be vested after 10 years when age and years of service total 45 years, followed in 5 years by 100 percent vesting (all employees must be 50 percent vested after 10 years and fully vested after 15 years of service).

3. Plan termination insurance is established up to a certain level for employees whose plans terminate with insufficient funds.

4. Individual retirement accounts (IRAs) may be established by workers without private or public employee pension coverage. There are limits on the annual investment allowed.

5. Employees may transfer vested pension rights (portability) on a tax-free basis from one employer to another or to an IRA.

ERISA contains quite specific reporting and disclosure requirements for private pension plans. In addition, amendments have been made since 1974. For example, ERISA now mandates that all pension plans subject to its provisions provide workers with a *joint and survivor option* at the time of retirement. If chosen, this option provides income to the surviving spouse in an amount equal to some percentage of the income payable during the time the employee and spouse were both alive. In the absence of such a provision, the surviving spouse often loses his or her interest in the pension benefit.

ERISA has not solved all the pension problems of individuals or their employers. For example, coverage is not mandatory, state and local governmental pension plans are not covered by the law, the value of pension rights is not assured for workers who change jobs, and survivors' provisions are thought to be weak. Thousands of court cases over pension rights have been brought forth under the ERISA law. In a 1991 case involving one of the largest ERISA settlements ever, Continental Can Company agreed to pay $415 million to settle a suit in which the company was charged with deliberately firing employees before they became eligible for benefits. More than 3,000 former employees were awarded an average of $90,000 each. The case is particularly noteworthy on several counts. It dates back to a 1977 labor contract agreed upon by the company and shows how workers must be vigilant against companies that promise the pension with one hand and take it away with the other (Schulz, 1995).

Special concerns remain for women in the arena of private pensions. As Table 11–9 shows, women are still not as likely as men to receive private pension benefits; 50 percent of men and 43 percent of women have private pension coverage in their current job. In part, the relatively low rates of coverage experienced by women is a function of the fact that they are more likely to be employed in low-wage jobs, small firms, and low-coverage occupations. In her review of recent trends, Korczyk (1993) reports that the good news is that differences between men and women almost disappear when level of earnings is controlled for (see Table 11–10), but the bad news is that women's coverage rates remain below those of men.

TABLE 11–10 Pension Participation Rates by Earnings and Gender

	All Workers		Pension Participants	
Earnings	Men	Women	Men	Women
Less than $10,000	10%	23%	13%	13%
$10,000–19,999	31	46	36	46
$20,000–29,999	27	21	63	64
$30,000–49,999	23	9	74	75
$50,000 or more	8	1	79	77

Source: S. M. Korczyk, Gender and pension coverage. In J. A. Turner & D. J. Beller (Eds.), *Trends in Pensions, 1992* (Washington, DC: U.S. Government Printing Office, 1993).

Private pensions have generally been designed as supplements to Social Security. Thus, it is no surprise that average benefits are quite low. A U.S. Department of Labor (1989) study of pension benefit levels in 1986 reported private pension benefits under $3,000 per year for 66 percent of women and 41 percent of men. Excluding the 8 percent of all persons who received both a government employee pension and a private pension benefit, median dollar income from a private pension in 1986 was $1,940 for women and $3,800 for men.

Such low replacement ratios are inadequate for the great majority of retirees. Benefit levels may improve as these plans mature; most private pension plans are *not* on a pay-as-you-go basis (as is Social Security) but are funded. Yet, in many plans, benefit levels are subject to collective bargaining agreements. Kassachau (1976) points out that unions are often dominated by younger workers, making retirees and their needs relatively unimportant. Retired persons who are "double dippers"—drawing both private pension and Social Security retirement benefits—are considerably better off than others.

Figure 11–5 depicts the results of a recent calculation by the U.S. Department of Labor Statistics of hypothetical replacement rates for long-service workers. Private pension levels were based on a representative sample of plans in firms employing 100 or more workers. Pension replacement rates ranged from 35 percent in lower-wage earners ($15,000) to 29 percent in higher-wage earners ($55,000). As Figure 11–5 shows, when Social Security benefits are added, the combined benefits do a good job of meeting replacement rate targets discussed earlier in the chapter.

The United States is likely to continue to have a mixture of public and private pension systems. Some of the advantages of Social Security—including almost universal coverage, cost-of-living adjustment, and financing backed by the federal government—have already been discussed. In addition, administrative costs are quite low. In 1987, administrative costs for Social Security amounted to less than 1 percent of contributions and reimbursements. Private pensions provide greater flexibility for different worker groups as well as the potential for investing pension funds in the national economy. Some disadvantages of private pensions

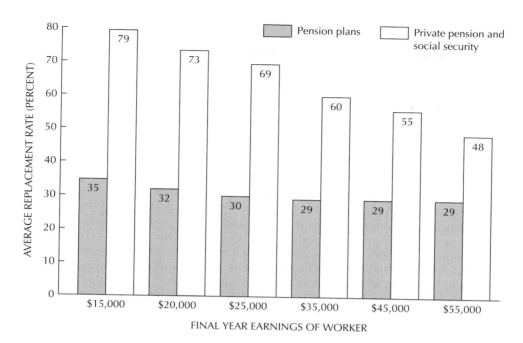

FIGURE 11–5   Income Replacement Rates of Pension Plans, 1989
Source: Employee Benefits in Medium and Large Firms, 1989 (Washington, D.C.: U.S. Bureau of Labor Statistics, 1991).

include higher administrative costs, a general absence of indexing to protect retirees against inflation, and the difficulty involved in achieving portability, among others mentioned earlier.

Robert Butler (1975) has suggested what seems to be an ideal pension system based on current standards of living: universal coverage; immediate 100 percent vesting; portability; full insurance, including survivors' benefits; and two benefit escalators—one tied to the cost of living and another tied to the nation's economic growth. Historian David Fischer (1977) believes that instead of supporting the aged with pensions at the end of life, it would be cheaper and easier to give each American a grant of capital at the beginning of life. He proposes that every American receive at birth a "national inheritance gift" in the amount of $4,400. The gift would be surrounded by restrictions. It would have to be invested in a savings account or government security and could not be spent, loaned, borrowed, or employed as collateral in any way. The money would not be taxed and would be left to earn interest until the infant who originally received it reached the age of 65. At 6 percent annual interest over 65 years, the original $4,400 would grow to $200,000. The average aged couple would have nontaxable income of more than $25,000 a year. On their death, the money would return to the United States Treasury. According to Fischer, supporting such a program would cost less than current government expenditures for the aged and might actually reduce inflation because the plan would be funded before the money was spent. (This is the opposite of deficit spending.) The likelihood of either of these proposals receiving serious consideration in the near future, however, is quite small.

SUMMARY

The major sources of income for the elderly are Social Security, asset income, and earnings. A considerable proportion of the elderly receive in-kind income in the form of goods and services they obtain free or at reduced expenditure. Examples include housing subsidies, health care, and food stamps. It is difficult to estimate how much in income these programs are worth to the aged. Since the mid-1960s, the median income of elderly has increased at a faster pace than for the population as a whole. By 1990, the median income of an aged couple was $23,352. Retirement status, age, and race are factors associated with income variation among the elderly. Tax advantages received by the elderly would seem to be of more help to property owners and those with higher incomes. Inflation has adverse implications for all people, although Social Security benefits, some private pensions, SSI, and in-kind programs such as food stamps are now indexed to the rate of inflation. This gives the aged an advantage relative to other age groups.

The elderly show a pattern of expenditures quite like that of other low-income groups. Poverty has been declining among the elderly, although aged African Americans are more than three times as likely as aged whites to be deemed officially poor in the U.S. in 1990 (30.8 percent vs. 9.6 percent, respectively). Orshansky (1978) argues that the government's poverty index is set too low and is not applied to those aged who are institutionalized or living with relatives. Adjusting the poverty index and applying it to these hidden poor might show as many as 40 percent of the aged to be living in poverty.

The Social Security Act of 1935 signaled a new era in financial arrangements for life after retirement. Nine out of ten workers are covered, and over 90 percent of the elderly receive some income from Social Security. Social Security is an earnings-based program; for the designated groups, participation is compulsory. Workers with lower earnings are favored by a weighted benefit schedule. Retirement is defined through a retirement test that withholds pension benefits if earnings are above a specified amount. Average benefits are relatively low because of the popularity of the early retirement option. Early retirement benefits (to those who retire at ages 62 to 64) are reduced because of the longer period over which they will be paid. It is generally believed that women are disadvantaged by the Social Security system, although, as a proportion of the total of all benefits, the amount paid on the earnings of women is slightly greater than that paid on the earnings of men. At least for now, the Social Security Amendments of 1983 appear to have put off fears about the financial status of the Social Security system well into the twenty-first century.

Private pension plans have generally been designed as supplements to Social Security. About 45 percent of U.S. workers are covered by one sort of private pension plan or another. In 1974, the Congress passed important legislation (ERISA) establishing minimum standards for these plans. Previously, the policing of private pension programs was irregular and ineffectual. Still, ERISA has not solved all the pension problems of individuals or their employers. For example, ERISA does not make private pension coverage mandatory.

Private pensions have generally been designed as supplements to Social Security.

As a result, average benefits are low. For those workers who have both Social Security and a private pension, the combined benefits do a good job of replacing preretirement earnings.

STUDY QUESTIONS

1. Discuss the economic position of U.S. elderly with regard to variation by age, race, and retirement status.

2. List and explain the various forms of indirect or in-kind income available to the elderly through federal programs.

3. Explain some of the ways in which inflation can have a detrimental impact on the economic situation of the elderly.

4. Discuss the *poverty index* and explain how it is used to determine the adequacy of elderly income. What are the problems inherent in using this measure of income adequacy?

5. With the passage of the Social Security Act of 1935, the United States became one of the last industrialized nations to execute a federal old-age pension program. Discuss the principles behind this legislation.

6. Explain why the Social Security payroll tax schedule is considered by many to be regressive.

7. Discuss the advantages and disadvantages women experience with respect to Social Security benefits.

8. Explain why ERISA was deemed a necessary piece of legislation. What are some of the major provisions of this act?

9. Why are average private pensions so low?

REFERENCES

Achenbaum, W. A. (1978). *Old age in the new land.* Baltimore: John Hopkins University Press.

Bondar, J. (1993). Beneficiaries affected by the annual earnings test, 1989. *Social Security Bulletin, 56,* 20–28.

Bromley, D. (1974). *The psychology of human ageing.* Middlesex, England: Penguin Books.

Butler, R. (1975). *Why survive?: Being old in America.* New York: Harper and Row.

Calhoun, R. (1978). *In search of the new old.* New York: Elsevier.

Chen, Y. P. (1985). Economic status of the aging. In R. Binstock & E. Shanas (Eds.), *Handbook of aging and the social sciences.* New York: Van Nostrand Reinhold.

Dowd, J., & Bengtson, V. (1978). Aging in minority populations: An examination of the double jeopardy hypothesis. *Journal of Gerontology, 33,* 427–436.

Drazaga, L., Upp, M., & Reno, V. (1982, May). Low-income aged: Eligibility and participation in SSI. *Social Security Bulletin, 45,* 28–35.

Fierst, E. U., & Duff, N. (Eds.). (1988). *Earnings sharing in Social Security: A model for reform*. Report of the Technical Committee on Earnings Sharing. Washington, DC: Center for Women Policy Studies.

Fischer, D. (1977). *Growing old in America*. New York: Oxford University Press.

Flowers, M. (1977). *Women and social security: An institutional dilemma*. Washington, DC: American Enterprise Institute for Public Policy Research.

Fox, A. (1982, October). Earnings replacement rates and total income: Findings from the Retirement History Study. *Social Security Bulletin, 45*, 3–24.

Gist, J. R., & Mulvey, J. (1990). Marginal tax rates and older taxpayers. *Tax Notes* (November 5), 679–694.

Grad, S. (1990). Earnings replacement rates of new retired workers. *Social Security Bulletin, 53* (10), 2–19.

Grad, S. (1992). *Income of the population 55 and over, 1990*. Washington, DC: U.S. Department of Health and Human Services, Social Security Administration.

Grad, S. (1994). *Income of the population 55 and over, 1992*. Washington, DC: U.S. Department of Health and Human Services, Social Security Administration.

Hardy, D. R. (1987). The future of Social Security. *Social Security Bulletin, 50* (8), 5–7.

Hollister, R. (1974). Social mythology and reform: Income maintenance for the aged. *Annals of the American Academy of Political and Social Sciences, 415*, 19–40.

Horlick, M. (1970). The earnings replacement rate of old-age benefits: An international comparison. *Social Security Bulletin, 33*, 3–16.

Institute of Life Insurance. (1975). *Pension facts*. New York: Author.

Kassachau, P. (1976). Retirement and the social system. *Industrial Gerontology, 3*, 11–24.

Korczyk, S. M. (1993). Gender issues in employer pensions policy. In R. V. Burkhauser & D. L. Salisbury (Eds.), *Pensions in a changing economy*. Washington, DC: Employee Benefits Research Institute.

Lapkoff, S. (1981). Working women, marriage and retirement. In President's Commission on Pension Policy, *Coming of age: Toward a national retirement policy*. Washington, DC: U.S. Government Printing Office.

Lawton, M. P. (1985). Housing and living environments of older people. In R. Binstock & E. Shanas (Eds.), *Handbook of aging and the social sciences* (2nd ed.). New York: Van Nostrand Reinhold.

Munnell, A. (1977). *The future of Social Security*. Washington, DC: Brookings Institution.

National Commission on Social Security. (1981). *Social Security in America's future*. Report of the Commission to the President. Washington, DC: Author.

National Council on Aging (1976). *The myth and reality of aging in America*. Washington, DC: Author.

Orshansky, M. (1978). Testimony in U.S. House Select Committee on Aging. *Poverty among America's aged*. Washington, DC: U.S. Government Printing Office.

Packard, M. D. (1990). The earnings test and the short-run work response to its elimination. *Social Security Bulletin, 53* (9), 2–16.

Palmer, B. A. (1989). Tax reform and retirement income replacement rates. *Journal of Risk and Insurance, 56*, 702–725.

Pattison, D., & Harrington, D. E. (1993). Proposals to modify the taxation of Social Security benefits: Options and distributional effects. *Social Security Bulletin, 56*, 3–21.

Poverty Studies Task Force. (1976). *The measure of poverty*. Washington, DC: U.S. Department of Health, Education and Welfare.

Putnam, J. K. (1970). *Old-age politics in California: From Richardson to Reagan*. Stanford, CA: Stanford University Press.

Radner, D. B. (1989). The wealth of the aged and nonaged, 1984. In R. E. Lipsey & H. S. Tice (Eds.), *The measurement of saving, investment and wealth*. Chicago: University of Chicago Press.

Ross, C. M., Danziger, S., & Smolensky, E. (1987). Interpreting changes in the economic status of the elderly, 1949–1979. *Contemporary Policy Issues, 5,* 98–112.

Schulz, J. (1992). *The economics of aging* (5th ed.). Westport, CT: Auburn House.

Schulz, J. (1995). *The economics of aging* (6th ed.). Westport, CT: Auburn House.

Schulz, J., Carrin, G., Krupp, H., Peschke, M., Sclar, E., & Van Steenberge, J. (1974). *Providing adequate retirement income—Pension reform in the U.S. and abroad.* Hanover, NH: New England Press.

Skolnick, A. (1974). Pension reform legislation of 1974. *Social Security Bulletin, 37* (12), 35–42.

Smeeding, T. (1982). *Alternate methods for valuing selected in-kind transfer benefits and measuring their effects on poverty.* Technical Paper No. 50. Washington, DC: U.S. Bureau of the Census.

Social Security Administration. (1986). *Income and resources of the population 65 and over.* Washington, DC: U.S. Government Printing Office.

Torrey, B. B., & Taeuber, C. M. (1986). The importance of asset income among the elderly. *The Review of Income and Wealth Series, 32,* 443–449.

U.S. Bureau of the Census. (1982). *Statistical abstract of the United States: 1982–83.* Washington, DC: U.S. Government Printing Office.

U.S. Bureau of the Census. (1985). *Statistical abstract of the United States: 1986.* Washington, DC: U.S. Government Printing Office.

U.S. Department of Health and Human Services. (1986). *Social Security programs throughout the world—1985.* Research Report No. 60. Washington, DC: U.S. Government Printing Office.

U.S. Department of Labor. (1989). *Trends in pensions.* Washington, DC: Pension and Welfare Benefits Administration.

U.S. House Committee on Ways and Means. (1967). *President's proposals for revision in the Social Security system: Hearings Part I.* Washington, DC: U.S. Government Printing Office.

U.S. Senate Committee on Finance. (1977). *The Supplementary Security Income Program.* Washington, DC: U.S. Government Printing Office.

U.S. Senate Special Committee on Aging. (1975). *Women and Social Security: Adapting to a new era.* Washington, DC: U.S. Government Printing Office.

Woods, J. R. (1989). Pension coverage among private wage and salary workers: Preliminary findings from the 1988 Survey of Employee Benefits. *Social Security Benefits, 52,* 2–19.

CHAPTER 12

WORK, RETIREMENT, AND LEISURE

Jacob Jensen[1] (a fictitious name) had been a happy, successful man. Thirty-seven years ago he had begun as a stock boy, and today he was the number-two man in the company. A fine family, plenty of money, good health, and respect in the community reflected his success. Yet, as he approached age 60, he was given a stark choice by the board chairman: Because of a restructuring of the company, he could retire or be transferred to a lesser position in a distant city. Jensen had never given thought to retirement, because it seemed there would always be time to prepare for such a distant event. Now he found himself in great psychological pain. A psychiatrist, later writing Jensen's case history, described him as depressed, suicidal, and a prime candidate for a debilitating physical illness such as a stroke.

Jimmy Kilpatrick[2] is another story. He worked in a factory in Detroit touching up paint on new Cadillacs. According to Mr. Kilpatrick, he had been working since he was 10 years old—and it was time to rest. At age 51, he retired from the assembly line at Cadillac. His monthly pension is about $900; the mortgage payment on the house he bought 25 years ago is only $175 a month. His children are grown and self-supporting, and his wife is considering going back to work. Kilpatrick says that if money gets a little short, "I'm not bragging, but I'm pretty good with paints."

Explaining the different responses of these two individuals toward retirement is not simple. Both cases represent aspects of the American experience with retirement. Mr. Jensen represents the situation of being at the top of his profession one day and then, the next, because of a corporate restructuring, anticipating himself

---

[1]From A. Rosenfeld, "The Willy Loman Complex," in R. Gross, B. Gross, and S. Seidman (Eds.), *The New Old: Struggling for Decent Aging* (Garden City, NY: Anchor Books, 1978).

[2]From J. Flint, "Early Retirement Is Growing in the U.S.," *New York Times,* July 10, 1977.

outside the arenas of achievement and competition. Mr. Kilpatrick, on the other hand, represents what has become a significant trend in the work style of Americans—early retirement. Growing numbers of workers have an opportunity to retire early, and many are taking it.

Most Americans, men and women, who are in the labor force or about to enter it, will face retirement. This itself is a radical transformation from the past. What researchers know about changes in survivorship rates alone should support this fact. Retirement requires longevity; if people do not live long enough to work and still have years left over, there can be no retirement. According to the gerontologist Robert Atchley (1976), three additional conditions are necessary for the emergence of retirement as a social institution. These include the following:

1. An economy that produces enough surplus to support adults who do not hold jobs
2. The presence of mechanisms, such as pensions or Social Security, to divert part of the surplus to support retired people
3. The acceptance in a society of the idea that people can live in dignity as older adults without working at a job

Other factors have contributed to the appearance of retirement in the United States. These include the decline of agriculture as a provider of jobs to U.S. workers and the increasing importance of formal education as an asset valued over experience (Achenbaum, 1978).

Still, the United States has been described by many as a work-oriented society where what a person does determines what a person is. Pollster Daniel Yankelovich (1974), on the basis of survey studies, says that the majority of Americans associate four ideas with work:

1. Being an adult in U.S. society means being a good provider for your family.
2. Work earns one freedom and independence.
3. Hard work leads to success.
4. A person's worth is reflected in the act of working.

Various national groups make competing claims about who works hardest, but there may be no people for whom work means more than it does for Americans. Ethel Shanas (1968) found, in a comparison of men age 65 and over living in Denmark, Britain, and the United States, that, although aged Americans were as likely to retire as were aged citizens of the other two countries, retired Americans were much more likely to say that they missed some aspect of their work. Interestingly, although they did not miss the work itself, they missed the sense of feeling useful that their jobs had provided, the people they had met at work, and the money they had earned—more than the Danes or the British did.

Why do people attach this special importance to work? Eminent German sociologist Max Weber offered one explanation, which is rooted in the religious ideals of Calvin and his followers. Calvin, following Luther, believed that man (and, no doubt, woman as well) had a calling to God in this world, and that this calling included one's work. Whatever that work was, it was a person's duty to do the best he (or she) could in order to please God. Calvin added the notion of predestination to the Lutheran theology. According to Calvin, God had already decided on the future course of humankind, including who would be saved and who would be damned. Thus, although one could still have a calling to God, following it no longer necessarily meant salvation.

Rather than simply accepting their fate, Calvinists sought signs of God's determination for them. Success in earthly endeavors became an indication of God's favor. Hard work (and the financial success it often brought) meant being in God's good graces. In early Christianity, by contrast, hard work reflected condemnation related to original sin.

Historically, the religious context for work eroded. Despite this secularization process, however, work still remained "the stuff of life." The Protestant ethic became the work ethic. Some argue that this work ethic has become increasingly outmoded in the twentieth century. Calhoun (1978) believes that technological progress, population growth, the accompanying contraction of work-force needs relative to availability, and increasing ability to influence, if not control, the business cycle have caused a devaluation of the work ethic.

It may be an oversimplification to call U.S. society work oriented. Given the enormous range of jobs in the United States and the different skills required to carry out these jobs, there may not be enough equivalent meaning among jobs to speak of a common meaning attached to work. Simpson, Back, and McKinney (1966) found that the type of job had a strong impact on a person's commitment to the identification with the job. Upper-white-collar jobholders (e.g., executives and professionals) were oriented toward autonomy and self-expression in their jobs, whereas semiskilled workers were oriented toward job security and income. Another early study along these lines found very few steelworkers or coal miners viewing their jobs as sources of meaningful life experiences (Friedmann & Havighurst, 1954). Williams and Wirths (1965), in their study of Kansas City adults, found that the world of work was the central element in the life-style of only 15 percent of their cases.

Much work in the United States *is* highly routinized, boring, exhausting, and without satisfaction. Mike Lefevre, a steel mill worker, talked to Studs Terkel (1972) about his "alienation" from work:

> It's hard to take pride in a bridge you're never gonna cross, in a door you're never gonna open. You're mass-producing things and you never see the end result of it.... My attitude is that I don't get excited about my job. I do my work, but I don't say whoopee-doo. The day I get excited about my job is the day I go to a head shrinker. How are you gonna get excited when you're tired and want to sit down.

Karl Marx saw the potential for alienation from work in industrial societies. According to Marx, work constitutes a person's most important activity—in fact, he called it *life activity*. Marx said that work is "creative" and that through it people create their world and, as a consequence, create themselves. Swedish sociologist Joachim Israel (1971) summarizes the conditions under which work is truly creative:

1. Work must be freely chosen.
2. It must allow an expression of capabilities.
3. It must allow an individual to express his or her social nature.
4. It should be *more* than a means for maintaining subsistence.

For Marx, any other kind of work is "forced" and alienating. Alienating work produces estrangement from one's labor and, perhaps more important, from oneself and the social world. "What is true of man's relationship to his work, to the product of his work and to himself, is also true of his relationship to other men" (Marx, quoted in Israel, 1971).

One does not have to be a Marxist to recognize that many workers, old and young, are doing "forced labor." Yet, the relationship between people and their jobs is a complicated one. How people feel about their jobs (and themselves) and how central their work is to their life-styles will strongly affect how they view the prospect of retirement. These factors may also determine how prepared a person is to deal with the demands of retirement. The next section surveys the complicated and changing relationships between aging and work, retirement and leisure. It begins by describing the status of elderly Americans in the labor force and how this status has changed in the twentieth century.

THE OLDER WORKER

Older people have always worked. In fact, it was not until sometime between 1930 and 1940 that the rate of labor-force participation by elderly U.S. males dipped below 50 percent. This rate has continued to decline and, as Table 12–1 shows, in 1990, about one-sixth (16.4 percent) of all males aged 65 and older were in the labor-force. Among males aged 55 to 64 (those approaching "normal" retirement age), labor-force participation rates have declined during the twentieth century and are quite in line with overall employment trends among males. In 1970, 79.7 percent of all males 16 years old and over were in the labor force; this figure dropped to 76.1 percent by 1990. The comparable figures for males aged 55 to 64 years were 83.0 percent and 67.7 percent, respectively.

The percentage of women 65 years old and over employed outside the home has not exceeded 11 percent in this century. Table 12–1 shows the narrow range within which the labor-force participation rate of older females has fluctuated since 1970. This is despite the fact that the proportion of gainfully employed women of all ages has increased dramatically during the twentieth century. About 18 percent of all women were employed in 1890; this figure has risen to 57.5 percent in 1990. The labor-force experience of women aged 55 to 64 reflects

TABLE 12–1   Civilian Labor-Force Participation Rates by Sex and Age, 1970–2000

	Males		Females	
	55–64 Years	**65+ Years**	**55–64 Years**	**65+ Years**
1970	83.0%	26.8%	43.0%	9.7%
1980	72.1	19.0	41.3	8.1
1990	67.7	16.4	45.3	8.7
2000	69.1	15.0	50.3	8.5

Source: Statistical Abstract of the United States: 1994 (114th ed.) (Washington, DC: U.S. Bureau of the Census, 1994), Table 615.

this phenomenon. Since 1950, labor-force participation rates for this group have increased from 27.0 to 45.3 percent in 1990 and are projected to exceed 50 percent in 2000.

Nonwhites (old and young) have had labor-force experiences similar to those described here. The labor-force participation rates of all nonwhite males have declined slightly, whereas those of elderly nonwhite males have fallen dramatically in this century. Almost 85 percent of aged African American men were employed in 1900 (Achenbaum, 1978), 40 percent in 1955, 21 percent in 1975, and 13.8 percent in 1990. Aged African American women have always had higher rates of employment than their white counterparts, although the difference in rates has narrowed. By 1990, only 9.4 percent of aged African American females were employed—a modest decline from the 10.5 percent in 1975, though a more significant decline from the employment rate of 16.5 percent in 1950. Aged Hispanic males had a labor-force participation rate of 15.9 percent, between that for whites and African Americans in 1990; the rate for aged Hispanic females was 7.8 percent.

Rose C. Gibson (1987) points out that despite the formal definition of retirement employed by the U.S. Bureau of the Census and other government agencies, for many older African Americans, the line between working and being retired is not so clear. Work in low-status jobs is a necessity for many aged blacks, and this continues a disadvantaged work pattern from youth through old age. As Gibson describes it, "This sameness of sporadic work patterns over the life course . . . may create for older blacks a certain ambiguity between work and retirement which, in turn, may affect the ways in which blacks define retirement" (1987, p. 691). Using data from the National Survey of Black Americans, Gibson identifies four factors that, in combination, contribute to many older African Americans thinking about themselves as being in an "unretired-retired" status:

1. An indistinct line between work in youth and work in old age
2. The receipt of income from other than private pension sources
3. The knowledge that one must work during old age
4. The benefits of defining oneself as sick or disabled rather than retired

More recently, Gibson (1991) has written of how the economic and psychological benefits of the worker who is disabled, in combination with perceptions of a discontinuous work life, discourages a self-definition of retirement among older African Americans.

What kind of work do older workers do? Historically, farming was the occupation in which most elderly men found work; it was a lifelong occupation. Retirement on a farm was rare. An older worker physically unable to perform some duties could assume other less demanding, though equally important, chores. This was especially true for white farmers. A greater proportion of African Americans than whites were in farming, but whites were much more likely to be owners or managers. Thus, they were in a position to remain in charge of planning and overseeing farm activities when they themselves were no longer able to carry out more physical farm duties.

Obviously, farming has diminished in importance as a source of jobs, not just for older men but for younger men as well. Still, older workers are more likely to be found in farming than is the total population of employed persons. Older workers are less likely than all workers to have blue-collar jobs. Many of these jobs are in industries where mandatory retirement has been the rule and where private pension plans are available. Moreover, many blue-collar jobs are physically arduous—truck driving and construction work, for example. Also, since 1970, opportunities for older workers have been undermined by economic restructuring concentrated in manufacturing industries. Between 1970 and 1987, the share of workers age 55 and over employed in goods-producing industries fell from 36 to 30 percent (Sum & Fogg, 1990).

Many older workers are self-employed or work for small businesses. These include accountants, lawyers, and tavern keepers, who simply continue at the same work beyond normal retirement age. Sales and clerical work offer part-time employment and are thus amenable to elderly individuals attempting to supplement retirement income, and this is especially the case for women.

Elderly workers are more likely than all workers to be found in service jobs: gardeners, seamstresses, practical nurses, washroom attendants, night guards, ticket takers, and domestics, for example. A *New York Times* article (Collins, 1987) reports that the child-care industry has begun to turn to older Americans to help care for the nation's preschool children. Although McDonald's, the giant fast-food firm, gained attention for a television advertising campaign involving older adult employees, the largest national chain of child-care centers, Kinder-Care Inc., estimated that about 10 to 12 percent of the company's work force is over the age of 55. It has been recruiting older workers through community groups and local and national organizations for the elderly.

Through the course of the twentieth century, increased longevity and changing social and work patterns have contributed to changes in the time people devote to life activities such as education, work, and retirement. Compared to 1900 (see Table 12–2), children today are spending more time in school, both males and females spend more time in work, and older people (especially males) are spending more time in retirement (U.S. Senate, 1987–1988).

TABLE 12–2   Life Cycle Distribution of Education, Labor Force Participation, Retirement, and Work in the Home, 1900–1980

	Number of Years Spent in Activity					
	1900	**1940**	**1950**	**1960**	**1970**	**1980**
Male						
Average life expectancy	46.3	60.8	65.6	66.6	67.1	70.0
Retirement/work at home	1.2	9.1	10.1	10.2	12.1	13.6
Labor force participation	32.1	38.1	41.5	41.1	37.8	38.8
Education	8.0	8.6	9.0	10.3	12.2	12.6
Preschool	5.0	5.0	5.0	5.0	5.0	5.0
Female						
Average life expectancy	48.3	65.2	71.1	73.1	74.7	77.4
Retirement/work at home	29.0	39.4	41.4	37.1	35.3	30.6
Labor force participation	6.3	12.1	15.1	20.1	22.3	29.4
Education	8.0	8.7	9.6	10.9	12.1	12.4
Preschool	5.0	5.0	5.0	5.0	5.0	5.0

	Percentage Distribution by Activity Type					
	1900	**1940**	**1950**	**1960**	**1970**	**1980**
Male						
Average life expectancy	100	100	100	100	100	100
Retirement/work at home	3	15	15	15	18	19
Labor force participation	69	63	63	62	56	55
Education	17	14	14	15	18	18
Preschool	11	8	8	8	7	8
Female						
Average life expectancy	100	100	100	100	100	100
Retirement/work at home	60	60	58	51	47	40
Labor force participation	13	19	21	27	30	38
Education	17	13	14	15	16	16
Preschool	10	8	7	7	7	6

Source: U.S. Senate, Special Committee on Aging (1987–1988). *Aging America. Trends and projections* (1987–1988 ed.) (Washington, DC: U.S. Government Printing Office).

On average, males spent almost seven more years (6.7 years) in the labor force in 1980 than in 1900. Nonetheless, a smaller proportion of their lives was spent working, 55 percent, than in 1900, when males spent 69 percent of their lives working. Since 1900, the average number of years women spent in the labor-force increased from 6.3 to 29.4 years and from 13 to 38 percent of average life expectancy.

The portion of life spent in retirement also has increased substantially since the beginning of the twentieth century. In 1900, average life expectancy for males was 46 to 47 years, and only 1.2 years (about 3 percent of that time) was spent in retirement. By 1980, the average male spent almost 14 of his 70 years in retirement (19 percent). Thus, although average life expectancy increased by 50 percent since 1900, average years in retirement increased by 1100 percent!

Although the twentieth century has brought with it increased life expectancy, increased work life expectancy, and an increased expectation of retirement, it has also brought significant decline in labor-force participation rates among older men. How can the declining employment level of older persons be explained? What factors have become important in setting that employment level?

Several explanations for the decline in labor-force participation of older men have been offered. A growing number of studies identify health status and the development of pension systems (including Social Security) as the most significant factors influencing the labor supply of older workers. Research also shows changes in the population age structure, changes in the occupational structure, and age discrimination in employment to be contributors to the declining employment rates of older workers. Each factor deserves some attention.

77-YEAR-OLD HASN'T MISSED A DAY IN 59 YEARS
Lisa Green, *USA Today*

Herbert Christiansen has worked at a Chicago hardware store since 1936 and never taken a sick day. That's 59 years—roughly 14,160 workdays. His only time off: holidays and three weeks of vacation each year. And two years in the Army at the end of World War II. Didn't the 77-year-old Chicago native ever catch the flu, sprain an ankle or spend the day in bed with a headache? "I've never had an instance where I even thought of calling in," he says. The only times injuries sent him to emergency rooms for treatment: when he was on vacation.

As Labor Day weekend gets under way, Christiansen's record has even Cal Ripken Jr. looking on with awe. Ripken, the Baltimore Orioles shortstop who Wednesday is expected to break Lou Gehrig's record of 2,130 consecutive baseball games, has some days off when his team isn't playing. And his career is seasonal. So of workers such as Christiansen, Ripken says: "That's phenomenal. I mean I get all this attention for consecutive game streak and in reality, I'm not going 365 days a year."

Three weeks ago, USA TODAY asked readers to nominate their "Cal Ripken at Work," and Christiansen's name was among more than 400 responses. The top nominees' records were verified by employers. Christiansen's 59 years without calling in sick put him at the head of the list. Of the 391 nominations mailed by the August 15 deadline, three others had a streak of 50 or more years. The number of days the average worker calls in sick each year: 5.6, finds CCH Incorporated research.

What drives people such as Christiansen and the other Cal Ripken at Work nominees to never take a sick day? Three common denominators: They love to work; they love the places they work; and they've been incredibly healthy.

Christiansen started April 1, 1936 as a salesman with Clark & Barlow Hardware in Chicago. A purchasing agent, his expertise is sought out by other employees. "He's the one everyone turns to. He's kind of like the icon," says John Sullivan, assistant vice president of Clark & Barlow, which has three other Illinois stores.

From his home in suburban Mundelein, he has a 15-minute drive to another suburb where he catches the train to Union Station in Chicago. From there, he has a 1-¼-mile walk to the store. He considers the walk one of the highlights. "I think it keeps me in pretty good shape. I do it pretty fast," he says.

Christiansen has seen up to 500 other employees come and go. The roll call brings some sadness. "There's got to 200 who have died since I've been there," he says.

Christiansen has slowed down lately. He used to work six days a week. Now, he works four. Some days are better than others. "These days, you don't always feel 100% but I fight it," he says. On days he doesn't feel right: "I just let nature take care of it. I don't take pills or anything. I get maybe a sniffle once a year. It usually lasts two or three days and then it's gone."

Christiansen credits his good health to the walking. Also, he doesn't drink and has never smoked. He has a banana every day—and perhaps some chocolate ice cream. Marjorie Christiansen doesn't mind her husband working. He spends time with the family and even helps baby-sit one of their great-grandchildren on Mondays. "I don't tell him to retire because I don't want him to stay home and be unhappy," she says. "He has to make that decision for himself."

Christiansen says he's devoted to his job in part because Clark & Barlow has treated him well. When he went into the Army in 1944, he was concerned about his mortgage payment. John Barlow, one of the store owners at the time, told him not to worry and assumed the responsibility. "I thought I was going to lose my house, but they paid my mortgage. It was a surprise," says Christiansen.

Although Clark & Barlow is a big part of Christiansen's life, he leaves his work at the store. He rarely talks hardware with friends, or even about his long tenure. "He doesn't think that this is a big deal," says Steve Johnson, who attends the same church as Christiansen. But Johnson does. "I have people who work under me and I don't have anybody with that kind of longevity or faithfulness," says Johnson, an administrator at a Chicago area hospital.

Few people can boast of having perfect attendance, says Marty Cohen, vice president of the Work in America Institute, a think tank on labor and management cooperation. Many companies, particularly those with 24-hour assembly lines, have incentives—such as $100–$125 per quarter—to show up every day. "There is a small group of Cal Ripken-like people who work through pain or despite grief," Cohen says. But they're in the minority.

Not all experts think long-serving workers are doing the right thing. Some may be "addicted and afflicted," says Pierre Haber of the Psychology Society, Inc. He says there's a time to work and a time to retire. "For most people, work is not that pleasant," Haber says. "It's a habit. People never consider the alternative. Many of these people are very narrow in their daily lives and look forward to the annual vacation." If they just gave in and retired in their 60s, he says, they could essentially be on vacation 52 weeks a year.

But even if their commitment to work may not be healthy in some cases, the Cal Ripkens and Herbert Christiansens do provide bottomline advantages for their employers. CCH Incorporated's 1995 survey shows absenteeism at companies rose about 3.5% last year. Since 1992, absenteeism—calling in on short notice to take the day off—is up 14.1% and costs as much as $668 per employee each year.

Ripken isn't sure he could match a streak such as Christiansen's. "I would like to think if I didn't make it (in baseball) that I would look to try to find something else, some other way to make a living, something that I really enjoy doing," Ripken says. "And if you really enjoy something, then it's easy to come to work. It's easy to go to the ballpark. It's easy to go to the office..."

Christiansen says he's happy. And he has yet to set a retirement date. "As long as I have good health," he says, "I'll be plugging along."

Health Status

One interpretation of the decline in labor-force participation of older persons has to do with the decline in death rates during this same period. This interpretation assumes that, compared with today's elderly, those in the past were healthier and thus better able to work. This assumption is based on recognition of the increasing numbers of chronically ill and physically debilitated people who today survive well into old age.

This proposition is difficult, if not impossible, to test empirically. Although life expectancy has increased dramatically and mortality rates are down significantly since 1900, it is not known whether the elderly are healthier or less healthy now than in the past. The National Health Survey, which reports on the health status of Americans, was not initiated in the United States until 1956. Also, older people vary considerably in their ability to describe symptoms and in the symptoms to which they give attention. Misattribution of illness symptoms is a problem among the elderly (Kart, 1981), as is underreporting of illness. And, as one prominent medical sociologist points out, "Information obtained from respondents tends to be highly discrepant from information obtained from clinical evaluations of the same populations" (Mechanic, 1968, p. 230). Further, changes over time and differences among the elderly in the reported incidence of illness may actually reflect variations in access to medical information, health beliefs, and availability of formal health services.

Despite the methodological difficulties involved in determining whether the current elderly population is as healthy as past elderly populations, a body of literature shows poor health to be a correlate of retirement. The 1968 Survey of Newly Entitled Beneficiaries (SNEB) conducted by the Social Security Administration found that 44 percent of wage and salaried male workers attribute health problems as the main reason for leaving their last jobs (Bixby, 1976). This influence declined with age, however; 57 percent of men aged 62 gave this reason, whereas only 23 percent of those aged 65 did so.

Parnes and colleagues (1975), reporting on results from the National Longitudinal Study (NLS) of older men, found that men who reported health problems in 1966 were twice as likely to have retired between 1966 and 1971 as men who were free of health impairments. This study is particularly important because it reflects a *causal* sequence of events: Health problems lead to retirement. Other studies are open to the charge that respondents cite health as a reason for retirement because they deem it to be a socially acceptable response. Kingson (1981) used this data set in studying men who retired before age 62 between 1966 and 1975 (U.S. Senate, 1981). He found the labor-force withdrawal of these very early retirees to be involuntary; 80 percent of the black and 66 percent of the white very early retirees did so involuntarily. Of these early withdrawees, 87 percent claimed disability or poor health.

The legitimacy of reported health problems is sometimes questioned. Reporting a health problem provides a socially acceptable reason for leaving work; thus, it was important for Kingson to determine the validity of such claims. One such test involves looking to the mortality rates of those claiming poor health as a reason for retirement and comparing the rates with those of healthy retirees. As Kingson (1981) notes, unfortunately for these early retirees, their claims of ill health were validated by their deaths. For example, by 1975, among white early retirees, the unhealthy group had died at a rate (42 percent) almost three times that of the healthy group (15 percent).

Not only do early retirees leave work voluntarily as a result of health problems, but, according to Kingson (1981), the research also shows these men to be among the most financially vulnerable retirees. One study of newly eligible beneficiaries for Social Security found that only one in four of all nonworking men entitled to Social Security benefits at age 62 retired voluntarily and had pension income in addition to Social Security; 45 percent had no pensions and did not want to retire when they had to leave their jobs. It seems that early retirees can be divided into two groups: those who leave work voluntarily (retirees in good health and with adequate pension income) and those—more numerous—with opposite characteristics.

Changing Retirement Policies

By 1990, 90 percent of all persons over the age of 65 were receiving money from one retirement program or another. This is a different picture from that in 1935, when Congress passed the Social Security Act. The increasing number of people eligible for Social Security benefits, the rising payment level of the benefits, and the growth of other public and private pension plans not only have provided security to many people in old age but also have permitted many older people to afford retirement.

The availability of early retirement benefits built into Social Security and other public and private pension programs has obviously contributed to the decline in old-age work participation rates. In 1956, the Social Security Act was amended to allow female workers to receive actuarially reduced benefits for early retirement between the ages of 62 and 64. This amendment was extended to men beginning in 1962. What resulted was a major increase in the number of men accepting early retirement benefits.

Employer-sponsored pension plans have had an increasingly powerful influence on the retirement decision. Schulz (1992) points out that it has become common practice in recent years for employers to encourage early retirement by setting a normal age for retirement in the pension plan that is below age 65. Many employers have also provided early retirement options to their employees. Sometimes, this takes the form of companies absorbing all the added costs of paying pensions out over a longer period of time, thus allowing workers the opportunity to retire early while at the same time assuring them of full pension benefits. For example, in 1986, Exxon Corporation, the largest oil company in the United States, offered immediate retirement to its employees aged 50 and over who had more than 15 years of service. The offer granted credit for an extra 3 years of service in calculating retirement benefits (Meier, 1986).

Kotlikoff and Wise (1989) show that the "pension stick" has sometimes taken the option out of the worker's decision to retire. Using data on pension plans in 1979, they show that workers who refused the early retirement option and continued working could experience up to a 30 percent reduction in pension benefits. Rather than emphasizing sanctions, other companies have developed incentive programs to encourage early retirement. In this case, workers who retire early may receive either a lump-sum cash payment equal to six months or a year's salary or additional pension credits aimed at increasing their pension benefit levels. During the 1980s and into the 1990s, many large multinational corporations—including General Motors, AT&T, and IBM—have employed these mechanisms to downsize and change the age structure of their labor force.

Changing Occupational Structure

Two theories related to changes in the composition of the labor-force often surface as explanations for the changes in the work status of elderly people in the twentieth century. The first is the argument that changing technology places older persons at a disadvantage. Occupational skills may become outmoded with technological innovation, and emphasis on assembly-line production may place a greater premium on speed and physical stamina than on work experience.

At first glance, the theory may seem credible, although evidence in support of it is difficult to obtain. Technological change that makes work skills obsolescent would seem to do so for all workers in an occupational category—not just the old. Moreover, older workers may be in a stronger position to hang on in such situations through recognition of seniority. Work careers sometimes involve shifts from one occupational group to another. Managers and administrators often are recruited from clerical and sales personnel. Typically, such a career pattern might tend to favor an older worker under conditions of changing technology. Additionally, in occupations where opportunities are undergoing contraction (because of technological change or otherwise), the greatest impact often is felt by young workers attempting to enter the occupation. Frequently, this is seen in the way craft unions regulate apprenticeship when demand for a particular skill is declining.

Although new technology makes some job skills unnecessary, it also prolongs working lives and opens up careers to some. Machines and automation often reduce the physical burdens and stress associated with industrial jobs and open the jobs to women who were previously excluded, justly or not, on the basis of insufficient physical strength. Bowen and Finegan (1969) have suggested that the reduction in the work week, itself often associated with automation in the labor force, may have *offset* the decline in elderly men's labor-force participation rates by as much as 3.5 percent between 1948 and 1965.

One place where older workers may have had special difficulty in the face of automation is in rural areas. Historically, rates of employment among older men have declined more in rural than in urban places. In rural areas, nonfarm employment opportunities for older people are minimal, and it seems likely that elderly men who followed the migration to urban areas did not do well. How much the population migration from rural to urban areas contributed to declining labor-force opportunities for older workers is difficult to discern, although it appears less than might have been expected. On the basis of his labor-force analysis, Long (1958) concluded that the effect of population migration between 1890 and 1950 on the elderly male labor-force rate was relatively little. According to one study, rural to urban migration accounted for about a 3 percent decline in elderly male workers between 1948 and 1965 (Bowen & Finegan, 1969).

A second theory regarding changes in labor-force composition is that the decline in the importance of farming as a source of jobs has had a depressing effect on the employment of older people. In 1890, almost 61 percent of all employed aged men were farmers; by 1980, this figure was only 11.3 percent. Yet, older workers were not the only ones affected by the twentieth-century revolution in agriculture. The increased technology and science involved in farming, the consolidation of small farms, and the development of multinational agribusiness had significant impact on farming employment for people of all ages. In 1900, about 36 percent of all those in the labor force were employed in agriculture, compared with about 2.7 percent in 1992.

These changes have affected younger and older men differently. Rapid expansion of the nonfarming components of the labor force has been a source of opportunities for younger workers, but no concomitant compensatory expansion of opportunities has occurred for older workers. Further, occupational longevity is greater for farmers than for other workers: "Age grading" is less relevant in agriculture. Retirement on the farm does not have the same meaning it does in other industries. The decline in the number of persons engaged in farming has been large enough to affect appreciably the labor-force participation rates of older men. In 1910, over 12 million workers were engaged in farming; by 1992, this figure had dropped to about 3 million.

A variation on this second theory is the effect the decline in manufacturing has had on the employment opportunities of older workers. Plant closings and layoffs resulting from corporate downsizing has disproportionately reduced opportunities for older workers in manufacturing industries. Applebaum and Gregory (1990) report that between 1981 and 1988, among all workers who lost their jobs because of plant closings or employment cutbacks, fully 33 percent of those over age 55 left the labor force compared to 14 percent of younger workers.

Age Discrimination in Employment

No one really knows the extent of age discrimination in employment that exists in U.S. society, although it is considered pervasive and is drawing increasing attention. A 1964 Department of Labor study reported that over one million worker-years of productive output are lost each year in the United States because of age discrimination. The Congress passed the Age Discrimination Employment Act

(ADEA) in 1967 and amended it in 1974, 1978, 1986, and 1990. The federal law prohibits the following:

1. Discrimination in the hiring of an employee on the basis of age
2. Discrimination in discharging a person on the basis of age
3. Discrimination in pay and other privileges and conditions of employment because of age
4. Instructions to a employment agency not to refer a person to a job or to only certain kinds of jobs because of age
5. Placement of any advertisement that shows preferences based on age or that specifies an age bracket

All employers with more than 20 employees are subject to the provisions of ADEA, as are employment agencies, labor organizations, and states and their agencies and subdivisions. With the 1986 amendments, virtually all employees aged 40 or older are protected, including firefighters, law-enforcement officers, and tenured faculty at institutions of higher learning, who, until December 31, 1993, may have been discharged on the basis of age at age 70 or older.

One study of employed aerospace workers 45 years old and over reported that *half* of them had at least one personal experience with discrimination in employment due to their age (Kasschau, 1976). Many workers suffer from age discrimination but do not identify it as such; others may be unaware of their protection under ADEA.

Age discrimination may occur in different forms. Employers may offer training opportunities only to younger workers. As a result, younger workers may receive salary increases and promotions at a faster pace than older workers. Older applicants may be told they are overqualified or that, because they have too much experience, they would be unhappy in a position. (In this regard, ADEA has been deemed ineffectual in promoting hiring of older workers [Ventrell-Monsees, 1991]). Companies may reorganize or restructure, thereby combining or consolidating functions and eliminating positions previously filled by older workers. However, 1990 amendments to ADEA, referred to as the *Older Workers Benefit Protection Act*, prohibits employers from treating older workers differently from younger workers during a reduction in force.

One theory of age discrimination, sometimes referred to as a *decrement theory of aging* (McEvoy & Cascio, 1989), is that employers assume decrement or decline in reaction time, in sensory and cognitive processes, in physical strength, and consequently in work performance. One recent survey of the literature on age and job performance reported little relationship between the two. In fact, older workers tend to have lower absenteeism, accidents, and turnover rates than do younger workers; typically, moreover, their commitment to the organization and job satisfaction is higher than that of younger workers.

Instances of age discrimination in employment can be difficult to identify. For workers not covered by federal law, states may vary in the protection they offer older workers. According to one report, although state laws generally are not as broad as the federal ADEA, many states do offer better protection to public than private employees (Goldberg, 1978). This same report found only four states having coverage equal to or better than federal laws.

Because the ADEA covers all employees aged 40 or older, discrimination based on age is not as clearly defined or obvious as race or sex discrimination (where unchanging characteristics are involved). When race or sex discrimination is proven, it usually affects the protected group as a whole. Age discrimination, on the other hand, may be directed at a subgroup of the protected class. For example, in one case brought before the U.S. Court of Appeals in Denver in 1980 (*Equal Employment Opportunity Commission v. Sandia Corporation*), the trial court found that in the company's layoff decisions, a pattern and practice of age discrimination began to appear at age 52. The inference that age was a factor became stronger after age 55, increasing to age 58, where it remained a steady influence in decisions until age 64.

RETIREMENT

Retirement as a mass phenomenon is a modern industrial creation. People certainly retired in preindustrial times, but only if they could generate income by performing some productive function or if they owned enough property to provide income. People who stopped working because they were too old and/or sick led difficult lives. They were "dead weight"—often treated, at least figuratively, like the Eskimo grandmother who, when she could no longer function, was abandoned or walled up in an igloo to await death (Donahue, Orbach, & Pollak, 1960).

Richard Calhoun (1978) points out that, in the sense of giving up "business or occupation in order to enjoy more leisure or freedom," the *Oxford English Dictionary's* first example of retirement comes from a 1667 entry in Samuel Pepys's diary. The example makes clear, through reference to pensions and "competences," that retirement was a status available only to nobility or mercantile elites. Working people of the day did not retire. Generally, they did not have access to pensions. Also, retirement was not valued.

In the U.S. context, Achenbaum (1978) explains that the word *retirement*, meaning stopping work at some prescribed age, was literally absent from pre–Civil War vocabulary. When people spoke of retiring, they were referring to "retiring" from winter storms to the warmth of a family circle. Webster, in the first edition of *An American Dictionary* (1828), defined *retirement* as "1. the art of withdrawing from company or from public notice or station; 2. the state of being withdrawn; 3. private abode; 4. private way of life." Obviously, old age was no prerequisite to retirement; anyone might retire. By the 1880 edition, however, a new meaning was attributed to the verb *to retire*: "to cause to retire, specifically to designate as no longer qualified for active service, as to retire a military or naval officer."

According to Achenbaum (1978), the first federal retirement measure became law in December 186l, when Congress passed an act requiring any naval officer below the rank of vice admiral who was aged 62 or older to resign his commission; the retirement age for naval officers was raised to 64 in 1916. Also noteworthy in the 1880 definition is the implicitly negative attitude toward old age. People were retired when they were no longer qualified for employment because of age.

From the mid-nineteenth to the mid-twentieth century, retirement policies became more prevalent in both public and private sectors. During this period, much debate surrounded issues of a standard age for defining retirement, mandatory versus voluntary retirement, and the adequacy of pension income. Debaters differed on the advantages and disadvantages of various retirement policies to older workers and to the national economy. Business, for example, regarded the issue of adequacy of pension as the price of management gaining prerogative over setting retirement age. Such power was essential for manipulating the size of the labor pool during business upturns or declines. Organized labor, on the other hand, viewed pension adequacy as a bread-and-butter issue—a right of every worker. Academicians and social reformers saw pension reform as extraneous, an issue used to exclude older workers from the labor force and deny them the freedom to work as long as they are able and desirous of doing so (Calhoun, 1978).

Many older workers saw retirement as a threat. They recognized that retirement (particularly forced retirement) might create an economically disadvantaged situation. Some believed the myth that death comes at retirement. Others believed in work as the American way of life.

In 1949, novelist James Michener published a short story in *Nation's Business* that he believed reflected the attitude of Americans toward retirement. The fictitious John Bassett was the head accountant at J. C. Gower and Company. The story involved his last day of work at the firm, which was forcing Mr. Bassett into retirement. He plotted revenge, but his employer—concerned about the impact of the forced retirement on Bassett and aware of the accountant's work record—waived the company's 65-and-out rule. Bassett stayed on the job, though at half pay. Gower also gave the employee a set of woodworking tools in an effort to increase the accountant's avocations. Bassett gave the tools to his grandson and, in doing so, summed up the attitude that Michener believed to be prevalent among U.S. workers: "Such substitutions for paid employment are for kids; what a man needs is a job."

Nevertheless, by the 1960s, something had changed. Retirement was becoming an accepted part of the life cycle for a greater proportion of the population. Ash (1966), studying the attitudes toward retirement among steelworkers, found that in 1951, retirement was justified only if an individual was physically unable to continue. By 1960, however, retirement was justified as a reward for a lifetime of work. Gerontologist Robert Atchley (1974) also found that retirement had become an overwhelmingly favorable concept. In his research, he discovered that people saw retirement as an active, hopeful, meaningful, healthy, relaxed, and independent time.

Even early retirement became acceptable. Apparently, when workers are provided adequate income for retirement before age 65, even to age 50, there is little resistance to retirement. Whereas in the immediate postwar environment, unions debated whether to set the retirement age at 65, by the 1960s, 30 years' service and out by age 55 was not atypical of union demands. The United Auto Worker's (UAW) 1965 collective bargaining agreement with the Big Three (Chrysler, Ford, and General Motors) had the effect of reducing retirement age to 60. Under the plan, an auto worker aged 55 with 30 years of service retired on a monthly pension plus a supplement until such time as the worker qualified for full Social Security benefits; at age 60, with at least 10 years of service, an auto worker could retire with a reduced benefit.

Ekerdt, Vinick, and Bosse (1989) provide formal support for the view that retirement—early or otherwise—has been institutionalized as an anticipated and orderly event in the life course. These researchers found that 66 percent of workers participating in the Veteran's Administration Normative Aging Study accurately predicted their eventual date of retirement within plus or minus one year; 40 percent were exact to within three months.

Mandatory Retirement

Some attribute the choice of age 65 as the age for retirement to the Old Age and Survivors Pension Act that Otto Von Bismarck pushed through as the first chancellor of the German Empire in 1889. One unverifiable account of how this came to be suggests that Bismarck's actuaries recommended 65 as a safe age because life expectancy at birth during the 1880s was about 45 years and few people could be expected to reach age 65. The English, playing it even safer, passed similar legislation in 1908, using 70 as a retirement age; they later reduced the age to 65. The United States followed in 1935 with its own Social Security program. Wilbur Cohen (1957), former Secretary of Health, Education and Welfare and one of the staff members who helped draft the 1935 legislation, has written that the choice of age 65 as a boundary line for providing old-age assistance had no scientific, social, or gerontological basis. There was simply a general political consensus that 65 was an acceptable age.

Although the original Social Security Act of 1935 was not involved in establishing a compulsory retirement age, the choice of age 65 seems to have carried over from Social Security to mandatory retirement policies. As already pointed out, recent amendments to the Age Discrimination Employment Act (ADEA) have, for the most part, eliminated 65 as the age for mandatory retirement.

It is difficult to say who was affected by mandatory retirement policies. A 1961 Cornell University sample survey (Slavick, 1966) of industrial firms in the United States with 50 or more employees found that most establishments had flexible retirement policies. Almost 95 percent of firms without pension plans, almost 70 percent of those with profit sharing, and 60 percent of those with formal pension plans had flexible retirement policies. Brandeis economist James Schulz (1992) points out the relationship between flexible retirement rules and establishment size in this survey. For example, 68 percent of the firms with 50 to 99 employees had flexible rules, yet only 30 percent of those with 500 or more employees had such rules. Thus, it is possible that relatively few firms have had mandatory retirement rules, while at the same time many workers have been subject to such policies.

A 1972 survey of the largest state and local government retirement systems covering about 70 percent of all employees enrolled in such systems showed that most had a mandatory retirement age; for two-thirds of the plans, retirement age was set at age 70 or later. Schulz (1992) has developed the tabulations of responses from this survey that show the incidence of mandatory retirement. Although 54 percent of male retirees were subject to mandatory retirement rules, only 7 percent of the total cohort of retired workers were able and willing to work but unable to find a new job. This small proportion of workers affected by mandatory retirement policies supports data on this issue provided by some of the largest corporations in the United States.

Why the fuss over mandatory retirement practices in light of how relatively few workers were forced out of work because of them and given that such practices are now against the law? One reason may be that although mandatory retirement practices are gone, so-called encouraged or forced retirement practices remain quite prevalent. Quadagno and Hardy (1996) describe how defined-benefit pension plans (DB)—plans that promise workers a specified benefit that the firm is obliged to pay—discourage staying in the work force. The value of DB plans typically does not grow smoothly with gradual, regular deposits. Rather, pension wealth remains low in the early years of tenure and increases rapidly as the worker approaches the early or normal retirement age (age 55 or 60 or 65). Once the worker actually exceeds the designated normal retirement age, pension accrual values decline sharply and may even turn negative. As a result, workers who remain with the firm beyond the early or normal retirement age may actually lose pension wealth.

Mandatory, forced, or encouraged retirement may have a number of different effects on retirees. Butler (1975) describes these as a *retirement syndrome*. Although not all retirees develop these characteristics, many formerly healthy workers do develop headaches, irritability, nervousness, lethargy, and the like in connection with retirement. Susan Haynes of the National Heart, Lung, and Blood Institute found that the mortality rate of workers who were in good heath when mandatorily retired at age 65 was 30 percent higher than expected three and four years following retirement.

Another reason for concern over forced or encouraged retirement may have to do with the traditional arguments made for and against mandatory retirement. These are often based on misconceptions and myths associated with the aging process and the employment of older people. Many studies indicate that older workers produce a quality of work as good as or better than that of younger workers. As already pointed out in Chapter 7, there is no reason to expect a decline in intellectual capacities with age and every reason to assume that older workers in good health are capable of learning new skills when circumstances require it.

The argument that forced or encouraged retirement of older workers opens needed jobs for the young may be especially appealing to some. Yet, no study can be cited that demonstrates that the termination of an older worker because of mandatory retirement directly caused the hiring of a young worker. Given the high rate of early retirement and the small proportion of retirees who would have continued working without mandatory retirement, it does not appear that the elimination of mandatory retirement policies would have any substantial impact on the labor supply or the unemployment rate.

Adjustment to Retirement

Adjustment to retirement can be difficult for many people, although most studies show that a majority of people adjust reasonably well. Finances, health and physical mobility, social involvement, and the specific circumstances of the retirement appear to top the list of factors researchers have identified as affecting adjustment to retirement. For example, Beck (1982) has identified poor health, lower income, and earlier-than-expected retirement as main determinants of a negative evaluation of retirement. Boaz (1987) implies some anxiety about retirement in her study of work as a response on the part of retirees to low and decreasing real retirement income. Findings from this research suggest that work during retirement among men *and* women "is a response to low or moderate levels of nonwage income at the beginning of retirement and, for men, work is also a response to a decrease in the real value of such income during retirement" (p. 437).

Reitzes, Mutran, and Pope (1991) identify a location effect among retired men, with those living in the suburbs having the highest average well-being scores. Fillenbaum, George, and Palmore (1985), however, found few consequences of retirement. Blacks and men with income at the poverty level were minimally affected by retirement, perhaps as a result of government-provided income supports.

Evans, Ekerdt, and Bosse (1985) used data from 816 male workers participating in the Normative Aging Study of the Veterans Administration in Boston to investigate the preretirement socialization process. These researchers found a strong linear relationship between proximity to retirement and informal preretirement involvement (measured by how often the preretiree had talked with his wife, his relatives, his close friends, or people on the job, or had read articles about retirement). This finding indicates that an anticipatory self-socialization to retirement was underway at least 15 years prior to the retirement itself. In addition, other factors—such as attitudes toward retirement, job characteristics, and personal resources (especially the existence of an already retired good friend)—were of relevance in explaining variation in preretirement involvement.

Attitudes toward retirement may directly determine adjustment. A study of college professors showed that about three-quarters of them looked forward to retirement; one-fourth did not have a positive attitude. A professor of the biological sciences held this negative view:

The problem I see about retirement is the failure of our society to appreciate the worth of all the education . . . packed into an academic. One can be a professor one minute, then a park bench occupant the next. . . . The greatest tragedy of retirement is the lack of imagination of our institutions including universities to develop a plan whereby individuals' worth and self-esteem can be maintained in a meaningful way. (Patton, 1977, p. 350)

The feelings of worth and self-esteem referred to by this professor may be at the core of discussions about adjusting to retirement. Miller (1965) has taken the position that retirement brings with it an identity crisis. He argues that retirement is basically degrading because it implies that the individual is no longer able to carry out the work role. This is especially problematic, Miller says, because occupational identity is so much a part of a person's life. It affects how all the other roles (spouse, parent, friend, etc.) are played. Leisure roles cannot replace work as a source of self-respect and identity because society does not support them in the same way it supports work roles. According to Miller, leisure is not sufficient replacement for work as a source of worth and self-esteem. The crisis comes because the individual's former claims to prestige and status are negated by retirement, and no replacement sources of prestige and status are available. This embarrasses the individual and causes withdrawal from social life.

In response to Miller's "identity crisis theory," Robert Atchley (1971) proposed an "identity continuity theory" of adjustment to retirement. Atchley points out that few people rest their entire identity on a single role. Rather, most people have several roles in which to base identity. The probability that retirement will lead to identity crisis or breakdown is slim because the roles (e.g., parent, grandparent, spouse) are maintained well into old age. Also, retired workers will likely continue to identify with their occupations even though they no longer play the role. Thus, the retired professor will continue to see himself or herself as a professor beyond the retirement age.

Furthermore, Atchley (1971) argues that people *can* gain self-respect from leisure pursuits in retirement, especially if they have sufficient financial resources available and a cohort of retired friends who accept full-time leisure as a legitimate enterprise. A final point of identity continuity theory is that many people develop skills during the course of their occupational careers that are quite useful in retirement and do provide a degree of identity continuity. Skill in interpersonal interaction developed in careers in sales or teaching, for example, may serve a person well in leisure activities and at the same time facilitate a sense of continuity in his or her life.

Although it does not appear to be a typical pattern, some people, especially those forced to retire, do undergo the identity crisis described by Miller. The retirement syndrome Butler referred to may reflect this identity crisis. Ellison (1968) suggests that this crisis can be an important precipitating factor in the adoption of the sick role. Having come to define illness as a more legitimate role to occupy than being retired, retirees may become "sick" (that is, behave as if they were ill). It may be easier for a person to say he or she has retired because of poor health than to explain that the employer no longer considers him or her competent to do a job.

A more typical pattern of adjustment in retirement involves those whose experiences fit the continuity perspective. Snow and Havighurst (1977) studied the careers after age 60 of administrators in U.S. higher education. Those with a life-style pattern that they identified as *maintainers* were able to hold onto their professional activities successfully, even after formal retirement, pursuing part-time assignments and filling time with other activities. Interestingly, the maintainers were contrasted with another group, the *transformers*. The transformers changed their life-styles with retirement, reduced their professional activities (by choice), and created a new pattern of living that often emphasized a nonprofessional area of activity (hobbies, arts and crafts, or travel). As one transformer put it:

> At the time of my full retirement, I was confronted by a series of invitations and opportunities to engage in continued professional work in various cities and as far away as Taiwan. . . . My wife and I decided to reject all of them. . . . We wished to stay here among our good friends. This would give me opportunity to activate a long smoldering interest in painting. The painting now claims my primary interest and labor, and I have become President of our local Art League. . . . I have opened up a new career which beckons me on to achievement and a new kind of fulfillment. (Snow & Havighurst, 1977, p. 548)

Older people can gain and maintain self-respect from their leisure-time pursuits.

Mutran and Reitzes (1981) have added to this discussion of "identity crisis" versus "identity continuity" through their secondary analysis of the 1974 national survey data collected by the National Council on Aging. In particular, they were interested in the way retirement (and a series of background variables) affects participation in community activities, visiting friends, self-identities, and feelings of well-being among men aged 55 and older in the survey. These researchers found that retirement was not directly associated with visiting friends, self-identities, or well-being, although it did *indirectly* encourage older self-identities and discourage well-being through its effect on community activities. Lack of involvement in community activities was the strongest predictor of older self-identities for both working *and* retired men, whereas involvement in community activities has the strongest effect on the well-being of both working men and retirees.

Mutran and Reitzes suggest that "involvement in community activities emerges as a possible intervening variable between retirement and social psychological measures" (1981, p. 739)—self-identity and well-being. Further, they point out the impact of retirement on other roles, such as active community participant, that may affect well-being but go unnoticed if researchers are not careful about how retirement is operationalized in their analyses.

Preretirement programs have been around since early in the post–World War II period. In general, their appearance is evidence of the belief that the work role is central and an important source of self-identity and status. As already discussed, some believe that the notion of work as central to self-identity has been given undue consideration in research on adjustment to retirement. Almost despite this ongoing discussion in the gerontological literature, there has been a substantial growth in the prevalence of preretirement programs. Two important questions are: Do workers participate in such programs? and Do preretirement programs work?

Campione (1988) has used data from the National Longitudinal Survey of Mature Men to estimate the probability of participation in a retirement preparation program. The final sample employed in the study included 294 retired men who reported having had the opportunity to participate in a preretirement program and for whom longitudinal data were available. Most workers who do participate in such programs do so within two years of their retirement. Campione finds that those individuals who prepare for retirement during their working lives are more likely to participate in formal retirement preparation programs. In addition, those who are married and have families to plan for, those who have minimal health problems, and those of higher occupational status are more likely to plan for retirement. She concludes that program sponsors are failing to attract a broad cross-section of employees into preretirement preparation programs. Apparently, those most likely to succeed in retirement anyway are those most likely to be given an opportunity in such programs (Beck, 1984).

Glamser (1981) has reported on a longitudinal study to determine the longer-term impact of two different preretirement programs. Two experimental groups and one control group were used to test the merits of a "comprehensive group discussion program" and an "individual briefing program." Those male industrial workers in the group discussion program met eight times during a one-month period, with sessions lasting approximately 90 minutes each. Those assigned to the individual briefing program met with the plant personnel officer for 30 minutes and received four booklets to read dealing with retirement planning, income, health, and leisure activities.

Questionnaire data were collected prior to program initiation and again six years later. The results showed no significant effect on the retirement experience of individuals by either program. Further, no substantive differences with the control group were noted in the length of the adjustment period, accuracy of expectations, level of preparation, life satisfaction, attitude toward retirement, or job deprivation. Glamser (1981) suggests that the major impact of preretirement programs may be of considerably shorter duration than six years. Further, their primary value may actually be in the period before employees leave the work setting.

Retirement in Cross-Cultural Perspective

As already indicated, retirement is a modern industrial phenomenon—with the emphasis on *industrial.* There are numerous examples of retirement patterns in contemporary preindustrial societies that are different from those in the United States. Holmes (1972) reports that in Samoa, there is the concept of retiring from the position of household head, an influential position in the village council. Sometimes, this is done to allow younger men to achieve status and power, but stepping down does not mean a complete withdrawal from village council activities. Often, the former chief will become an elder statesman and function in an advisory capacity with the council.

Among the !Kung San of the Kalahari Desert in southwestern Africa, the aged are held in high esteem. They act as the following:

1. Stewards of rights to water and resources in the area
2. Storehouses of knowledge, skills, and lore
3. Teachers and minders of children
4. Spiritual specialists and healers
5. Ritually privileged figures

In this subsistence economy, these roles are based on reciprocal obligations across the life cycle, not on the accumulation of economic power and resources (Biesele & Howell, 1981). Adult men are hunters, and many are healers. They do not know retirement. Aging men carry out these roles as long as they can and then replace them with less strenuous activities such as trapping, gathering, making artifacts, telling stories, and visiting. Women are gatherers, and many of them are healers also. With age, they also continue these roles and gradually move to less physically arduous activities, including child care and handicrafts work (Biesele & Howell, 1981).

Japan provides an interesting case study of retirement in an advanced industrial society much like that of the United States (Palmore, 1975). Older Japanese men are more likely to work than are older American men. According to the 1965 census, 60 percent of the employed older men in Japan were between the ages of 65 and 69, compared with 37 percent for the United States. Most older Japanese workers are self-employed or work in a family business; over 50 percent are farmers, lumbermen, or fishermen. One survey reported that 41 percent of workers over age 60 gave "duty" as the reason for continuing work in advanced age; 36 percent of those surveyed cited financial necessity as a reason for working (Palmore, 1975).

About 75 percent of Japan's industries have compulsory retirement, and the most frequent retirement age is 55. Yet, almost all Japanese firms maintain the pattern of "permanent employment," which motivates the firms to provide some kind of employment for older workers even after compulsory retirement. This may take the form of extending the old job, creating a new job not subject to compulsory retirement, or offering a step-down job at reduced pay. Workers who retire to another job in the same company usually show a smaller decline in earnings than if they moved to another company.

There are arguments in Japan about raising the retirement age and doing away with mandatory retirement. These arguments center on the needs of older people to work and maintain an adequate standard of living and the needs of the nation to utilize the productive capacities of older Japanese. Management specialist Peter Drucker (1971) believes that the Japanese system of retirement—mandatory retirement at age 55 and "permanent employment"—is an important contributor to Japan's economic growth. He says that the system reduces labor costs at no decline in worker productivity.

Women and Retirement

Most research on retirement has emphasized the experience of men, who traditionally have dominated in the labor force. The employment experience of women is changing, however, especially among younger cohorts. As these women enter old age, an increasing proportion will have participated in the labor force and will have done so for a longer period of time. This will have a positive effect on the economic position of women in old age; they will have accumulated more primary Social Security credits and more private pension benefits (Uhlenberg, 1979). Further, retirement is likely to become more salient as an experience of older women.

In the short run, employment in the labor force will not be a major activity for older women. As Table 12–1 showed, the proportion of women 65 years and over participating in the labor force has declined since 1970; in 1990, only 8.7 percent of these women were working. The table also shows a slight decline in labor-force participation rates among women 55 to 64 between 1970 and 1980, but an increase to 45.3 percent by 1990. By the year 2000, 50.3 percent of women aged 55 to 64 are expected to be participating in the labor force.

In the past, data on the retirement experiences of female workers were culled from studies of male workers. Today, there is an emerging literature on women's retirement. There is some evidence that women have different attitudes toward retirement than men do, even when these men are their husbands (Campbell, 1979). For example, based on their analysis of a national personal interview survey, Barfield and Morgan (1978) report that husbands are more likely to plan early retirement than their wives. Wives plan to work longer and think about early retirement only when there is a high family income and no mortgage payments or commitments to children.

Campione (1987) has used data from the University of Michigan's Panel Study of Income Dynamics to study the retirement decisions of married women aged 55 to 70. She found the married woman's decision to be influenced significantly by changes in financial status, including Social Security wealth, wage wealth, pension wealth, and age. In addition, the married woman's retirement decision was significantly influenced by her spouse's labor-force status. Thus, the retirement of her husband does increase the likelihood of the wife's retirement.

Working women seem to be opposed to mandatory retirement. Many do not start working until age 40 or 45 and are not ready to retire by age 62 or 65 (as long as they remain healthy and capable of job performance). Concentrated in occupations and industries where pensions are inadequate or nonexistent, working women receive lower wages, on average, than men do, and the gaps in their work histories translate to low Social Security payments (Campbell, 1979). Add to these conditions the probability of an older woman being widowed, divorced, or married to a man with a low income, and it becomes understandable that older women workers are willing to struggle to delay the years of reduced income that accompany retirement. Eliminating the mandatory retirement age should have the dual effect of allowing a large population of low-income older women to continue working, while reducing the strain on Social Security and pension funds by keeping this population contributing to these funds rather than withdrawing from them.

Finally, some research suggests that men and women do not differ substantially in their adjustment to retirement. Schnore and Kirkland (1981), in their study of retirement in London, Ontario, report no sex differences in life satisfaction, satisfaction with the decision to retire, happiness, and attitudes toward work and retirement.

Is a woman's satisfaction with retirement different if she is married as opposed to widowed? Dorfman and Moffett (1987) addressed this question in their study of older women in two rural Iowa counties. The sample included women who reported that they had retired from a paying job in the last 10 years. Two factors—self-perceived health status and increases in social participation in voluntary associations—were predictors of retirement satisfaction for married *and* widowed rural women. Perceptions of financial status and the frequency and perceived certainty of receiving aid from friends were predictors of retirement satisfaction among married women, whereas maintenance of preretirement friendships and frequency of contacts with friends predicted retirement satisfaction for widowed women. Should one be surprised by the fact that retirement satisfaction among rural widows seemingly was not affected by concerns about financial status or whether aid from close friends could be counted on in a crisis? According to Dorfman and Moffett (1987), these findings may simply reflect rural values of independence and the acceptance of unfavorable conditions of life without complaint.

Kroeger (1981) has provided what she aptly describes as a "tantalizing piece of data" on the relationship between duration of work experience and women's adjustment to retirement. The data come from a survey of recent retirees of all occupational classifications from the merchandising industries (major department stores, small retail shops, buying offices, etc.) in New York City. Adjustment to retirement was measured with a 14-item scale, including statements on job satisfaction, social relationships, personal identity, and changes in activities since retirement. The average scores for women who reported having worked all their lives and those who reported having worked for about two-thirds of their lives were virtually identical. The average score for women who reported working only about one-third of their adult lives (about fifteen years) was lower (though not at a statistically significant level), reflecting greater dissatisfaction with retirement.

How does one explain the greater satisfaction with retirement experienced by those women who have worked all their lives? Do they really relish a return to house and hearth? Perhaps they do, at least in comparison to the more traditional housewife who, having had her fill of "good housekeeping" but only a taste of work life, finds less satisfaction in returning home.

LEISURE

The conventional wisdom was that older people spent more time in leisure activities, on the average, than middle-aged people (Riley & Foner, 1968). The assumption was that old age brings retirement for men and a reduction in obligatory pursuits for women. This would leave more time free for leisure pursuits.

However, as Cutler and Hendricks (1990) point out, much cross-sectional research shows a decline in overall leisure and recreation participation with age. This is especially the case when participation is measured in terms of frequency or time spent in particular activities. Table 12–3 shows the decline in participation in various sports activities across age categories. The sports activities with the highest percentage of participants aged 65 years and older include exercise walking (29.1 percent), swimming (8.6 percent), and fresh-water fishing (7.7 percent). Still, there is variability across different types of activities. Gordon, Gaitz, and Scott (1976) have reported that activities involving high physical exertion and intensity

TABLE 12–3   Percentage Participating in Sports Activities by Age, 1992

	Age			
Activity	35–44 yrs	44–54 yrs	55–64 yrs	65+ yrs
Aerobic exercising[1]	12.3%	9.6%	5.5%	3.7%
Bicycle riding[1]	20.9	12.8	13.1	6.8
Bowling	18.7	11.4	7.2	4.9
Calisthenics[1]	4.2	3.8	2.4	2.9
Camping	24.8	16.3	12.2	5.5
Exercise walking	35.4	38.5	40.2	29.1
Fishing—fresh water	20.8	18.0	13.8	7.7
Golf	11.6	10.9	8.9	7.4
Hunting	10.8	8.7	5.1	2.9
Running/jogging[1]	8.3	6.0	2.2	1.1
Swimming[1]	27.5	15.7	13.3	8.6
Tennis	6.2	4.7	2.5	0.5

Source: U.S. Bureau of the Census. 1994. *Statistical abstract of the United States, 1994* (114th ed.) (Washington, DC: Bureau of the Census, 1994), Table 406.
[1]Participant engaged in activity at least six times in the year.

conform to age patterns, but that moderate-intensity activities, especially those that are home-based, show more consistency across the life course. Kelly (1987) reports marked decreases with age in physically active outdoor recreation but much smaller age differences for social, home-based, and family activities.

There is considerable controversy in the gerontological literature concerning leisure-time pursuits. One argument is that leisure roles are not adequate substitutes for the work role. This is because leisure roles are not supported by norms that would legitimate the replacement (Miller, 1965). Basic to this argument is the notion that work (and not leisure) is the dominant value in the United States; thus, individuals are unable to develop self-respect from leisure-time pursuits.

An opposing position is that leisure can, in fact, replace the work role and provide personal satisfaction in later life (Atchley, 1971). This may be the case especially in the presence of adequate income and good health.

Thompson (1973) has tested the relative merits of these two positions. Data from personal interviews with almost 1,600 older men were analyzed in this study. The results challenged the position that argues for the centrality of work as a value in the lives of older Americans. Those retirees in the sample who were found to have low self-respect (the actual variable employed in the study was labeled "morale") were also found to be older, to have negative evaluations of their health, and to have more disability and less income. The research suggests that low self-respect is related to these factors, not to their lack of work role. Thompson writes, "It appears that given relative youth, an optimistic view of health, a lack of functional disability, and an adequate income, the retirement years can be pleasant as the years of employment for a great many men and that leisure roles can adequately substitute for that of worker."

One reason that many people may have difficulty occupying leisure roles is simply that they lack the practice. Television, gardening, visiting, and reading are so popular precisely because older people have had so much practice time with these activities. Atchley (1977) points out that many people are reluctant to engage in leisure activities because they feel incompetent at them. Miller (1965) argues that the prospect of embarrassment keeps many older people from participating in new leisure pursuits.

Efforts should be made to prepare people for the life of leisure, because once people are already old, it is too late for such preparation. Older people tend to retain activity patterns and preferences developed earlier in life. Leisure competence should be learned early; doing so may be the only way to assure leisure competence in later life. In recent years, preretirement planning programs have been used to help workers identify activities and roles that may be rewarding after retirement, but such programs do little to enhance a lifelong learning approach to leisure.

Understanding the relationship between participation in leisure and recreational pursuits and aging requires placing leisure in some life-course perspective (Cutler & Hendricks, 1990). In doing so, one may identify how structural factors differentially affect leisure participation levels of successive cohorts of older people. For example, Riley (1987) points out that differences in leisure-time pursuits among successive cohorts of older people may simply reflect differences in normative expectations, other social roles, occupational stages, and personal resources. Table 12–3 gives the impression that there is a negative relationship between bicycle riding and age. However, longitudinal data, not yet developed, may show that younger cohorts maintain a level of participation in this particular leisure-time pursuit that is consistent with changes in normative expectations for older people or in the social roles adopted by future cohorts of elderly.

Finally, it is useful to remember that much of the research on leisure-time pursuits of older people is based on frequency counts or time-use studies. Missing from this literature are studies that take the view of the actor and attempt to specify the symbolic value of leisure. Kelly, Steinkamp, and Kelly (1987) argue, for example, that leisure, like work, is a central life focus that deserves more serious attention.

SUMMARY

Labor-force participation rates of old people have declined throughout the twentieth century. Currently, about one-sixth of aged males and fewer than 9 percent of aged females are in the labor force. Factors that have contributed to this decline include the health status of older people, new pension systems, changes in the population age structure, changes in economy characteristics, and age discrimination in employment.

Retirement is a modern industrial creation. According to Atchley (1976), the emergence of retirement as a social institution in a society requires four factors: longevity, economic surplus, pension systems, and acceptance of the idea of retirement. Recently, early retirement has become more acceptable. This reflects a changing attitude (increasingly positive) toward retirement on the part of industrial workers. Most current retirees did not wait to be "forced" into leaving the work force.

Adjusting to retirement is seldom easy. Adequate finances, good health, and social activities may positively affect that adjustment. Some gerontologists believe that retirement necessarily brings an identity crisis. Others argue that self-respect can be gained

from leisure pursuits. In the future, retirement is likely to become an issue that is salient to the experiences of older women as well.

Finally, although older people seem to prefer solitary leisure activities, it may be that most older people simply have more practice with such activities. Americans need to be educated for leisure, and this should begin early in life. Leisure needs to be placed in a life-course perspective. Doing so may help identify structural factors useful for explaining age-based differentials in leisure and recreational participation.

STUDY QUESTIONS

1. Discuss the social conditions necessary for the emergence of retirement as a social institution.

2. In what types of jobs are older workers likely to be employed? How has the occupational distribution of the elderly work force changed during the twentieth century?

3. Discuss the relationship between health status and retirement.

4. Discuss age discrimination in employment in the United States, with emphasis on the Age Discrimination Employment Act. Why are age discrimination cases sometimes more difficult to prove than race or sex discrimination?

5. Within a historical context, describe changing attitudes toward retirement in the United States.

6. Discuss the many social and psychological factors that contribute to or detract from adjustment to retirement.

7. Compare and contrast the *identity crisis* and *identity continuity* theories of adjustment to retirement.

8. Explain why leisure time can actually create problems for some older people. What can older people do to prepare for more effective use of their leisure time?

REFERENCES

Achenbaum, W. A. (1978). *Old age in the new land.* Baltimore, MD: John Hopkins University Press.

Applebaum, E., & Gregory, J. (1990). Flexible employment: Union perspectives. In P.

Doeringer (Ed.), *Bridges to retirement: Older workers in a changing labor market.* Ithaca, NY: ILR Press.

Ash, P. (1966). Pre-retirement counseling. *The Gerontologist, 6,* 97–99, 127–128.

Atchley, R. (1971). Retirement and leisure participation: Continuity or crisis. *The Gerontologist, 11,* 13–17.

Atchley, R. (1974). The meaning of retirement. *Journal of Communication, 24,* 97–100.

Atchley, R. (1976). *The sociology of retirement.* New York: Halsted.

Atchley, R. (1977). *Social forces in later life* (2nd ed.). Belmont, CA: Wadsworth.

Barfield, R., & Morgan, J. (1969). *Early retirement: The decision and the experience.* Ann Arbor: Institute for Social Research, University of Michigan.

Barfield, R., & Morgan, J. (1978). Trends in planned early retirement. *The Gerontologist, 18* (1), 13–18.

Beck, S. H. (1982). Adjustment to and satisfaction with retirement. *Journal of Gerontology, 37* (5), 616–624.

Beck, S. H. (1984). Retirement preparation programs: Differentials in opportunity and use. *Journal of Gerontology, 39,* 596–602.

Biesele, M., & Howell, N. (1981). The old people give you life: Aging among !Kung hunter-gathers. In P. T. Amoss & S. Harrell (Eds.), *Other ways of growing old: Anthropological perspectives.* Stanford, CA: Stanford University Press.

Bixby, L. (1976). Retirement patterns in the United States: Research and policy interaction. *Social Security Bulletin, 39* (8), 3–19.

Boaz, R. F. (1987). Work as a response to low and decreasing real income during retirement. *Research on Aging, 9* (3), 428–440.

Bowen, W., & Finegan, T. (1969). *The economics of labor force participation.* Princeton, NJ: Princeton University Press.

Butler, R. (1975). *Why survive? Being old in America.* New York: Harper and Row.

Calhoun, R. (1978). *In search of the new old.* New York: Elsevier.

Campbell, S. (1979). Delayed mandatory retirement and the working woman. *The Gerontologist, 19* (3), 257–263.

Campione, W. A. (1987). The married woman's retirement decision: A methodological comparison. *Journal of Gerontology, 42* (4), 381–386.

Campione, W. A. (1988). Predicting participation in retirement preparation programs. *Journal of Gerontology, 43* (3), S91–95.

Cohen, W. (1957). *Retirement policies under Social Security.* Berkeley: University of California Press.

Collins, G. (1987). Wanted: Child-care workers, age 55 and up. *The New York Times,* December 15, pp. 1, 8.

Cutler, S. J., & Hendricks, J. (1990). Leisure and time use across the life course. In R. H. Binstock & L. K. George (Eds.), *Handbook of aging and the social sciences,* (3rd ed.). San Diego, CA: Academic Press.

Donahue, W., Orbach, H., & Pollak, O. (1960). Retirement: The emerging pattern. In C. Tibbitts (Ed.), *Handbook of social gerontology.* Chicago: University of Chicago Press.

Dorfman, L. T., & Moffett, M. M. (1987). Retirement satisfaction in married and widowed rural women. *The Gerontologist, 27* (2), 215–221.

Drucker, P. (1971). What can we learn from Japanese management? *Harvard Business Review, 49,* 110–122.

Ekerdt, D. J., Vinick, B. H., & Bosse, R. (1989). Orderly endings: Do men know when they will retire? *Journal of Gerontology, 44* (1), 528–535.

Ellison, D. (1968). Work, retirement and the sick role. *The Gerontologist, 8,* 189–192.

Evans, L., Ekerdt, D. J., & Bosse, R. (1985). Proximity to retirement and anticipatory involvement: Findings from the Normative Aging Study. *Journal of Gerontology, 40* (3), 368–374.

Fillenbaum, G. G., George, L. K., & Palmore, E. B. (1985). Determinants and consequences of retirement among men of different races and economic levels. *Journal of Gerontology, 40* (1), 85–94.

Friedmann, E., & Havighurst, R. (1954). *The meaning of work and retirement.* Chicago: University of Chicago Press.

Gibson, R. C. (1987). Reconceptualizing retirement for black Americans. *The Gerontologist, 27* (6), 691–698.

Gibson, R. C. (1991). The subjective retirement of black Americans. *Journal of Gerontology, 46* (4), S204–209.

Glamser, F. D. (1981). The impact of preretirement programs on the retirement experience. *Journal of Gerontology, 36* (2), 244–250.

Goldberg, D. (1978). Mandatory retirement and the older worker. *Aging and Work, 1,* 264–267.

Gordon, C., Gaitz, C. M., & Scott, J. (1976). Leisure and lives: Personal expressivity across the life span. In R. H. Binstock & E. Shanas (Eds.), *Handbook of aging and the social sciences.* New York: Van Nostrand Reinhold.

Holmes, L. (1972). The role and status of the aged in changing Samoa. In D. Cowgill & L. Holmes (Eds.), *Aging and modernization.* Englewood Cliffs, NJ: Prentice-Hall.

Israel, J. (1971). *Alienation: From Marx to modern sociology.* Boston: Allyn and Bacon.

Kart, C. (1981). Attribution (and misattribution) of symptoms among the elderly. In M. Haug (Ed.), *Elderly patients and their doctors.* New York: Springer.

Kasschau, P. (1976). Perceived age discrimination in a sample of aerospace employees. *The Gerontologist, 18,* 166–173.

Kelly, J. R. (1987). *Peoria winter: Styles and resources in later life.* Lexington, MA: D. C. Heath.

Kelly, J. R., Steinkamp, M. W., & Kelly, J. R. (1987). Later life satisfaction: Does leisure contribute? *Leisure Sciences, 9,* 189–200.

Kingson, E. (1981). Involuntary early retirement. *Journal of the Institute for Socioeconomic Studies, 6* (3), 27–39.

Kotlikoff, L. J., & Wise, D. A. (1989). *The wage carrot and pension stick.* Kalamazoo, MI: W. E. Upjohn Institute.

Kroeger, N. (1981). *Women in retirement: Good housekeeping revisited.* Paper presented at the annual meeting of the Gerontological Society of America, Toronto, Ontario.

Long, C. D. (1958). *The labor force under changing conditions of income and employment.* Princeton, NJ: Princeton University Press.

McEvoy, G. M., & Cascio, W. F. (1989). Cumulative evidence of the relationship between employee age and job performance. *Journal of Applied Psychology, 74* (1), 11–17.

Mechanic, D. (1968). *Medical sociology.* Glencoe, IL: Free Press.

Meier, E. L. (1986). Employment experience and income of older women. *American Association of Retired Persons #8609.* Washington, DC: AARP Public Policy Institute.

Miller, S. (1965). The social dilemmas of the aging leisure participant. In A. Rose & W. Peterson (Eds.), *Older people and their social world.* Philadelphia: F. A. Davis.

Mutran, E., & Reitzes, D. C. (1981). Retirement, identity and well-being: Realignment of role relationships. *Journal of Gerontology, 36* (6), 733–740.

Palmore, E. (1975). *The honorable elders.* Durham, NC: Duke University Press.

Parnes, H., Adams, A. V., Andrisani, P. J., Kohen, A. I., & Nestel, G. (1975). *The preretirement years. Volume 4. A longitudinal study of the labor market experience of men.* U.S. Department of Labor, Manpower Research and Development Monograph No. 15. Washington, DC: U.S. Government Printing Office.

Patton, C. (1977). Early retirement in academia: Making the decision. *The Gerontologist, 17* (4), 347–354.

Quadagno, J., & Hardy, M. (1996). Work and retirement. In R. H. Binstock & L. K. George (Eds.), *Handbook of aging and the social sciences* (4th ed.). San Diego, CA: Academic Press.

Reitzes, D. C., Mutran, E., & Pope, H. (1991). Location and well-being among retired men. *Journal of Gerontology, 46* (4), S195–203.

Riley, M. W. (1987). On the significance of age in sociology. *American Sociological Review, 52,* 1–14.

Riley, M. W., & Foner, A. (1968). *Aging and society. Volume One: An inventory of research findings*. New York: Russell Sage Foundation.

Schnore, M. M., & Kirkland, J. B. (1981). *Sex differences in adjustment to retirement*. Paper presented at joint meetings of the Canadian Association of Gerontology and the Gerontological Society of America, Toronto, Ontario.

Schulz, J. (1992). *The economics of aging* (5th ed.). New York: Auburn House.

Shanas, E. (1968). The meaning of work. In E. Shanas et al. (Eds.), *Old people in three industrial societies*. New York: Atherton Press.

Simpson, I., Back, K., & McKinney, J. (1966). Orientation toward work and retirement, and self-evaluation in retirement. In I. Simpson & J. McKinney (Eds.), *Social aspects of aging*. Durham, NC: Duke University Press.

Slavick, F. (1966). *Compulsory and flexible retirement in the American economy*. Ithaca, NY: Cornell University Press.

Snow, R., & Havighurst, R. (1977). Life style types and patterns of retirement of educators. *The Gerontologist, 17* (6), 545–552.

Sum, A., & Fogg, W. N. (1990). Profile of the labor market for older workers. In P. Doeringer (Ed.), *Bridges to retirement: Older workers in a changing labor market*. Ithaca, NY: ILR Press.

Terkel, S. (1972). *Working: People talk about what they do all day and how they feel about what they do*. New York: Random House.

Thompson, G. (1973). Work versus leisure roles: An investigation of moral among employed and retired men. *Journal of Gerontology, 28*, 339–344.

Uhlenberg, P. (1979). Older women: The growing challenge to design constructive roles. *The Gerontologist, 19* (3), 236–241.

U.S. Senate, Special Committee on Aging. (1981). *The early retirement myth: Why men retire before age 62*. Washington, DC: U.S. Government Printing Office.

U.S. Senate, Special Committee on Aging. (1987–1988). *Aging America: Trends and projections, 1987–88 edition*. Washington, DC: U.S. Government Printing Office.

Ventrell-Monsees, C. (1991). Enforce the age discriminations laws. In A. Munnell (Ed.), *Retirement and public policy*. Washington, DC: National Academy of Social Insurance.

Williams, R., & Wirths, C. (1965). *Lives through the years*. New York: Atherton Press.

Yankelovich, D. (1974). The meaning of work. In J. Rosow (Ed.). *The worker and job*. Englewood Cliffs, NJ: Prentice-Hall.

CHAPTER 13

THE POLITICS
OF AGING

This chapter takes the view that age issues have become a substantial element in U.S. politics in recent years. Demographic trends already in place suggest that many future political issues are likely to be centered on questions of age. Do old people stick together in their voting attitudes and behavior? Will long-standing bases of political conflict such as race and social class be superseded by questions of age? Have old people become a favored political constituency in the United States? What is the future of the political economy of aging? These important questions have only recently become substantive concerns for gerontologists. Some of these questions have fragmentary and incomplete answers; on others, a growing body of literature is emerging.

Before beginning a discussion of these questions and of the answers emerging in the gerontological literature, it seems useful to remind readers of the discussion in Chapter 2 about the age/period/cohort problem. Interpretation of the political attitudes and behavior of older people involves the ability to understand and elicit the effects of the distinct perspectives represented by these three concepts (Hudson & Binstock, 1976).

1. One must consider the possibility that the political attitudes and behavior of older persons can be explained by developmental patterns inherent in the processes of human aging. This consideration describes what could be called the *age effect*.

2. One must look at the possibility that changes in the political attitudes and behaviors of older people simply mirror the impact of historical or period effects on an entire population. If older people have become more conservative over a period of time, perhaps this tendency can be explained by showing that people in *all* age groups have become more conservative over the time period examined (Hudson & Binstock, 1976). This describes the *period effect*.

3. It is possible that the political attitudes and behaviors of older people result from the shared experiences and perceptions of a particular older generation. This perspective describes the *cohort effect*.

Only recently has gerontological research used quantitative techniques to distinguish among these three analytical perspectives effectively. Much of the work discussed in this chapter overlooks this important methodological and conceptual problem. Nevertheless, the reader must not be insensitive to these issues as the chapter begins with a discussion of the relationship between political participation and age.

POLITICAL PARTICIPATION AND AGE
Voting Behavior

A basic indication of participation in the political process is voting behavior. A variety of factors affect an individual's voting participation. Historically, it seems that men were more likely to vote than were women at all ages, and those with more education voted more frequently than those with low levels of education.

Table 13–1 presents data on voting behavior by age, race, sex, region, employment status, and education for the United States in the 1992 presidential election. Race, employment status, education, and age seem the most important contributors to variation in voting behavior in 1992. Whites were more likely to vote than African Americans (59.1 percent vs. 51.5 percent, respectively), and more than twice as likely to vote as those of Hispanic origin (28.8 percent). The employed were about 50 percent more likely to vote than the unemployed (58.4 percent vs. 38.6 percent, respectively). Interestingly, however, the proportion of those reporting they voted among the employed was only slightly greater than the proportion voting among those who had been unemployed so long that they were considered to be out of the labor force. College graduates report voting at a higher rate in the 1992 presidential election than any other group (77.6 percent).

The proportion of individuals reporting they voted in the 1992 election is lowest in the youngest age group. Voter participation increases with successive age levels until old age. This pattern seems consistent with generalizations about the relationship between chronological age and voting behavior made by Milbrath (1965) in the mid-1960s.

Milbrath (1965) identified three factors that may help explain the relationship between age and voting exhibited in Table 13–1. First, younger people are typically not as well integrated into the communities in which they reside as are mature and older adults. Those who own homes, have families, enroll children in the local schools, and pay local taxes may be more affected by political issues (both local and national) and thus are more likely to vote. Second, as children grow up, become more independent, and leave home, mature and older adults may have

TABLE 13–1   Voting-Age Population, and Percentage Reporting Registered and Voted, 1992 Presidential Election

Characteristic	Voting-Age Population (Mil)	Percentage Reporting They Registered	Percentage Reporting They Voted
Total	185.7	68.2	61.3
18–20 years old	10.7	44.9	33.2
21–24 years old	14.8	50.6	38.3
25–34 years old	42.7	57.8	48.0
35–44 years old	35.2	69.3	61.3
45–64 years old	45.9	75.5	67.9
65 years old and over	28.8	78.4	68.8
Male	84.5	65.2	56.4
Female	93.6	67.8	58.3
White	152.9	67.9	59.1
African American	19.7	64.5	51.5
Hispanic	12.9	35.5	28.8
Northeast	37.9	64.8	57.4
Midwest	43.3	72.5	62.9
South	60.7	65.6	54.5
West	36.2	63.0	55.6
8 yrs or less of school	19.1	47.5	36.7
1–3 years high school	21.1	52.8	41.3
4 years high school	70.0	64.6	54.7
1–3 years college	34.3	73.5	64.5
4 yrs or more of college	33.6	83.1	77.6
Employed	113.8	67.1	58.4
Unemployed	5.8	50.4	38.6
Not in labor force	58.5	67.2	57.3

Source: U.S. Bureau of the Census, 1994, Table 448.

more available leisure time to become active in the political process. Finally, although most older people are in good health with little activity limitation, age does bring an increased risk of deterioration in mental and physical health. The greater likelihood of experiencing a health impairment later in the life cycle may be associated with reduced participation in a variety of forms of social behavior, including the political process. This final point makes the high rate of voting among older adults even more impressive.

Active Participation in Politics

Voting is a relatively passive form of political participation, occurring infrequently and requiring minimal effort on the part of an individual. It is a far cry from active involvement in the political process through community or campaign activity.

Two often cited investigations of older people's political involvement have been carried out by Verba and Nie (1972) and Nie, Verba, and Kim (1974). In general, these authors find (1) that the level of older people's participation in the political process is higher than the population average and (2) that when variation in socio-economic status is controlled for, older people show even higher participation scores. In fact, when this variation is controlled for, these authors find the peak period of political activity to occur in the sixth decade of life.

Verba and Nie (1972) created a political participation typology and looked to the distribution of those aged 65 and over across the six types in this categorization schema. The six types are as follows:

1. *Inactives:* No political activity
2. *Voting specialists:* Regular voters
3. *Parochial participants:* Those who make occasional contact with a public official
4. *Communalists:* Those working actively in community organizations
5. *Campaigners:* Those working actively around campaigns, including working for a party or a candidate and contributing money
6. *Complete activists:* Those highly involved in each of the preceding activities

The aged are overrepresented among the inactives, the voting specialists, and parochial participants. They are moderately underrepresented among the communalists and the campaigners and highly underrepresented as complete activists. Data reported by Nie, Verba, and Kim (1974) provide some support in a cross-national context for the findings presented here.

Glenn and Grimes (1968) suggest that older people turn to political activity because they have few other absorbing interests or activities. From the point of view of these authors, older people's involvement in politics may have more to do with attempting to achieve personal fulfillment than with achieving some instrumental political end. Schmidhauser (1968) has provided support for such a hypothesis by showing that age brings an increase in interest in politics while at the same time it brings an increase in cynicism about the ability of individual political action to have impact on the broader political process. Still, Binstock and Day (1996) point out that contacting public officials by mail and/or telephone is a demanding form of political participation engaged in by older people at the same rate as the nonelderly. These activities can be carried out within the quiet of one's own home. Older people, who are the beneficiaries of many government programs, have valid reasons for staying in contact with their governmental representatives.

Approximately 1,800 Americans 18 years of age and older were interviewed by the National Opinion Research Center (NORC) for the 1982 General Social Survey. Respondents were asked how much confidence they had in the executive branch of the federal government and whether they believed government should do more or less. For purposes of presentation here, respondents were divided into three approximately equal-sized age groups: 18 to 32 years, 33 to 54 years, and 55

LOCAL SENIOR POLITICAL POWER: REAL OR ILLUSORY?

Metro Seniors in Action is a Chicago-based grass-roots coalition of 77 community and church groups (serving the aged) begun in 1974 and incorporated in 1978. It was founded as a citywide organization aimed at pursuing issues related to municipal and county government, including health and social service programs that would be beyond the scope of any single neighborhood organization. The affiliated groups served black, white, and Hispanic neighborhoods, with predominantly middle- and lower-class members of diverse religious backgrounds. The organization stopped functioning as a coalition in 1987. Reitzes and Reitzes (1991) followed the coalition through its rise and fall, and identified six lessons that may aid future senior citizen political organizations.

1. Political organizations with ties across neighborhoods and communities require continuous maintenance.

2. Coalitions require a knowledgeable, experienced, professional organizer, especially after the initial developmental phase.

3. Achieving financial solvency through foundation grants and entrepreneurial fund-raising has a down side: The organization is not accountable to its local affiliates and therefore to its members; local affiliates and their aged members may have less of a commitment to the coalition.

4. A broad-based democratic organizational structure requires the vigilance of officers and committees but enables the organization to act quickly and decisively.

5. Groups such as Metro Seniors can benefit from engaging with other similar groups in statewide coalitions, expanding vistas and participating in actions by the local affiliates.

6. Confrontation and protest actions can be very effective political tools.

In its initial development period, Metro Seniors engaged in protest activities that highlighted inhumane treatment of the elderly. They generated strong emotional support for them, scorn for opponents, and wide media attention. As Reitzes and Reitzes (1991) point out, however, the coalition failed to take full advantage of these situations to advocate broad policies and programs to improve the quality of life for seniors.

In the United States, municipal governments continue to act as basic service providers to seniors as well as other constituencies. As a result, involvement in neighborhood groups and other citywide organizations is important for seniors. Although Metro Seniors lost a sense of purpose and mission, its experiences demonstrate the potential of local senior political organizations.

years and older. In general, older people pay more attention to government and public affairs than do the young; 43.1 percent of those aged 55 and older compared to 23.5 percent of those 18 to 32 answered that they followed what was going on in government most of the time. Only 22 percent of the older respondents reported having a great deal of confidence in the executive branch of the federal government; 13.4 percent of the younger adults and 18.7 percent of the middle-aged reported similarly. Among the older respondents, there is no support for Schmidhauser's hypothesis mentioned previously. In fact, 24.2 percent of those with the most interest in government affairs had a great deal of confidence in the executive branch; only 14.8 percent of those with the least interest in government had a great deal of confidence in the executive branch.

Political Leadership

Perhaps the most intense form of political participation involves occupying an office or holding a position of political leadership. It is widely believed that persons in late middle-age and old age disproportionately occupy positions of leadership in the United States and other advanced industrial nations. The visibility of national political leaders such as former Senate majority leader and 1996 Republican presidential candidate Bob Dole provides support for these beliefs. In a wide variety of political contexts in the United States—presidents, senators, U.S. representatives, governors, Supreme Court justices, U.S. ambassadors, cabinet members—positions of political leadership have been held by relatively old persons. In the 94th Congress (1975), 39 percent (39/100) of the senators and 21 percent of the representatives (91/435) were 60 years of age or over. Eighteen years later, the 103st Congress showed fewer aged members of the U.S. Senate (34/100) aged 60 years or over, but an increase in the number of representatives 60 years of age or older (104/432).

Lammers and Nyomarkay (1980) have shown a changing age pattern among the appointees to cabinet-level positions in five advanced industrial nations, including the United States. These authors find a growing concentration of middle-aged cabinet members, with aging populations increasingly underrepresented in the political leadership in these five nations. Table 13–2 shows the representation of the age 65-and-over group in the cabinets of Canada, France, the United Kingdom, Germany, and the United States over the last 100 years or so. Through the 1950s, the general pattern was clearly toward overrepresentation. Only in France and the United States were the aged slightly underrepresented in cabinet positions in the late nineteenth century. By the 1960s (and through the 1970s), a significant and uniform shift had taken place: The underrepresentation of the elderly in cabinet positions has been the case in every country.

How do Lammers and Nyomarkay (1980) explain the increasing underrepresentation of the aged in the leadership groups of these advanced industrial societies? One answer is found in greater bureaucratization, which has caused career patterns to become more routinized. This has brought a more focused age structure, resulting in the exclusion of older cabinet appointees and a greater uniformity of ages at time of appointment and departure.

Will the aged suffer as a function of this underrepresentation? As these authors point out, it is certainly possible that more youthful leaders will develop an identification with the problems of the old age, perhaps out of a belief that they constitute a significant voting block. On the other hand, if it is true that "the wearer is the best judge of the shoe," then there are fewer individuals who both directly experience the vagaries of aging and are directly responsible for making public policy that affects the aged.

TABLE 13–2 Representation: Individuals 65 Years of Age or Older in Total Population and in Cabinets (in Percentages)

Year	Canada			France		
	Population 65+	Cabinet Members	Difference	Population 65+	Cabinet Members	Difference
1870s	4	6	+2	7	19	+12
1880s	4	16	+12	8	5	-3
1890s	5	16	+11	8	5	-3
1900s	5	14	+9	8	9	+1
1910s	5	19	+14	9	14	+5
1920s	5	13	+8	9	11	+2
1930s	5	12	+7	10	13	+3
1940s	5	15	+10	11	7	-4
1950s	8	16	+8	11	7	-4
1960s	8	8	0	12	7	-5
1970s	8	1	-7	13	6	-7

Year	United Kingdom			Germany			United States		
	Population 65+	Cabinet Members	Difference	Population 65+	Cabinet Members	Difference	Population 65+	Cabinet Members	Difference
1870s	5	17	+12				3	8	+5
1880s	5	19	+14				4	12	+8
1890s	5	25	+20				4	0	-4
1900s	5	18	+13				4	17	+13
1910s	5	13	+8				4	10	+6
1920s	7	17	+10	6	6	0	5	28	+23
1930s	8	17	+9	7	7	0	6	30	+24
1940s	10	21	+11				7	22	+15
1950s	11	13	+3	10	15	+5	8	9	+1
1960s	12	4	-8	12	12	0	9	4	-5
1970s	14	3	-11	14	1	-13	10	2	-8

Source: W. W. Lammers & J. L. Nyomarkay, "The Disappearing Senior Leaders," *Research on Aging, 2* (3), 1980, pp. 329–349. Copyright © 1980 by Sage Publications, Inc. Reprinted by permission of Sage Publications, Inc.

POLITICAL ORIENTATIONS AND ATTITUDES OF OLDER PERSONS

One indicator of political orientation is party affiliation. As Table 13–3 shows, people of all age groups report more identification with the Democratic party than with the Republican party. And, although identification as a Republican appears *not* to change across the life course, in general, older cohorts show more identification as Democrats than do younger cohorts. Older people report less identification as Independents than do the young. Does this mean that aging brings with it conversion to the Democratic party? Hardly. What seems more likely is that the association between the Democratic party and aging is a function of cohort or generational differences. Thus, it is possible that early socialization experiences have made many of today's aged cohorts (those 66 to 81 years and those 82 years and older) Democrats.

Although a disproportionate number of older people compared with the young say they support the Democratic party, a view persists that older people are more politically conservative than are the young. Is this the case? Campbell and Strate have addressed this question while analyzing data from 14 American National Election Studies conducted by the Center for Political Studies at the University of Michigan from 1952 to 1980. After using a variety of measures of political attitudes available in these studies, these authors warn against facile generalizations:

> If one takes these results as a whole a general conclusion does emerge. The political orientations of older people are not peculiar. Knowing that someone is old will not help very much in predicting how conservative he or she is, in most important respects. The elderly are very much in the mainstream of American political opinions. (1981, pp. 590–591)

Cutler, Leutz, Muha, and Riter (1980) have studied this issue by examining the relationship between age and attitudes about legalized abortion. They found that, if controls for cohort differences are employed, little variation exists among the different age groups. Looking at changes over time in specific cohorts, they found

TABLE 13-3   Political Party Identification of the Adult Population by Age, 1992

Age	Total	Democrat[1]	Republican[2]	Independent	Apolitical
Under 34 years old	100	46	38	15	2
34–49 years	100	49	39	11	1
50–65 years	100	52	38	11	1
66–81 years	100	56	35	8	—
82–97 years	100	53	37	10	—

Source: U.S. Bureau of the Census, 1994, Table 446.

[1]Includes those who identify as weak Democrat, strong Democrat, and independent Democrat.
[2]Includes those who identify as weak Republican, strong Republican, and independent Republican.

that people who are now old had more conservative views when they were younger than currently younger cohorts do, but that their attitudes have become more liberalized at the same rate as those of the younger group.

Are old people more conservative? Aging per se does not appear to bring with it a set of conservative positions on prominent political issues. Yet, a different set of self-interests may be associated with age than with youth. In this respect, the answer to the original question (Are old people more conservative?) would seem to be both yes and no!

According to Binstock and Day (1996), older voters departed from their usual pattern in the 1992 Presidential election. Using data from the Portrait of the Electorate (1992), they describe that the elderly voted for Republican George Bush in the same proportion as did other age groups, but they voted for Democrat Bill Clinton at a higher rate and for Independent Ross Perot at a lower rate than did younger voters. One explanation is that older voters did not take the Perot candidacy seriously. Another is that their greater attachment to traditional political institutions make them less supportive of independent parties, regardless of the candidate.

ARE THE AGED
A FAVORED CONSTITUENCY?

The aged have been a favored social welfare constituency in the United States; that is, across the last 30 years or so, older persons have done relatively well in the arena of public policy in comparison with other population groups whose needs can be argued to be equally pressing. Binstock and Day (1996) report over 100 national organizations, mass membership groups, as well as organizations of professionals and service providers, focused on aging policies and concerns. Many of these groups also have local chapters. Among the largest and/or most well known are the 35-million member American Association of Retired Persons (AARP), the National Council for Senior Citizens (5 million members), and the Gray Panthers (40,000 members).

Federal programs benefiting the elderly are plentiful. The program categories represented include employment and volunteer, health care, housing, income maintenance, social services, training and research, and transportation. Virtually every agency in the executive branch and many independent agencies are represented. Many of these programs involve mandatory spending at the federal level. For example, mandatory spending accounts for approximately 56 percent of net federal outlays for fiscal year 1995, including Social Security retirement benefits and Medicare.

Robert Hudson of Brandeis University distinguishes between breakthrough and constituency-building policy enactments that may bring favored status upon a special-interest group. *Breakthrough* policies consist of those pieces of legislation that involve the federal government in providing or guaranteeing some fundamental benefit. *Constituency-building* policies are those that recognize that different groups have common interests and give these interest groups a voice in the making of public policy. The aged have been the principal beneficiaries and most functional constituency in the federal government's involvement in breakthrough legislation to ensure health care financing for high-risk populations (Medicare and Medicaid) and to guarantee minimum income for the impoverished (e.g., Supplemental Security Income) (Hudson, 1978).

Still, several commentators have described the differential success of federal intervention on behalf of the elderly. Kutza points out that minority older persons and older women have not shared in the gains experienced by other elderly in this recent period of concentrated assistance provided to older people. She describes this as follows:

> Since 1969, elderly white women have made remarkable gains; their poverty rate has dropped to 14.4 (compared to 8.3 for elderly white males). Elderly black women cut their rate nearly in half, moving from 77 percent in 1969 to 41.2 percent in 1977. Yet, that two out of every five elderly black women live below the poverty level today points up the serious differential impact our federal income-support programs have had in the past ten years. While great progress has been made in providing a more adequate income standard for most older retired persons, several subgroups within the population—most especially nonwhites and women— remain seriously disadvantaged. (1981, p. 85)

Beth Hess (1983) has identified what she describes as a gerontological "gender gap" in the application of federal programs to the elderly. Three areas where older women are especially disadvantaged are income, health, and housing. As Hess reports, because of their lower incomes, increasing frailty, and singlehood, old women are the prime market for subsidized rental housing. During the administration of President Reagan, the major federal programs for the construction of such facilities—Section 8 and Section 202—lost funding. In addition, eligibility was limited, and the share paid by renters was increased. Hess argues that "public programs have been shaped by assumptions based on the life experience of men.... Yet, not only are the real problems of old age disproportionately experienced by women, but it is women who are increasingly expected to bear the brunt of dealing with these problems."

Despite this growing recognition of the differential impact of public-policy efforts for the elderly, there is currently considerable debate about the economic costs of this favored status for the elderly. This may be part of a resistance to social welfare expenditures in general. Some writers see the costs of programs for the elderly as the dominant factor shaping federal spending and taxing decisions. In 1978, one analyst characterized the cost of an aging America as having the potential to "bust the U.S. budget" (Samuelson, 1978). Almost 15 years later, this characterization was clearly still in play when a cover story in the national magazine, *Fortune,* offered that "the tyranny of America's old ... is one of the most crucial issues facing U.S. society" (Smith, 1992). Such characterizations deserve careful scrutiny.

Spending for Social Security and Medicare alone amounted to about one-quarter (25.5 percent) of the federal budget in 1980; by fiscal year 1995, this figure had increased to 33.9 percent of projected outlays in the federal budget. If, as some suggest, expenditures for Social Security and Medicare represent 80 percent of all federal spending for the elderly, then the outlay of programs for the elderly represents about 42 percent of the projected 1995 federal budget.

There will be continued pressure on the federal budget in coming years. By 1990, federal outlays for Social Security and Medicare alone had more than doubled from 1980 (an increase of about 130 percent) and accounted for more than the entire outlay of federal spending for the elderly in that year. Social Security expenditures increased by about 110 percent between 1980 and 1990, but Medicare spending tripled during this time. As the size of the elderly population increases, the government must either raise taxes and reduce funding for other programs, run increasingly larger deficits, or cut programs. With current annual federal deficits of approximately $150 to 200 billion, the prevalent political scenario at this time would seem to be one involving sharp cuts in federal spending, including so-called entitlement programs such as Social Security, Medicare, and Medicaid. Current efforts at balancing the federal budget and reducing federal taxes suggests an upcoming age of scarcity for education, urban, and social welfare constituencies. The specter of these needy and powerful political interest groups battling for scarce federal dollars is not inviting, but it is one that many policy analysts consider will become a reality.

Not everyone has ascribed to the age of scarcity scenario. Jack Ossofsky (1978), executive director of the National Council on the Aging, takes exception to characterizations of the federal budget as ready to bust and to calculations of expenditures on the aging in the federal budget. For example, Ossofsky stresses that the Social Security program provides income to many millions of younger men, women, and children as part of its dependents', survivors', and disability programs. Over seven million people alone received survivor benefits in 1990 under Social Security. For 1993, about 38 percent of Social Security recipients were *not* themselves retired workers and included workers who are disabled, wives and husbands of retired workers or workers with disabilities, and the children of retirees and of workers who are deceased or disabled.

In addition, remember that workers "buy in" to Social Security (as do employers): To include employee contributions when computing government expenditures on behalf of the aged makes little sense. Beyond simply confusing matters, it creates the impression that Social Security is just another government welfare program, rather than a return of money put aside during the course of a person's working years. This holds true as well for the Federal Civil Service Retirement System; redistributed employee contributions should not be counted as government expenditures. Finally, as Ossofsky (1978) points out, playing hocus pocus with the federal budget figures creates the impression that the elderly are receiving lavish treatment from the federal government. This is clearly not the case; 12.2 percent of the U.S. aged have incomes below the poverty level (1990 figure), and the proportion in near-poverty is substantial as well.

Robert Butler (1978) takes a different tack. He suggests that the discussion over expenditures in the federal budget for the elderly is misdirected—a case of blaming the victims. Butler makes three important points:

1. The need for all those dollars in retirement systems might be lessened somewhat if people were not pressured to leave the work force while they are still able and willing to continue working. If people were free to continue working after age 65 or 70, as is now the case by law, they could continue to contribute to retirement systems, and the budget would become less menacing.

2. A considerable proportion of the federal budget reflects the existence of illness and disability in the aged population. What if one could identify the biomedical and socioenvironmental factors that produce illness and disability and that prompt people to retire? If these illness factors could be minimized in any way, it would reduce expenditures made through the Medicare and Medicaid programs.

3. Government expenditures for health care services have increased dramatically in recent years. Nevertheless, the elderly now pay as much out of pocket for health care as they did before Medicare. To what extent is the increasing cost of health care to be attributed to the elderly? To what extent should it be attributed to the providers of health care services?

What are the political consequences of this debate over federal expenditures for the elderly? Will proposed funding for programs for the aged face opposition in the future? Can the aged mobilize political pressure to serve their interests?

Comments by Ossofsky and proposals such as those by Butler get little attention today in the popular media and press. More fashionable are proposals to ration health care for older people, most of which is financed through government programs, as a means for reducing health care costs and providing care to other groups such as poor children (Callahan, 1987; Preston, 1984). As Binstock and Day (1996) point out, in 1990, the Ford Foundation convened a distinguished panel that proposed a series of social policies for the U.S. future costing $29 billion in the first year alone. They suggested funding it out of reduction in or taxes on Social Security benefits (Ford Foundation, 1990).

ARE THE ELDERLY A POLITICAL FORCE?

One commonly held image of the aged is as a political force capable of playing interest-group politics. Political scientist Robert Binstock, former president of the Gerontological Society of America, believes this image to be inaccurate, though nurtured by several aging-based membership organizations:

> There is little reason to believe that a phenomenon termed "senior power" will significantly increase the proportion of the budget devoted to the aging, or redirect that portion of the budget toward solving the problems of the severely disadvantaged. Whatever senior power exists is held by organizations that cannot swing decisive voting blocs. (Binstock, 1978)

Evidence of this may have been present in the 1976 Carter campaign for the presidency. The "seniors' desk" had the lowest budget and the fewest paid personnel among the 11 desks established by the Democratic Presidential Campaign Committee (Binstock, 1978).

More recently, Binstock's assessment of the senior lobby has changed only slightly. He suggests that the proliferation of old-age interest groups has mostly followed, rather than preceded and/or influenced, the creation of major governmental programs for the elderly. Further, he argues that the power of these interest groups is mostly defensive, "aimed at protecting existing programs and fighting tax hikes" (Binstock & Day, 1996, p. 373).

One reason the image of senior power persists lies in the belief that the elderly are a homogeneous group and thus a homogeneous political constituency. This is just not the case. The elderly are as heterogeneous politically as they are socially and economically. Binstock argues that most older voters do not primarily identify themselves, and hence their self-interests, in terms of aging. When a person

Many older people are actively involved in the political process through community and campaign activity.

reaches age 65, retires, or is widowed, he or she does not suddenly lose all prior self-identities; self-interest is still derived from race, education, religion, community ties, and so on.

Not everyone sees senior power as illusory, however. Pratt (1976) notes that the elderly have come to expect some degree of income security as well as adequate health care. Theirs may be a revolution of rising expectations. Pratt cites the 1971 White House Conference on Aging as the watershed for old-age political influence. Through the Conference, he argues, national groups such as the National Retired Teachers Association (NRTA), the American Association of Retired Persons (AARP), and the National Council of Senior Citizens (NCSC) developed the political acumen necessary for effecting legislation that benefits the aged. Pratt credits the NCSC with helping to formulate and pass the Social Security Amendments of 1972. These amendments pegged increases in Social Security benefits to the rate of inflation and replaced welfare programs for the aged, blind, and disabled with SSI.

Can an old-age political movement become institutionalized? According to Achenbaum (1983), such a "gray lobby" would differ from other interest groups in at least two important ways. First, there are ideological and political schisms within and among the organizations that purport to represent and work for the elderly. Second, the gray lobby is the only interest group to which every American can hope to aspire. Hence, it is especially important for leaders of these organizational entities to weigh the future ramifications of current policy decisions. What looks good in the short run may have devastating implications for the elderly of the next century.

Hudson sees great potential surrounding the organization of a political agenda "of and for the able elderly." Presumably, the *able elderly* are those not frail, not in poverty, and not dependent; the concept captures a growing number of older people who are integrated, vigorous, affluent, and well. They constitute a political and economic generation "caught between the demands of a frailer generation ahead of it and the pressures of a command generation behind it" (1987, p. 406). Still, as Hudson correctly notes, formalizing the concept of the able elderly and organizing a political agenda around this group creates potential problems for the less able old as well as for those who may properly be described as able. For example, in the area of employment, the concept of an able elderly highlights the contradiction between the desire to eliminate mandatory retirement rules (and thus allow older workers to continue in place) and to take early retirement. In areas such as income support and medical care, the improved education and economic status associated with being able is likely to bring new proposals. These would include self- and private financing of pension and health benefits, as well as the imposition of more means-tested and needs-tested standards to better target services for the elderly.

How willing will current and future aged be to identify themselves as old? The development of a widespread *aging group consciousness* would bring recognition among the elderly of their common interests. Bengtson and Cutler (1976) present evidence that older people who identify themselves as "old" are more liberal, particularly on issues affecting the aged (e.g., government intervention in inflation and medical care). As Hudson (1987) notes, the development of an aging group consciousness may have important consequences beyond helping to create and sustain an old-age political movement. Not the least of these would be a lessening of the stigmatization and isolation of the aged, the maintenance of self-esteem, and a viewing of intergenerational policy proposals in a more favorable light (Wisensale, 1988).

THE FUTURE OF OLD-AGE POLITICS: AGE VERSUS NEED ENTITLEMENT

Much of the material contained in this book is aimed at describing a new set of realities regarding the aged and aging. In general, it has been argued that many of the conditions prevalent in the early part of the twentieth century led one to see old age as a social problem (e.g., incapacity, isolation, and poverty). These conditions have changed dramatically as a result of collective political action that took the form of governmental legislation to create programs of income maintenance, housing, transportation, health services, social services, and tax benefits.

In creating these programs, which emanated from real concern about the welfare of older people, chronological age was used as a convenient indicator of need. Remember that older people in the United States were seen as a homogeneous population. Even through the 1950s and 1960s, they were described as poor and lacking in access to health services and the like. As Neugarten (1982) indicates, programs based on age eligibility did catch a large proportion of persons in need. Today, however, the situation is different. The elderly are currently described as a heterogeneous group, in many respects indistinguishable from the general population. For example, the proportion of those 65 years and over with incomes below the poverty line is approximately the same as the proportion of the total population with incomes below the poverty line. Further, some subpopulations of the aged that have been differentially advantaged by governmental programs, and other groups such as minority elderly and older women, remain relatively disadvantaged despite these programs.

Rather than emphasizing the special disadvantages of minority elderly and older women, Nelson (1982) examines the relationship between social class and public policy for the elderly. Essentially, he argues that government programs for the aged act to perpetuate the existence of socioeconomic differences among the elderly that existed prior to old age. According to Nelson, three classes of elderly beneficiaries of governmental initiatives can be identified:

1. The marginal elderly
2. The downwardly mobile elderly
3. The integrated elderly

Each class of elderly receives a different level of support that, in total, serves to sustain the social class inequalities that were present prior to the experience of old age. I will briefly describe these three classes of elderly and exemplify how government provides different levels of support for the different classes.

1. *Marginal Elderly:* The marginal elderly are characterized by absolute need and poverty. For most of them, poverty in old age is a continuation of a life of poverty. They are more likely to be living alone, female, minority, and old-old. Their work careers were in unskilled, semiskilled, or domestic labor that has been transient or interrupted during the adult years. Many such jobs were not covered by Social Security or other pension programs. These individuals represent the truly needy.

2. *Downwardly Mobile Elderly:* This class of elderly corresponds most closely to those who were considered middle class or lower-middle class prior to old age. The downwardly mobile elderly experience need as a sense of relative deprivation. They are trying to maintain a preretirement life-style on more limited resources. Some are at risk of falling into poverty. They may prevent this by using available sources of public support.

3. *Integrated Elderly:* These individuals are presumed to be continuing a middle- or upper-middle-class life-style. The integrated elderly are likely to be able to do this by marshaling personal and private resources together with public support. Because these individuals are able to maintain their socioeconomic status—including social values, roles, and group and community memberships—they are referred to as the socially integrated elderly.

How does this three-tiered approach to the elderly affect government support for income-transfer programs? The central income-transfer program for the marginal elderly is SSI. As already noted, eligibility is determined by meeting certain income and assets standards. The program establishes a common minimum income benefit for the approximately 2.1 million marginal or poor elderly receiving SSI benefits in December 1993. (An additional 4 million children and adults who are blind and disabled also were receiving SSI benefits in December 1993.) Some states (29, including the District of Columbia, in 1993) provide an additional supplement to the federal benefit. The average monthly amount of combined federal and state SSI payments in the United States was a paltry $236.52 in December 1993. The average federal payment was $204.11; the average state supplementation was $114.74. Still, many who are eligible for SSI do not receive it, and many who are receiving it are clearly still living below the poverty level. It seems reasonable to conclude, as Nelson (1982) does, that the marginal elderly are guaranteed the most meager subsistence under the SSI income-transfer program.

The second tier of income support for the elderly is Social Security. Most of the work force is covered by this program, which is underwritten by the collected contributions of workers and their employers. Average monthly benefit amounts payable in December 1993 were $674 for retirees and $642 for workers who are disabled. The *downwardly mobile elderly* include most recipients of Social Security who were average wage earners. Members of this group have a special reliance on the Social Security check plus accumulated private savings. For most of them, the Social Security check is a guarantee against falling into near- or absolute poverty.

The third tier of income support programs for the elderly includes those that are directed at the integrated elderly. Many of the integrated elderly receive Social Security; they are also recipients of (1) government-supported public (railroad retirement, civil service, state and local governments) and private pensions; (2) cash benefits from government-supported private savings plans (annuities, 401(k)s, individual retirement accounts, and Keogh plans); and (3) favorable tax policies, including property tax reductions. These tax preferences, in conjunction with private and public pension supplements to Social Security, act to maintain the socioeconomic position of the higher income elderly.

The federal government's cost of maintaining the integrated elderly at a life-style consistent with that prior to retirement is staggering in comparison with the costs, for example, of maintaining the marginal elderly. In 1990, federal expenditures for all elderly on SSI amounted to approximately $2.5 billion. In that same year, almost $49 billion was contributed on a pretax basis by wage earners to their qualified retirement plans (sometimes referred to as 401(k) plans). If these contributions were taxed at only a 15 percent marginal federal tax rate, the yield would be $7.35 billion or almost three times the cost of providing SSI to the poorest aged Americans in 1990. Many who contribute pretax dollars to their 401(k) plans are high-wage earners whose marginal federal tax rates are 28 or 31 percent, or higher. Comparable examples of higher government expenditures and subsidies for those least in need are also available in the areas of health care and social services.

As Nelson's (1982) use of the term *integrated elderly* implies, the higher-income elderly are more likely to be socially integrated into the broader society than are other classes of elderly. Yet, as already noted, age entitlement programs cause a considerable proportion of government resources to be directed at those elderly who are least in need. Is this fair? Shouldn't public policy benefits be redistributed on the basis of need?

The obvious answers seem to be *no*, it is not fair, and *yes*, benefits should be redistributed on the basis of need. Still, who is to decide who is needy and how? Some readers might say to redistribute benefits to just the marginal elderly or to some combination of the marginal and downwardly mobile elderly. One problem with such a reform is that it continues to employ age as a basic organizing principle in the development of policies and programs. After all, the elderly do not have a monopoly on need in the United States. As Elizabeth Kutza describes it, "No problem occurs in old age that does not occur also in other age groups, whether it be poverty, mental or physical disability, isolation, or malnutrition" (1981). Further, she quotes from an Administration on Aging study in which researchers were struck not by the differences among the young, the middle-aged, and the old but by the similarities: "When the picture is examined as a whole, the most striking aspect is how much alike were the values placed on quality of life factors regardless of age and how relatively little people's needs seem to change over time."

Reorganizing the distribution of federal policy benefits on the basis of need rather than age is an effort fraught with political liability. Benefits to the aged have been remarkably popular, especially those aimed at the downwardly mobile and integrated elderly. In part, this may result from the high value placed on independence by the elderly and their family members. It also may result from an understanding that the aged are a unique group—the one minority group to which *all* people anticipate belonging!

It seems likely that political support for the basic needs of the elderly will continue to be strong (Crystal, 1982). In the current political environment, however, federal budgets are under constant pressure. As Crystal describes it, "If human services are to be cut, it is poor policy to slash benefits for the needy aged and spare those aiding mostly the middle-class and higher-income elderly" (1982).

Binstock and Day (1996) suggest that a trend is already in place to combine age and economic need as policy criteria in old-age benefit programs. The Social Security Reform Act of 1983 made 50 percent of Social Security benefits subject to taxation for the first time; this affected individuals with incomes exceeding $25,000 and married couples with incomes exceeding $32,000. The Tax Reform Act of 1986 eliminated the extra personal exemption available to persons 65 years and older filing their federal income tax returns and provided new tax credits to low-income elderly. The Omnibus Budget Reconciliation Act of 1993 increased the proportion of Social Security benefits subject to taxation to 85 percent for individuals with incomes over $34,000 and married couples over $44,000. Most recently, President Clinton's 1994 proposal for health care reform differentiated among older people by income level; those with higher income were asked to pay more for certain services within Medicare, including long-term care.

SUMMARY

Age-related issues have become a substantial element in U.S. politics, and the demographics of aging suggest that this trend will continue. Understanding the relevant questions and answers emerging from research into the politics of aging requires a sensitivity to the methodological and conceptual issues inherent in the age/period/cohort problem.

In the 1992 Presidential election, the percentage of people reporting they voted was lowest in the youngest age groups; the proportion of people reporting that they voted increased with age. Only 33.2 percent of voters aged 18 to 20 reported voting in 1992, whereas 68.8 percent of those 65 years of age and older reported similarly. Factors contributing to this pattern include (1) the increased social integration of mature and older adults, (2) the increased leisure time available to adults, and (3) the greater likelihood of the elderly experiencing a health impairment.

The aged are actively involved in partisan politics. They seem more likely than the young to make occasional contact with a public official. Many older people are also involved in working for community organizations and in political campaigns. Some suggest that older people's involvement in politics has more to do with their attempting to remain active and fulfilled than with a desire to achieve particular political goals.

The general impression many people have is that the elderly are overrepresented in positions of political leadership. Former Presidents Ronald Reagan and George Bush notwithstanding, the trend in advanced industrial nations seems toward an underrepresentation of the aged in leadership positions. This is likely a result of a greater bureaucratization of government, which causes career patterns to become more routinized.

Are the elderly politically more conservative than the young? This is difficult to say. A higher proportion of the older cohorts—those 66 to 81 years old and those 82 and older—identify with the Democratic party than is the case for the youngest cohorts (those under 34 years of age and those 34 to 49 years old). Rather than aging bringing with it a change in positions on prominent political issues, it is more likely that today's older people, when younger, had different political views than currently younger cohorts.

There is considerable debate about the impact of a growing aged population on the federal budget. Some analysts view increased outlays for the elderly as being about to bust the budget. Others believe this characterization of the budget to be inaccurate. Unfortunately, it may create the impression that the federal government gives lavish treatment to the elderly. There is considerable debate about whether the aged constitute a political force that can mobilize to serve their own interests.

Several groups of aged—including the poor, minority elderly, and older women—have not been advantaged by government initiatives on behalf of older people. Public policy appears to perpetuate the existence of social class differences among the elderly that existed prior to old age. There was a time when age entitlement programs seemed necessary to identify a large proportion of elderly persons in need. The current question, however, is whether a change to need entitlement would more effectively target government programs for the truly needy elderly. Evidence is mounting that suggests that public policy is already on a course that combines age and need as important policy criteria for old-age benefit programs.

STUDY QUESTIONS

1. Explain how age, employment status, education, and race influence voting behavior in the United States.

2. Discuss how the three factors identified by Milbrath explain the relationship between age and voting.

3. List the six categories described by Verba and Nie in their typology of political participation. In which categories are the elderly overrepresented, and what could explain their overrepresentation?

4. Discuss the changing trend of political participation of the elderly in leadership positions in advanced industrialized nations.

5. Explain the difference between *breakthrough* and *constituency-building* policy enactments. Give examples.

6. Distinguish among the *marginal, downwardly mobile,* and *integrated* elderly. How does the distribution of policy benefits act to perpetuate social class differences among the elderly?

7. Discuss the concept of *senior power.* How does it relate to the presence or absence of *aging group consciousness?*

8. Discuss the relative merits of providing programmatic support to older people on the basis of age and need.

REFERENCES

Achenbaum, W. A. (1983). *Shades of gray: Old age, American values, and federal policies since 1920*. Boston: Little, Brown.

Bengtson, V., & Cutler, N. (1976). Generalizations and intergenerational relations: Perspectives on age groups and social change. In R. H. Binstock & E. Shanas (Eds.), *Handbook of aging and the social sciences*. New York: Van Nostrand Reinhold.

Binstock, R. H. (1978). Federal policy toward the aging—Its inadequacies and its politics. *National Journal* (November 11), 1838–1845.

Binstock, R. H., & Day, C. L. (1996). Aging and politics. In R. H. Binstock & L. K. George (Eds.), *Handbook of aging and the social sciences* (4th ed.). San Diego, CA: Academic Press.

Butler, R. (1978). The economics of aging: We are asking the wrong questions. *National Journal* (November 4), 1792–1797.

Callahan, D. (1987). *Setting limits: Medical goals in an aging society*. New York: Simon and Schuster.

Campbell, J. C., & Strate, J. (1981). Are old people conservative? *Gerontologist, 21* (6), 580–591.

Crystal, S. (1982). *America's old age crisis: Public policy and the two worlds of aging*. New York: Basic Books.

Cutler, S. J., Leutz, S. A., Muha, M. J., & Riter, R. N. (1980). Aging and conservatism: Cohort changes in attitudes about legalized abortion. *Journal of Gerontology, 35,* 115–123.

Ford Foundation. (1990). *The common good: Social welfare and the American future*. New York: Ford Foundation.

Glenn, N. D., & Grimes, M. (1968). Aging, voting and political interest. *American Sociological Review, 33,* 563–575.

Hess, B. (1983, September). *Aging policies and old women: The hidden agenda*. Paper presented at the 78th Annual Meeting of the American Sociological Society, Detroit.

Hudson, R. (1978). The 'graying' of the federal budget and its consequences for old-age policy. *Gerontologist, 18* (5), 428–439.

Hudson, R. (1987). Tomorrow's able elders: Implications for the state. *Gerontologist, 27* (4), 405–409.

Hudson, R., & Binstock, R. H. (1976). Political systems and aging. In R. H. Binstock & E. Shanas (Eds.), *Handbook of aging and the social sciences*. New York: Van Nostrand Reinhold.

Kutza, E. A. (1981). *The benefits of old age: Social-welfare policy for the elderly*. Chicago: University of Chicago Press.

Lammers, W. W., & Nyomarkay, J. L. (1980). The disappearing senior leaders. *Research on Aging, 2* (3), 329–349.

Milbrath, L. W. (1965). *Political participation*. Chicago: Rand McNally.

Nelson, G. (1982, March). Social class and public policy for the elderly. *Social Service Review,* 85–107.

Neugarten, B. L. (1982). Policy for the 1980s: Age or need entitlement? In B. L. Neugarten (Ed.), *Age or need? Public policies for older people*. Beverly Hills: Sage.

Nie, N., Verba, S., & Kim, J. (1974). Political participation and the life-cycle. *Comparative Politics, 6,* 319–340.

Ossofsky, J. (1978). Through the aging budget—One more time. *National Journal* (March 11), 408–409.

Portrait of the Electorate. (1992). *New York Times,* (November 5), B9.

Pratt, H. (1976). *The gray lobby*. Chicago: University of Chicago Press.

Preston, S. H. (1984). Children and the elderly in the U.S. *Scientific American, 251* (6), 44–49.

Reitzes, D. C. & Reitzes, D. C. (1991). Metro Seniors in Action: A case study of a citywide senior organization. *Gerontologist, 31* (2), 256–262.

Samuelson, R. (1978). Busting the U.S. budget—The costs of an aging America. *National Journal* (February 18), 256–260.

Schmidhauser, J. (1968). The political influence of the aged. *Gerontologist, 8* (1), 44–49.

Smith, L. (1992). The tyranny of America's old. *Fortune, 125* (1), 68–72.

Social Security Administration. (1991). Social security programs in the United States. *Social Security Bulletin, 54* (9), 2–82.

Verba, S., & Nie, N. (1972). *Participation in America: Political democracy and social equality.* New York: Harper and Row.

Wisensale, S. K. (1988). Generational equity and intergenerational policies. *Gerontologist, 28* (6), 773–338

CHAPTER 14

RELIGION AND AGING

Writing in 1972, Heenan described the literature on religion and aging as "empirical lacunae." Have things changed in the 25 years since? Although the literature on death and dying (see Chapter 19) has grown dramatically in the last decade or so, empirical research on the religious attitudes and behavior of older people is still relatively scarce. One explanation for the scarcity of such research is that this aspect of older life is taken for granted. Elders are consistently portrayed as both more superstitious and more religious than younger people, and the assumption is that the role of older people in religious activities remains strong and enduring (Hess & Markson, 1980; Orbach, 1961).

Another explanation is that the relative scarcity of research on religion and aging may have roots in methodological concerns. First, most research in social gerontology is cross-sectional in design. Thus, it is difficult to disentangle age, cohort, and period effects on a wide variety of behaviors and attitudes, including religious behavior and attitudes (Maddox, 1979). As Moberg observes:

> Whether the differences in religious beliefs between the generations are a result of the aging process or of divergent experiences during the formative years of childhood and youth, which are linked with different social and historical circumstances, is unknown. Longitudinal research might reveal considerably different conclusions from the cross-sectional studies which provide the foundation for current generalizations about age variations in the ideological dimensions of religion. (1965, p. 8)

Second, certain concepts are difficult to define in the area of religion. What constitutes a religious individual, anyway? And how should religiosity be measured: by church or synagogue attendance or by engagement in private devotional activities?

Third, though religious groups "differ in terms of the amount of participation and interest demanded of their adherents, the degree of organization they possess and the opportunities they offer for the individual to achieve his or her goals" (Atchley, 1980, p. 331), there seems to be a general insensitivity within the field of gerontology toward the need to distinguish among religious groups. Thus, what few studies there are make no basic attempt to separate Protestants, Catholics, and Jews, and further subdivision among these groups is even more rare. One review of the measures used in studies of age and religiosity indicates that most are Christian and church oriented (Payne, 1982). Insensitivity toward religious diversity among the aged may simply be an extension of the development of the broader field of social gerontology. Only recently has recognition of the ethnic and racial diversity present in the aging experience begun to infiltrate the field.

Young and Dowling (1987) suggest that a period effect accounts for a vacillating interest in religion on the part of researchers. Following World War II and peaking in 1965, considerable work focused on religiosity and old age, with particular emphasis on attendance at religious services. During the 1980s and into the 1990s, interest in religion has once again increased on college campuses and among the U.S. population at large. One chronicler corroborating this perceived resurgence indicates that researchers in the field of aging have increasingly incorporated religion-related variables in their research designs (Fecher, 1982). Thus, Heenan's "empirical lacunae" appear to be closing.

Coloring the execution and any interpretation of this empirical research, however, is a richness of history and myth. Many contemporary beliefs and attitudes toward older people are built on an orientation first recorded in Scripture. This chapter uses such chronicles of life and humanity to assess the relationship between religion and aging. Following Achenbaum's (1985) lead, the chapter begins with a review of perceptions of age among the ancient Hebrews and early Christians as these may be reflected in the Old and New Testament. Subsequently, the functions that organized religion provides to society and to its aged constituents are identified. Literature on the relationship between age and religious commitment is reviewed, although, as already indicated, such studies generally have not distinguished among individuals of different religious affiliation. Finally, the interactions among age, religion, and health are examined.

IN THE BEGINNING...

As many commentators have pointed out, the images of old age presented in the Old Testament are generally quite positive: "The hoary head is a crown of glory, it is found in the way of righteousness" (Proverbs 16:31). Longevity is presented as the reward for service to the Lord. This is especially evident in Moses's discourses on the religious foundations of the Covenant. For example, "Ye shall walk in all the way which the Lord your God hath commanded you, that ye may live, and that it may be well with you, and that ye may prolong your days in the land which ye shall possess" (Deuteronomy 5:30).

In Genesis 5, the book of the generations of Adam, a list of individuals who lived abnormally long lives is provided. Adam is said to have lived 930 years, Seth

912 years, Enosh 905 years, and so on. Most biblical scholars doubt the accuracy of this chronology, however. Maimonides holds that only the distinguished individuals named in this chapter lived these long years, whereas others lived a more or less normal span (Hertz, 1981).

The general respect and favorable position of the elderly in ancient Hebraic culture was a function of three vital roles they played (Achenbaum, 1985). First, the elderly were often instruments of the Lord's will. Noah exemplifies this function. In the face of God's decision to cleanse the earth of corruption and violence, Noah is instructed to "make thee an ark of gopher wood" (Gen. 6:14) and bring "all thy house into the ark" (Genesis 7:1). Noah was 600 years old when "the flood of waters was upon the earth" (Genesis 7:6) and 601 years when instructed to "be fruitful, and multiply, and replenish the earth" (Genesis 9:1); he died at the age of 950 (Genesis 9:29).

The second function fulfilled by the elderly was that of wielder of political influence and power. The Book of Numbers describes the wanderings of the Israelites after their departure from Egypt. In Chapter 11, Moses complains to the Lord that he is unable to bear alone the burden of all these people. The Lord instructs Moses as follows:

> Gather unto Me seventy men of the elders of Israel, whom thou knowest to be the elders of the people, and officers over them; and bring them unto the tent of meeting, that they may stand there with thee. And I will come down and speak with thee there; and I will take of the spirit which is upon thee, and will put it upon them; and they shall bear the burden of the people with thee. (Numbers 11:16–17)

Finally, the elderly are viewed as custodians of the collective wisdom of the years. Job, who had his family and material possessions stripped from him and his body covered with boils, asks, "Is wisdom with aged men, And understanding in length of days?" (Job 12:12). One answer he receives is as follows: "Days should speak, And multitude of years should teach wisdom" (Job 32:7).

It is difficult, if not impossible, to discuss the positive themes attached to old age and aging in ancient Hebraic culture without speaking to the conception of parent/child relations presented in the Old Testament. The Fifth Commandment provides the basic guideline: "Honor thy father and thy mother, as the Lord thy God commanded thee; that thy days may be long, and that it may go well with thee, upon the land which the Lord thy God giveth thee" (Deuteronomy 5:16). As Achenbaum (1985) points out, however, the Old Testament may have been written in a time when ideals were not always realized. Thus, the Fifth Commandment can be juxtaposed with descriptions of the severe punishments assigned to children if a parental order was disobeyed or if a child cursed a parent. For example, an incorrigible son, whom milder measures failed to reclaim, might be tried by the elders at the gate of the city, and be liable to death by stoning (Deuteronomy 21:18–21).

New Testament perspectives on old age and aging were built on Old Testament precedents. Honor to parents specifically and to the older generation generally is a device for expressing obedience toward God (Ephesians 6:1–4). Yet, distinctively Christian views of age and aging are put forth in the New Testament. For the most part, these are intertwined with the conception of the personhood of Christ:

> But grace was given to each of us according to the measure of Christ's gift...until we all attain to the unity of the faith and of the knowledge of the Son of God, to mature manhood, to the measure of the stature of the fulness of Christ;...speaking the truth in love, we are to grow up in every way into him who is the head, into Christ, from whom the whole body, joined with which it is supplied, when each part is working properly, makes bodily growth and upbuilds itself in love. (Ephesians 4:7, 13–16)

This image of aging posits that the goal of human development is to grow into the "mature manhood" of Christ. The theme of growth and continuity stretching through the course of human life is accentuated in the New Testament (Achenbaum, 1985). Still, no Christian, no matter how old, can attain full maturity in this world. Presumably this results when one becomes fully incorporated into the Body of Christ. Achenbaum (1985) suggests that this may explain why no older person in the New Testament is portrayed as vividly or with the same stature as the patriarchs of the Old Testament; the central figure of the New Testament is a vigorous middle-aged Christ.

Another important difference between the Old and New Testaments is the portrayal of the relationship between death and aging. The Old Testament offers little comfort or consolation for the reality of death. Afterlife or immortal life was not a substantive issue for the ancient Hebrews—nor is it one for contemporary Jews, for that matter. For Christians, Old Testament teaching has been transformed by the story of Christ's death, resurrection, and ascension. The New Testament proclaims victory over death, although, as Achenbaum notes, different Christian sects have come to visualize the afterlife in different ways.

FUNCTIONS OF RELIGION

As a social institution, religion fulfills several basic functions within human societies. For example, religion defines the spiritual world and provides explanation for events and occurrences that seem difficult to understand. On a more mundane level, religious institutional services provide a meeting ground for unattached and otherwise disaffiliated individuals. Three functions of religion worthy of discussion here include integration, social control, and the provision of social support.

Social Integration

According to French sociologist Emile Durkheim (1912/1965), ideas about the ultimate meaning of life and ritual ceremonies that express these ideas arise out of the collective experience of individuals. Beliefs, including religious beliefs, depend on agreement among people for their meaning. The content of religious belief systems—ideas expressed, ritual ceremonies enacted, and values held sacred—all express the shared fate of the believers. For Durkheim, all systems of religious belief "have the same objective significance and fulfill the same function everywhere.... There are no religions that are false. All are true in their own fashion; all answer, though in different ways, to the given conditions of human existence" (1912/1965).

The sharedness of religious bonds, the common adherence to a religious belief system, can overcome personal and divisive forces (Koenig, George, & Siegler, 1988). It can act as a societal glue, holding together individuals and social groups with diverse interests and aspirations. It is exemplified in ritual ceremonies of passage such as confirmation, bar and bas mitzvahs, weddings, and funerals. The integrative function of religion is, perhaps, most apparent in traditional, preindustrial societies where agricultural events such as seeding and harvesting, kin relationships, and even the exercise of authority by leaders are governed by religious beliefs and rituals (Schaefer, 1986).

Religion can be a powerful integrative force for older people in a society. In their analysis of aging and modernization in 14 societies, Cowgill and Holmes (1972) listed nine universals of human aging. *Universals* represent common denominators or constants of behavior that are found in the same form in most societies around the world. One of these universals is as follows: *Societies rich in ceremonialism and religious ritual tend to honor the aged and accord them prestige seldom found in less formalistic societies.* Old people can be the caretakers of ritual tradition. Not only can they teach the details of the ceremonies but they also represent a liaison between the affairs of earth and the realm of the supernatural (Holmes, 1983). De Beauvoir adds:

> As the custodian of the traditions, the intercessor, and the protector against the supernatural powers, the aged man ensures the cohesion of the community throughout time and in the present.... Generally speaking, the services, taken as a whole, that the old are enabled to render because of their knowledge of the traditions, mean that they have not only respect but also material prosperity. They are rewarded with presents. The gifts that they receive from those whom they initiate into their secrets are of particular importance—they are the surest source of private wealth, a source that exists only in societies that are insufficiently well-to-do to have an advanced culture. (1972, p. 83)

Many of the ceremonial and ritual roles performed by the elderly are described by Simmons

> They have served as guardians of temples, shrines, and sacred paraphernalia, as officers of the priesthood, and as leaders of the performance of rites associated with prayers, sacrifices, feast days, annual cycles, historic celebrations, and the initiation of important and hazardous enterprises. They also have been prominent in ceremonies with critical periods in the life cycle—such as birth, puberty, marriage and death. (1945, p. 164)

Amoss (1978, 1981) has described the Coast Salish Indians of Washington State and British Columbia as a society in which the aged have continued to be valued because of their knowledge of ritual and ceremonial detail. According to Amoss, contact with the white world in the late nineteenth century was initially devastating for the Coast Salish aged. With the shift to wage labor (away from hunting and gathering), old people's knowledge and skills became outdated and irrelevant. Religious leadership passed to younger men, and the supernatural powers of the old were challenged.

Since World War II, the Coast Salish have faced economic hardship, jobs have been difficult to come by, and many individuals have been on welfare. During the 1940s and 1950s, many sought relief in revivalistic Christianity. Christian churches, however, were not able to offer them the opportunity to feel dignity as Native Americans, and some ministers were even antagonistic toward Native American belief systems. Traditional religious ceremonies, including the revival of traditional-type spirit dancing rituals, began to reappear. These traditional rituals emphasized solidarity with past generations as well as among present-day Coast Salish. Old men and women became the focus of this new revivalism. The young wanted to be proud of their traditional culture, and it was the elderly who had preserved traditions from the past.

Similarly, Sinclair (1985) reports that older Maori (a culture indigenous to New Zealand) women have achieved a degree of equality if not dominance in modern society through their participation in a religious movement referred to as *Maramatanga*. Affiliated with the Catholic Church in New Zealand, the ideology of this movement draws heavily on traditional Maori religion and the Maori prophetic tradition. Although men participate in the movement, it is the women who receive messages from the "spirits of the dead," who return as these spirits, and who monitor relations between humans and spirits. Middle-aged and older women, freed of the responsibilities of domestic life, participate most vigorously in the Maramatanga movement and often experience an enhancement of status within both the Maori and European communities. Some of the women become effective culture brokers, comfortable with the Maori traditions of the past but simultaneously accommodating themselves to modern directions dominated by the Europeans.

As Spencer and Jennings (1977) report, societies without a ceremonial tradition may provide little or no opportunity for the prestige or the participation of the elderly. Among the Chipewyns of the western subarctic region of North America, elderly men no longer able to hunt command little respect. There is minimal interest in myth or legend about the past, and there are few, if any, remaining religious rituals. As a result, the elderly are left with almost no opportunities for participation in the society.

Social Control

Karl Marx agreed with Durkheim's view of the collective and socially shared nature of religious behavior. But Marx (1844/1963) was also concerned that religion produced an "otherworldly" focus that diverts attention from the circumstances and realities of life in this world. From this perspective, religion supports the status quo and helps to perpetuate patterns of social inequality. Long-held religious beliefs and practices enforce taken-for-granted beliefs that sometimes act as significant barriers to new or different ways of thinking and behaving. Traditional practices, handed down from previous generations, become defined as God-approved ways of doing things and are resistant to change. This is so, even when the results of such traditional practices include inequalities and inequities. Racism, sexism, and, to some extent, ageism have been linked to religion, and when this occurs, the social control functions of religion may be enhanced. For example, Vander Zanden (1988) quotes Louisiana State Senator W. M. Rainach in defending racial segregation in 1954: "Segregation is a natural order—created by God, in His wisdom, who made black men black and white men white."

Marx portrayed religion as a painkiller for the suffering experienced by all oppressed peoples, including the poor and indigent of all ages. Like other painkillers, it may suppress the symptoms for a while but the underlying condition remains.

> Religious suffering is at the same time an expression of real suffering and a protest against real suffering. Religion is the sigh of the oppressed creature, the sentiment of a heartless world, and the soul of soulless conditions. It is the opium of the people. (1844/1963)

From a Marxist perspective, religion keeps people from understanding their living conditions in political terms. Marxists argue that religion induces a "false consciousness" among the disadvantaged that lessens the possibility of collective political action to change the material conditions of people's lives. Have the elderly experienced a false consciousness that hides from them the possibility of changing the material conditions of their lives? Or have they, in fact, enjoyed political and legislative successes far beyond their relative proportion in the U.S. population? These remain much-debated questions among students of aging (see Chapter 13).

Social Support

Religious institutions bring together people of all ages and help reduce the isolation of the elderly. For many elderly residing in smaller communities, religious pursuits help instigate and provide nurturance for social relationships. Friendships, opportunities for reciprocal exchanges, sympathy, empathy, encouragement, and reassurance all represent supportive aspects of religious organizational environments and may contribute to well-being in later life (Koenig, Kvale, & Ferrel, 1988). Even when capacities for firsthand participation in religious services and activities diminish, the importance of continued interaction with representatives of the religious institution cannot be underestimated.

Another option has become available in recent years—that of the electronic church. Almost one in three U.S. viewers say they watch religious programming on television. These viewers are disproportionately older, female, southern, from small towns, and are less well educated than are people who do not watch religious programs (Clymer, 1987). Although most use television as a supplement to participation in local religious activities, many elderly shut-ins use it as a substitute for attendance at religious services. Television allows viewers to "privatize" religious worship, to gain a feeling of immediate and personal help in coping with their troubles, and to enjoy the illusion of a face-to-face relationship with a dynamic religious leader (Hadden & Swann, 1981).

AGE AND RELIGIOUS COMMITMENT

Data from the 1993 General Social Survey (GSS) show a strong relationship between age and several different dimensions of religious commitment. Carried out by the National Opinion Research Center at the University of Chicago, the GSS is a survey taken annually of the attitudes and opinions of a representative sample of noninstitutionalized adults 18 years of age and older in the United States. For example, survey results for 1993 show that although a majority of Americans have confidence in the existence of God, age differences do exist. Three of four (74.5 percent) people aged 65 years and older have confidence in the existence of God; at the same time, 62.7 percent of respondents aged 18 to 44 years indicate a similar belief. One place where age differences do not appear is in the proportion of GSS respondents who believe in life after death. Approximately 81 percent of all Americans believe in life after death with differences between the oldest and youngest respondent groups at less than two percentage points (81.8 percent vs. 80.1 percent). Additional results are reported in Tables 14–1 through 14–3.

According to Table 14–1, older people are more likely than younger people to characterize themselves as being strongly religious. More than one-half (51.5 percent) of GSS respondents aged 65 and over described themselves as being strongly religious. This compares with 36.4 percent of those 18 to 44 years and 45.6 percent of those 45 to 64 years of age who make the same claim.

TABLE 14–1   Strength of Religious Affiliation, by Age, 1993

	Age		
	18–44	**45–64**	**65+**
Strongly religious	36.4%	45.6%	51.5%
Not very strong	47.0	40.5	33.5
Somewhat strong	16.6	13.8	14.9

Source: Data from the 1993 General Social Survey by the National Opinion Research Center at the University of Chicago.

Does this relationship between age and strength of religious affiliation hold up in a review of patterns of attendance at religious services? A decline in attendance at religious services and participation in organized religious activities is sometimes associated with physical limitations or disability as well as the lack of transportation. According to Moberg:

> Persons who have commuted to church for as much as half a century blame their declining participation on poor eyesight, 'old age,' or failing health. Driving to church, especially at night, has become an arduous task, and they do not wish to be a 'bother' or to become a burden upon someone else by 'begging' rides to all of the church's meetings. (1965)

Table 14–2 provides data on the variation by age in attendance at religious services among GSS respondents in 1993. People 65 years and over are nearly twice as likely as those aged 18 to 44 to attend religious services once a week or more frequently (43.4 percent vs. 23.8 percent, respectively). However, there is only a modest difference in patterns of attendance at religious services between the old and middle-aged; 51.7 percent of those 44 to 64 and 58.3 percent of those aged 65 and over report attending religious services more frequently than once a month.

Table 14–3 shows that compared with young and middle-aged adults, the old pray more often. More than three-fourths (76.4 percent) of the GSS respondents aged 65 and over reported engaging in prayer once a day or more. It is interesting

---

TABLE 14–2   Attendance at Religious Services, by Age, 1993

	Age		
	18–44	**45–64**	**65+**
Once a week or more	23.8%	29.3%	43.4%
Once a month or more	24.6	22.4	14.9
Once a year or more	26.2	21.7	18.6
Less than once a year/never	25.4	26.7	23.1

Source: Data from the 1993 General Social Survey by the National Opinion Research Center at the University of Chicago.

TABLE 14–3   Frequency of Prayer, by Age, 1993

	Age		
	18–44	**45–64**	**65+**
Several times a day	19.9%	31.8%	38.2%
Once a day	25.6	31.4	38.2
Once a week or more	28.2	15.7	8.6
Less than once a week/never	26.3	21.1	15.1

Source: Data from the 1993 General Social Survey by the National Opinion Research Center at the University of Chicago.

AGE DIFFERENCES IN MYSTICAL EXPERIENCE

Have you ever had a mystical experience? Thought you were somewhere you had not been before? Felt as if you were in touch with someone who had died? Are such experiences associated with aging? And, if so, how? Are you more or less likely to have such an experience as you grow older?

As Levin (1993) reports, the 1988 General Social Survey (GSS) contained five measures of mystical experience, grouped together after the question, "How often have you had any of the following experiences?" These included *déjà vu* ("Thought you were somewhere you had been before, but knew that it was impossible"), *ESP, clairvoyance, spiritualism* ("Felt as though you were really in touch with someone who had died"), and *numinous experience* ("Felt as though you were very close to a powerful spiritual force that seemed to lift you out of yourself").

On average, GSS respondents reported experiencing each of the mystical phenomena roughly once or twice in their lives, with déjà vu and ESP being considerably more common than the other experiences. At the high end, 67.3 percent of respondents indicated that they had experienced déjà vu once or more in their lives; at the low end, 28.3 percent of respondents indicated that they had had a clairvoyant experience once or more in their lives.

Levin divided GSS respondents into four roughly equal-sized age groups: 18–30, 31–40, 41–60, and 61+. Statistically significant age differences were revealed in 2 of the 5 mystical experiences. Lifetime prevalence of déjà vu steadily declined across age cohorts from younger to older, as did prevalence of clairvoyance, although the decline is less steep. Also, the overall mysticism scale (made up of the five items) was lowest in the oldest group.

Religiosity (measured in different ways) appears to exert statistically significant effects on mystical experience in each age group, although the pattern of significant effects varies across the age groups. For example, among young adults (18–30 years), mystical experience is more likely to occur among *subjectively* (strength of religious preference) and *nonorganizationally* religious people (those who say grace after meals or read the Bible at home). It is less likely among *organizationally* religious people (those who attend religious services and take part in various religious activities). Among the oldest respondents (61+ years), only subjective religiosity predicted mystical experience—that is, people who defined themselves as strongly religious and feeling close to God were more likely to have mystical experiences.

The same five items were asked in the 1973 GSS. In the 15 years that passed, the percentage of respondents who reported ever having experienced mystical phenomena increased for four of the five indicators, declining only slightly for numinous experience. Thus, both aging and cohort effects could be thought to be operating: Mystical experience may decline with age but simultaneously be increasing over the years. As Levin points out, "If the past few decades represent a period of increasing secularization of culture...then perhaps an increase in certain mystical experiences with successively younger age cohorts reflects a successive substitution of engagement of the psychic world for organized, institutional religious practice" (1993, p. 511). Or, perhaps, "It may be that, among those whose religious expression is predominantly organizational, regular participation in public worship discourages paranormal involvement (or at least reports of such experiences to survey researchers)" (1993, p. 512).

to note, however, that more than 60 percent (63.2 percent) of middle-aged respondents reported praying at least once a day, whereas less than one-half (45.5 percent) of all younger respondents reported doing similarly.

General Social Survey data for 1993 provides a single snapshot of the relationship between age and religious commitment. Just what is really known about how aging affects religious behavior and commitment? Bahr (1970) analyzes prior research in this area and suggests that the relationship between aging and church attendance be interpreted with reference to four distinct models: (1) traditional, (2) lifetime stability, (3) family life cycle, and (4) progressive disengagement.

According to the *traditional* model, there is a sharp decline in religious activity during young adulthood, with the lowest point in the life cycle being between ages 30 and 35. Beyond age 35, this model posits a steady increase in church activity until old age.

The *lifetime stability* model alleges that aging and church attendance or religious activity are not related. One interpretation of this model is made by Lazerwitz: "Perhaps church attendance is based upon patterns established fairly early in life and subject to little (if any) change with aging" (1962, p. 433). Wilensky's (1961) review of studies of the variations in religious participation by age supports this interpretation. He found that church membership and attendance was fairly stable in the middle years and did not drop off until after age 70 or 75.

A third model derives from the view that religious participation is related to stage of *family life cycle*. In general, family life cycle seems to be a euphemism for presence or absence of children. According to this model, when children are young and tied to the home, parental involvement in religious services peaks; with children no longer in the home, regularity of religious participation falls off. Although this model speaks to the influence of the presence of children on parental involvement in organized religion, there is general agreement that parents' religious orientations are particularly important influences on young people's development (Hoge & Petrillo, 1978). Hunsberger (1985) reports that mothers have the strongest proreligious influence.

The *progressive disengagement* model is tied to the disengagement theory of aging. From the perspective of this theory, aging is seen as "an inevitable mutual withdrawal or disengagement," resulting in decreased interaction between the aging person and others in his or her social systems (Cumming & Henry, 1961). Applied to participation in religious activities, the theory suggests a model of decline following middle age. Riley and Foner (1968) conclude that "the evidence, though slight, suggests that more individuals decrease than increase their attendance as they reach old age."

Bahr's (1970) own interviews with more than 600 men from three distinctive socioeconomic strata (skid row, urban lower class, and urban middle class) show substantial religious disaffiliation during adult life in all three groups. The progressive disengagement model is most congruent with the pattern of church attendance reported by Bahr's respondents. With advancing age, church attendance is increasingly less important as a source of voluntary affiliation among both well-to-do and poor men (Bahr, 1970). As Bahr himself suggests, however, it may be that age brings a qualitative change in the nature of religiosity such that the decline in attendance is not matched by declines in religious belief or feeling.

Wingrove and Alston (1974) have argued that support for each of Bahr's four models varies by the type of sample and methodology used and by the year of data collection. Applying cohort analysis to data collected by the Gallup Poll between 1939 and 1969, these authors found that, although church attendance appears related to age, no consistent support for any one of the four models was provided. Each cohort was found to show its own church attendance pattern. Gender and social environment seemed to have greater impact on church attendance than did age.

Blazer and Palmore (1976) report the results of a longitudinal study of the religious attitudes and activities of 272 community residents over an 18-year period. Subjects were interviewed at two- to three-year intervals beginning in 1957. Measures included church attendance and Bible reading, among others. They found that positive religious attitudes remain fairly stable over time. If individuals were religious or nonreligious when young, chances are they will continue to have the same basic religious orientation when they become old. As Figure 14–1 shows, Blazer and Palmore's findings do show a gradual decline in religious activities in the later years.

Criticism of these and other studies of the relationship between age and religious behavior often centers on the fact that researchers have too narrowly conceptualized religiosity in terms of attendance or participation in formal

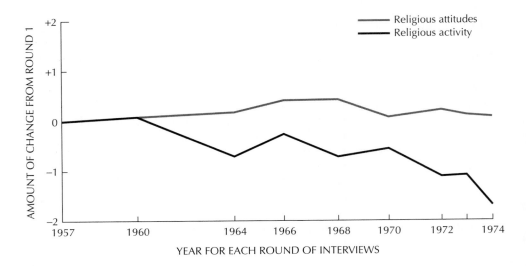

FIGURE 14–1   **Religious Attitudes and Activities Over Time**

Source: Dan Blazer and Erdman Palmore, "Religion and Aging in a Longitudinal Panel," *The Gerontologist, 16* (1), 1976, Part 1, p. 84. Copyright © The Gerontological Society of America.

organizations. As Mindel and Vaughn (1978) point out, the role of "religious person" encompasses more than simple participation in a religious organization and may include private or nonorganizational religious behavior. Some even suggest that, with aging, these more private and nonorganizational religious expressions increase in importance (Moberg, 1972). Stark (1968) found that greater piety among the elderly compared with the young was manifested in the reported frequency of praying.

Employing a small sample of elderly from Central Missouri, Mindel and Vaughn (1978) observed that, although a majority did not attend religious services frequently, a majority of sample members maintained that they were nonorganizationally religious "very often." For the purposes of this study, examples of nonorganizational religious activity included engaging in individual or family prayer and listening to religious music or a religious service on the radio or television.

Young and Dowling (1987) have attempted to extend the work of Mindel and Vaughn by identifying factors that account for the variation in dimensions of religious participation. They sampled American Association of Retired Persons (AARP) members in El Paso, Texas, who were fairly evenly split between large "liberal" Protestant denominations (e.g., Methodist, Presbyterian, or Episcopal) and "conservative/traditional" churches (e.g., Baptist, Mormon, or Roman Catholic). Strength of religious conviction was the strongest predictor of organized religious activity and private religious behavior. These authors hypothesized that indicators of social or personal deprivation (including poor health, low income, reduced activity, and living alone) would predict higher levels of nonorganizational or private religious behavior. The assumption is that private religious behavior *compensates* for these deprivations. The researchers were forced to reject this hypothesis. Interestingly, they did find that strong kin and friend networks predict high levels of private devotion. Young and Dowling contend that frequent interaction in an informal social network contributes to the spiritual well-being of older persons through nonorganizational religious participation.

Kart, Palmer, and Flaschner (1987) studied the relationship between age and religiosity among Jews in northwest Ohio. Religiosity was measured in a variety of ways under two broad categories: organizational religious commitment and nonorganizational, or individual, religious commitment. Indicators of *organizational* religious commitment included synagogue attendance and the number of Jewish organizational memberships reported by each respondent. Indicators of *individual* religious commitment included whether the respondent follows religious dietary laws and keeps a kosher home, whether the respondent recites prayers of mourning for deceased parents and other family members, whether the respondent posts mezuzahs (parchment scrolls) on the doors of the household, whether female respondents light sabbath candles, and whether male respondents ritually pray over a cup a wine to consecrate the Sabbath. Respondents were also asked a question aimed at determining the strength of their religious beliefs.

For men in this sample, no statistically significant age differences could be observed on the array of organizational and individual measures of religious commitment. This is in contrast to Orbach's (1961) report made more than 35 years ago from the Detroit area study in which Jewish men showed increased synagogue attendance with age. In northwest Ohio, only the number of Jewish organizational memberships showed age-related differences. Older men were much more likely to report holding multiple memberships in Jewish voluntary associations or organizations than were younger men.

Women in this study provide a different picture. Statistically significant age differences can be observed on a number of organizational and individual measures of religiosity, including synagogue attendance and the use of mezuzahs on the doorposts of the home. In all cases, older women evidence stronger religious commitment than do younger women. Only on a single scale made up of two items—observance of dietary laws and the lighting of Sabbath candles—did Kart and colleagues (1987) find no apparent age differences.

Analyzing data from a large sample of Washington State residents, Finney and Lee (1976) found that age had a small, positive influence on private devotional practices but no effect on four other dimensions of religious commitment: belief, ritual, knowledge, and experience (Glock, 1962; Glock & Stark, 1965; Stark & Glock, 1968). Finney and Lee suggest that older people may tend to employ religion as a means of reducing or alleviating anxieties, and the researchers point to the small effect of age on several dimensions of religious commitment as indicative of the need "to raise questions about recent thought in both social gerontology and the sociology of religion."

RELIGION, AGING, AND HEALTH

The general hypothesis that social ties may protect individuals from a variety of disease outcomes has received support from numerous researchers. The effect of marriage (e.g., Gove, 1973), contacts with relatives and friends (Zuckerman, Kasl, & Ostfeld, 1984), and group membership (Berkman & Syme, 1979) all have been reported as significantly associated with health status; those individuals most isolated (fewest contacts with others) have an increased risk to their health and greater mortality. Greater religiousness has been associated with lower levels of functional disability and symptoms of depression (Idler, 1987). Researchers have reported an association between religious involvement and lower levels of hypertension (Graham et al., 1978) and myocardial infarction (Medalie et al., 1973), as well as lower risk of mortality (Berkman & Syme, 1979; House, Robbins, & Metzner, 1982; Schoenbach et al., 1986; Zuckerman, Kasl, & Ostfeld, 1984). It is unclear, however, how or why health benefits may be derived from social ties.

Idler (1987) suggests focusing on the structure and support-giving characteristics of particular unique institutions, such as the church or synagogue, in order to discover the linking mechanisms between individual health status and involve-

Religion can be a powerful integrative force for older people in society.

ment in the social environment. Presumably, benefits from social ties are not only differentially distributed among social institutions in terms of frequency of occurrence but potential benefits may be qualitatively unique as well.

The question remains as to how and why social ties generate health benefits. Classical sociological theory holds at least four explanations for the influence of religiosity or participation in religious organizational activity over health status (Idler, 1987; Norgard & Kart, 1989).

1. Religious organizations are comprised of distinctively normative patterns from which individuals may structure their behaviors and attitudes. Religious guidelines may influence health status through restrictive behavioral habits associated with health risk such as smoking, drinking, or diet (*health behaviors hypothesis*).

Mormons have been shown to have low cancer rates. This likely reflects adherence to their Church doctrines advocating abstention from the use of tobacco and alcohol. All Mormons do not adhere equally to the health practices of the Church, however. Gardner and Lyon (1982a) studied cancer in Utah Mormon men in relation to their adherence to Church doctrines. Cancer rates for 1966–1970 indicate that the most devout group had lung cancer rates 80 percent lower than those of the least devout group. The same was seen for all smoking- and alcohol-associated cancer sites combined. Cancer rates of the stomach and the leukemias and lymphomas also were lower in the most devout group. Mormon women classified as having the strongest adherence to Church doctrine had lung cancer rates during 1966–1970 much lower than did women with the weakest adherence (Gardner & Lyon, 1982b).

2. Religious involvement may also influence health status by giving individuals an opportunity to participate in a "moral community" (Durkheim, 1897/1951), whereby religious involvement is seen as an affirmation of belonging to a group of like-minded people. Belonging may provide emotional as well as material support (*social cohesiveness hypothesis*).

Graham and colleagues (1978) examined the relationship between blood pressure levels and church attendance patterns in a group of white male heads of households in the 1967–1969 follow-up examination of the Evans County, Georgia, Cardiovascular Epidemiologic Study. A consistent pattern of lower systolic and diastolic blood pressures was found among frequent church attendees. The findings held up when controls for age, obesity, cigarette smoking, and socioeconomic status were employed.

3. Another functional aspect of religion, as a "unified system of beliefs and practices relative to sacred things" (Durkheim, 1897/1951), is to define the spiritual and give meaning to the divine. A belief system that emphasizes people's relationships to a spiritual world provides an explanation for events that may otherwise seem unexplainable. Religious involvement may, therefore, provide a coherent framework for interpreting uncertainties associated with day-to-day experiences, and may provide support in stressful, out-of-the-ordinary situations (*cognitive coherence hypothesis*).

Zuckerman, Kasl, and Ostfeld (1984) reviewed mortality data during a two-year follow-up of some 400 elderly poor residents of three Connecticut cities in 1972 and 1974. Religiousness, measured by frequency of attendance at services and by two measures of religious strength and intensity, had an important protective effect among the elderly of both sexes in poorest health. This is the case when sociodemographic variables and health status measures are controlled. Among the religious, 19 percent of the males and 12 percent of the females who were ill died; the comparable mortality figures for the nonreligious in poor health were 42 percent of the males and 20 percent of females. Virtually no differences in death rates were apparent between the religious and nonreligious elderly in good health. Borrowing from Antonovsky, the authors suggest that religiosity may provide individuals with a *sense of coherence* that events "are predictable and that there is a high probability that things will work out as well as can reasonably be expected" (Antonovsky, 1979, p. 123).

4. Finally, religious involvement may act to modify how individuals perceive particularly stressful situations, including hospitalization, disability, or other traumatic events. Typically, religious belief systems provide a variety of contexts for understanding and interpreting individual human suffering. In part, this function of religion may be an extension of the social support and cognitive coherence functions just mentioned (*theodicy hypothesis*).

Norgard and Kart (1989) have investigated the relationship between religiosity and health status using older white respondents 55 years and older in the 1984 and 1987 General Social Surveys. Because of their insufficient numbers, nonwhites were excluded from the study. The four hypotheses identified here were tested in this work. The dependent variable, health status, was operationalized in two ways: a subjective evaluation of health status ("Would you say your health in general is excellent, good, fair, or poor?") and a subjective evaluation of psychological well-being ("Would you say that you are very happy, pretty happy, not too happy?"). Self-assessment of health status has been reported as correlating well with other measures of health status and in predicting general emotional states and behavior (Maddox & Douglas, 1973). A number of researchers have identified a positive relationship between religiosity and happiness or life satisfaction (Blazer & Palmore, 1976; Hunsberger, 1985).

Religiosity was also measured in two ways: the frequency of attendance at religious services and an attitudinal measure of strength of religious belief. Demographic variables and measures relevant to each of the four hypotheses were also used. These included age, education, income, sex, and marital status.

In general, and as predicted, religiosity was positively associated with subjective health and happiness among the elderly GSS respondents. In addition, some empirical support was provided for each of the four hypotheses. These hypotheses are not mutually exclusive. There is nothing exclusive or inconsistent, for example, about encouraging people to be supportive of their family members and friends and at the same time encouraging them not to smoke. Religious institutions have multiple functions, and individuals, including elderly individuals, have a relationship to the social environment that is multifaceted. Certainly an older person may receive qualitatively different positive contributions to perceived health and happiness from their religious beliefs and attitudes.

SUMMARY

The relative scarcity of research on religion and aging may have roots in methodological concerns. Most research is cross-sectional in nature, making it difficult for researchers to disentangle age, cohort, and period effects. Religiosity is a difficult concept to operationalize: Are organizational affiliations and attendance of more importance than measures of private devotional activity? Finally, most research simply does not distinguish between and among religious groups.

Contemporary beliefs and attitudes toward older people have roots in Scripture. Images of aging presented in the Old Testament are quite positive. Longevity is often presented as a reward for service to the Lord. The elderly often played vital roles as instruments of God, wielders of political power and influence, and custodians of the collective wisdom of the years. The Fifth Commandment offers the basic guideline in parent/child relationships. New Testament perspectives on old age and aging built on the Old Testament precedents. Distinctively Christian views of age and aging are intertwined with the conception of the personhood of Christ. Another important difference between the Old and New Testaments is the portrayal of the relationship between death and aging.

Major societal functions of religion include social integration, social control, and social support. Religion can be a powerful integrative force for older people in society. Societies rich in ceremonialism and religious ritual tend to honor the aged and accord them prestige seldom found in less formalistic societies. Religion can also be a powerful force for social control. It can provide barriers to new ways of thinking and behaving. It can also force people to focus on otherworldly issues rather than the material conditions of their lives. Has religion induced a false consciousness among the elderly?

Data from the 1993 General Social Survey show a strong relationship between age and religious commitment Older people are more likely than young adults to describe themselves as being strongly religious. There is only modest difference between the old and middle-aged when it comes to attendance at religious services, but the old report praying more often than the young or middle aged.

Early research on age and religious commitment provided four distinct models: traditional, lifetime stability, family life cycle, and progressive disengagement. Criticism of the early work centered on the narrow conceptualization of religiosity strictly in terms of attendance at religious services. The distinction between organizational religious commitment and private or individual religious commitment has become relevant. In addition, different researchers have identified different dimensions of organizational commitment.

Religiosity may influence the health status of older people in at least four ways: health behaviors hypothesis, social cohesiveness hypothesis, cognitive coherence hypothesis, and theodicy hypothesis. Some empirical support exists for each hypothesis.

STUDY QUESTIONS

1. What methodological issues help explain the relative scarcity of research on religion and aging?

2. What is the general position of the elderly in ancient Hebraic culture as reflected in the Old Testament? How do the Old and New Testaments differ in their conception of the aging process and the elderly?

3. Describe three major functions of religion. Give examples.

4. Distinguish the old from young and middle-aged adults with regard to strength of religiousness, attendance at religious services, and frequency of prayer.

5. Describe Bahr's four models of the relationship between aging and church attendance. Which model does Bahr's own data support?

6. List some measures or dimensions of religiosity that are alternatives to attendance at religious services. What is the importance of being able to identify these alternative measures?

7. How may religion affect the health status of older people?

REFERENCES

Achenbaum, W. A. (1985). Societal perceptions of the aging and the aged. In R. H. Binstock & E. Shanas (Eds.), *Handbook of aging and the social sciences* (2nd ed.). New York: Van Nostrand Reinhold.

Amoss, P. (1978). *Coast Salish spirit dancing.* Seattle: University of Washington Press.

Amoss, P. (1981). Coast Salish elders. In P. Amoss & S. Harrell (Eds.), *Other ways of growing old.* Stanford, CA: Stanford University Press.

Antonovsky, A. (1979). *Health, stress, and coping.* San Francisco: Jossey-Bass.

Atchley, R. (1980). *Social forces in later life* (3rd ed.) Belmont, CA: Wadsworth.

Bahr, H. (1970). Aging and religious disaffiliation. *Social Forces, 49*, 59–71.

de Beauvoir, S. (1972). *Coming of age.* New York: G. P. Putnam's Sons.

Berkman, L. F., & Syme, S. L. (1979). Social networks, host resistance, and mortality: A nine-year follow-up study of Alameda County residents. *American Journal of Epidemiology, 109*, 186–204.

Blazer, D., & Palmore, E. (1976). Religion and aging in a longitudinal panel. *Gerontologist, 16* (1), 82–85.

Clymer, A. (1987). Survey finds many skeptics among evangelists' viewers. *New York Times* (March 31), 1, 14.

Cowgill, D., & Holmes, L. 1972. *Aging and modernization.* New York: Appleton-Century-Crofts.

Cumming, E., & Henry, W. (1961). *Growing old: The process of disengagement.* New York: Basic Books.

Durkheim, E. (1897/1951). *Suicide.* New York: Free Press.

Durkheim, E. (1912/1965). *The elementary forms of religious life.* New York: Free Press.

Fecher, V. (1982). *Religion and aging: An annotated bibliography.* San Antonio, TX: Trinity University Press.

Field, M. (1968). *Aging with honor and dignity.* Springfield, IL: Charles C. Thomas.

Finney, J. M., & Lee, G. R. (1976). Age differences on five dimensions of religious involvement. *Review of Religious Research, 18* (2),173–179.

Gardner, J. W., & Lyon, J. L. (1982a). Cancer in Utah Mormon men by lay priesthood level. *American Journal of Epidemiology, 116,* 243–257.

Gardner, J. W., & Lyon, J. L. (1982b). Cancer in Utah Mormon women by church activity level. *American Journal of Epidemiology, 116,* 258–265.

Glock, C. Y. (1962). On the study of religious commitment: Review of recent research bearing on religion and character education. *Religious Education* (July–August), 98–110.

Glock, C. Y., & Stark, R. (1965). *Religion and society in tension.* Chicago: Rand McNally.

Gove, W. (1973). Sex, marital status and mortality. *American Journal of Sociology, 79,* 45–67.

Graham, T. W., Kaplan, B., Cornoni-Huntley, J., James, S., Becker, C., Hadden, J. K., & Swann, C. E. (1978). Frequency of church attendance and blood pressure elevation. *Journal of Behavioral Medicine, 1,* 37–43.

Hadden, J. K., & Swann, C. E. (1981). *Prime time preachers: The rising power of televangelism.* Reading, MA: Addison-Wesley.

Heenan, E. F. (1972). Sociology of religion and aged. *Journal of Scientific Study of Religion, 11,* 171–176.

Hertz, J. H. (Ed.). (1981). *Pentateuch and haftorahs: Hebrew text, English translation and commentary.* London: Soncino Press.

Hess, B., & Markson, E. (1980). *Aging and old age.* New York: Macmillan.

Hoge, D. R., & Petrillo, G. H. (1978). Development of religious thinking in adolescence: A test of Goldman's theories. *Journal for the Scientific Study of Religion, 17,* 359–379.

Holmes, L. D. (1983). *Other cultures, elder years: An introduction to cultural gerontology.* Minneapolis: Burgess.

House, J. S., Robbins, C., & Metzner, H. L. (1982). The association of social relationships and activities with mortality: Prospective evidence from the Tecumseh community health study. *American Journal of Epidemiology, 116,* 123–140.

Hunsberger, B. (1985). Religion, age, life satisfaction, and perceived sources of religiousness: A study of older persons. *Journal of Gerontology, 40* (5), 615–620.

Idler, E. L. (1987). Religious involvement and the health of the elderly: Some hypotheses and an initial test. *Social Forces, 66* (1), 226–238.

Kart, C. S., Palmer, N. P., & Flaschner, A. B. (1987). Aging and religious commitment in a midwestern Jewish community. *Journal of Religion and Aging, 3* (¾), 49–60.

Koenig, H. G., George, L. K., & Siegler, I. C. (1988). The use of religion and other emotion-regulating coping strategies among older adults. *The Gerontologist, 28* (3), 303–310.

Koenig, H. G., Kvale, J. N., & Ferrel, C. (1988). Religion and well-being in later life. *The Gerontologist, 28* (1), 18–28.

Lazerwitz, B. (1962). Membership in voluntary associations and frequency of church attendance. *Journal of Scientific Study of Religion, 2,* 74–84.

Levin, J. S. (1993). Age differences in mystical experience. *The Gerontologist, 33* (4), 507–513.

Maddox, G. (1979). Sociology of later life. *Annual Review of Sociology, 5,* 113–135.

Maddox, G., & Douglas, E. (1973). Self-assessment of health: A longitudinal study of elderly subjects. *Journal of Health and Social Behavior, 14,* 87–92.

Marx, K. (1844/1963). Estranged labour—economic and philosophic manuscripts of 1844. In C. W. Mills (Ed.), *Images of man.* New York: George Braziler.

Medalie, J. H., Kahn, H. A., Neufeld, H. N., Riss, E., & Goldbourt, U. (1973). Five year myocardial infarction incidence II: Association of single variables to age and birthplace. *Journal of Chronic Disease, 26,* 329–349.

Mindel, C. H., & Vaughn, C. V. (1978). A multidimensional approach to religiosity

and disengagement. *Journal of Gerontology, 33,* 103–108.

Moberg, D. O. (1965). Religiosity in old age. *Gerontologist, 5* (2), 80–85.

Moberg, D. O. (1972, January). Religion and the aging family. *The Family Coordinator,* 47–60.

Norgard, T., & Kart, C. S. (1989, April). *Religiosity and health status among the elderly: Replication with national samples.* Paper presented at the annual meeting of the North Central Sociological Association, Akron, OH.

Orbach, H. (1961). Aging and religion. *Geriatrics, 16,* 534–540.

Payne, B. (1982). Religiosity. In D. J. Mangen & W. A. Peterson (Eds.), *Research instruments in social gerontology: Vol. 2. Social roles and social participation.* Minneapolis: University of Minnesota Press.

Riley, M., & Foner, A. (1968). *Aging and society: Vol. 1. An inventory of research findings.* New York: Russell Sage.

Schaefer, R. T. (1986). *Sociology* (2nd ed.). New York: McGraw-Hill.

Schoenbach, V., Kaplan, B., Fredman, L., & Kleinbaum, D. G. (1986). Social ties and mortality in Evans County, Georgia. *American Journal of Epidemiology, 123,* 329–349.

Simmons, L. (1945). *The role of the aged in primitive society.* New Haven, CT: Yale University Press.

Sinclair, K. P. (1985). Koro and Kuia: Aging and gender among the Maori of New Zealand. In D. A. Counts & D. R. Counts (Eds.), *Aging and its tranformations: Moving toward death in Pacific societies.* Pittsburgh, PA: University of Pittsburgh Press.

Spencer, R., & Jennings, J. D. (1977). *The native Americans.* New York: Harper and Row.

Stark, R. (1968). Age and faith: A changing outlook as an old process. *Sociological Analysis, 29,* 1–10.

Stark, R., & Glock, C. Y. (1968). *American piety: The nation of religious commitment.* Berkeley: University of California Press.

Vander Zanden, J. W. (1988). *The social experience: An introduction to sociology.* New York: Random House.

Wilensky, H. L. (1961). Life style, work situation, and participation in formal associations. In R. W. Kleemeier (Ed.), *Aging and leisure.* New York: Oxford University Press.

Wingrove, C. R., & Alston, J. (1974). Age, aging and church attendance. *The Gerontologist, 11* (4), 356–358.

Young, G., & Dowling, W. (1987). Dimensions of religiosity in old age: Accounting for variation in types of participation. *Journal of Gerontology, 42* (4), 376–380.

Zuckerman, D., Kasl, S., & Ostfeld, A. M. (1984). Psychosocial predictors of mortality among the elderly poor: The role of religion, well-being, and social contacts. *American Journal of Epidemiology, 119,* 410–423.

CHAPTER 15

RACIAL AND ETHNIC AGING

The United States has been described as a *melting pot* in which ethnic minorities lose their distinctive character and become assimilated into the broader culture. Recently, the ideology of the melting pot has been challenged by those who emphasize the pluralism of U.S. society. Cultural pluralism exists in a society when ethnic and racial groups are able to retain their unique character and when they are also able to participate equally in key roles in the society. Unfortunately, U.S. society cannot be characterized as a place where opportunities to participate in key roles in society have been distributed equally. Still, whether the United States is a melting pot or a culturally pluralistic society may be an academic question. Clearly, as much as any society in the world, the United States has retained enormous ethnic and racial diversity.

Andrew Greeley (1974) uses the notion of ethnogenesis to explain this diversity. *Ethnogenesis* describes a model of ethnic relations in which pressures to assimilate exist alongside pressures to maintain ethnic identification. In this model, maintaining an ethnic identity becomes a device for expressing group interests and maintaining group identity. Glazer and Moynihan, in their book *Beyond the Melting Pot,* anticipated the ethnogenesis perspective. They recognized, for example, that European immigrants often lost original customs and ways by the third generation yet still "voted differently, had different ideas about education and sex, and were still, in many essential ways, as different from one another as their grandfathers had been" (1963).

Recognition of the ethnic and racial diversity present in the U.S. experience has only recently begun to have an impact on the field of social gerontology. Clearly, much of what has been learned about aging stems from studies of working- and middle-class whites. Robert Kastenbaum has written in characterizing the great majority of studies carried out on aged white samples, "Any resemblance to the aging non-Caucasian is accidental and unintentional" (1971).

Is there really anything to learn from studying the aging experiences of U.S. minorities? After all, there are many commonalities among the elderly that appear to cut across racial and ethnic lines. The greater number of older women and the higher remarriage rates of males, to cite two examples, appear in all elderly groups in the United States, regardless of racial and ethnic identification. Noted gerontologist Donald Kent (1971a, 1971b) believed that the study of minority patterns of aging was important for practical as well as theoretical reasons. According to Kent, from a practical point of view, it is important to remember that the aggregate number of minority aged is substantial, and these individuals are underrepresented among the prosperous and healthy. Thus, humanitarian considerations urge the study of minority aged. From a theoretical point of view, it is important that ideas about the aging process be generalizable across cultural groups. There is no way to accomplish this without studying a variety of aged groups. In addition, researchers often learn most about how their ideas work when they observe them in "extreme" situations. The position of minority aged in the United States makes it possible to test principles of aging in just such extreme situations.

MINORITY AGING—A CASE
OF DOUBLE JEOPARDY?

Minority aging has been characterized by many as a case of *double jeopardy* (Jackson, 1970, 1971; U.S. Senate, 1971).[1] This term is used to reflect the idea that the negative effects of aging are compounded among minority group members. The suggestion is that aged minority group members suffer age *and* race discrimination. Inherent in the concept of double jeopardy is the idea of comparison. Generally, researchers and policymakers have employed the concept to determine whether minority group members are more disadvantaged than are whites in the same age groupings. For example, the U.S. Senate Special Committee on Aging reported that, compared to the white aged, minority aged "are less well educated, have less income, suffer more illnesses and earlier death, have poorer quality housing and less choice as to where they live and where they work, and, in general, have a less satisfying quality of life" (1971). The Senate Committee followed this up by suggesting that social policy be generated to reflect these differences.

Dowd and Bengtson (1978) have empirically tested the hypothesis of minority aging as a double jeopardy. These authors analyzed data collected as part of a larger survey of adult (ages 45 to 74) African American, Mexican American, and Anglo residents of Los Angeles County. The researchers divided each group into

---

[1]Some social scientists have used the term *triple jeopardy* to represent the position of minority aged. The reference is to being old, poor, and a member of a minority group. Jackson (1971) has used the designation *quadruple jeopardy* to represent those who are black, female, old, and poor.

three age strata—45 to 54, 55 to 64, and 65 to 74 years old—and compared them on a series of variables that included (1) total family income, (2) self-assessed health, (3) two measures of life satisfaction, and (4) a series of social interaction items.

Income

The data gathered by Dowd and Bengtson (1978) showed that, although the incomes of all groups decline with age, the mean income reported by the oldest (ages 65 to 74) African American and Mexican American respondents is considerably lower than any other group. The relative decline in income from ages 45 to 74 was also substantially greater for minority respondents than it is for whites. This decline was 36 percent for whites, 55 percent for African Americans, and 62 percent for Mexican Americans.

Health

Older minority respondents reported poorer health than white respondents when asked, "In general, would you say your health is very good, good, fair, poor, or very poor?" The average health scores of African Americans and Mexican Americans declined 13 and 19 percent, respectively, across the age strata represented in the sample. The decline for whites was only 9 percent. The data on self-assessed health is quite consistent with observed differences on so-called objective measures of morbidity and mortality. Dowd and Bengtson (1978) attribute these health differences to past and present policies of racial discrimination, which have caused nonwhites to have lower incomes, inadequate nutrition, and poorer health than whites.

In general, the data on income and self-assessment of health from this study support the double-jeopardy hypothesis.

Life Satisfaction

Two measures of life satisfaction were analyzed in this study: *tranquility* and *optimism*. Both measures reflect different configurations of responses to 11 items concerning life satisfaction. A typical item related to optimism was: "As you get older, do you feel less useful?" A negative response indicated life satisfaction. An item related to tranquility was: "Do you worry so much that you can't sleep?" Presumably, a negative response here would indicate life satisfaction.

The tranquility scores of Mexican Americans ages 65 to 74 are significantly lower than those of whites and African Americans. The decline in scores across the three age strata for Mexican Americans is so slight, however, it questions the impact of age on tranquility scores. This indicates that, at least with regard to this dimension, aging is not jeopardizing the life satisfaction of Mexican Americans. The pattern is different for the second measure of life satisfaction, optimism, and clearly supports the double-jeopardy hypothesis. Mexican Americans show a significant decline in optimism with age; their optimism scores are significantly lower than the scores of whites; and the differences in scores when compared to whites increases with age. Whites show a 2-percent decline in average optimism scores between those aged 45 to 54 and those aged 65 to 74, whereas the decline for Mexican Americans is 23 percent.

When African Americans and whites are compared on the two measures of life satisfaction, the differences present between younger respondents *narrow* and almost disappear entirely with age. This *leveling* phenomenon will be discussed in more detail later.

Social Interaction

One measure of social interaction involved asking respondents the frequency with which they had contact with children and grandchildren. This measure can be considered a quality-of-life variable. The reliable presence of family members can be an important social support for people making the transition to old age in U.S. society (Dowd & Bengtson, 1978).

Mexican Americans at every age report the most frequent contact with their children and grandchildren. Relative to whites, African Americans maintain an advantageous position on this measure in all but the oldest age stratum. A similar pattern exists on a second measure of social interaction, which asked respondents about their contacts with other relatives. Younger whites had fewer contacts with relatives than either African Americans or Mexican Americans, although the dif-

The reliable presence of family members can be an important social support for people as they age.

ferences become smaller in the older age groups. The result is a *leveling of differences* across the ethnic groups.

Finally, a third measure of interaction asked respondents about the frequency of their contacts with neighbors and friends. Whites report higher levels of contact with friends and neighbors than African Americans and Mexican Americans at all ages, and their contacts increase with age. The lower social interaction of African Americans and Mexican Americans on this measure remains essentially stable across the age groups. Thus, although ethnic differences are present in frequency of contact with friends and neighbors, the absence of age as an influence on this variable for African Americans and Mexican Americans creates a situation that does not constitute a double jeopardy.

In summary, Dowd and Bengtson's (1978) study finds the notion of double jeopardy to characterize accurately the situation of minority aged (African Americans and Mexican Americans) on selected variables (especially income and self-assessment of health). Interestingly, the data also suggest that aging influences some variables in ways that *reduce* ethnic differences that existed in midlife. Kent (1971a, 1971b; Kent & Hirsch, 1969) has written of age as a *mediator* of racial and social differences. From this perspective, the problems faced by old people are seen as very similar regardless of ethnic or racial background. Kent states, "This is not to say that the same proportion of each age group faces these problems; obviously they do not. The point, however, is that if we concentrate on the group rather than on the problem, we shall be treating symptoms rather than causes."

Some believe that too much attention continues to be focused on the concept of double jeopardy. They argue that, at best, the concept may be period bound and unable to capture the most recent social and political changes in the status of minority group members. At worst, investigators who have used the concept can be accused of providing very little useful information about age changes "in the statuses, roles, interpersonal relationships, attitudes, and values of adult minority individuals or populations as they age in their later years" (Jackson, 1985).

Data on the comparative average disadvantage of minority aged may not be particularly useful for recognizing diversity in the total minority aged population or within a specific subgroup such as aged African American males (Kart, 1990). The concept of double jeopardy has been employed in many studies in a fashion that suggests insensitivity to issues of aging and social change. Most researchers interested in measuring double jeopardy have used cross-sectional data that confound age and cohort effects. For example, income differences between young-old and old-old African American males are not a function of age alone, but also of differences in educational achievement and occupational and wage histories of males in different birth cohorts. Further, although there is abundant literature on racial differences in patterns of aging, very little attention has been paid to the issue of how social change differentially affects racial groups.

Schaie, Orchowsky, and Parham (1982) have used data on the life satisfaction of white and African American respondents in the 1973 and 1977 General Social Surveys to show "the interacting effect of race not only with age, but also with cohort and period effects." They determined that there were significant cohort effects in life satisfaction favoring earlier-born cohorts, regardless of race (even while controlling for health and income). Nevertheless, there were race differences across the period studied, with life satisfaction increasing for African Americans and remaining stable for whites. The authors speculate that this finding may result from African American respondents, on average, "beginning to perceive positive societal changes, which affect their overall levels of life satisfaction." This work may provide a model for moving beyond the double-jeopardy concept.

Manuel (1982) argues that people need to move beyond the assumption that application of a minority group label can be used as an indication that an individual has experienced the sociocultural events generally thought to be associated with the label. Given the complexity of racial and ethnic identity, the experience of some individuals may more closely resemble that of members of the majority than it will the experience of other members of what is only a nominal reference group. Clearly, there may be diversity within a minority group with regard to the extent and manner in which group members have been victimized by their minority group status. To paraphrase a question asked by Manuel, Can one assume that all aged African American males, for example, have had significantly less of a chance than their white counterparts to participate fully in U.S. institutions? To the contrary, he answers. It can be expected that there will be differential circumstances of aging within minority groups (Manuel, 1982).

AGING AND THE
MINORITY EXPERIENCE

This section describes the situation of aged members of selected racial and ethnic minority groups. In each case, demographic statistics are presented, followed with a discussion of some special aspects of the aging minority experience.

The African American Elderly

The diversity of experience represented in the population of older African Americans cannot be overstated. Each cohort of African Americans in the United States has been exposed to different cultural practices and social and political conditions (Greene & Siegler, 1984). Wilson (1978) has identified three major stages that African Americans in the U.S. have experienced historically. The first stage includes slavery and the post–Civil War period. Stage two is the period of industrial expansion beginning in the last quarter of the nineteenth century and continuing through World War II. The third stage comprises the contemporary era since the end of World War II.

During stages one and two, racial barriers were explicit and designed to systematically deny African Americans access to economic, political, and social resources. Efforts to minimize, neutralize, and even negate the voting privileges of African Americans exemplify these barriers (Simon & Eitzen, 1982). According to Wilson (1978), very few African Americans were employed in industrial plants prior to World War I. In the South, African American labor was restricted largely to agricultural work and domestic services. The emergence of Jim Crow segregation effectively prevented the employment of African Americans in industry. Mechanization reduced the need for farm labor during the 1920s and 1930s, thereby increasing African American unemployment. Along with working-class members, the self-employed, and recent immigrants, African Americans experienced particular hardship during the Great Depression.

The third stage brought change. World War II instigated a wave of African American migrants to the industrial cities of the North. Following the war, this concentration of African Americans in cities increased the likelihood of group actions in response to oppressive conditions in housing, employment, and the like. Increased educational opportunities allowed for the development of a cadre of African American leaders. The civil rights movement of the 1950s and 1960s helped reduce overt discrimination in employment, housing, education, and transportation, and provided African Americans with access to economic and social resources (Eitzen, 1986).

As Greene and Siegler (1984) point out, gains that occurred during the post–World War II period came too late to make appreciable impact on the educational level or economic condition of the oldest cohorts of African American elderly. An African American man who was 85 years of age in 1985 was already completing his work career by the time of the passage of the Civil Rights Act of 1964. Many in the younger cohorts of African American aged have benefited, however, so that social and economic differentiation is greater among the young-old than the old-old.

By 1990, African American elderly made up about 8 percent of the total U.S. elderly population; about 12 percent of the total U.S. population is African American. In general, the U.S. African American population is younger than the population of whites. As Table 15–1 shows, the proportion of the African American population that is old is considerably smaller than that of the white population. Most people attribute this to the lower life expectancy of African Americans. Although the differential in life expectancy between the two races contributes moderately to the relative youthfulness of the African American population, the key factor is the higher fertility among African Americans. Based on fertility during 1990, the number of births a woman could be expected to have in a lifetime was 1.96 for whites and 2.58 for blacks. A total fertility rate of 2.11 represents "replacement level" fertility for the total population. This disparity in fertility rates contributes to the fact that approximately 45 percent of all African Americans are under the age of 25, whereas only about 35 percent of all whites are in this age grouping. The median age of African Americans is roughly 6 years younger than for whites; in 1992, African Americans and whites had median ages of 28.5 and 33.4 years, respectively.

TABLE 15–1   Age Distribution by Race, 1990

Age	Total	White	Black	Hispanic[1]
All ages	100%	100%	100%	100%
0 to 54	80	77	84	90
55 to 64	8	9	7	5
65 to 74	7	8	5	3
75 to 84	4	4	3	2
85+	1	1	1	0
55+	20	22	16	10
65+	12	13	9	5

Source: Statistical Abstract of the United States, 1994 (114th ed.) (Washington, DC: U.S. Bureau of the Census, 1994), Table 20.

[1]Hispanics may be of any race.

As an aside, it is useful to note that the phrase *racial crossover in mortality* describes the fact that the death rate for African Americans in virtually all age groups, except the very aged, is significantly higher than the rate for whites. In the older years, the racial differential declines and, among people in their 80s, a crossover occurs in which the reported death rates of African Americans of both sexes falls below those of whites (Zopf, 1986). Several hypotheses for this crossover effect have been put forth, although hard data are scarce. Some suggest that the effect is an artifact of age misreporting in older African American cohorts, while others argue that genetic and environmental factors combine to produce hardier older African Americans (Jackson, 1988).

Readers should be reminded that the size and age composition of the African American population show wide geographical variation. For example, 26 percent of the total Atlanta metropolitan statistical area (MSA) population was made up of African Americans in 1990; the San Diego MSA was composed of only 6.4 percent African Americans in 1990. Thus, one might expect that the aged African American population of Atlanta is larger by numbers and proportion than is the case for San Diego. These differences reflect the residential patterns of African Americans. Approximately 53 percent of all African Americans live in the South; only 9.4 percent live in the West. Most aged African Americans residing in the North and West have their roots in the South. Moreover, these southern roots have greatly affected African American cultural patterns, including religion, culinary habits, language, and life-style.

Despite the historical situation, African Americans have become urbanites. In 1980, about 85 percent of all African Americans lived in metropolitan areas, and 75 percent of these resided in central cities. By 1990, 68 percent of all African Americans in the United States resided in the 51 metropolitan areas with the largest African American population. African American urbanization has come about at the same time as white suburbanization, leaving many areas in central cities without a sufficient tax base to support programs for the less affluent minority aged.

Aged African Americans fare worse than aged whites across a variety of socioeconomic indicators. Elderly blacks have fewer years of education, lower incomes, and lower occupational status. Census data comparisons for the older population show that 38 percent of African American men and 18 percent of African American women had completed less than five years of formal education, as compared with 8 percent of white men and 7 percent of white women (Taylor & Taylor, 1982).

The median income of older African American couples and singles was only 60 percent of the median income of white couples and 70 percent of white singles (Chen, 1985). This disparity in income levels is reflected in the higher incidence of poverty among elderly African Americans. As was reported earlier in Chapter 11, the poverty rate for aged African Americans is about three times that for aged whites.

A study derived from the 1972 Social Security Survey of the Status of the Elderly (STATEL) shows the relationship between education and income for African Americans (Abbott, 1977). In general, the data indicate that education yields a lower economic return for African Americans than for whites. At all education levels, white elderly were likely to have achieved a higher economic status than African Americans. Among those with a high school diploma or more, African American elderly were twice as likely (20 percent vs. 10 percent for whites) to be found in the lowest quintile of annual income and half as likely (19 percent vs. 36 percent for whites) to be located in the highest quintile. Many African Americans achieved economic status despite less education. The proportion of African Americans in the highest annual income quintile with less than eight years of schooling was 44 percent, whereas for whites, this figure was 8 percent.

Older African Americans are found in the labor force in about the same proportion as older whites; as with African Americans at all other ages, however, their work brings them less income. The work histories of many African Americans have clearly had impact on their retirement income. African American unemployment has been significantly higher than that of whites. African Americans have also been overrepresented in jobs (e.g., domestic service) and industries (nonunionized) that did not afford protection from the whims of the marketplace. Interestingly, Belgrave (1988), using data gathered from African American and white women aged 62 through 66 in Cleveland, Ohio, found that African American women were more likely than whites to have worked steadily most of their adult lives, more likely to be eligible for pensions, but less likely to have retired. Gender is probably the most widely studied predictor of socioeconomic status among aged African Americans. In summarizing this body of work, Taylor and Chatters report that "elderly black women tend to have more years of education than older black men" (1988, p. 436). Despite this educational advantage, however, older African American women have lower levels of occupational prestige, lower incomes, and a higher incidence of poverty.

The health status of older African Americans is generally thought to be poorer than that of older whites (Ferraro, 1987). Krause (1987) made a similar finding, although he identified different stress-related correlates of health status for whites and African Americans. Chronic financial strain was found to be associated with ill health among older whites, while crisis events in the social support network were related to poor health among older African Americans. Krause argues that older African Americans may be more integrated into their communities than are older whites. This social involvement often occurs within the context of family ties and church-related social networks. Still, as Krause points out, social support entails reciprocity and greater involvement in the lives of others. Such involvement in the lives of others can be stressful and detrimental to health, especially when network members experience stressful events.

The disadvantaged health status of older African Americans also is displayed in reduced life expectancy, particularly among males. As a result, many African Americans do not live long enough to collect the benefits of Social Security and other programs for the elderly—even those to which they have contributed through many years of taxation.

Income—or more accurately the lack of it—is probably the most serious problem faced by aged African Americans in the United States. The high rate of poverty among aged African Americans reduces their capacity to deal effectively with other major concerns, including health, crime, transportation, housing, and nutrition. Borrowing from Dancy, one can put a human face on such dry assertions:

> Mrs. Mary C. was a widow. She eked out her existence on a tiny allotment from Social Security.... Mrs. C. had suffered chronic health problems for ten years...regular check-ups by the doctor were important.... On one occasion, after Mrs. C had left the doctor's office and returned to the car, she remarked that the doctor...had written a prescription for her. Mrs. C.'s friend immediately turned her car in the direction of the drugstore. Seeing where her friend was headed, Mrs. C. said, "Oh, no, I'm not going to get the prescription filled now...I'm going to wait until the first of the month." (1977, pp. 12–13)

An unfilled prescription can do nothing to keep Mrs. C. healthy. Lacking resources, however, she must wait until the first of the month when the Social Security check arrives before filling the physician's prescription.

Income is not the only factor affecting the health status of elderly African Americans. Elderly African Americans in San Diego were asked why they did not utilize available health services. They offered several categories of response in addition to finances: fear of illness and consequences, mistrust of physicians and hospitals, language barriers, and transportation (Stanford, 1978).

Fear of crime is a problem for elderly people of all races. Nevertheless, a Michigan survey reports 62 percent of elderly African Americans worried about crime, compared to only 28 percent of whites (Michigan Offices of Services to the Aging, 1975). Many African American elderly reside in poorer inner-city neighborhoods. Often, the official crime statistics simply do not reflect all the victimization of the elderly in such neighborhoods. Old people fear attacks and robberies but also may feel that going to the police is useless. Many remember a time when they were accorded less than first-class citizenship by police and the courts. A similar feeling often arises in another context. One crime-prevention measure suggested by local police departments is direct-deposit mailing. This involves having Social Security and pension checks sent directly to a bank so they cannot be stolen from mailboxes at home. Many African American elderly, however, do not have extensive experience dealing with banks; in addition, many mistrust bank personnel for sometimes failing to treat African Americans with the same respect granted to whites.

About 43 percent of all African American households in the United States were owner occupied in 1991; this compares with 68 percent for whites. Given that homeownership increases with age, it is reasonable to assume that more than 43 percent of the African American elderly own their homes (Stanford, 1990). Still, many elderly African Americans are housing-poor. A M.I.T.-Harvard study on housing in America (Birch et al., 1973) found that in 1970, almost 13 million families (one-sixth of all American families) were in this condition. *Housing-poor* was defined as living in a housing unit with a deficiency in one or more of the following: (1) the ability of the household to afford the unit, (2) the location of the unit, (3) the physical condition of the unit, and (4) the degree of overcrowding.

Housing costs constitute a substantial portion of regular income. According to the Department of Housing and Urban Development (HUD), renters who spend more than 30 percent of before-tax income on housing and homeowners with housing expenditures in excess of 40 percent of income have *excessive housing costs*. The 1987 American Housing Survey estimates that 17 percent of male and 25 percent of female homeowners who live alone have excessive housing costs; 59 percent of the male and 69 percent of the female renters who live alone also have excessive housing costs. Many low-income elderly are simply unable to keep up with the rising rents and maintenance costs.

African American aged are residentially concentrated in central cities and low-income areas; thus, they are somewhat more likely to reside in older housing. Many of the homes owned by the elderly, in general, were built before World War II. In fact, 18.4 percent of all housing units in the U.S. were built before 1940. Many of these units are of high quality, but some are substandard. The slowed rate of housing construction in the early 1990s means that many physically substandard units that might otherwise have been removed from the housing inventory are necessary to provide some degree of shelter for individuals. This undersupply of housing, especially in the inner city, also means that the housing-poor are often crowding two or three generations together in their homes or apartments and are at great risk for homelessness.

Although, in general, the problems of aged African Americans are related to income deprivation, two areas of strength emerge in which participation is not affected by income status: family and religion. These deserve special mention.

African American Family Ties. It has become part of the conventional wisdom that family ties are a source of strength among African Americans. Interestingly, however, much evidence suggests that in the African American experience (particularly the urban experience), the notion of family extends beyond the immediate household. Stack (1970) has shown how family functions are carried out for urban African Americans by clusters of kin who may or may not reside together. She offers the example of Viola Jackson's brother, who, after his wife died, "decided to raise his two sons himself. He kept the two boys and never remarried. His residence has been consistently close to one or another of his sisters who have fed and cared for his two sons" (Stack, 1970).

Elderly African Americans, especially the women, play an important role in this extended kin network which so well characterizes the family life of many urban African Americans. Hill (1971) reports that 48 percent of elderly black women have other related children living with them—in contrast to only 10 percent of similar white families. Another study shows 26 percent of African American aged taking grandchildren into their homes, compared to 15 percent of the white aged (Jackson & Wood, 1976).

One reason African Americans may rely so heavily on family members is that they have little expectation of receiving effective service from social service agencies. This may especially be the case for older African Americans, who have a painful history of inequality, rejection, and ejection when it comes to dealing with such agencies (Dancy, 1977). Furthermore, as Dancy (1977) points out:

1. Elderly blacks often lack full knowledge or understanding of the service or benefits to which they are entitled.
2. They are cynical about promised services.
3. Most older blacks have no influence whatsoever on programs and services.
4. Few meaningful and needed services are located in their communities.

Family members often value their aged relations because they serve as important role models. Dancy (1977) lists four strengths of the African American elderly that may be useful to remember.

1. The accumulation of wisdom, knowledge, and common sense about life comes not only from age but from the experience of hardship and suffering.
2. A creative genius allows them to do much with little.
3. The ability to accept aging results from their belief that old age is a reward in itself. They are less likely to deny their age than those in the dominant society. Many elderly African Americans voice this sentiment: "I thank the Lord that He spared me!"
4. They maintain a sense of hope and optimism for a better day.

The African American Church. In general, religion is a source of strength to African American elderly. Historically, the church has been a frame of reference for African Americans in coping with racial discrimination, and it has played a role in their survival and advancement. The church is one institution that African Americans control locally; it has remained relatively free from white authority.

AGING AFRICAN AMERICANS AND THEIR CHILDREN
Gender Issues

Surprisingly, the literature on the position of the elderly within African American kin networks has ignored issues of gender. Several reviews do assert that elderly African American women are more integrated into extended kin networks, but few studies have actually focused on gender differences in interaction between older African American adults and their children.

Spitze and Miner (1992) studied contact between aging African American parents and their adult children using a subsample of over 500 respondents aged 55 and over from the 1984 Supplement on Aging to the National Health Interview Survey. Each respondent had at least one child but lived independently of their children. Respondents were asked how frequently they visited with any child and how frequently they talked on the telephone with any child.

Men received substantially fewer visits and telephone calls, on average, per year than did women. Men who lived alone had fewer visits and less telephone contact with children than men who lived with others, and fewer of both types of contact with children than women who lived alone. For many of these men, isolation from children is not related to aging; because of divorce or nonmarital birth, many of these men may have had little contact with children for years.

Women with higher levels of education had less contact in person with children. Distance from nearest child also had nega-tive impact on contact. Women's visits were affected positively by both the number of their sons and daughters; their telephone contacts were also affected by the number of daughters. Men's visits with children were affected only by the number of daughters they had.

The process of determining contact with children, Spitze and Miner argue, is highly similar for both men and women, with the exception of living alone. They suggest that this effect is related to marital status and reflects historical differences in living arrangement with children.

A number of researchers have already started to specify the potential for future isolation from children among middle-aged Baby Boom fathers who have not had custody of children following divorce. Until now, most of the focus has been on the consequences to the children of growing up without much contact with their fathers. Spitze and Miner shift that focus to the consequences on aging parents and their relations with their adult children.

Do elderly African American men who are not married, live alone, and are also less involved with their children find that their needs for social interaction and assistance go unmet? Is the pattern observed by Spitze and Miner in the African American community simply precursor of what is yet to come in the population at large? Only time, data sets with better information on marital and custodial histories, and contact with adult children will tell.

The so-called African American church is really many churches, including traditional Protestant denominations such as Baptists and Methodists as well as fundamentalist groups. Religious behavior within these churches often differs from that in comparable white churches. The African American church is a place of expression, and worship frequently takes the form of celebration.

Religion is a main involvement of many African American elderly. For most, this simply reflects the continuation of a lifelong trend. Church attendance and participation in church activities were important early in life and continue to be so in later life. Participation in church activities provides an opportunity for many to "be somebody." African American elderly receive high status and respectability in the community as a function of such participation.

> Mr. John Jordon worked as a baggage handler. . . . He was in his late fifties and had worked for twenty-five years for the same company. . . . He had been passed over. . . for promotion to a job with more pay and responsibility. . . . He was told that he was "not ready" or lacked the skills or was given other excuses. Yet he saw whites with the same education as his—tenth grade—get better opportunities. What kept Mr. Jordon from becoming demoralized and bitter was his church. . . . Now he was also treasurer of the church—a job of enormous responsibility. . . . Mr. Jordon's church appreciated his talents, and Mr. Jordon was a faithful man and loved his church. There he was somebody. (Dancy, 1977)

Finally, considering the influential position of the church in the African American community, it is essential that service providers understand the roles the church plays in the lives of African American elderly. The church is not only a place where large numbers of elderly can be reached but it is also a place where needs can be assessed and services delivered.

The Hispanic Aged

In 1990, Hispanic Americans constituted 9 percent of the U.S. population, or over 22 million people. Next to African Americans, they make up the largest minority in the United States. The Hispanic population is fast growing, with birthrates and immigration rates relatively high. Officially, this population increased by 50 percent between 1970 and 1980, and by 53 percent between 1980 and 1990. Few doubt that the actual rate of growth has been higher as a function of illegal immigration. Current U.S. Bureau of the Census projections show the Hispanic population exceeding the African American population in the U.S. by the year 2010, making it the nation's largest minority group.

The Hispanic population is a heterogeneous group. About 63 percent of all Hispanic Americans are Mexican, 11 percent are Puerto Rican, and 24 percent are of other Hispanic heritage, including Cubans and those from Central and South America. The diversity of the population has created real problems for researchers and helps explain why so little systematic research is carried out on Hispanic Americans. Hispanic Americans are not easily categorized; attempts to generalize from Cubans in Florida to Puerto Ricans in New York and Mexican Americans in California is likely to bear little fruit. In addition, Hispanics are one of the youngest ethnic groups in the United States; as seen in Table 15–1, the elderly account for only about 5 percent of the total Hispanic population. In light of the major problems faced by the population, in general, the special concerns of the elderly have not emerged with a visibility in any way comparable to the situation among Anglos. Until this changes, gerontologists are forced to rely on widely and varied sources for relevant materials. Because much of this available (although scarce) literature concerns itself with Mexican Americans, they dominate the discussion here. This is the case, despite the fact that the proportion of Mexican Americans who are 65 years or older is lower than for Cubans, Puerto Ricans, and other Hispanics (see Table 15–2).

The Hispanic population is concentrated largely in the southwestern states of California and Texas, where 54 percent of all Hispanics were projected to be living in 1995. Most of these people are of Mexican descent. A majority of Puerto Ricans live in New York and New Jersey; in 1990, 15.4 percent of the 18 million or so residents of the New York consolidated metropolitan area were of Hispanic origin. Cubans have settled primarily in Florida; in 1990, 33.3 percent of the 3.2 million residents of the Miami-Fort Lauderdale metropolitan area were of Hispanic origin. A majority of the Hispanic population resides in urban areas, with most living in central cities.

About half of the Hispanic elderly are foreign born. Cubans and Puerto Ricans are more recent migrants than Mexican Americans, many of whom are descendants of original settlers of territories annexed by the United States in the Mexican-American War. The Hispanic American population is an even younger population than African Americans (30 percent under 15 years of age vs. 27.2 percent for African Americans in 1990). High fertility and large family size, in addition to immigration of the young and repatriation of the middle-aged, contribute to the youthfulness of this group.

Overall, a lower proportion of Hispanic Americans than African Americans were college educated by 1993 (9.0 percent vs. 12.2 percent, respectively). However, a higher proportion of Hispanics than African Americans are employed (58.9 percent vs. 54.4 percent, respectively, in 1993) and Hispanics have a higher 1993 median income than blacks ($23,912 vs. $21,161, respectively) (U.S. Bureau of the Census 1994, Tables 49 and 53). One in five (22.0 percent) Hispanic elderly persons lived below the poverty level in 1992. The proportion of Hispanic Americans holding professional or technical jobs is less than half the proportion for whites. As Hendricks and Hendricks (1977) point out, however, there are marked differences

TABLE 15–2   Age Distribution of Hispanic Population, 1993

Age	Hispanic Total	Mexican	Puerto Rican	Cuban	Central and South American	Other Hispanics
Under 5 years	11.7%	12.2%	10.4%	4.6%	10.0%	8.3%
5 to 14 years	18.5	20.1	20.6	7.9	15.1	14.1
15 to 44 years	50.7	50.9	48.4	40.1	56.7	47.5
45 to 64 years	14.4	12.6	14.8	27.2	14.3	21.5
65 years +	5.4	4.2	5.7	20.3	3.9	8.4

Source: U.S. Bureau of the Census, 1994, Table 53.

between Cubans and other Hispanic people, who more frequently hold high-paying jobs, and Mexican Americans and Puerto Ricans found in lower-income manual labor occupations. Many elderly Hispanics work in unskilled labor or as farm workers. According to Barrow and Smith (1979), they stay in the labor force longer than white elderly. Few have had lengthy work careers in settings that provide retirement preparation. Others either entered the country illegally or have failed to maintain certification of their residential status as aliens. In either case, they forfeit benefits and services for which they might otherwise be eligible.

It would make sense that, as with African American elderly, the problems of Hispanic elderly emanate from their deprived income status. Yet, an early study of the expressed needs of a Hispanic elderly population showed income to be fourth on the list (Valle & Mendoza, 1978). For these elderly Hispanics in San Diego, health, transportation, and concerns about children preceded income as a "present cause of greatest concern." Steglich, Cartwright, and Crouch (1968) also found health to be a priority need among Mexican American elderly in Lubbock, Texas. Torres-Gil (1976) indicated lack of money, inadequate transportation, and health as major areas of concern among elderly Mexican Americans in San Jose.

Often, the special needs of Hispanic elderly are understated because of the popular assumption that they are properly cared for within the context of the extended family. Aged Hispanics are seen as receiving positive emotional and social support because of their unique position as older family members. Historically, this popular view of Mexican Americans may have been correct; today, however, it is incomplete and misleading. For example, many widowed women over age 75 do live in an extended family household. Those who live alone, however, are often found in inadequate housing, with the incidence of substandard housing greater among Hispanics than among whites (Cuellar, 1990).

The traditional Mexican American family has been described as a supportive and flexible structure that assumes a variety of functions in dealing with the environment and with the emotional and psychological aspects of the family unit and individuals (Sotomayor, 1971). Such a family pattern maintains the elderly within the physical and social life of the family, thus reducing the likelihood of isolation. In general, the aged person holds high status and has considerable influence in the family's social life.

Recognition of the concept of *machismo* has led many to characterize the Mexican American family as a patriarchal structure. The most emphasized aspect of *machismo* has to do with sexual prowess (Alvirez & Bean, 1976). From early childhood, males are given more freedom than females and are socialized into "manliness." This includes playing the dominant role in the family. Women are expected to be submissive and to subordinate their needs to those of the husband and other family members (Alvirez & Bean, 1976).

Maldonado (1975) argues that this division of labor in the Mexican American family often changes as family members grow older. Close observation, he says, reveals that the woman plays an increasingly more active role as she grows older, to the point that the grandmother may be dominant in the extended family. In part, this may reflect the higher early death rate among Mexican American males.

To a great extent, the foregoing describes a picture of the Mexican American family that *does not* take into account the rapidly changing situation in the Mexican American community (Maldonado, 1975). These changes, which may have a negative impact on the elderly, include the increased urbanization of Mexican Americans ("barrioization") and the gradual movement toward a stronger nuclear family. Many elderly now find themselves either in a small town or rural community isolated from their children, or in a barrio where, because of the social and educational mobility of the young, their status and influence have declined significantly. This generation gap leaves elderly Chicanos misunderstood by the society at large and by younger members of their own families. In addition, the general society, with its obsolete understanding of Chicano culture, believes that the Chicano family will provide for its older members, which the younger Chicano generation is having an increasingly difficult time doing (Maldonado, 1975). Although patterns of intergenerational assistance remain strong, especially in comparison to white populations, more older Mexican Americans are reporting unfulfilled expectations of filial responsibility by their adult children (Markides, Boldt, & Ray, 1986; Markides, Liang, & Jackson, 1990).

Despite the tension between the generations instigated by social changes in the Mexican American community, there is still some evidence that Chicano families are maintaining respect for the elderly. One example of this is reflected in the underutilization of nursing home facilities by Mexican American elderly. Eribes and Bradley-Rawls (1977) attribute this underutilization to the fact that nursing homes are not as yet viewed as a culturally viable alternative to the Mexican-American family handling the housing and medical care of their elderly.

Nursing home placement may truly be the choice of last resort for Hispanics (Eribes & Bradley-Rawls, 1978). Reviewing the records of admission to one nursing home in New York City, Espino and colleagues (1988) found Puerto Rican/Hispanic patients to be younger and more impaired than their non-Hispanic counterparts. These researchers argued "that Puerto Rican/Hispanics are cared for in the community longer in that higher degrees of disability are reached and that these levels are reached at a younger age. At that point they or their families are forced to choose institutionalization" (1988, pp. 823–824).

The Native American Aged

The aged Native American population is small and relatively invisible. Despite the enormous diversity among Native American cultures (500 federally recognized tribes and nearly 200 native languages spoken), they suffer deprivation by any social or economic indicator employed. To a great extent, this reflects the special history of Native Americans and their relationship with the U.S. government. Certainly, no other minority group has been as physically and socially isolated from the mainstream of U.S. life.

The total population of Native Americans in 1990 (including Eskimos and Aleuts) was approximately 2.0 million. A century or so ago, anthropologists estimated that the aboriginal population of North America before contact with the Europeans (circa 1600) was between 500,000 and 1.5 million persons. Some critics have suggested that these figures are too low and were generated for the purpose of legitimating European conquest of an allegedly unoccupied land (Feagin, 1984). A considered estimate by Dobyns (1966) puts the number of Native Americans in North America at near 10 million at the time of the initial European contact. European diseases and firepower sharply reduced the number of Native Americans to a low point of about 200,000 in 1850.

Benedict (1972) considers this decrease to be a unique occurrence in American history. He has written, "Although other minority groups have experienced involuntary relocation and social and economic discrimination, none seems to have been subjected to a similar assault on life itself" (1972). Despite general agreement that high fertility and reduced mortality has contributed to an increase in the Native American population, current estimates should be regarded as crude. The Bureau of Indian Affairs (BIA) and the U.S. Census Bureau often disagree on their respective estimates. As an additional problem, the 1970 census initiated self-designation as an enumeration technique for the category "Native American."

About 48 percent of the Native American population resides in the western United States, although the largest concentrations of native people are found in Oklahoma, Arizona, California, and New Mexico. Oklahoma, California, and Arizona all had in excess of 200,000 Native Americans in 1990. Almost two-thirds of the native population resides on or near a reservation; the remainder are urbanized. This is the only minority group that is less urbanized than the U.S. population as a whole. Los Angeles has the most Native Americans of any urban area, approximately 87,000. Tulsa, New York, Oklahoma City, and San Francisco all had over 40,000 Native Americans in 1990. The urbanization of this population is a relatively recent phenomenon. Bahr (1972) suggests this migration was triggered by the push factors of poverty and unemployment on reservations and the pull factor of expanding economic opportunities located in the cities.

The Native American population is quite young. The median age in 1980 was 23; by 1992, it was 26.4 years. Women live longer than men. About 5.2 percent of this population is 65 years or older. The fertility rate for 1993 was 2.8, higher than that of either white (2.0) or African Americans (2.5). Life expectancy among Native Americans has increased to 71.1 years by 1980, according to the Indian Health Services (1990). If this is true, it is a remarkable improvement likely resulting from control of infectious diseases and making acute medical care available (John, 1991). Several researchers have pointed out that Native Americans exhibit a mortality crossover with the white population at about age 65, much earlier than for African Americans (John, 1991). High mortality rates at younger ages may be associated with selective survival of healthier elderly Native Americans (Kunitz & Levy, 1989; Markides & Machelek, 1984).

The contemporary Native American experience is characterized by poverty; the official poverty rate among this group in 1980 was 23.7 percent; some estimate the real rate at closer to 50 percent (Kramer, 1991, 1992). Typically, Native Americans are concentrated in unskilled, semiskilled, and low-wage service jobs. Work in these job categories is often seasonal. Unemployment is considerably higher than the national average. Historically, the unemployment rate among Native Americans was more than double that of whites—and these rates do not include the large numbers who have given up looking for work. Retirement is both a luxury and a hardship for this population. For many, there has been no work from which to retire. As Benedict (1972) points out, old age is simply a continuation of a state of economic deprivation to which Native Americans have had ample time to accustom themselves.

Formal educational attainment levels for Native Americans of all ages lag behind those of whites. Remember, however, that aged Native Americans were of school age at a time when only a small percentage attended any type of formal school. Schooling took place within informal tribal circles. The few boarding schools (run by the BIA) and mission schools were often oppressive environments that attempted to enforce acculturation. Students were punished for speaking native languages, and Native American values were denigrated. Until very recently, this remained an accurate characterization of the educational environments in which Native Americans found themselves.

Although the diversity of tribal cultures makes generalization difficult, it is fair to say that the status of elderly Native Americans has undergone enormous change in the last 100 years or so. According to Simmons (1945), most North American Indian societies ensured respect for the aged—at least until they were obviously powerless and incompetent. Close inspection, however, shows that respect was given not simply as a function of age but rather on the basis of some particular asset that an older person possessed. The range of avenues that afforded access to homage was great. An individual might be respected for extensive knowledge, seasoned experience, expert skill, power to work magic, control of property rights, or skill in games, dances, songs, and storytelling. The Iroquois associated long life with wisdom. A common prayer began, "Preserve our old men among us. . . ." Among the Chippewa, the elderly men held the central positions in council gatherings where the young were expected to sit in silence. Aged Navaho women were custodians of much property and highly regarded in both family and public life.

Much has changed. Today, elderly Native Americans are, for the most part, ministered to by government bureaucracies. Social and financial services are provided by the Bureau of Indian Affairs; health needs are provided by the Public Health Service (In the 1990s, Native American health conditions are among the worst in the United States.) The way these programs are operated often denies the old their traditional position in tribal society. According to Native American advocates, the Bureau of Indian Affairs expends 90 percent of its annual $3 billion budget on maintaining and supporting the bureaucracy, with only 10 percent going to services for Native American people (Cook, 1990).

No program can immunize the Native American elderly from a lifetime of inadequate nutrition, housing, and health services. These deprivations usually take their toll long before old age. Clearly, many changes must be made before future generations of elderly Native Americans can expect a better day.

The Pacific Asian Aged

The median family income of Pacific Asian Americans was $43,418 in 1992—higher than for all other racial groups, including whites. No wonder, then, that Pacific Asian Americans are characterized as being a successful model minority. This concept of *model minority* describes the general belief that Pacific Asian families—and communities, for that matter—are stable and in full command of their social and economic concerns.

Kim (1973) argues that this view of Asian Americans as a model minority supports a myth and is a convenient device for excluding them from programs related to education, health, housing, and employment. He suspects that behind the prosperous shops of the Chinatowns and Little Tokyos are thousands of disaffiliated old people waiting out their remaining years in poverty and ill health. This view is supported by a White House Conference on Aging report:

> The Asian American elderly are severely handicapped by the myth that pervades society at large and permeates the policy decisions of agencies and governmental entities . . . that Asian American aged do not have any problems, that Asian Americans are able to take care of their own, and that Asian American aged do not need or desire aid in any form. (1972)

This report characterizes older Asian Americans as:

1. Having problems that are, in many respects, more intensive and complex than the problems of the general senior citizen population
2. Being excluded by cultural barriers from receiving their rightful benefits
3. Committing suicide at a rate three times the national average
4. Being among the people most neglected by programs presumably serving all elderly

Kalish and Moriwaki (1973) believe that the situation of older Asian Americans cannot be grasped without an understanding of four factors: (1) their cultural origins and the effects of early socialization, (2) their life history in the United States, (3) those age-related changes that occur regardless of early learning and/or ethnicity, and (4) their expectations concerning what it means to be old. These factors are integrated with brief discussions of two of the largest elderly Asian American populations: the Japanese and the Chinese. First, however, is a description of the general characteristics of the older Pacific Asian American population.

Over 7 million Pacific Asian Americans were recorded in the 1990 census; this is equivalent to 2.9 percent of the total population and about 15 percent of the non-white population in the United States. Among the largest Asian American groups in the United States are the Chinese, Filipinos, Japanese, Asian Indians, and Koreans. Most Pacific Asian Americans are urbanites, residing in ethnic enclaves in cities such as Los Angeles, San Francisco, New York, and Honolulu. Each of these metropolitan areas is home to over 500,000 people of Asian or Pacific Islander descent. About 15 percent of the San Francisco metropolitan area population is composed of Asian and Pacific Islanders.

Although the sex ratio among Japanese American elderly is comparable to that for whites, a majority of Chinese elderly and Filipino elderly are males. This reflects historically restrictive immigration laws, especially for Chinese and Filipinos, which often denied entry to women and children. Like earlier immigrants, without language and labor skills, Asian men were exploited. They were used as cheap labor in mining, canning, farming, and railroad work. Even now, this experience has an impact on elderly men who survived the exploitation. One study of the Chinese carried out under the auspices of the Community Service Society (CSS) of New York reported that nearly one-third of the older unattached men in the CSS caseload had no contact with a public or voluntary agency. Many were eligible for public support and needed it, but refused to apply when they discovered the sort of personal information they were required to provide (Cattell, 1962, cited in Fujii, 1976).

Despite earlier comments about the exalted income status of Asian Americans in general, the income status of older Pacific Asian Americans is quite low. Poverty rate estimates vary among different groups of Pacific Asian elders from 14 percent to over 40 percent for oldest-old female heads of households (Gould, 1989; Liu, 1986). Most elderly Asians have spent considerable employment time in low-paying jobs or in jobs not covered by Social Security or other pension programs. In a study of Chinese elderly in San Diego (Cheng, 1978), median monthly income was reported to be $214. Many elderly Asians are still employed as farmers or in small businesses. Occupations commonly held by the women included garment factory or cannery work, helping their husbands in a family business, semiskilled labor, and office/clerical work.

Elderly Japanese Americans. The significant migration of Japanese to the United States occurred after 1890. Many came to this country as sojourners with an intent to stay a while, establish themselves financially, and then return home. Migrants were young, uneducated, and unskilled. Hostility against the Japanese was great. Racist attitudes were prevalent: The Japanese were said to be wily, lacking in morals, and inassimilable. Discriminatory laws and local nuisance ordinances were used to limit the activities of Japanese. Unions were successful in excluding Japanese, and city governments were pressured into refusing permits to Japanese businesses. In 1913, California passed an Alien Land Law, which disallowed land purchase or lease on the part of Japanese Americans. The Immigration Act of 1924 placed severe restrictions on Japanese immigration to this country. This hostility culminated during World War II, when all people of Japanese ancestry were evacuated from their homes along the West Coast and placed in "relocation camps." No people of Italian or German ancestry were similarly evacuated.

After the war, the camps were closed, and treatment of Japanese Americans improved. In general, the group has made enormous progress since 1950; they are upwardly mobile. This success has been attributed to Japanese American family life (Kitano & Kikumura, 1976).

In traditional Japan, families occupied a central position. The extended family was an associational and supportive institution and most important for early socialization and upbringing. Marriage was often arranged by a father intent on maintaining family solidarity. The father/son relationship was preeminent in the family; women were dutiful and deferred to men. Caring for aged parents was the responsibility of the eldest son in particular, although clearly all adult children were expected to bear some responsibility in this area.

Among the first Japanese American families (called *Issei*), this traditional family picture survived in some modified form. As Kitano and Kikumura (1976) point out, there were no grandparents to serve as reminders of old traditions, and many immigrants felt free to Americanize. One powerful constraint on assimilation was the norm of *enyro* brought from Japan and still in existence in the United States. This norm is related to power and regulates how those who have power are to behave toward those without it (and vice versa). In the Japanese family and community, power and privilege were associated with the father. In the U.S. context, the norm *enryo* helped reinforce this association, even when the Japanese father was subject to the humiliation and abuse of whites outside the family. Montero (1979) has described the continued importance of the family to Issei elderly. He points to data showing the disengagement of elderly Japanese Americans from many social and organizational ties, but the continued existence of a strong family support system. It is the adult children with whom Issei visit regularly and frequently who form the foundation of this family support system (Montero, 1979).

Pressures to assimilate increased for subsequent generations of Japanese (*Nisei* and *Sansei*). Data presented earlier on the income status of Japanese Americans reflects their successful economic assimilation. Cultural assimilation, particularly in regard to language and religion, also advanced among Nisei and Sansei. Feagin and Fujitaki (1972), in a 1969–70, study, found Nisei and Sansei showed significant acculturation with respect to speaking English at home, not reading Japanese literature, and not feeling it was essential to maintain Japanese traditions.

Kalish and Moriwaki (1973) have written of the problems created as different generations of Japanese come to reflect different degrees of assimilation to the U.S. context. As an example, they use the theme of filial piety—"honor thy father and thy mother"—which is common in Western as well as East Asian literature. Kalish and Moriwaki argue that the theme of filial piety is undermined by other themes in U.S. culture—independence, self-reliance, and mastery over one's own fate. This creates a situation whereby first-generation elderly retain expectations consistent with the theme of filial piety, while the second- and third-generation members become assimilated into a society "where future potential is more important than past accomplishments in evaluating the worth of a person, [and] the wisdom and the accomplishments of the elderly were often perceived as irrelevant or were forgotten and ignored" (1973). As Nisei and Sansei move into old age, these intergenerational incongruities should lessen. Increased interracial marriage and upward social mobility are also likely to reduce the relevance of traditional values among Japanese Americans. The Japanese American elderly in the future are likely to be more diversified in terms of social class and geographical distribution (Osako & Liu, 1986).

Elderly Chinese Americans.   The Chinese began to arrive in California during the middle of the nineteenth century. Railroad and mining agents often went to China to recruit laborers with promises of work, higher wages, and free passage. Racism was rampant against the highly identifiable Chinese. Violence and murder were not uncommon and rarely punished by the authorities. Efforts to expel Chinese from California and other western states began almost with their arrival. California passed exclusion laws in 1852, 1855, and 1858; each was declared unconstitutional by the U.S. Supreme Court. Taxes and other discriminatory devices were used against the Chinese. Article XIX of the California State Constitution, initiated in 1879, prohibited corporations from directly or indirectly employing Chinese (Burkey, 1978). Chinese were considered sinister and inassimilable, with vices bred into them over generations (Burkey, 1978). Federal laws eventually passed in 1882, 1888, 1902, and 1904 severely limited Chinese immigration into this country until World War II. During this period, the Chinese retreated into invisibility. Chinese Americans benefited somewhat from the war, however, because China was an ally of the United States. They were granted citizenship, exempted from land restriction, and permitted to enter professional and commercial activities that previously had been denied to them (Lyman, 1974).

Many Chinese who arrived in the United States had no intention of staying. They came in order to provide for a family left behind with the expectation of returning in order to enjoy the fruits of their labors (Huang, 1976). This may explain why they were able to withstand the racism and hostility encountered in the United States.

Before 1949, when the People's Republic of China assumed control of the mainland, it was the practice of many older immigrants to return to China after they retired. One of the traditional values of the Chinese family is filial piety. Thus, retired immigrants could enjoy a period of old age filled with respect and obedience and surrounded by children and grandchildren they may have never seen. Since 1949, the luxury of returning to the homeland has been taken away from the elderly Chinese immigrant (Huang, 1976).

Like the Japanese, older Chinese Americans may have difficulty adjusting to the American values of children and grandchildren. Huang reports an anecdote in this respect:

> Recently a mother confided in this writer that she and her husband were shocked to receive a letter from their son and Caucasian daughter-in-law. They were happy to hear from them, but not to be addressed as "Dear Jeanie and Jack." "At least she

could address us as Father Wong and Mother Wong," she stated, meaning that undoubtedly it was the American daughter-in-law who instigated such a big dose of democracy in their new relationship. (1976, p. 141)

More serious problems beset aged Chinese Americans as a result of the changing values of the young. For example, drug abuse is apparently high among older Chinese American men, especially those isolated from family and community.

Another problem for older Chinese Americans may involve a new sense of relative deprivation. These feelings result from the recognition that a new glory period for the aged has begun in China where, unlike their U.S. counterparts, the elderly are better off than other segments of the population. A *New York Times* report in 1979 suggests that elderly in China are the beneficiaries of both the traditional Chinese chivalry toward old age and a munificent Communist retirement policy (Butterfield, 1979). According to this report, a retiring worker may bring in one of his or her children as a job replacement. This is a very important consideration under conditions of high unemployment among the young and serves to support the position of aged persons in the family. In addition, early retirees (at age 60) may find a second job, particularly if they are skilled or technical workers in much demand. Between pensions and a second income, earnings can exceed preretirement income. Women may retire at age 50, and many remain at home to care for grandchildren. As another benefit, if retired people agree to move to the countryside, where many of them came from, they receive a stipend from the state to build a new house. In general, it appears that policy decisions in areas such as employment, retirement, and housing have had the consequence of underscoring rather than undermining the position of the aged in the Chinese family and community.

China is no utopia for the old, however. Disparities do exist among the elderly. For example, the oldest segment of the aged, who have not worked in state enterprises, are disadvantaged because they are generally not covered by retirement benefits. In addition, large numbers of older people are left with little to do, because no formally organized recreation programs exist for those elderly not in old-age homes. As one Chinese social researcher interested in the problems of old age commented, "Many are just waiting to die" (Goldstein & Goldstein, 1986).

Assimilation of Elderly Asian American Immigrants. Immigration of Pacific Asian elderly to the United States has continued through the 1970s, 1980s, and into the 1990s, and includes Koreans as well as newer groups such as the Vietnamese and Thai from southeast Asia. How do these elderly immigrants who have grown old in a traditional Asian culture adjust to life in the contemporary United States? Kim and Schwartz-Barcott (1983) did periodic participant observation over seven years with 14 Korean American elderly women ranging in age from 55 to 68 at the time of initial contact. Their results suggest that this small group of women did unexpectedly, though exceptionally, well. All these women arrived in the United States in the early 1970s. They were all from urban areas; seven were widows, two were separated from their husbands, and five were married and came to the United

States with their husbands. They all initially lived with either their son's or daughter's families in Providence, Boston, Los Angeles, and Toronto.

Most of these women experienced a typical progression of adjustment from an initial period of high involvement in family life to a series of steps involving employment in nontraditional roles, movement into a single or shared apartment, and, finally, development of social ties based on friendship rather than family networks. All the women expressed satisfaction at residing with their children's families, although this may have represented the socially acceptable response. Traditionally, it is assumed that women (especially widows) prefer to live with their children rather than alone. Yet, within a year or two of their arrival, many of these women began talking about living independently of the family.

The results of this study suggest (at least in this group of women) that having a living arrangement that allows a peer-group social network to develop along with financial independence provides a greater degree of satisfaction with life than when only either one of these conditions is possible. Interestingly, it appears that after a short period of adjustment to life in the United States, elderly Korean women in this study began to realize that there might be a wide array of options available for independence and social ties outside of family life and traditional roles for elderly women. For these women, achieving independence was an attraction that provided a high level of self-esteem and satisfaction with life.

SUMMARY

Most studies of aging are carried out on samples of whites. Recognition of the ethnic and social diversity present in the U.S. experience has only recently begun to be presented in social gerontology.

Many have characterized minority aging as a case of double jeopardy. This term is used to reflect the idea that the negative effects of aging are compounded among minority group members. Although, in general, research supports the notion of double jeopardy among African American and Mexican American aged, some data suggest that aging may reduce ethnic differences that existed in middle life. Recently, some have contested the importance of a double-jeopardy concept of minority aging.

Lack of income is probably the most serious problem faced by aged African Americans in the United States. Approximately one-third of aged African Americans remain in poverty. This has major impact on the health status of elderly African Americans and underscores problems related to transportation and housing. Two areas of strength that have emerged for African American elderly that are not related to income deprivation are family and religion.

Next to African Americans, Hispanic Americans make up the largest minority in the United States. This population is quite heterogeneous, although about 63 percent of all Hispanic Americans are of Mexican heritage. As with African American elderly, the problems of Hispanic American elderly emanate primarily from their deprived income status. However, a growing generation gap between old and young leaves many elderly Hispanic Americans misunderstood by the society at large and by the young in their own families.

The aged Native American population is quite small and relatively invisible. Their special history has clearly contributed to their deprived situation. No simple social program can immunize the Native American elderly from a lifetime of inadequate nutrition, housing, and health service.

Pacific Asian Americans have been described as a model minority. This may be myth. Despite the successful economic assimilation of Japanese and Chinese Americans, the accommodation of younger generations to U.S. values has left many aged Asian Americans isolated from family and community. If this pattern continues, one can expect future generations of elderly Asian Americans to have expectations and experiences more like those of elderly whites than is currently the case.

STUDY QUESTIONS

1. Define *double jeopardy* as it relates to the minority aged. According to the study by Dowd and Bengtson (1978), how accurately does this term describe the social situation of the U.S. minority aged. Write a brief critique of the double-jeopardy concept.

2. Explain the term *housing-poor*. Why is it so central to any discussion of the African American elderly in the United States?

3. Despite the economic problems that still confront African American elderly, two major strengths of African American culture should not be ignored. Identify and discuss the importance of these strengths.

4. The special needs of Hispanic American elderly are often understated because of the belief that this group takes care of its own. Give a more realistic picture of the modern Hispanic American family.

5. How has the status of elderly Native Americans changed over the last 100 years?

6. Explain what is meant by the concept of *model minority* in referring to Pacific Asian Americans. In what way has this view of Asian Americans been detrimental to the social conditions of their elderly?

REFERENCES

Abbott, J. (1977, July). Socioeconomic characteristics of the elderly: Some black-white differences. *Social Security Bulletin*, 16–42.

Alvirez, D., & Bean, F. (1976). The Mexican-American family. In C. Mindel & R. Habenstein (Eds.), *Ethnic families in America.* New York: Elsevier.

Bahr, H. (1972). An end to invisibility. In H. Bahr, B. Chadwick, & R. C. Day (Eds.), *Native Americans today.* New York: Harper and Row.

Barrow, G., & Smith, P. (1979). *Aging, ageism and society.* St. Paul, MN: West.

Belgrave, L. L. (1988). The effects of race differences in work history, work attitudes, economic resources, and health on women's retirement. *Research on Aging, 10* (3), 383–398.

Benedict, R. (1972). A profile of Indian aged. In *Minority aged in America.* Ann Arbor: University of Michigan.

Birch, D., et al. (1973). *America's housing needs: 1970 to 1980.* Cambridge, MA: Joint

Center for Urban Studies, M.I.T. and Harvard University.

Burkey, R. (1978). *Ethnic and racial groups: The dynamics of dominance.* Menlo, Park, CA: Cummings.

Butterfield, F. (1979). China's elderly find good life in retirement. *New York Times* (July 29), 1, 13.

Cattell, S. (1962). *Health, welfare and social organization in Chinatown.* New York: Community Service Society of New York.

Chen, Y. P. (1985). The economic status of the aging. In R. H. Binstock & E. Shanas (Eds.), *Handbook of aging and the social sciences* (2nd ed.). New York: Van Nostrand Reinhold.

Cheng, E. (1978). *The elder Chinese.* San Diego: Campanile Press, San Diego State University.

Cook, C. D. (1990). American Indian elderly and public policy issues. In M. S. Harper (Ed.), *Minority aging.* DHHS Pub. #HRS (P-DV-90-4). Washington, DC: U.S. Government Printing Office.

Cuellar, J. (1990). Hispanic American aging: Geriatric educational curriculum development for selected health professions. In M. S. Harper (Ed.), *Minority aging.* DHHS Pub. #HRS (P-DV-90-4). Washington, DC: U.S. Government Printing Office.

Dancy, J. (1977). *The black elderly: A guide for practitioners.* Ann Arbor: Institute of Gerontology, University of Michigan-Wayne State University.

Dobyns, H. (1966). Estimating aboriginal American populations. *Current Anthropology, 7,* 395–416.

Dowd, J., & Bengtson, V. (1978). Aging in minority populations: An examination of the double jeopardy hypothesis. *Journal of Gerontology, 33,* 427–436.

Eitzen, D. S. (1986). *Social problems* (3rd ed.). Boston: Allyn and Bacon.

Eribes, R. A., & Bradley-Rawls, M. (1978). *The underutilization of nursing home facilities by Mexican American elderly in the southwest.* Paper presented at 30th annual meeting of the Gerontological Society, San Francisco.

Espino, D. V., Neufeld, R. R., Mulvihill, M., & Libow, L. S. (1988). Hispanic and non-Hispanic elderly on admission to the nursing home: A pilot study. *Gerontologist, 28* (6), 821–824.

Feagin, J. (1984). *Racial and ethnic relations.* (2nd ed.). Englewood Cliffs, NJ: Prentice-Hall.

Feagin, J., & Fujitaki, N. (1972, February). On the assimilation of Japanese Americans. *American Journal, 1,* 15–17.

Ferraro, K. F. (1987). Double jeopardy to health for black older adults? *Journal of Gerontology, 42* (5), 528–533.

Fujii, S. (1976, March). Elderly Asian Americans and use of public services. *Social Casework,* 202–206.

Glazer, N., & Moynihan, D. P. (1963). *Beyond the melting pot.* Cambridge, MA: Harvard University Press and The M.I.T. Press.

Goldstein, A., & Goldstein, S. (1986). The challenge of an aging population: The case of the People's Republic of China. *Research on Aging, 8* (2), 179–199.

Gould, K. H. (1989). A minority-feminist perspective on women and aging. *Journal of Women and Aging, 1,* 195–216.

Greeley, A. (1974). *Ethnicity in the United States.* New York: John Wiley & Sons.

Greene, R. L., & Siegler, I. C. (1984). Blacks. In E. B. Palmore (Ed.), *Handbook on the aged in the United States.* Westport, CT: Greenwood Press.

Hendricks, J., & Hendricks, C. (1977). *Aging in mass society.* Cambridge, MA: Winthrop.

Hill, R. (1971). A profile of the black aged. *Los Angles Sentinel* (October 7).

Huang, L. J. (1976). The Chinese American family. In C. Mindel & R. Habenstein (Eds.), *Ethnic families in America.* New York: Elsevier.

Indian Health Services. (1990). *Trends in Indian health—1990.* Washington, DC: U.S. Government Printing Office.

Jackson, J. J. (1970). Aged negroes: Their cultural departures from statistical stereotypes and rural-urban differences. *Gerontologist, 10,* 140–145.

Jackson, J. J. (1971). Negro aged: Toward needed research in social gerontology. *Gerontologist, 11,* 52–57.

Jackson, J. J (1985). Race, national origin, ethnicity, and aging. In R. H. Binstock & E. Shanas (Eds.), *Handbook of aging and the social sciences* (2nd ed.). New York: Van Nostrand Reinhold.

Jackson, J. S. (1988). Growing old in black america: Research on aging black populations. In J. S. Jackson & others (Eds.), *The black American elderly: Research on physical and psychological health.* New York: Springer.

Jackson, M., & Wood, J. (1976). *Aging in America, No. 5: Implications for the black aged.* Washington, DC: National Council on the Aging.

John, R. (1991). The state of research on American Indian elders' health, income security, and social support networks. In *Minority elders: Longevity, economcis, and health.* Washington, DC: Gerontological Society of America.

Kalish, R., & Moriwaki, S. (1973). The world of the elderly Asian American. *Journal of Social Issues, 29* (2), 187–209.

Kart, C. S. (1990). Diversity among aged black males. In Z. Harel, E. A. McKinney, & M. Williams (Eds.), *Black aged: Understanding diversity and service needs.* Newbury Park, CA: Sage.

Kastenbaum, R. (1971). The missing footnote. *Aging and Human Development, 2,* 155.

Kent, D. (1971a). Changing welfare to serve minority. In *Minority aged in America.* Ann Arbor: Institute of Gerontology, University of Michigan–Wayne State University.

Kent, D. (1971b). The elderly in minority groups: Variant patterns of aging. *Gerontologist, 11,* 26–29.

Kent, D., & Hirsch, C. (1969). *Differentials in need and problem solving techniques among low income Negro and White elderly.* Paper presented at the International Congress on Gerontology, Washington, DC.

Kim, B. (1973, May). Asian Americans: No model minority. *Social Work, 18,* 44–53.

Kim, H. S., & Schwartz-Barcott, D. (1983). Social network and adjustment process of Korean elderly women in America: Some unexpected findings. *Pacific/Asian American Mental Health Center Research Review, 2* (3), 1–2.

Kitano, H., & Kikumura, A. (1976). The Japanese American family. In C. Mindel & R. Habenstein (Eds.), *Ethnic families in America.* New York: Elsevier.

Kramer, B. J. (1991). Urban American Indian aging. *Cross-Cultural Gerontology, 6,* 205–217.

Kramer, B. J. (1992). Cross-cultural medicine a decade later: Health and aging of urban American Indians. *The Western Journal of Medicine, 157* (3), 281–285.

Krause, N. (1987). Stress in racial differences in self-reported health among the elderly. *Gerontologist, 27* (1), 72–76.

Kunitz, S. J., & Levy, J. E. (1989). Aging and health among Navajo Indians. In K. S. Markides (Ed.), *Aging and health: Perspectives on gender, race, ethnicity and class.* Newbury Park, CA: Sage.

Lacayo, C. (1977). *Research and the Hispanic elderly.* Paper presented at the Texas State Department of Public Welfare Conference, January 14, McAllen, TX.

Liu, W. T. (1986). Health services for the Asian elderly. *Research on Aging, 8,* 156–175.

Lyman, S. (1974). *Chinese Americans.* New York: Random House.

Maldonado, D. (1975, May). The Chicano aged. *Social Work,* 213–216.

Manuel, R. C. (1982). The dimensions of ethnic minority identification: An exploratory analysis among elderly black Americans. In R. C. Manuel (Ed.), *Minority aging: Sociological and social psychological issues.* Westport, CT: Greenwood Press.

Markides, K., Boldt, J. S., & Ray, L. A. (1986). Sources of helping and intergenerational solidarity of Mexican-Americans. *Journal of Gerontology, 41,* 506–511.

Markides, K., Liang, J., & Jackson, J. (1990). Race, ethnicity and aging: Conceptual and methodological issues. In R. Binstock &

L. K. George (Eds.), *Handbook of aging and the social sciences* (3rd ed.). New York: Academic Press.

Markides, K. S., & Machelek, R. (1984). Selective survival, aging, and society. *Archives of Gerontology and Geriatrics, 3,* 207–229.

Michigan Offices of Services to the Aging. (1975). *The Michigan comprehensive plan on aging.* Lansing, Mich.: Offices of Services to the Aging.

Montero, D. (1979). Disengagement and aging among the Issei. In D. E. Gelfand & A. J. Kutzik (Eds.), *Ethnicity and aging: Theory, research, and policy.* New York: Springer.

Osako, M. M., & Liu, W. T. (1986). Intergenerational relations and the aged among Japanese Americans. *Research on Aging, 8* (1), 128–155.

Schaie, K. W., Orchowsky, S., & Parham, I. A. (1982). Measuring age and sociocultural change: The case of race and life satisfaction. In R. C. Manuel (Ed.), *Minority aging: Sociological and social psychological issues.* Westport, CT: Greenwood Press.

Simmons, L. (1945). *The role of the aged in primitive society.* New Haven, CT: Yale University Press.

Simon, D. R., & Eitzen, D. S. (1982). *Elite deviance.* Boston: Allyn and Bacon, Inc.

Sotomayor, M. (1971, May). Mexican-American interaction with social systems. *Social Casework, 5,* 321.

Spitze, G., & Miner, S. (1992). Gender differences in adult child contact among black elderly patients. *The Gerontologist, 32* (2), 213–218.

Stack, C. (1970). The kindred of Viola Jackson: Residence and family organization of an urban black American family. In N. Whitten & J. Szwed (Eds.), *Afro-American anthropology.* New York: The Free Press.

Stanford, E. P. (1978). *The elder black.* San Diego, CA: Center on Aging, San Diego State University.

Stanford, E. P. (1990). Diverse black aged. In Z. Harel, E. A. McKinney, & M. Williams (Eds.), *Black aged: Understanding diversity and service needs.* Newbury Park, CA: Sage.

Steglich, W., Cartwright, W., & Crouch, B. (1968). *Study of needs and resources among aged Mexican-Americans.* Lubbock: Technological College.

Taylor, R. J., & Taylor, W. H. (1982). The social and economic status of the black elderly. *Phylon, 43,* 295–306.

Taylor, R. J. & Chatters, L. M. (1988). Correlates of education, income, and poverty among aged blacks. *Gerontologist, 28* (4), 435–441.

Torres-Gil, F. (1976). *Political-behavior: A study of political attitudes and political participation among older Mexican-Americans.* Unpublished doctoral dissertation. Brandeis University, Waltham, MA.

U.S. Bureau of the Census. (1994). *Statistical abstract of the United States, 1994.* Washington, DC: U.S. Government Printing Office.

U.S. Senate Special Committee on Aging. (1971). *The multiple hazards of age and race.* Washington, DC: U.S. Government Printing Office.

Valle, R., & Mendoza, L. (1978). *The elder Latino.* San Diego, CA: Center on Aging, San Diego State University.

White House Conference on Aging. (1972). *The Asian American elderly.* Washington, DC: U.S. Government Printing Office.

Wilson, W. J. (1978). *The declining significance of race: Blacks and changing American institutions.* Chicago: University of Chicago Press.

Zopf, P. (1986). *America's older population.* Houston, TX: Cap and Gown.

CHAPTER 16

LIVING ENVIRONMENTS OF THE ELDERLY

Elderly Americans, like people of all ages, reside in a variety of settings—from single-room-occupancy hotels to Palm Springs condominiums, from urban homes and apartments to isolated rural farmhouses. Although the first public housing units designated explicitly for the elderly were mandated in the 1959 Housing Act, not until about 1966 did gerontologists begin to focus on the special problems of the elderly in securing physically adequate housing at a reasonable cost. Most recently, gerontologists have addressed themselves to broader questions about the relationship between behavior and living environments. In particular, some have asked: How and to what extent is the physical, social, and psychological functioning of an elderly individual influenced by the kind of environment in which he or she lives? This chapter summarizes some of the growing body of literature that has appeared in response to this question. It begins by addressing some general issues important to understanding the impact of the environment on older people.

THE IMPACT OF ENVIRONMENT ON OLDER PEOPLE

According to the 1971 White House Conference on Aging, housing is probably the single most important element in the life of an older person, aside from his or her spouse. Still, as Carp (1976) points out, one sign of the growing maturity of this subfield of gerontology is recognition of the limited utility of considering housing out of context. Gerontologists have come to understand that, although number of rooms, square footage, and closet space are important, so is the broader living environment in which the housing unit is located.

The main elements of this living environment include characteristics of the neighborhood and community, such as (1) the age and ownership of the dwelling unit, (2) the physical condition and availability of funds for maintenance and repair, (3) the location of the dwelling unit with regard to services needed by older people, (4) the proximity to commercial and recreational activities, (5) the proximity to relatives and age peers, (6) the accessibility and usability of transportation, and (7) the congeniality or threat in the surrounding environment—for example, poor street lighting or high crime rates (Carp, 1966; Havighurst, 1969).

What kind of neighborhood environment is most supportive for older persons? Chapman and Beaudet (1983) have explored the relationship between the neighborhood as a physical and social context and the well-being of a sample of relatively frail elderly persons living independently in a variety of community settings within Multnomah County (Portland), Oregon. Measures of the physical and social environments of the sample groups, the personal characteristics of the respondents, and their well-being were developed out of personal interviews. Environmental variables used in the analysis were house type, neighborhood quality, crime rate, age concentration of the neighborhood, distance to services, the social status of the neighborhood area, and distance to the city center.

The important part of this analysis involved determining whether, when personal characteristics are controlled for, environmental variables are useful predictors of the well-being of frail elderly people. Using a measure of life satisfaction as a global indicator of well-being, Chapman and Beaudet (1983) found that people living in higher-quality neighborhoods were significantly more satisfied with their lives. How satisfied were people with their neighborhoods? Living in a higher-quality neighborhood and living relatively far from downtown were two factors that significantly increased satisfaction with the neighborhood.

Three additional indicators of well-being were employed. Each provides a measure of social interaction with others. Interaction with neighbors was highest among those individuals residing in good-quality neighborhoods, relatively far from the center of the city, and with a low percentage of older people in the area. Frequent social contact with friends and relatives was associated with the environmental variables of good neighborhood quality, relatively low social status of the neighborhood, a low crime rate in the area, and relatively greater distance from the city center. No environmental variables were predictive of a general activity level, measured by the frequency of visits to the bank, grocer, and other families.

The environmental variables most consistently associated with well-being were increased distance from the center of the city and the quality of the neighborhood. Quality of the neighborhood is a composite measure reflecting a residential area that is quiet, has little traffic, and is well maintained and landscaped. Such attributes suggest a neighborhood that is especially well suited to the competence levels of the frail elderly. One surprising finding is the failure of distance to services to show any value in predicting well-being. As Chapman and Beaudet (1983) point out, however, this may simply result from members of the study population having available social contacts and supports on whom they can rely to provide transportation.

Lawton and Nahemow (1973) have attempted to classify living environments on the basis of the demands they place on older people. Some living environments make greater physical, social, and psychological demands on people than others do. As a result, it is possible to place living environments on a hypothetical continuum from "very demanding" to "not demanding at all." Following the terminology of the noted psychologist Henry Murray (1938), Lawton and Nahemow (1973) use the term *environmental press* to describe this continuum. They posit that when a person of a given level of competence behaves in an environment of a given press level, the outcome can be placed on a scale from positive to negative (Lawton, 1980a). Another way of describing this is to talk of the *fit* between an individual's competence and the environment in which that individual resides. When the fit is good, the competence of an individual will be consistent with the demands of the environment, and adaptation is positive. This may be the case for the great majority of older people. When environmental demands are too great, adaptation is poor and the outcome is negative.

An example may be useful. Mrs. L. is 74 years old and resides with her never-married brother. Mrs. L. has been a diabetic for 30 years and suffers from heart disease as well. She requires frequent medical care, including in-home personal care. When Mrs. L. began to show signs of mild confusion and forgetfulness, she was no longer able to meet the demands of the living environment. She was less able to participate in her own care and often found it difficult to navigate her way through the small house in which she and her brother lived. Her brother tried to find some home assistance, but this was scarce and expensive. Because he feared for his sister's safety, the brother reluctantly sought a nursing home.

A small change in the environment, such as the presence of a homemaker, might have reduced the environmental press and made it compatible with Mrs. L.'s competence. She might have been able to defer entrance to the institution. Lawton and Simon (1968) stated this relationship between environmental press and individual competence in the form of a principle referred to as the *environmental docility hypothesis*: The less competent the individual, the greater the impact of environmental factors on that individual.

This principle is particularly relevant to older people because of the broad way in which Lawton (1980a) has chosen to view competence. Competence not only is reflective of characteristics within the person—such as biological health, sensorimotor coordination, and cognitive skills—but also reflective of external processes, including age discrimination, social isolation, mandatory retirement, and reduced income. These social deprivations may be suffered by any person as he or she ages, although the elderly are particularly vulnerable to them. The occurrence of one or more of these phenomena may say nothing about the inherent competence of the individual who experiences them. Yet, the individual often experiences these occurrences as reductions in competence. Although the deprivation occurs outside the person, it may significantly affect his or her ability to deal with the environmental press (Lawton, 1980a).

The environmental docility hypothesis has a positive side. If features of the broader living environment can deprive individuals of competence, then perhaps

Sometimes, small accommodations in a living environment allow an elderly individual to maintain competence and elevate the quality of life.

there are features of the living environment that can increase competence and elevate the quality of life. As Lawton has stated, "If we could design housing with fewer barriers, neighborhoods with more enriching resources, or institutions with higher stimulating qualities, we could improve the level of functioning of many older people more than proportionately" (1980a).

Achieving the ideal fit between the individual and the living environment may be difficult in the real world. This is reflected in Lawton's (1980c) discussion of two contrasting developmental models of independent living environments: the constant model and the accommodating model. The *constant model* attempts to maintain the essential character of the environment and assumes that the needs of residents remain relatively stable over time. The *accommodating model* assumes that all aspects of the environment (including the resident) change over time.

According to Lawton (1980c), characteristics of the constant model are:

1. Admission criteria for replacement tenants are the same as those for original tenants.
2. Criteria for continued residence are established so that administrators may initiate termination of residence when a tenant's physical or mental condition declines below a specific level.

3. Termination of residence because of reduced independence leads to transfer to either the home of a family member, congregate housing, or an institution. Some individuals will experience multiple transfers—to the home of a family member and then again to an institution. Much research (to be discussed) demonstrates that such late-life relocations are undesirable.

4. The community continues to regard the housing environment as a place for independent living; thus, there is a continuation of the effort to recruit replacement tenants who are fully independent.

In some contrast, a typical accommodating environment might be characterized as follows:

1. Criteria for continued residence in the environment are considerably less stringent than those applied to the original applicants.

2. Changes in tenants' physical and mental conditions require the addition of a variety of services, including on-site health services.

3. The provision of such services requires alteration in the physical environment to provide for the delivery of such services.

4. The needs of tenants do not change at an equal rate; thus, at first, new services provided are not cost effective. Moreover, there will be a mix of independent and less independent residents.

5. Admission criteria for replacement tenants may be relaxed as the service environment changes to be able to provide for less independent tenants.

6. The community image of the housing changes such that more marginally independent people apply in greater numbers. Over an extended period of time, such an accommodating environment could evolve into a long-term care institution.

As Lawton (1980c) points out, most housing environments are not as extreme as the two types characterized here. Still, housing that attempts to become accommodating certainly may face difficulty in remaining financially viable while attempting to provide services in physical settings not originally planned to function in this way. At the same time, those environments that attempt to remain constant and resist accommodation face the unpleasant task of terminating residence because of lack of services or of maintaining marginal tenants without being able to provide them with needed services.

Ehrlich, Ehrlich, and Woehlke (1982) completed a needs assessment that examined the tenant population of the Delcrest Apartments for the Elderly in St. Louis, Missouri. Essentially, they asked, "Can a congregate housing program remain constant over a long period of time (13 years) without making some attempt to accommodate to an aging population?" Their findings failed to support an accommodating environment concept. Yet, the constant model embodied in the original program was not sufficient to take into account the diverse needs represented in a population of young-old and old-old residents.

The authors (Ehrlich, Ehrlich, & Woehlke, 1982) put forth what is described as a balanced environmental model that would allow for the maintenance of the traditional mobile-well independent environment while still guaranteeing some support for those with need. In many respects, this balanced model sits midway between the constant and the accommodating models described by Lawton. In particular, Ehrlich and colleagues emphasized the importance of strengthening informal support networks, as evidence suggests the feasibility of elderly people assisting each other in all basic supportive tasks, such as crisis intervention, activities of daily living, and advice giving.

WHERE DO THE ELDERLY LIVE?

This section describes the living arrangements of older people, the characteristics of their housing, and their degree of satisfaction with their housing situations. Earlier, Chapter 3 discussed the geographical distribution of the elderly in the United States, including their residential mobility and concentration.

Living Arrangements

Nearly all of the elderly live in independent households. In 1990, approximately two-thirds of the elderly were living with family, with the great majority of these married and residing with a spouse (54.1 percent). Table 16–1 presents data on the living arrangements of the elderly, by sex and age, for 1990. In 1990, only 5.3 percent of the elderly were in institutions on any given day. Chapter 17 discusses the elderly in old-age institutions.

There is a striking difference in the household composition of elderly men and women, reflecting differences in marital status between the sexes. In 1990, elderly women were about 2.7 times as likely to live alone as men (42.0 vs. 15.7 percent, respectively), whereas almost three-quarters (74.3 percent) of all aged men were married and living with their wives. Only about 4 in 10 elderly women (39.7 percent) were married and living with a spouse. (The proportions are even lower for African American and Hispanic American women.) Even among the oldest-old (those 85 years of age and older), almost half (47.0 percent) of all men were married and living with a spouse.

The proportion of the elderly living alone is increasing. In 1965, for example, 29.9 percent of aged women lived alone as compared with 42.0 percent in 1990. In addition, the proportion of older men and women who live alone increases with age. This seems to be chiefly the result of the increasing number of widows among the elderly and the fact that more elderly persons today can afford to live alone than in the past. Among men, the percentage living alone increases from 13.0 at ages 65 to 74 to 28.1 among those 85 years and over. Among women, the percentage living alone increases from 33.2 at ages 65 to 74 to 56.8 at ages 85 and over. The high proportion of the very-old living alone does not portend well for them. A

TABLE 16–1   Living Arrangements of the Noninstitutionalized U.S. Elderly

Elderly Group	Number	1990 Percentage Distributions			1980–1990 Percentage Change		
		Total	Male	Female	Total	Male	Female
Age 65+	29,566,000	100.0	100.0	100.0	22.4	24.7	20.8
Living alone	9,176,000	31.0	15.7	42.0	29.8	34.2	28.7
Living with spouse	16,003,000	54.1	74.3	39.7	25.2	23.1	28.2
Living with other relatives	3,734,000	12.6	7.7	16.1	−4.1	14.5	−9.1
Living with non-relatives only	653,000	2.2	2.3	2.2	56.6	66.3	50.0
Age 65 to 74	17,979,000	100.0	100.0	100.0	17.5	21.0	14.8
Living alone	4,350,000	24.2	13.0	33.2	16.0	30.7	12.1
Living with spouse	11,353,000	63.1	78.2	51.1	20.3	18.5	22.6
Living with other relatives	1,931,000	10.7	6.6	14.1	2.2	21.1	−3.6
Living with non-relatives only	345,000	1.9	2.2	1.7	52.7	72.8	35.8
Age 75 to 84	9,354,000	100.0	100.0	100.0	30.4	31.5	29.7
Living alone	3,774,000	40.3	19.3	53.3	41.7	36.2	42.9
Living with spouse	4,145,000	44.3	71.2	27.7	39.2	34.8	46.8
Living with other relatives	1,237,000	13.2	7.4	16.8	−11.3	−2.6	−13.3
Living with non-relatives only	198,000	2.1	2.0	2.2	44.5	46.0	43.7
Age 85+	2,233,000	100.0	100.0	100.0	32.7	35.4	31.3
Living alone	1,051,000	47.1	28.1	56.8	60.9	46.9	65.0
Living with spouse	505,000	22.6	47.0	10.2	37.2	29.9	59.6
Living with other relatives	567,000	25.4	21.1	27.5	−6.7	28.0	−15.9
Living with non-relatives only	110,000	4.9	3.8	5.5	103.7	81.3	113.2

Source: U.S. Bureau of the Census, 1991.

study conducted on behalf of the Commonwealth Fund Commission on Elderly People Living Alone concluded:

> The elderly person living alone is often a widowed woman in her eighties who struggles alone to make ends meet on a meager income. Being older, she is more likely to be in fair or poor health. She is frequently childless or does not have a son or daughter nearby to provide assistance when needed. Lacking social support, she is at high risk for institutionalization and for losing her independent life style. Finally, like one-half of all elderly people living alone, she may have lived alone for ten years or more. Many elderly people living alone are poor; one-quarter have income below the federal poverty level. The elderly living alone are likely to be dependent on Social Security; overburdened with health care bills; lack pensions;

are less likely to own their own home; and are unlikely to be receiving Supplemental Security Income assistance and Medicaid. (Louis Harris & Associates, 1987, p. i)

In 1990, only 12.6 percent of persons aged 65 and over lived with a relative other than a spouse; another 2.2 percent lived with nonrelatives only. The incidence of such living arrangements has declined steadily since the end of World War II. Still, such data must be viewed cautiously. Percentages reflecting a single point in time typically understate the likelihood of the arrangement occurring over the lifetime of the older person. Also, data describing those 65 years and over may mask substantial differences among the subgroups. For example, as Table 16–1 shows, 27.5 percent of women age 85 or over live with other relatives, and another 5.5 percent live with nonrelatives only. Also, according to the U.S. Senate Special Committee on Aging (1991), older African Americans and Hispanic Americans (and especially women) are more likely than older whites to live with a relative other than a spouse.

Serious physical illness or disability that make remaining alone safely without supervision impossible is the most important factor that may determine the choice of a shared household, even one with nonfamily members (Horowitz, 1985). Other important influences include poverty, widowhood, or loneliness. Beth Soldo (1979) found that older people living with relatives were twice as likely to have low incomes as older people living independently. When the low income of the elderly person is pooled with that of the household in which he or she resides, a higher quality of living may be afforded all. Figure 16–1 shows the relationship between living alone and poverty status in 1990. Some 24 percent of the elderly living alone were poor, compared with 14 percent of those who live with others. An additional 27 percent of elderly people living alone have incomes between 100 percent and 149 percent of the poverty level.

Living in the household of a nonrelative or a relative other than one's spouse sometimes implies greater limitations in mobility and activity than living with a spouse or alone. Although differences are not extraordinarily large, data from the National Health Interview Surveys do suggest that a shared household may act as protection when circumstances preclude maintaining an independent household.

Housing Characteristics

Most Americans, including the elderly, live in single-family owner-occupied homes. Of the 20 million households headed by older persons in 1990, 76 percent were owner occupied, and 24 percent were rental units. Among the elderly, however, there are wide variations in patterns of home ownership by age, sex, and living arrangements. Householders aged 75 years and over are more likely to rent than those 65 to 69 years (27.3 vs. 20 percent, respectively), as are elderly persons living alone when compared with those living with a spouse (38 vs. 12 percent, respectively). Elderly men are more likely than women to own their own home (83 vs. 65 percent, respectively).

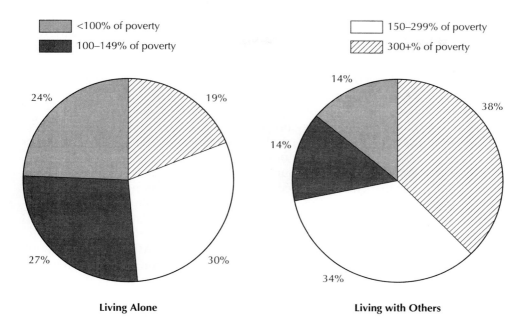

FIGURE 16–1   Economic Status of People 65+ Living Alone or with Others, 1990
Source: U.S. Special Committee on Aging, *Aging America: Trends and Projections* (Washington, DC: U.S. Government Printing Office, 1991).

Homes owned by the elderly are older than those owned by younger people. In 1987, 43 percent of elderly householders lived in structures built before 1950; another 15 percent lived in structures built before 1920. There is a difference in the age of the structures in which different cohorts live. For example, only 25 percent of younger homeowners lived in pre-1950 housing, whereas only 8 percent lived in units constructed before 1920 (U.S. Senate Special Committee on Aging et al., 1991).

Despite the high visibility accorded elderly migrants to the South and West, most elderly people remain in the homes they have long lived in. Among persons 65 years and over, high percentages have been living in their houses for 30 or more years, and these percentages increase in each successive cohort.

Housing Quality. There has been poignant evidence of elderly persons living in dirty, unsafe, and thoroughly wretched conditions. In general, however, there is no consensus on what measures should be included in a definition of adequate housing.

A commonly used indicator of inadequate housing is "incomplete plumbing." The U.S. Census category "with all plumbing facilities" comprises those housing units that have hot and cold piped water, a flush toilet, and a bath or shower—all within the structure and for the exclusive use of the occupants of the unit. Because of urban/rural differences—and because, for example, residents of an otherwise delightful lodging house may share shower facilities—"incomplete plumbing" does not always tell much about housing quality.

A study completed by the Joint Center for Urban Studies of the Massachusetts Institute of Technology and Harvard University estimated that 31 percent of all homes with incomplete plumbing are also dilapidated, with such defects as "holes, open cracks, substantial sagging of floors and roof," and so on (Birch et al., 1973). The study provided no comparable estimate for the incidence of dilapidation among homes with complete plumbing.

The 1987 American Housing Survey employed "physical problems" as an indicator of inadequate housing. Specified housing flaws falling under the definition of physical problems included those related to plumbing, kitchen, maintenance of physical structure, public hall/common area, heating, and electrical systems.

According to the 1987 American Housing Survey, older African Americans (23 percent) and Hispanic Americans (15 percent) were much more likely than whites and those of other races (5 percent) to live in housing with physical problems. Other groups at risk of having physical problems in their housing included older rural householders, those living in the oldest housing units, and the poorest older householders.

Struyk and Soldo (1980) used six indicators of deficiencies in their study of the quality of elderly housing. These indicators of housing inadequacy were related to plumbing, kitchen facilities, sewage, heat, maintenance, and public halls. For example, a housing unit would be declared deficient if it lacked a complete kitchen, or if the household had to share kitchen use, or if the heating system was completely unusable for six or more hours at least three times during the past winter. The elderly were found to have a higher incidence than the nonelderly of incomplete plumbing and kitchen facilities. Elderly and nonelderly households had a similar proportion of heating system and sewage breakdowns, but elderly owners had slightly more maintenance deficiencies than their nonelderly counterparts, and elderly renters had fewer.

What quality indicators do older people themselves identify as most salient in their housing? Lawton (1980b) lists two that appear stronger than the others. Having more bathrooms characterizes luxury dwelling units and is probably related to newness of housing. Central heating is also important and is strongly related to housing satisfaction. In fact, Lawton suggests that if we are to choose a system whose improvement will add most to older occupants' perceived satisfaction with housing, it is the heating system that should be given highest priority.

High-quality living environments can show up in the most unlikely places. J. Kevin Eckert (1980) has studied the "unseen elderly" who reside in single-room-occupancy (SRO) hotels in San Diego. A distinguishing feature of these living environments for older people is that men outnumber women. In virtually every other residential setting for older persons, older women predominate.

Ten women reside in one SRO, the Ballentine Hotel, on a permanent basis. Four of the women have lived in the hotel for more than 10 years. They are old

OLD AND HOMELESS

Estimates of the number of homeless people in the United States are numerous; advocacy groups identify between one and three million. Only three scientific studies have been carried out for the nation as a whole. The U.S. Department of Housing and Urban Development (HUD) estimates between 250,00 and 350,00 homeless on any given night in the United States. The Urban Institute estimates as many as 600,000 homeless Americans, whereas the United States Census Bureau counted 250,000 in the 1990 census. What proportion of the homeless population is made up of elderly people? Buss (1991) reviewed almost 100 studies and found between 1 and 7 percent of the homeless population estimated to be elderly. Why does this proportion seem so low when, after all, many homeless people on the streets of the nation's cities appear to be elderly? One explanation offered by Buss (1991) is that with age, survivorship becomes difficult. Many homeless may die prematurely; others may find their way into public or Veterans' Administration nursing homes or other long-term care facilities.

Another explanation for the low proportion of homeless who are elderly is that the safety net works more efficiently for older people than it does for other age groups. The health and human service delivery system program environment is relatively rich for older people and these programs may do a better job of preventing homelessness among the elderly than programs for younger and middle-aged adults. Also, as Buss (1991) reminds us, the homeless come from a variety of backgrounds and are exposed to extremely hostile environments. As a result, they may give the appearance of premature aging. This may especially be the case for long-term substance abusers, alcoholics, and the chronically mentally ill.

Homelessness is not confined to bag ladies and skid row bums. Buss offers the example of "Blondie" to put a personal face on homelessness:

> They call her "Blondie" on the streets, but she says her real name is Nancy. She hangs out at a downtown street she calls "Main Street." Nearby is a soup kitchen that serves a meal every day except Wednesdays, Saturdays, and Sundays. On Sundays, Blondie goes to another place that serves meals only on that day. She does not eat on Wednesdays and Saturdays.
>
> Blondie is 52 years old but looks older. She is very thin, her remaining teeth are rotten, and her straight blond hair touches her shoulders. She complains of arthritis in her neck and shows how she stays bundled up in the bitter cold of this winter.
>
> Blondie says she was 28 when her "nerves let go." At the time, she spent about six weeks in a state mental hospital . . . where, she claims, they gave her lemon juice as medicine, then released her. She had no income, no family, and lost the house she occupied before her breakdown. She has not been hospitalized in recent years.
>
> Usually when it gets cold, Blondie rents a room above a downtown tavern for $91 a month. She receives a General Assistance check for $117 a month and $78 in food stamps. But when the weather turns warm, she is on the streets again. Her checks stop coming because, she says, she can never get a check when she does not have a residence. During the warm months, she carries a bag containing her belongings.
>
> When Blondie goes into the welfare office, she "prepares for the worst," because "they are not nice to me." She says "the public" has done barbaric things to her. "There is not one thing they have not done to me." (1991, pp. 13–14)

and retired. As a group, the women view the hotel as home and prefer it to other living arrangements they have experienced. Why would the SRO be preferable to an apartment? One woman answers:

> The advantages are that you have a lot of people. If you get tired of staying in your room, you can go to the lobby, then back to your room. I don't like apartments because here if you get sick or anything happens you get help right away. If you live in an apartment by yourself, you can drop dead and no one will know the difference. That's what I like about living here. I can get help right away if something happens, which is good health-wise.

The availability of social supports in the SRO is a theme expressed by both older men and women. As Eckert (1980) points out, living in the hotel gives them instant access to a helping network. Women seem more likely than men to be involved in social networks and to have worked out supportive arrangements with others. Such arrangements are more likely worked out with other women, although, because the SRO is a predominantly male environment, the women do have a large pool of older men from which to choose relationships. For many of these older women, living in a hotel is an adaptive strategy that provides benefits over and above those of other living environments.

An indicator of housing adequacy related to the availability of social supports is the presence of a telephone in the housing unit. Data from the 1987 American Housing Survey show that elderly renters are more than twice as likely to be without a telephone as older homeowners (7 vs. 3 percent, respectively). Elderly impoverished households were three time more likely than the nonpoor to have no telephone (9 vs. 3 percent, respectively).

Finally, Lane and Feins (1985) estimate that over one-third of U.S. elderly households are "overhoused." That is, they had at least one extra bedroom and more than two extra nonsleeping rooms given the size of the household. Older widows living alone were predictably the most likely to occupy overhoused accommodations. The disadvantages of overhoused situations include the extra physical maintenance that may be required to keep the home fit and clean, and the higher dollar costs of maintenance and utilities. Advantages include the ability to accommodate return visits by adult children and their families or a home office/storage area. Also, the costs of maintaining these dwellings (with low rent or paid-up mortgage) may still be less than if the household relocated to smaller accommodations.

Cost of Housing. A principal problem for the elderly is that they have to pay too large a portion of their incomes to meet housing expenses. The U.S. Department of Housing and Urban Development (HUD) defines 40 percent or more of total income devoted to housing as a criterion for a excessive housing burden for homeowners and 30 percent as an excessive burden for renters. Housing costs include gross rent or mortgage, basic utility costs (for all owners and for renters if such fees are not included in rent), and real-estate taxes and insurance for owners. As

Figure 16–2 shows, in all three categories of housing tenure, older householders are more likely to experience excessive housing costs than are householders under 65 years of age. Among the elderly, 36.5 percent of renters, 26 percent of owners with a mortgage, and 17.1 percent of owners with no mortgage experienced excessive housing cost burdens.

Estimates of those elderly experiencing financial burden related to housing may be both understated and overstated. Those understating the size of the elderly population experiencing financial burdens may be excluding large one-time maintenance expenditures such as a new roof or heating system. They may also have no way of factoring in how many older people reduce food consumption or use of utilities to the detriment of their health in order to cope with overly costly housing. At the same time, estimates of the financial burden of housing may be overstated if they fail to include the value of wealth of elderly people as well as benefit assistance from governmental programs, such as food stamps, Medicare, and Medicaid.

Three important points on the housing costs of the elderly are evident from review of additional data on housing costs (U.S. Senate Special Committee on Aging, 1985, 1991):

1. Lower-income households pay a higher proportion of their income for housing, regardless of age, sex, or home ownership status.

2. At more advanced ages, people pay a higher proportion of their income for housing. This is consistent for males and females, and home ownership category.

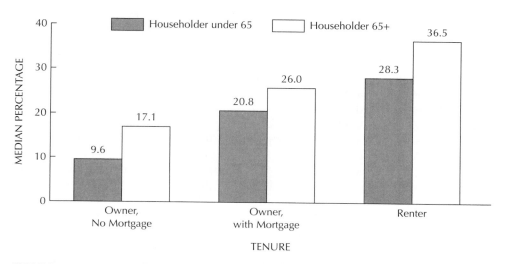

FIGURE 16–2   **Monthly Housing Costs as Percentage of Income, by Age and Tenure of Householder, 1987**

Source: U.S. Bureau of the Census and U.S. Department of Housing and Urban Development. "American Housing Survey of the United States in 1987," *Current Housing Reports,* H-150-87, December 1989.

3. Female householders pay proportionately more for their housing than do male householders, at all ages and in all home ownership categories.

Satisfaction with Housing. The American Association of Retired Persons (AARP, 1990) commissioned nationwide surveys of older adults in 1986 (those aged 60 years and over) and in 1989 (those aged 55 and over), asking about housing arrangements and housing concerns. The findings emphasize that the majority of older people are satisfied with their housing arrangements. Over 70 percent of older respondents indicated being "very satisfied" with neighborhood or location of home (75 percent), physical condition of the home (71 percent), personal safety in the home (74 percent), type of home (76 percent), and general comfort of home (80 percent). Small minorities expressed that they were "very dissatisfied" with the cost of utilities (11 percent), cost of property taxes (8 percent), and lack of public transportation (7 percent). Most significant housing concerns included failing health (61 percent were "very concerned"), losing independence (56 percent), and keeping the home in good condition (59 percent). One explanation for the generally high satisfaction with housing expressed by older people may be the strong attachment they have to their homes and neighborhood. After all, a great proportion of the elderly have spent the better part of their adult lives in their present homes and neighborhoods.

Another explanation for the high satisfaction elderly people have with their living environments reflects the options available. When an individual has no options, assessments of even highly deficient environments may be satisfactory. Several studies report favorable ratings by residents of housing that "objective" investigators rated as poor (Britton, 1966; Hamovitch, Peterson, & Larson, 1969). One explanation for this difference is that the ratings of elderly residents include an element of psychological defense. This view is supported by Carp's (1976) report of changes in evaluations of housing that occurred when another option became available. In each of two situations of public housing, before anyone moved in, evaluations of current housing became more negative among applicants who were offered apartments and remained stable for those who were not.

This is not to say that there is no correlation between subjective assessments of housing by the elderly and more objective indicators of housing quality. Using data in the Annual Housing Survey, Lawton and Hoover (1979) found a modest correlation (.36) between older people's subjective ratings of housing quality and a summed index based on households with higher socioeconomic status, owner-occupied structures, and newer housing.

O'Bryant (1982) investigated the housing satisfaction of elderly people living in a large midwestern metropolitan area. She was particularly interested in whether subjective or objective factors better explained satisfaction with housing. She found that subjective factors (e.g., feelings of competence and emotional security that can be derived from a home) explained more of the variation in housing satisfaction than did demographic characteristics of residents or objective housing characteristics.

When controlling for individual differences, Golant (1985) identified six social and physical environmental experiences that helped explain life satisfaction among a sample of aged respondents in Evanston, Illinois. In the order of their contribution (from high to low), these measures were:

1. Feeling bored in dwelling
2. Thinking about memories of personal things
3. Having a good time in the community or neighborhood
4. Feeling satisfaction with stores and shopping in the community
5. Feeling lonely
6. Feeling annoyed because appliances have broken down

As Golant (1985) points out, these social and physical environmental experiences that influence life satisfaction emphasize the multidimensional content of the environment that impinges on the lives of older people.

In an overall assessment of the neighborhood, Struyk and Soldo (1980) report that the distinction between homeowners and renters appears to be more salient than that between elderly and nonelderly; 25 to 30 percent of renters rate their neighborhood as "fair" or "poor"; only 12 to 13 percent of homeowners give such ratings. Interestingly, the elderly and nonelderly both viewed the lack of adequate public transportation as the greatest service inadequacy in their neighborhoods. In general, the elderly found fewer bothersome conditions in their neighborhoods than did the nonelderly. Street noise and neighborhood crime led the list of complaints for both groups.

Fear of Crime. Over the past 20 years or so, numerous writers and researchers have reported on the reality and pervasiveness of fear of crime among the elderly. Not all investigations agree, however (Akers et al., 1987). Some have described the elderly as living under "house arrest." Many have pointed out, however, that such fear is out of proportion to the actual probability of an elderly person being a victim of crime. Generally, older people are victimized least often, but the rate for larceny with contact (e.g., purse snatching and wallet stealing) is selectively high for older people (Yin, 1980). Also, although they are victimized less than the young, crimes against them are more serious, result in larger losses, are more likely committed by strangers who are armed, and occur close to their homes (Whitaker, 1989).

The relationship between age and fear of crime continues to be a subject of scrutiny, as a result of two different motivations. On the one hand, researchers have sought to distinguish segments of the elderly population that are more or less fearful of crime. On the other hand, investigators have employed a variety of test factors, including residential location and income, to explain the relationship between age and fear of crime. For example, Braungart, Braungart, and Hoyer (1980), using a nationwide sample, found that the elderly were only somewhat more fearful of crime than their younger and middle-aged counterparts. These researchers identified gender as more strongly related to fear of crime than either age or community size. Using Washington State residents, Lee (1982) reports that elderly urban dwellers showed more fear of walking alone in their own neighborhoods than did elderly residents of rural areas, although they did not estimate their chances of being victimized much differently. Interestingly, when the actual incidence of recalled victimization was introduced into the analysis, the statistical significance of residential location disappeared.

Petee, Kart, and Palmer (1985) used 1982 General Social Survey data to test the effects of age, sex, income, and residential location on fear of crime. Several different analyses yielded the same final results. Sex and residence had direct effects on fear of crime. Females and big-city dwellers tended to show fear; males and rural residents tended not to show fear. There were no effects of age.

FEDERAL SUPPORT OF HOUSING FOR THE ELDERLY

In 1908, a presidential housing commission examined the problem of slums in U.S. cities. Appointed by President Theodore Roosevelt, the commission was particularly interested in those eastern seaboard cities that had become the entry point for masses of new immigrants (Jacobs et al., 1986). Federal intervention in housing in the country's major cities was recommended. But not until 1918, after World War I, did Congress intervene by authorizing a loan program for housing construction for shipyard workers. In 1918, Congress also created the U.S. Housing Commission and authorized the development of 25 community housing projects for defense workers.

The Great Depression of 1932 marked the beginning of large-scale federal intervention in housing. Between 1932 and 1937, several important government initiatives were begun. For example, direct funding of low-income housing and slum clearance was provided under the Emergency Relief and Construction Act of 1932. The National Housing Act of 1934 created the Federal Housing Administration (FHA) to provide government insurance for mortgages made by private lenders.

Jacobs and colleagues describe the Housing Act of 1949 as the beginning of the modern era in federal housing and development programs. This act declared that the quality of life of the nation's people required "housing production and related community development sufficient to remedy the serious housing shortage, the elimination of substandard and other inadequate housing through the clearance of slums and blighted areas, and the realization as soon as feasible of the goal of a decent home and a suitable living environment for every American family" (1986).

The Housing Act of 1959 provided public housing specifically for the elderly, with the creation of two new programs. Section 231 of the National Housing Act provided Federal Housing Administration mortgage insurance for rental projects for the elderly, and Section 202 created a direct-loan program for elderly rental housing developed by private nonprofit corporations. Since that time, a considerable amount of construction has taken place. At the end of the 1980s, more than 1.9 million elderly households were living in housing subsidized in some manner by the federal government. This represented about 9.6 percent of the nation's older households. To the uninformed, these numbers seem impressive. Yet, the 1971 White House Conference on Aging called for the annual production of 120,000 units of new housing for the elderly. By 1983, one estimate was that a minimum of 136,000 replacement units (new and rehabilitated) would be needed annually to supply the elderly in the United States over the next 20 years (Handler, 1983). The need certainly exists, but these goals were unrealistically high. One problem is that, as Lawton (1980a) points out, most federal housing programs lead a precarious existence. They may be initiated and terminated within the time of one or two national political administrations. The Reagan-Bush years (1981 through 1992) were noteworthy for the absence of a federal housing policy, with no new initiatives for the low income and elderly. In the current budget-cutting environment of the 1990s in Washington, DC, the likelihood of new initiatives for subsidized housing for the poor and elderly is small.

Another kind of barrier to the development of housing for the elderly can be called *community resistance* (Mangum, 1985). Lawton and Hoffman have observed that "community response to the announcement of plans to construct elderly housing in a neighborhood is frequently hostile, sometimes to the point of a local group's taking legal action to bar the construction" (1984, p. 42). Community resistance may result from (1) threats associated with perceived change in the characteristics of people in the area, (2) concern about the development of stigmatizing service facilities, (3) concern that neighborhood may be disturbed by a secondary set of resource users, and (4) the fact that any increase in density is threatening (Winkel, cited in Lawton & Hoffman, 1984).

Mangum (1985) makes four recommendations for sponsors of housing for the elderly to help overcome possible community resistance:

1. If possible, build in a "nice" semicommercial area.

2. If housing can be built only in a residential area of predominantly single-family homes, obtain community input.

3. If there is opposition from the community, make efforts to reach a compromise with opposing residents.

4. If a compromise cannot be reached, look for an alternative site.

Most public housing construction has involved low-cost, high-rise apartment buildings. To be eligible for public housing designed specifically for the elderly, a person must be 60 years or over, the spouse of a person 62 years or over, or disabled (without age restrictions). Restrictions on income and assets are usually set at the local level. Almost uniformly, tenants pay rent on a sliding scale up to a maximum of 30 or 35 percent of total income. According to the U.S. Senate Special Committee on Aging (1991), 1.9 percent of families with any member age 65 years or over and 11.9 percent of single-person households lived in publicly supported rental housing in 1988. Almost one-quarter (23.3 percent) of single-person households with incomes below the poverty level lived in publicly subsidized housing in 1988.

Federal programs responsible for rent-subsidized apartment units occupied by the elderly (age 62 and over) are briefly described here. These include the Low-Rent Public Housing Program, Section 202, Section 8, and several programs of the Farmers Home Administration.

Low-Rent Public Housing

The federal Public Housing Program was established through The Housing Act of 1937. It was the first public agency to finance construction of apartment units for low-income elderly and nonelderly persons. Today, eligible tenants must have an income that is 50 percent or less of their locality's median income and pay 30 percent of their net income on rent and utilities. There are approximately 1.2 million units in the current inventory, located in low-rent projects. About 480,000 of these apartments were occupied by the elderly in 1990. The low-rent projects are owned, operated, and maintained by nonprofit housing authorities in localities throughout the United States. Most units were produced prior to the 1980s, although the housing authorities can finance additional construction or modernization of units on their own. Thus, in most cases, apartment units become available as a result of vacancies.

Section 202

This program, enacted as part of the Housing Act of 1959, was designed to provide independent living for the elderly as well as the nonelderly disabled. Suspended because of criticism in 1969, the program was revived in 1974 under an amendment to the Housing and Community Development Act of that year.

The program authorizes direct loans to nonprofit organizations so that they can develop and operate multifamily housing projects. These housing projects are expected to be small in scale (no more than 300 units) and aimed primarily at low- and moderate-income elderly persons. Following 1978 legislation, some proportion of new rental units is reserved for the nonelderly disabled. The number of annual units produced under Section 202 peaked at about 20,000 in the late 1970s and has declined steadily to under 10,000 in 1990. By the end of the 1980s, about 3,200 projects had been funded with approximately 230,000 units; 95 percent of these units are occupied by the elderly.

Most Section 202 projects are located within cities and in predominantly residential neighborhoods that offer little or no other public or subsidized housing. The residents of these neighborhoods tend to be white and with income that is low but higher than persons supported by the Public Housing Program (U.S. Department of Housing and Urban Development, 1979). The program appears to be serving primarily white, elderly females of middle socioeconomic status and current incomes that, though low in absolute terms, are above the poverty level. According to the U.S. Department of Housing and Urban Development, males, African Americans and other minorities, the disabled, and persons with the lowest incomes are not as well served by the program (U.S. Department of Housing and Urban Development, 1979). Nevertheless, experts consider Section 202 to be among the more successful housing programs for the low-income elderly (U.S. House of Representatives, 1989).

Since 1978, Section 202 housing has been involved in a demonstration project that attempts a marriage between housing and services to meet the needs of frail elderly persons in subsidized housing. It is a direct effort to put off premature institutionalization. In the Congregate Housing Services Program (CHSP), federal funds were given directly to the managers and administrators of public housing and Section 202 projects who had to deal with the problem of "aging in place" (Nachison, 1985). In 1990, the demonstration covered 59 projects in 33 states and served about 1,500 people. Eligible elderly needed help with three or more activities of daily living (ADLs) and were an average age of 77. The CHSP is generally thought to be a success, perhaps in part because it is such a small program. According to Nachison (1985), costs are less than the delivery of services through agencies in the general community and there seems a real and measurable impact on unnecessary institutionalization.

Section 8

The Section 8 program was created by the Housing and Community Development Act of 1974. This program is currently the principal federal means of providing housing assistance to the elderly. It offers rental assistance through four mechanisms: (1) construction or rehabilitation of rental units, (2) support of already-built rental units funded through other federal programs, (3) support of already-built private-sector rental units with Section 8 certificates, and (4) support of already-built rental units with housing vouchers (U.S. Congressional Budget Office, 1988).

Section 8 subsidies are designed to compensate a family for the difference between the cost of housing it can afford (some percentage of adjusted family income) and the cost of standard housing in the local area where it resides. To be eligible for Section 8 housing subsidies, families and single persons must have incomes below 50 percent of the area median (classified as lower-income households). The federal government pays the difference between the contract rent (an approximation of fair marker rent) and the rent paid by the tenant, usually 30 percent of adjusted family income. As of the end of 1989, it was estimated that approximately 2.4 million rental units were subsidized by Section 8 funds and about 48 percent of these were occupied by the elderly (U.S. Senate, 1990).

With the repeal of the statutory authority for new construction and substantial rehabilitation in 1983, moderate rehabilitation and existing housing constructed under the Section 202 program are the major components of the Section 8 program (Jacobs et al., 1986):

1. In 1978, at the request of the Department of Housing and Urban Development, Congress created a new moderate rehabilitation component of the Section 8 program for units needing some "fixing up" but not major repairs. Rehabilitation activities would include repair of leaky roofs and replacement and/or repair of heating, electrical, or plumbing systems. Typically, a local public housing agency (PHA) oversees the repair work.

2. The existing housing program, in which households find existing housing units in the private market, is the basic structure of the Section 8 program. A PHA determines the eligibility of applicants, based on their income. A Certificate of Family Participation is issued to eligible applicants. With this certificate, a family can look for housing on the private market, provided the housing meets standards of quality and is suitable for the family. The units are inspected by a PHA to make sure they are of standard quality. The PHA then makes rental payments to the owners on behalf of the households.

Under the Housing and Community Development Act of 1987, a Section 8 housing voucher program was started. The program is similar to the certificate program described earlier except that it arguably provides greater choice to the resident. The actual apartment rent is negotiated between the tenant and landlord. If the negotiated rent is greater than 30 percent of a tenant's monthly income plus the housing voucher, the difference must be paid out of the tenant's pocket or the tenant must look for less expensive housing. If the negotiated rent is less than 30 percent of the tenant's monthly income plus the housing voucher, the tenant is able to pocket the difference and use it for other purposes. According to the U.S. Senate (1991), about 250,000 families were using the vouchers in 1990. Unfortunately, the proportion of vouchers being used by elderly households is not available.

Farmers Home Administration

Assistance to the elderly can be provided under both of the Farmers Home Administration's (FmHA) programs: the Section 502 single-family and Section 515 rural rental housing assistance programs. Section 502 provides subsidized and unsubsidized direct loans and unsubsidized guaranteed loans. An unsubsidized Section 502 loan can be used to finance the construction or acquisition of a new, substantially rehabilitated, or existing home. Homes are limited to those that are modest in size, design, and cost. The maximum loan term is 33 years, and interest rates are adjusted periodically according to market changes.

In 1962, Congress added Section 515 in recognition of the need for rental housing in rural areas and small towns. This section authorizes loans to finance cooperative and rental housing projects. Nonprofit, limited-dividend, and profit-motivated sponsors may participate in the rental housing program. The 515 program is open to low- and moderate-income families and to those 62 years or older (Jacobs et al., 1986).

In recent years, there have a number of important state housing initiatives for the elderly (Council of State Housing Agencies et al., 1986). In part, these resulted from the abdication of federal responsibility in this area that characterized the 1980s. These state initiatives occur in the areas of leadership and planning, technical assistance, service development, and financial support. Programs and projects may be categorized as those that help older people remain in their own homes (including home equity conversion, home repair and improvements, property tax relief, rental assistance, and condominium conversion protection programs); those that help older people continue living near familiar supports and institutions (e.g., shared housing programs); and those that provide specific services along with shelter. Examples abound. Those presented here are taken from a publication of the Council of State Housing Agencies and the National Association of State Units on Aging (1986).

1. The state of Maryland awards grants to local entities—such as development corporations, local governments, and Area Agencies on Aging—for programs to provide minor repairs and maintenance of properties occupied by low-income elderly homeowners and homeowners who are disabled. These programs are administered by the Department of Economic and Community Development Office of Housing Assistance, part of the Division of Local Government Assistance.

2. The Senior Citizen Shared Housing Program is a project of the California Department of Aging and the California Department of Housing and Community Development. California has a critical shortage of senior housing. More than one-quarter of older renters pay more than 50 percent of their limited income for housing, and two-thirds of all elderly renters pay more than 25 percent of their income for housing. State general funds and local matching resources are used to provide information and referral about housing issues and to help older persons find a home-sharing partner. Funds are distributed primarily to nonprofit agencies to operate the services. Some government agencies and cities are also sponsors. Since 1981, when the program began, over 3,700 persons over age 60 have been matched with housemates.

3. Through a program started in 1983, the Ohio Housing Finance Agency (OHFA) has financed 19 congregate facilities. Mortgage funds come from tax-exempt bonds and HUD mortgage insurance. Tenant services include one or two meals a day, maid and linen service, transportation, and social services. Services are provided by the management company itself or in conjunction with a nearby nursing facility, using that facility's caterers and nursing staff. A minimum of 20 percent of the units must be occupied by low-income residents. Suggested rent levels are 30 to 80 percent of the area median income.

RETIREMENT COMMUNITIES

Increasingly, gerontologists are giving attention to the phenomenon of retirement communities. The term *retirement community* evokes an image of wealthy older people residing in a country-club setting. This is one type of retirement community, but a retirement community may also look like an urban ethnic neighborhood, a suburban town, or a single apartment building. Hunt and Gunter-Hunt (1985) describe naturally occurring retirement communities (NORCs) as housing developments that are not planned or designed for older people but that, over time, come to house largely older people.

Retirement communities may be defined more by their membership than by their geographic boundaries. Longino (1980) defines a retirement community as any living environment most of whose residents have relocated there since they retired. The essential elements of the definition are *retirement* and *relocation.* Although many residents of retirement communities still work, almost all who have worked have also retired from full-time employment at least once. In addition, the definition excludes communities of retirement-aged people who have aged in place; only the settings to which retired people *move* may be defined as retirement communities.

Retirement communities can be distinguished by the amount of conscious planning that goes into developing and operating them. Some are designed specifically for individuals of a certain chronological age. These *de jure* retirement communities are designed to take into account the more common needs of retirees. Planned communities may be separated into two types: subsidized and unsubsidized (Longino, 1980). A housing project built under the auspices of any of the federal programs described in the previous section can be classified as a subsidized retirement community. Unsubsidized planned communities for retirees range along a continuum from planning limited to housing alone, to life-care communities that attempt to provide a full range of services.

Some retirement communities place no age restrictions on new residents but nonetheless attract people who are retired. These *de facto* retirement communities are not designed as such, but in them a series of organizations and services arise that cater to older people (Longino, 1980).

Why do people move to retirement communities? According to Longino (1981), there are positive (pulls) and negative (pushes) triggering mechanisms in the relocation decision process. Residents of three different retirement communities in the Ozark region connecting the states of Missouri, Arkansas, and Oklahoma were all asked for the single most important reason for their move. In general, Longino reports a congruence between personal needs and community selection.

Residents of the Ozark Lakes County, a *de jure* retirement community that attracts relatively younger couples who are in better physical and financial health to the existing towns of the region, reported the outstanding natural beauty of the region as primary justification for relocating there. Some 54 percent of residents gave this as the most important reason for their relocation. Another 21 percent reported social needs as the most important reason for their move.

Horizon Heights is a *de facto* subsidized retirement community, part of a public housing facilities network in a midwestern city with a population of almost

200,000. It is exclusively for less affluent people of retirement age, who pay 25 percent of their adjusted income toward the rent. Almost one in four (23 percent) gave financial reasons as the most important reason for the move. Another 25 percent offered the push factor of wanting to leave an unhappy neighborhood situation.

Finally, over half (51 percent) of the residents of Carefree Village, a nonsubsidized life-care retirement community inhabited by upper-middle-class migrants, cited health needs as the major reason for selecting this community. Another 19 percent indicated the availability of other services as the primary reason for the move.

Planned communities specialize in providing services and meeting special needs of older people. They make their advantages known to prospective residents and they attract people who, because of unhappy events in their lives or changing circumstances, feel they must move. Such people generally show a higher push level of explanation for their relocation. People who reside in unplanned or *de facto* communities generally have more positive or pull factors as explanation for their move (Longino, 1981).

Although the literature on retirement communities is not large, several interesting ethnographic studies have been carried out. *Ethnography* is a branch of anthropology that studies and reports on everyday lives of particular cultural groups. Two of these studies are worth noting, for they help highlight a question of practical and theoretical importance to gerontologists today: Are older people better served by age-integrated or age-segregated environments?

Merrill Court

Merrill Court is an apartment building housing 43 retired individuals. Most of the residents are women who are widowed, fundamentalist Christians, and of working-class background. Hochschild (1973) worked at Merrill Court in a variety of jobs, including recreation director. When she began, Hochschild expected to find a disengaged, lonely group of individuals. Instead, she found an "unexpected community" of active and engaged older people who appeared to be quite satisfied with their lives. Residents have a great deal of interaction, much of which began with the installation of a coffee machine in the recreation room. Visitation among residents and between residents and their families occurs frequently. Having frequent contact with their neighbors provides these elders with the gratification of friendship, as well as an opportunity for relaying information about other people. Although the status equality among residents led Hochschild to characterize their relationships as a sibling bond, informal status distinctions are made among the residents.

According to Hochschild, within Merrill Court there is a status system based on a distribution of honor accumulated through holding offices in the service club. A parallel hierarchy existed based on the distribution of "luck": Being young-old, having good health, and living close to one's children were defined as having luck. Those who fall short on the criteria for luck are called "poor dears." This hierarchy ran in one direction. Someone who was a "poor dear" in the eyes of another seldom called that other person a "poor dear" in return. Many residents applied the term to those in nursing homes they visited. Hochschild explained the "poor dear" hierarchy as follows:

> The way the old look for luck differences among themselves reflects the pattern found at the bottom of other social, racial and gender hierarchies. To find oneself lucky within an ill-fated category is to gain the semblance of high status when society withholds it from others in the category. The way old people feel above and condescend to other old people may be linked to the fact that the young feel above and condescend to them. The luck hierarchy does not stop with the old. (1973)

Despite these informal status differences among the residents of Merrill Court, no one is isolated. The widows of Merrill Court are independent. They do not use "poor dear" when referring to themselves. They take care of themselves, fix their own meals, pay their own rent, shop for their own food, and make their own beds. And, when it is necessary, they do these things for others.

Fun City

Jacobs (1974, 1975) has written about Fun City, a pseudonym for a retirement community of about 6,000 residents located 90 miles from a large western metropolitan area. Fun City is a planned community of single-level ranch-style tract homes. A nearby shopping center caters to the needs of residents. An on-site activity center houses ninety-two clubs and organizations available to residents. Fun City residents are predominantly white and middle to upper class; the average age is 71 years.

Fun City bills itself as promoting "an active way of life." From Jacobs's reports, however, it seems clear that Fun City is a false paradise. The retirement community exhibits many of the negative aspects residents associate with life on the "outside." Fun City has no public transportation, no police department, and no adequate health care facilities. It is geographically isolated. Despite all the scheduled activities, fewer than 10 percent of the residents participated in any activity on a given day, and generally the same individuals participated in different activities on different days. Thus, inactivity is the norm for Fun City residents.

Jacobs concludes that many residents were withdrawing from society when they moved to Fun City and simply continued this withdrawal after arrival. Despite the promise of "an active way of life," the environment was organized in a way that promoted disengagement. No transportation, geographical isolation, and a lack of ties among the residents led to dissatisfaction with life on the part of many in Fun City. Those in the retirement community expressing the highest degree of satisfaction with Fun City were those whose financial situations allowed for travel, vacations, and visits with family.

Age Integration versus Age Segregation

Merrill Court and Fun City are both age-segregated living environments; nearly all the residents of both retirement communities are older people. Both are planned retirement communities. Merrill Court represents public housing for the elderly, whereas Fun City is an unsubsidized retirement community. In contrast, there are the Ozark lakes region retirement communities that developed on a *de facto* basis and remain age integrated.

Much discussion in the gerontological literature has evaluated the relative merits for older people of age-segregated and age-integrated housing. Very influential in this discussion has been the research of Irving Rosow (1967), who examined the social behavior of older people living in apartment buildings in Cleveland (privately developed and public housing). In particular, he was interested in how social behavior was affected by the concentration of age peers in the buildings. Rosow classified apartment buildings into three categories of age density: those buildings in which the elderly represented 1 to 15 percent of the residents, those in which 33 to 49 percent were elderly, and those in which 50 percent or more of the residents were elderly. For both working-class and middle-class aged, Rosow found that the presence of more age peers was positively associated with social interaction with neighbors. In addition, he demonstrated that this relationship was even more advantageous for those with lower status.

Generalizing from Rosow's evidence is difficult. For example, both Merrill Court and Fun City have age densities that are higher (almost 100 percent) than Rosow's highest category (50 percent plus). Yet, Merrill Court shows high sociability among its residents, whereas social interaction among Fun City residents is minimal. Accounting for this difference is no easy task. Carp (1976) cites five reasons that she believes generalizing from Rosow's work is so difficult. These reasons point to differences between Merrill Court and Fun City and may help explain why social interaction among residents was high in one and low in the other.

1. Rosow's work was not conducted in new housing for the elderly, but in older apartment buildings.

2. In the highest age density of Rosow's apartment buildings, only about half of the residents were elderly. In public housing for the elderly and other planned retirement communities such as Fun City, the percentage of elderly in the environment approached 100 percent.

3. Rosow studied long-time residents of apartment buildings, whereas tenants in newly constructed public housing or newly developed tract housing for the elderly are often the first in-movers.

4. Rosow studied people in old housing located in older established neighborhoods. In-movers to retirement communities have left accustomed living environments and have relocated, often in new housing in newer neighborhoods.

5. Rosow's respondents may have been a special population, and no one knows how it differs from the population of other age-segregated environments or from the general population of older people.

Certainly one important difference between Merrill Court and Fun City that affected the potential for social interaction is the physical layout. For example, it would be considerably easier for interaction to occur among the 43 residents of a five-story building at Merrill Court than among 6,000 residents distributed one or two to each home in the sprawling tract home community of Fun City (Jacobs, 1975). Hochschild makes this clear in her description of the design of the building:

> There was an elevator midway between the apartments, and a long porch extended the length of all the apartments. It was nearly impossible to walk from any apartment to the elevator without being watched from a series of living room windows that looked out into the porch.... A woman who was sewing or watching television in her apartment could easily glance up through the window or wave to the passerby. (1973, p. 4)

No such arrangement existed at Fun City. Other factors that likely contributed to the generation of an "unexpected community" at Merrill Court included the greater status similarity and "good health" that existed among Merrill Court residents compared to residents of Fun City.

Fun City notwithstanding, the evidence from most studies of age-segregated living situations show them to be satisfactory environments for aging. Generally, the studies show higher rates of activity and social interaction in age segregated housing. Research on morale or life satisfaction in age-segregated versus age-integrated housing is less clear. Messer (1967) measured morale and social interaction of elderly living in two public housing projects. One was age segregated, the other a mixture of older and younger families. In the age-integrated setting, there was an association between the morale of older tenants and the amount of social interaction they engaged in; no such association appeared in the age-segregated project. Messer believes morale was linked to activity in the age-integrated environment because the norms of that environment were based on standards of youth; the older person who did not succeed in becoming active would feel deficient in light of these standards. The age-segregated environment fostered social norms appropriate to the ages of its residents; lack of activity did not reflect a deficiency; and it was commonly recognized that some individuals preferred to be active, whereas others did not.

Data from two large-scale research studies (reported in Lawton, 1980a) show that older people *themselves* approve of age-segregated living arrangements. Still, there is great danger in concluding that achieving the ideal social situation for older persons is contingent on their residing in age-segregated housing. Although such environments do meet friendship and social needs for many elderly, others' needs may not be filled by such arrangements. Apparently, age segregation in Fun City did little to enhance the social relationships of many of the residents.

One special problem with much of the research on age-segregated versus age-integrated housing for the elderly is that it is virtually impossible to isolate the age composition of an environment from other variables that may be operating in that environment. As Carp (1976) points out, it is very difficult to locate sites for research that are otherwise equivalent and whose tenants are similar. Thus, it is possible (perhaps even likely) that reports of high satisfaction on the part of the elderly tenants of age-segregated housing have more to do with the *fit* of the physical and social environment than with age segregation in itself.

SUMMARY

Housing is an important element in the life of an older person. Yet, gerontologists have come to understand that the physical characteristics of housing represents only one part of the broader living environment in which an older person resides.

Lawton and colleagues have been particularly interested in the relationship between an older person's competence and the demands the living environment places on that individual. This relationship is stated in the form of a hypothesis: The less competent the individual, the greater the impact of environmental factors on that individual. Lawton sees competence in the broadest possible terms. It may be affected not only by internal biological or physiological factors but also by external social processes such as age discrimination and social isolation.

Nearly all elderly Americans live in independent households; the majority live with a spouse or other relatives, but women are more than twice as likely as men to live alone. Physical disability, poverty, widowhood, and loneliness have an important impact on the choice of living arrangements.

Most elderly Americans live in single-family owner-occupied homes. Homes owned by the elderly are older than those owned by younger people. The elderly live in household units that are more modest than those of the nonelderly and more likely to have incomplete plumbing and kitchen facilities.

Determining how many elderly persons live in inadequate housing is problematic, primarily because there is no consensus on what measures should be included in a definition of inadequate housing. A principal problem for the elderly is that a large proportion of their incomes are used to meet housing expenses. Housing costs, as a percentage of income, increase with age. Lower-income households pay a higher proportion of their income for housing.

In general, the elderly are quite satisfied with their housing arrangements. Over 70 percent of older respondents indicated being "very satisfied" with neighborhood locations of their homes, physical condition of their homes, personal safety in their homes, type of homes, and the general comfort of their homes. Small minorities expressed that they were "very dissatisfied" with the cost of utilities and property taxes, and the lack of public transportation. Housing concerns that topped the list of concerns included failing health, loss of independence, and keeping the home in good condition. The high level of satisfaction with housing accommodations is thought to reflect a strong attachment of older people to their homes and neighborhoods, as well as the limited housing options that may be open to them.

Federal involvement in housing for the elderly has increased in the last two decades. Nevertheless, the 1971 White House Conference on Aging called for an annual production of 120,000 units of new housing for the elderly. By 1983, estimates were that 136,000 replacement units would be needed annually to supply the elderly in the United States over the next 20 years. The principal federal housing programs for the elderly have been the Low-Rent Public Housing Program, Sections 202 and 8 of the National Housing Act, and several programs of the Farmers Home Administration. In recent years, the states have taken diverse initiatives in creating housing programs for the elderly.

Gerontologists have given increasing attention to retirement communities—living environments defined by the retirement and relocation experiences of the residents. Retirement communities may be planned or not, and planned communities may be subsidized or unsubsidized. There is considerable discussion in the gerontological literature about whether age-segregated or age-integrated housing is more advantageous for older people. Although the evidence from most studies of age-segregated environments show them to be satisfactory for aging, it is still too early to conclude that achieving the ideal social situation for older persons is contingent on their residing in age-segregated housing.

STUDY QUESTIONS

1. List the major neighborhood and community characteristics that influence the study of housing for the aged. How do these relate to the concept of *environmental press?*

2. Define and discuss the accommodative model of independent living environments. How does it differ from the constant model?

3. Discuss the living arrangements of the elderly in contemporary society. What is the impact of sex and marital status on those arrangements?

4. How do elderly homeowners and renters assess their living accommodations? What factors do they express the most satisfaction with? The least satisfaction?

What are their greatest concerns about housing?

5. Discuss the federal housing programs aimed at helping to provide for housing needs of the elderly.

6. Define *retirement community*. Distinguish between *de facto* and *de jure* communities. Describe the elderly who reside in this type of housing and reflect on the selection processes that operate to get them there.

7. In examining the relative merits of age-segregated and age-integrated housing for the elderly, why is it so difficult to generalize conclusively from current studies?

REFERENCES

Akers, R. L., LaGreca, A. J., Sellers, C., & Cochran, J. (1987). Fear of crime and victimization among the elderly in different types of communities. *Criminology, 25,* 487–505.

American Association of Retired Persons. (1990). *Understanding senior housing for the 1990s.* Washington, DC: AARP.

Birch, D., et al. (1973). *America's housing needs: 1970 to 1980.* Cambridge, MA: Joint

Center for Urban Studies, MIT and Harvard University.

Braungart, M., Braungart, R., & Hoyer, W. (1980). Age, sex, and social factors in fear of crime. *Sociological Focus, 13* (1), 55–66.

Britton, J. (1966). Living in a rural Pennsylvania community in old age. In F. Carp (Ed.), *Patterns of living and housing of middle-aged and older people.* Washington, DC: U.S. Government Printing Office.

Buss, T. F. (1991). *Meeting the health care needs of the homeless elderly.* Cleveland, OH: Western Reserve Geriatric Education Center.

Carp, F. (1966). *A future for the aged.* Austin: University of Texas Press.

Carp, F. (1976). Housing and living environments of older people. In R. Binstock & E. Shanas (Eds.), *The handbook of aging and the social sciences.* New York: Van Nostrand Reinhold.

Chapman, N. J., & Beaudet, M. (1983). Environmental predictors of well-being for at-risk older adults in a mid-sized city. *Journal of Gerontology, 38* (2), 237–244.

Council of State Housing Agencies et al. (1986). *State initiatives in elderly housing.* Washington, DC: Council of State Housing Agencies.

Eckert, J. K. (1980). *The unseen elderly: A study of marginally subsistent hotel dwellers.* San Diego, CA: Campanile Press.

Ehrlich, P., Ehrlich, I., & Woehlke, P. (1982). Congregate housing for the elderly: Thirteen years later. *The Gerontologist, 22* (4), 399–403.

Golant, S. M. (1985). The influence of the experienced residential environment on old people's life satisfaction. *Journal of Housing for the Elderly, 3* (¾), 23–49.

Hamovitch, M., Peterson, J., & Larson, A. (1969). *Perceptions and fulfillment of housing needs of an aging population.* Paper presented at the Eighth International Congress of Gerontology, Washington, DC.

Handler, B. (1983). *Housing needs of the elderly: A quantitative analysis.* Ann Arbor: University of Michigan, National Policy Center on Housing and Living Arrangements for Older Americans.

Havighurst, R. (1969). Research and development goals in social gerontology. *The Gerontologist, 9,* 1–90.

Hochschild, A. (1973). *The unexpected community.* Englewood Cliffs, NJ: Prentice-Hall.

Horowitz, A. (1985). Family caregiving to the frail elderly. *Annual Review of Gerontology and Geriatrics, 5,* 194–246.

Hunt, M. E., & Gunter-Hunt, G. (1985). Naturally occurring retirement communities. *Journal of Housing for the Elderly, 3* (3/4), 3–21.

Jacobs, B. G., Harney, K. R., Edson, C. L., & Lane, B. S. (1986). *Guide to federal housing programs* (2nd ed.). Washington, DC: Bureau of National Affairs.

Jacobs, J. (1974). *Fun city: An ethnographic study of retirement community.* New York: Holt, Rinehart and Winston.

Jacobs, J. (1975). *Older persons and retirement communities.* Springfield, IL: Charles C. Thomas.

Lane, T. S., & Feins, J. D. (1985). Are the elderly overhoused? Definitions of space utilization and policy implications. *The Gerontologist, 25,* 243–250.

Lawton, M. P. (1980a). *Environment and aging.* Monterey, CA: Brooks/Cole.

Lawton, M. P. (1980b). Housing the elderly: Residential quality and residential satisfaction. *Research on Aging, 2* (3), 309–328.

Lawton, M. P. (1980c). Social and medical services in housing for the aged. Rockville, MD: U.S. Department of Health and Human Services.

Lawton, M. P., & Hoffman, C. (1984). Neighborhood reactions to elderly housing. *Journal of Housing for the Elderly, 2* (2), 41–53.

Lawton, M. P., & Hoover, S. (1979). *Housing and neighborhood: Objective and subjective quality.* Philadelphia: Philadelphia Geriatric Center.

Lawton, M. P., & Nahemow, L. (1973). Ecology and the aging process. In C. Eisdorfer

& M. P. Lawton (Eds.), *Psychology of adult development and aging*. Washington, DC: American Psychological Association.

Lawton, M. P., & Simon, B. (1968). The ecology of social relationships in housing for the elderly. *The Gerontologist, 8,* 108–115.

Lee, G. (1982). Residential location and fear of crime among the elderly. *Rural Sociology, 47* (4), 655–669.

Longino, C. (1980). The retirement community. In F. Berghorn & D. Schafer (Eds.), *Dimensions of aging*. Boulder, CO: Westview Press.

Longino, C. (1981). The retirement community. In C. Kart & B. Manard (Eds.), *Aging in America: Readings in social gerontology* (2nd ed.). Sherman Oaks, CA: Alfred.

Louis Harris & Associates. (1987). *Problems facing elderly Americans living alone*. New York: Louis Harris.

Mangum, W. P. (1985). But not in my neighborhood: Community resistance to housing for the elderly. *Journal of Housing for the Elderly, 3* (¾), 101–119.

Messer, M. (1967). The possibility of an age-concentrated environment becoming a normative system. *The Gerontologist, 7,* 247–251.

Murray, H. (1938). *Explorations in personality*. New York: Oxford University Press.

Nachison, J. S. (1985). Congregate housing for the low and moderate income elderly—A needed federal state partnership. *Journal of Housing for the Elderly, 3* (¾), 65–80.

O'Bryant, S. L. (1982). The value of home to older persons: Relationship to housing satisfaction. *Research on Aging, 4* (3), 349–363.

Petee, T., Kart, C., & Palmer, N. (1985). *Fear of crime: Are there age effects?* Paper presented at the annual Meeting of the Gerontological Society of America, New Orleans.

Rosow, I. (1967). *Social integration of the aged*. New York: Free Press.

Soldo, B. (1979). The housing characteristics of independent elderly: A demographic overview. *Occasional papers in housing and urban development*, No. 1. Washington, DC:

U.S. Department of Housing and Urban Development.

Struyk, R., & Soldo, B. (1980). *Improving the elderly's housing*. Cambridge, MA: Ballinger.

U.S. Bureau of the Census. (1991). *Statistical Abstract of the United States, 1991* (111th ed.). Washington, DC: U.S. Government Printing Office.

U.S. Congressional Budget Office. (1988). *Current housing problems and possible federal responses*. Washington, DC: Superintendent of Documents.

U.S. Department of Housing and Urban Development. (1979). *Housing for the elderly and handicapped*. Washington, DC: Office of Policy Development and Research, U.S. Department of Housing and Urban Development.

U.S. House of Representatives, Select Committee on Aging. (1989). *The 1988 national survey of Section 202 housing for the elderly and handicapped*. Washington, DC: U.S. Government Printing Office.

U.S. Senate, Special Committee on Aging. (1985). *How older Americans live: An analysis of census data*. Washington, DC: U.S. Government Printing Office.

U.S. Senate, Special Committee on Aging. (1990). *Developments in aging, 1989* (Vol. 1 & 2). Washington, DC: U.S. Government Printing Office.

U.S. Senate, Special Committee on Aging. (1991). *Developments in aging, 1990* (Vol. 1 & 2). Washington, DC: U.S. Government Printing Office.

U.S. Senate, Special Committee on Aging, American Association of Retired Persons, Federal Council on Aging, & U.S. Administration on Aging. (1991). *Aging America: Trends and projections*. Washington, DC: U.S. Government Printing Office.

Whitaker, C. J. (1989). Elderly victims. In U.S. Senate, Special Committee on Aging, *Developments in aging, 1988: Volume 2—Appendixes*. Washington, DC: U.S. Government Printing Office.

Yin, P. (1980). Fear of crime among the elderly. *Social Problems, 27,* 492–504.

CHAPTER 17

LONG-TERM CARE

Ruth E. Dunkle and **Cary S. Kart**

In the minds of many Americans, the phrase *long-term care* is synonymous with *old age* or *nursing home,* in part because it is not so long ago when such facilities were the primary place for the provision of long-term care. Nursing homes are now viewed as just one point or place on a continuum of long-term care service options in the community. Also, they are shifting from a social service model of providing personal care toward a health care model that manages illness and dysfunction. At the same time, social service and home health care agencies are extending community services to include respite care and hospice programs, mental health counseling, visiting nurses and in-home care, as well as case management. These changes are a reflection of "an aging, increasingly disabled population in addition to a new regulatory focus on residents' rights, quality of life, and comprehensive assessment" (Levenson, 1993, p. 152). In this chapter, the concept of long-term care is used to describe a continuum of services from those delivered at home or in community settings to those delivered within institutional facilities. In addition, the chapter shows increasing awareness that the boundaries between and among various long-term care services (e.g., home care, institutional care, and other services) is increasingly blurred (Kane, 1995).

Long-term care involves the provision of "one or more services ... on a sustained basis to enable individuals whose functional capacities are chronically impaired to be maintained at their maximum levels of psychological, physical and social well-being" (Brody, 1984). Typically, long-term care is evoked when an individual is functionally disabled enough to require assistance in two or more activities of daily living (Kane & Kane, 1989).

Kane and Kane (1982) include provision for the following objectives in the spectrum of long-term care services:

1. Health and nursing care (e.g., physical care, medical treatments, medication injections)
2. Personal care (e.g., assistance with bathing, dressing, toileting)
3. Domestic services (e.g., housekeeping, cooking, shopping)
4. Housing (i.e., shelter in the least restrictive environment)
5. Social and emotional support (e.g., legal assistance, counseling, telephone assurance programs)
6. Services to informal care providers (i.e., services necessary for the caregivers, such as support programs)
7. Transportation (e.g., special cab services, volunteer drivers)

These services can be continuous or intermittent, and delivered over an extended period of time. According to the U.S. Senate Special Committee on Aging (1982), the goals of long-term care involve a three-part strategy: (1) to delay the onset of preventable disease in healthy adults, (2) to lengthen the period of functional independence in those elderly with chronic disease, and (3) to improve the quality of one's later life.

This chapter begins with a review of the long-term care needs and patterns of service utilization in the elderly population. Selected types of noninstitutional services are then described. The actual risks of an older person being institutionalized are discussed, as is the logic of institutional care in the United States, and the effects institutionalization may have on the aged individual. Policy issues related to long-term care are explored in Chapter 18.

LONG-TERM CARE NEEDS AND PATTERNS OF UTILIZATION

The U.S. National Center for Health Statistics estimates 1.7 million elderly in nursing homes at any given time (U.S. Bureau of the Census 1994, Table 192). This represents approximately 5.3 percent of the elderly population. It is generally believed that an additional 10 percent of elderly living in the community are homebound and as functionally impaired as those in institutions (Kemper, Applebaum, & Harrigan, 1987). Although the help needed by older people living in the community varies greatly, anywhere from 12 to 40 percent may require some kind of supportive services (Manton, 1989). The Pepper Commission (1990) estimates that between 9 and 11 million additional Americans of all ages are at risk for needing long-term care services.

Who are those most likely to need long-term care assistance? The type of person who receives services at various stages of the life course in various places on the long-term care service continuum is not well understood. This is particularly the case for those using community services. It is known, however, that people with limitations in activities of daily living are likely to use long-term care services. Currently, about 7 million elderly are limited in activities of daily living or instrumental activities of daily living. A little more than 3 million of these older people are severely disabled (in need of assistance in three or more activities of daily living), with approximately 4 million suffering from significant mental health problems as well (The Pepper Commission, 1990). Those elderly most likely to receive care in a nursing home are described as predominantly female, 80 years of age or older, widowed, and with income below the poverty level (Cohen, Tell, & Wallack, 1986; Jette et al., 1992).

Not every individual who needs long-term care assistance receives it. Service delivery barriers for older persons are numerous. Sometimes, the elderly are reluctant to admit need or accept help; many even deny using services. Generally, those services they do use are perceived by them as being earned (Moen, 1978).

Simply creating services and making them available is not enough to ensure that they are utilized. Information about available services distributed through the media, service providers, and informal sources are important determinants of service utilization (Silverstein, 1984). Ward indicates, "Making services objectively available to older people is not sufficient—they must perceive a need, know about the service, view it as appropriate, etc." (1977, p. 66). Who delivers the service, and where and when the service is delivered are also important dimensions of the service utilization issue (Little, 1982).

How older people choose the long-term care services they will use is determined by a complex set of interacting personal and environmental factors (McAuley & Blieszner, 1985). Personal factors include demographic, psychological, economic, and health-related characteristics. Environmental factors relate to the availability of informal support and of community and institutional services (Branch & Jette, 1982; Deimling & Poulshock, 1985; Soldo, 1981).

In a recent study of long-term care use (Mui & Burnette, 1994), race/ethnicity was found to be a significant predictor of service use. Whites reported more use of professional in-home service providers and nursing-home services, and racial/ethnic minority groups reported more care provided by informal helpers (e.g., family members, friends, and neighbors).

Although researchers have identified predictors of institutional versus home-based long-term care (e.g., Branch & Jette, 1982), few have examined how older people might select among various types of long-term care services (McAuley & Blieszner, 1985). Stoller (1982) asked elderly people living in the community what they would do if they were ill and needed constant care. Most frequently mentioned was the nursing home; 30 percent could offer no strategy for obtaining care. Dunkle and colleagues (1982) found that a majority of hospitalized elderly persons with long-term care needs had no idea what services were available in their own communities. Lack of knowledge about resources and services appears to reduce the search for information about what services do exist (Silverstein, 1984). In addition, knowledge about services does not mean that people are able to see the connection to their own needs. Older people may not know how to negotiate receiving services from agencies.

McAuley and Blieszner (1985) surveyed over 1,200 elderly Virginians on their attitudes toward different long-term care arrangements. Respondents favored paid in-home care, care from a relative in one's own home, and adult day care over nursing home care. When arrangements require a change of residence, however, people identify a nursing home as the residence of preference more often than moving into a relative's home. The nursing home was the long-term care arrangement of choice for nonwhites, single persons, and those with higher incomes who felt they did not have anyone to care for them for an extended period (McAuley & Blieszner, 1985). Adult day care was the choice of younger persons and nonwhites in better health; paid home care seemed more appealing for whites and those with emotional problems.

The preference of nonwhites for nursing homes described in the foregoing study is somewhat curious. Kart and Beckham (1976) have reported that nonwhites tend to be less likely than whites to be admitted to nursing homes. They suggest that this lower rate of utilization among nonwhites may result from whites, in general, being more able to pay for care in proprietary nursing homes and from discrimination in the admission of black elderly to nursing homes.

A body of research has developed suggesting that presence of family is an important factor in delaying, if not preventing, the institutionalization of a chronically ill elderly person (Brody, Poulshock, & Masciocchi, 1978; McAuley & Prohaska, 1982). Still, not enough is actually known about the views toward various long-term care arrangements held by family members of elderly who are prospective consumers of such services. It is not known if the views of the elderly and their family members differ with regard to the perceived efficacy of these various arrangements (Neu, 1982) or even if congruence of view is related in any way to successful outcomes for the elderly person.

The risks of needing long-term care are high for elderly Americans. The growth in the elderly population, coupled with longer age-specific life expectancy among the aged, will increase demand for long-term care services in the coming decades. Some argue that access to these needed services is already compromised for many elderly, especially as state and federal cost containment efforts increase. Some subpopulations of elderly, the poor, those with cognitive and/or neurological impairment, and those who generally have heavy care requirements may be at greatest risk to be denied access to needed long-term care.

THE DUALITY OF INFORMAL
AND FORMAL SUPPORTS

Many gerontological researchers and practitioners recognize the duality of informal and formal supports to the elderly (Cantor & Little, 1985). Litwak (1985), among others, argues that the needs of the frail and vulnerable elderly are best met if there is a proper balance between formal and informal support, with each system performing the tasks for which it is best suited.

The main source of informal support for older persons is the family. Silver-stone describes this support system as

> a rich fabric of informal relationships which envelopes the majority of elders in our society along a number of dimensions. This fabric is bonded most strongly by marriage, and adjacent generational and peer relationships and for racial minorities, by expanded kin as well. (1985, p. 156)

Yet, research findings indicate that residing with other relatives is not the living arrangement of choice for most elderly (Kobrin, 1981; Troll, Miller, & Atchley, 1979). Living with relatives is typically a result of impaired health or low income. Certain living arrangements are more satisfying than others. Johnson (1983) found that dissatisfaction with care-giving arrangements is more likely when the care-giver is a child rather than a spouse. She suggests that dissatisfaction may result from the change in the relationship between child and parent when the parent becomes ill.

Various family members seem to be used for care giving, depending on the type of help required. The likelihood is greater that the caregiver will be a spouse before an adult child (Hanson & Sauer, 1985), especially for the bedfast and home-bound. When children are available, they provide a second important source of help. Childless elders rely on other sources of informal support. A third tier of helpers includes siblings. This three-tiered preferential list of helpers has been termed the *hierarchical compensatory model* (Cantor, 1979).

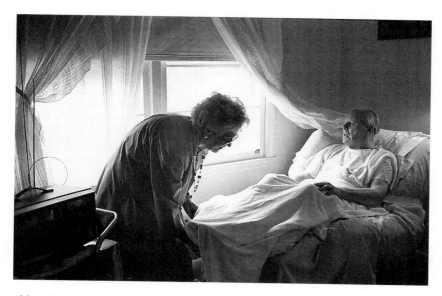

Although various family members may be available to provide support for older people, the first line of care giving is usually the spouse.

It is generally recognized that family and other informal supports frequently have difficulty providing help on a long-term basis to elders who are impaired and disabled (Brody et al., 1987). Emotional, physical, and financial strains appear associated with personal and situational characteristics of the caregiver, with emotional strain seemingly the hardest to bear (Cantor, 1981; Cicirelli, 1988; George, 1987). The isolation of a caregiver, as well as a decrease in emotional resilience and morale, may provoke many elderly persons and their families to turn to formal service providers for help.

The array of services available to older people outside of institutions covers a broad range, including health, housing, and nutrition. Services have been designed to aid the informal care-giving structure, and it has actually been demonstrated that the provision of formal services can prolong the duration and effectiveness of informal care (Chappell, 1990). The organization and delivery of these services are the result of complex policy and financial issues. Estes and Wood (1986) demonstrate that economic constraints, as well as hospital reimbursement policies primarily guided by Medicare and Medicaid regulations for community care, have begun both to medicalize services and to raise the possibility of limiting reimbursable services.

Measurable outcome benefits appear to be minimal for in-home care services and may cost more than is saved by prolonging time to institutionalization. Even in the face of these facts, however, home care has the promise of breaking even, financially, while benefiting more people, if appropriate subgroups are served and outcomes are measured appropriately (Weissert, 1991).

Some existing formal services are identified next in order to help define the range of services available. This listing is not all inclusive. Many communities have a substantial number of these services, but only a limited number of communities are providing a complete set of services. Services are presented in order from most to least restrictive.

Adult Day Care

The term *day care* applies virtually to any service provided during the day. Such services range from social to health-related care, from home care to hospital care, and include rehabilitation as well as physical and mental health care (Harder, Gornick, & Burt, 1986). Weiler and Rathbone-McCuan (1978) define *day care* as a unique service modality because it meets people's long-term care needs while allowing for individual differences. These tailor-made services can have a therapeutic objective of prevention, rehabilitation, or maintenance. Length of hospital stays may also be shortened when elderly adults can be discharged to take advantage of adult day-care centers (Chappell & Blandford, 1983). Table 17–1 depicts the services available under the rubric of day care. Four different service modalities are presented: day hospitals, social/health centers, psychosocial centers, and social centers. A wide range of services is offered to various types of clients in many different service settings. Geriatric day services help the older person placed in day care and can be used to provide respite care for caregivers as well.

TABLE 17–1   Geriatric Day Services

Modality	Major Service Objective	Type of Client	Service Setting
Day hospital	To provide daily medical care and supervision to help the individual regain an optimal level of health following an acute illness.	Individual is in active phase of recovery from an acute illness and no longer requires intense medical intervention on a periodic basis.	Extended-care facility or hospital
Social/health center	To provide health care resources when needed by chronically impaired individuals	Individual has chronic physical illness or disabilities; condition does not require daily medical intervention but does require nursing and other health supports.	Long-term care institution or free-standing center
Psychosocial center	To provide a protective or transitional environment that assists the individual in dealing with multiple problems or daily coping	Individual has a history of psychiatric disorder; could reactivate or suffer from mental deterioration (organic or functional) that places him or her in danger if not closely supervised.	Psychiatric institution or free-standing center
Social center	To provide appropriate socialization services	Individual's social functioning has regressed to the point where overall capacity for independent functioning would not be possible without formal, organized social stimuli.	Specialized senior citizen center

Source: P. Weiler & E. Rathbone-McCuan, *Adult Day Care: Community Work with the Elderly.* Copyright © 1978 by Springer Publishing Company, Inc., New York 10012. Used by permission.

Home Health Care

Home health care entails the provision of coordinated multidisciplinary services, including skilled nursing; therapeutic services; social casework; mental health, legal, financial, and personal care; and household management assistance (Applebaum & Phillips, 1990). Noelker and Harel state, "Its purpose is to aid the elderly person in the performance of activities of daily living which are essential for continued independence yet are problematic for many aged given their health problems and functional impairments" (1978, p. 37). Home health services include the in-home services of a homemaker, home health aid, or home aide assistant (Surpin, 1988). According to Benjamin, however, the term *home* includes any residential setting in which formal medical services are not provided as part of the housing component. Thus, *home* may "mean a detached home, an apartment in a family member's home, or a large complex, or a unit in a congregate housing arrangement with supportive services" (1992, p. 13).

Eligibility requirements for Medicare coverage limit access to this type of service at the same time need is growing with shortened hospital stays resulting from the prospective payment plan (diagnostic-related groups or DRGs) under Medicare (Seifer, 1987). Medicare requires the beneficiary of services to be homebound, to have rehabilitation potential, and to have a medically identified need for skilled care on an intermittent basis. Medicaid programs in most states mimic this model (Kane, 1995). About 80 percent of home care patients are posthospital referrals; the others are referred by a physician after an outpatient episode of illness or by family or friends who need help in providing care.

Home health services are available from proprietary and private service organizations, although use of such organizations may be limited by availability and cost. In 1991, there were approximately 7,000 home health care agencies in the United States; 38 percent reported proprietary ownership.

Historically, home health services were available only under voluntary or public auspices. Usually, this involved a visiting nurse service, public health or welfare department, and, on rare occasions, an extension of hospital services. With the increased profitability of this sector of the health care market, there has been increased development of profit-making agencies that function as local franchises of national organizations.

Foster Care

Foster family care approximates the normal living environment, with the added dimension of supervision. It allows the older person an element of privacy as well as freedom not possible in the larger protected environment of the nursing home. Adult foster care is considered among the least restrictive housing options available to help older persons remain in the community. It utilizes private residences for the care of a nonrelated elderly person who is in need of supervision and/or assistance with the activities of daily living. Definitions of foster care vary from state to state. In Ohio, only homes that have Supplemental Security Income recipients are subject to licensing regulations that control foster care, whereas in Oregon, for example, adult day care has gained respectability and is frequently used as an alternative to nursing homes (Ladd, 1986).

Certain problems are inherent in the provision of adult foster care. For example, unlike foster care for children, where the child moves toward independence and gains the capacity to contribute to the foster family, the elderly person is often viewed as only moving toward greater dependence. As a result, many potential care providers are reluctant to offer their foster homes to the elderly.

Hospice

Hospice is a concept of care for the terminally ill that is gaining popularity in the United States. It is a model of care that is more than a program of medical health care for the terminally ill. Hospice services are often directed by a physician with an interdisciplinary team to provide psychological, social, and spiritual services when needed by the patient and/or family members on a 24-hour, seven-day-a-week basis. These services can continue for family and friends after the patient's death. Of the approximately 1,000 hospice programs in the United States, the average patient is 75 years of age, female (55 percent), white (83 percent), and married (49 percent) (U.S. Bureau of the Census, 1994, Table 195). Whereas much hospice care is delivered in the patient's home, it can also be delivered in virtually any homelike or institutional setting. Additional material on hospice is located in Chapter 19.

Protective Services

Protective or surrogate services describe visits by a social worker, with supplemental community services such as visiting nurses, homemakers, clinical services, meals, telephone checks, and transportation. The myriad of needs addressed under protective services include daily living, physical health, psychosocial problems, household management, housing, economic management, and legal protection. These services are similar to those delivered through the social service delivery system, although their effects may vary because of the potential for legal intervention in the form of guardianship, placement, and commitment and emergency services.

Every older person who is incapacitated is not necessarily a candidate for protective services. The decisive factor appears to be the availability of a reliable person to help the needy individual. Thus, protective services encompass a wider range of considerations than just the condition of the individual alone.

There are three dimensions of protective services provided to older persons (Hall & Mathiasen, 1968): prevention, support, and surrogate service. Protective services strive to maintain the well-being of the older person through reducing or remedying conditions that place the older person at risk, thereby preventing unnecessary institutionalization. Support services provide the aid necessary for the impaired older person to maintain independence and self-direction to the maximum level possible. In providing surrogate services, the service provider is required to act in behalf of or assist someone to act in behalf of the impaired older person. The task is to provide the necessary supportive services, with or without the client's approval.

Respite Care

Respite care offers support to family caregivers so that they can continue to provide care for the frail elderly (General Accounting Office, 1989). This service aims to support the entire family by providing a break for the caregiver and a safe place for the care receiver. Coming in several forms, these programs can be delivered to the home or they can be temporary beds in the hospital or nursing home where the care receiver can stay for a few days. There is clear evidence that families express a need for respite care (Miller & Goldman, 1989) and that it may prevent or delay institutionalization (Townsend & Flanagan, 1976). Even with these noted advantages, respite care is not widely available to families caring for disabled elders.

There are four models of respite care: (1) home-based respite care, (2) group day care, (3) group residential care, and (4) residential programs providing respite care as an adjunct service (Upshur, 1983). *Home-based respite care* uses trained sitters who provide the service in the client's home or other homelike space and are matched with appropriate families. *Group day care* involves provision of daytime activities for brief time periods during the week so that family caregivers may shop or attend meetings. *Residential care* involves a residential facility that is established to provide overnight respite care to small groups of disabled persons (Upshur, 1983). More intensive care can be given in this setting to medically and behaviorally difficult clients. These services, offered in a facility designed and staffed for short stays, can also be given on an adjunct basis.

Board and Care Homes

Board and care facilities provide shelter, food, and protection to frail and disabled individuals (Subcommittee on Health and Long Term Care, 1989). The U.S. Bureau of the Census reports 18,000 licensed board and care homes accommodating approximately 360,000 residents (U.S. Bureau of the Census, 1994, Table 193). Most of these facilities have fewer than 10 beds. However, estimates run as high as one million Americans living in 68,000 licensed and unlicensed board and care homes, with an additional 3.2 million at risk for placement in such facilities. Two-thirds of all residents are old and female, with the majority coming to board and care facilities from mental institutions.

Mental illness is common to residents in board and care homes. Approximately one-half of elderly residents of these homes have been discharged from state mental institutions (Subcommittee on Health and Long Term Care, 1989).

Case Management

Case management is an administrative service that coordinates the delivery of multiple services to frail elders. The Omnibus Budget Reconciliation Act (OBRA) of 1981 introduced case management as a service package under Medicaid waivers. This service package is a combination of formal long-term care services and informal services provided by friends and family (Capitman, MacAdam, & Abrahams, 1991). It is recommended for clients with multiple problems that cut across traditional service delivery systems (Kane et al., 1991) and provides a channel for clients to gain access to other services as well (U.S. Health Care Financing Administration, 1984). It is the case manager's job to coordinate formal and informal, and traditional and nontraditional, services for a holistic approach.

The initial step involves the development of a traditional care plan, in which objectives are set in concert with the elderly client. It is important to determine who will be responsible for providing the various services. At times, it is the client, but it may also be family, friends, or the case manager.

Policymakers and practitioners alike have feared that the programs offered through case management would be overwhelmed by elders and families requesting service. This has not been the case.

In the actual running of these programs, there are staffing and service delivery problems. Recruitment and retention problems plague the staffing of case management programs. In part, lack of professional social work or nursing training may contribute to the retention problem. Under such circumstances, case managers do not have the skilled personnel available to them to do the job in an effective manner.

Unfortunately, given the differences among elderly clients in impairment level, living arrangements, and access to informal supports, the development of tailor-made service plans is difficult. If anything, case management can be accused of suffering from a "cookie cutter" approach, which frequently results in some elders receiving too much service while others receive too little (Capitman, MacAdam, & Abrahams, 1991).

There are numerous models of care that combine various types of case management care. The identification of benefits and disadvantages of these various models has begun to emerge. For instance, there is doubt that case management reduces inpatient hospitalization or costs (Capitman, Haskins, & Bernstein, 1986; Kemper, Applebaum, & Harrigan, 1987; Franklin et al., 1987). Targeting is the key to understanding which type of patient will benefit from which type of service. For instance, in some cases, only information and referral is offered, thus leaving the individuals themselves to coordinate these services. Case management can also be offered for limited periods of time or over an extended time period.

Unfortunately, there is no evidence, as yet, for the effectiveness of case managers in improving access to care, limiting costs, and coordinating services (Estes, Swan et al., 1993).

THE LOGIC OF FORMAL CARE

Formal supports consist of open and closed care (Little, 1979, 1982). *Open care* is provided in the community and encompasses all the formal social services aimed at allowing the individual to maintain life at home and avoid premature or unnecessary institutionalization. *Closed care* describes formal care in institutions such as acute care hospitals. Hospitals service more elderly than any other community agency (Brody & Persily, 1984). About 20 percent of all older people use inpatient facilities at least once a year. Based on discharge data for 1992, rates of hospital stays are 126 percent higher for patients 65 years of age and older than they are for people of all ages. The average length of stay is 44 percent longer for the elderly, consuming a total of 33 percent of total hospital bed days in the U.S. health care system (U.S. Bureau of the Census, 1994, Table 186). It is in the hospital setting that many older people make decisions about long-term care services. When the hospitalization is associated with physical or mental impairment, plans must often be made for nursing home care.

A sense of urgency typically accompanies discharge from the hospital, and this may interfere with usual patterns of problem solving. Moreover, the extent to which the elderly patient participates in arriving at a decision may be limited by the circumstances under which the plans are made (Brody, 1984).

The Risks of Institutionalization

As indicated earlier, approximately 1.7 million elderly, or 5.3 percent of those 65 years and older, are found in nursing homes at any one time. Estimates are that 3 million elderly (over 7 percent of those 65 years and over) will be in nursing homes by 2010 (Zedlewski et al., 1990). Disagreement exists over whether these figures represent overuse of nursing homes.

Kastenbaum and Candy (1973) were the first to point out the fallacy of assuming that the number or proportion of elderly in nursing homes could be used as an estimate of their cumulative chances for institutionalization. They reviewed 20,234 death certificates for those aged 65 and over filed in the metropolitan Detroit area during the 1971 calendar year. They found that 20 percent of all these deaths were reported in nursing homes, and approximately 24 percent were reported occurring in a larger category of institutions that included all identifiable extended-care facilities. Others were able to substantiate these findings, with a consensus opinion emerging by the mid-1970s that "the total chance of institutionalization before death among normal aged persons living in the community would be about one in four" (Palmore, 1976). More recently, it seems that the actual chance of residing in a nursing home at some point in old age has increased to almost one in three for men and about one in two for the women who turned age 65 in 1990 (Kemper & Murtaugh, 1991). The risks of institutionalization also increase with age. People 85 years of age and older represent only about 11 percent of the total elderly population in the United States but about 45 percent of the population of nursing home residents.

Presenting a picture that shows that one in three elderly men and one in two elderly women can expect to be institutionalized in a nursing home or rest home makes it easier to understand why a major fear of many older persons is that they will become dependent and have to face institutionalization. Such figures also make it easier to begin to understand the potentially high financial and human costs of institutionalization and the tremendous strain this phenomenon may place on public and private resources.

Who Gets Institutionalized?

A complex array of factors seems to influence who among the elderly gets institutionalized. Confusing matters is the fact that studies differ in focus, with some emphasizing new admissions, others characterizing residents currently in nursing homes, and still others focusing on discharges. Further, most research on institutionalization limits variables to characteristics of individuals, and neglects health care system and community characteristics. Of those individuals who are institutionalized, 75 percent of residents are female and widowed (Mezey & Knapp, 1993); 30 percent have no living children (National Center for Health Statistics, 1989); 45 percent are 85 years of age or older; 59 percent are dependent in four or five activities of daily living (Lair & Lefkowitz, 1990); and more than 60 percent have some sort of cognitive, mental, or behavioral disorder (Lair & Lefkowitz, 1990). Approximately one of three residents have been in a nursing home for less than a year; 21 percent have resided in a facility for five or more years.

The picture of the typical nursing home resident has been changing. Increasingly, the nursing home is shaped by regulatory and financial pressures, which encourage the admission of patients who are more incapacitated and have more complex medical problems (Karuza & Katz, 1994). There is also a prevalence of mental health problems among these residents (Rovner, Burton, & German, 1992), including chronic behavioral problems as well as acute problems of adjustment and coping (Karuza & Katz, 1994). Services need to be provided to meet these mental health needs.

Recent research results have reported characteristics of persons who are more likely to be discharged from nursing homes. This reality has been largely ignored until recently. Previously, it was believed that all those admitted to a nursing home would die there. Greene and Ondrich (1990) found the following characteristics to predict greater likelihood of being discharged alive from a nursing home: not being African American; owning a home; being younger; and having better health, cognitive capacities, and mental acuity.

Characteristics of Nursing Homes

According to the National Center for Health Statistics, there were 33,000 nursing and related care facilities in the United States in 1991. This is a 43 percent increase from 1980. Forty-five percent (44.6 percent) of these facilities are nursing homes;

the rest are board and care homes. The great majority of nursing homes (71.4 percent) are run for profit. Although nonprofit and government nursing homes make up only about 28 percent of the facilities, their greater capacity (an average of 112 beds versus 103 beds for proprietary facilities) enables them to serve about 30 percent of all nursing-home residents.

Nursing homes may also be classified according to their certification status. About two-thirds of all nursing homes (65.9 percent) in 1991 were certified as Skilled Nursing Facilities (SNFs). Certified for participation under Medicare, SNFs typically have transfer agreements with hospitals and provide skilled nursing care services for rehabilitation of people who are injured, disabled, or sick.

Over the past three decades, medical care prices rose much faster than prices in general. Nursing-home costs have been no exception. Through the 1980s to date, nursing-home charges have continued to rise at a faster pace than the Consumer Price Index (CPI). A November 1992 *Newsweek* story assessed the average cost of a nursing-home bed as $32,000 a year, with costs as high as $80,000 a year (Beck et al., 1992). Although specific data on nursing homes is not easily available, medical care costs increased, on average, 5.9 percent in 1993—the lowest level of increase since 1972–73. Still, this rate of increase was almost twice that of the total CPI in 1993 (3.0 percent).

THE DECISION TO INSTITUTIONALIZE AN OLDER PERSON

Old-age institutions have been described as dehumanizing and depersonalizing (Townsend, 1962). Nursing-home critics describe many facilities as human junkyards and warehouses (Butler, 1975). Studies of old persons residing in a variety of institutional settings have shown them to be more maladjusted, depressed, and unhappy; to have a lower range of interests and activity; and to be more likely to die sooner than aged persons living in the community (Lieberman, 1969; Mendelson, 1974; Townsend, 1970).

Despite the unfavorable reputation of old-age institutions and the negative attitudes of elderly citizens toward them, many elderly individuals need and seek out institutional care. Usually, this need is apparent to family members or is based on a physician's recommendation. In fact, in cases involving physical illness or debility, the need may be apparent to the elderly patient as well.

As already mentioned, the availability of adequate and applicable home care and community services can prevent the institutionalization of many elderly patients. Family members are often very much involved in decisions concerning the institutionalization of an elderly person. When an aged family member is placed into a nursing home, many of the responsibilities for caring for that individual shift from the family to the institution. Still, many families continue to remain involved with that family member.

What is the most effective way for a family to remain involved with an institutionalized relative so as to promote higher-quality nursing home care? What responsibilities do institutions have to provide support to families that want to stay involved? A first step in answering these questions and ultimately in providing optimal care is for both parties—families and nursing-home staff—to understand and accept their respective responsibilities in providing services to the institutionalized individual.

Shuttlesworth, Rubin, and Duffy (1982) have assessed the extent to which Texas nursing home administrators and relatives of institutional residents have congruous attitudes about whether the nursing home or the family is responsible for performing an inventory of tasks that are essential in nursing home care. Two findings are worthy of mention. First, administrators as well as relatives assigned responsibility to the nursing home for the majority of tasks that they see as vital to care. These include technical tasks involving medical care, security, housekeeping, cooking, and the like. Second, in most cases of discrepancies, relatives were more likely than administrators to assign responsibility to families. For the most part, these discrepancies involved nontechnical tasks such as room furnishings, leisure-time activities, clothing, and special foods.

This study suggests that a problem in engaging families in the care of institutionalized relatives is not with the willingness of families to claim responsibility for nontechnical aspects of care, but rather with administrators' insufficient recognition of family responsibility for nontechnical tasks. As a result, administrators may fail to communicate sufficient support for family involvement in such tasks. They may overlook possible policy or procedural changes in institutional arrangements that could better facilitate family involvement in overseeing the nontechnical aspects of care.

Lack of congruence of view between relatives of the institutionalized individual and nursing-home staff may result in aggressive behavior directed at nursing-home personnel by residents' family members. In a survey of 70 Florida nursing homes over a six-month period, administrators reported 1,193 cases of verbal aggression and 13 acts of physical aggression (Vinton & Mazza, 1994). Dissatisfaction over how the care needs of residents were being met was most frequently cited as the contributing factor. Social workers were often called on to help resolve conflicts, and discussing the incident with either the staff person or family member alone were the most frequently reported conflict resolution strategies.

INSTITUTIONAL EFFECTS: REAL OR IMAGINARY?

The gerontological literature is filled with descriptions of the institutionalized elderly as disorganized, disoriented, and depressed. Tobin and Lieberman (1976) review three explanations for this portrait: (1) relocation and environmental change, (2) preadmission effects, and (3) the totality of institutions.

Relocation and Environmental Change

The relationship of environmental change to mortality and morbidity has been investigated in mental hospitals, nursing homes, and homes for the aged. Much controversy exists regarding the effect of relocation on mortality and other health status outcomes (Horowitz & Schulz, 1983). Researchers generally agree, however, that moving an older person from a familiar setting into an institution leads to psychologic disorganization and distress, especially when the move is involuntary (Schulz & Brenner, 1977). Having a sense of choice over entering a nursing home and receiving visits from preferred visitors have been identified as predictors of well-being of the institutionalized aged (Harel & Noelker, 1982).

Some investigators argue that the disruption of life caused by relocating an elderly individual into new surroundings may create many of the effects attributed to living in that new setting (Tobin & Lieberman, 1976; Lieberman & Tobin, 1983). Others argue that it is not simply the stress of relocation, but, rather, environmental discontinuity—the degree of change between a new and an old environment—may explain the effects observed after institutionalization (Lawton, 1974). Interestingly, some evidence suggests that environmental change can elicit desirable behavior and increase the competence of the older individual. Carp (1966) and Lipman (1968) have both reported on favorable changes experienced by elderly individuals during the year after a move into an age-segregated housing situation. Important in such settings are the physical proximity of age peers and the development of behavioral expectations appropriate to the level of competence of the average resident (Lawton, 1974).

Preadmission Effects

Anticipating and preparing for the move into an institution can be very stressful. The effects of this stress on the older person before admission are often very similar to what are described as institutional effects. Tobin and Lieberman (1976) found old people who were awaiting institutionalization to be markedly different from those living in the community in cognitive functioning, affective response, emotional state, and self-perceptions. What is even more interesting is that the psychological status of the study sample awaiting institutionalization was not unlike the psychological status generally descriptive of aged persons in institutions: slight cognitive disorganization, constriction in affective response, less than optimal feelings of well-being, diminished self-esteem, and depression (Tobin & Lieberman, 1976, pp. 55–56). This evidence supports the existence of an anticipatory psychosocialization process in which forces are set into motion so that the individual comes to approximate the institutionalized elderly in frame of mind even before entering the institutionalized environment.

Another explanation that has been offered in the literature is that selection biases account for the usual portrait of the institutionalized elderly. In this context, the term *selection bias* refers to the fact that people who are admitted to institutions may have characteristics that sensitize them to respond negatively to living in those institutions. In this view, differences found between older persons living in the community and those living in institutions are not a function of institutional life but of population differences (Tobin & Lieberman, 1976). If selection is playing a role, then, in Tobin and Lieberman's words, "The institutionalized aged share some characteristics because of who they are and not where they are."

The Total Institution

What do institutions do to the old? A compelling answer has been offered by Erving Goffman (1961) in his characterization of the total institution. According to Goffman, a basic social arrangement in contemporary society is that the individual tends to sleep, play, and work in different settings with different coparticipants. A central feature of total institutions is the breakdown of the barriers that ordinarily separate these activities, so that all three activities take place in the same setting with the same people. One category of total institution includes those places that take care of persons who are perceived to be generally incapable of caring for themselves and harmless to themselves and others. Included in this category are nursing homes, homes for the aged, and homes for the poor and indigent.

Goffman argues that common to all total institutions is the fact that individuals in such institutions undergo a process of *self-mortification*. This process, which involves interacting with others in the institutional setting, strips the resident of his or her identity and reduces the control individuals perceive they have over events of daily life. Goffman (1961, pp. 14–43) identifies the features of an institutional environment that he suggests contribute to the mortification process. These features are discussed here with particular emphasis on nursing-home residents.

Admission Procedures. Admission procedures typically bring loss. The individual is often stripped of personal possessions, issued institutional clothing, and "shaped and coded" into an object that can be worked on smoothly by the institution. Such procedures are depersonalizing in that they serve to detach the individual from the social system at large. Jules Henry (1973) refers to this as "depersonalization through symbolic means," with a person losing his or her name or being addressed as "you" instead of as "Mrs. Jones."

Barriers. The total institution places barriers between the resident and the outside world that result in a loss of the roles that are a part of the resident's self. Most institutionalized individuals simply are not able to play the roles of mother and father, grandmother and grandfather, aunt or uncle, and friend in the way they played these roles on the outside. All institutionalized persons face the loss of a familiar way of living. Most describe it simply in terms of losing others and leaving their families' possessions at home.

Deference Obligations. Because total institutions deal with almost all aspects of a resident's life, there is a special need to obtain the resident's cooperation. Thus, the resident may be required to show physical and verbal deference to the staff members or be subject to punishment. Such deference may be humiliating and result in loss of self-esteem. Often, the individual is asked to engage in activities with symbolic implications that are incompatible with conceptions of self. Sharon Curtin describes the case of Miss Larson, at shower time in the Montcliffe Convalescent Hospital:

> I could hear Miss Larson. "No, no, I can bathe myself, just let me alone, I can do it.". . . Two aides, one on each side, would pick up the old carcasses, place them in a molded plastic shower chair, deftly remove the blanket, push them under the shower and rather haphazardly soap them down. . . . The aides were quick, efficient, not at all brutal; they kept up a running conversation between themselves about food prices, the new shoes one had bought, California divorce laws. They might have been two sisters doing dishes. Lift, scrub, rinse, dry, put away. And did you hear the one about. . . . (1972)

Verbal or Physical Humiliation.   Residents may have to beg or humbly ask for little things, such as a glass of water or permission to use the telephone. Staff or fellow residents may call residents obscene names, curse them, publicly point out their negative attributes, or talk about them as if they were not there. At the extreme, there may be loss of a sense of personal safety—beatings, shock therapies, or, in some cases, the understanding that one will be denied necessary treatment—which may lead residents to feel that they are in an environment that does not guarantee their physical integrity.

Contaminative Exposure.   On the outside, the individual can hold his or her feelings about self, actions, thoughts, and some possessions clear from others. In the total institution, these areas of self are violated. Facts about the residents' social statuses and past behaviors, including negative information, are collected upon admission and continually recorded and made available to staff. Physical contamination (such as unclean food, messy quarters, shoes and clothing soiled by previous users) as well as interpersonal contamination (such as forced social relationships and denial of privacy) may also occur.

Admission procedures, barriers, deference obligations, verbal and/or physical humiliation, and contaminative exposure represent the mortifying processes that patients are subject to in old-age institutions (and other institutions). The patient must adapt to these processes. Goffman (1961) identifies four modes of adaptation to the processes of mortification that take place in an institution. The first, *situational withdrawal,* occurs most frequently in old-age institutions and can be described in terms previously used to describe institutional effects. The patient withdraws attention from everything around him or her, and there is a drastic curtailment of involvement in interaction. Regression occurs and is often irreversible. A second mode of adaptation is what Goffman calls the *intransigent line*: The inmate intentionally challenges the institution by flagrantly refusing to cooperate with staff members. This mode of adaptation can lead to patient abuse.

Two other modes of adaptation to the total institution, described by Goffman, are *colonization* and *conversion*. Patients who take a colonization tack accept the sampling of the outside world provided by the institution and build a stable, contented existence by attempting to procure the maximum satisfaction available in the home. Such patients turn the institution into a home away from home and may find it difficult to leave. As Goffman (1961, p. 63) points out, the staff who try to make life in total institutions more bearable must face the possibility that doing so may increase the likelihood of colonization. Patients who convert take on the staff view of the patient and often attempt to act out the role of perfect patient. A patient employing this mode of adaptation might adopt the manner and dress of the attendants while helping them to manage other patients.

THE QUALITY OF LONG-TERM CARE

Goffman (1961) implies that mortification of the self is characteristic of all total institutions (no matter how therapeutic the environment). It makes intuitive sense, however, that some institutional settings are less mortifying than others and provide higher-quality care. How such evaluations are made is often difficult to determine. Health care practitioners and researchers find the issue of evaluating institutional care to be extraordinarily complex. What is a good nursing home? Should quality be measured in terms of resident satisfaction or professional nursing care? Given limited resources, is it more important to spend money on gardeners, interior design, janitorial services, food quality, or an abundance of aides, orderlies, and health professionals?

A number of researchers have looked to the relationship between institutional characteristics and quality of care (see Kart & Manard, 1976, and Lemke & Moos, 1986, for detailed reviews of this literature). Characteristics of institutions thought to be related to quality of care include ownership status, size, socioeconomic status, social integration, and staff professionalism.

Can high-quality care be assured in nursing homes? Some cynics argue that even the inspectors and regulators themselves admit regulation is a poor tool for assuring high-quality institutional care. Approaches suggesting administrative change and accountability through greater community involvement have been offered in the past. In recent years, government efforts to control abuse have been aimed primarily at reducing costs rather than improving quality of care. Still, cost containment efforts by the federal government could force better compatibility of patient needs and long-term care services. One approach involves some efficient substitution of long-term care services for acute services (Vladeck, 1985). Another is the single or channeling agency, an organizational reform intended to provide opportunities for better matching resources in the community with the needs of the area's elderly population (Brecher & Knickman, 1985).

Little is known about the best ways to deliver long-term care services. For the most part, the lack of homogeneity within the nursing-home population requires flexibility in service delivery. For example, the needs of the short-stay rehabilitation patient differs from the short-stay terminally ill person or the long-term cognitively ill patient. Many times, a patient's needs are not primarily medical. The interdisciplinary nature of service delivery personnel allows for these diverse needs to be potentially met within one setting. Still, variability in the course of long-term care makes it problematic to determine which long-term care services can be delivered most effectively to which patients and where.

Within the long-term care service delivery system, certain measures are commonly identified as appropriate criteria to study service efficacy. These include mortality, morbidity, functional deficits of residents, overall health condition, appropriateness of use of health facilities (e.g., emergency rooms and acute care hospitals), and resident complaints (Mezey & Knapp, 1993).

The lack of firm consensus on an outcome measure for long-term care has resulted in staffing being used as a measure of quality of care in nursing facilities

---

IN SEARCH OF THE RIGHT HOME

According to *Consumer Reports* (1995), a long stay in a nursing home can consign a resident's family to financial hardship, even poverty. Choose the wrong nursing home, however, and you may also consign your loved one to physical and emotional hardship, premature dependency and incontinence, even premature death. Unfortunately, finding the wrong nursing home is easy; it is the good ones that appear difficult to find (*Consumer Reports,* 1995). Little objective guidance is available for families who are pressed to make a decision when a sudden illness or disability requires a nursing-home stay. Sometimes, the government's patchwork payment system dictates the choice of facility, or a hospital discharge planner forces a quick decision in an effort to move patient's out of expensive hospital beds as quickly as is possible.

Consumer Reports offers that there is no substitute for your own firsthand investigation in selecting a nursing home. Where to start?

1. Federal law requires that nursing homes make their latest inspection report (conducted every 12 to 15 months)

available and readily accessible to residents and the public. It is essential to read these reports. They detail deficiencies and violations of federal law. If the report is unavailable, hidden, out of reach, out of date, locked up, or unreadable, assume the facility has something to hide.

2. No matter how good the inspection report, it is necessary to inspect the facility yourself. Visit unannounced at different times of the day and week. Avoid the guided tour. Talk with staff and residents, where possible.

3. Decor counts for little. Appearance of residents' rooms is more important. Does the home allow residents to personalize their rooms? Furniture? Photos? Books? Curtains? Plants?

4. The best facilities have no lingering stench. Accidents will happen, but generally smells should be confined to certain rooms. "If intense odors waft from several rooms at, say 10 A.M., it could mean that staff hasn't changed residents' diapers since the night before" (*Consumer Reports,* 1995, p. 523).

5. Assess safety hazards. Are mops and brooms propped about in the hallways? Are spills and wet towels on the floors ignored?

6. Is staff turnover high? Many facilities are understaffed, so job stress is high. Are staff responsive to residents? Do you observe interaction between staff and residents? And, if so, what is the quality of this interaction? Is it rude and unpleasant or warm and abundant?

7. Are residents well groomed? According to *Consumer Reports,* a sure-fire sign of neglect is the failure to keep residents clean, well dressed, and well groomed. Are residents wearing soiled clothing? Are they appropriately dressed for the season? Do they have on shoes?

8. Visit at mealtime and taste the food. Is it attractively served? Tasty? Served at the proper temperature? Dining rooms should be pleasant and attractive. Menus should be posted and followed. Are between-meal and bedtime snacks available?

9. Is there an activities calendar that is followed? Are residents actively engaged? Is socialization encouraged? Do residents have reason to come out of their rooms?

10. Federal law prohibits nursing homes from using restraints, unless there is medical justification or the order of a physician. "If you see a high proportion of residents in a sitting room or at an activity who are restrained, alarms should go off" (*Consumer Reports,* 1995, p. 524). Freedom to move about is central to quality of life in a nursing home. If you find a facility that is restraint free, it is likely a good one.

11. *Consumer Reports'* review of inspection reports found 25 percent of facilities cited for deficiencies for allowing the development of bed sores. Almost one-third failed to give appropriate treatment for bed sores that had developed. You cannot observe the development of bed sores and you may have no way of knowing whether a facility is moving residents frequently enough to prevent sores from forming. If the inspection report notes a problem with bed sores, this should be a red flag. Ask questions.

12. Are patients with cognitive deficits (e.g., demented or with Alzheimer's) separated from or mixed with other residents? According to *Consumer Reports* (1995, p. 526), many nursing homes are pushing special-care units for demented patients at extra cost. The magazine cites the Alzheimer's Association indicating that these special-care units "may too often be an expensive marketing technique." Is controlled space available for residents to wander outdoors? Is there a special place for those residents who are agitated? Those with sleep disturbances?

13. Finally, nursing homes are required to complete an assessment of each patient who enters. This should include physical, mental, and social abilities. This assessment is the basis of a care plan. Are care plans written and carried out? Is there a care plan conference? Follow-up conferences? And can you attend? If the care plan requires particular behavior or activities (e.g., walking twice a day), it may be necessary for you or other family members to assume the role of policeman to be sure the activity is done.

No clear consensus exists on what exactly contributes to or reflects quality of care in a nursing home. There is no substitution for visiting, observing, and speaking up. If you believe care is poor, it probably is. Confirm your perceptions with reports from the local ombudsman or citizens advocacy group, where these are available.

(Mezey & Scanlon, 1988). Staffing personnel characteristics alone do not ensure high quality of care, but without good professional and paraprofessional staff, the quality of care provided to residents does suffer (Institute of Medicine, 1986; Mohler & Lessard, 1991).

One complex aspect of viewing staffing as an indicator of quality of care is that organizational, managerial, and professional staffing characteristics that may influence quality of care in nursing homes are mediated through nursing aides and assistants. These are the staff members who provide the greatest amount of direct care to residents (Bowers & Becker, 1992; Kruzich, 1990).

Nursing aides and assistants are often described as poorly trained, with high turnover, and low job satisfaction (Chartock et al., 1988). This is particularly problematic in the case of mentally ill elders. Estimates of mental illness among residents of nursing homes run in excess of 50 percent, yet nursing aides and assistants constitute about 63 percent of the primary caregivers for mentally ill elderly. Since nursing assistants have become *de facto* mental health technicians, additional training in mental health and aging is clearly required to maintain some semblance of quality of care (Spore, Smyer, & Cohn, 1991). Almost by definition, without such training, most nursing-home residents could be defined as inappropriately placed relative to the resources available in that nursing home.

SUMMARY

Assessing the long-term care needs of the elderly and matching services to those needs can be difficult. There are many service delivery barriers for older people. Sometimes, the elderly are reluctant to admit that they have needs, and many even deny using services. The mere fact that services are created and made available to the elderly does not mean that those services will be utilized. How older people choose the long-term care services they will use is determined by a complex set of interacting personal and environmental factors.

The main source of support for older persons is the family. A body of research suggests that the presence of family is an important factor in delaying, if not preventing, the institutionalization of a chronically ill elderly person. Still, some argue that the needs of the frail and vulnerable elderly are best met if there is a proper balance between formal and informal support. A broad array

of services is available to older people in the community, including health, housing, and nutrition services. A limited number of these noninstitutional services are discussed in this chapter. These include adult day care, home care, foster care, hospice, protective services, board and care homes, and respite care.

Currently, more than 1.7 million elderly individuals (about 5.3 percent of the aged population) reside in nursing homes in the United States. The risk of an elderly person in the United States being institutionalized is currently about one in three for men and one in two for women. Typically, the nursing home population is white, female, widowed, age 80 or over, poor, and has lived in an institutional facility for about two years. Over 80 percent of nursing-home residents were admitted primarily for physical reasons. There are more than 33,000 nursing and personal care homes in the United

States today. The great majority of these are run for profit.

Nursing homes have an unfavorable reputation, and elderly individuals often have strong negative feelings toward being institutionalized, even when institutional care is absolutely necessary. In part, this may result from the portrait the gerontological literature paints of the institutionalized elderly. This population is overwhelmingly characterized as disorganized, disoriented, and depressed. Three explanations for this negative portrait are discussed. These include problems of relocation, preadmission effects, and the totality of institutions.

Quality nursing-home care is difficult to define and assess. Some characteristics of nursing homes—such as nonprofit status, wealth of resources, and staff with positive attitudes toward the residents—are thought to be related to quality of care. In recent years, government has emphasized cost containment. A better approach might emphasize compatibility between resources and the needs of the elderly population. In the nursing home, such compatibility would require additional training for nursing aides and assistants—those staff persons who have the most direct contact with residents.

STUDY QUESTIONS

1. Identify the goals of long-term care.
2. Profile the long-term care service user. Does every individual who needs long-term care assistance receive it? Explain. What are the service delivery barriers?
3. What is known about how older people select among long-term care alternatives?
4. What role does the family play in providing long-term care assistance?
5. Identify the following:
   a. Adult day care
   b. Home care
   c. Foster care
   d. Hospice
   e. Protective services
   f. Respite care
   g. Board and care homes
   h. Case management
6. Why can't the institutionalization rate for the elderly be used as an estimation of their cumulative chances for institutionalization?
7. Describe the so-called typical nursing-home resident. How would you explain the disproportionate number of women and the underrepresentation of nonwhites in nursing homes.
8. List some major organizational dimensions along which nursing homes vary. How have nursing-home costs increased in relation to prices in general? Why might you expect significant variation in charges among nursing and personal care homes?
9. What is the process of "self-mortification" as defined by Goffman? List and explain the features of an institutional environment that Goffman suggests contribute to the mortification process.
10. Why is quality of care in nursing homes so difficult a concept on which to get a handle? Is staff a quality-of-care indicator? If so, how do many U.S. nursing homes shape up on this dimension?

REFERENCES

Applebaum, R., & Phillips, P. (1990). Assuring the quality of in-home care: The "other" challenge for long-term care. *The Gerontologist, 30* (4), 444–450.

Beck, M., Hager, M., Springer, K., & Barrett, T. (1992). Planning to be poor. *Newsweek* (November 30), 66–67.

Benjamin, A. E. (1992). In-home health and supportive services. In M. G. Ory & A. P. Duncker (Eds.), *In-home care for older people: Health and supportive services.* Newbury Park, CA: Sage.

Bowers, B., & Becker, M. (1992). Nurse's aides in nursing homes: The relationship between organization and quality. *The Gerontologist, 32* (3), 360–366.

Branch, L. G., & Jette, A. M. (1982). A prospective study of long-term care institutionalization among the aged. *American Journal of Public Health, 72,* 1373–1379.

Brecher, C., & Knickman, J. (1985). A reconsideration of long-term care. *Journal of Health Politics, Policy and Law, 10,* 245–273.

Brody, E. M., Kleban, M. H., Johnson, P. T., Hoffman, C., & Schoonover, C. B. (1987). Work status and parent care: A comparison of four groups of women. *The Gerontologist, 27* (2), 201–208.

Brody, S. J. (1984). Goals of geriatric care. In S. Brody & N. Persily (Eds.), *Hospitals and the aged: The new old market.* Rockville, MD: Aspen.

Brody, S. J., & Persily, N. (Eds.). (1984). *Hospitals and the aged: The new old market.* Rockville, MD: Aspen.

Brody, S. J., Poulshock, W., & Masciocchi, C. (1978). The family caring unit: A major consideration in the long-term support system. *The Gerontologist, 18,* 556–561.

Butler, R. N. (1975). *Why survive? Being old in America.* New York: Harper and Row.

Cantor, M. (1979). Neighbors and friends: An overlooked resource in the informal support system. *Research on Aging, 1,* 434–463.

Cantor, M. (1981). *Factors associated with strain among family, friends and neighbors caring for the frail elderly.* Paper presented at the Annual Scientific Meeting of the Gerontological Society of America, Toronto, Canada.

Cantor, M., & Little, V. (1985). Aging and social care. In R. Binstock & E. Shanas (Eds.), *Handbook of aging and the social sciences* (2nd ed.). New York: Van Nostrand Reinhold.

Capitman, J., Haskins, B., & Bernstein, J. (1986). Case management approaches in community oriented long term care demonstrations. *The Gerontologist, 26* (4), 398–404.

Capitman, J., MacAdam, M., & Abrahams, R. (1991). Case management roles in emergent approaches to long-term care. In P. Katz, R. Kane, & L. Mezey (Eds.), *Advances in long-term care.* New York: Springer.

Carp, F. M. (1966). *A future for the aged.* Austin: University of Texas Press.

Chappell, N. (1990). Aging and social care. In R. Binstock & L. George (Eds.), *Handbook of aging and the social sciences* (3rd ed.). San Diego, CA: Academic Press.

Chappell, N. L., & Blandford, A. A. (1983). *Adult day care: Its impact on the utilization of other health care services and on quality of life.* Ottawa, Ontario: NHRDP, Health and Welfare Canada.

Chartock, P., Nevins, A., Rzetelny, H., & Gilberto, P. (1988). A mental health training program in nursing homes. *The Gerontologist, 28,* 503–507.

Cicirelli, V. G. (1988). A measure of filial anxiety regarding anticipated care of elderly parents. *The Gerontologist, 28* (4), 478–482.

Cohen, M. A., Tell, E. J., & Wallack, S. S. (1986). Client related risk factors of nursing home entry among elderly adults. *Journal of Gerontology, 41,* 785–792.

Consumer Reports. (1995). Nursing homes: Covering the cost. *Consumer Reports, 60* (9), 591–597.

Consumer Reports. (1995). Nursing homes: When a loved one needs care. *Consumer Reports, 60* (8), 518–528.

Curtin, S. (1972). *Nobody ever died of old age.* Boston: Little, Brown.

Deimling, G. T., & Poulshock, S. W. (1985). The transition from family in-home care to institutional care. *Research on Aging, 7* (4), 563–576.

Dunkle, R., Coulton, C., Mackintosh, J., & Goode, R. (1982). The decision making process among the hospitalized elderly. *Journal of Gerontological Social Work, 4* (3), 95–106.

Estes, C. L., Swan, J. H., & associates. (1993). *The long term care crisis: Elders trapped in the no-care zone.* Newbury Park, CA: Sage.

Estes, C. L., & Wood, J. B. (1986). The non-profit sector and community based care for the elderly in the U.S.: A disappearing resource? *Social Science and Medicine, 23,* 175–184.

Franklin, J., Solovitz, B., Mason, M., Clemons, J., & Miller, G. (1987). An evaluation of case management. *American Journal of Public Health, 77,* 674–678.

General Accounting Office. (1989). *Respite care insights on federal, state and private sector involvement.* GAO/HRD-89-12, April 6.

George, L. K. (1987). Easing caregiver burden: The role of internal and formal supports. In R. A. Ward & S. S. Tobin (Eds.), *Health in aging: Sociological issues and policy directories.* New York: Springer.

Goffman, E. (1961). *Asylums.* New York: Doubleday.

Greene, V., & Ondrich, J. (1990). Risk factors for nursing home admissions and exits: A discrete-time hazard function approach. *Journal of Gerontology, 45,* S250–258.

Hall, G., & Mathiasen, G. (1968). *Overcoming barriers to protective services for the aged: Report of the National Institute on Protective Services.* New York: National Council on Aging.

Hanson, S. M., & Sauer, W. J. (1985). Children and their elderly parents. In W. J. Sauer & R. T. Coward (Eds.), *Social support networks and the care of the elderly.* New York: Springer.

Harder, W. P., Gornick, J. C., & Burt, M. R. (1986). Adult day care: Substitute or supplement? *The Milbank Quarterly, 64* (3), 414–441.

Harel, Z., & Noelker L., (1982). Social integration, health and choice: Their impact on the well-being of institutionalized aged. *Research on Aging, 4,* 97–111.

Henry, J. (1973). Personality and aging—With special reference to hospitals for the aged poor. In J. Henry (Ed.), *On shame, vulnerability and other forms of self-destruction.* New York: Random House.

Horowitz, M. J., & Schulz, R. (1983). The relocation controversy: Criticism and commentary in five recent studies. *The Gerontologist, 23,* 229–234.

Institute of Medicine. (1986). *Improving the quality of care in nursing homes.* Washington, DC: National Academy Press.

Jette, A. M., Branch, L. G., Sleeper, L. A., Feldman, H., & Sullivan, L. M. (1992). High-risk profiles for nursing home admission. *The Gerontologist, 32* (5), 634–640.

Johnson, C. (1983). Dyadic family relations and social supports. *The Gerontologist, 23* (4), 377–383.

Kane, R. A. (1995). Expanding the home care concept: Blurring distinctions among home care, institutional care, and other long-term care services. *The Milbank Quarterly, 73* (2), 161–186.

Kane, R. L., & Kane, R. A. (1982). Long term care: A field in search of values. In R. L. Kane & R. A. Kane (Eds.), *Values and long term care.* Lexington, MA: Lexington Books.

Kane, R. L., & Kane, R. A. (1989). Transitions in long term care. In M. Ory & K. Bond (Eds.), *Aging and health care: Social Science and policy perspectives.* New York: Routledge.

Kane, R., Pernod, J., Davidson, G., Moscovice, I., & Rich, E. (1991, June). What cost case management in long-term care? *Social Service Review,* 281–303.

Kart, C., & Beckham, B. (1976). Black-white differences in the institutionalization of the elderly: A temporal analysis. *Social Forces, 54*, 901–910.

Kart, C., & Manard, B. (1976). Quality of care in old-age institutions. *The Gerontologist, 16* (3), 250–256.

Karuza, J., & Katz, P. (1994). Physician staffing patterns correlates of nursing home care: An initial inquiry and consideration of policy implications. *Journal of the American Geriatrics Society, 42*, 787–793.

Kastenbaum, R., & Candy, S. (1973). The 4 percent fallacy: A methodological and empirical critique of extended care facility population statistics. *International Journal of Aging and Human Development, 4*, 15–21.

Kemper, P., Applebaum, R., & Harrigan, M. (1987). Community care demonstration: What have we learned? *Health Care Financing Review, 8* (4), 87–100.

Kemper, P., & Murtaugh, C. M. (1991). Lifetime use of nursing home care. *New England Journal of Medicine, 324*, 595–600.

Kobrin, F. (1981). Family extension and the elderly: Economic, demographic and family cycle factors. *Journal of Gerontology, 36*, 370–377.

Kruzich, J. (1990). *Assessing the influence of organizational characteristics on resident adjustment.* Paper presented at the 43rd annual scientific meeting of the Gerontological Society of America, Boston.

Ladd, R. C. (1986). Oregon's long-term system for the elderly and disabled. In R. A. Kane & R. L. Kane (Eds.), *Long-term care: Principles, programs, and policies.* New York: Springer.

Lair, T., & Lefkowitz, D. (1990). *Mental health and functional status of residents of nursing and personal care homes.* (DHHS Pub. No. (PHS) 90-3470). Agency for Health Care Policy and Research. Rockville, MD: Public Health Service.

Lawton, M. P. (1974). Social ecology and the health of older people. *American Journal of Public Health, 64*, 257–260.

Lemke, S., & Moos, R. H. (1986). Quality of residential settings for elderly adults. *Journal of Gerontology, 41* (2), 268–276.

Levenson, S. A. (1993). The changing role of the nursing home medical director. In P. R. Katz, R. L. Kane, M. D. Mezey (Eds.), *Advances in long term care* (Vol. 2). New York: Springer.

Lieberman, M. (1969). Institutionalization of the aged: Effects of behavior. *Journal of Gerontology, 24*, 330–340.

Lieberman, M., & Tobin, S. S. (1983). *The experience of old age: Stress, coping, and survival.* New York: Basic Books.

Lipman, A. (1968). Public housing and attitudinal adjustment in old age: A comparative study. *Journal of Geriatric Psychiatry, 2*, 88–101.

Little, V. (1979). For the elderly: An overview of services in industrially developed and developing countries. In M. Teicher, D. Thursz, & J. Vigilante (Eds.), *Reaching the aged: Social services in forty-four countries: Vol. 4. Social service delivery systems: An international annual.* Beverly Hills: Sage.

Little, V. (1982). *Open care for the aging.* New York: Springer.

Litwak, E. (1985). *Helping the elderly.* New York: Guilford.

Manton, K. G. (1989). Epidemiological demographic, and social correlates of disability among the elderly. *The Milbank Quarterly, 67* (2-1), 13–58.

McAuley, W., & Blieszner, R. (1985). Selection of long-term care arrangements by older community residents. *The Gerontologist, 25* (2), 188–193.

McAuley, W., & Prohaska, T. (1982). Professional recommendations for long-term placement: A comparison of two groups of institutionally vulnerable elderly. *Home Health Care Services Quarterly, 2*, 44–57.

Mendelson, M. A. (1974). *Tender loving greed.* New York: Random House.

Mezey, M., & Knapp, M. (1993). Nursing staffing in nursing facilities: Implications for achieving quality of care. In P. R. Kane, R. L. Kane, & M. D. Mezey (Eds.), *Advances in long term care* (Vol. 2). New York: Springer.

Mezey, M., & Scanlon, W. (1988). *Registered nurses in nursing homes: Secretary's Commission on Nursing.* Washington, DC: Department of Health and Human Services.

Miller, D. B., & Goldman, L. (1989). Perceptions of caregivers about special respite services for the elderly. *The Gerontologist, 29* (3), 408–410.

Moen, E. (1978). The reluctance of the elderly to accept help. *Social Problems, 25,* 293–303.

Mohler, M., & Lessard, W. (1991). *Nursing staff in nursing homes: Additional staff needed and cost to meet requirements and intent of OBRA'87.* Washington, DC: National Committee to Preserve Social Security and Medicare.

Mui, A., & Burnette, D. (1994). Long term care service used by frail elders: Is ethnicity a factor? *The Gerontologist, 34* (2), 190–198.

National Center for Health Statistics. (1989). *The national nursing home survey: 1985 summary for the United States.* (Vital and Health Statistics, Series 13, No. 97, DHHS Pub. No. [PHS] 89-1758). Public Health Service. Washington, DC: U.S. Government Printing Office.

Neu, C. R. (1982). Individual preferences for life and health: Misuses and possible uses. In R. L. Kane & R. A. Kane (Eds.), *Values and long term care.* Lexington, MA: D. C. Heath.

Noelker, L., & Harel, Z. (1978). Aged excluded from home health care: An interorganizational solution. *The Gerontologist, 18,* 37–41.

Palmore, E. (1976). Total chance of institutionalization among the elderly. *The Gerontologist, 16,* 504–507.

Pepper Commission Hearing. (1990). Washington, DC: U.S. Government Printing Office.

Rovner, B., Burton, L., & German, P. (1992). The role of mental morbidity in the nursing home experience. *The Gerontologist, 32,* 152–158.

Schulz, R., & Brenner, G. (1977). Relocation of the aged: A review and theoretical analysis. *Journal of Gerontology, 32,* 323–333.

Seifer, S. (1987). The impact of PPS on home health care: A survey of thirty-five health agencies. *Caring, 6* (4), 1–12.

Shuttlesworth, G. E., Rubin, A., & Duffy, M. (1982). Families versus institutions: Incongruent role expectations in the nursing home. *The Gerontologist, 22* (2), 200–208.

Silverstein, N. M. (1984). Informing the elderly about public services: The relationship between sources of knowledge and service utilization. *The Gerontologist, 24,* 37–40.

Silverstone, B. (1985). Informal social support systems for the frail elderly. In Institute of Medicine/National Research Council (Ed.), *America's aging: Health in an older society.* Washington, DC: National Academy Press.

Soldo, B. J. (1981). The living arrangements of the elderly in the near future. In S. B. Kiesler, J. N. Morgan, & V. K. Oppenheimer (Eds.), *Aging: Social change.* New York: Academic Press.

Spore, D. L., Smyer, M. A., & Cohn, M. D. (1991). Assessing nursing assistants' knowledge of behavioral approaches to mental health problems. *The Gerontologist, 31,* 309–317.

Stoller, E. P. (1982). Sources of support for the elderly during illness. *Health and Social Work, 7,* 111–122.

Subcommittee on Health and Long Term Care, Select Committee on Aging, United States House of Representatives (1989, March). *Board and care homes in America: A national tragedy.* Washington, DC: Government Printing Office.

Surpin, R. (1988). The current status of the paraprofessional in home care. *Caring, 4* (1), 4–9.

Tobin, S., & Lieberman, M. (1976). *The last home for the aged.* San Francisco: Jossey-Bass.

Townsend, C. (1970). *Old age: The last segregation.* New York: Grossman.

Townsend, P. (1962). *The last refuge*. London: Routledge & Kegan Paul.

Townsend, P. W., & Flanagan, J. J. (1976). Experimental pre-admission program to encourage home care for severely and profoundly retarded children. *American Journal of Mental Deficiency, 180*, 562–569.

Troll, L., Miller, S., & Atchley, R. (1979). *Families in later life*. Belmont, CA: Wadsworth.

U.S. Bureau of the Census. (1994). *Statistical abstract of the United States: 1991*. Washington, DC: U.S. Government Printing Office.

U.S. Department of Health, Education and Welfare. (1977). *Characteristics, social contacts, and activities of nursing home residents, U.S. 1973 National Nursing Home Survey*. DHEW Publication. No. (HRA) 77-1778, Public Health Service. Hyattsville, MD: U.S. Government Printing Office.

U.S. Health Care Financing Administration. (1984). *Report to Congress: Studies evaluating Medicaid home and community based waivers*. Baltimore, MD: Department of Health and Human Services.

U.S. Senate Special Committee on Aging. (1982). *Developments in aging* (Vol. 1). Report 97-314, 97th Congress, Second Session. Washington, DC: U.S. Government Printing Office.

Upshur, C. (1983). Developing respite care: A support service for families with disabled members. *Family Relations, 31*, 13–20.

Vinton, L., & Mazza, N. (1994). Aggressive behavior directed at nursing home personnel by residents' family members. *The Gerontologist, 34*, 528–533.

Vladeck, B. (1985). Reforming Medicare provider payment. *Journal of Health Politics, Policy and Law, 10*, 513–532.

Ward, R. (1977). Services for older people: An integrated framework for research. *Journal of Health and Social Behavior, 18*, 61–70.

Weiler, P., & Rathbone-McCuan, E. (1978). *Adult day care: Community work with the elderly*. New York: Springer.

Weissert, W. G. (1991). A new policy agenda for home care. *Health Affairs, 10* (2), 67–77.

Zedlewski, S. R., Barnes, R. O., Burt, M. R., McBride, T. D., & Meyer, J. A. (1990). *The needs of the elderly in the 21st century*. Washington, DC: Urban Institute Press.

CHAPTER 18

HEALTH POLICY AND AGING

This chapter begins by identifying the patterns of health and medical service utilization among the elderly. Of particular interest are physician visits and the use of nonphysician professional and hospital inpatient services. In addition, policies, programs, and funding mechanisms available for the health and medical care of the elderly are assessed. The chapter concludes by placing health care in a broader political economy of aging perspective.

USE OF SERVICES

Figure 18–1 presents data on physician contacts per person per year by age for 1992. The average number of physician contacts by persons 65 years and over was 10.6 visits, compared with 5.9 visits for persons of all ages. As the figure depicts, with the exception of children under 5 years of age, the average number of physician contacts per person increases with age. The likelihood of seeing a doctor at least once during a given year also increases with age. About 73 percent of people aged 15 to 44 years of age reported seeing a doctor in the last year, compared to 78 percent of those 45 to 64 years of age and 88.2 percent of those 65 years of age and older. The elderly account for a disproportionate amount of the physician utilization in the United States. In 1992, they represented between 12 and 13 percent of the nation's noninstitutionalized population and accounted for 23.3 percent of the office visits to physicians.

The average number of physician contacts per person 65 years of age in a year are up over 58 percent since 1964. In 1964, the average number of physician contacts among those 65 years and over was 6.7. The change in this indicator for the entire elderly population masks changes that have taken place within the popula-

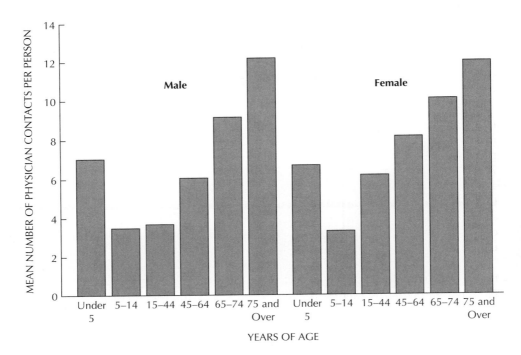

Sex	Under 5 Years	5–14 Years	15–44 Years	45–64 Years	65–74 Years	75 Years and Over
Male	7.1	3.5	3.7	6.1	9.2	12.2
Female	6.7	3.3	6.2	8.2	10.1	12.1

FIGURE 18–1   **Physician Contacts by Sex and Age of Patient: United States, 1992**

Source: Centers for Disease Control and Prevention, National Center for Health Statistics, National Health Interview Survey. See related *Health, United States, 1993,* table 85.

tion. According to the U.S. Department of Health and Human Services, the number of physician contacts per person per year has *increased* for the elderly poor and *decreased* for the nonpoor. This finding suggests that differences in the rate of physician utilization by the poor and nonpoor elderly have been narrowed or eliminated in recent years. One problem with this suggestion is that it fails to distinguish the differential need for health and medical services in various income groups. The inference here is that eight or nine physician contacts a year may be sufficient, given the need for services of an average elderly individual with income at or above the median for the total population. Nevertheless, 10 office visits may not meet the needs of the average elderly individual with income at or below the poverty level. According to the National Center for Health Statistics, in 1990–92, women age 65 years and over with income below the poverty level had an average of 11.2 physician contacts per year, while their counterparts with incomes of 200 percent or greater than the poverty level had 9.9 contacts. Interestingly, among those in these groups who assessed their health status in negative terms (fair or poor), nonpoor elderly women reported 18.2 physician contacts per year, on average, and poor elderly women reported 16.6 physician contacts per year.

Physician visits also vary by race and sex. In 1992, elderly African Americans reported more physician contacts per person than did elderly whites (13.7 vs. 12.0, respectively, among those 75 years and over); elderly women also reported more physician visits than do elderly men (10.1 vs. 9.2, respectively, among those 65 to 74 years of age). Differences in health and medical service use by race are generally explained by racial differences in socioeconomic status. The gender differential in utilization of physician services exists in all age groups except for those ages at which a mother usually makes the health care decisions. The largest differential occurs between the ages of 15 and 44, when women are most likely to be making use of obstetrical and gynecological services.

Explanations for these sex differences in utilization of medical services (and in morbidity rates) have focused primarily on the social situation of women. Nathanson (1975) groups these explantions into three categories:

1. Women report more illness than men and utilize medical services more frequently than men because it is culturally more acceptable for them to be ill.

Elderly women report more physician visits than do elderly men.

2. A woman's role is relatively undemanding; thus, reporting illness and visiting the doctor is more compatible with her other role responsibilities than is the case for men.

3. Women's assigned social roles are, in fact, more stressful than those of men—consequently, they have more real illness and need more care.

As Nathanson points out, insufficient data are available to evaluate the merits of these explanations. The elderly have higher rates of usage than people under age 65 for a whole array of health services, including prescription drugs, vision aids, medical supplies and equipment, and nonphysician health care providers (including optometrists, podiatrists, psychologists, chiropractors, and physical therapists, among others). For example, according to the National Center on Health Statistics, in 1991, elderly people were more likely to receive a drug prescription during an office visit with a physician than is the case for any other age group. In 68.2 percent of their office contacts with physicians, older people were given a drug prescription; 58.9 percent of physician contacts made by those aged 15 to 44 similarly yielded a drug prescription. In 1988, the elderly accounted for 34 percent of all outpatient prescription drugs used in the United States.

Dental problems increase with age. More than one-fourth of persons aged 45 to 64 have lost all their teeth; almost 90 percent have diseases of the tissues supporting or surrounding remaining teeth (Shanas & Maddox, 1977). Yet, in 1989, elderly individuals averaged only 2.0 dental visits a year, up from 1.5 dental visits in 1983 and 0.8 visit in 1964. Only about 43 percent of those 65 years and over have visited a dentist in the past year, according to National Health Interview Survey data for 1989; this compares with about 57 percent of people 45 to 64 years who have visited the dentist in the past year.

Unlike medical care, dental care is rarely financed by public programs or private health insurance. Thus, financial barriers to dental care are still substantial. Data from the National Health Interview Surveys suggest that those with higher income make substantially more dental visits per year, on average, than do those at or below the poverty level. In 1989, individuals in families with income at $50,000 or more reported 3.1 dental visits a person while those in families with less than $14,000 in income reported 1.3 dental visits a person.

The lack of dental care among the elderly is serious. Fully 50 percent of the elderly have no natural teeth. Of those, 10 percent have no false teeth or an incomplete set. Even those with false teeth do not use them all the time; many report that their dentures are improperly fitted. Increasing availability of dental services could improve the quality of life of many older people. Fear and embarrassment about socializing because of oral health problems has led many old people to isolation. This could be overcome if dental care services were made available to more elderly people. Nutritional status could also be improved by making it possible for those people who are edentulous or who have periodontal disease (and thus are restricted in diet) to eat a wider variety of foods.

The elderly are the heaviest utilizers of hospital care; in 1992, they accounted for 35 percent of all hospital discharges. Discharge rates for those 65 years and

TABLE 18–1   Utilization of Short-Stay Hospitals for Selected Age Groups, 1992

Age Group	Discharges (per 1,000)	Days of Care (per 1,000)	Average length of stay (days)
Under 5 yrs	77.3	422.8	5.5
5–14 yrs	26.8	123.5	4.6
15–44 yrs	65.6	340.5	5.2
45–64 yrs	120.6	801.5	6.6
65 yrs +	255.5	2045.2	8.0
75 yrs +	304.9	2667.2	8.7

Source: National Center for Health Statistics, Data from National Health Interview Survey.

over (255.5 per 1,000 population) were more than twice as high as those for individuals 45 to 64 years (120.6 per 1,000) and almost four times those for individuals 15 to 44 years of age (65.6 per 1,000). Hospital utilization rates vary by age and other demographic variables. As shown in Table 18–1, starting at age 5, both the discharge rate and the average length of stay increase with age. Discharged patients aged 45 to 64 years spent 6.6 days in the hospital, on average, per episode of hospitalization; for patients aged 75 and over, the average length of hospital stay was 8.7 days.

In 1983, Medicare introduced a prospective payment system (PPS) that was expected to produce shorter lengths of stay and greater admission rates. Discussed in more detail later, this new system paid hospitals a fixed amount per admission according to the diagnostic-related group (DRG) the patient was assigned to on the basis of an admitting diagnosis. As expected, the length of hospital stays decreased. However, as Figure 18–2 graphically shows, with discharge data from nonfederal short-stay hospitals, admission rates surprisingly declined between 1983 and 1992 for each age group shown, and have likely continued to decline since 1992. One explanation for this decline is that the PPS caused a shift from in-hospital care to treatment in outpatient facilities. Today, many surgeries and other specialized procedures and treatments can be delivered without hospitalization. In 1983, patients aged 75 years or older averaged 10.2 days per stay; this indicator fell to 9.1 days in 1987, then fell again to 8.7 days by 1992.

The elderly have lower rates of admission to inpatient psychiatric facilities than all other age groups except those under 18 years of age. Data for 1986 (National Center for Health Statistics, 1993) show lower rates of admission for the aged for all diagnoses in state and county mental hospitals and private psychiatric hospitals. In general, only for organic disorders do those 65 years and older have higher rates of admission to psychiatric facilities than is the case for the total population.

EXPLAINING USE OF HEALTH AND MEDICAL SERVICES

Although I have concentrated on the impact of age on utilization of health and medical services, other variables are included as well. Certainly, health beliefs or

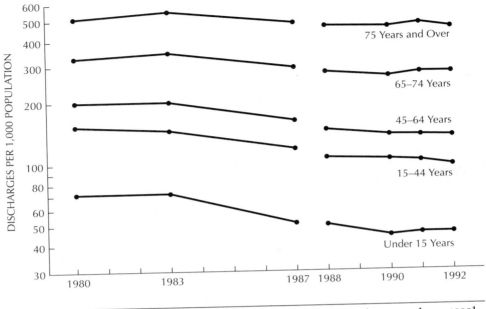

Age	1980	1983	1987	1988[1]	1990[1]	1991[1]	1992[1]
Under 15 years	71.6	70.8	51.3	49.2	43.9	45.3	45.2
15–44 years	150.2	140.3	115.1	104.0	101.7	99.3	96.0
45–64 years	194.8	192.2	156.9	140.5	133.1	132.2	131.0
65–74 years	315.9	334.2	280.9	262.8	253.9	264.2	264.5
75 years and over	489.1	529.3	451.6	436.5	430.0	443.5	432.6

FIGURE 18–2 Hospital Discharge Rates for Nonfederal Short-Stay Hospitals by Age: United States, 1980–92

Source: Centers for Disease Control and Prevention, National Center for Health Statistics, National Hospital Discharge Survey. See related *Health, United States, 1993,* table 94.

[1]Comparisons of data from 1988 to 1992 with data from earlier years should be made with caution as estimates of change may reflect improvements in the design . . . rather than true changes in hospital use. Excludes newborn infants.

values and knowledge about health and the health care system are related to use of health services (Andersen & Newman, 1973). What Ward (1977) calls *community variables* also affect utilization. These include location of residence (central city, suburban, or rural [Andersen et al., 1972]); density of age peers; availability of local transportation; and availability of neighborhood-based services and social supports (Cantor, 1975; Carp, 1975; Lopata, 1975).

Writers and researchers have looked at how the health care delivery system itself affects patterns of utilization. Many criticize the current system of service delivery as being too fragmented and disorganized. Such critics emphasize the extent to which financing programs are predisposed to fund inpatient care at the expense of community-based or home care and the way public funding mechanisms discourage preventive care and mental health services.

Determining the conditions under which people use health care services is a difficult enterprise. The presence of an impairment or a self-assessment of poor health does not necessarily indicate a need for medical care. Even an objective indication of need for medical care may not be a foolproof predictor of whether an individual will use available health services.

A number of studies have implicated structural, social, and psychological factors in utilization behavior. The costs of medical care (Berki & Ashcraft, 1979), the level of psychological distress (Tessler, Mechanic, & Dimond, 1976), and the availability of social support (Shuval, 1970) are among those variables that apparently have an effect on the utilization of health services among the population at large.

Andersen (1968) and colleagues (Aday, Andersen, & Fleming, 1980; Aday, Fleming, & Andersen 1984; Andersen & Newman 1973) have generated a conceptual framework within which to sort factors that contribute to the use of health services. Referred to as the *health behavior model,* this framework is arguably the most widely used for studying health services utilization. Basically, the health behavior model views the use of health services as a function of the predisposing, enabling, and need characteristics of the individual.

The predisposing element of the model reflects the idea that some individuals have a greater propensity for using health services than do others. Presumably, these propensities can be predicted prior to an illness episode from knowledge of the personal characteristics of elderly individuals. *Predisposing factors* include three dimensions that represent the sociocultural component of the model: demographics, social structure, and health beliefs. Indicators of demographics usually include age, sex, marital status, and other life-cycle indicators. Social-structural measures more typically reflect life-styles and routinely include education, employment, and ethnicity, among other such indicators. Health beliefs are assessments of attitudes about medical care, physicians, and disease.

The enabling element of the model comes from the idea that even if an individual is predisposed to employ health services, he or she must have some means for doing so. Thus, this element contains factors that make health services available to individuals. *Enabling factors* include two dimensions that represent the economic component of the model: familial resources and community resources. Familial resources are measured by income, the availability of health insurance, and the availability of sources of health care. Indicators of community resources typically include physician and hospital service-to-population ratios, geographic location, and population density indices.

The need element of the model is the most immediate cause of health service use. It assumes that, even in the presence of predisposing and enabling factors, individuals will not use health services unless they have or perceive themselves to have some illness. *Need factors* tap the individual's recognition of a present health problem or one in the making and consist of two dimensions. The first includes subjective perceptions of overall health status; the second includes professional evaluations of illness symptoms and need for service.

Using this categorization schema in an early study in Sweden, Andersen, Anderson, and Smedby (1968) found that the social class (a predisposing factor) and income (an enabling factor) of an individual were important predictors of the use of health services. More recently, Wolinsky and Johnson (1991) have carried out what is arguably the most complete test of the health behavior model. Including a broad array of predisposing, enabling, and need factors, 29 in all with interaction between race and need, they used the first wave of the National Center for Health Statistics' Longitudinal Study on Aging ($N = 5,151$ people age 70 and over) to test the health behavior model. Nine different measures of health services utilization were employed, tapping formal as well as informal services. Examples include measures of physician and hospital use, as well as bed disability and home health service use, among other factors. Three important themes emerge from this analysis.

First, in Wolinsky and Johnson's (1991) analyses, the health behavior model typically explains between 10 and 25 percent of the variation in health service utilization by a population of elderly people. This is consistent with other studies in the literature. These authors suggest a number of ideas for future research that may increase the robustness of the findings. For example, some research shows that older people are relatively consistent users of health care services (Mossey, Havens, & Wolinsky, 1989), thus it would seem advantageous to incorporate some measure of prior use patterns into the model. Some insist that the consistent pattern of physician services is physician driven. The argument here is that elderly patients are particularly compliant with physician insistence on regular visits. Others argue that a core group of elderly are reliant on informal or lay networks of friends, relatives, or indigenous leaders and that these networks are particularly resistant to the use of professional health services (Freidson, 1989). Measures that tap compliance with physician instruction for subsequent visits as well as reliance on informal networks for service referrals also might increase the power of the health behavior model in future research. Along these same lines, it is useful to recall that Wolinsky and Johnson's test of the model was on a cross-sectional data set. Use of longitudinal data are necessary to test whether the model is sensitive to changes in health services utilization over time.

A second theme to emerge from these analyses involves the dominance of need factors in explaining variation in use of health services. Andersen and his colleagues (Aday, Andersen, & Fleming, 1980; Aday, Fleming, & Andersen, 1984) have used the model to assess the equitable nature of the health delivery system. They employ evidence that utilization appears to be primarily a function of need to conclude that equitable access to health care has been achieved in the United States. Wolinsky and Johnson (1991), among others (Berki et al., 1985; Mechanic, 1985), urge caution in arriving at such a conclusion. They point out that most of the variation in health services utilization remains unexplained. As a result, researchers still do not know what accounts for most of the health service use by older people. Another concern of these researchers has to do with the differential effects of need characteristics for white versus minority older adults. A number of recent reports, for example, document the fact that, compared to whites, minority elderly are far more constrained by and sensitive to the need characteristics in their use of health services (Blendon et al., 1989; Freeman et al., 1987). Such findings are not consistent with conclusions of equity. Kart (1993) adds that until more is known about how and why older people employ community and home-based long-term care services, it is premature to declare the health delivery system to be equitable.

A third theme from this research involves the identification of important effects from previously absent or improperly measured factors. Several of these are worthy of mention. Wolinsky and Johnson found that worrying about one's health resulted in greater levels of health services utilization. This suggests that among both well and ill elderly, worrying about health places greater demands on the health delivery system than need characteristics alone would indicate.

Contrary to expectations from previous research (e.g., Brody, 1985), non-kin rather than kin supports appear to substitute for the use of formal health care services. Interestingly, however, both kin and non-kin supports were found to have positive effects on rates of physician contact. Wolinsky and Johnson suggest that in the course of discussions with friends and family about health matters, older people receive encouragement for going to see the doctor.

Finally, in operationalizing need characteristics, Wolinsky and Johnson distinguished between basic household activity of daily living (*basic ADLs* including the need for help with bathing, dressing, getting out of bed, walking, and toileting) and *advanced ADLs* that focused more precisely on cognitive capacities (needing help with managing money, using the telephone, and eating). Only the advanced ADLs had consistent effects on health services outcomes, predicting the taking of bed disability days, hospital use, and mortality. These results highlight the importance of identifying cognitive deficits in assessing functional status, prognosis, and placement of older adults (Folstein, Folstein, & McHugh, 1975).

Roos and Shapiro (1981), using data from a sample of Manitoba (Canada) elderly, suggest that a relatively few elderly account for a disproportionate share of health service utilization. The majority of older people in their study use services at approximately the same rate as younger people. Having advanced age, low self-perceived health status, and several self-reported health problems seem to place individuals at a higher risk for the use of hospital services. Still, although the very old were at greater risk to be hospitalized, they used only marginally more physician services than their younger counterparts. This finding is in opposition to a widely held belief that advancing age significantly increases the consumption of *all* types of health care (Roos & Shapiro, 1981).

Several studies have tried to identify additional sociodemographic determinants of medical care use among the elderly. Haug (1981) has found that older persons, in general, are more likely to get physical checkups and more likely to overutilize the health care system for minor complaints than younger persons. Yet, they are little different from the younger in underutilization for conditions that should receive a doctor's attention. Interestingly, currently married elderly are more likely than younger married persons to overutilize the health care system. As Haug points out, this may be due to what Eliot Freidson (1961) has described as the *lay-referral system:* A person who is ill turns first to a spouse for advice; it appears that spouses are more likely to recommend contacting a physician when an older husband or wife has a complaint.

Wan (1982) has studied the use of health services among almost 2,000 elderly individuals residing in low-income areas of Atlanta, Kansas City, and Boston, among other selected cities. He describes the regular user of neighborhood health centers as being African American, with low incomes, relatively uneducated, and on some form of public assistance. Persons using a hospital ambulatory clinic as a regular source of health care have a similar profile, although they seem more likely to be younger (65 to 69 years), male, and suffering from acute episodes of illness and a chronic disability.

In a multivariate analysis of his data, Wan (1982) found health status (as measured by number of acute illnesses experienced by an individual and level of chronic disability) to account for more variation in physician contacts than did access to a regular source of medical care. Access to medical care (as measured by the availability of a usual source of care and insurance coverage) did correlate with more frequent visits to physicians. Those with a regular source of care were three times as frequent users of ambulatory care as those with no regular source.

Interestingly, Wan's (1982) analysis showed Medicaid recipients and those with access to neighborhood health centers to be the most frequent users of physician care. African Americans also had a greater number of physician contacts than whites. Previously, a number of studies had indicated that the poor have less access to health care services. At least in the United States, this was the case prior to the implementation of Medicare and Medicaid, when, for example, the lowest socioeconomic groups had fewer physician visits than those with more income (Mechanic, 1978). According to Wan, poor elderly African Americans appear to have benefited significantly from the advent of Medicaid and other forms of public assistance. They have also taken advantage of various services provided by neighborhood health centers. Wan concludes, "One inference that can be drawn is that the removal of financial barriers, coupled with a concerted effort toward making health services readily available to the medically needy, has greatly facilitated the use of ambulatory physician care" (1982, p. 104). This does not necessarily mean, however, that equity or parity in the use of health care services in the United States has been achieved.

SELF-HEALTH CARE AMONG THE ELDERLY

Self-health care includes all the actions and decisions that an individual takes to prevent, diagnose, and treat personal ill health. While concentrating on formal health care services—doctor contacts, hospital utilization, and the like—researchers have generally neglected the issue of health care that older persons provide to themselves. Most illness symptoms do not lead to a medical consultation. Self-evaluation of symptoms and self-treatment are the basic and predominant forms of primary health care. They represent efforts on the part of people to take control of their health.

Most older people live at home in their communities, function well, and maintain a capacity to provide care for themselves. Still, there are forces, biological and social, that act to increase the problems associated with remaining healthy and providing self-care during illness while growing older. Certainly, biological changes may occur in later adulthood that create deficits in one's actual ability to provide self-care. These deficits may also produce feelings of helplessness which limit the range of outcomes actually attainable by an older person.

The social and psychological changes experienced as one grows older—role loss, dimunition of reference group, and a view of aging as an irreversible decline—lead to a sense of vulnerability. The elderly person may grow more dependent on the external definition of the situation and begin to doubt his or her competence. With increasing health problems and functional limitations, doubts about competence may turn into dependencies. Negative stereotypes about the aging process remain prevalent and contribute to behaviors among older people that confirm these stereotypes and lead to diminished feelings of control and self-esteem.

The medical treatment model and the resultant organization of health-care services are pervasive and pernicious influences on older people. Implicit in the logic of the medical model is a biological determinism that promotes professionals and lay people alike into a pathological model of old age. Attributing illness to biological changes or "pathological aging" focuses an elderly person and his or her physician away from situational and social factors that are stress-inducing and, consequently, affect the individual's health. As we have seen in this text, much gerontological literature is concerned with the impact on health status of retirement, changes in economic status, and changing living environments, among other stressful factors.

A number of writers have identified irrationality as a feature of the health-care system in the United States. One manifestation of this irrationality is the incompatibility of the acute care capabilities of medicine with the increasingly chronic nature of illness. Clinical medicine, with its emphasis on in-hospital, high-technology "sickness care," misses the focus on "health care" and, thus, negates efforts at increasing levels of individual responsibility for personal health.

The relation between control and health may actually be heightened in old age. Three factors may be at play. First, experiences related to control and health seem to increase markedly in old age. Retirement, widowhood, loss of friends and family members, for example, all challenge individual competence. Second, the association between control and certain indicators of health, such as immunologic function, is altered by aging. Finally, frequent medical care contacts may actually reduce opportunities of control (at any age). Professional providers seem to prefer patients who are most manageable—conforming, obedient and deferential—and those most receptive to the helping efforts of others.

Can these factors be overcome? Can self-health care be taught to older people? Self-care training programs may be no more effective than the improvement in health gained from engaging in "normal" health promotion and illness prevention practices. This assumes, however, that self-care programs may be defined as effective if some proportion of participants can be encouraged to achieve a "normal" level of engagement in health practices. In addition, it is important to note that desired outcomes of self-care programs need not be measured in terms of gains in physical health status but rather in terms of "perceived control" or "life satisfaction" or "morale."

Source: Kart, C. S. 1992. *Self-health care among the elderly: Does it reduce or increase reliance on professional health-care providers?* Toledo, OH: Final Report to the AARP Andrus Foundation.

PAYING FOR MEDICAL CARE

During the fiscal year 1974, the total cost of health care in the United States reached over $116 billion, for an average of $521 per person. By 1993, these numbers had increased over six times. National health care expenditures were in excess of $884 billion, with per-capita expenditures reaching approximately $3,299. Health expenditures were projected at 13.9 percent of gross domestic product (GDP) in 1993. For 1993, the annual percentage increase in health care costs was about 8 percent; expectations are that medical spending will increase at this rate or higher, on an annual basis, over the next five years. This is a radically different picture from that of 1965, the year Congress passed the Medicare and Medicaid legislation. In 1965, total health care expenditures amounted to $42 billion, 6.1 percent of the GDP, or $207 person.

Health costs for the elderly have increased as rapidly, if not more so. The amount of money expended on Medicare alone increased more than 19 times between 1970 and 1993 ($7.6 vs. $147.5 billion). The source of funds to pay for health care of the elderly has also changed dramatically. During 1966, the year Medicare and Medicaid were implemented, only 30 percent of these funds were public; since then, the percentage of expenditures from public funds has increased by almost one-half again, to 44 percent.

The largest single item on the health care bill of elderly individuals is hospital care. In 1981, this item cost $36.6 billion and accounted for 44 percent of all personal health care expenditures for the aged. By 1993, Medicare expenditures for hospital insurance alone exceeded $93.5 billion.

Hospital care, nursing-home care, and physicians' services together account for most of the dollars spent on health care for the elderly. Items such as drugs, dental services, eyeglasses, and appliances constitute a very small part of the total bill and are mostly funded by the elderly out of pocket. Generally, expenditures for these latter items are thought to be low because many elderly people are going without them. As costs continue to rise and such services continue to remain outside the scope of most public funding mechanisms for health care of the elderly, one can expect continued low utilization. About 8.5 percent of all health care expenditures in 1993 went to drugs and related medical supplies. How many older people go without needed drugs because public funding mechanisms typically do not underwrite the costs of drugs and personal funds are unavailable?

Payments for health care are made under a variety of public and private programs designed to provide care or access to care for specified population groups. The two largest programs are Medicare and Medicaid. They are the principal public funding mechanisms for health care of the elderly.

Medicare

In 1965, the *Social Security Act of 1935* was amended to provide health insurance for the elderly. This amendment, which became effective July 1, 1966, is known as *Title XVIII* or *Medicare*. It marked the inauguration in the United States of a national system of financing individual health services on a social insurance basis. It was not, however, the country's first attempt at establishing national health insurance. Such attempts and their failures date back to the beginning of the century. The historical record is worthy of a brief review.[1]

Between 1915 and 1918, a group of academics, lawyers, and other professionals who were organized under the American Association for Labor Legislation attempted to push a model medical care insurance bill through several state legislatures. They had no success. The American Medical Association (AMA) opposed the bills, as did the American Federation of Labor (AFL). The AFL feared that any form of compulsory social insurance might lead to further government control of working people. Not until the Great Depression did interest in governmental health insurance reappear on a sustained basis.

In 1934, President Roosevelt created an advisory Committee on Economic Security. In the climate of destitution and poverty that accompanied the Great Depression, this committee was charged with drafting a social security bill providing a minimum income for the aged, the unemployed, the blind, and the widowed and their children. The result was the Social Security Act of 1935. The Social Security Act was originally intended to include health insurance provisions also. Nevertheless, as Feingold (1966) points out, the extent of this intention was little more than one line in the original bill that suggested that the Social Security Board study the problem and report to Congress. When opposition to this line became so strong that it appeared to jeopardize the Social Security bill itself, the line was dropped.

Although advocates of compulsory health insurance proposed congressional bills from 1939 on, it was not until Truman's "Fair Deal" that the possibility of passing such a bill became strong. In the interim (1939 to 1949), private health insurance—through Blue Cross, Blue Shield, and commercial insurance carriers—was endorsed by the AMA and became firmly established in the United States as a way of paying for medical expenses.

In 1949, President Truman requested congressional action on medical care insurance. In order to placate the AMA and its allies, it was specified that doctors and hospitals would not have to join the plan. In addition, doctors would retain the right to refuse to serve patients whom they did not want. This was not enough. The American Medical Association was adamantly opposed to so-called socialized medicine, and despite Truman's characterization of the AMA as "the public's worst enemy in the efforts to redistribute medical care more equitably," efforts at passing a national health insurance bill were defeated.

What were the major objections to these early national health insurance proposals? According to Marmor (1973), they were as follows:

1. Medical insurance was a "giveaway" program that made no distinction between the deserving and undeserving poor.

---

[1]Historical material on Medicare comes primarily from Marmor (1973) and Feingold (1966).

2. Too many well-off Americans who did not need financial assistance in meeting their health needs would be helped.

3. Utilization of health care services would increase dramatically and beyond capacity.

4. There would be excessive control of physicians, establishing a precedent for socialism in the United States.

Clearly, another strategy was necessary. The one that developed shifted attention away from the health problems of the general population to those of the aged. There was great appeal in focusing on the aged, for, as a group, they were needy yet deserving. Most had made a contribution to the United States. Still, through no fault of their own, many suffered reduced earning capacity and higher medical expenses. Proponents of this new strategy waged a public war of sympathy for the aged and a private war of pressure politics from 1952 until 1965. Not until then was the political climate ripe for amending the original Social Security Act to provide health insurance (Medicare) for the U.S. aged.

Medicare consists of two basic components. Part A is a compulsory hospital insurance (HI) plan that covers a bed patient in a hospital and, under certain conditions, in a skilled nursing facility or at home after having left the hospital. It is financed by employer/employee contributions and a tax on the self-employed. Most of the elderly are automatically eligible as a result of their own or a spouse's entitlement to Social Security. Currently, over 30 million persons aged 65 years and over are covered by Medicare. If for any reason a person is not eligible for HI at age 65, it can be purchased on a voluntary basis. The monthly premium was $261 in 1995.

Part B represents a voluntary program of supplemental medical insurance (SMI) that helps pay doctor bills, outpatient hospital benefits, home health services, and certain other medical services and supplies. Financing is achieved through monthly premiums paid by enrollees and matching funds by the federal government. As of January 1, 1995, the monthly premium was $46.10, or $553.20 for the year.

Hospital insurance (Part A) benefits are measured by periods of time known as *benefit periods*. Benefit periods begin when a patient enters the hospital and end when he or she has not been a hospital bed patient for 60 consecutive days. This concept is important because it determines the amount of care to which a Medicare beneficiary is entitled at any particular time. Medicare will help pay covered services for a patient for up to 90 days of in-hospital care, for up to 100 days of extended care in a skilled nursing facility, for posthospital home health care in each benefit period, and for hospice care for terminally ill beneficiaries who have a life expectancy of less than six months. If an individual runs out of covered days within a benefit period, he or she may draw on a lifetime reserve of 60 additional hospital days. Use of these days within the lifetime reserve, however, permanently reduces the total number of reserve days left. For example, if a patient has been in the hospital for 90 days and needs 10 more days of hospital care, he or she may draw 10 days from the reserve of 60, leaving a reserve of 50 days.

Part A Medicare benefits will pay for such services as semiprivate accommodations, including meals and special diets, regular nursing services, laboratory tests, drugs furnished by the hospital, and medical supplies and appliances furnished by the hospital. It will not pay for convenience items, such as a private room or private-duty nurses.

A Medicare patient is financially responsible, through copayments and deductibles, for various components of his or her hospital insurance plan. As a bed patient in a participating hospital, he or she is responsible for the first $716 of costs in each benefit period (the 1995 figure). After this, Part A pays for covered services for the first 60 days of hospital care. From day 61 through day 91 in a benefit period, hospital insurance pays for all covered service except for $179 per day (in 1995). If more than 90 days of inpatient care are required, reserve days may be used. The copayment after 90 days of care is $358 a day in 1995. Beyond 150 days in a hospital, Medicare pays nothing.

Extended-care benefits provide for covered services for the first 20 days in a benefit period. After the first 20 days, the recipient must pay $89.50 (1995 figure) per day for up to an additional 80 days in a benefit period. Home health care, from a home health agency participating in Medicare, covers part-time nursing care by a registered nurse or under her or his supervision, physical or speech therapy, and medical supplies and appliances. It does not cover services of part-time health aides at home. Currently, 210 or more days of hospice care are available to beneficiaries certified as terminally ill.

The medical insurance program (Part B) of Medicare is a voluntary one; an individual must pay a monthly premium in order to be eligible for coverage. In addition, the subscriber pays a deductible each year (currently $100) and 20 percent of the remainder. Although Part B pays for a broad array of outpatient hospital services, doctors' services, home health benefits, and other medical supplies, it does *not* routinely cover such things as regular physical examinations, eye and/or hearing examinations, eyeglasses or hearing aids, prescription drugs, false teeth, or full-time nursing care. However, such coverage may be provided to Medicare beneficiaries who opt to participate in special coordinated care plans such as health maintenance organizations (HMOs).

Medicaid

Medicaid, or *Title XIX* of the Social Security Act, passed also in 1965 and became effective July 1, 1966. According to Stevens and Stevens (1974), some observers of the time saw Title XIX as the "sleeper" of the 1965 legislation. After all, Medicare is limited in terms of who is covered (primarily the aged), the types of services covered (described previously), and the presence of deductibles and copayments. Medicaid was intended as a catchall program to handle the medical expenses not covered by Medicare as well as to provide medical assistance to needy groups other than the aged. The program is jointly funded by federal and state governments, with the federal government contributing in excess of 50 percent in poorer states. Eligibility varies from one state to another, as states have broad discretion in determining which groups their Medicaid programs will cover. The federal government does mandate certain Medicaid eligibility groups, including recipients of Aid to Families with Dependent Children (AFDC), Supplementary Security Income (SSI) recipients, children in poor families, pregnant women in families with income below 133 percent of the poverty level, and certain other protected groups.

Financial criteria for Medicaid eligibility is also somewhat variable, although one requirement seems to be almost universal. Wherever an individual qualifies for Medicaid, "pauperization" has preceded qualification. All persons, including the elderly, may find themselves eligible for Medicaid only after they have drained their resources and qualified as a member of the poor. Effective September 30, 1989, Medicaid eligibility was accelerated for some nursing home patients by protecting more income and assets for the institutionalized person's spouse living at home. Also, new limits were placed on the amount of assets and income of a married couple that must be "spent down" before Medicaid will pay for nursing home care.

HEALTH POLICY: IS THERE A CRISIS IN MEDICAL CARE FINANCING?

The Medicare program has made and continues to make various medical services available to many persons who would not receive them otherwise. Older people living on low, relatively fixed incomes might not be able to secure the services of a physician, a hospital, a skilled nursing home, or a home health care program without Medicare. Nevertheless, the Medicare program is riddled with various out-of-pocket deductibles and copayments for its beneficiaries, not to mention limitations in services provided.

Many elderly Americans supplement their Medicare with some private health insurance plan. The Omnibus Budget Reconciliation Act of 1990 directed that standards be set for Medicare supplemental insurance (Medigap) policies. Further, Medigap policies may not be canceled or a renewal refused by an insurer solely on the basis of the health of the policyholder.

In 1988, Congress passed the largest expansion of Medicare benefits since the program's inception in 1965. Elderly and disabled beneficiaries were to be protected from the costs of catastrophic medical bills. Also provided was the program's first coverage of outpatient prescription drugs. The new benefits were to be paid for with two premiums. First, all beneficiaries would pay for increases in Medicare Part B premiums. Second, all Part A enrollees would be assessed a "supplemental" premium based on their amount of federal income tax liability, subject to an annual limit.

This supplemental premium for Part A enrollees broke new ground. All other Part A benefits are funded from payroll taxes, as described in Chapter 11. For the first time, older people alone (and really only those with annual income tax liability) were being asked to underwrite an expansion in the Medicare benefits. Faced with pressure from politically active older adults and their organizational representatives, who were upset about the funding mechanisms for these expanded benefits, the Congress passed the Medicare Catastrophic Coverage Repeal Act of 1989 and repealed the Medicare catastrophic benefits legislated in 1988. Also repealed were the proposed premium increases.

In addition to limits in coverage, Medicare focuses too narrowly on providing acute care. The maintenance of chronic health conditions and quality-of-life issues do not receive appropriate attention. Eye examinations for eyeglasses, hearing examinations for hearing aids, orthopedic shoes, and false teeth are all excluded from coverage. Under this system, Medicare patients could not take advantage of geriatric consultation clinics that are concerned with the prevention of illness and the maintenance of chronic conditions. Such clinics could exist only for private, paying patients.

The language employed throughout the Medicare regulations refers to medical need, medical care, and medical necessity. Health teaching, health maintenance, prevention of illness, aspects of rehabilitation, and personal care are related to health care but not necessarily to medical care. The elderly often need health care services in far greater proportion than medical care services (Schwab, 1977). If the health needs of the elderly population are to be served and if suitable health maintenance programs are to be developed, then a financing system must be initiated that allows for funding of services that prevent illness and maintain health.

Because Medicare and Medicaid result from legal entitlements to services, there has been some concern that expenditures from these programs are uncontrollable. The costs of providing medical care under these programs has increased at a rate exceeding the growth of the federal economy and the Consumer Price Index. Medicaid may be more problematic in this respect than Medicare. In 1993, skilled nursing facility services for the elderly accounted for 25 percent of all Medicaid payments; the average annual payment for nursing home care for the elderly was $15,798 per person. The federal outlay for Medicaid has increased from $2.5 million in 1970 to $72.3 billion in 1993. State contributions in 1993 approached another $53.5 billion. The compound rate of growth for Medicaid is projected to be 12.7 percent per year between 1993 and 2000.

Frustration over apparently uncontrollable costs has led to major reform in Medicare and Medicaid. Starting in October 1983, a new system began that fixed Medicare hospital payment rates in advance. Under this *prospective payment system,* hospitals know in advance what Medicare will pay them for treating a patient with a particular ailment. A fee is set for the treatment of illnesses and injuries categorized into *diagnosis-related groups* (DRGs). Fees vary by region, according to whether the hospital is in an urban or a rural setting and according to the prevailing wage rate in the area. Rates are adjusted annually. Psychiatric care, long-term care, rehabilitation, and children's hospitals were initially excluded from this prospective payment system.

The fixed fee will have to be accepted as payment in full for treatment of a Medicare patient who has been hospitalized, although hospital administrators may be able to choose the best paying DRG justified by the clinical picture presented by the patient. Those hospitals that can provide the care for less than the fixed payment rate will be allowed to keep the extra money. Hospitals unable to provide the care for the fixed payment rate may charge patients only for the deductibles and copayments that already are part of the Medicare payment system. Some argue that this prospective payment system provides incentives to hospitals to admit patients at a later stage in the progress of illness and discharge them at an earlier stage of illness recovery (Blumenthal, Schlesinger, & Brown Drumheller, 1988). Kane and Kane argue that the DRG system runs directly contrary to the goals of geriatrics:

> Whereas geriatrics addresses the functional result of multiple interacting problems, DRGs encourage concentration on a single problem. Extra time required to make an appropriate discharge plan is discouraged. Use of ancillary personnel, such as social workers, is similarly discouraged, except to expedite discharges from the hospital. (1990, p. 420)

In 1989, Congress revised the Medicare physician payment system. Beginning in 1997, the new schedule is based on a "resource-based relative value scale" that measures the time, training, and skill required to perform a given service. The new schedule allows adjustments for overhead costs and geographical differences, and limits what doctors may charge beneficiaries over and above the Medicare allowed fee.

Medicaid has also experienced reform. As Rabin (1985) reports, states have been given greater program autonomy over which services to provide. They may limit the freedom to select a medical care provider, develop new formulas for hospital reimbursement, and emphasize community-based alternatives to institutional care. Furthermore, states are now in a position to negotiate with providers about the organization and price of health and medical care delivery.

Despite these reforms, Medicare and Medicaid still represent legal entitlement to medical care. Although the price of medical care is more regulated than in the past, costs continue to rise. Combined spending for Medicare and Medicaid in 1993 (federal and state contributions) was $219.3 billion. The actuarial status of the Hospital Insurance (HI) and Supplementary Medical Insurance (SMI) Trust Funds suggest that in the absence of additional asset funds, services and costs will need to be cut. The Social Security Administration reports $128 billion in trust funds available for the HI program at the end of 1993—an increase of 29 percent since the end of 1990. However, expenditures have increased almost 41 percent in this period, suggesting that the present financing schedule for the HI program is sufficient to ensure the payment of benefits through entry into the twenty-first century but not much beyond. The SMI program is actuarily more problematic. Trust fund assets actually declined by a small fraction between the end of 1992 and 1993 to $24 billion. At the same time, benefit payments increased by 13 percent.

Argument can be made to expand eligibility and enduring services for both Medicaid and Medicare. However, there is also great pressure to reduce deficits and balance the federal budget and to limit state budget expenditures for Medicaid as well. As a balance for these considerations is sought, the likelihood for changes in federal laws is likely. As a result, one can expect both programmatic as well financial changes in Medicaid and Medicare.

HEALTH POLICY: LONG-TERM CARE ISSUES

Services that are delivered across the continuum of long-term care are fragmented. Community based long-term care programs, including those described in Chapter 17, comprise a heterogeneous collection of agencies, institutions, and programs dominated by public funding. In particular, Medicaid, which accounts for about one-third (34 percent) of all long-term care expenditures for the elderly in the United States, does attempt to meet the acute and long-term care needs of the elderly poor (Davis & Rowland, 1986).

In addition to home health care and nursing-home care, chore services, homemaker aid, and other types of social services are now covered by Medicaid under a waiver provision if a state can demonstrate that total expenditures are not increased by the use of this type of service. States vary widely in their approaches to determining eligibility for long-term care services. However, one early study by the U.S. General Accounting Office (1982) found that expanded home health services do not necessarily reduce nursing-home or hospital use or even total service costs. Even with the appearance of such expanded service benefits, public spending has, for the most part, reinforced the use of institutions for providing long-term care (Davis & Rowland, 1986). Medicare accounted for about 18 percent of all nursing-home and home care expenditures in the United States in 1993. Home health care benefits under Medicare have been liberalized to cover some part-time health care or therapy on an intermittent basis if the beneficiary is housebound and under a physician's care. Recent amendments to Medicare have shown increased sensitivity to connecting acute care services to long-term care services. It is not unusual for long-term care patients to be frequently moved back and forth between hospital and nursing home. In fact, Kane and Kane suggest that "hospitalizations might be more accurately viewed as phases of acute care within the long-term care episode" (1990, p. 235).

Anticipating relationships between acute care and long-term care service use should help meet needs and control costs. Improved patient assessment can identify high-risk cases, reduce subsequent long-term care utilization and mortality, and improve function (Rubenstein et al., 1984). Providing postacute care is an area of service need that requires greater recognition. How this care will be provided in local communities is a frequent problem.

Short-term long-term care is considered care that is offered for a period less than 90 days. *Step-down* services, which range from outpatient rehabilitation to community outreach services, can be used. Brody and Magel (1986) recommend the use of step-down services to cross traditional service lines where settings are organized to respond to a hierarchy of patient care needs. When short-term care is used, case management is frequently called into play: It is a "method of providing comprehensive, unified, coordinated, and timely services to people in need of them through the efforts of a primary agent who, together with the client (and the client's family), takes responsibility for providing or procuring the services needed" (Kemp, 1981, p. 213).

Posthospital care is often provided by long-term care service agencies. Although Medicare usually pays for these services, there has been discussion to explore ways to tie these costs to the prospective payment system now used in reimbursing hospitals (Kane & Kane, 1989). A total capitation system may be a device for recognizing episodes of care in payment policies. Within such a system, a single payment would cover all care, including long-term care (Kane & Kane, 1989).

Medicaid and Medicare are *not* the only public payers for long-term care for the elderly. At the federal level, the Social Services Block Grant, Title III of the Older Americans Act, and the Veterans Administration (VA) accounted for about 3 percent of all long-term funding for the elderly in the United States in 1993 (Wiener, Illston, & Hanley, 1994). The largest of these public programs is the VA, which maintains nursing homes, domiciliary care facilities, and hospital-based home health care programs for low-income veterans.

According to the Health Insurance Association of America, about 2.9 million private long-term care insurance policies were sold in 1992, many to nonelderly (Coronel, 1994). Thus, while approximately 97 percent of those 65 years and older had Medicare coverage, and over 60 percent had supplementary insurance to Medicare, about 5 percent of the aged had private insurance to cover the catastrophic costs of long-term care.

In addition to the public programs and private insurance, long-term care recipients have considerable out-of-pocket costs, perhaps as much as 44 percent of all expenditures in the United States in 1993. Still, Hanley, Wiener, and Harris (1994) estimate that fewer than 10 percent of elderly nursing home users could afford to pay for a year of nursing home care out of income. Average out-of-pocket costs for nursing home care in 1993 were over $28,000, and one estimate is that about 36 percent of all nursing home admissions spent more than 40 percent of their income and assets for long-term care in 1993.

Policy proposals and initiatives for reforming the system abound. Until relatively recently, these proposals were for expanded or additional services, including additional homemaking and other community-based services to reduce the rate of institutionalization, providing transportation to or centralizing the location of needed services, or even providing direct payment or tax incentives to family caregivers for their services (Benjamin, 1985; Doty, 1986; Hamm, Kickham, & Cutler, 1983).

Some policy suggestions contain latent functions that may be difficult to anticipate. One special concern involves the possibility that a new program or a program change might act as a disincentive to continuation of family care or that a newly developed service would simply act as a substitute for family care. Although there is no research to support this concern, no family policy for older people has been developed in the United States. The future trend in family support of older people is somewhat unpredictable as a result of uncertain family rates. Changes in family composition and/or dependency ratios may cause changes in the quantity and types of care families can offer their elders. Nevertheless, commitment to the American ideal of individuals taking responsibility for themselves and their family members is likely to remain strong.

Most people agree that reform is needed in the current system for financing health and long-term care services for the elderly, as this current system appears to satisfy no one. Clearly, there is some conflict between the need for acute and chronic health services, long-term care, and budgetary constraints. Other flaws include a lack of public and private insurance, high catastrophic out-of-pocket costs, an institutional bias, lack of services in many communities, and a finance system oriented toward welfare rather than the assumption that the need and use of long-term care services is a normal life risk (Wiener & Illston, 1996).

Tapping home equity and employing private insurance are two private-sector approaches to financing long-term care. Money accumulated in home equity could be released to older people through reverse annuity mortgages and other sale-leaseback arrangements. According to *Consumer Reports,* however, by mid-1992 only about 3,000 individuals nationwide had taken advantage of an FHA program to promote reverse annuity mortgages.

Private insurance is being marketed to enable people who can afford to pay for services to have access to some sort of saving insurance mechanism (Brody & Magel, 1986). Tax-deductible or tax-deferred medical or long-term care retirement accounts, medical or long-term care versions of IRAs, are also being promoted, especially for those upper-middle and upper-income individuals with discretionary incomes. This assumes that working-age adults will prepare for the risk of needing long-term care. Many have competing demands, deny the risk, or mistakenly believe that Medicare will cover these costs (Wiener & Illston, 1996). Even if private insurance and/or LTC IRAs are available and grow in the near future, they are unlikely to have impact on Medicaid spending (Wiener, Illston, & Hanley, 1994).

Unfortunately, in the current political environment, reform is often simply a euphemism for reducing costs. As of this writing, Democrat and Republican leaders in the Congress, and President Clinton, are recommending cuts in the federal matching funds for Medicaid and reductions in the growth of Medicare spending. As a result, efforts will likely increase at moving elderly individuals into managed care arrangements. Such options would be widely available under both Medicare and Medicaid. About 25 percent of Medicaid beneficiaries are currently enrolled in managed care, although most are mothers and children (Riley, 1995); only 18 states are currently enrolling noninstitutionalized people in risk-based managed care. About 2.3 million Medicare beneficiaries (7 percent) were enrolled in managed care programs in 1994, and most of these were in California, Oregon, Arizona, New Mexico, Nevada, and Florida.

Arizona may have the longest experience enrolling older people in managed care. According to Riley (1995), over the past nine years, Arizona found costs to increase at a slower pace in their managed care program than was the case in the fee-for-service Medicaid program. Minnesota has most currently received the first waiver to operate a managed care demonstration for elders dually enrolled in Medicare and Medicaid. Conflicts in the rules that govern the two programs remain. Also, as other states proceed with applications for the waiver, it is not clear whether they will be held accountable for providing certain mandatory services. And, if not, which critical services are most likely to be jeopardized by cost controls?

TOWARD A POLITICAL ECONOMY OF HEALTH AND AGING

In attempting to understand the relationships among aging, health, and health services utilization, students of aging in the United States have directed their analyses primarily at the individual older person. Resultant research has been concerned with biomedical, psychological, and social-psychological models of aging. Much of the material presented in this book can be located in one or more of these models. Thus, one might ask, How do individuals adjust to the aging process? Why are certain aged persons healthier than others? Why do some elderly people avail themselves of health services and others do not?

As Estes and colleagues point out, questions like these make the economic and political structure of the society residual in explaining old age. These authors offer an alternative approach that "starts with the proposition that the status and resources of the elderly and even the trajectory of the aging process itself are conditioned by one's location in the social structure and the economic and social factors that affect it" (Estes, Swan, & Gerard, 1984).

From this *political economy* perspective, the structure and operation of the major societal institutions (including the family, the workplace, the medical and welfare institutions) shape both the subjective experience and objective condition of the individual's aging. In the area of health and aging, Estes, Swan, and Gerard (1984) note that the political economy perspective emphasizes the following:

1. The social determinants of health and illness
2. The social creation of dependency and the management of that dependency status through public policy and health services
3. Medical care as an ideology and as an industry in the control and management of the aging

4. The consequences of public policies for the elderly as a group and as individuals

5. The role and function of the state vis-à-vis aging and health

6. The social construction of reality about old age and health that both undergirds and reinforces the institutional arrangements and public policies concerning health and aging in the society

Political economy provides a critical approach to the study of aging that does *not* attempt to psychologize the health problems of the aging. An analysis of health and aging from a political economy perspective emphasizes the broad implications of economic life for the aged and for society's treatment of the aged and their health. This view also examines the special circumstances of different classes and subgroups of older persons. It is a systematic view based on the assumption that old age cannot be understood in isolation from other problems or issues raised by the larger social order.

From this perspective, the future seems grim for positive health policy initiatives for the elderly. Minkler (1984), for example, sees a continuation of victim blaming and scapegoating of the elderly for economic problems and fiscal crises such as the federal budget deficit, although the character of victim blaming is changing. She describes how earlier efforts at victim blaming defined the elderly as a social problem, and, consequently, solutions were devised for dealing with that problem. Medicare and Medicaid represent but two highly visible programs generated to deal with the problems of the aged. Victim blaming in the 1980s defined these solutions as part of the problem. Not only are the elderly themselves seen as a problem, but programmatic efforts to address their needs are characterized as "budget busting" and in need of being dismantled entirely or privatized.

The terms of discussion have shifted to proposals for allocation of health care. For example, Longman (1987) argues that each new generation inherits valuable new medical technologies without the dedicated capital to pay for their use. The result is accumulating debt that can only be discharged by younger, coming generations. The pattern is exacerbated by efforts to prolong life to an advanced age. Implicit is the suggestion that those who benefit from such advances (the aged) are not those who will have to pay (the young).

Blank (1988) identifies three obstacles that stand in the way of traditional reform of U.S. medical care system: (1) the belief that individuals have the right to unlimited medical care should they choose it, (2) the traditional acceptance of this maximalist approach by the medical community, and (3) the insulation of the individual from feeling the cost of treatment. He asks not whether we must ration health care, but how.

Callahan (1988) similarly argues that the "happy days" strategies are no longer working. The nation can no longer maintain the illusion of a health care system that will be all things to all people. Presumably, rationing will help restore the balance. And *age* may be the first standard that is employed for the rationing or limiting of medical care.

The political economy perspective raises a whole new set of questions that need to be asked *and* answered as the country proceeds into the future. These questions and their answers will provide a significant opportunity for students of aging to rethink the relationship between society and its elderly constituents.

SUMMARY

The average number of physician visits per person increases with age. Although differences in the rate of physician utilization by the poor and nonpoor elderly have been narrowed or eliminated in recent years, the poor likely continue to use fewer services relative to their needs than do those in higher socioeconomic circumstances.

There is a gender differential in the utilization of physician services in all adult age groups. Explanations have focused primarily on the social situation of women. In general, the utilization of dental services by older people is lower than among younger groups, despite the fact that dental problems increase with age. Few third-party reimbursement plans for health care include dental services, thus, financial barriers to dental care are still substantial. The elderly are the heaviest utilizers of hospital care; they accounted for 35 percent of all hospital discharges in 1992.

Andersen and colleagues have generated a conceptual framework within which to sort factors that explain variation in the use of health services. Referred to as the *health behavior model*, this framework is arguably the most widely used for studying health services utilization. Basically, the health behavior model views the use of health services as a function of the predisposing, enabling, and need characteristics of the individual. Generally, researchers employing the model have been able to explain between 10 and 25 percent of variation in health services utilization among the elderly at any one point in time.

Health care expenditures have increased rapidly in recent years. The amount of money expended on Medicare alone has increased 19 times between 1970 and 1993. The source of funds to pay for health care for the elderly has also changed. Increasingly, more of the health care dollars expended are public monies. The largest single item on the health care bill of elderly people is hospital care. Public funds, including Medicare and Medicaid, pay for most of this service.

The Medicare program for the elderly contains many out-of-pocket deductibles and copayments, as well as limitations in services, and focuses too narrowly on acute care problems. The language employed throughout the Medicare regulations refers to medical need, medical care, and medical necessity. The elderly are often in greater need of health promotion and illness prevention services than they are in need of medical care services. Some reforms of Medicare have recently been made. Arguably, the most notable among these are the institution of a prospective payment system for hospitals and the payment for hospice care for the dying. Despite reforms, Medicare and Medicaid still represent legal entitlement to medical care and costs continue to rise. Pressures to rein in costs are likely to result in congressional revision of federal law regulating these programs.

The political economy perspective is a newer critical approach to understanding the relationships among aging, health, and health services utilization. Rather than "biologizing" or "psychologizing" the problems of health and aging, this perspective tries to place problems of health and aging in the broader context of the economic and political life of the society. Whereas earlier victim-blaming efforts identified the elderly as a social problem, current victim blaming defines programmatic efforts to address the health care needs of the elderly as part of the problem. Consequently, suggestions to ration health care by age seem in some favor.

STUDY QUESTIONS

1. How does use of physician services vary by sex? What are some possible explanations for this difference in utilization of medical services between men and women?

2. What is the apparent relationship between age and dental problems? Dental visits? How can the low rates of utilization of dental services among the aged be explained?

3. Identify the three factors in Andersen's categorization schema that contribute to the use of health services. Give an example of each of these factors. How do the three factors rank in their ability to account for variation in health care utilization by the elderly?

4. How have programs such as Medicare and Medicaid influenced the amount of physician contact among poor elderly?

5. Distinguish between Medicare and Medicaid. What are the major gaps in these programs?

6. Is there a crisis in medical care financing? What reforms have been instituted in the past to ensure the financial integrity of Medicare?

7. What reforms are needed in the current system of long-term care services for the elderly?

8. What is the value of the political economy perspective in understanding the relationships among aging, health, and health services utilization? Why do you think that the allocation of health care resources continues to be an issue today?

REFERENCES

Aday, L. (1975). Economic and non-economic barriers to the use of needed medical services. *Medical Care, 13,* 447–456.

Aday, L., Andersen, R. M., & Fleming, G. V. (1980). *Health care in the U.S.: Equitable for whom?* Beverly Hills: Sage.

Aday, L., Fleming, G. V., & Andersen, R. M. (1984). *Access to health care in the U.S.: Who has it, who doesn't?* Chicago: Pluribus Press.

Andersen, R. M. (1968). *A behavioral model of families' use of health services,* Research Series 25. Chicago: Center for Health Administration Studies.

Andersen, R. M., Anderson, O., & Smedby, B. (1968). Perceptions of and response to symptoms of illness in Sweden and the U.S. *Medical Care, 6,* 18–30.

Andersen, R. M., Greenley, R., Kravits, J., & Anderson, O. 1972. *Health service use: National trends and variations: 1953–71.* Chicago: Center for Health Administration Studies.

Andersen, R. M., & Newman, J. (1973). Societal and individual determinants of medical care utilization in the U.S. *Milbank Memorial Fund Quarterly, 51,* 95–124.

Benjamin, A. (1985). Community based long-term care. In C. Harrington, R. Newcomer, C. Estes, & associates (Eds.), *Long term care of the elderly: Public policy issues.* Beverly Hills: Sage.

Berki, S. E., & Ashcraft, M. (1979). On the analysis of ambulatory utilization. *Medical Care, 17,* 1163–1179.

Berki, S. E., Wyszewianski, L., Lichtenstein, R., Gomotty, P., Bowlyow, J., Papke, E., Crane, S., & Bromberg, J. (1985). Health insurance coverage of the aged. *Medical Care, 223,* 847–854.

Blank, R. H. (1988). *Rationing medicine.* New York: Columbia University Press.

Blendon, R. J., Aiken, L. H., Freeman, H. E., & Corey, C. (1989). Access to medical care for black and white Americans. *Journal of the American Medical Association, 261,* 278–281.

Blumenthal, D., Schlesinger, M., & Brown Drumheller, P. 1988. *Renewing the promise: Medicare and its reform.* New York: Oxford University Press.

Brody, E. M. (1985). Parent care as normative family stress. *The Gerontologist, 25,* 19–29.

Brody, S. J., & Magel, J. (1986). Long term care: The long and short of it. In C. Eisdorfer (Ed.), *Reforming health care for the elderly: Recommendations for national policy.* Baltimore, MD: Johns Hopkins University Press.

Callahan, D. (1988). Allocating health resources. *Hasting Center Report, 18* (2), 14–20.

Cantor, M. (1975). Life space and the social support of the inner city elderly of New York. *The Gerontologist, 14,* 286–288.

Carp, F. (1975). Life-style and location within the city. *The Gerontologist, 15,* 27–34.

Cohen, M. A., Kumar, N., McGuire, T., & Wallack, S. S. (1992). Financing long-term care: A practical mix of public and private. *Journal of Health Politics, Policy and Law, 17* (3), 403–424.

Coronel, S. (1994). *Long-term care insurance in 1992.* Washington, DC: Health Insurance Association of America.

Davis, K., & Rowland, D. 1986. *Medicare policy.* Baltimore, MD: Johns Hopkins University Press.

Doty, P. (1986). Family care of the elderly: The role of public policy. *The Milbank Quarterly, 64* (1), 34–75.

Estes, C. L., Gerard, L. E., Zones, J. S., & Swan, J. H. (1984). *Political economy, health, and aging.* Boston: Little, Brown.

Estes, C. L., Swan, J. H., & Gerard, L. E. (1984). Dominant and competing paradigms in gerontology: Towards a political economy of aging. In M. Minkler & C. L. Estes (Eds.), *Readings in the political economy of aging.* Farmingdale, NY: Baywood.

Feingold, E. (1966). *Medicare: Policy and politics.* San Francisco: Chandler.

Folstein, M. F., Folstein, S., & McHugh, P. R. (1975). Mini-mental state: A practical method for grading the cognitive state of patients for the clinician. *Journal of Psychiatric Research, 12,* 189–198.

Freeman, H. E., Blendon, R. J., Aiken, L. H., Sudman, S., Mullinix, C. F., & Corey, C. (1987). Americans report on their access to health care. *Health Affairs, 6,* 6–18.

Freidson, E. (1961). *Patient views of medical practice.* New York: Russell Sage Foundation.

Freidson, E. (1989). Client control and medical practice. In E. Freidson (Ed.), *Medical work in America: Essays on health care.* New Haven, CT: Yale University Press.

Gibson, M. (1984). Family support patterns, policies and programs. In C. Nusberg (Ed.), *Innovative aging programs abroad.* Westport, CT: Greenwood Press.

Gibson, R., Waldo, D., & Levit, K. (1983). National health expenditures, 1982. *Health Care Financing Review, 5* (1), 1–31.

Hamm, L. V., Kickham, T., & Cutler, D. (1983). Research, demonstrations and evaluations. In R. Vogel & H. Palmer (Eds.), *Long term care: Perspectives from research and demonstrations.* Washington,

DC: Health Care Financing Administration.

Hanley, R. J., Wiener, J. M., & Harris, K. M. (1994). *The economic status of nursing home users*. Washington, DC: Brookings Institute.

Haug, M. (1981). Age and medical care utilization patterns. *Journal of Gerontology, 33*, 103–111.

Kamerman, S. (1976). Community services for the aged. *Gerontologist, 16* (6), 13–18.

Kane, R. L., & Kane, R. A. (1990). Health care for older people: Organizational and policy issues. In R. H. Binstock & L. K. George (Eds.), *Handbook of aging and the social sciences* (3rd ed.). San Diego, CA: Academic Press.

Kart, C. S. (1993). Community-based, noninstitutional long-term care service utilization by aged blacks: Facts and issues. In C. M. Barresi & D. E. Stull (Eds.), *Ethnic elderly & long-term care*. New York: Springer.

Kemp, B. (1981). The case management model of human service delivery. In E. Pan, T. Barker, & C. Vash (Eds.), *Annual Review of Rehabilitation* (Vol. 2). New York: Springer.

Longman, P. (1987). *Born to pay: The new politics of aging in America*. Boston: Houghton Mifflin.

Lopata, H. (1975). Support system of elderly urbanites: Chicago of the 1970's. *The Gerontologist, 15*, 35–41.

Marmor, T. (1973). *The politics of medicare*. Chicago: Aldine.

Mechanic, D. (1978). *Medical sociology* (2nd ed.). New York: Free Press.

Mechanic, D. (1985). Cost containment and the quality of medical care: Rationing strategies in an era of constrained resources. *Milbank Memorial Fund Quarterly, 63*, 453–475.

Minkler, M. (1984). Blaming the aged victim: The politics of retrenchment in times of fiscal conservatism. In M. Minkler & C. L. Estes (Eds.), *Readings in the political economy of aging*. Farmingdale, NY: Baywood.

Mossey, J. M., Havens, B., & Wolinsky, F. D. (1989). The consistency of formal health care utilization. In M. Ory & K. Bond (Eds.), *Aging and the use of formal health services*. New York: Routledge.

Nathanson, C. (1975). Illness and the feminine role: A theoretical review. *Social Science and Medicine, 9*, 57–62.

Rabin, D. L. (1985). Waxing of the gray, waning of the green. In Institute of Medicine/National Research Council (Eds.), *America's aging: Health in an older society*. Washington, DC: National Academy Press.

Rabin, D. L., & Stockton, D. (1987). *Long-term care for the elderly: A factbook*. New York: Oxford University Press.

Riley, P. (1995). Long-term care: The silent target of the federal and state budget debate. *The Public Policy and Aging Report, 7* (1), 4–5, 7.

Roos, N., & Shapiro, E. (1981). The Manitoba longitudinal study on aging: Preliminary findings on health care utilization by the elderly. *Medical Care, 19*, 644–657.

Rubenstein, L. Z., Josephson, K. R., Wieland, G. D., English, P. A., Sayre, J. A., & Kane, R. L. (1984). Effectiveness of a geriatric evaluation unit: A randomized clinical trial. *New England Journal of Medicine, 311*, 1664–1670.

Schwab, M. (1977). Implications for the aged of major national health care proposals. *Journal of Gerontological Nursing, 3*, 33–36.

Shanas, E., & Maddox, G. (1977). Aging, health, and the organization of health resources. In R. Binstock & E. Shanas (Eds.), *Handbook of aging and the social sciences*. New York: Van Nostrand Reinhold.

Shuval, J. (1970). *The social functions of medical practice*. San Francisco: Jossey-Bass.

Stevens, R., & Stevens R. (1974). *Welfare medicine in America: A case study of Medicaid*. New York: Free Press.

Tessler, R., Mechanic, D., & Dimond, M. (1976). The effect of psychological distress on physician utilization: A prospective study. *Journal of Health and Social Behavior, 17*, 353–364.

Trager, B. (1981). *In place of policy: Public adventures in non-institutional long-term care.* Unpublished paper presented at the American Public Health Association Annual Meeting, Los Angeles.

U.S. General Accounting Office. (1982). *The elderly should benefit from expanded home health care but increasing these services will not insure cost reductions.* Public No. GAO/IDE-83–1. Washington, DC: U.S. Government Printing Office.

U.S. Senate Special Committee on Aging et al. (1991). *Aging America: Trends and projections.* Washington, DC: U.S. Government Printing Office.

Van Gelder, S., & Johnson, D. (1991). *Long-term care insurance: A market update.* Washington, DC: Health Insurance Association of America.

Wan, T. (1982). Use of health service by the elderly in low income communities. *Milbank Memorial Fund Quarterly, 60,* 82–107.

Ward, R. (1977). Services for older people: An integrated framework for research. *Journal of Health and Social Behavior, 18,* 61–70.

Wiener, J. M., Hanley, R. J., & Illston, L. H. (1992). Financing long-term care: How much public? How much private? *Journal of Health Politics, Policy and Law, 17* (3), 425–434.

Wiener, J. M., & Illston, L. H. (1996). The financing and organization of health care for older Americans. In R. H. Binstock & L. K. George (Eds.), *Handbook of aging and the social sciences* (4th ed.). San Diego, CA: Academic Press.

Wiener, J. M., Illston, L. H., & Hanley, R. J. (1994). *Sharing the burden: Strategies for public and private long-term care insurance.* Washington, DC: Brookings Institute.

Wolinsky, F. D., & Johnson, R. J. (1991). The use of health services by older adults. *Journal of Gerontology, 46* (6), S345–357.

CHAPTER 19

DEATH AND DYING

Cary S. Kart and Eileen S. Metress

Age is an important variable in the study of a wide array of issues relating to death and dying. These issues include the relationship between age and the meaning of death, study of the grief and bereavement process, characterizations of the dying process, and decisions about where death should take place and who should decide about the access of older people to life-sustaining medical treatments. This chapter presents an overview of a selection of such issues as they pertain to the older adult.

AGING AND THE MEANING OF DEATH

The meanings that individuals give to death vary as a function of age. Nagy (1959) studied postwar Hungarian children and argued that the child's idea of death develops in three stages, each marked by a different view of death. She found that children under age 5 did not recognize death as irreversible; they viewed it as a temporary departure or sleep, a type of separation. Between the ages of 5 and 9, death was often personified and seen as a contingency. Although viewed as irreversible, it was not necessarily inevitable, at least as far as the child was concerned. Death existed but was remote. By age 9 or 10, the children understood death to be inevitable, final, and less remote, a part of the life cycle of all living organisms.

Some have questioned the universal application of Nagy's findings. McIntire, Angle, and Struempl (1972) found that, unlike Hungarian children, U.S. children are able to conceptualize "organic decomposition" as early as age 5 and in some cases as early as age 3. The tendency to personify death noted by Nagy during stage 2 is not a common finding in more recent studies (Kastenbaum, 1991). Kastenbaum considers that, since Nagy's research, children may have developed a fashionably scientific outlook in response to death. He notes one 7-year-old who likened death to "when the computer is down." Perhaps the children's tendency to personify is masked by contemporary images and terms. In addition, such work demonstrates the need to examine variations within cultural groups.

Likewise, the work of anthropologist Bluebond-Langner (1974, 1989) illustrates the need to consider children's personal experiences in relation to their understanding of death. Her work with hospitalized, terminally ill children showed them capable of a more sophisticated death awareness at a younger age than early researchers thought possible. Such awareness included the perception that death is final, inevitable, and happens to everyone—including them!

Bluebond-Langner (1977) summarizes research on the relationship between social class and children's views of death as follows: Children from lower socioeconomic groups are more likely to cite violence as the general and specific cause of death, whereas middle-class children are more likely to cite disease and old age as the general cause and the arrest of vital functions as the specific cause of death. These variations seem to reflect differences in the life experiences of the children.

Two meanings of death with particular significance for the elderly are suggested by a large body of literature: death as an organizer of time and death as loss. To the elderly and the terminal patient, death is a clearly perceived constraint that limits the future (Kalish, 1976). Anticipating the end of one's life may bring a reorganization of time and priorities. In work done nearly thirty years ago, Kastenbaum (1991) found that older persons projected themselves into a much more limited time frame than did younger persons when asked to report coming important events in their lives and the timing of these events.

Death also makes all possessions and experiences transient. For many elderly persons, the anticipation of death may generate feelings of meaninglessness. There is nothing meaningful to do because whatever is attempted will be short lived or unfinished (Kalish, 1976). Kurt Back (1965) asked residents of rural communities in the West what they would do if they knew they were to die in 30 days. The elderly were less likely than younger respondents to indicate that their activities would change at all. A more recent study by Kalish and Reynolds (1976) supported Back's findings. Using respondents in three age groups and extending the duration to the time of death to six months instead of 30 days, more of the older group were found unwilling to change their life-styles. Nearly three times as many older persons as younger reported they would spend their remaining time in prayer, reading, contemplation, or other activities that reflected inner life, spiritual needs, or withdrawal.

Perception by the elderly of the finitude of life comes not only from within. Older persons receive many reminders of their impending death from other individuals and from social institutions. Society tends to perceive the older person as not having sufficient futurity to deserve a major investment of the resources of others.

GRIEF AND BEREAVEMENT

Bereavement refers to the state of having sustained a loss. For the elderly, losses accumulate and become very much a part of life. *Grief* is the reaction to loss. It is a painful yet necessary process that facilitates adjustment to the loss. Its course is quite variable; it may be short or long, taking months to a few years for the loss to be resolved and a normal life to resume. It may vary in its intensity. In addition to depression, reactions may include anger, guilt, anxiety, and preoccupation with thoughts of the deceased.

In his pioneering work, Lindemann (1944) described the physical symptoms of grief, which may include sensations of somatic distress lasting from 20 minutes to an hour. Stomach upset, shortness of breath, tightness in the throat, frequent sighing, an empty feeling in the abdomen, lack of muscular power, and "subjec-

DEATH IN THE SOUTH PACIFIC

Among the Managalase of Papua New Guinea in the South Pacific, death is central to cultural ideology and key concepts of power and exchange (McKellin, 1985). Managalase dead continue to participate in the life of the society. Because so few people achieve old age, longevity requires explanation. Why does a person outlive his or her contemporaries? The answer lies in the strength of one's soul. A strong soul may avoid or withstand attacks by sorcerers or bush spirits, the main explanations of death among the young. Responsibility for a younger person's death also rests with family and community. In part, death reflects failed obligations to protect the victim from assault. It suggests unsatisfactory exchanges and offerings to ancestral ghosts.

Death in youth and adulthood can be enormously disruptive to social life. Exchange relations are interrupted and alliances may end. The death of a man may be less problematic than that of a woman as his siblings assume his responsibilities. Multiple deaths in a village threatens the life of the village itself. In one case described by McKellin,

> After the death of...the village councilor and area bigman, the whole web

of political alliances in Siribu and surrounding villages began to unravel. After two or three more deaths, the village was pronounced *derahar* "dead", and over the course of several years the people dismantled their houses and established three new villages at different sites. (1985, p. 193)

Death from old age is described as "passing away." It reflects the end of participation in village life and is explained as a failure of the soul to return to the body after long and distant travels. Ultimately, the strength and magic of soul which contributed to longevity fail the older person and cause his or her death.

Death of the old is much more conclusive for village life than death of a younger person. The old have lost power by outliving their contemporaries; they come to rely on younger relatives for food and sustenance. Surviving kin have already developed exchange relations with ghosts and others in the village and are not dependent on ties with the recently deceased. In fact, by the end, the reverse has occurred. Prior to passing away, the position of the old has typically come to mirror that of a dependent child.

tive distress" were found to be common among the grieving. Confusion, disorganization, absentmindedness, and insomnia were also expressed.

In part, the loss reaction is shaped by cultural norms and experiences. In less-developed societies with extended families, the trauma of death is only minimally disruptive. In preliterate families, the primary relationships involving parents, children, and spouses may be extended to other relatives. In this way, others may serve to compensate for a loss. For instance, among the Trobrianders, the role of the father is assumed by the mother's brother. Such is *not* the case in the smaller nuclear family units that characterize industrialized societies. Nuclear family members are customarily left to their own resources to adjust to the psychological and social impact of loss.

In many societies, including that of the United States, established rituals determine how life crises such as death are to be managed. Rituals have important social functions as well as utilitarian value to those who are grieving. They serve to channel and legitimize the normal expression of grief, as well as to rally emotional support for the bereaved through the participation of friends and relatives. *Mourning,* the culturally patterned manner by which grief is managed, is quite variable from one society to another and among subcultures within U.S. society as well.

Many believe that among African Americans, funerals provide a number of psychological mechanisms that facilitate the grief process (Masamba & Kalish, 1976). One factor that permits emotional expression at funerals in African American churches is the visual confrontation with the deceased. This is carried out in at least two ways. First, the picture of the deceased uniformly appears on the program of the order of the service. According to a member of one deceased person's family, printing the picture in this fashion helped him accept the reality of the loss and generated a feeling of the spiritual presence of the deceased in the church (Masamba & Kalish, 1976).

Second, the visual confrontation with the deceased is especially vivid when the remains are viewed by the living. In almost all the funerals attended by Masamba and Kalish (1976), caskets were closed at the beginning of the service and opened at the end of the concluding sermon. Those present were asked to view the body. Responses varied: Some walked by silently; others touched and even talked to the deceased. Members of the family were always last to view the body, although this is usually done by bringing the body closer to where they are seated so that they can see the body without standing up. Overt expression can be quite strong, including vehement physical motion.

According to Masamba and Kalish (1976), emotion may not be expressed when (1) there is a feeling that such expression may be seen as masculine inadequacy, (2) there is belief that such expressions should not be made in front of people who are not family members or friends of the family, and (3) the minister expresses a belief that such behavior implies a lack of acceptance of resurrection and hope in Christ.

Expression takes a different form in the funeral rites of American Jews. For example, the service begins with the cutting of a garment or a black ribbon. As

Cytron (1993) describes it, this rite symbolizes the individual being "cut away" from loved ones. Children make the cut in a garment above the heart; others do it on the right side of the garment. At the grave site, many family members choose to participate personally in placing some earth on the lowered coffin. It symbolizes both acceptance of the finality of death and assurance of a proper burial (Cytron, 1993). Typically, the Jewish service ends with a recitation of the "homecoming" prayer called *kaddish*. This prayer makes no overt reference to death, yet offers an affirmation of life through "an ancient formula praising God as the author of life and its wonderous ways" (Cytron, 1993, p. 119).

The elderly in U.S. society are not always provided an outlet for the expression of grief. Goodstein (1984) asserts that because of their own significant longevity, the elderly may be expected to grin and bear their losses rather than to grieve. Loss is expected with old age. When held by family, friends, and practitioners, such an attitude may compel older persons to act strong out of fear that doing otherwise might label them as weak.

Various types of losses accumulate with age, underscoring the possibility of severe grief reactions after the loss of a spouse, relative, friend, home, employment, financial security, or health, as well as the loss of personal belongings such as a domestic pet (Keddie, 1977). Attachments to remaining people and objects may take on increasing value. Their loss may generate an intense response.

Symptoms of grief in the elderly may be mistaken for other conditions in what is referred to as a *devious pattern of grief* (Goodstein, 1984). The clinician may

Losses accumulate with age, making remaining attachments to people, pets, and objects especially valuable. Such losses may generate an intense response.

attribute the symptoms to another physical illness or to dementia. As the grief remains ignored, episodic exacerbation of symptoms may result. Unresolved grief is one of the most frequently misdiagnosed illnesses in the elderly. Continued physical and emotional pain, if verbalized by the victim, may be dismissed as hypochondriasis.

Physical and emotional symptoms of grief usually subside in time, but some bereaved individuals are at increased risk for illness and possibly death (Osterweis, 1985). Existing illness may worsen, and new illnesses may be precipitated. Frederick (1976, 1982–1983) has suggested a pathway by which illnesses might be triggered. He has proposed that a chain of hormonal responses to the stress of loss leads to depression of the body's immune system; if the response pattern continues, the immune suppression can lead to the development of infection and even cancer. Until about age 75, widowed men are one and one-half times more likely to die than are married men (Helsing & Szklo, 1981). Morbidity, hospitalization, and mortality exceed expected rates in the two-year period following a loss of spouse (Greenblatt, 1978; Rowland, 1977).

A number of factors appear to exert significant influence on the resolution of grief (Lieberman, 1978; Osterweis, 1985; Osterweis, Solomon, & Green, 1984). The nature of the lost relationship is important. Loss of spouse has received considerable attention. More research needs to be directed at the loss of friends, siblings, and adult children. Gorer (1965) posits that the loss of an adult child would seem to be the most distressing and long lasting of all griefs. Besides exerting emotional trauma, the death of an adult child might leave the older person without a caregiver. Yet, research focusing on such a loss is extremely limited (Levav, 1982). How the death occurred, the availability of a social support system, experiencing several deaths within a short period of time, the existence of illness prior to or at the time of the loss, and life changes necessitated by the loss can all influence the intensity, duration, and consequences of the grieving process.

Although it is almost always best to allow the bereaved to experience the grieving process, problems may arise if the grieving appears interminable. In old age, the depression involved in bereavement may not be self-limiting (Brocklehurst & Hanley, 1976). Treatment may be necessary. Care may involve simple encouragement, personal warmth, understanding, and compassion; or it may require antidepressant drug therapy and psychiatric management. Life decisions related to finances, living arrangements, and personal care may have to be made. Counsel should be given carefully, lawfully, and together with the physician and family members. No irrevocable decisions involving such important matters should be made until the main period of grieving has passed.

Bereavement is a significant contributing factor to suicide. Suicide is more frequent among the widowed. The resolution of grief goes hand in hand with the resumption and development of interpersonal relationships. The psychosocial environment of the aged widow or widower may not furnish the opportunity for reestablishing relationships or building important new links (Bromberg & Cassel, 1983). Older persons who are married and who maintain contact with their children and other relatives are less likely to commit suicide (Robbins, West, & Murphy, 1977).

The elderly are more likely than the young to complete a suicide effort (Maris, 1981). Perhaps the older person who attempts suicide is less ambivalent about doing so and more likely to use a more lethal technique. Chapter 6 includes additional material on suicide and the mental health of the elderly.

THE DYING PROCESS

Death and the dying process itself are being seen more and more as the terminal phase of the life cycle. Professionals who work with the dying and those who study death and dying have made attempts to understand this final stage. It is hoped that such understanding will help health care professionals to enrich the lives of the dying and their families and to provide personalized care for those who have been defined as terminally ill.

The Dying Trajectory

The Glaser-Strauss research team was the first to study and clarify the various sequences and distinctive characteristic of the terminal course. They observed the social process of dying in six medical facilities in the San Francisco area. The majority of their findings are published in two books: *Awareness of Dying* (1966) and *Time for Dying* (1968). Although their research was not limited to older patients, the results of their work are relevant to the elderly dying patient.

According to Glaser and Strauss (1968), staff members working with the ill must answer two questions for themselves about every patient: Will he or she die? And, if so, when? These questions are important because the staff generates expectations about a patient's death and takes its treatment and other attitudinal cues from the answers that are developed.

Perceptions about the course of dying are referred to as *dying trajectories*. The nature of staff interaction with the patients is closely related to the particular expectations the staff have formed about the patient's dying. This is the case regardless of whether the staff happens to be correct in its expectations. Patients' expectations about their own dying trajectories are greatly affected by staff expectations as well.

Two important cues that contribute to the perception of the dying trajectory are the patient's physical condition and the temporal references made by medical staff members. Physical cues are easiest to read and help establish some degree of certainty about the outcome. Temporal cues are more difficult to read, in part, because they have many reference points. Doctors' expectations about the progression of a disease ("It's going fast," "He's lingering"); length of hospital stay; and even the work schedule, (e.g., whether the patient continues to be bathed, turned and/or fed, etc.) are temporal cues that contribute to expectations about how much longer the patient will live (Glaser & Strauss, 1968, p. 10).

In perceptions of a lingering trajectory, custodial care predominates. Aggressive treatment is rare. Health care professionals tend not to find the support of such patients challenging or rewarding. Lower-paid staff may provide the majority of care for such patients (Friedman & DiMatteo, 1982).

When staff perceive patients as being in a lingering death trajectory, these patients may suffer a loss in their own perceived social worth and relinquish control over their care (Kastenbaum, 1991). Staff members may feel that they have done everything that is possible to care for the patient, and they may view a downhill course as inevitable. Death of one who has been on a lingering trajectory may seem appropriate to the staff, who rationalize that the patient's life held limited value. Intense emotional reactions at the death of such a patient may serve to confuse those who have made assumptions about the patient's present limited social worth. Or stress may result when the lingering patient does not die on schedule.

In contrast, the expected quick trajectory typically involves acute life-or-death crises. The patient's perceived social worth can influence the type of care delivered. The unexpected quick trajectory involves an unanticipated crisis that may challenge the professional caregiver's defenses regarding anxiety about death.

Dying: The Career Perspective

Julius Roth has written that "when people go through the same series of events, we speak of this as a career and of the sequence and timing of events as their career timetable" (1963, p. 93). Roth used the institutionalized tuberculosis patient as his career model. He argued that individuals involved in a career try to define when certain salient things will happen to them, developing time norms against which to measure their individual progress. The benchmarks on this timetable are the significant events that occur in the average career (Gustafson, 1972).

Gustafson (1972) has applied Roth's notion of career timetables to the nursing-home setting. She views the last phase of life as a career that moves in a series of related and regressive stages toward death. These stages, she argues, are defined by a series of benchmarks, which, for elderly patients, consist of the degree of deterioration indicated by their social activity, mobility, and physical and mental functioning. A successful career, in this sense, consists of the slowest possible regression from one stage to another.

Bargaining is an important aspect of the career timetable, according to Gustafson (1972), although she identifies it in a way that contrasts with Roth's original model. Roth depicts the tubercular patient as bargaining with medical and hospital authorities to move as quickly as possible toward the goal of restored health. Gustafson sees the elderly nursing-home patient as bargaining with God, the disease, and the nursing-home staff in an attempt to slow down the movement toward death.

By use of this perspective, the dying process is not conceptualized as an undifferentiated, unbroken decline toward death. Rather, the dying career is viewed as comprising a social stage and a terminal stage. In the social stage, the elderly patient is fighting against the tendency of society (as represented by relatives, staff, visitors, and peers) to impose a premature social death. Bargaining may involve holding on to status symbols that indicate the possibility of a future. An elderly woman may never read, but she indignantly demands a new pair of eyeglasses, for example, or an elderly man may not be able to walk, yet he demands a new walker or cane. In the terminal phase, when the signs of death are more dependable and its imminence cannot be avoided, the patient may begin bargaining directly with God or the disease in an effort to secure additional time.

According to Gustafson (1972), a nursing-home patient's dying career can be made less difficult if the staff adopts a view of the dying process as consisting of a social stage and a terminal stage. A nursing staff with this view might try to extend the social stage as long as possible and be supportive during the terminal stage. Later, this chapter discusses some ways in which health professionals, family members, and others can help ease the dying process for terminal patients.

The Stages of Dying

The best known conceptualization of the dying process is that proposed by Elizabeth Kubler-Ross (1969) in her landmark best-seller, *On Death and Dying*. In her view, various stages or emotional reactions mark an awareness of dying. The patient may experience denial, anger, bargaining, depression, and acceptance. The applicability and universality of these five stages are still empirical questions. Kubler-Ross (1974, pp. 25–26) points out that patients may skip a stage, exhibit two or three simultaneously, or experience them out of order. Kalish contends that Kubler-Ross's stages are in danger of becoming self-fulfilling prophecies: "Some health caretakers have been observed trying to encourage, or even manipulate, their dying patients through Kubler-Ross's stages; patients occasionally become concerned if they are not progressing adequately" (1976, p. 38).

The first stage, *denial,* is most evident during the early period of awareness of impending death. It may be viewed as a coping mechanism to buffer the shock of such news ("No, not me, it can't be true"). Kubler-Ross offers the case of a patient who went through a long and expensive ritual to support her denial:

> She was convinced that the x-rays were "mixed up." She asked for reassurance that her pathology report could not possibly be back so soon and that another patient's report must be marked with her name. When none of this could be confirmed, she quickly asked to leave the hospital, looking for another physician in the vain hope "to get a better explanation for my troubles. . . ." She asked for examination and re-examination, partially knowing that the original diagnosis was correct, but also seeking further evaluations in the hope that the first conclusion was indeed in error. (1969, p. 38)

When the first stage of denial cannot be maintained any longer, it is often replaced by feelings of *anger* or *rage*. The patient finally realizes that denial is fruitless ("It is me, it was not a mistake"). The next question becomes, Why me? This stage is perhaps the most difficult for staff and family members to deal with. Anger may be displaced and projected on anyone and everyone who comes into contact with the patient. Much of this anger is rational and should be expected. Place yourself in the terminal patient's position. You, too, would be angry if your life's activities had been interrupted and you could no longer enjoy life, especially if you had been kept too long in a hospital, subjected to unpleasant tests and treatments, and constantly being reminded that you could no longer carry out your own affairs.

The third stage, *bargaining*, is really an attempt on the part of the patient to postpone the inevitable. As Kubler-Ross indicates, the terminal patient in this stage uses the same maneuvers as a child; he or she asks to be rewarded "for good behavior" (1969, p. 82). Most bargains are made with God and almost always include wishes for the removal of pain or discomfort and for life extension. Kubler-Ross presents the case of a woman quite dependent on injections for painkillers. The woman had a son who was to be married, and she was sad at the prospect of being unable to attend the wedding. With great effort, she was taught self-hypnosis and was able to be comfortable for several hours at a time.

> She had made all sorts of promises if she could only live long enough to attend this marriage. The day preceding the wedding she left the hospital as an elegant lady. Nobody would have believed her real condition. She was "the happiest person in the whole world" and looked radiant. (1969, p. 83)

Patients rarely hold up their end of the bargain. This same woman returned to the hospital and remarked, "Now don't forget, I have another son."

When the terminally ill person is unable to continue to deny the illness, when the rage and anger are dissipated, and when bargaining efforts are seen as hopeless, *depression* may begin. This fourth stage is characterized by feelings of loss, and two types of depression may be evident. *Reactive depression* is a result of the various other losses that accompany illness and dying. For instance, the patient may mourn the loss of a limb that has been amputated, or the cancer patient may mourn the loss of her beautiful hair to radiation therapy. The second type of depression, *preparatory depression*, takes impending losses into account; that is, it prepares the individual for loss of all love objects. It facilitates the final stage of acceptance.

Acceptance should not be mistaken for happiness or capitulation. The dying patient can accept his or her imminent death without joy and without giving up the life that remains. According to Kubler-Ross, this is often a time when the dying individual will "contemplate his coming end with a certain degree of quiet expectation." This stage may represent "the final rest before the long journey" (1969, pp. 112–113).

Although many researchers and practitioners find Kubler-Ross's conceptualization of the dying process extremely valuable, others are critical (Corr, 1992,

1993; Feigenberg, 1977; Kastenbaum, 1991; Metzger, 1979; Schulz & Aderman, 1974; Shneidman, 1980; Weisman, 1992). Weisman (1972), for example, rather than using the notion of *acceptance of death,* encourages the concept of *appropriate death.* Such a death means that the person has died in a fashion that resembles as much as possible the way that he or she wished to die. The totality of the person's life can be ignored in strict adherence to the stages of dying. The effects of age, gender, ethnic background, and one's life experience have not been studied as they apply to Kubler-Ross's stage theory (Kastenbaum, 1991). Remember as well that the process of dying may be very strongly influenced by the behavior and attitudes of those persons in the dying individual's social milieu.

Consider the inhabitants of the Etal Island in the Caroline Islands (Micronesia). They have no formal theory of dying, yet it is important to them that some resolution be achieved. "Dying is the last important social act an old person can perform. Past conflicts must be resolved. Also, this is the time for the old person to make a final decision about the disposition of property" (Nason, 1981).

Islanders believe that the dying should pass on in an atmosphere of peace and solitude. A new ancestor, pleased with attention and respect provided by kin while he or she was alive, is likely to aid and protect islanders. On the other hand, a person who dies angry or dissatisfied with the inattention of relatives might take revenge on them. Actually, an older person might be driven to suicide to make a public protest against ill treatment by relatives. To prevent this, relatives may stay constantly with the dying person. Such a suicide would bring public shame on the relatives and would cause trouble with the final settling of the estate, because suicides often make no final distribution of their property (Nason, 1981). Just the threat of suicide by a dying person (or any elder, for that matter) can quickly bring about a change in relations with extended kin members.

Kubler-Ross's work has been of tremendous value in sensitizing people to the needs and rights of the dying. Shortcomings in the application of her work or its uncritical acceptance by some should not lead to a dismissal of her many useful insights or of the need for further research in this area (Kastenbaum, 1991). Kubler-Ross argues that the physician can help the patient reach a calm acceptance of death. Schulz (1978) summarizes a body of literature that finds that physicians avoid patients once they begin to die. The nature and impact of the doctor/ dying patient relationship on the dying process would seem an area ripe for additional research.

THE WHERE OF DYING

Today, most people die in health care institutions of one kind or another. In hospitals, rest homes, and nursing homes, the dying process has become bureaucratized and, to a great extent, depersonalized. Such institutions, while treating the terminally ill, also isolate them from the rest of society. These institutions have routinized the handling of death for their own benefit. This may reduce disturbance and disruption for the institution. Standardized procedures render death nearly invisible. To protect relatives and other visitors, bodies may not be removed during visiting hours. When death appears imminent, the patient may be moved to a private room to protect other patients.

Many people, health professionals and laypeople alike, are aware of the depersonalized treatment provided to the terminally ill in many health facilities. On the basis of their study of individuals in four ethnoracial communities in Los Angeles, Kalish and Reynolds (1976) report that most people of all ages would prefer to die at home, particularly those under age 40 and over age 59. Although many dying patients and their families wish for death in the home, the wish is not often realized. One recent study clearly indicates that even when plans for home death have been made, they may be precluded by many factors, the most prominent of which appears to be the emotional and physical exhaustion of the family (Groth-Junker & McCusker, 1983).

New options for caring for the dying are becoming available. One such option, called a *hospice,* combines the technical expertise for caring for the ill that is available in health care bureaucracies with the personalized attention of home care. The most widely known is St. Christopher's Hospice in London, founded by Dr. Cicily Saunders.

A hospice is not a place; rather, it is a concept of care that combines various elements. It emphasizes *palliative care* rather than cure. Control of pain and distressing symptoms is viewed as a treatment goal in its own right. If a patient's preoccupation with suffering is of such intensity that everything else in life is excluded, then self-control, independence, human dignity, and interpersonal relations are sacrificed. Each patient is seen as a part of a family whose total well-being and life-style may be affected by the circumstance of having a terminally ill member. Caring does not stop when the patient dies, but the hospice continues to help the family during bereavement. The hospice concept also views the home as a suitable domain for patient care. An interdisciplinary team involving physician, nursing, social work, counseling, and volunteer services provides hospice care.

The first hospice in the United States became operative in 1974. Known as the Connecticut Hospice (originally Hospice, Inc.), it provides both inpatient and home care services. Since its inception, hospice programs have developed in every state in the nation. They now take several forms in their organization. Home care programs have been preferred in the United States. The Connecticut Hospice began as a home care program and later added an inpatient facility. Some hospitals are developing hospice units within their walls to deliver hospicelike care or other separate or freestanding facilities.

In the United States, hospice has evolved from a fringe alternative led by a group of idealistic professionals and volunteers to an accepted mainstream approach to terminal care (Tehan, 1985). Much of this change has been precipitated by legislation that allows terminally ill patients over the age of 65 to receive Medicare reimbursable services from certified hospice programs.

The National Hospice Study, conducted between 1980 and 1984, was spawned by a concern for the feasibility of a hospice Medicare benefit (Greer & Mor, 1985). Its results represent the largest collection of carefully controlled data on hospice care in the nation. In general, results of the study demonstrate that hospice care tends to be less expensive than traditional hospital care and that hospice patients spend more time at home during the course of their terminal illness.

Medical anthropologist Robert Buckingham and colleagues (1976) have, through participant observation, compared the relative merits of standard hospital versus hospice care for the dying. Using an elaborate and deceptive scheme that was aided by physicians, Buckingham played the role of a cancer patient. He prepared himself in a number of ways before entering the hospital. He went on a severe six-month diet and lost 22 pounds from his already spare frame. Exposure to ultraviolet rays made it appear that he had undergone cancer radiation therapy. Puncture marks from intravenous needles on his hands and arms indicated that he had also had chemotherapy cancer treatment. A cooperative surgeon performed minor surgery on him in order to produce biopsy scars, indicating that exploratory surgery had been performed. Buckingham reviewed medical charts and maintained close contact with patients dying of cancer of the pancreas. He was thus able to observe and imitate suitable behavior. A patchy beard and the results of several days of not washing or shaving completed the picture. He spent two days in the holding unit, four days on a surgical care ward, and four days on the hospice or palliative care ward of Royal Victoria Hospital in Montreal.

Buckingham's findings lend empirical support to the assumption that the hospice system of care for the terminally ill is effective. He lists certain hospital staff practices that were observed in the surgical care ward that should be sources of concern in attempting to develop an optimal environment for the dying. These practices are as follows:

1. The tradition of physicians making their patient rounds in groups (This fostered social and medical discussion between the doctors but completely prevented doctor/patient communication on any but the most superficial level.)

2. The lack of eye contact between staff members and patient (Patients walked in the halls close to the walls, greetings were rare, and staff frequently crossed to the other side of the hall and walked by with heads averted.)

3. Reference to a patient by the name of his or her disease rather than by the name of the person

4. The accentuation of negative aspects of a patient's condition

5. The lack of affection given to the complacent patient

6. The discontinuity of communication among medical and nursing staff

Staff/patient and staff/family relationships were qualitatively different on the hospice care ward. Buckingham and associates (1976) describe Buckingham's arrival on this ward as follows:

> The initial nursing interview was conducted by a nurse who introduced herself by name, sat down so that her eyes were on a level with [the patient's] and proceeded to listen. There was no hurry, her questions flowed from [the patient's] previous answers, and there was acceptance of the expression of his concerns. She asked questions such as "What do you like to eat?" and "Is there anything special you like to do?"
>
> In the hospice care unit Buckingham observed relatives enquiring for the doctor five times. On each occasion the doctor was reached and either came or spoke to the family on the phone . . . families also spent much time at the bedside participating in the care of the patient. They changed the bed linen, washed and fed the patient, brought the urinal and plumped the pillows frequently. The staff encouraged the family to experience the meaning of death by allowing them to help in the care of the dying. (1976)

A greater effort is necessary to accomplish total care of the terminally ill. Four observations made by Buckingham (Buckingham et al., 1976) that are often overlooked by health care professionals may facilitate consummating the total care effort. These are:

1. The sharing and help provided by other patients form a powerful social support system for patients with terminal disease.
2. The need for the patient as a person to give and thus retain his or her individuality should be recognized.
3. The care given by families is a source of support for patients that must be recognized and emphasized.
4. The interest and care given by student nurses and volunteers is important, particularly in bringing the person out of the patient.

TERMINATION OF TREATMENT
Who Decides?

Central issues concerning who decides or exerts control in matters related to death and dying are exemplified in a series of recent court cases about the access of older people to life-prolonging medical treatments. One such case worthy of attention here is that of Earle Spring (Kart, 1981).

Earle Spring was born in 1901. In his working years, he was a chemist and metallurgist at a tool-and-die plant in Greenfield, Massachusetts. He was an avid outdoorsman who retired in 1966. In November 1977, Mr. Spring hurt his foot, developed an infection, and was hospitalized. He subsequently suffered pneumonia and then developed kidney failure and nearly died. Early in 1978, he was transferred to a hospital closer to his home, where hemodialysis treatments began. Within several weeks, Mr. Spring was returned to his home, where he received dialysis treatments three times a week, on an outpatient basis, at a private facility in the community.

According to the court record, Mr. Spring began showing signs of mental deterioration in conjunction with his progressive kidney failure. At home, he became destructive and was unable to care for himself. After being diagnosed as having chronic organic brain syndrome, he was admitted to a nursing home. By early 1979, his mental deterioration had continued to the point that he failed to recognize his wife and son. Yet, he was ambulatory and, except for his kidney failure, in good physical condition.

On January 25, 1979, Mr. Spring's son and wife petitioned a local probate court for an order that hemodialysis treatments be terminated. The medical consensus was that Mr. Spring might live for four or five weeks following the termination of these treatments. The probate judge appointed a guardian for Spring in this case, who opposed the petition. Yet, in May 1979, the judge ordered the temporary guardian to "refrain from authorizing any further life-prolonging medical treatment." The guardian appealed; but after a stay of the order, the judge ruled that the attending physician, together with the wife and son, were to make the decision to continue or terminate the dialysis treatments.

The guardian appealed this decision to the Appeals Court of Massachusetts, where it was affirmed. A further appeal was made to the Massachusetts Supreme Judicial Court, where, on May 13, 1980 (approximately one month after Earle Spring's death), it was reversed and remanded to the lower court. The Massachusetts Supreme Judicial Court acknowledged the substance of the lower court's decision, yet opined that the ultimate decision-making responsibility should not have been shifted away from the probate court by delegating the decision to continue or terminate care to the physician and Mr. Spring's wife and son.

Who should decide in this matter? The court itself? The physicians? Spring's family members? What about Earle Spring himself? A close examination of some underlying issues in this case is noteworthy. A careful reading of the transcript of the probate court's hearing in the matter of Earle Spring shows that the court found that Mr. Spring would "if competent, choose not to receive the life-prolonging treatment." In so finding, the court followed a standard applied in another Massachusetts case, *Superintendent of Belchertown State School* v. *Saikewicz* (370 N.E. 2d 417, 1977), and invoked the principle of *substitute judgment*.

Joseph Saikewicz was 67 years old, had a mental age of approximately 3 years, and had been a resident of the Belchertown State School for 48 years. He was well nourished and ambulatory, could make his wishes known through gestures and grunts, but was suffering from leukemia. In April 1976, the superintendent of the school filed a petition in local probate court asking for the appointment of a guardian for purposes of making a decision about Saikewicz's care and treatment for the leukemia. The judge did so, and the guardian filed a report with the court, stating that the illness was incurable, that the indicated treatment would cause adverse side effects and discomfort, and that Saikewicz was incapable of understanding the treatment. In sum, it was the view of the guardian that the negative aspects of the treatment situation outweighed the uncertain and clearly limited extension of life the treatment could bring; in the guardian's opinion, treating Saikewicz would not be in his best interests.

In May 1976, the probate judge entered an order agreeing with the guardian; the Massachusetts Supreme Judicial Court concurred, and later that summer, Joseph Saikewicz died without pain. It is noteworthy that in November of that year, the Supreme Judicial Court handed down a written decision in the *Saikewicz* case. In this written opinion, the court argued that, like competent persons, incompetents must also have the right to refuse medical treatment. In making this argument, the court recognized what may currently be a widely held view—that medical treatment does not always further the best interests of the patient. The central problem the court faced, however, was in deciding how to determine what is in the best interest of an incompetent person (Glantz & Swazey, 1979). The standard adopted was the substitute judgment test, which, according to the court, seeks "to determine with as much accuracy as possible the wants and needs of the individual involved."

In the case of Joseph Saikewicz, the use of the substitute judgment test would seem a "legal fiction" (Glantz & Swazey, 1979). How is it possible to know the wishes of a 67-year-old man who has been severely retarded all his life? In effect, the court substituted its own judgment for that of the incompetent person. Earle Spring's case, however, is another matter. He was competent for the greater part of his adult life. Nevertheless, how did the *Spring* court ascertain that "if competent, Spring would choose not to receive the life-sustaining treatment"? Mr. Spring had never stated his preference regarding continuing or terminating life-sustaining medical treatment.

The probate court substituted the judgment of Earle Spring's wife, who indicated that, on the basis of their long years of marriage, she believed "he wouldn't want to live." In doing so, the court employed a variant of the substitute judgment standard used by the Supreme Court of New Jersey *In re Quinlan* (355 A. 2d 647, 1976). Karen Quinlan was an adult woman in a persistent vegetative state from which her physicians felt she could not recover. Her father sought to be appointed her guardian so that he could have the power to authorize the discontinuance of all extraordinary medical procedures for sustaining his daughter's vital processes. The *Quinlan* court assumed that, if Karen were competent and perceptive of her irreversible condition, "she could effectively decide upon discontinuance of the life-sustaining apparatus, even if it meant the prospect of natural death." Because the patient was not competent, the court concluded that her father and other family members, with the concurrence of a hospital ethics committee, could assert this decision for her.

This variant of the substitute judgment test was applied by the probate court in the *Spring* case, even though Spring's wife could offer no evidence in support of her conclusion about his wishes. No evidence was put forth that might provide a basis for believing that Earle Spring would reject life-sustaining medical treatment. Nothing was made of the fact that when Spring first began hemodialysis treatments, before he was believed to be incompetent, he cooperated in taking these treatments. In fact, the court took testimony from family members that Earle Spring's activity level had fallen off considerably before the diagnosis of organic brain syndrome. He was no longer able to hunt and fish, as was the case in his younger years. This is precisely what some gerontologists argue is supposed to happen in old age. From this view, activity reduction in the later years is natural, expected, and even looked forward to by the aging.

The Massachusetts Supreme Judicial Court rejected the lower court's delegation of authority to withhold life-sustaining medical treatment to Earle Spring's wife, family, and physicians. In effect, the higher court rejected the approach employed in the *Quinlan* case and reasserted the standard employed in the *Saikewicz* case: "When a court is properly presented with the legal question, whether treatment may be withheld, it must decide the question and not delegate it to some private person or group" (Mass., 405 N.E. 2d 115, 122).

Is there basis in relevant literature for rejecting the substitute judgment of family members for that of an incompetent organic brain syndrome patient? Some would say yes. Several recent papers suggest that great stress is felt by family members of organic brain syndrome patients (Mace, Rabins, & Lucas, 1980; Schneider & Garron, 1980). Mace and colleagues report that more than 90 percent of the families they studied showed anger—at the situation, the patient, other family members, or professionals—as a response to the presence of a dementia patient in the family. Other stress responses include depression, grief, conflict with family members, withdrawal from social activity, and the like. Such research suggests that family members may not be in the best position to substitute their judgment for that of an incompetent in the question of whether to continue life-sustaining medical treatment.

Some would argue that the decision about whether to continue medical treatment in cases like Spring, Saikewicz, and Quinlan should be based on quality-of-life issues. Defining the issue in these terms may serve to exclude physicians, given that there is nothing inherently medical about a quality-of-life decision. Rather, it seems, as some have indicated, cases that raise quality-of-life questions are the ones that need to be resolved by a court of law.

Traditionally, decisions about how long to maintain a hopeless patient have been made by the physician, sometimes in concert with family members, and less frequently with input from the dying person. Many dying patients, particularly those who are very old and extremely deteriorated, have no input whatsoever into decisions about their own death. There have been several recent attempts to better represent the patient's wishes in such a decision through the use of *advance directives (AD)*.

Living wills, sometimes referred to as *instructional advance directives,* are being used by some to specify the conditions under which they would prefer not to be subjected to extraordinary measures to keep them alive. In 47 states (as of 1995) and the District of Columbia, living wills have legal standing. With them, a competent person can instruct a physician not to use heroic measures to prolong life when "there is no reasonable expectation of recovery from physical or mental disability."

Still, controversy exists over the meaning and application of the document. In particular, some argue, difficulties may arise out of uncertainties of clinical prognosis that allow for misinterpretation of the living will. Two safeguards are in order. First, the details of the living will should be discussed with the personal physician at the time it is completed. This may lessen the chances of misinterpretation. If the physician refuses to carry out the wishes expressed in the will, the individual who wrote the will should consider finding another doctor. Second, the will should name someone who can interpret the exact wishes of the writer should he or she ever be unable to express them. This provision, more commonly known as a *Durable Power of Attorney for Health Care (DPAHC)*, is afforded in the proxy advance directive. It is especially important should the writer become incompetent. Such a person can then make decisions as to specific measures to be taken or not taken on the writer's behalf. Presently, over 30 states recognize the DPAHC.

The major purpose of the Patient Self-Determination Act (PSDA) is to inform patients of their right to participate in decisions about the use of life-sustaining medical treatment and to execute advance directives. Under this federal law, implemented in 1991, designated health care institutions receiving Medicare and/or Medicaid funding must inform their adult patients in writing about:

1. Their right under state law to take part in medical decisions including accepting or rejecting medical and surgical treatment;
2. Their right under state law to execute advance directives such as a living will or durable power of attorney for health care; and
3. The policies and procedures the institution has formulated to honor these rights. (Fulton & Metress, 1995)

The law requires the institutions (which include hospitals, skilled nursing facilities, home health agencies, and health maintenance organizations) to provide this information to patients upon admission to their programs. Additionally, they must document in the medical record whether a patient has an AD. In the case of a hospital or skilled nursing facility, an existing AD must be made part of the patient's medical record.

Removal of Food and Fluids

As Steinbock (1983) indicates, a substantial body of legal opinion views the disconnection of all life-support apparatus from irreversibly comatose patients as morally and legally permissible. Nevertheless, many fear that such permissiveness leads to the "slippery slope" whereby the lives of all individuals who are terminally ill and disabled are endangered. Steinbock (1983) asks, for example, "If it is permissible to remove a feeding tube from a permanently comatose patient, why not from a barely conscious, senile and terminal patient?"

In January 1985, the Supreme Court of New Jersey ruled that artificial feeding, like other life-sustaining treatment, may be withheld or withdrawn from an incompetent patient if it represents a disproportionate burden and would have been refused by the patient under the circumstances. This decision was made in the case of Claire Conroy, an 84-year-old nursing-home resident who had suffered irreversible physical and mental impairments. She could move to a minor extent, she did groan, and she sometimes smiled in response to certain physical stimuli. She had no cognitive ability and was unaware of her surroundings.

She had been placed in a nursing home after having been declared incompetent. Eventually, she was transferred to a hospital for treatment of a gangrenous leg (a complication of her diabetes). Amputation was recommended, but Ms. Conroy's nephew, who was her legal guardian, refused consent. He maintained that she would have refused treatment. Surgery was not performed, but while she was in the hospital, a nasogastric tube was inserted. Her nephew requested that its use be discontinued in the hospital and, likewise, in the nursing home where she eventually returned. On both requests, permission was denied by her attending physician.

Conroy's nephew filed suit to obtain court permission to remove her feeding tube. A lower court granted permission. The decision was appealed and reversed by the appellate court in a declaration that termination of feeding constituted homicide. Ms. Conroy died during the appeal with the nasogastric tube still in place. Her guardian carried the case to the state supreme court.

The New Jersey Supreme Court ruling is consistent with that of the *Barber* case decided by the California Court of Appeals in 1983. In this case, the cessation of intravenous feeding was equated with the removal of a respirator. The *Conroy* case represents the first time that a state supreme court eliminated a distinction between artificial feeding and other artificial life supports (Nevins, 1986). Four years later, in the now well-known and much discussed *Cruzan* case, the United States Supreme Court agreed that artificial feeding and hydration constituted medical treatment that could be refused.

Nancy Cruzan, a young woman grievously injured in an automobile accident, had been unconscious and in a persistent vegetative state for more than four years when her parents requested that her feeding tube be removed. The Missouri Supreme Court had denied this request, emphasizing the lack of clear and convincing evidence of Ms. Cruzan's own wishes in this matter. At the same time, the court also stated that artificial feeding or hydration could not be refused in Missouri. The importance of advance directives was seemingly underscored by the United States Supreme Court's upholding of the state of Missouri's right to demand evidence that treatment cessation is what the patient would choose for herself or himself. Nancy Cruzan had never executed an advance directive. Ms. Cruzan's parents ultimately prevailed when they returned to the Missouri court with several new witnesses who testified that conversations with the young woman convinced them that, under the circumstances, she would not want treatment of any kind, including feeding or hydration. Her feeding tube was removed, and Ms. Cruzan died, after having been unconscious for almost eight years.

While recognizing the legal rights of all patients to self-determination, the New Jersey court, in the *Conroy* case, also imposed very strict requirements in providing previously competent patients the right to exercise treatment refusal by proxy. Through the application of a "best-interest test," the court must ascertain the patient's known or suspected personal attitude toward life-sustaining treatment and the burden of pain.

The New Jersey court apparently felt a special duty to protect the rights of the now-incompetent nursing-home patient. It maintains that the patient's guardian, next of kin, the attending physician, two consulting physicians (unaffiliated with the nursing home), and the state Office of the Ombudsman for the Institutionalized Elderly must all concur in the decision to remove life-sustaining treatment. The procedural portion of the New Jersey court decision has received considerable criticism on the basis that it fosters a climate of distrust, is difficult to implement, and artificially distinguishes between nursing-home and hospital patients (Annas, 1985a, 1985b; Nevins, 1985, 1986; Olins, 1986).

The court does heavily involve the state ombudsman, an office charged with guarding against and investigating allegations of elder abuse in conjunction with the state's Elder Abuse Statute. The ombudsman must be notified before any such decision to terminate treatment is rendered and must consider every such decision as a possible case of abuse.

The court asserts that special precautions are necessary because elderly nursing-home patients present special problems. Indeed, the court's holding is restricted to nursing-home patients. Reasons cited are the patients' average age, their general lack of next of kin, the limited role of physicians in nursing homes, reports of inhuman treatment and understaffing in nursing homes, and the less urgent decision making that occurs within these facilities allowing for more time to review options.

It has been held by others that nursing-home decisions can confound ethical considerations in a number of ways (Besdine, 1983):

1. Personal autonomy may be lost because nursing-home admission might result in a new physician providing care rather than one who has previously treated the patient and is familiar with the patient's wishes.

2. The patient may view that life is diminished by virtue of entry into the nursing home.

3. The possibility of dementing illness does not allow for informed consent.

4. The typical advanced age of the residents may influence decisions concerning treatment limitations.

Annas (1985b) charges that the court's strict differentiation between nursing-home and hospital patients regarding life-sustaining treatment decisions is artificial. He states that almost all nursing-home patients will be transferred to hospitals when invasive treatment is required. He adds that if ombudsman intervention is appropriate, it should apply in both settings. More appropriately, the ombudsman should be available to investigate cases of suspected abuse. Otherwise, the Conroy approach requires that time be wasted on cases that do not need investigation. Annas also posits that the court decision may create confusion in its applicability to nursing-home residents who are temporarily hospitalized.

Changes in Medicare funding are moving patients from hospitals to nursing homes "sooner and sicker." Although differences exist, problems of the two patient populations promise to become more similar. Nevins concludes, "So although their rhythms may differ, the two populations and their problems are becoming more homogeneous. No doubt differences exist, but to devise a totally new mechanism to resolve the same clinical issues depending on the locus of decision-making is unnecessary and unwise" (1986, p. 143).

The court's ruling is binding only in New Jersey. Ultimately, how it influences decision making there rests largely with how the ombudsman's office interprets and applies the court's rulings in the *Conroy* case. Although the mechanism set forth to allow incompetent patients to exercise the right to refuse treatment is cumbersome and restrictive, it stands testimony to a sensitive concern for human dignity and patient autonomy for people of all ages.

SUMMARY

Death is something that must inevitably be faced by everyone. The deaths of friends, relatives, and others are more frequent occurrences for older adults. Yet, death may have different meanings for people of different ages. Two meanings of death with particular significance for the elderly include death as an organizer of time and death as loss.

Bereavement refers to the state of having sustained a loss, whereas *grief* is a term that describes the reaction to loss. In part, this reaction is shaped by cultural norms and experiences. *Mourning,* the culturally prescribed manner in which grief is managed, varies from group to group within a society as well as between societies. A wide variety of factors appear to exert influence on the resolution of grief.

A number of conceptualizations of the dying process have been offered as attempts to understand this final stage of life. Dying has been described as a *trajectory,* a *career,* and a *five-stage process.* It is hoped that added understanding of the dying process will allow health care professionals and family members to provide for personalized care to the dying.

Today, most people die in health care institutions. One response to this practice is the development of hospice—a new caring community that provides medical and psychosocial care to the dying and their bereaved family members. The *Earle Spring* case involves the question of whether the decision to continue life-prolonging medical treatments should be in the hands of the individual, the family, the physicians, or the courts. This is especially problematic in cases involving incompetent patients. Advance directives, such as a living will, represent a possible solution to such dilemmas in the future.

Recently, the morality of withholding food and hydration in the case of severely demented or comatose elderly has emerged. Do such provisions constitute life-sustaining medical treatment? In the case of Claire Conroy, the Supreme Court of New Jersey ruled that artificial feeding, like other life-sustaining medical treatment, may be withheld from an incompetent patient if it represents a disproportionate burden.

STUDY QUESTIONS

1. Explain how the meanings individuals give to death vary as a function of age. Describe the two meanings of death found to have particular significance for the elderly.

2. Note some symptoms associated with the grieving process. Differentiate *bereavement, grief,* and *mourning.*

3. What factors might influence the expression of grief among the elderly? What is meant by a devious pattern of grief? Note various factors that might influence the resolution of grief.

4. Define the *dying trajectory.* What role does perception play in staff and patient definitions of the dying trajectory? What cues contribute to the perception of the dying trajectory?

5. Discuss Gustafson's concept of dying as a career timetable. How is bargaining used to manipulate the timetable?

6. List and explain the five stages of the dying process as conceptualized by Elisabeth Kubler-Ross. What has been the reaction to the stage theory of dying?

7. Define *hospice,* tracing its development in the United States. Explain how a hospice provides care for the terminally ill patient and his or her family.

8. Discuss the conflicting private and public interests involved in decisions about the continuance of life-prolonging medical treatments. Use the *Spring* and *Saikewicz* cases in your answer.

9. Explain the purpose of advance directives such as the living will. What are the arguments against the use of these instruments?

10. Present an overview of the *Claire Conroy* case. What has been the reaction to the Supreme Court of New Jersey's ruling in this case?

REFERENCES

Annas, G. (1985a). Fashion and freedom: When artificial feeding should be withdrawn. *American Journal of Public Health, 75,* 685.

Annas, G. (1985b). When procedures limit rights: From Quinlan to Conroy. *Hastings Center Report, 15,* 24–26.

Back, K. (1965). Meaning of time in later life. *Journal of Genetic Psychology, 109,* 9–25.

Besdine, R. (1983). Decisions to withhold treatment from nursing home residents. *Journal of the American Geriatrics Society, 31,* 602.

Bluebond-Langner, M. (1974). I know, do you? Awareness and communication in terminally ill children. In B. Schoenberg & associates (Eds.), *Anticipated grief.* New York: Columbia University Press.

Bluebond-Langner, M. (1977). Meanings of death to children. In H. Feifel (Ed.), *New meanings of death.* New York: McGraw-Hill.

Bluebond-Langner, M. (1989). World's of dying children and their well siblings. *Death Studies, 13,* 1–6.

Brocklehurst, J., & Hanley, T. (1976). *Geriatric medicine for students.* Edinburgh: Churchill Livingston.

Bromberg, S., & Cassel, C. (1983). Suicide in the elderly: The limits of paternalism. *Journal of the American Geriatrics Society, 31,* 698–703.

Buckingham, R., Lack, S., Mount, B., Mac-Lean, L., & Collins, J. 1976. Living with the dying. *Canadian Medical Association Journal, 115,* 1211–1215.

Corr, C. (1992). A task-based approach to coping with dying. *Omega, 24,* 81–94.

Corr, C. (1993). Coping with dying: Lessons that we should learn and should not learn from the work of Elisabeth Kubler-Ross. *Death Studies, 17,* 69–83.

Cytron, B. D. (1993). To honor the dead and comfort the mourners: Traditions in Judaism. In D. P. Irish, K. F. Lundquist, & V. J. Nelsen (Eds.), *Ethnic variations in dying, death and grief: Diversity in Universality.* Washington, DC: Taylor & Francis.

Feigenberg, L. (1977). *Terminalvard.* Lund: Liber Laromedel.

Frederick, J. (1976). Grief as a disease process. *Omega, 7,* 297–306.

Frederick, J. (1982–1983). The biochemistry of bereavement: Possible basis for chemotherapy. *Omega, 13,* 295–304.

Friedman, H., & DiMatteo, M. (1982). Interpersonal issues in health care: Healing as an interpersonal process. In H. Friedman & M. DiMatteo (Eds.), *Interpersonal issues in health care.* New York: Academic Press.

Fulton, G., & Metress, E. (1995). *Perspectives on death and dying.* Boston: Jones and Bartlett.

Glantz, L., & Swazey, J. (1979, January). Decisions not to treat: The Saikewicz case and its aftermath. *Forum on Medicine,* 22–32.

Glaser, B., & Strauss, A. (1966). *Awareness of dying.* Chicago: Aldine.

Glaser, B., & Strauss, A. (1968). *Time for dying.* Chicago: Aldine.

Goodstein, R. (1984). Grief reactions and the elderly. *Carrier Letter, 99,* 1–5.

Gorer, G. (1965). *Death, grief and mourning.* New York: Doubleday.

Greenblatt, J. (1978). The grieving spouse. *American Journal of Psychiatry, 135,* 43–47.

Greer, D., & Mor, V. (1985). How Medicare is altering the hospice movement. *Hastings Center Report, 15,* 5–9.

Groth-Junker, A., & McCusker, J. (1983). Where do elderly patients prefer to die? Place of death and patient characteristics of 100 elderly patients under the care of a home health care team. *Journal of the American Geriatrics Society, 31,* 457–461.

Gustafson, E. (1972). Dying: The career of the nursing home patient. *Journal of Health and Social Behavior, 13,* 226–235.

Helsing, G., & Szklo, M. (1981). Mortality after bereavement. *American Journal of Epidemiology, 114,* 41–52.

Kalish, R. (1976). Death and dying in a social context. In R. Binstock & E. Shanas (Eds.), *Handbook of aging and the social sciences.* New York: Van Nostrand Reinhold.

Kalish, R., & Reynolds, D. (1976). *Death and ethnicity: A psychocultural study.* Los Angeles: University of Southern California Press.

Kart, C. (1981). In the matter of Earle Spring: Some thought on one court's approach to senility. *The Gerontologist, 21,* 417–423.

Kastenbaum, R. (1991). *Death, society and human experience.* Columbus, OH: Charles E. Merrill.

Keddie, K. (1977). Pathological mourning after the death of a domestic pet. *British Journal of Psychiatry, 139,* 21–25.

Kubler-Ross, E. (1969). *On death and dying.* New York: Macmillan.

Kubler-Ross, E. (1974). *Questions and answers on death and dying.* New York: Macmillan.

Levav, I. (1982). Mortality and psychopathology following the death of an adult child: An epidemiological review. *Israel Journal of Psychiatry and Related Sciences, 19,* 23–38.

Lieberman, S. (1978). Nineteen cases of morbid grief. *British Journal of Psychiatry, 132,* 159–163.

Lindemann, E. (1944). Symptomatology and management of acute grief. *American Journal of Psychiatry, 101,* 141–148.

Mace, N., Rabins, P., & Lucas, M. (1980). *Areas of stress on families of dementia patients.* Paper presented at the annual meeting of the Gerontological Society of America, San Diego, CA.

Maris, R. (1981). *Pathways to suicide*. Baltimore, MD: Johns Hopkins University Press.

Masamba, J., & Kalish, R. (1976). Death and bereavement: The role of the Black church. *Omega, 7* (1), 23–34.

McIntire, M., Angle, C., & Struempl, L. (1972). The concept of death in Midwestern children and youth. *American Journal of Diseases of Children, 123,* 527–532.

McKellin, W. H. (1985). Passing away and loss of life: Aging and death among the Managalase of Papua New Guinea. In D. A. Counts & D. R. Counts (Eds.), *Aging and its transformations: Moving toward death in Pacific societies*. Pittsburgh, PA: University of Pittsburgh Press.

Metzger, A. (1979). A Q-methodological study of the Kubler-Ross stage theory. *Omega, 10,* 291–302.

Nagy, M. (1959). The child's theories concerning death. In H. Feifel (Ed.), *The meaning of death*. New York: McGraw-Hill.

Nason, J. D. (1981). Respected elder or old person: Aging in a Micronesian community. In P. T. Amoss & S. Harrell (Eds.), *Other ways of growing old: Anthropological perspectives*. Stanford, CA: Stanford University Press.

Nevins, M. (1985). Big brother at the bedside. *New Jersey Medicine, 82,* 950.

Nevins, M. (1986). Analysis of the Supreme Court of New Jersey's decision in the Claire Conroy case. *Journal of the American Geriatrics Society, 34,* 140–143.

Olins, N. (1986). Feeding decisions for incompetent patients. *Journal of the American Geriatrics Society, 34,* 313–317.

Osterweis, M. (1985). Bereavement and the elderly. *Aging, 348,* 8–13.

Osterweis, M., Solomon, F., & Green, M. (1984). *Bereavement: Reactions, consequences and care: A report of the Institute of Medicine*. Washington, DC: National Academy Press.

Robbins, L., West, P., & Murphy, G. (1977). The high rate of suicide in older white men: A study testing ten hypotheses. *Social Psychiatry, 12,* 1–20.

Roth, J. (1963). *Timetables*. Indianapolis, IN: Bobbs-Merrill.

Rowland, K. (1977). Environmental events predicting death for the elderly. *Psychological Bulletin, 84,* 349–372.

Schneider, A., & Garron, D. (1980). *Problems of families in recognizing and coping with dementing disease*. Paper presented at the annual meeting of the Gerontological Society of America, San Diego, CA.

Schulz, R. (1978). *The psychology of death, dying and bereavement*. Reading, MA: Addison-Wesley.

Schulz, R., & Aderman, D. (1974). Clinical research and the stages of dying. *Omega, 5,* 137–144.

Shneidman, E. (1980). *Voices of death*. New York: Harper and Row.

Steinbock, B. (1983). The removal of Mr. Herbert's feeding tube. *Hastings Center Report, 13,* 13–16.

Tehan, C. (1985). Has success spoiled hospice? *Hastings Center Report, 15,* 10–13.

Weisman, A. (1972). *On dying and denying*. New York: Behavioral Publications.

Weisman, A. (1992). Commentary on Corr's "A task-based approach to coping with dying." *Omega, 24,* 95–96.

EPILOGUE:
CAREERS IN THE
AGING NETWORK

There is no clear consensus on what a degree or certificate in gerontology especially qualifies a person to do. Certainly, there are very few jobs titled "gerontologist." Does this mean that students in gerontology degree programs, or those interested in a career in aging, are being prepared for jobs that do not exist? Not at all! Hundreds of thousands of Americans earn their livelihood working with and for aged people.

Virtually every department in the executive branch of the federal government and a number of independent agencies are responsible for policies and programs meant to serve the elderly either directly or indirectly. These include the Departments of Health and Human Services (Medicare and Medicaid), Agriculture (food stamps), Housing and Urban Development (housing for the elderly and disabled), and the Veterans Administration (pensions and health care). Transportation, Labor, Energy, Treasury, and Commerce also administer or monitor programs affecting the elderly. Moreover, state and local governments sponsor, monitor, and administer programs for older people.

Following the passage of the Older Americans Act in 1965, the Administration on Aging (AoA) was founded for the express purpose of carrying out the provisions of the act. As a result, federal dollars, mandated for community-based services to help older people, travel through AoA to State Units on Aging, which pass the funding on to local Area Agencies on Aging (AAA). These federal dollars fund jobs in the "aging network," requiring some knowledge of aging, including directors, program planners, program specialists, program executors, training officers, and researchers, among others. The private sector also provides job opportunities in aging, including preretirement and retirement counselors, financial and investment advisors, nursing home and health care administrators, travel agents and recreation specialists, writers and reporters, among many others who are actively employed on behalf of older people.

The elderly population continues to grow, with dramatic increases in the populations over 75 and over 85 years of age. And, as you no doubt recall from your reading in the previous chapters, these populations will continue to grow at a rapid pace. Does this mean that finding a job in the aging field will be easy? Not necessarily. Recognition of the work-force needs in gerontology is widespread, and in recent years, many students have sought training to prepare for entry into this job market. As the nation prepares to enter the twenty-first century, about 1,200 college and university campuses are offering at least one credit course in gerontology during the academic year. In 1990, a survey identified 40 master's, 35 bachelor's, 25 associate, and 2 doctoral programs in gerontology (Connelly, 1990).

No doubt these numbers have increased since then, although growth is probably constrained by insufficient faculty with expertise in gerontology. Professionals in social work, occupational therapy, counseling, and recreation leadership report that most current professionals do not have adequate gerontology training to serve their clients (Peterson & Wendt, 1990).

How can students best be prepared for the gerontological job market? First, they must obtain a clear picture of career alternatives in aging early enough in their academic lives so that they can obtain the best preparation for entry into the labor force. Part of this early preparation should involve contact with a general gerontological curriculum that contains information essential for all persons who will work with or for the elderly.

Finding a general gerontological curriculum, however, may not be as easy as it seems. A collaborative project of the Gerontological Society of America (GSA) and the Association for Gerontology in Higher Education (AGHE) (Johnson et al., 1980) found a consensus (defined by 90 percent agreement) to exist around the inclusion of only three topical areas in such a generalized curriculum: *psychology of aging* (with emphasis on normal changes), *health and aging,* and *biology of (normal) aging.*

In a survey of gerontology programs carried out by AGHE and the University of Southern California (USC), four courses were identified as most commonly offered and required in gerontological instruction programs in U.S. colleges and universities. An introductory course in social gerontology was the most frequently reported; 51 percent of gerontological instruction programs required it. Psychology of aging (50 percent) was second, with biology/physiology of aging (42 percent) and sociology of aging (42 percent) following (Peterson et al., 1987).

Generally, content areas required by gerontology programs differ according to a program's level of instruction. The core courses listed here were more likely to be required at the associate-degree level than at the bachelor's or master's level. For example, a social gerontology course was required by 75 percent of the associate-degree programs, 67 percent of the bachelor's-degree programs, and 39 percent of the master's-degree programs. This suggests that students moving from an associate to a bachelor's-level program, or from a bachelor's to a master's-level program, are likely to experience some repetition of course material.

Beyond the core courses, gerontological instruction programs show some variation in program level in substantive emphases. For example, associate-degree programs are likely to include courses on death and dying (43 percent), nutrition (41 percent), and counseling (38 percent). On the other hand, master's programs provide more content in research methods (55 percent), public policy (36 percent), and statistics (26 percent).

Second, students must be made to understand the growing specialization in the field of gerontology and the fact that different preparation may be necessary as careers in aging become further specialized. The collaborative project involving the GSA and the AGHE (Johnson et al. 1980) has defined four different career clusters in gerontology. The *biomedical* career cluster involves direct contact with older people. Among the targets of activity or inquiry are the biological aspects of aging and their effects on the health and physical functioning of the older person. Career examples include dieticians, nurses, physicians, and speech therapists. The *psychosocial* career cluster also involves direct contact with older people. Here, the emphasis is on the psychological characteristics of the aged, the interplay among these characteristics and economic and familial situations, and the effects of this interplay on the well-being of older people. Possible careers include clinical psychologist, social worker, retirement counselor, and legal advisor.

A third career cluster involves professional activities in the realm of the *socioeconomic environment.* Such professional activities may involve direct contact with older people, but the emphasis is on the social, economic, and cultural aspects of the community and broader society and the effects of these on older people. Educators, program administrators, government officials, social workers, and sociologists exemplify professional groups concerned with the socioeconomic environment of older people.

A fourth career cluster involves the *physical environment* of older people. The main professional activity of careers in this cluster has to do with the natural and manufactured physical environment and the effects of this environment on older people. Architecture, safety engineering, and transportation planning are careers in which professional activities revolve around the relationship between people (including the elderly) and the physical environment.

Each career cluster demands different educational preparation, with some overlap. Table E–1 presents a comparison of areas of study considered essential for inclusion in a core curriculum and the curricula of three of the career clusters. Those topics included in the core curriculum (psychology of aging, health and aging, and the biology of aging) overlap somewhat with actual course offerings in U.S. gerontology programs referred to previously and are also uniformly found in the curricula of the three career clusters. Only one additional topical area on the list, the demography of aging, is similarly included in the curricular content of all three career tracks. It is important to recognize that the consensus criterion used for inclusion in the curricular content of the career clusters is the same 90 percent agreement among experts used by GSA-AGHE in identifying topics to be included in a core gerontological curriculum. This standard is an arbitrary one. A number of additional topics were deemed essential for inclusion in the core curriculum (as well as in career clusters) by a relatively large proportion of experts in the GSA-AGHE project. Clearly, with a different standard (85 percent, for exam-

TABLE E–1   Comparison of Substantive Areas Deemed Essential for Inclusion in the Core Gerontological Curriculum and Curricula of Three Career Clusters

Topics	Core	Biomedical	Psychosocial	Socioeconomic Environmental
Psychology of aging	yes	yes	yes	yes
Health and aging	yes	yes	yes	yes
Biology of aging	yes	yes	yes	yes
Demography of aging		yes	yes	yes
Mental health and illness		yes	yes	
Adaptive mechanism		yes	yes	
Sociology of aging		yes		yes
Environment and aging		yes		yes
Marital and family relationships			yes	yes
Sensory change		yes		
Health care and services		yes		
Nutrition and aging		yes		
Behavioral changes		yes		
Stress		yes		
Physiology of aging		yes		
Chronic conditions		yes,		
Diseases of old age		yes		
Exercise physiology		yes		
Physical needs		yes		
Pathology		yes		
Pharmacology and aging		yes		
Cognition			yes	
Personality development			yes	
Economics of aging				yes
Attitudes toward aging and aged				yes
Public policy for aged				yes
Sociocultural context of aging				yes
Legislation concerning the aged				yes

Source: Adapted from H. R. Johnson et al., "Foundations for Gerontological Education," *The Gerontologist, 20* (3), 1980, p. 25, Table III-9. Copyright © The Gerontological Society of America.

Note: Inclusion is based on 90 percent agreement.

ple), additional topics would have been included in the core curriculum. Sensory change, sociology of aging, and mental health and illness are examples of topic areas that would have been included in the core curriculum if the arbitrary standard employed had been at 85 percent agreement.

Despite the emphasis on specialized training in gerontology, students should not lose sight of the value of a well-rounded, multidisciplinary undergraduate education. This undergraduate education should provide an appropriate grounding in the humanities and the social and natural sciences. Effective writing and communication skills, understanding of the research process and statistics, and familiarity with humanistic values should inform a student's gerontological expertise. In fact, given the availability and even the necessity of more specialized graduate training in gerontology for many positions in the field, the development of writing, communication, research, and statistics skills—as well as broad contact with the humanities—should not be subordinate to specialized training in gerontology in the undergraduate curriculum.

A third component of proper preparation for entry into the gerontology job market includes job experience. Many college graduates, regardless of their field of study, often run into the barrier caused by their lack of experience when they seek their first professional-level job. Gerontology students are no exceptions. They may attempt to gain experience by taking a job below their level of training, or they may become discouraged and take a position unrelated to their field of study.

Field placements or job internships are frequently part of basic and specialized programs in gerontology. Such placements can give students a chance to sample work in the field of aging while at the same time providing excellent job experience. Field placements and job internships that most effectively fulfill these functions are those that involve direct contact with older people while providing close supervision and allowing for continued evaluation of student progress. Table E–2 lists a variety of strategies for ensuring the most desirable characteristics in field placements and job internships. Obviously, careful planning is important, although an additional important point is the need for "open and continuous communication between and among program faculty, staff of the placement institution and . . . students" (Johnson et al. 1980, p. 36).

A cautionary note about field placements is in order as well. Experience with the elderly may not be the most effective teacher. Placements in which students see older people only as dependent and sick may serve to reinforce already held stereotypes. As described in Chapter 1, the consensus of third-year medical students was that 50 percent of the elderly are in ill health and as many as half of these were in institutional settings. Clearly, this is not the case. Just as clearly, however, such an estimate was consistent with the nature of the contact these students had with older people in the hospital clinics where students received the bulk of their medical training. How many other students in job placements or internships associated with preparation for a career in the service of older people are similarly affected?

Field placements and job internships are likely to become more important components of gerontological education programs in the future. Effective use of such program components may be an appropriate strategy for dealing with the concerns often expressed by different constituencies in the gerontological community. For example, some express dissatisfaction with the quality of personnel serving the elderly, including health care personnel. Concerns about quality of personnel are often indirect criticisms of a lack of training and experience. Moreover, many in the gerontological community (including educators, policymakers, and program administrators) discuss the viability of licensure requirements based on gerontological/geriatric training, especially for those in the health care field, including physicians and nurses.

TABLE E–2   Ways Suggested to Ensure Desired Field Placement Characteristics

---

Communication
Install written "contract" between educational institution and placement institution regarding
   expectations, content, and supervision.
Have faculty present written objectives to agency and to students.
Require three-way agreement between student, school, and agency, plus ongoing communication.
Clearly define procedures between university and agency.
Arrange regular contact between agency staff and university.

Supervision
Use faculty as supervisor or as liaison.
Monitor continuously.
Put multidisciplinary program committee in charge.
Make field coordinator (liaison) a full-time position.
Make randomly timed visits.
Develop criteria for supervisors at setting.
Give adjunct university appointments to field work supervisors.
Hold periodic conferences between university and supervisor.
Have good people in charge—person with rank, pay, motivation, and intelligence.
Assess student's progress regularly.

Planning
Contract placements thoughtfully.
Establish accreditation procedures, criteria for placements.
Conduct on-site observation before assignment.
Match student and placement carefully.
Have people knowledgeable about agency do the planning.
Involve older persons in planning.

Commitment
Arrange performance contract between university and agency.
Reward faculty who are good teachers of practice.
Educational institution should assist agency, give time and effort to build mutuality.
Pay agency (dollars, consulting time, tuition breaks) for their cooperation.
Agency must be committed to student; they should assign responsibility for students to their own staff.
Obtain student stipends.

Other
Develop field manuals.
Use stable agencies, not ones in survival struggle.
Hold regular class periods to discuss topics of mutual interest.
Use student's abilities to fullest.
Require interview between student's adviser and agency.
Involve students in activities relevant to their goals.

Source: H. R. Johnson et al., "Foundation for Gerontological Education," *The Gerontologist, 20* (3), 1980, p. 37, Table III-18. Copyright © The Gerontological Society of America.

Preparation for entry into the gerontology job market is likely to be affected by a number of future trends in gerontological education identified by Rich, Atchley, and Douglass (1990).

1. Gerontological education is likely to continue to expand. There are still more colleges and universities without course work in gerontology than there are

with it. Continued growth may be constrained, however, by an absence of qualified faculty with training in gerontology.

2. By definition, many programs with gerontology content are already special-ized. These include gerontological nursing and social work, geriatric medicine and dentistry, nutrition and aging, and the like. Still, pressure is likely to con-tinue to push general curricula in the direction of specialization. Already, some degree programs are moving to focus on specific issues such as long-term care, program administration, and public policy.

3. As a result of the increased emphasis on specialization, there is increased interest in identifying competencies and outcomes for different gerontological specialties. This may allow for greater articulation between gerontological training programs and job descriptions within the aging network.

4. There has been an allocation of resources (public and private) within higher education toward the health sciences, including biomedical research and training of health-related personnel. This is likely to continue. In some pro-grams, this allocation of resources has caused a shift away from behavioral and social science professions. In other programs, it has provided new oppor-tunities for program development.

I will briefly describe some careers in aging in one field: health care. Much has been written about the inadequacy of health care for the elderly. One crucial factor in the delivery of geriatric health care is the lack of availability of adequately trained personnel. Further, a criticism of proposals for national health policies in the United States is that they concentrate on the problem of paying for health care and ignore the need to produce additional health services for those populations, including some subpopulations of the elderly who do not have access to health-care services. Gerontology careers in health care include social workers, counse-lors, psychologists, and other allied mental health workers; dentists and dental hygienists; optometrists; podiatrists; physicians; nurses; dietitians and nutrition-ists; speech pathologists and audiologists; occupational therapists; medical records specialists—the list goes on. Next, the needs for physicians, nurses, and social workers are reviewed.

PHYSICIANS

As Figure E–1 depicts, the number of active doctors of medicine, specialists and primary care physicians, has increased between 1970 and 1992. Approximately 315,000 doctors of medicine were active in the United States in 1970. This number grew to almost 575,000 by 1992; projections by the Bureau of Health Professions are to 685,000 by the year 2000.

Although there is no shortage of physicians in the United States, only a small number practice geriatric medicine. A 1977 physician survey conducted by the American Medical Association found that fewer than 0.6 percent of the respon-

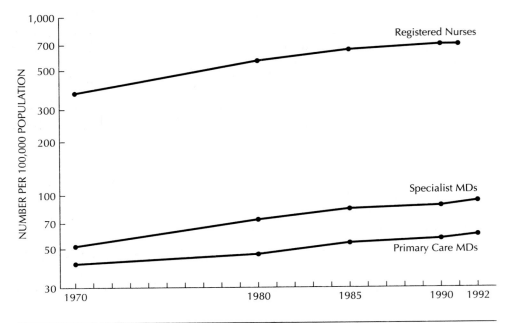

Health Personnel	1970	1980	1985	1990	1992[1]
Registered nurses	368.9	560.0	641.4	690.0	697.3
Nonfederal office-based specialist MD[2]	51.1	73.0	83.7	87.6	93.0
Nonfederal office-based primary care MD[3]	41.0	46.6	53.8	56.7	59.9

FIGURE E–1   Active Doctors of Medicine and Registered Nurses: United States, 1970–92

Source: Health Resources and Services Administration, Bureau of Health Professions. See related *Health, United States, 1993,* tables 110 and 111.

[1]Registered nurse data are for 1991.

[2]Specialist MDs include medical specialties other than primary care.

[3]Primary care MDs are defined as general and family practitioners, internists, and pediatricians. Sub-specialists are included.

dents indicated an interest in geriatrics. Traditionally, the specialty of geriatrics has lacked prestige and has been seen by prospective physicians as an unrewarding area in which to work.

Libow (1977) believes attitudes toward geriatrics are changing. He surveyed students in eight medical schools and found 75 percent of them desirous of having a full course in geriatrics; 72 percent wanted to take an elective course dealing with the elderly at some time in their clinical training. Libow recommends a department of geriatrics in every medical school and hospital. Despite these attitudinal data, the geriatrics specialty training programs have not yet attracted large numbers of candidates (Committee on Leadership for Academic Geriatric Medicine, 1987) and some reports continue to document the lack of enthusiasm among medical students for interaction with elderly patients (Duthie, Donnelly, &

Kirsling, 1987). Some medical educators have reported success with gamelike interventions in which medical students personally experience sensory and functional deficits as a result of simulated physical, psychosocial, and economic losses (Galanos, Cohen, & Jackson, 1993).

Geriatrics seems to be a field that should grow, if only to keep pace with growing numbers of elderly. One forecast suggests that soon almost every other patient in a doctor's office will be elderly (Kane et al., 1981). Kane and colleagues (1981) attempted work-force projections on the need for geriatricians in the United States. Actually, they made four sets of projections based on four different levels of geriatric activity in the United States, as follows:

1. A continuation of the current care delivery pattern, with essentially no specially trained geriatricians

2. Geriatricians trained primarily for academic positions, but with some inevitable spillover into practice

3. Academic geriatricians plus a trained cohort of geriatric consultants, as are found in much of western Europe

4. Geriatricians in academic roles and actively involved in practice as both consultants and providers of substantial amounts of primary care

At the time, Kane and associates (1981) believed that about 1,500 geriatricians needed to be trained just to staff existing training programs in internal medicine and family practice, as well as to provide a core group of geriatricians in each medical school. In addition, they projected a need for 16,000 geriatricians during the 1990s if geriatricians were to render some primary care to those in the population who are 65 years of age and older. A more intermediate estimate of need was for about 8,000 additional geriatricians by 1990, though even this estimate assumed that most specialized geriatric care would be directed at persons 75 and older; that there would be a moderate degree of delegation of care to nurse practitioners, clinical specialists, physician's assistants, and social workers; and, finally, that there would be some increment of improved care for the elderly.

Internists and family practitioners are probably providing the bulk of primary medical care to older people in the United States. While the number of active general and family practitioners increased 15 percent from 1970 (50,816) to 1992 (58,603), those practicing internal medicine increased almost threefold across this same time period (22,950 vs. 65,073). General and family practitioners and specialists combine to make up about one-third of all active physicians in the United States. Approximately 4,000 of these specialists took the first national certifying examination in geriatrics in 1988, and over half of them passed (Kane & Kane, 1990). Still, this suggests a substantial shortfall of geriatricians remains.

Although geriatrics is not identified as high-technology medicine innovation has emerged around the development of geriatric assessment units, which are multidisciplinary in orientation and multifunctional in purpose. Geriatricians do sophisticated diagnostic work, develop effective care plans, mobilize community resources, and keep older people in their homes.

NURSES

In 1968, a geriatric nursing practice division was established by the American Nurses' Association (ANA). In 1974, the *Guidelines for Geriatric Nursing Practices* were developed, and the ANA now certifies qualified nurses and nurse practitioners in geriatrics. Although geriatrics courses are being added to nursing curriculums, too few schools have a specialty in geriatrics. Three types of programs awarding different credentials prepare their graduates for licensure as registered nurses:

1. Hospital-based programs are usually three academic years in length and lead to a diploma.
2. Programs located at community colleges are two academic years in length and lead to an associate degree.
3. Programs located in colleges and universities most often lead to a four-year baccalaureate degree.

As Figure E–1 shows, the supply of active registered nurses has increased between 1970 and 1991. Almost 1.75 million registered nurses were active in 1992—a million more than in 1970. All three programs described here have grown since 1980, with baccalaureate and graduate-degree programs showing the greatest proportional increase. Registered nurses (RNs) with the baccalaureate degree or beyond constituted 28.6 percent of all active RNs in 1980 and 37.4 percent by 1991.

The trend in nursing education is toward preparation in academic institutions, including community colleges. The number of baccalaureate programs has continued to increase over the past 20 years. These programs differ from diploma and associate-degree programs in two important ways: They prepare students to function as public health nurses in community settings as well as to provide service in institutional facilities, and they provide the basis for advanced study in a clinical or functional area like geriatrics.

Qualified geriatric nurses are at a premium at all levels of training, especially at the baccalaureate, master's, and doctoral level. A 1982 report on nurse supply, distribution, and requirements made by the U.S. Department of Health and Human Services to the Congress projected that the supply of baccalaureate nurses in 1990 would be significantly less than what would be required (747,000). The organization, Alliance for Health Reform, projects a continued undersupply of baccalaureate-trained nurses, with the need being an additional 400,000 by the year 2000. The actual number of baccalaureate-trained RNs in 1991 was 533,500. For the master's and doctoral group, the 1991 number (124,700) was less than one-half of the projected need (270,000). The majority of nurses in practice across all specialties are prepared only at the entry level (associate degree or hospital-based diploma). In 1991, only 7.1 percent of nurses were estimated to hold a master's degree or beyond in nursing.

Geriatric nurses can form the backbone of care for the elderly in the community as well as in the institutionalized setting. The geriatric nurse is in a position to

Geriatric nurses form the backbone of care for the elderly in the community as well as in the institutional setting.

oversee primary nursing care of the institutionalized elderly and thus to upgrade the care provided in nursing homes. Similar opportunities exist for visiting nurses for the homebound elderly.

Although they constitute a very small fraction of the registered nurse work force, nurse practitioners also have significant potential for serving the elderly in a variety of settings. Nurse practitioners are registered nurses whose additional formal training prepares them for expanded nursing care functions, especially in the diagnosis and treatment of patients. In addition to delivering traditional nursing services, they are qualified to perform some services more often delivered by physicians, such as managing self-limiting conditions and stabilized chronic illness. Their potential for serving the elderly is great because the scope of their practice is necessarily broad; they can facilitate movement into the health care delivery system and provide continuity within the system as the patient moves from one part of the system to another (U.S. Department of Health and Human Services, 1982; Mezey, Lynaugh, & Cartier, 1989).

There are more than 200 nurse practitioner training programs in the United States. The majority of these programs lead to a certificate, although many do lead to a master's degree, and the rate of growth in the latter type has been greater in recent years. It is noteworthy that programs established in the early years of the nurse practitioner movement focused primarily on pediatric practice. Since the early 1980s, the specialty emphasis has shifted to family and adult health, which encompasses the geriatric population (U.S. Department of Health and Human Services, 1982). This trend is likely to continue.

A very small proportion of currently employed nurses describe themselves as *nurse clinicians* or *clinical nurse specialists*. As the titles imply, these nurses are expected to be expert in a clinical practice area. Nurse clinicians and clinical nurse specialists provide patient care and, through teaching and by example, develop the competencies of less experienced nurses and students to meet the needs of patients whose nursing care management requires special knowledge and skills. This career title is likely to increase in importance within the nursing profession. Indeed, there is already some pressure to increase the supply of nurse clinicians with advanced training. One recommendation made by the U.S. Department of Health and Human Services in its 1982 report to the Congress, mandated by the Nurse Training Act of 1975, was as follows: "The number of nurses with advanced nurse training should be augmented to assure sufficient numbers of expert clinicians, particularly in acute care settings, to direct the learning and clinical practice of students and to effect changes in the delivery of services both in institutions and community settings."

An important growth area here is likely to be the nursing-home sector, where expertise in geriatric nursing is a vital element in maintaining patients at a maximum level of productive functioning. Unfortunately, like other health professionals, many nurses still maintain a generally negative stereotype about nursing homes, making it more difficult to find adequate nursing staff for this vital sector (Cotler & Kane, 1988).

GERIATRIC SOCIAL WORKERS

The vulnerability of many older people; the impact of their problems on family, community, and the broader society; and their relative lack of knowledge about how to secure the services they require make the aging population a prime concern of social work. As Elaine Brody indicated, "On all levels, social work is an essential ingredient of health care and welfare systems and should have a major role in the identification of problems and in the delivery of preventive, supportive, and restorative services" (1977, p. 73). Nevertheless, as recently as 1977, the National Association of Social Workers (NASW) issued a policy statement acknowledging that social work, along with some other disciplines, had "failed to recognize its unique contributions among the professions to the improvement of the quality of life for older Americans" (NASW, 1977). In 1981, social work educators interested in gerontology and geriatric social work formed the National Committee for Gerontology in Social Work Education. Its purpose was to promote the development of a gerontological focus in social work education (Nelson, 1983).

In all its traditional forms—individual and group services, community organization, policy formulation, education, and research—social work can participate in recognizing the potential of older people and in helping them overcome the prominent myths about the aged. The social worker who works with the elderly, sometimes referred to as a *geriatric social worker,* will likely require a master of social work degree (M.S.W.) and, no doubt, some positions will demand a specialization in geriatric or medical social work. Such specialization will be developed through course work and experience in the M.S.W. curriculum or through a certificate program. This individual will be an expert on the variety of human resources available in the local community. These include nutrition programs, transportation services, home health services, homemaker services, and income sources. The social worker affiliated with a health care institution assumes responsibility for all intake procedures, case work, and group work with patients and their families.

The geriatric social worker is often able to assume the role of an objective patient advocate. The aged (especially those who are ill) may be economically, socially, or psychologically vulnerable. They have little power or connections to power. One satisfaction of working in this field is that frequently the social worker can get the system that oppresses to work for the people who are most often oppressed. As Nelson (1983) has indicated, work-force demands for gerontological and geriatric social workers will be a product of the growth of the aging population and governmental and private-sector responses to the needs of the elderly. The Administration on Aging, the National Institute of Aging, and other agencies have provided training monies to institutions as part of the effort to encourage institutions and individuals to enter the field of gerontology. Social work majors led the list of those receiving these training monies and, according to one report (cited in Nelson, 1983), approximately half of those who received gerontological training were working in the field of gerontology after graduation.

The most frequently identified employment locations were human service agencies, hospitals and nursing homes, mental health organizations, educational institutions and libraries, and government. What these people were actually doing included planning, evaluation and advocacy, direct service provision, counseling the elderly, supervision of direct services, provision of specialized service, research, and teaching (Nelson, 1983). According to one government report, the number of social workers employed on the staff of mental health organizations in the United States increased by 47 percent from 1984 to 1990 (36,397 vs. 53,487). This included employees of state and county mental hospitals, private psychiatric hospitals, nonfederal general hospitals' psychiatric services, Department of Veteran Affairs psychiatric services, and residential treatment centers.

What about the future? Recently, the Bureau of Labor Statistics published a list of the 12 fastest-growing occupational titles. Geriatric social work was identified as one of the leading growth areas. The majority of jobs were in high-technology areas, including industrial robot production, but geriatric social work was projected to account for 700,000 jobs by the mid-1990s. Cutbacks in the funding of social and health service programs during the 1980s have taken some of the sheen off these projections. Nevertheless, there definitely seems to be a place for gerontological and geriatric social work in the field of aging and in the future job marketplace.

Many allied health specialists and others work with an elderly clientele. These include nurse practitioners, physician assistants, occupational therapists, speech therapists, geriatric aides, home health aides, physical therapists, recreation therapists, family and spiritual counselors, and a long list of other professions. Persons holding these positions have wide and varying educational requirements and responsibilities on the health care team. Although a detailed description of the career opportunities in each category cannot be provided, with patience, proper evaluation, and realistic goals, each can make an important contribution to geriatric health care.

REFERENCES

American Nurses' Association. (1987). *Facts about nursing 1986–87.* Kansas City, MO: Author.

Brody, E. M. (1977). Aging. In J. B. Turner (Ed.), *Encyclopedia of social work* (17th ed.). Washington, DC: National Association of Social Workers.

Committee on Leadership for Academic Geriatric Medicine. (1987). Report of the Institute of Medicine: Academic geriatrics for the year 2000. *Journal of the American Geriatrics Society, 35,* 2771–2775.

Connelly, J. R. (1990). Gerontology program development. In T. A. Rich, J. R. Connelly, & E. B. Douglass (Eds.), *Standards and guidelines for gerontology programs* (2nd ed.). Washington, DC: Association for Gerontology in Higher Education.

Cotler, M., & Kane, R. L. (1988). Registered nurses and nursing home shortages: Job conditions and attitudes among RNs. *Journal of Long-Term Care Administration, 16* (4), 13–18.

Duthie, E. H., Donnelly, M. B., & Kirsling, R. A. (1987). Fourth-year students' preference for geriatrics as a career. *Journal of Medical Education, 62,* 511–514.

Galanos, A. N., Cohen, H. J., & Jackson, T. W. (1993). Medical education in geriatrics: The lasting impact of the aging game. *Educational Gerontology, 19,* 675–682.

Johnson, H. R. (1982). Perspectives on the 1981 White House Conference on Aging: Education. *The Gerontologist, 22* (2), 125–126.

Johnson, H. R., Britton, J., Lang, C., Seltzer, M., Stanford, E., Yancik, R., Maklan, C., & Middleworth, A. (1980). Foundations for gerontological education. *The Gerontologist, 20* (3), i–61 (whole issue).

Kane, R. L., & Kane, R. A. (1990). Health care for older people: Organizational and policy issues. In R. H. Binstock & L. K. George (Eds.), *Handbook of aging and the social sciences* (3rd ed.). San Diego, CA: Academic Press.

Kane, R. L., Solomon, D. H., Beck, J., Keeler, E., & Kane, R. (1981). *Geriatrics in the United States.* Lexington, MA: Lexington Books.

Libow, L. (1977). The issues in geriatric medical education and postgraduate training: Old problems in a new field. *Geriatrics, 32* (2), 99–102.

Mezey, M. D., Lynaugh, J. E., & Cartier, M. M. (1989). *Nursing homes and nursing care: Lessons from the teaching nursing homes.* New York: Springer.

National Association of Social Workers. (1977). *NASW News, 22* (3), 17–18.

Nelson, G. M. (1983). Gerontological social work: A curriculum review. *Educational Gerontology, 9,* 307–322.

Peterson, D., Douglass, E., Bolton, C., Connelly, J., & Bergstone, D. (1987). *Gerontology instruction in American institutions of higher education: A national survey.* Washington, DC: Association for Gerontology in Higher Education and the University of Southern California.

Peterson, D. A., & Wendt, P. F. (1990). Employment in the field of aging: A survey of professionals in four fields. *The Gerontologist, 30,* 679–684.

Rich, T. A., Atchley, R. C., & Douglass, E. B. (1990). Future trends in gerontological ed-

ucation. In T. A. Rich, J. R. Connelly, & E. B. Douglass (Eds.), *Standards and guidelines for gerontological programs* (2nd ed.). Washington, DC: Association for Gerontology in Higher Education.

U.S. Department of Health and Human Services. (1982). *Nurse supply, distribution and requirements: 3rd report to the Congress.* Hyattsville, MD: U.S. Public Health Service, Division of Nursing.

GLOSSARY

Abkhasians The long-lived people of the Soviet state of Georgia; they attribute their longevity to practices in sex, work, and diet.

accommodating environment A model that assumes that all aspects of the environment (including the resident) will change over time.

accommodation A term used by Piaget to describe the method of processing incoming information by changing the knowledge base to make it a better approximation of the environment.

active life expectancy Operationally defined as the period of life free from limitations in activities of daily living.

activity limitation Limitations in activities of daily living, work outside the home, and housekeeping.

activity theory Often referred to as the implicit theory of aging, this theory states that there is a positive relationship between activity and life satisfaction: The individual who is able to maintain the activities of the middle years for as long as possible will be well adjusted and satisfied with life in the later years.

acute brain syndrome Reversible organic brain syndrome due to impairment of brain cell function. Specific cause may include alcoholism, drug abuse, and malnutrition.

acute illness A condition, disease, or disorder that is temporary.

Administration on Aging An administrative unit within the Department of Health and Human Services that oversees the operation of various services and programs provided in the Older Americans Act.

age composition Involves a quantitative description of the proportions of young and old people in a society. A population's age composition depends first on its level of fertility and only secondarily on mortality.

Age Discrimination Employment Act A federal law passed in 1967 and amended several times since. The law prohibits discrimination in hiring, firing, and conditions of employment on the basis of age.

age stratification A concept that perceives society as divided on the basis of age with each age stratum having its own set of rights, obligations, and opportunities.

age-integrated environments Those environments in which people of all ages live, work, and interact together.

age-related macular degeneration Visual impairment as a result of damage to the macular area of the retina; the leading cause of blindness among older adults in the U.S.

age-segregated environments Those environments in which people of certain age groups live separated from individuals of other ages.

age-specific life expectancy The average duration of life expected for an individual of a given age.

aged family Family in which the head of household is age 65 or older.

aged subculture Concept proposed by sociologist Arnold Rose. It is based on the premise that because of changes in the aged population and U.S. society, the aged have developed their own norms, system of stratification, and consciousness.

ageism A term coined by Robert Butler to describe negative attitudes toward aging and the aged.

aging group consciousness Arnold Rose believed that the development of an aged subculture would stimulate a group identification and consciousness among older people with the potential for social action.

Alzheimer's disease A progressively deteriorating form of dementia of unknown etiology. It involves a diminution of intellectual capabilities, memory loss, impaired judgment, and personality change.

ancestry group Defined by individuals in terms of the nation or nations of family origin.

antediluvian theme Involves the belief that people lived much longer in the past.

aphasia A term used to denote impaired ability to comprehend or express verbal language, and a clinical feature of stroke in many elderly victims.

appropriate death A concept developed by Avery Weisman. Such a death means that the person has died in a fashion that resembles as much as possible the way that he or she wished to die.

arteriosclerosis A generic term indicating a hardening of or loss of elasticity of the arteries.

arthritis Inflammation or degenerative joint change often characterized by stiffness, swelling, and joint pain. Some forms of arthritis are believed to be autoimmune diseases.

assimilation Piaget's term for method of processing incoming information by fitting it into the existing knowledge base.

atherosclerosis A condition whereby the inner wall of an artery becomes thickened by plaque formation.

autoimmune theory This theory maintains that because of "copying errors" in repeated cell divisions, protein enzymes produced by newer cells are literally not recognized by the body. This brings the body's immunologic system into play, forcing it to work against itself.

average life expectancy at birth Defined as the average number of years a person born today can expect to live under the current mortality conditions.

Baby Boom A term often used to describe the higher fertility rates in the years immediately following the Second World War.

benefit periods Hospital insurance benefits under Part A of Medicare are measured by periods of time known as benefit periods. Benefit periods begin when a patient enters the hospital and end when he or she has not been a hospital patient for 60 days.

bereavement Refers to the experience of getting over another person's death. In part, the character that bereavement takes is shaped by society. Physical symptoms such as shortness of breath and psychological distress may accompany bereavement.

biological aging A term often used to describe the postmaturational changes in physical appearance and capability.

brain death A recently formulated conception of death that replaces the traditional heart death definition. Criteria include coma, apnea, cerebral unresponsivity, dilated pupils, absence of reflexes, and electrocerebral silence.

breakthrough policy A piece of governmental legislation that involves the federal government in providing or guaranteeing some fundamental benefit.

cataracts The most common disability of the aged eye. The normally transparent lens of the eye becomes opaque and interferes with the passage of rays of light to the retina.

centenarians Those who live 100 years or more.

cerebrovascular disease A term used to describe impaired brain cell circulation. When a portion of the brain is completely denied blood, a cerebrovascular accident or stroke occurs.

chronic illness A condition, disease, or disorder that is permanent or that will incapacitate an individual for a long period of time.

cohort The term used for a group of persons born at approximately the same time. Although defined broadly, no two birth cohorts can be expected to age in the same way; each has a particular history and arrives at old age with unique experiences.

cohortcentric Describes the fact that people in the same place on the life-course dimension experience historical events similarly and, as a result, may come to see the world in a like fashion.

collagen A protein fiber distributed in and around the walls of blood vessels and in connective tissue, which has been implicated in age-related changes in physiological functions.

compression of morbidity When the length of time between onset of disease and death is shortened.

conductive hearing loss Hearing loss resulting from the interrupted conduction of sound waves.

congestive heart failure A state of circulatory congestion produced by the impaired pumping action of the heart.

constant environment A model of the physical and social environment that assumes that the needs of residents remain relatively stable over time.

constituency-building policy A governmental policy that recognizes that different groups can have a common interest and allows "space" for these interest groups in the making of policy.

content analysis A research technique that involves analyzing the content of records or documents.

context of mutual pretense A phrase used by Glaser and Strauss that describes a situation in which both patient and staff know that the patient is dying but pretend otherwise.

continuity theory Put forth by Robert Atchley, this theory argues that few people rest their entire self-identities on the work role. Most people have several roles in which identity is based; thus, they are able to adjust to retirement and gain self-respect and self-esteem from leisure time pursuits.

cross-cultural study A method that involves gathering comparable data from different societies to test hypotheses—for example, about the status of the aged.

cross-sectional research Studies based on observations representing a single point in time. Studies employing this research design are useful for emphasizing differences.

crystallized intelligence Intelligence obtained through experience and formal education.

cultural pluralism A situation in which ethnic groups may be able to retain their cultural uniqueness.

day care Includes a wide range of services for older people who have some mental or physical impairments but can remain in the community if supportive services are provided.

deductive logic Reasoning from the general to the specific or from certain premises to a logically valid conclusion.

delayed retirement credit (delayed benefit credit) Increase in social security benefits payable to workers who postpone retirement past age 65 up to age 70.

dementing illness Any disease that produces a decline in intellectual abilities of sufficient severity to interfere with social or occupational functioning (memory disorder is usually prominent).

demographic transition A three-stage conceptual model of population growth and change.

demography The study of the size, territorial distribution, and composition of population and the changes therein.

dependency ratio The ratio of the population of ages too young or too old to work to the population of working age.

depression The most common functional psychiatric disorder among older people; it can vary in duration and degree and show psychological as well as physiological manifestations.

diabetic retinopathy Vascular changes in the retina that may result in diminished vision or blindness.

diagnostic-related groups (DRGs) A categorization scheme for illnesses and injuries that forms the basis for the prospective payment system that fixes Medicare hospital payment rates in advance.

disengagement theory Developed by Cumming and Henry, this theory postulates that aging involves a mutual withdrawal between the older person and society.

double jeopardy A term used to reflect the idea that the negative effects of aging are compounded among minority group members.

dying career A concept used by Gustafson, who views the last phase of life as a career that moves in a series of related and regressive stages toward death.

dying trajectory A term used by Glaser and Strauss to describe the dying process. All dying processes take time and can be visualized as having a certain shape through time. The combination of duration and shape can be charted as a trajectory.

early retirement Retirement before that mandated by age or tenure.

ego integrity Key concept in Erikson's eighth age that describes a basic acceptance of one's life as appropriate and meaningful.

empirical method A broad category that includes quantitative and qualitative research techniques that can be replicated by many.

empty nest period Period of time after grown children have left home, sometimes referred to as *postparental period*.

enabling factors A term used by Andersen to describe individual characteristics and circumstances (e.g., family income, accessibility of health service) that might hinder or accelerate use of a health service.

enculturation The process by which new generations come to adopt traditional ways of thinking and behaving.

enryo A norm brought from Japan and still in existence in America. It is related to power and regulates how those with it are to behave toward those without it. In the Japanese family and community, power and privileges are associated with the father.

environmental discontinuity The degree of change between a new and an old environment that may explain the effects observed after institutionalization.

environmental docility hypothesis The less competent the individual, the greater the impact of environmental factors on the individual.

ERISA The Employee Retirement Income Security Act, passed by Congress in 1974, to establish minimum standards for private pension programs.

error catastrophe Maintains that aging results from mutations.

ethnogenesis Describes a model of ethnic relations in which pressures to assimilate exist alongside pressures to maintain ethnic identification.

exchange theory A social-psychological theory recently applied to the situation of the aged. The basic assumption of the theory is that people will attempt to maximize benefits from an interaction while incurring the least costs.

extended-care facility Long-term care facility equipped to provide skilled nursing care around the clock.

extended family Three or more generations living together in one household.

external attribution Ascribing causality to factors outside the individual.

family dependency ratio Defined in simple demographic terms (for example, population 65–79 years/population 45–49), this ratio crudely illustrates the shifts in the ratio of elderly parents to the children who would support them.

family life cycle A concept used by family sociologists to characterize the changes that families undergo from their establishment through the postparental stage.

family of orientation The family into which one is born.

family of procreation The family that adults form at the time of marriage.

fertility rate The number of births that occur in a year per 1,000 women of childbearing age.

fibroblasts Embryonic cells that give rise to connective tissue.

field research A research strategy that is "observation centered" and allows the researcher to establish close contact with subjects and their actions.

filial piety Reflects the respect and deference owed to one's elders, perhaps especially to a father. Filial piety is most often present in traditional societies dominated by a patriarchal social order.

fluid intelligence Innate information processing skills independent of acquired experience and formal education.

foster care Use of private residences for the care of a nonrelated elderly person who needs supervision or assistance with daily living activities.

fountain theme Based on the idea that there is some unusual substance that has the property of greatly increasing the length of life.

free radicals Highly unstable molecules that contain an unpaired electron. Their presence reduces cellular efficiency and causes an accumulation of cellular waste that may lead to cell aging.

fund of sociability hypothesis According to this idea, there is a certain quantity of interaction with others that people require and that they may achieve in a variety of ways—either through one or two intense relationships or through a larger number of less intense relationships.

generational stake theory Perspective that argues that the older generation is more invested in the parent/child relationships than are the young.

generativity The desire to become a productive and caring member of society.

geriatric day center An alternative to an extended care facility; such a center may provide care on an eight-hour-a-day, five-day-a-week basis.

geriatrics A subfield of gerontological practice; the medical care of the aging.

gerontological gender gap Term used by Hess to describe the differential application of federal programs to the elderly such that older women are disadvantaged in the areas of income, health, and housing.

Gerontological Society of America The dominant professional society in the field of gerontology. Incorporated in 1945, it publishes the *Journal of Gerontology* and *The Gerontologist.*

gerontology The systematic study of the aging process.

gerontophilia Respect and reverence for the aged.

gerontophobia A fear of and negative attitude toward the aged.

glaucoma The most serious eye disease affecting the aged. It results from an increase in pressure within the eyeball.

gray lobby A term used to describe all the groups and organizations that purport to represent the interests of the elderly.

health Defined by the World Health Organization as "a state of complete physical, mental, and social well-being and not merely the absence of disease or infirmity."

health behavior model Conceptual framework within which to identify predisposing, enabling, and need factors that contribute to the use of health services.

hidden poor Those living in institutions or with relatives and not counted among the aged poor.

home health care The provision of coordinated multidisciplinary services, including skilled nursing and therapeutic services as well as social casework; mental health; legal, financial, and personal care; and household management assistance.

hospice   A facility that specializes in caring for and treating terminally ill patients and their families.

housing inadequacy   Housing unit with a deficiency in the physical condition, a high degree of overcrowding, or an inability of the household to afford the unit.

housing poor   Living in a housing unit with a deficiency in the physical condition of the unit, a high degree of overcrowding, or an inability of the household to afford the unit.

Hunza   A group of allegedly long-lived people in the mountains of Kashmir, Pakistan.

hyperborean theme   Involves the idea that in some remote part of the world, there are people who enjoy a remarkably long life.

hypertension   High blood pressure.

hypochondirasis   Overconcern for one's health, usually accompanied by delusions about physical dysfunction or disease.

identity crisis theory   Because occupational identity is so much a part of a person's life, Stephen Miller argues, retirement necessarily brings an identity crisis. According to this theory, leisure roles cannot be expected to replace work as a source of self-respect and identity.

income replacement rate   A term often used to describe the income position of a retiree relative to the income position of the individual before retirement. A replacement rate of 50 percent would indicate that a retiree received an income that was 50 percent of his or her preretirement earnings.

index of correlation   A measure of the relationship between two interval-level variables. The strength of a correlation ranges from .00, meaning no correlation, to 1.0, meaning a perfect correlation.

infant mortality   Often used as a simple measure of the general welfare of a population, it usually reflects the number of infant deaths in a given year by the number of live births registered during that year.

in-kind income   Income received indirectly or in the form of goods and services that are free or at reduced cost.

innate heat   Believed by Hippocrates to be the essential factor in life. Individuals were believed to have a fixed quantity of this life force and aging was equated with its continuous diminishment.

interiority of the personality   Concept used by Neugarten (1968) to describe age-related increase in introspection, contemplation, reflection, and self-evaluation as characteristic forms of mental life.

intermediate nursing care   Provision of health-related care and services (often in an institution) to those who need less than skilled nursing care but more than custodial care.

internal attribution   Ascribing causality to factors inside the individual (e.g. disease or biological aging).

ischemic heart disease   Another term for coronary artery disease. Tissue that is denied adequate blood supply is called ischemic.

laboratory experimentation   A research technique that involves the systematic observation of phenomenon, under controlled conditions.

life course   A schedule or sequence of roles and group memberships that individuals are expected to follow as they move through life.

life review   Postulated by Robert Butler to describe an almost universal tendency of older persons toward self-reflection and reminiscence.

life span   The extreme limit of human longevity; the age beyond which no one can expect to life.

life-span construct   A person's unified sense of the past, the present, and the future.

life story   A personal narrative history that organizes past events into a coherent sequence.

life table Shows what the probability is of surviving from any age to any subsequent age based on the death rates at a particular time and place.

liquid assets Financial assets (e.g., stocks or bonds) easily convertible to goods, services, or money.

living will A device used by some to attempt to specify the conditions under which they would prefer not to be subjected in order to keep them alive.

longitudinal research Studies designed to collect data at different times. This research design emphasizes the study of change.

lysosomes Saclike structures in the cell cytoplasm containing digestive enzymes that implement the breakdown of fats, proteins, and nucleic acids. Lysosomes have been implicated in cellular aging.

machismo An exaggerated manliness, with emphasis often placed on sexual prowess. From early childhood, Mexican American males, for example, are given more freedom than females and are expected to play a dominant role in the family.

maladjustment Behavior that does not completely satisfy the individual and social needs of the person.

malignant neoplasms Cancerous growth.

mandatory retirement Forced retirement, usually at age 65 or 70.

Medicaid A public welfare program for indigent persons of all ages paid for with matching federal and state funds. Medicaid has become the principal public mechanism for funding nursing-home care.

Medicare A federal insurance program financing a portion of the health care costs of persons age 65 and over.

melting pot A term often applied to the United States to describe a situation in which ethnic minorities lose their distinctive character and become assimilated into the broader culture.

menopause A term used to describe the conclusion of long-term changes in the female genital system. These changes usually progress at different rates in each individual. Menopause marks the end of childbearing potential.

middle knowledge A concept used by Weisman to describe the sense that dying patients have about a diagnosis even before they are told.

migration Refers to the movement of populations from one geographical region to another.

minimum adequate diet Lowest-cost food budget that could be devised to supply all essential nutrients using food readily available in the U.S. market.

modernization theory Attempts to describe the relationship between societal modernization and the changes in role and status of older people. It holds that with increasing modernization, the status of older people declines.

modified extended family A term used to describe several related nuclear families who do not share the same household but who do maintain strong kinship ties and have frequent social interaction and helping patterns.

morbidity The condition of being ill; often used to refer to the rate of illness per some unit of population in a society.

mortality crossover A concept used to describe the higher life expectancy and lower death rates of nonwhites of advanced ages relative to whites of similarly advanced ages.

mortality rate The total number of deaths in society in a year per 1,000 individuals in the society.

mourning Culturally patterned process by which grief is managed or resolved.

myth of desexualization One stereotype of ageism: If someone is old (or getting old), he or she is finished with sex.

National Institute of Aging One of the institutes within the National Institutes of Health. Established in 1974, its mandate is to support research in the biomedical, social, and behavioral aspects of aging.

need factors A term used by Andersen to describe subjective perceptions and judgments about the seriousness of illness symptoms and the need for health care services.

nonliquid assets Assets that are not easily convertible into cash.

normal distribution Concept used to describe that there is an average or central tendency around which are distributed higher and lower measurements.

nuclear family A family unit composed of husband, wife, and children.

nutrition The science that deals with the effects of food on the body.

obesity Excessive body fatness, generally defined as 15 to 20 percent overweight.

old-age dependency ratio Ratio of the population of those too old to work to the population of working age.

old-age institution A general term used to describe the entire array of rest homes and long-term care facilities for the aged.

old-old Those 75 years of age and older.

organic mental disorder (OMD) Designates a particular organic brain syndrome that has a known or presumed cause.

organic mental syndrome (OMS) A constellation of psychological or behavior signs and symptoms without reference to etiology.

organization Concept in Piaget's theory describing how people's thinking is put together.

osteoarthritis Degenerative joint change that takes place with aging. It is often referred to as "wear and tear arthritis."

osteopenia A gradual loss of bone that reduces skeletal mass and is associated with the aging process.

osteoporosis A demineralization of bone, often associated with aging.

palliative care Care directed at symptom control rather than cure. Term is often used synonymously with hospice care.

paranoia Form of psychopathology that involves delusions, usually of a persecutory nature.

Parkinson's disease A common movement disorder among the elderly.

participant observation A type of field research that includes observing and participating in events in a group.

pathological aging As individuals grow older, they are more likely to become afflicted with diseases. Changes that occur as a result of disease processes may be categorized as relating to pathological aging.

period The period of historical time a person lives through influences how that person ages. Those who experience a historical point in time at different times in the life cycle may be influenced differently.

pneuma A term used by Francis Bacon in place of the Greek notion of innate heat. Every body part was believed to contain a spirit; with use, the spirits dissolved and, alas, old age ensued.

political economy Critical approach that allows for broadly viewing old age and the aging process within the economic and political context of the society.

"poor dear" hierarchy A status system based on the distribution of luck. Being young, healthy, and close to one's children may be defined as having luck.

Poor Laws Relief for the poor, passed during the reign of Elizabeth I.

population pyramid A technique used to graphically depict the age and sex composition of a societal population.

portability A term used to describe the rights of employees to transfer pension credits on a tax-free basis from one employer to another.

postformal thought Stage of cognitive development with increased tolerance of ambiguity and acceptance of the possibility of more than one correct answer.

postparental family That state of the family life cycle that occurs after the children have left home.

poverty index An index developed by the Social Security Administration and based on the amount of money needed to purchase a minimum adequate diet as determined by the Department of Agriculture; it is the most frequently used measure of income adequacy.

predisposing factors A term used by Andersen to describe social structural variables (e.g., race, religion, ethnicity) as well as family attitudes and health beliefs that may affect the recognition that health services are needed.

preindustrial society A premodern society characterized by a lack of technological sophistication.

preparatory depression A type of depression, associated with the stages of dying, that takes impending losses into account. This depression prepares the individual for loss of all love objects.

presbycusis Impaired hearing associated with aging.

presbyopia Degenerative changes that occur in the aging eye.

primary memory Short-lived memory of information while it is being used.

primary mental abilities Includes number, word fluency, verbal meaning, inductive reasoning, and space.

principle of substitution Rule that elderly in need of support are likely to receive it in serial order, depending on availability, from a spouse, then a child, then from siblings, other relatives, and friends and neighbors.

prolongevity A term used to describe attempts to significantly extend the length of the human life span.

proprietary nursing homes Old-age institutions that are operated for profit.

prospective payment system Medicare-based reimbursement system that fixes, in advance, how much payment a hospital will receive for care provided.

prostrate gland A small gland that surrounds the base of the urethra in the male. It secretes a fluid that is discharged into the urethra at the time of emission of semen.

protective services Visits by the social worker with supplemental community services such as visiting nurses, homemakers, clinical services, meals, telephone checks, and transportation.

psychological aging A term often used to describe all the developmental processes, such as intellectual functioning and coping, that may be related to aging.

psychological autopsy A method of inquiry in which researchers draw together medical, social, and psychiatric information about a patient in an attempt to understand the psychosocial context in which death occurs.

R.D.A. Recommended Daily Allowance; refers to nutrient needs.

reaction time Measure of psychomotor performance affected by familiarity of task, practice at a task, task complexity, and other factors.

reactive depression A type of depression evident during the dying process that is a result of past losses (e.g., the patient may have lost a job because of an inability to work).

respite care Temporary services that use trained sitters to provide relief for permanent caregivers of the frail elderly.

Retired Couple's Budget A measure of the adequacy of aged income used by the Bureau of Labor Statistics.

retirement community Any living environment to which most of whose residents have relocated since retirement.

retirement test A system employed by the Social Security Administration to determine whether a person otherwise eligible for retirement benefits can be considered retired.

reverse annuity mortgage Mortgages under which a homeowner may sell some equity in his or her house and, in return, receive a fixed monthly sum based on a percentage of the current market value of the house.

rheumatoid arthritis A type of arthritis characterized by serious inflammation and joint destruction.

rites of passage Ceremonial rituals that mark an individual's move from one social position to another (e.g., single person to married person).

role loss Effect of life changes that involve loss of important social relationships and roles typical of adulthood.

role theory One of the earliest frameworks within which researchers in gerontology attempted to understand the adjustment of the aging individual. According to the theory, role loss (e.g., retirement, widowhood) leads to maladjustment.

scheme Piaget's term that describes cognitive structures that people develop for dealing with specific situations in their environment.

scenario Expectations a person has for the future.

schizophrenia Chronic psychiatric disorder manifested by psychotic thinking, withdrawal, apathy, and impoverishment of human relationships.

secondary analysis A reanalysis of data produced by someone else.

secondary memory Type of memory that holds a great deal of information for an extended period of time.

selection bias Used in this context to describe those old people who may have characteristics that sensitize them to respond negatively to living in institutional settings.

self-mortification A process, associated by Erving Goffman with institutional settings, by which an individual is stripped of his or her identity.

senescence The term used by biological gerontologists to describe all the postmaturational changes in an individual.

senile psychosis A common form of organic brain syndrome in the elderly. It is often characterized by progressive intellectual and cognitive impairments and by personality disorganization. The cause remains unknown. This condition is distinct from senility—that all too frequently used term that refers to mental incapacities believed to be associated with increased age.

senility A term often inappropriately used that describes all the age-related changes in intellectual functioning.

sensorineural hearing loss Hearing loss related to disorders of the inner ear where conducted sound vibrations are transformed into electrical impulses.

sex ratio The number of males for every 100 females ($\times$ 100).

shared household Two or more older persons (relatives or nonfamily members) who share a residence.

skilled nursing care Typically offered in a specially qualified facility that has the staff and equipment necessary for providing high-level nursing care and rehabilitation services as well as other health services.

social gerontology The study of the impact of social and sociocultural factors on the aging process.

social security The colloquial term used to describe the Old Age Survivors, Disability, and Health Insurance (OASDHI) program administered by the federal government. The most well known aspect of this program is the public retirement pension system, which provides income support to over 90 percent of U.S. elderly.

Social Security Act of 1935 The original piece of legislation, put forth by an advisory committee created by President Franklin D. Roosevelt, that created the so-called social security system. It has been amended and expanded numerous times. For example, Medicare and Medicaid represent Titles XVIII and XIX of the Social Security Act.

socialization Learning process through which one masters language, gestures, values, and beliefs of the culture into which one is born.

societal modernization Perspective that looks to changes in the role and status of older people as society modernizes (in general, with increasing modernization, the status of older people declines).

socioenvironmental theory A theory that is directed at understanding the effects of the immediate social and physical environment on the activity patterns of aged individuals.

sociological aging   A term often used to connote the role changes and adjustments associated with aging.

stages of dying   The most well-known conceptualization of the dying process. Prepared by Kubler-Ross, dying is seen as a five-stage process through which most dying persons proceed.

status passage   Process of negotiating a passage from one age-based status to another; may have both an objective and a subjective reality.

substitute judgment   A legal standard that allows for the substitution of another's judgment when a person is determined to be incompetent.

Sunbelt   Made up of those states in the South and southwestern regions of the United States.

Supplemental Security Income   A federal assistance program envisioned to supplement the existing incomes of eligible aged to bring them up to a minimal income level.

support system   System of relationships (friends, neighbors, and family) in which health and social services are provided to the aged.

survey research   A currently popular form of social science research that involves collecting data directly from a representative sample of a relatively large population.

symbolic interactionism   A theoretical orientation based on the premise that people behave toward objects and others according to perceptions and meanings developed through social interaction.

tertiary memory   Very long-term storage of information, presumably learned earlier in life.

total institution   An institutional setting within which the barriers that ordinarily separate the activities of work, play, and sleep are broken down so that all these activities take place in the same setting with the same people.

transient ischemic attack (TIA)   A small or mini-stroke that may signal the onset of a more substantial stroke.

very-old   Those 85 years of age and older.

vesting   The nonforfeitable right of an individual to receive a future pension based on his or her earned credits, even if the individual leaves the job before retirement.

Vilacabamba   A village in the Andean mountains of Ecuador where there is purported to be a high proportion of centenarians.

wear and tear theory of aging   Theorists using this biological model of aging often employ machine analogies to exemplify the theory's underlying assumption that an organism wears out with use or stress.

widowhood   Stage of life experienced more by aged women than aged men, defined by death of a spouse.

young-old   Those aged 55 to 74 years.

INDEX